New Dutch Swing

Kevin Whitehead

An imprint of Watson-Guptill Publications/New York

for Susanna von Canon and Erik van den Berg
that's friendship

and

in memory of Chuck Whitehead 1915-1997
thanks

Senior Acquisitions Editor: Bob Nirkind
Edited by: Sylvia Warren
Book and cover design: Jay Anning, Thumb Print
Production Manager: Ellen Greene
All photos by: Francesca Patella

First published 1998 in hardcover by Billboard Books, an imprint of Watson-Guptill Publications,
a division of Billboard Productions, Inc., at 1515 Broadway, New York, NY 10036

Library of Congress Cataloging-in-Publication Data

Whitehead, Kevin.
    New Dutch Swing / Kevin Whitehead
        p. cm.
    Includes bibliographic references, discography, and index.
    ISBN 0-8230-8348-9
        1. Jazz--Netherlands--Amsterdam--History and criticism. 2. Swing
    (Music)--Netherlands--Amsterdam--History and criticism. I. Title.

    ML3509.N4 W55 2000
    781.65'09492--dc21

                                                                    99-045231

Manufactured in the United States of America

First Paperback Printing, 2000

1 2 3 4 5 6 7 8 9 / 08 07 06 05 04 03 02 01 00

Acknowledgments

Foremost, thanks to 50-plus interviewees: Maarten Altena, Louis Andriessen, Ab Baars, Han Bennink, Steve Beresford, Peter van Bergen, Sean Bergin, Eric Boeren, Willem Breuker, Peter Brötzmann, Joost Buis, Allan Chase, Curtis Clark, Peter Cusack, Leo Cuypers, Daniele D'Agaro, Tobias Delius, Franky Douglas, Hans Dulfer, Martin van Duynhoven, Cor Fuhler, Jodi Gilbert, Ernst Glerum, Arjen Gorter, Ig Henneman, Fred Hersch, Terrie Hessels, Tristan Honsinger, Maurice Horsthuis, Bernard Hunnekink, Guus Janssen, Wim Janssen, Wilbert de Joode, Steve Lacy, George Lewis, Theo Loevendie, Willem van Manen, Misha Mengelberg, Pino Minafra, Gregg Moore, Michael Moore, Butch Morris, Alan Purves, Ernst Reijseger, Huub van Riel, Giancarlo Schiaffini, John Tchicai, Paul Termos, Michael Vatcher, Bert Vuijsje, Michel Waisvisz, Wolter Wierbos and Jan Wolff.

Some are not quoted at length in the text, and a few not at all; all helped shape my views, not always in ways they'd endorse. Many opened their archives, homes, kitchens, and record and tape collections to me, helped track down or made presents of rare materials, and patiently endured multiple and increasingly meticulous interrogations. While I've freely condensed or rearranged their comments, or lightly tidied makeshift English, I've tried to let them speak in their own voices.

Less formal conversations with Chris Abelen, Carlo Actis Dato, Frank Baldé, Richard Barrett, Erik van den Berg, Gilius van Bergeijk, J. Bernlef, Nico Bes, Barre Bouman, Giny Reijseger Busch, Jean Busch, Allison Cameron, Roy Campbell, Susanna von Canon, Alex Coke, Tom Cora, Lol Coxhill, Andrew Cyrille, Jetske de Die, David Dramm, Ray Edgar, Huib Emmer, Burton Greene (when's his book coming out?), Thomas Heberer, Klaas Hekman, Werner Herbers, Frank van Herk, Geert van Keulen, Anne La Berge, Ot Louw, Yo-Yo Ma, Ad Peijnenburg, Boy Raaymakers, Jaap de Rijke, Claudio Roditi, Roswell Rudd, Martin Schouten, Jimmy Sernesky, Jan Cees Tans, Sylvia Warren and others left their marks. The helpful staff at the Dutch Jazz Archive came up with a few hard-to-find documents and recordings. I'd also like to thank writers Schouten, Vuijsje, Kees Stevens, the late Rudy Koopmans and others for making my job easier by covering the scene so well over the years. Van den Berg,

Dramm, Vuijse, and Wierbos also read portions of the manuscript and ferreted out numerous errors.

I always had Francesca Patella's photographs in mind to illustrate the book, partly because the idea of using another foreigner covering the same scene seemed appropriate — she's from Bologna — but mostly because of her knack for capturing a musician's spirit with an image.

Many many people in Holland (and out) helped me in myriad ways while work progressed, especially when I was new in country. Honor roll: Erik and Susanna; Ernst, Giny and Janna; Jodi, Michael and Reuben; Francesca; Michael; Karin, Sofie and Jamie; Eric and Maria; Huub; Hope Carr, Karin Klooster, Dick Lucas and Larry Stanley. For favors large and small, I'm indebted to Bas Andriessen, Konrad Boehmer, John Corbett, Pedro Costa in Liston, Francis Davies, Jellie Dekker, Dominique Eade, Anne Cantler Fulwiler, Pim Gras, Terry Gross, Holly Halvarson, Ben and Ruby Lucas, Jacob Lucas, Jim Macnie, Marijke Lijnkamp, Suzanne Mikesell, Michael Nieuwenhuizen, Bob Nirkind, Mary Oliver, Gabriël Oostvogel, Cyriel Pluimakers, Peter Pullman, J.R. Rich, Jan Schretzmeijer, Tim Scully and Karen Pryor, Frans Sedee, Roberta Shorrock, Massimo Somonini, Chuck Stephens, Dane and Anne and Elizabeth Tiffany, Saskia Törnqvist, Anna Urbano, Marc Weidenbaum, all the Whiteheads, Peter Niklas Wilson, and the folks at Zaal 100.

Modest but timely grants from the SJIN/Dutch Jazz Foundation covered travel within Holland and numerous sessions poring over documents with my able and amiable translator Herman te Loo, who bears no responsibility for any spin I put on them. After the book was completed, funds were raised to assist publication from several Dutch sources: BUMA Fonds, Prins Bernhard Fonds and the OC&V — the Ministry of Culture, Education and Welfare. None of them asked me to change a word, and I didn't. Special thanks also to Stichting Buschplein, Howard Mandel, and two folks I should never forget to be grateful to, my dear New York mentors Irving and Stephanie Stone.

Contents

Introduction

When I started listening to jazz obsessively in the mid-'70s, the music was coming from everywhere. Fifty years of jazz records had seen to that; people all over the world knew how it sounded and worked. In the 1970s, major record labels all but ignored jazz. Musicians, undaunted, sought out independent labels, or started their own, in St. Louis, San Francisco, Amsterdam or New York.

Then as now, I saw that decentralization as healthy, prima facie evidence of jazz's adaptability and universal appeal. In New York, then as now, decentralization was taken as a sign the music was in trouble. The center would not hold—a problem only if you assumed the need for one center. (What is the current capital of classical music?) The oft-heard claim that Wynton Marsalis saved jazz in the 1980s implied a touching naivete about the impact the music was making around the world, and an odd lack of confidence in its durability—unless independent thinking and initiative were bad things. The diversity of modern jazz has been used to support the counter-intuitive claim that the music is under siege. Jazz is a democracy, we're told, but some conservatives believe it can survive only under a one-party system.

In reality, musicians in different places have always developed regional accents, and resisted tidy textbook models. Love him or hate him, critics have made much of how white Bix Beiderbecke sounded. But trombonist Wilbur De Paris, born in 1900, once testified, "[T]he type of trumpet playing that came to be identified later with Bix Beiderbecke was quite common in the Midwest among Negro musicians. I came from Indiana, and I can name half-a-dozen trumpet players who were playing that style." He adds, "Jazz was growing up in different parts of the country without one part necessarily knowing what the other part was doing. . . . " Jabbo Smith told Whitney Balliett of jamming on the street as a kid, in Charleston before 1920.

When jazz began cropping up all over—spreading to or being independently created in New Orleans, the Midwest, San Francisco and New York—every region had a different take, valid no matter how they might feed the mainstream later. Jazz grabbed whatever it could use; purity could never be an issue for a music synthesized or cob-

In 1875, the Fisk Jubilee Singers toured Europe, did a command performance for the Dutch king and queen. That would have been Holland's first exposure to African-American music.

The first jazz records were made in New York in 1917. Two years later a society combo called The Original Jazz Syncopators was working in the Hague. More Dutch jazz bands—or at least bands that called themselves such—followed within the year. Musicians knew jazz was the next big thing, but weren't so sure what it sounded like. Records were not yet easy to come by. Will Marion Cook's Southern Syncopators played Amsterdam in 1919—the same tour on which its clarinetist Sidney Bechet elicited Swiss conductor Ernest Ansermet's famous praise—but that was it for top American talent for awhile. (Paul Whiteman came in 1926, before Bix joined up; Ellington didn't make it till '33.) Dutch musicians traveled however. Around 1920 the Blue Band, a quintet from Leiden, recorded ten sides in Berlin and London, for Odeon and Columbia; titles included "Alabama Lullaby," "How Ya Gonna Keep Em Down on the Farm" and the future dixie standard "Jada."

In 1921 the Royal Dancing Band, a quintet, began a six-year stand at a club in the Hague. That city was a hotspot for the new music, but by the mid-'20s jazz bands had cropped up all over the country, on the radio, on records, on gigs: the Queen's Melodists, Savono's Superior Orchestra, Whimsical Whimperers, the Syncopated Harmony Four. . . . In 1926, the pianist from the Original Jazz Syncopators, Theo Uden Masman, assumed leadership of The Ramblers, Holland's most famous big band by far, which lasted in some form or other into the 1960s.

A very few black musicians were part of the mix from early on. Nedly Elstak, who we'll meet later, said that when trumpeter Teddy Cotton blew his horn at Amsterdam's Nieuwmarkt he could be heard some noisy blocks away at Central Station: a (typically miniaturized) Dutch version of Buddy Bolden blasting cornet clear across Lake Ponchartrain. Teddy Cotton came from Surinam, the Dutch colony on the northern hump of South America, a place with its own riot of African, Caribbean, Brazilian and other influences. In the '30s he opened his own Amsterdam nightspot: inevitably, the Cotton Club. In that same decade trumpeter Louis de Vries made records in England and Germany, became known to hot music initiates even in the States. Louis Armstrong called him the best trumpeter in Europe, but of course he hadn't heard them all. The Dutchman cut a "St. Louis Blues" in England in 1935. First he plays a striking countermelody, then a double-tongued solo chorus, what Armstrong would have sounded like coming out of the academy. De Vries was a conservatory jazzman before his time.

As 1935 began Coleman Hawkins was in England, working as featured soloist with Jack Hylton, whose band embarked on a continental tour, which is how Hawk came to Holland in early January. They'd come from Paris, would continue on to a string of German gigs, but first they played ten days at the Scala theater in the Hague, and one-nighters north and south: Groningen, Rotterdam, Nijmegen.

The Dutch countryside must have looked familiar to a Missourian and itinerant musician who'd criss-crossed the American midlands. He knew the look of a flat agricultural landscape on guard against high water. What the locals called a dike he called a levee.

By now American jazz records were easy to obtain; in the Hague he snapped up new sides by Ellington, the Boswell Sisters, and the Casa Loma Orchestra, a Canadian band he liked a lot.

When Hylton moved on to Germany, Hawkins was left behind, black folk unwelcome in Hitler country. Theo Uden Masman offered him a guest slot with the Ramblers. They did a week at a Rotterdam dance hall for starters, continued to play together off and on for months. The Dutch musicians were struck by Hawk's drinking whiskey straight from the bottle, and how the booze didn't seem to hurt his playing.

In February, Hawkins cut four standards with the Ramblers. Soloing on "I Wish I Were Twins," he hammers at the alternation of strong and weak accents, stomping up and down on the beat, as if kidding their slightly stiff phrasing.

Hawkins would hop around Europe from now till summer 1939—England, France, Switzerland, Belgium—and frequently revisited Holland. (John Chilton tells the story well in *The Song of the Hawk.*) When Hawkins recorded with the Ramblers again in August '35, they were readier. Trumpeter/composer/arranger Jack Bulterman brought "Meditation," nothing much—one chord and four pulsing beats per bar—but an effective backdrop for Hawkins's rhapsodic tone and time. At the session Hawkins wrote a nice testimonial to the piece on the back of Bulterman's music, and he wasn't known for doling out praise to be polite. On the same date they waxed the sentimental "What Harlem Is to Me." Kees Kranenburg's two-to-the-bar press rolls are firm and driving, bespeak a Euro-percussionist's martial-music roots, and in retrospect symbolize the sound of jackboots approaching from the east.

But war was still a few years off. Hawkins was in Holland a couple of times in '37, to play with Benny Carter—then based in London himself—and the Ramblers, and expat pianist Freddy Johnson, who'd been in Holland since '34 and Europe since the late '20s. (He'd come over with Sam Wooding). Johnson could lay down a relatively solid four- or eight-beat bass. With the Ramblers he'd sung "Zuiderzee Blues": "There's no place in this wide wide world like good old Rembrandtplein / And if you ever go there, you'll find it just the same." Jazz had made English the default language of entertainment music.

Carter laid some arrangements on the Ramblers, and guested on trumpet, clarinet, alto and tenor, usually more than one per track. Hawk had figured out how to sound good in front of them, but Carter made the whole band snap to: made them sound like they were playing a Benny Carter chart. Having Freddy Johnson sit in on piano didn't hurt; he was no Earl Hines, but he was hotter than Theo Uden Masman. The BBC broadcast the results.

By 1931, there were enough Dutch jazz bands and fans to support a magazine, *De Jazzwereld* (The Jazz World). The Ramblers were the most extensively documented band by far, thanks to Decca. Listening to them, you can hear that Dutch musicians mastered the rudiments of swing before the '30s was over, which is to say they weren't trailing their American colleagues by much. The idea, clearly, was to play just like the Yanks. "I'm Gonna Clap My Hands," from the same period—a novelty with stop-time breaks for handclaps, fingerpops, footstomps and whistling—showed how deftly The Ramblers could manage rhythmic and formal intricacies.

Carter and Hawkins had both dug the alto and clarinet player in Freddy Johnson's quartet, a Surinamese immigrant in his mid–20s, Arthur Parisius, a.k.a. Kid Dynamite. (Teddy Cotton was born Theodoor Kantoor; Surinamese musicians found American-sounding stage names didn't hurt business any.)

In '39 Hawkins went back to New York, cut "Body and Soul." The press wasn't too interested in what he'd heard in Europe, and Hawk didn't tout any finds. But it may say something for the state of jazz in Europe that Hawk was surprised New Yorkers hadn't made more progress in his absence. After the War he'd record the radical "Picasso," as rich with European atmosphere as anything in American jazz, a structured improvisation for unaccompanied tenor saxophone.

Back in Holland, saxophonists who aimed for his barrel-round sound mushroomed: tenors Piet van Dijk, Jan Cieremans, Hans van Assenderp, Ab Witteboon, altoist Red Debroy. Also Kid Dynamite, who'd switched to tenor, and was working for Teddy Cotton. Holland is so small, it takes musicians very little time to find each other.

Now come the jackboots. The Germans occupied the country, and because Anne Frank kept a diary everyone remembers Amsterdam's Jewish population was wiped out. Jews were penned up in public squares and then railroaded to the camps. The Germans started their own umbrella artists' organization—the Kultuurkamer, the Chamber of Culture—which musicians, painters, architects and others resisted joining at their peril. Sometimes refusing meant a trip to a detention camp; the composer Hendrik Andriessen was one such internee. Theo Uden Masman fired but supported in hiding his Jewish trumpeter. Many other Jewish musicians were taken away and never came back. Eventually the Surinamese bands got shut down too.

In Germany, jazz was suppressed but not defined, which left some wiggling room for musicians and jazz-loving or humanitarian officials. Pianist and composer Peter Kreuder slipped blue notes into his music for German pop films.

In Holland, curiously, the music was more tightly regulated. In *De Jazzwereld*'s final issue in 1940, seven months after the occupation, assistant editor Will Gilbert (co-author of the book *Jazzmuziek*) took over to say the magazine had never thought white folks should play this (Jewish degradation of) primitive Negro music, listenable as it might be. Gilbert wrote the Kultuurkamer's three-page pamphlet of guidelines for dance and entertainment music issued in 1942. It was mostly a detailed roster of forbidden devices and practices: plunger mutes, growls, smears and other dirty timbres, blue notes, scatting, drum solos, stop-time breaks, off-beat accents, boogie and other ostinato basses, background riffs repeated more than three times, charts written by black musicians, washboards, the use of the word "jazz" were all off-limits. Musicians were instructed to play good European music instead.

The Ramblers recorded straight through the War, in Hilversum, already the Dutch broadcasting capitol, and in Brussels. Uden Masman made the necessary compromises, but like other groups, the Ramblers kept performing American tunes under bogus Dutch or French titles. (Pianist Charlie Nederpelt waxed the all-Jewish "Oh! Lady Be Good" as "Kareltje in De Bocht.") The culture cops sent Uden Masman stern letters, instructing him to feature more German and fewer French lyrics. Some other Dutch musicians spent the war years working and recording in Berlin.

In Holland record collectors kept collecting, and small combos kept playing and making a few records.

So, in a sense, musical life went on as before. The Concertgebouw Orchestra's powerful conductor Willem Mengelberg made his peace with the enemy. He'd been partial to German music since the 'teens, hated the 12-tone Viennese, and was a tyrant
by temperament. Willem wasn't pure evil. He protected his musicians, saving Jewish
and other lives in the process. But he also set himself up to be a handy scapegoat after
the War, when his longtime nemesis—hostile critic and progressive composer
Matthijs Vermeulen—would find himself lionized.

The Canadians liberated Amsterdam.

Will Gilbert put out an update of *Jazzmuziek* in 1947; there was no mention of the
War.

What severed the connection between the old musical world and the new was less
the War itself than the slow recovery. Physical destruction accounted for only part of
Holland's depression. The independent Dutch had been overrun, and some of the
people whose country was built on commercial savvy had taken the quick fix and sold
out.

But even in those dark days, there were gropings toward an indigenous jazz style.
For instance, there were a few accordion players, such as Johnny Meyer and Harry
Mooten, who learned to swing passably on that not-very-responsive instrument. On a
January 1941 cover of "In the Mood" Jacques Gerlagh plays the familiar three-note riff
on accordion, while guitarist Eddy Christiani sweeps the chords with a heavy broom,
and heavy reverb: one culture's artifact remade in another culture's terms. On "Three
Little Words" by the sextet Secco's Gitanos, Jaap Valkhoff's accordion solo floats rhythmically above guitars' two-beat, Djangoesque cachunk. Accordionist Mat Mathews
(born Matthieu Schwartz) went to the States in the early '50s, formed his own quartet
with the young Herbie Mann, made records with Oscar Pettiford and Kenny Clarke.
(Mathews eventually returned to Europe, like emigre pianist Nico Bunink, who'd
record with Mingus for Candid and Columbia around 1960.) But that ur-European
squeezbox tradition dried up; there are few accordions on the modern Dutch scene.

Some trails proved truer. The Ramblers' '39 trifle "Flip de Fluiter" (Flip the
Whistler) is a harbinger: the instrumental choruses are for three unisono Tonettes—
kids' plastic flutes—played in close harmony (the melody squashed in the middle), the
better to accent those little recorders' imprecise intonation. Their pale blur is the
piece's main color, its reason to be. In retrospect, it's very Dutch.

Eddy Christiani's 1952 "Hilversum Express" begins with a moment of pure disori-
entation: heavily processed electric guitar enters, solo: slashing single chord, silence,
the chord again, silence. Again. Finally the chord is repeated faster, and you recognize
the terrain: a train song's stock accelerating-locomotive opening.

A genre gesture defamiliarized; frozen grating guitar chords; conceptual and timbral severity: it's the music of Peter van Bergen's LOOS, 40 years ahead of schedule.

That steam engine throttling up is our segue to modern Holland, which emerged
from the mud after the disastrous floods of 1953. Think of that disaster as Biblical
metaphor for a fresh start. By the late '50s Holland was a clean slate: a shiny new place,
remodeled, sleek as a Mondrian, headed for prosperity.

Prologue:
What Hawk Found

"I think 'Meditation' is one of my best recordings in late years, and I think it is a great number."

—COLEMAN HAWKINS, 1935

For clues to how influences flow in Amsterdam, get out of town. Grab a bicycle, the preferred mode of transport locally, and pedal west toward Haarlem. Not that there's a mystical connection to its new world namesake—New York of course being full of names from Dutch colonial days, Staten Island to Schermerhorn Street. The point is you pass through very low Lowlands to get there. The Dutch throw cigarette butts on the sidewalk like everyone else but in a sense every Hollander is an ecologist because the environment is always in your face. There are pockets of farmland and modestly moated sheds-and-shrubs community gardens (private and increasingly upscale) within city limits, and full cow and waterfowl country outside the beltway north of the harbor, out where you tell one hamlet from another by the shape of its centuries-old church tower.

You cross a lot of water out here, begin to differentiate canals as Inuits do snow: drainage ditches, irrigation trenches, boundary markers, shipping canals, back alleys and more, sometimes running side by side, with strikingly different water levels. You cross lots of canals in Amsterdam, their names sometimes a key to former function: a singel was once the city's moat, a schans a defensive trench.

Outside town, a ringvaart is serious high water. Much of Holland is old marshland, drained bit by irregular bit. A ringvaart is where all the water pumped out goes when you drain the area inside the ring, reclaimed land now called polder. A high earthen dike on either side of the vaart holds the water in. There was a lot of inland water to be gotten out of the way—old maps reveal more lakes than land—and the Dutch are still at it.

Head west through suburban Slotermeer to the tree-shaded country lanes beyond, and halfway to Haarlem is Halfweg. You climb, coming into town, level after level, a giant staircase. As bicyclist in flat Holland you become sensitive to slight variations in elevation; you feel the approach of a dike in legs' extra effort, in the tug against your established rhythm. Swing is motoric in a country where everyone has a bicycle (including drummers, who devise kits with skinny bass drums, breaking down and nestling small enough to be carried on the back of a bike); it's all about maintaining a tempo, graceful transitions, interrupting momentum only when absolutely necessary, knowing how to pace oneself and save energy for later. The rhythm of 4/4 swing is in every revolution of the feet. (When canals freeze you get another perspective on same: the scrape of alternating blades on ice is the rhythm of Han Bennink's brushes on snare drum.)

Cross the ringvaart from Halfweg into Zwanenburg, follow the road atop the dike a little south and look back toward Amsterdam. What you see is less Ruysdael than de Chirico, disorienting. The dike you are on, the water at your feet, sit far higher than the greenhouses beyond, set at angles to lead your eye further on, to still-lower fields, every far row of trees and odd quadrangle of land receding to a different vanishing point. Through a break in the trees you can see modern buildings in the distance— that's Osdorp—which given how the land recedes before you seems to be sitting on a hill. Your eye returns to the ringvaart, full as a bathtub, all that water above all that land. At such moments it's hard not to think about the shell game the Dutch play with water. Living below sea level is Holland's glory and peril: the water so soothing to contemplate everywhere stands ready to swallow you up.

Head to Haarlem, hit the art museums, learn something about Dutch self-absorption. Half the paintings are Haarlemscapes, the spire of St. Bavo's somewhere on view, even when sailing ships heel on roiling waves in the foreground. A couple of hundred years ago, most of the area east of this inland city was the Haarlemmermeer, the Haarlem Lake. Now it's Schipol airport.

Returning to Amsterdam cut across the polder from Halfweg to Osdorp, specimen slice of history. You're deep in farmland one minute, cross a ditch and you're in a suburb, pale brick apartment and rowhouse complexes through which the old watercourses still pass, reminders this all used to be fields acrop and wetland or seabed before that.

Osdorp is a big post–1960 suburb lying next to the Sloterplas, placid lakelet two kilometers by half a kilometer big. First the polder was drained. Later more sand was needed to build houses on nearby, so they dug it out of this newly drained sea bottom, and then dug a canal to the nearest higher water to refill the hole. Sloterplas water is about four feet below Amsterdam city canals.

(If you cut south from there, to Sloten, new suburb where following Dutch custom streets are named by theme—trees, mayors, Nobel Prizewinners—you might find the 'hood commemorating jazz musicians: Chet Bakerstraat, Count Basiestraat, and streets for Coltrane, Ellington, Holiday, Charlie Parker, Ben Webster, Boy Edgar and Wessel Ilcken.)

First you wring water from the land, then you carve out more negative space, and then you put water back. Now let it all be symbolic. Let polder be indigenous Dutch culture, and water be the outside world: irresistible, but capable of being rechanneled, or let in one trickle at a time.

bled together from sources as diverse as field hollers, Sousa marches and opera. Sleek 4/4 swing developed in the Southwest, a porous-border region where Mexican *corrida* singers strummed their guitars evenly, on the beat. Jack Teagarden came out of Oklahoma and Texas playing blues trombone and singing like a cowpoke.

In early days New York was out of step. Jazz in the Mississippi basin was marked by a feel for the blues and the oral transmission of information. New York was a weak blues town and a music-publishing center. (Not that there weren't black work songs to be heard; Willie the Lion Smith heard them in the brickyards of Haverstraw on the Hudson. The borders between north and south are porous too.) In New York, piano was the incipient jazz musician's tool, ragtime and pop songs the shared language of everyone from Eubie Blake through the '20s stride pianists. Their music was not about the crushed blues intervals of the south, but streamlining the natty syncopations of the page: making ragtime swing. At the end of the stride cycle stands compleat musician Fats Waller, whose jolly persona you can read as ironic commentary on the blues, a southern regional dialect alien (but adaptable) to his northern experience.

Regional dialects intermingled as musicians moved around. Jazz musicians have always been itinerants; Sidney Bechet spent all of 1920 in Paris and London. Canadian historian Mark Miller says the music was thriving north of the border before most Americans knew it existed. Foreign-born improvisers found acceptance in the States—Oscar Peterson, George Shearing, Toshiko Akiyoshi . . . —but usually had to move there to get it.

Some folks dismiss jazz abroad—in Europe especially—as one more ripoff of black culture. Wrong. Not ripoff but great triumph of: the world adopts the diasporan esthetic. Jazz has the fingerprints of African and African-American cultures all over it. Oral traditions valuing improvisation, paraphrase and flexible forms go back to the old world. Slavery made the systemic subversion of established beliefs and institutions necessary for survival; that's a handy description of what jazz did to European harmony and instruments too. (It's how I know in my bones black people invented it, no matter how fast everyone else jumped on the idea.) To play jazz right, you have to absorb some African-American attitudes, and those attitudes may affect ways you interact with people in nonmusical settings as you improvise your life. As far as that goes, Europeans who decry the Americanization of the continent are right.

In the '50s, when Armstrong and Ellington did their first State Department tours, commentators spoke of jazz as a great cultural export, but few Americans have checked up on what musicians overseas did with it. Outside of S. Frederick Starr or Bill Minor, who've written about jazz in Russia, no American has written extensively about a foreign jazz scene. Wilfrid Mellers' 1964 book *Music in a New Found Land*, an English scholar's meditation on American music, made me see the possibilities. Mellers misses some connections obvious to Americans, but makes others that native commentators had missed.

Amsterdam was a logical choice to study for a few reasons. It's a good city to live in, which is fortunate because the five months I'd planned to spend there writing this book stretched out to two years. A lot of the musicians involved are outsize characters; their lives make a good read. The Dutch as a rule speak good English. Also, the music is awfully good—distinct, funny, polished and innovative, swinging and bluesy when it wants to be—and well-documented on CDs. There's a discography in the back; please verify my claims for yourself.

The Amsterdam scene is small, relatively self-contained, and very specific, but this story is meant to convey some larger truths about how jazz eddies outward and interacts with other musical strains, how ideas enter and permeate the music—that's why the book follows two generations in some detail. But it also touches on a few broader matters, like the birth of the European free-jazz movement in the '60s, and the origins of game pieces, and conducted improvising, and other modernist ideas.

Even so, delving into Amsterdam music in such detail required a trade-off; it meant largely neglecting the vibrant music coming from other Dutch scenes, in the Hague, Rotterdam and elsewhere.

Dutch improvised music is a reflection as well as refraction: jazz seen in a distant, distorting mirror. You can recognize the figure in the glass, even if some limbs are too big or too little. Tracking how it did and didn't sound just like American jazz, it didn't take long to see I'd have to delve far into the realm of composed music to follow all the influences at play. The musicians didn't worry about distinctions among genres, so neither did I, except to examine what happens when the modern taboo against mixing jazz and classical music is violated. As influences in Holland, Charles Ives and Terry Riley loom as large as Thelonious Monk.

That said, one testament to jazz's power is how hard it can be to escape. In the '60s, even European improvisers who renounced links with jazz played long saxophone solos propelled by contrabass and trap set.

Too many Americans think of jazz overseas as like Japanese baseball: worth noting as a curiosity but not worth looking at. A better analogy is to the Italian western, an ingenious transformation of a genre, where some aspects are immutable and others undergo radical shifts in style and tone. The films of Sergio Leone don't supplant those of John Ford, but knowing the work of one makes the other's more enjoyable.

Folks sometimes ask me, why is Dutch improvised music better than some other kind, or, why did certain developments only happen in Holland. Kindly note I do not make such assertions of superiority or exclusivity. If the tone of the book does seem overwhelmingly positive—well I wouldn't waste your time dwelling on dull music of which Holland like everyplace has plenty.

Part I

Founders

Chapter One

How the Dutch Tell Time

"Jazz is a kind of teacher in the field of improvisation of this century in industrial towns. You can learn a kind of precision from it, and it's the standard of how to think about certain musical problems. To that extent it can be part of everybody's improvisation."

— MISHA MENGELBERG, 1980

One Sunday afternoon at the end of summer 1995, there's an exhibit in a gallery in the Hague's prewar Gemeentemuseum, a building which looks like it was made to house Mondrians—which it does, dozens—from the lean-brick facade to the orange ceramic squares which line each gallery's ceiling, in turn echoed by the rectangular light panels above, and by the Berlage-designed piano bench in the exhibition space where a tall man sits quietly.

Like Mondrian's paintings architect H. P. Berlage's building is about geometric order. The works in this room, however, look dragged in from a barn. It's one way you recognize the several styles on view as the work of one mind. The artist's media are the stuff other people set on the curb after clearing the attic. Old vegetable crates have been converted into misterioso dioramas; broken drumsticks ferment in old bottles full of what looks like bongwater; a statuette of RCA's trademark dog Nipper is graced with a huge ceramic erection.

One work is a horrid mass-produced forest scene, a painted metal sheet, a hart by a stream—but the deer has a suction-tipped arrow sticking from its side, and a glued-on broken drumstick echoes a painted felled tree, and a bas-relief blimp bulges from the blue sky. The surreal protrusions draw you in, somehow make the world of the ready-made more real.

The artist can recapitulate a motif as obsessively as Berlage or Mondrian, but he's averse to right angles. True, the surfaces on which he's drawn look like blank LP sleeves, but the distinctive calligraphy with which he covers them—repetitions of Dutch-phonetic bird calls, TAK, DJEK, KIK, KWIK, KWIE, KEH—is all slants and bold diagonals and long curving 'S's like a sloop's mainsail in a headwind. His G, R and j have tails as long as a raccoon's.

Along the wall to the quiet man's left are two rows of worn or broken drum heads, some adorned with broken sticks or worn out brushes. In one case he's glued a tiny feather to the end of a wayward tine. On a couple of heads he's inscribed the names of cities, those in which he played them before they broke. The lists are not long.

Suddenly there is the sound of a huge explosion.

Han Bennink on the Berlage bench, behind his traps, at three o'clock hits his snare drum so hard six tots sitting on the floor before him jump in surprise. So do a third of the adults crowded into the room, standing or sitting against the walls.

Within seconds, Bennink's fusillade shakes loose one of the mounted drum heads; it crunches onto the floor. Han freezes in mid-gesture—one arm raised to strike—and then walks over, picks the object up. When he does so the attached stick comes off in his hand. He drops both pieces to the floor instantly; they've returned to what they once were, trash. He goes back to the drums, resumes playing where he left off, but now there is a hole in the symmetrical pattern of circles on the wall, an imperfection that nags him. He keeps glancing over. After a few measures he rises again, strides back to the wall and plays that empty space—plays the imaginary circle the object left as its afterimage: plays the wall, plays the museum itself, plays Berlage as other drummers play Gretsch. He pours the music into the hole his art leaves, just as he'd made art of the holes his drum sticks tore.

He strikes the wall—click, triple-click triple-click triple-click triple click click click click click click—in fast and headlong double-sticking patterns he keeps developing even after he quits the wall and returns to his kit, missing barely a beat. By now his accomplices have joined in: Sean Bergin on tenor saxophone, Ernst Reijseger on cello. They improvise. Some drummers ride a rhythm, caught in the same wave as the other players. Some push a group from behind. Han pulls musicians along with him, and heaven help those who don't keep up.

Sean slides from free improvisation into a repeater riff, tilts the trio into a simple happy tune: Ornette Coleman's "School Work," a.k.a. "Theme from a Symphony," one melodic figure turned this way and that, playful and nursery rhymey. It fits the space and the kids at Han's feet. Sean Bergin is from South Africa, and you can hear echoes of highlife music in a couple of his tunes they play, accent on the fourth beat. Reijseger picks out a walking bass line, Han trades his sticks for brushes and slips into emphatic 4/4 swing, feathering each beat on his bass drum.

We begin with Bennink to dispel a lingering (American or otherwise) prejudice that foreign jazz musicians don't swing. Bennink's 4/4 flexing is so in your face you can't miss it. The complaint some make is that he doesn't do it all the time—that he's pre-occupied with antics which lead him away from the drums. But the spectacle, the time when swingtime is literally suspended, heightens the suspense. The time (dura-tion) away from the drums is the frame for his time (pulsation) at the drums, which is all the stranger as it derives from and speaks to another era.

Han Bennink has perfect time—when he doesn't rush from excitement—and the chops of a very hip prebop swing-band drummer. (His favorite bebop drummer is the original one, bass-drum bomber Kenny Clarke, who grew from the same roots.) Bennink can chingaching on ride cymbals with the best, and his snare accents prod and poke, cuff you about the head: *I'm doing something, why don't you?* He always discounts the idea his music is aggressive—the only one I'm battling up there is myself—but behind it is the idea of jazz as a joust: cutting contests where cuts draw blood. One reason is that he is very, very loud: too loud, he says, but that's too simple. Han hits drums hard because he's concerned with (a) timbre, and that's one way to make a drum truly sing, and (b) dynamics, because a loud hit stands in contrast to every softer stroke. (He's also preoccupied with pitch, raising the tone of a drum about a third, stretching the head taut by applying one stick while beating it with the other.) When he plays with brushes, his attack is slap not caress.

His sticking combinations: stick slams head and rim microsecond before other stick slams the first stick and the head, an instant before he slams the hi-hat shut, then slams bass drum and lets hi-hat fly open. Do all that at once, you make a loud sound. Stagger them as described and you have narrative, a zigzag line, time moving forward, propulsion: after I play these four or five events, how will you extend our sequence? This is one way of looking at the old jazz advisory to tell a little story with a solo.

Such precisely irregular phrasing is an essential of the too-frequently mystified phenomenon of swing, which players often arrive at intuitively: you either hear how to sway with it or you don't. Dutch musicians had been listening to Americans swinging on records almost as long as Americans had been doing it. By the '50s there were a number of Dutch drummers who sounded at ease with that rhythmic concept, enough to make one wonder if there's a cultural predisposition toward subdividing time so.

In Holland as in much of Europe there are public clocks everywhere: lampposts, steeples, watchtowers, municipal buildings. There is a cuckoo clock and mechanical instrument museum in Utrecht. Composer Peter Schat has devised a "tone clock," a way of thinking about harmonic relationships using a clock face as a visual aid, each note of the tempered scale represented by a different hour. Digital clocks are few; clocks with faces are the rule.

Here is how the Dutch talk about time. The hour 2:15 is simple enough, *kwart over twee*, quarter past two. Likewise 2:45, *kwart voor drie*, quarter before three. But 2:30 is *half drie*—halfway to three—and from here the orientation toward quarter and half hours gets complicated: 2:37 is *zeven over half drie*: seven minutes past halfway to three, and 2:20 is *tien voor half drie*—ten minutes before halfway to three.

An hour divided into four strong and weak beats around which all other fractions of time are oriented—a little ahead, a little behind, you never forget where you are in relation to them—and in which time is so forward-looking that 2:20 is described in relation to the hour 40 minutes ahead: that sort of thing can be useful, playing jazz where each bar is structured the same way. Don't some drummers picture the hands of a clock, sweeping through a full rotation once a bar, in order to orient themselves to the time in an environment of shifting beats? Charles Mingus called it "rotary perception."

Han is big, athletic—strapping—ruddy faced, white hair crew cut, lumberjack shirts, workman shoes, his head a proud Easter Island monument with promontory nose. He towers over the flatlands, physically and conceptually.

There are a number of traits peculiar to Dutch improvised music, not all of them on this list: an ability to abstract from the music of American jazz masters; an impulse toward theater, role play, humor and ironic distance from one's own creations; killer chops that make all the horsing possible, the virtuosity that assures any fuck-up is deliberate; a certain clunkiness Louis Andriessen calls "lousy Dutch wooden-shoe timing." Bennink embodies all of them.

Often comes a moment when Han, swinging, shuts down, full stop. The rest of the music continues, then BLAM a fast four-stroke combination like a filing cabinet loose in a stairwell. The musical emblem of a silent-movie pratfall becomes the pratfall itself. Bennink has slapstick timing, deft simulacrum of uncoordination. A Bennink schtick: sitting at the traps on a cramped stage, he'll entwine himself in the curtain behind him, struggling to escape, graceful as W. C. Fields tidying a pyramid of light bulbs. There is also, when this very loud drummer lays out, the suspense that comes waiting for the other shoe to drop, for the inevitable crash that can still make you jump no matter how often you've heard him. Han has said he got into music and art because he was verbally awkward, and there is a slight stammer in that timing too. When the hammer is cocked and the trigger taut the tension can be unbearable.

♪

"My father was an orchestra percussion player who also sounded like Benny Goodman on clarinet, and played tenor saxophone in the Coleman Hawkins style. Even my mother went to see Hawkins when he was with Freddy Johnson, because she was already in love with my father, who really admired him. My father was a very clean guy, always cleaning his clarinet, his horn, cleaning everything. He also did repairs for the reed section in the orchestra. One day he went into a repair shop, and the saxophone of Coleman Hawkins was there, because it was leaking. My dad thought it must be a fantastic clean horn, because of his sound. The guy said, 'You know why it is leaking? There was a toothbrush and this other shit in the bell.' Very nice."

Han was born in Zaandam, across the harbor from Amsterdam, 17 April 1942. When he was ten his father moved the family a half hour east of the city, to Hilversum. Rein Bennink was already working as percussionist in AVRO broadcasting's orchestra. The early '50s is when the radio industry really took off in Holland, and is part of the reason Hilversum is known still as a town for folks with money. It and the surrounding area, close to what was once the innermost reach of the ocean—until it was closed by construction of a huge dike in the '30s, the water behind it slowly turning from salt to fresh—is as near as Holland gets to Beverly Hills or Long Island's north shore, which is not very. The Dutch are not ostentatious—they call themselves Calvinists so often it co-opts that reading of the culture for outsiders—but some folks in Hilversum had swimming pools, power boats, water skis.

Musicians from all over Holland gravitated to the area. There were five broadcast organizations time-sharing two frequencies, and if only AVRO and VARA carried any jazz, they all needed musicians, some of whom played jazz after hours. The mid-'50s anthologies called *Jazz Behind the Dikes* show what they were up to. West Coast cool is a conspicuous model. The rhythm sections swing lightly and politely, the tenors sound like Stan Getz, the arranging like Shorty Rogers, which is to say *Birth of the Cool* is behind it as well. True, pianist Rob Madna was in the thrall of Bud Powell. But in general Hilversum jazz was as clean and tidy as a good hospital.

The teenaged Han played field hockey and began making art, including early versions of the wooden-crate dioramas on view in the Hague. (Rein Bennink was a weekend impressionist, taking Han along when he pedaled out in the country to paint the landscape: "Music and drawing both come from the influence of my father.") In his early teens Han also played clarinet a minute, and discovered percussion.

"For years and years I played a Thonet-style chair, made with a very thin plywood. When the nails get loosened it has a very nice vibrating sound. Then when I was about 16 my father gave me a wooden snare drum he'd had hand-built for me. He said that was more than enough, and of course he was right." Even now, on stage, he might grab his snare drum, come down to the footlights, play it alone for a few numbers. "That drum was really howling like BAAOOWW! when you hit it, so fucking loud. Later we sold it so I could get a Ludwig snare. Now I look and look for a sound like that and can't find it. But most of the time I had second-hand stuff. We were not rich, but he always had a way of finding good used stuff for me. The second thing was the hi-hat, then the cymbal, and then the bass drum."

Before he assembled a full kit, he might accompany Rein to orchestra gigs, play dad's traps during intermission. This could drive the other musicians nuts.

"I wasn't so interested in technique, but I tried to swing all the time. First I was inspired by Max Roach, then Kenny Clarke—I saw him at the Concertgebouw with Phineas Newborn in 1958, playing very very loud. There were a few Dutch drummers I liked a lot: John Engels, Cees See, and Joop Korzelius, a studio percussionist who was always borrowing my dad's drum kit. On Saturdays, Wessel Ilcken played with Pim Jacobs on the lakeshore in Loosdrecht near Hilversum, in a boathouse rebuilt as a jazz club. I'd ride there on my bicycle, and had to be home by nine o'clock. Watching Wessel Ilcken, I saw how it was done: how he played the hi-hat on 2 and 4.

"He was good but Cees See was much better. He had a little shed in his garden where Hans Dolman and I would visit him and we would all play. We studied all the bop licks with Cees. He must have been 15 years older than I was." Eight, in fact.

"We had an attic where I could study the drums. You could hear me playing blocks away, but the next-door neighbors were old and deaf, and very nice to me, so I could practice. I used to play with my record player, all the time, very loud. Bob Cooper and Wessel Ilcken live in Zaandam, Wessel was playing good on that. One of my favorite records to play with was—and is—*Concert by the Sea* by Erroll Garner, with Denzil the doctor Best, great brushes player. I know all his accents on it by now. I also played along with the modern stuff. Once when my father came home from a bad day in the studio and was really hating music, he ran up to the top floor, said, 'Stop it now! Goddamn nonsense.' He said Ornette Coleman sounded like a chicken coop.

"My father never gave me any instruction, but he supported me tremendously. The only thing that bugged him was that I couldn't read. 'If you can read notes, you will always have something to eat.' When I was about 14, he sent me to a friend of his, the percussion player of the Concertgebouw Orchestra, who was supposed to be the best teacher. He asked me to play a roll, and as soon as he saw it said, 'This is bullshit, you're playing nothing.' I never went back."

Han Bennink has played duets with everybody: Willem Breuker, Misha Mengelberg, Sonny Rollins, J. R. Monterose, Derek Bailey, René Thomas, Peter Brötzmann, Conrad Bauer, Peter Kowald, Steve Beresford, Fred Frith, Irene Schweizer, Andrew Cyrille, Myra Melford, David Moss, Dave Douglas, Marc Ribot, Eugene Chadbourne, Ray

Anderson, Ellery Eskelin. . . . Rein Bennink was his first duet partner, very early. Han felt like Krupa when Rein played "Sing, Sing, Sing" on clarinet.

Rein Bennink was as Han says super-clean; in old photographs his drums glisten like a new Buick. He was a tinkerer, refurbishing old equipment for Han (who inherited this nexus of attitudes: thrift, economy of means, recycling). Rein was well-plugged into the Hilversum scene, and picked up a lot of little gigs at army bases and the clubs sprouting up in the area: the boom years were coming.

Those Hilversum bands could be rhythmically shaky, one reason Han debuted early. Before he was 18, the Benninks played together as a duo and also in little swing/mainstream combos, often with bassist Arend Nijenhuis and Utrecht saxophonist Gijs Hendriks. (War memories were fading: Rein drove them around in a VW bus.) "I was gigging at army bases with seven people who all came out of the semi-classical radio band where my father worked. They could do all these different shows, Hungarian style, Honolulu style, all this sort of bullshit. I was always much too loud. Once when the rhythm section stayed on and a famous singer came out, my father was behind the curtain, whispering 'Softer, softer!'"

In 1959, he won first prize in a radio jazz concours—one of several period jazz competitions, not unlike the old Notre Dame Jazz Festival in Indiana—playing "Opus de Funk," "Nice and Easy" and "St. Thomas," a familiar folk tune to Surinamers, many of whom wrongly believed Sonny Rollins had swiped it from Kid Dynamite. "I was very very successful," Bennink wrote in his scrapbook. (He has a bunch of these, going way back: large, spiral-bound books full of journal entries, clippings, programs and photographs.)

Also during the late '50s, Han sat in at sessions at Sheherazade, Amsterdam's premier jazz venue, and also hung out on Sunday afternoons—an awful lot of Dutch jazz history gets made on Sunday afternoons—at a club in Bussum where he didn't play with but got to hear a piano player in his early 20s who played Monk tunes and always had a cigarette going, Misha Mengelberg.

♪

Han Bennink sits at the drums, takes a sheet of newspaper and begins tearing it into long thin strips. He crumples them, stuffs them into his lower hi-hat cymbal, a deep-dish item from Tibet he uses sometimes 'cause it's loud. When he's got a good pile of paper in there, he produces a box of matches, lights one, and holds it up to a frayed paper end. The match goes out, and the audience laughs. They think that's the joke: funny man pretends to light what looks like kindling in what looks like an ashtray. He strikes another, and one tongue of paper ignites; Han blows gently on the ember until more paper catches. Pretty soon he has a real fire going, from which thin wisps of smoke rise. Now that the fire takes care of itself, he begins to play, first just skins, then working in cymbals, then hi-hat. He loudly stomps it shut, strikes it rattattattat ata ratta tatt, and when he opens it again, the smothered newsprint yields black inky smoke billowing out the sides. Now he plays a fast sequence, opening and closing hi-hat quickly, syncopated pattern of choked versus resonating cymbals. Each clampdown squeezing out air forms a perfect smoke-ring, which drifts slowly toward the ceiling, out-of-tempo counterpoint to the music roaring below. Close your eyes, it's just great busy

8 *Founders*

drumming. Open them, you see a man calmly manufacturing cartoon smoke signals, each circle expanding as it rises.

⚜

"I had always heard drummers on the radio or on a record. You just have to touch a button in order to grab it. But to see people play, really see them, helped me a lot.

"In 1960 I went to New York, playing with the Gijs Went trio on the *Maasdam* of the Holland-America line, which many emigrants from Holland used in the '50s to go to America and Canada. I was seasick for three days but we still had to play. There were some strange moments. When we played below decks for the working people, they fought till there was blood on the wall. Incredible! And we had to play in a sort of storm, because people still wanted to dance. I stayed in room 462, the same cabin Gene Krupa had when he had traveled to Europe. The cabin was awful, there was no natural light. I was not smoking marijuana then, but the guy who looked after the cabins said, 'Gene Krupa always stayed in his room, that's all right, but he was always smoking these morphine cigarettes!'

"The port of entry for New York was Hoboken, across the river. I arrived July 21, 1961, and we sailed again on July 24. I remember standing on the corner of Bleecker Street, and a guy yelled, 'Hey McCoy!' and then I realized, 'Wow, I'm in America; somebody's yelling "McCoy" and it's McCoy Tyner.' That was a miracle for me.

"I saw many many bands. Opposite the Village Gate on Bleecker Street was a little joint called Cafe Ruffio. We arrived too early because we did not want to miss anything—real European jazz fans. (The trio went everywhere together, like cattle.) The drum kit was sitting there, just a bass drum and a snare, and a hi-hat, very old cymbals, one with a screw in it. The stage was so small, it looked like they'd sawed an octave off the piano to make it fit. The first guy who came in was wearing a white plastic shirt, he didn't look that fantastic to me. He just started touching the drums, and it was great: Billy Higgins. The piano player was Sonny Clark, it was his birthday; he had a glass of awful red wine from a little bottle that I later found out is only used by junkies, or drunkies. And then the soprano player came, and I met Steve Lacy.

"I went to the Village Gate. Aretha Franklin opened, with just a drummer. She accompanied herself on upright piano, with a microphone stand between her legs. Very very good. The second part of the show was John Coltrane, with I think Stuart Davis on bass, and Elvin, and McCoy Tyner. Before Coltrane went on, you could hear him already playing the scale of 'My Favorite Things.' He walked on stage, played it for an hour, and that was it." He means Art Davis, not painter Stuart, but it's a nice slip. And yes, Sonny Clark's birthday is July 21.

"I also went to the old Five Spot. Ornette was there, with Bobby Bradford, Jimmy Garrison and Charles Moffett. The second group was Walt Dickerson, who I knew from time he had spent in Holland. He had a quartet with quite a good drummer, Edgar Bateman. By the time I got back to the ship, I'd drunk so many Coca-Colas that I had to vomit.

"I saw Phil Woods and Gene Quill, and Art Farmer, Benny Golson and Albert Heath. Bob Cunningham, the bass player, was at the Half Note, possibly with Jimmy Giuffre. And Gene Krupa played at the Metropole, you just walked in off Broadway and heard him playing. That was a very weird joint, disappointing in a way. All that sort of stuff was weird to see for me, you know?" The musicians played on a platform behind the bar, in a line.

"That first trip to America changed me a lot—at least that's what Misha says. Back in Europe, the drummers seemed too nice all the time: more like they were polishing the drums." This quest for fire is the great creation myth of Dutch improvised music. Listening to Han's early records suggests he didn't really come into his own till a few years later. "It meant a lot to me, to see people really playing, on the job. That's the first time that I realized we had been aping the American musicians in a way: that it was their language, their music."

Later in the year, after their weekly matinee in Hilversum, Han accompanied bassist Nijenhuis to his other regular Sunday gig, at the club Persepolis in Utrecht. Han was subbing for the usual drummer, played far too loud, but the pianist heard something new to him: a drummer who knew Monk's "Off Minor."

"In art school, during drawing lessons we always listened to Monk. So we did 'Misterioso,' all these Monk tunes, and I could play them better than all the other drummers he used before.

"From that moment me and Misha stuck together."

Stooped potbellied buttless bald on top wearing a moth-eaten sweater and old droopy jeans, with his three props, cigarette dangling from his mouth giving him that smoker's light squint, snifter of cognac cradled in the left hand, coffee cup rattling atop saucer clutched in the right, Misha Mengelberg shambles on stage to a mostly empty BIMhuis, far too early. No one begins a nine o'clock set at 9:12. He sets down his drinks on the ledge above the piano keyboard, places the cigarette on the saucer, pulls his sweater over his head, and drapes it casually on the strings.

Real Zen stuff.

Looks at it a moment, then drapes it casually on a slightly different section of the strings.

Cancel the Zen stuff. Misha hates anything even remotely smacking of mysticism.

Sits down and inventories a couple of octaves, creeping up note by note to hear what the sweater's good for, and then begins to play.

When Misha Mengelberg was in New York in February '94 to record his trio album *Who's Bridge*, he played two nights at the Knitting Factory. He got a good crowd, still didn't make any money. (He was charged for the piano rental.) He began Friday night with a long themeless improvisation that had no trace of blues in it, and ended Saturday romping on "Lover Man" and a B-flat blues. In a way it took him two nights to get from one place to the other, but then he has spent a lifetime making such slow crossings.

"We went to the zoo from time to time. The zoo, yes. All kinds of wolves. Black. White. Wolves." He likes to talk, slowly, over Indonesian coffee—a cup half-filled with ground mocha, covered with boiling water, stirred like hell and left to settle: you sip an inch of ridiculously bracing sap off the top. He sits in his dining room on the Olympiaplein (not far from the stadium built for the 1928 Olympics), hunched over a table and under a lamp that looks designed for poker, his cigarette smoke obscuring him as it's caught in the glare, streetcars rattling by every few minutes. He savors certain words. Zoo. Wolves. He speaks of them as evidence he remembers something of Kiev, where he was born and left forever at 3.

Misha's father Karel Mengelberg came from Utrecht, studied music in Berlin in the '20s. There he met his future wife Rahel, a German harpist, and a younger fellow student from Enschede, Holland, named Kees van Baaren. Kees and Karel both played some jazz piano—there's a photo of them playing four hands on one instrument—and dug Gershwin, and worked their way through college, working in cinemas, playing and writing pieces for silent films.

Karel conducted the opera in Königsberg, Germany in the early '30s; he was the nephew of the dreaded Concertgebouw conductor Willem, his political opposite. Karel never joined the Party, but he was a devout lifelong communist. He and Rahel went to Spain in 1934, to enjoy its enlightened republican government, but different factions had begun shooting at each other. (While there Karel composed the orchestra piece *Catalunya Renaixent*, which sounds less optimistic than its title. But his pieces show a lyrical gift and light melodic touch much like his son's.) While in Spain Rahel heard about a harpist's job; it was remote, but Europe like the States was in a severe depression, and you took what you could get. She went to work in the orchestra in Kiev. "I think part of it was a political commitment; you wanted to build socialism together with the Russians."

There was no work for Karel at first, and he returned to Holland, although Rahel was pregnant. He was still there when Misha was born—5 June 1935—but soon after that Karel came to Kiev to work at a state film studio, scoring collective-farm epics.

The Mengelbergs joined Kiev's free-thinking artistic community.

They skipped to Amsterdam in 1938 when their free-thinking bohemian pals began to disappear without warning. Karel still thought they should give Stalin a chance; Rahel said, pack.

Misha was a coddled child, slept with his stuffed animals Beestebeest and Hertie. He played field sports as a boy but says he always tried to avoid physical contact. "As soon as we came to Amsterdam there was a piano I could play. I improvised, I would say, as a reaction against the contemporary music I heard a lot when I was very young: four, five, six." By his own recollection, he began composing at 4. Karel transcribed for him a little ditty the boy kept playing at the piano; it sounds rather like a precocious child's conception of Beethoven.

Then came the War, and times got tough for most everyone. Misha's Jewish grandmother was sent to a camp, "not as demonic as other camps where Jews went." She survived. (The Mengelbergs were traditionally Roman Catholic, but Karel had turned from the church as a child, when his own father was carted off to an asylum.) At around age 8, Misha began his lifelong passion for chess.

"I remember in '45—I was ten at the time—we had some jazz records at home. We had some Ellington from before the War. They were among my favorites, along with Stravinsky's *Firebird*. For me it was all dance music. I danced on *Firebird* but I also danced on 'The Mooche.' It had that rhythm for me at the time." Slow, with nice tight dissonant voicings. He tried to irritate his parents a little by trying to play boogie-woogie, but they didn't get so upset.

After the War Karel looked for conducting work but as Willem Mengelberg's nephew and front-row red he was double-jinxed. (Later he'd guest-conduct some-times—the Residentie Orchestra, the Amsterdam Philharmonic. "I have seen my father do things with orchestras which were amazingly good. I don't think I'm being subjective. He was a nice and dear person to me, but I could distinguish very well between being a nice person and making good music.")

"When I was 12 or 13 I went to all those terrible Sunday afternoon concerts at the Concertgebouw, chamber music, I listened to that a lot. And then at a certain point I said, 'I won't go with you anymore, I've had enough.'" As he told John Corbett, he was impatient with the pace composers set: "I thought, 'What arrogant idiots, they can say all they're saying there in five or ten minutes.'"

Karel reviewed concerts for the socialist paper *Het Vrije Volk* (The Free People); he'd go to concerts, write them up overnight, then sleep till afternoon. (Misha is well-known to keep Dracula hours too; Karel by the way had bad posture, smoked con-stantly—cigars—and was habitually late for important engagements.) "I'd read what he wrote. Sometimes we agreed, at other times not at all. But he had a very open mind to jazz music, and wrote about it."

One Concertgebouw concert was different: Duke Ellington and the orchestra. The house was nearly empty; no one had money and tickets were expensive. Misha enjoyed the first half, went to the lobby at intermission, got bored, went back inside: there was Ellington, sitting at the piano, playing alone for a few minutes before the band straggled back on, his way to avoid waiting for the tardy.

Here was a guy who let himself be dissed by his audience and his band, who by blurring the distinction between the performance and the pause spilled the music out of its normal box, as it were.

Misha thought, this is an interesting development.

"I started studying piano when I was six I think. I'd already been playing for years, but then I had to adapt to those stupid little children's pieces, which I did with great reluctance. There are interesting pieces for children, Bartok's *Mikrokosmos* for instance, but I was not able to play them. Then I found out that I had to have some kind of technique to deal with certain musical material. That hadn't occurred to me before. Then I thought, maybe if I just go on improvising, I will find solutions, and I did. You could say my technique is my own technique.

"I started playing boogie-woogie in the '40s, at home. Those were the first steps. The later steps were being interested in Charlie Parker and Thelonious Monk. I was interested in what the Americans had done, during those years that we didn't hear their music. I heard Charlie Parker in '47 I think. He was a big influence on me imme-diately, but I couldn't do anything with it because I lacked the technique to do any-thing he may have done." He laughs. "I could whistle it. The funny thing was, even then I recognized that nobody was able to do what Charlie Parker was doing. Absolutely nobody. There are generations after him who tried but nobody succeeded.

"I was interested in Bud Powell, but not as much as Monk. I heard Monk very early also, about 1950 or '51. I had a Stravinsky education, so funny chords were something I found a lot of fun in. The first thing I heard was 'Humph.' It was what I had been waiting for. Then there was a piece which I later identified as 'Carolina Moon,' with the trumpet in the Salvation Army style.

"A little later I was also interested in Dave Brubeck. His being a pupil of Darius Milhaud had some positive effect; sometimes his harmonies were more daring than in most jazz music I listened to. I thought, 'Jazz music is very nice, but the harmonies are uninteresting.' That's what I usually thought about the music of the '30s. I thought, 'Art Tatum can play the piano very well, but he has no sense for developing something out of the harmonies. When I play jazz, I will do that for him.'

"I did not have a perfect idea of what was interesting at the time. Whatever was more interesting than not, I grabbed, kept in mind, and tried to use. I formed my opinions about all those things later. When I really got into analyzing some of the stuff, I came to some conclusions. Thelonious stood out because for me he had the most interesting harmonic ear, very well developed. But that realization came somewhere around '56 or '7. Almost at that same time, the Herbie Nichols records appeared, the trio things for Blue Note. That also sounded very impressive to me.

"I started playing jazz in high school, with an idea that except for blues there was no form in jazz music. On standards I would play perhaps 73 bars instead of 32, stretching the 32-bar form.

"The Monk pieces I attacked furiously from the moment I entered the conservatory. Before that it was just looking into sounds, certain moments. There was no reason to know about forms when I was mostly playing alone. I learned to play jazz because that was the way to play together with other people. When I started playing with people who knew about those forms, I adapted very quickly. The only problem was, I could not play any fast pieces, and still cannot. Some of the inventions I have allow me to play fast, but I was not one of the tigers who could play 'Cherokee.'"

He sat in at Sunday jam sessions at the Sheherazade, on Wagenstraat off the Rembrandtplein. (A plein is a town square.) "I could play a slow blues. I was thrown out, always, when some more fancy piano players arrived. I agreed with that. I wanted to be thrown off. But around 1958, they let me play on sessions.

"I tried to convince everybody to play some Monk music, but that was not easy because Monk was considered a very lousy piano player who had made one nice piece—that ballad even Miles Davis played, with the wrong chords. But I always wanted to play free music in a way: to just improvise, with no preestablished rules.

"In those times I was looking for role models. I was also into inventing things, but I drew distinctions between compositions and improvisation. I didn't think you could combine the two."

♫

One Saturday night in October '95, Mengelberg plays with the SOSA-Band in Soest, a mile from the queen mother's palace. In Holland, where the arts are government-subsidized, most little towns have an arts center presenting dance and chamber music and jazz and stuff. Eventually a musician gets to play them all. In Soest the venue is Artishock, a big old building with a modern disco built out back—the boom of bass drum wafts over all night—and where improvisers play in a room one flight up which boasts grotesque jazz murals: shades and berets. There is a quiet bar just outside the room, where bassist Ernst Glerum and alto saxophone and clarinet player Michael Moore have a drink, half listening to Misha, whom they can hear through the door, warming up on the little upright piano. They stop talking to try to identify one item: "Melancholy Baby," a tune one doesn't hear much in this half of the century.

SOSA is a silly acronym, stands for something like Success for the Downtrodden of Amsterdam. The rest of the quintet is trumpeter Evert Hekkema, and a drummer Misha used before Han Bennink came along, Harry Piller. They're pretty mainstream players—Piller plays the melody all through his solos, so the rest of the band always knows when to come back in—while Glerum and Moore, maybe 20 years younger, play with Misha in his freewheeling ICP Orchestra, so the band has a curious conceptual/generational split. Nobody really writes for the group, they don't rehearse—it's a traveling version of the band Misha played with at the artists' club the Kring, on Amsterdam's Leidseplein.

First tune is Herbie Nichols's "House Party Starting," and the pianist's opening solo immediately lags so far behind the time your stomach tightens—how does anyone get so lost so fast?—until he finally alights on a chord change right on time.

His piano skills have been shortchanged by just about everybody, including his musicians and himself. Misha has no time, they say; I can't even read my own music he says. Like Monk he likes to set up his chords with care—it takes a second to get the fingers properly bunched—but for this particular theater-conscious Dutch musician part of the schtick is never to be in a hurry.

(Later in the show, he'll vanish into the bar during a bass solo, come walking back in with a beer in his hand to arrive at the piano at the precise moment to hit the last chord in Glerum's last chorus. If you'd happened to spy him entering the room you'd have caught him fine-tuning his pace to hit his mark on time.)

Second number is "In Walked Bud," Moore bouncing down the wide intervals on bass clarinet, the leaps more than his plaintive sound suggesting Dolphy. Harry's brushes are very polite. The trumpeter solos, and Misha chimes in with his comments: comping for soloists, he really shows his Monkish splayed chords. (Listen to "Off Minor" on the 1987 recording *Dutch Masters* for the flavor of his playing with SOSA, and to the excellent *Who's Bridge* for a sampling of the vintage Mengelberg tunes they play.)

Evert Hekkema was a friend and admirer of Chet Baker (who lived for awhile in Holland, and died of a fall from an Amsterdam hotel window) and like Chet doesn't believe in playing too many notes too forcefully too far in the stratosphere. The way he holds the horn to the side of his mouth, it's almost like he's embarrassed to be seen with it. Misha comps by finishing the ideas Evert doesn't. (And sometimes, it's almost as if Moore heckles him, blowing empty air loudly through his alto during a retiring trumpet solo.) Now the pianist is warmed up; Glerum's arco solo becomes a dialogue for bass and piano, then a trio, when a large dog heretofore sitting quietly by its master starts harmonizing with bass's bowed moan.

By the third tune, Billy Strayhorn's ballad "Chelsea Bridge," fault lines appear. Trumpet takes the melody, aggressively goosed by bass clarinet—now Moore really sounds Dolphian. Glerum, seated, playing a three-quarter-size bass tonight, holds his bow stationary and rakes his instrument back and forth in time, a giant metronome in the face of the drummer whose time may wander. During Moore's solo, Michael and Misha play a little game: whenever one hits an obvious note the other harps on it, hard. When the pianist takes his solo turn, he interrupts his own gossamer Strayhorn chords with clunky chromatic scales, derived from and corroding the melody.

For the Dutch, one attractive thing about standards, your own or anyone else's, is that they're indestructible. No matter how much you trash them tonight, tomorrow they're still good as new, ready for the next respectful reading or raking over.

First three pieces of the night: Nichols, Monk, Ellington's book.

♪♫

When it was time for college Misha studied architecture for a year. The buildings he designed were all underground, of limited use below sea level—tribute to his low opinion of modern design. "At some early stage I started writing music instead of going to classes. So then I thought, in that case it's better to go to the conservatory."

Karel's old running buddy Kees van Baaren had been living in Amsterdam; Misha knew and liked him. In the 1970s he recalled, "When I was 17, van Baaren did a four-part setting for me of 'All the Monkeys Love It in the Water,' after I showed up one day with my own setting of the song. Two visits: one to bring it, one to fetch it. The second time we talked about it for awhile. That's a lovely memory."

Kees had just become director of the Royal Conservatory in the Hague, and Misha enrolled. He became pals with another son of a composer, Louis Andriessen—Hendrik's boy, born 1939—who remembers his conservatory years as richly bohemian. Somewhere in there, says Louis, he and Misha and their friend Boudewijn Leeuwenberg went to Paris, lived in an attic, crowded the piano bench to play five-hand versions of bebop tunes: "Boudewijn also transcribed some records by the Gerry Mulligan quartet with Chet Baker, a lot of work. Then we'd play the three-part counterpoint, three hands on the piano."

Misha: "We were mainly involved in teasing Louis. He composed and he also improvised, but his improvising was . . . too much, too heavy. But also we improvised in a style I think had more links to Stravinsky or to American composers of the time, like Copland or Virgil Thomson."

Louis had seen close up that one could pursue two separate musical styles. In 1956, his brother Jurriaan, a pianist 14 years older and already an established composer, had made a five-song jazz EP with a three-piece Hilversum rhythm section, under the name Leslie Cool. There his pretty block chords, springy rhythm, and the little motifs he'd develop in a solo didn't place him so far from his idol Nat Cole or even Herbie Nichols; one downward-skipping whole-tone row suggests he knew his Monk.

Kees van Baaren was a champion of long-suppressed serial music in Holland. The Nazis had forbidden it, but Willem Mengelberg had already suppressed it before the War; afterwards, even his nemesis Matthijs Vermeulen couldn't accept it. Some other aspects of van Baaren's life suggest a lingering influence on Misha. He considered himself an anarchist, albeit a gentle one, and he believed in keeping a cool head when composing, because writing music is emotional enough. He also saw every school of composition in the rearview mirror.

Van Baaren accepted the notion that tonal music had played itself out: that as soon as the laws of harmony had been codified, it was all over. His former student Hein Kien wrote in 1976, "he presented this subject as a dead language, the grammar of an important but past period." But, says Kien: "It was . . . impossible for him to ignore the most striking quality of Western European music, the constantly changing form in which it manifested itself, and to regard any one single stage of development as fixed and final. As long as music showed signs of life the time for experimentation was not yet past." In Berlin, van Baaren had also learned strict Palestrinian counterpoint, in which the voices relate only to each other and are not dependent on underlying harmony. Even atonalists could use that.

Misha had a splendid ear, could parse those Monk chords, hear the ingenuity behind the deliberate lack of polish. What some heard as fumbling, thick fingers crushing so many adjacent notes, Misha heard simply as a liberal use of minor seconds; Monk in a way took diatonic harmony to its extreme, hiding every basic triad in an obfuscatory thicket. Van Baaren nurtured Misha's love of analytical thinking, but Misha came to reject Kees's belief that any good piece of music is analyzable. Mengelberg's music tends to ignore or defy rules or expectations. In architecture certain realities must be recognized, but even the most sloppily constructed piece of music can be safely executed. People may be bored, a musician may get hit by a tomato, but nobody gets hurt.

In 1958, already a student, Misha went to the summer music courses at Darmstadt—hotbed of new composition that had spawned and came to be dominated by serialist Stockhausen—and there met John Cage, whose more open approach to form and content was a revelation. Pianist David Tudor performed Cage's "Water Music," playing octaves and other bland intervals while doing various water tricks. It was greeted with nervous laughter. And Cage gave a lecture Misha later described to Peter Cusack:

"He was smoking six cigarettes at a time but also manipulating them, burning them or laying three on an ashtray and burning the fourth. I remember the manipulating more than the lecture. His talking was also interfered with by David Tudor playing. I remember thinking that the lecture, manipulating and playing should appear as one. . . . I hated musical theater in the classical sense, but there were new possibilities." Misha was unaffected by Cage's hostility toward jazz.

Louis Andriessen: "Misha came back from Darmstadt with all these stories of Cage doing crazy lectures, and we were very excited. We started reading koans, studying Zen Buddhism at that time. We were 18!" But Misha's inherited mistrust of religion kept him at arm's length from that beatnik creed.

"When I was 11 or 12 I got hold of the Tao Te Ching, and I think that has influenced me all my life, on a very low level. I wasn't very fond of the philosophy, just the book. I thought, here we have a kind of world religion based on a little storybook. Everything you can say about Taoism is denied by the book, reduced to nonsense. It's nothing you can ever define. To say, 'This or that is very much Tao' is unthinkable.

"This is all related to my ideas about dadaism and surrealism, which I think were the most profound things added to the possibilities in this century.

"At the conservatory I studied some Beethoven, some Bach, Anton Webern, and I learned to play those pieces, but it took me six years of practice. I had to play some chords with cross-fingering, all kinds of things. I found ways to play some of the Debussy Preludes, and that's it, that's all the technique I've got. Plus the things I found out about piano playing myself, even at the conservatory. To this day I feel more like an autodidact than a product of classical training." Every Friday afternoon, all the students were required to sing in a choir. Misha never showed.

Louis Andriessen: "Apart from this liberal approach to what was interesting and what was not, there was an anarchist element to van Baaren too. He taught us Charles Ives, for instance; he was the first person in Holland who had even heard about that kind of music.

"Misha was not conformist enough for the school. He didn't compromise, and got a lot of criticism from other teachers. The reason he was kept on as a student was because Kees protected him."

You hear what he wrote then, you hear why they thought him frivolous. Mengelberg's *Musica per 17 strumenti* from 1959 allows each instrument only one note (or gesture: the harpsichord's permitted a chord, one string can gliss). From tuba to woodblock they cover almost the entire range of the piano, its point of origin. The pace is so slow, the texture so spare—two instruments sounding simultaneously at most—it's barely there. The musicians might fairly feel toyed with. Willem Breuker remembers a performance where the tubist is always picking up a mute, putting it in the horn, blowing one note, taking the mute out and putting it on the floor, blowing another note, picking up the mute and putting it back in—visual comedy divorced in a way from musical content, à la Bennink. It won first prize at Amsterdam's Gaudeamus Music Week—a sort of young composers trade fair—in 1961. (The composer says the version heard on a 1982 Composers' Voice LP of three of his composed pieces was edited together by him from isolated notes, recorded separately by members of the student ensemble credited.)

17 strumenti is a bit too cute and maybe Cagey too, but then Misha was only 24. His 1962 string quartet "Medusa" was a more graceful joke: the austerity of Cage sliding into the peeping of birds sliding into slow baroque music, just a hint of style-quotation, a new fad for new composers.

Van Baaren could be critical too. Misha's *Three pieces for piano* (1961) outCage Cage the way he'd outMonked Monk. A lone note every once in awhile: empty boxes.

As Misha recalled years later, he brought them to Kees, who sat at the piano and raced through them six times too fast, and said, 'Well, that's that!'

"And it was. I never went to van Baaren with a composition again."

There was a fourth short piano piece that got separated from the other three: a cluster piece, heavy. But it didn't occur to Misha to play like that on a jazz gig—not until later, when he heard Cecil Taylor improvising the kinds of things he'd been writing years before.

♫

In 1959, the year Han Bennink heard him jamming in Bussum, Misha's trio won the jazz concours at Loosdrecht. (This contest open to Dutch groups, elimination rounds held on six consecutive summer Sundays, ran in this form from 1958 through '72.) The 15-year-old Willem Breuker heard them: "He was copying Thelonious Monk better than Monk could play himself." For Phonogram, Mengelberg recorded two original tunes in Hilversum with Harry Piller and American bassist Earl Freeman but they were never issued.

Misha's piano has sounded like Monk for as long as anyone can remember, to everyone except Misha anyway. As he himself heard it (he later told interviewer Bert Vuijsje) his timing was Monklike but there was a heavy dose of Nichols in there, and some Parker, and some Tommy Flanagan-like agility.

While at school Misha learned orchestration hands-on. He was commissioned to arrange a Monk piece for radio orchestra, was delighted when it was announced, fore and aft, as "Monkey's Dream." He says Rein Bennink played his part well.

But for the Hilversum crowd, Misha was too out even then. One reedman upbraided him for writing a clarinet part—outmoded, it's all saxophones now. Still, before hooking up with Han, Misha formed a partnership with tenor saxophonist Toon van Vliet, 13 years his senior. (On *Jazz Behind the Dikes* he comes off as a frank Stan Getz fan, but like other Hilversumers he was making a switch from cool to East Coast hard-bop.) They liked and respected each other, stayed together a few years, played some Monk. There was one German bass player Misha liked then, Joop Cristoffer, but mostly he worked with well-behaved rhythm players: drum-polishers.

Misha had been intrigued by the leader's liner notes to *Herbie Nichols Trio*, released in 1956—notes which incidentally revealed him to be a fellow chess player. Nichols theorized about the relationship between drums and piano, starting with the notion that drums sound with overtones of fifths, and drawing a connection with the prevalence of cycles of fifths in jazz harmony. It makes the band "sound," the verb, Nichols says, and that's why bebop drummers like Kenny Clarke started to "drop bombs" on bass drum. "Each bomb created a newly rich and wholly unexpected series of overtones beginning in the lower registers. These rich syncopations"—i.e., the placement of the bombs—"were fitting accompaniments to the supplemental overtones played by the horns in the higher registers. This is why pianists became so percussive with their left hands." In truth this is as murky as an awful lot of musicians' theoretical pronouncements, but at least part of it deals with the simple idea that pounding the drums will make a piano ring sympathetically, come alive in a way it wouldn't otherwise.

Mengelberg interprets it the opposite way: the piano activates the drums. You're playing, you suddenly perceive that the ride cymbal sounds a D-flat, so now you have one note in every octave to color the crash, set the cymbal humming. It's a theory.

Misha had heard Bennink before he went to the States, was not so impressed. The new too-loud Han who sat in that Sunday in Utrecht was another story. Now Misha heard his chance to have his piano, his bandstand, resonate in sympathetic vibration.

Han and Misha, one evening in the musicians' bar De Engelbewaarder—the Guardian Angel—after a rehearsal at the BIMhuis a few blocks away, grab a chess board and settle in at a table in the back room. They begin: speed chess for 20 moves, clearing the underbrush, then Misha abruptly gets up and goes to a neighboring table, where an Italian musicologist waits to interview him in English. Han spends the next 20 minutes contemplating his next move, tentatively setting up a few possibilities. Ten

minutes after he commits, Misha returns, takes a minute and a half to size up the situation and respond. Han moves maybe 30 seconds later, then Misha in 15, then it's
speed chess again till without warning he returns to his interview.

That's what their duo concerts had become by the early '90s: exercises in blocking
each other's moves and throwing off each other's rhythm. Like chess itself, stylized
warfare.

Like other lifelong partners, Han and Misha have always had a talent for driving
each other nuts. And as with other jazz partners—Hawkins and Roy Eldridge for
instance—people tend to assume they are closer than they are. They do not visit each
other's homes; their families do not socialize. They are married musically, but it is a
troubled marriage.

♫

One day Misha says something like, "The cigarette has always been part schtick."
—The cup of coffee too?
"Yes."
—And the cognac?
"No, that is something else."

In the early '60s he used a long slim debonair cigarette holder. Only other guy that
decade used one was Burgess Meredith as The Joker. One night a very attractive young
woman originally from Indonesia came into a club in the Hague where he was playing, saw him standing in the doorway, and said to herself, "That's a guy I like." They
had their first real conversation a few months later. Amy Chattelin and Misha
Mengelberg have been together ever since.

Another night out in the Hague, Misha discovered alto saxophonist Piet Noordijk.
"He was playing a kind of bebop music, but he was doubling on bass, and I think
singing. He was a real nightclub musician playing for strippers and all that. But there
was something about his approach to jazz music; he was rhythmically interesting, not
playing those endless sequences of 8ths or 16ths like everybody else. He tried to copy
Parker, which of course he didn't do very well, but it had some blues in it."

In short, more hardbop than bebop, with that searing Jackie McLean or
Cannonball Adderley quality. He eventually replaced Toon van Vliet as Misha's saxophonist. Piet, three years older than Misha, was already a Hilversum guy, had been a
professional for years, and would only work with other pros—which means he would-
n't play at first with that too-loud art student drummer.

Fall '61, back from New York, Han Bennink went into his second year of art school
in Amsterdam, where he'd made friends with a funny, verbal student named Wim T.
Schippers, before Schippers got kicked out. Han was heavily into Ornette and Monk,
and still living in Hilversum, where he attracted the attention of Pim Jacobs, jazz
pianist, studio kingpin, TV host, and husband of singer Rita Reys, widow of Wessel
Ilcken (who'd died of a brain hemorrhage in 1957). She was then Holland's major jazz
celebrity not least for recording with the Blakey/Horace Silver/Hank Mobley Jazz
Messengers in New York in 1956. Han began appearing on Jacobs's TV show *Djezz
Zien*—the title reflecting a period mania for transliterating English into phonetic
Dutch: "jazz scene."

With Pim and younger brother Ruud Jacobs on bass, Han played with lots of visiting Americans: Mobley, Johnny Griffin, Clark Terry and Wes Montgomery among them. Bennink worked with the Jacobs brothers a lot: "They asked me for the television program, for the school concerts, for spectacular things, but never for the trios with Rita."

All that playing too loud: Han has always had a lot of energy. Early '60s, he's going to art school and painting, a lot. He's playing day or night with various Hilversum types. By now he's also playing with American soloists at Sheherazade and has become house drummer at Persepolis. Over a few months he plays with Misha and Arend Nijenhuis; with pianist Kenny Drew (living in Copenhagen) and the French saxophonist Barney Wilen; with Toon van Vliet; in quartet with saxophonist Theo Loevendie, pianist Gijs Went, and Arend; with Belgium's blazing post-Django electric guitarist René Thomas; with Johnny Griffin, with whom he did three tours in 1963 alone, and who liked to play ridiculously fast.

Han reads a March '63 journal entry: "'Johnny Griffin was quite heavy'—meaning up-tempos. 'For now I can't take it anymore. He was really heavy on me. After intermission I refused to play. So Johnny Engels had to play. . . . That was not such a good idea of Johnny Griffin's, because after the first tune he had to stop, and he was shouting very loud through the Sheherazade, "Where is Han Bennink?"

—Who finished the set?

"Me. Griffin was fast, I played with Tubby Hayes who was also very quick, but Lucky Thompson and Don Byas were much faster than Johnny. Don Byas, incredible. He used to smoke three big reefers and have a couple of shots of whiskey before he went on. He was very much into bodybuilding, looked very good, and was very good at checkers. I did some interesting gigs with him and with Lucky Thompson at that time."

Despite all the gigs Han did with the Jacobs brothers—whose group might also include guitarist Wim Overgaauw—Pim rarely used a drummer on his many combo records, and when he did, it was someone else. (The one exception is a frothy 45-rpm single from '66 where Han backed singers Reys and Rob de Nijs.) Han's first record is a 7-inch EP by altoist Tony Vos's trio, with Nijenhuis on bass: "Ridiculous band—a bit like the Sonny Rollins trio but very soft." True enough, save for the loud and frequent brushes-on-snare-drum accents.

By the '60s itinerant American jazz musicians were becoming common, and pianists Jacobs and Cees Slinger usually got the call to lead the pickup band. Misha might get the gig when a slightly more advanced pianist was desired. In 1963 his trio backed Johnny Griffin at Persepolis, which makes sense in one way—Griffin had played with Monk—and no sense in another, since Misha doesn't play quick. "He counted off very fast, yes, but I can play chords at that tempo, that's not a problem. When it was my turn to play a solo, the first thing I did was break the tempo down to half. A very slow piano solo following him. After my solo, the tempo returned to up, because they all wanted to play those fast pieces. Han Bennink certainly did." One night in Rotterdam, Griffin was playing "Rhythm-a-ning" at an insane clip. Came time for the piano solo, Misha waved Han to a halt, began playing a slow "Getting Sentimental over You."

At the end of May '64, Misha's trio was hired to play with Eric Dolphy on a short series of Dutch gigs, in Alkmaar, Rotterdam, and Eindhoven. (Eric also squeezed in a rehearsal and Concertgebouw concert with Boy Edgar's chaotic but spirited big band. Misha's trio joined Dolphy for a few numbers.) Eric had been in Amsterdam in April, on the famous tour with Charles Mingus where a bootleg recording seemed to've been made at every gig. Dolphy elected to stay in Europe at tour's end, settled in Paris.

"We had a very good personal relationship. I was reading John Cage's *Silence* at the time. Dolphy borrowed it, read it in a few days, and then we talked about it. He liked the book. Me too. Especially the questions, 180 or something, it's a lecture: 'If a car goes along the street, is it music when it goes along the conservatory?' Those kinds of questions."

(There are 74. One reads: "Which is more musical, a truck passing by a factory or a truck passing by a music school?")

"I was very interested in playing with him, but I didn't like the compositions very much. In my opinion the pieces were not advanced at all. The playing was advanced, and I think the thing he needed was to be hooked up with Nichols's music, for instance. Dolphy was doing things that Nichols suggested with his pieces: finding alternate ways to the simple construction of chords. He could deal with shortcuts and things in a Nichols-like way, but he didn't know Nichols, was not aware of what he had written for the Blue Note sessions. But not everybody can know everybody."

The first released Misha record and the first of Han's anyone ever heard of is Eric Dolphy's *Last Date*, 2 June 1964, Hilversum. (Years later Han and Misha's ICP label brought out a crudely recorded but spirited "Epistrophy" which a fan had recorded in Eindhoven the day before. The piece on the flipside was by Misha and a parrot, but that's for later.) Dolphy had been contracted to do a radio concert on Wednesday the 3rd, but he was due back in Paris by then, so it was taped a day early instead of going out live. This became a record after Dolphy suddenly died of diabetic shock a month later in Berlin. The Hilversum session wasn't in fact his last date, but for a long time it was the last Dolphy available, its main point of interest. Compared to *Iron Man*, *Conversations*, and *Out to Lunch* made over the previous year, it's a step back. He plays with a pickup group, and it sounds it. His helpers were Han, Misha, and straight-ahead, conservatory-bred bassist Jacques Schols, who two days before had cut two tunes in another Hilversum studio with the mainstream Diamond Five. As for how much attention accrued to the Netherlanders on *Last Date*, we quote Simosko and Tepperman's Dolphy biography: "The Scandinavian musicians perform admirably, and Mengelberg's solos are particularly fine."

Misha's sportive side is plainly evident. He plays the chords called for, shows he gets the point of the harmonic motion, but his impatience with the material shows too. Soloing on "Miss Ann," first he sounds engaged by the line, then defaults, feeding chords; he ends his feature chorus quoting the beginning of "I Got Rhythm" (a joke he likes enough to repeat, later). There's nice interaction with Dolphy on the Hilversum "Epistrophy," Misha answering bass clarinet leaps with top-of-the-keyboard dapples, blurring the line between comping and dialogue. Most of the material is fast, but the piano solo on the ballad change-up "You Don't Know What Love Is" suggests he did-n't much care for that choice either; he hints at Randy Weston's bubbly "Hi-Fly." Nor did Misha like Eric's flute, which he also plays there and on "South Street Exit."

"South Street Exit" illustrates Misha's strategies for dealing with fast tempos: spack-ling lone staccato notes over the upper registers, a rhythmical hunt-and-peck with impeccable drummer's time; little repeating treble figures that sound trained to come quickly to the fingers; short lines in octaves, for structural support; very even and dex-terous single-note runs, from which he'll pull up short with some deflating gesture: bebop suddenly become children's song. Monk is obvious in the timing and narrow-interval chords (which have not yet collapsed into clusters) but Mengelberg's har-monic color has a deeper blush, more Nichols-like. On this album a certain line of influence is laid bare: Misha is a major source of the ironic stance which is a defining characteristic of Dutch music, and Monk is one source of same for Misha.

Oddly, one of the faster pieces is Misha's "Hypochristmutreefuzz" which like its portmanteau title is designed to keep you from coming up for breath. Irked at being confronted with (fast) material he had to struggle with—the rehearsals had been diffi-cult for the sidefolk—Mengelberg brought a piece whose rapid-ripple line lacks breath pauses. Dolphy made adjustments: carved it into chewable phrases, capped those phrases with low notes for variety. Mengelberg's own solo is on Monk's dime, but his increasingly implosive harmonies parallel the still-tonal mid-'50s Cecil Taylor.

At the end of "Hypochristmutreefuzz" is a lovely mishap. After the second bass clar-inet solo comes a bass solo—well, it would be a bass solo if Schols did anything besides walk, which he doesn't. Misha chimes in, Basie-like, but when he realizes Schols isn't going for anything, he decides to fill in, but what to play that's in keeping with the nothing he's played already? More of the same. The result is a chorus more Cage-spare than Monk-.

Han isn't quite Han yet: the heavy ride cymbal swing is there, but he drops few of the snare drum bombs that are Bennink the bebopper's specific accent. On the fast "South Street Exit" he shimmers beautifully on the cymbals, keeps up chattering answers on snare, but he's nowhere near as intense as his mature self. (He's more assertive on the boisterous Eindhoven track.) In his own way, Misha is more aggressive.

A month later, Dolphy is gone. Universally cited bittersweet coda: A few days after Eric's passing Han gets a letter from him, inviting him to join his band with vibist Bobby Hutcherson and bassist Niels-Henning Ørsted-Pedersen for a two-week engagement in Denmark—the Scandinavian country occasionally confused with Holland.

Preparing a memorial broadcast in July for the same radio series on which Dolphy had just appeared, producer Michiel de Ruyter ended with a snippet of a Dolphy inter-view from April, when he'd come through with Mingus: "When you hear music, after it's over, it's gone, in the air. You can never capture it again." When the broadcast became an album, Eric's spoken comment became its famous coda and his unofficial epitaph. Never mind that the words being preserved on tape and then vinyl refute Dolphy's point. The sidefolk were paid 200 guilders each, rather less than 75 dollars. They had been told the LP would be a limited edition, but it's been reissued many times since. Misha says he's never seen any royalties for "Hypochristmutreefuzz."

—Would *Last Date* be so well remembered if Dolphy hadn't died soon after?

"No. The record would not have been released at all."

—When it was did you expect some recognition from the States?

"I felt there might be people who'd say, 'Maybe there is some interesting piano play-ing.' But it's too far away from Oscar Peterson to have an impact in America."

Around the same time Misha assembled his new quartet, with Noordijk and Bennink and any of several bassists: Schols, Ruud Jacobs, Rob Langereis. But on their first recording the bassist was Gary Peacock, who'd been in the same Hilversum studio a month earlier, while on tour with Albert Ayler, Don Cherry, and Sunny Murray. (Han and Misha would like to have played with Ayler, but he didn't seem much interested in the Europeans. After his early '63 Copenhagen recording you can understand why—he and his Danish pickup band are from different worlds, clash mightily.) Peacock had the kind of versatility Misha could use. He had recently worked also with leaders Shorty Rogers, Paul Bley, Bill Evans, and Jimmy Giuffre.

Three of four tunes on Mengelberg's album *Driekusman Total Loss* (released many years later on VARAJAZZ) are from a December 4th broadcast with Peacock, whose bass sounds beautiful, by the way—plump and woody—and who gets plenty of space to demonstrate the all-over-the-fingerboard style he helped found. Wide-interval leaps are the order of the day; Noordijk reels audibly from Dolphy's impact (he had played with him in Boy Edgar's band), scaling his alto in jagged ascents, and Misha evokes Monk's broken-field runs. All the above happens on the tune "Driekusman Total Loss," a mess of contradictions; the title mixes current slang with the name of a cen-turies-old Dutch dance form.

"At that point I liked very much to combine certain contradictory elements, at least in the titles."

Contradictions ran deeper. The thumping oompah bass says 2/4, but it's clearly a 16- not 32-bar tune, which it would be in duple meter. If anyone else hears it as I do, it means thinking of individual bars as being in one time signature and the whole form as being in another. As for the AABA melody itself—rollicking little riff relieved by a standard little bridge—is this Cannonball hardbop or rock-and-roll jump? Whatever, only someone who saw the world split-screen could compose this and the four Cagean piano solos and *Musica per 17 strumenti*.

The other tunes with Peacock are standards, a slow "Nature Boy" with Piet's anguished alto lurching toward bathos, and "If I Had You," where Misha's Tommy Flanagan strain finally shows itself alongside Monk. Somehow, Misha acquits himself less well than with Dolphy. His playing is more defined on the fourth track, "Remember Herbie" (recorded in June '66 with Langereis), an elegaic melody that twists slowly in on itself, although it doesn't sound much like Nichols.

Bennink's snare chatter and its propulsive power are increasing; the density of the web is more Bennink-like, but relative to his sound now, he still sounds shackled.

"I think it was at the end of '64 that I played three weeks in the Jazz Gallery in Berlin, where Eric Dolphy got sick before he died. I played with the American saxophonist

Herb Geller, Martial Solal on piano, and a good Danish bass player. I stayed about 14 days, but I couldn't stand to stay with Herb Geller, he was so boring. He had to get up at eight o'clock in the morning because of his studio job, and he had the radio on, with people shouting all the time: American baseball. I felt horrible.

"I was stealing marijuana out of the Berlin botanical garden, which helped me through that week. That was the first time for me, although of course many many other people smoked it already, and I loved the smell. Johnny Griffin used to call me the Milk Drinker. I didn't drink till I was I think 25. Now I like wine, but not too much. I had a feeling that you wake up in the morning with a headache from drinking. Still after all these years in this profession I like to get up early."

Reconstructing from recordings, over 1966–68, the drummer really becomes Han Bennink. It was time, for him, approaching his mid–20s. Those were also the years when he married his beloved Masje, jazz fan he met at the Persepolis, and they moved into the houseboat on the Vecht river where they still live, and had the first of their three kids: Suki, who became an artist. (Her cover for Han's 1982 solo album *Tempo Comodo*—line drawing, side view of a stylized bird, which you can identify by its plumage once you color it by the numbers—is childlike, deconstructive, reconstructive: dad's daughter.)

March 4 1966, Misha's quartet—Noordijk, Langereis, Bennink—recorded the first Mengelberg album to be released, on Holland's Artone records, a pop label which was staunch for improvised music in the mid-'60s. The band recorded many takes, spent their day in the studio tinkering with different approaches.

It's a step beyond the '64 radio date; Peacock is a better bassist than Langereis (who according to de Ruyter's liner notes had little jazz experience), but the band is better integrated, maneuvers better over varied terrain. The music's obviously in transition. Opening "Journey" Han adopts the loose-limbed time of Elvin Jones; that and Piet's modal planing belie the influence of one of Misha's least favorite major jazz figures, Coltrane. "Driekusman" is reprised, a little faster, and the Monk strain is still clear in "Peer's Counting Song," a slow Misha tune recalling "Reflections" (but based on a march from *Peer Gynt*) albeit with a hiccup; the A section is 9 bars, A1 9½. On the appropriately blues-drenched swinger "To John Hodjazz," Piet's slinky, but the rhythm section's brisk interplay is in Monk's pocket.

With "Samba Zombie" for trio Mengelberg makes rare reference to his boogie-woogie origins; the time is straight-eight; smashing chords get the spirit of the root music, Monk's and his. There is a hint of Brazilian accent in Han's playing, but no cookie-cutter bossa-nova; before the master take he'd switched to a Tunisian clay drum, crisp, dry sound, desert-baked not jungle-steamed.

Misha sprung "Auntie Watch Your Step" on the band at the session: a couple of themes, mostly open solos, plenty of elbow room for Han. Overall the variety and formal quirks give a sense of bebop dissolving rather than evolving.

By now Noordijk is less caught up in Dolphyisms, but retains some of the sputtery attack, along with his flailing hardbop and pure Parker phrases. John Zorn once told Han Bennink that Noordijk is his idol as alto player—Zorn's 1987 program of vintage Mengelberg numbers (like "Hodjazz," which he recorded as "Number One") speaks for his familiarity with the material—and the resemblance is sometimes striking. Zorn's sputters are Dolphy thirdhand.

The Artone record is called *The Misja Mengelberg Quartet as heard at the Newport Jazz Festival 1966*. (His first name got the same variant spelling on *Last Date*.)

That July Han made his second trip to the U.S., and Misha his first, when the quartet with Noordijk and Langereis got booked at Newport. They flew to New York and drove to Rhode Island. The New York correspondent for the fine new Dutch magazine *Jazzwereld* (no relation to the prewar magazine) also turned up, said the few folks on hand to listen were attentive. (The quartet played early Sunday afternoon, before the main program.) She informally polled a few listeners for reactions: nice to hear Europeans who get away from bebop; not enough tension; maybe they should try New York awhile. The quartet might have increased the tension if Han had announced the tune title "Paper Tiger," as he wanted to. Piet nixed that.

Misha filed his own festival report for *Jazzwereld*. He was unmoved by what he called Coltrane's snake-charmer music—Misha blames him for popularizing one-chord jams—and liked Bill Dixon even less, but dug Charles Lloyd's pianist for his collage-like choruses, mix of clusters, bop and rumba riffs, and his hands-on work under the hood: Keith Jarrett.

Han: "We played very early, not many people were there, and George Wein didn't want to pay us. That made Piet Noordijk, who was very money-conscious, furious. But then, it turned out that people liked it, and we got a good review, and George Wein said, 'Will you guys play another night?' Piet said, 'Of course we'd like to play a second night, how much are you paying?' And that was absolutely wrong. So we didn't play a second time.

"We went to George Wein's party, at one of the gorgeous houses there in Newport, and I saw Archie Shepp playing piano, jamming with Gerry Mulligan on saxophone. My whole view of things changed in a second. I thought, 'It's about fucking music. Everybody's playing together.' Black and white, everybody playing with each other; that was very nice."

Same party, Misha was struck negatively by how rich white folks had black servants.

On the way home they laid over in New York, sat in on a Jaki Byard gig in the Village. Out of the blue Misha called Herbie Nichols's friend Roswell Rudd to enquire about the whereabouts of the pianist's grave, but Rudd hadn't been invited to the cemetery and didn't know the answer. They didn't meet till years later.

Newport parties aside, Shepp-Mulligan jams were rare; back then mainstreamers and new-thingers were at loggerheads. Holland, same way. And yet Bennink increased his cross-genre activities. In 1967, he recorded LPs with Marion Brown, with Willem Breuker, and with the long-running Stork Town Dixie Kids, though there's little to betray his identity. Han stayed with them about a year.

"Piet Noordijk was also in the Stork Town Dixie Kids, and we played much too mainstream sometimes for the dixieland cats. I like well-played dixieland very much. But I was too loud and still too modern, I can see that now. But they always asked me, because I was a swinging and steady drummer, and not a drunkie, and came precisely on time. They could depend on me."

—Did it seem odd you could move back and forth in this way other people didn't?

"Maybe a bit. But I never really thought like that. It was completely natural for me. But when I tried to play pop music at that time, I was not able to do that."

—Did you get flak from people on either side?

"All the time, from both sides, over and over.

"Once I played a very nice set with Ben Webster, and then I had a duo with Misha during the intermission, and then a set with Ben again. For my set with Misha I would use a completely different drum kit then, and we took the music far out, too far for Ben. Ben was drunk for the second set, as usual unfortunately, and I got into an argument with him, and he really wanted to beat me up. Anyway we played a great second set and he was kissing me afterwards. No problems." Ben was living in Amsterdam then. Han told him he heard a connection between his tenor playing and Albert Ayler's but Webster wasn't buying it.

In '67 Bennink and Ruud Jacobs did a few Dutch dates with Sonny Rollins. Sonny modulated through various keys a lot, prompting the bassist to lay out, so it became a de facto duo. There was a broadcast, but no bootleg or legit album ever surfaced.

—Does your duo with J. R. Monterose give an idea of how you sounded with Rollins?

"Yeah in a way it does, to me. I always had a good time with J.R. I also played with J.R. and René Thomas quite a lot, they also went together like this." He meshes his fingers. "Sometimes we played with Ruud Jacobs, and we did a couple of gigs with other players, but he liked to be open, completely, not dependent on the bass player, just drums."

Zooming ahead a bit: in 1969 American tenor J. R. Monterose made a record at Paradiso, locus of A'dam counterculture, psychedelic cannabis club in an old church in the Leidseplein theater district; the LP was put out by the guy who ran weekly jazz concerts there, gruff fast-talking new-car salesman from Amsterdam West named Hans Dulfer, who then lived a few miles upriver from Han, and who the Benninks saw a lot of: daughters Candy Dulfer and Femke Bennink are the same age.

Part of the album *J. R. Monterose Is Alive in Amsterdam (Paradiso)* is a duo ramble for tenor saxophone and drums, through "Sonnymoon for Two" and "Giant Steps." It's a perfect example of Bennink stoking a soloist, changing up his phrases to deflect his partner from his patterns, constant accents inspiring a constant volley of ideas—high stakes, high energy. This is great jazz drumming by any standard. Except maybe that it's too loud.

Back to 1966: Misha was a judge at a jazz concours in the Hague, where he didn't much like one finalist, heavy on the Ayler tenor—Hans Dulfer—but was impressed by a kid of 18 he'd been hearing about, Willem Breuker. "Of course I wanted to give Willem first prize, but the other people on the jury said, 'He doesn't play jazz music.' I said, 'Well, that's the last of my concerns, if he plays jazz music. But he improvises, and does his thing, and I think that is more interesting than anything you can say about the competition.'"

As Misha tells it, they started playing together almost immediately. They would be associated for the next seven years, during which time they barely recorded together, and mostly drove each other nuts.

Chapter Two
City Kids

"The big thing about Charles Ives's music is, those clashing orchestras came from real life. If it happens in real life, why not in art? Ives 'steps in and out of art.' Sometimes it's just chaos, then he steps back into the form. That's what interests me about American art, music, literature: to let the chaos in, but try to operate in the field between chaos and order. It's what makes American art fresh and exciting."

DUTCH AUTHOR J. BERNLEF

"Willem Breuker showing up was one of the first signs that things were going to change in the Dutch scene."

MISHA MENGELBERG

Soon as the topic of Dutch improvised music's homegrown roots comes up, the talk turns to Amsterdam street culture, public music. The center—the old canal-ring city, the easy walk from Central Station—is where ambient sound gets dense enough to reach critical mass, to become clear music. Carillons chime out belodies old and new. So many churches: steeples peak the low skyline. In the fall of '95, one church on the west side rang out Ellington's "Come Sunday," including the bridge. It's a bell town: trams clangalang, instantly recognizable, when inching into traffic.

Saturday, every shopping street and outdoor market, you see the little trailer with the steam-driven doohickey on it wheeled slowly along, barrel organ wheezing calliope melodies accompanied by the rack rack rack of the guy shaking his change cup, in case you've forgotten what brings him out. The church-bell and barrel-organ spiel is a writers' favorite outside Holland (look at any 750-word newspaper piece on Breuker) and within.

"The son of a market stall-holder, he would prick up his ears as a child at the booming cries of the Jewish onion vender: 'Onions in wine-vinegar; cucumbers, only one cent!'" This is Erik Voermans writing in the English language/Dutch music magazine *Key Notes*, about saxophonist and composer Theo Loevendie. "In these same days he was also captivated by the polyrhythmic structures he heard daily in the tolling church

26

bells of his Kinkerbuurt neighborhood in Amsterdam. Another early musical impression was the driving rhythms of the drums and bugle bands he heard in the streets and, particularly, the physical sensation of their pounding drums. The story goes that the young Theo was so captivated by their din that he would often follow them through the streets and later have to be retrieved from some other part of the city by his worried mother."

Loevendie, born in Amsterdam 17 September 1930, started writing music at eight, after a school teacher took him to some Bach organ recitals. He wrote little pieces for his classmates to play on toy xylophones, and "inverted" children's songs by having the kids play the xylophones turned backward.

"I think I was about 16 or 17 when" — his cat jumps on the keys of his piano, twice, a thin repeated treble cluster, distracting him — "I started to feel attracted to jazz. Friends in school played boogie-woogies and I tried to play them on the piano with another guy. I didn't play very well, but that's what people do when they're 16 or 17. Boogie-woogie was one of those things that appeared just after the War. During the War, there was nothing. Of course you had guys older than I was who listened to records in secret, but I had no contact with that."

He got a guitar, learned a few chords, strummed rhythm. "I remember at 16 another guy who played guitar said, 'Let's go to a jazz club, the IJsbreker on the Amstel.' There I saw a dixieland band for the first time in my life. I was 16, maybe 17. I saw Mike de Ruyter play in that band. I found the atmosphere fantastic, something completely new to me.

"At 17 I didn't know what to do, so I went to the PTT, the post office, and there I had training in Morse code. I don't think I ever really used it, but a year or two later I went into military service, and again had training as a telegrapher. In my composed music, very often you'll find tone repetition" — he sings one note, in a lively rhythm that sounds a little Morse and a little Turkish — "which must have to do with that."

He joined the post office harmonie — a sort of brass band including reeds — and was given a clarinet. "Immediately I tried to improvise on it, while my friend played guitar. Now because I was playing clarinet I listened to the Benny Goodman trio with Teddy Wilson. I was fascinated by that. And for some reason I knew Ellington, which I suppose you couldn't hear every day.

"Then from the radio programs of Mike de Ruyter or Pete Felleman I discovered Dizzy Gillespie, Charlie Parker, Howard McGhee, Miles Davis, Thelonious Monk and so on. That was really a revolution to me." It would have been Felleman. He'd made friends with transoceanic travelers — KLM employees, merchant sailors, American GIs — and got them to bring the latest records back from the States. "This must have been '48, '49, the beginning of bebop. So we followed it pretty close, but back in '45 we hadn't known anything about it.

"My alter ego in jazz, you might say, was Nedly Elstak. My first professional things were with him. Sometimes he played in my group, or I in his, or we didn't know whose group it was. We had a quintet and found a cafe — the Cafe de Looier, still there under that name — on the Looiersgracht where we played every night. I played clarinet at first, and as soon as I had the money bought an alto. Because there was some talk about it in the newspapers, customers came. Some of them were artists themselves —

writers, painters, poets like Remco Campert—but we didn't know those people then."
J. Bernlef remembers coming up from Utrecht once a week to hear them at
Sheherazade, a little later.

Trumpeter Elstak, one year younger than Theo, was born in Semarang, Central
Java, but his parents were from Surinam. They moved to Holland when he was five.
At eight he began studying violin, later taking up trumpet on the side, and was active
in Surinamese dance bands at the Palace on the Thorbeckeplein.

Nedly Elstak died in 1989; he was a character even by local standards, and in the
local mold: given to drink, to gambling, to excess (and rash pronouncements: some
folks say Teddy Cotton wasn't much of a trumpet player, that if he was, he would have
crossed over to jazz bands as Nedly did). In 1968 he recorded an LP for ESP, *The
Machine*, quartet with Martin van Duynhoven on drums, Maarten Altena on bass, and
singer Sophie van Lier. Everyone remembers him as a gentle, likable soul, but he and
Loevendie must have been a strange match.

At 65 Loevendie is thin, fringe of white hair close-cropped, has a natty goatee; he's
almost bubbly. He is also an idealist. He named an album for Nelson Mandela long
before most people ever heard of him. He once said composers might benefit from
spending a year working on a farm in Bangladesh or Kenya. Talking to him, you can
see how someone like Misha or party-guy Nedly might find him a little square. Can't
picture Misha hauling water from the well, ear cocked to a rice-grower's rhythm song.

In 1954 Loevendie and Elstak went to Turkey to play at a NATO base with an international dance band: two Turks, two Greeks, an Italian, and an English-German black
guy. On the boat back Theo met a Turkish student on her way to school in
Switzerland; she moved to Amsterdam and married him instead. Loevendie learned
the Turkish language, got into the culture.

"The first experiments I did were with modal improvisation. It was very different
from what was happening in the mid–1950s, because in Holland then the prevailing
idiom was West Coast–oriented. What we did was in a sense less civilized and a little
wilder than was common here, before the revolution.

"I think in our playing, there was a kind of—well I hate the word but maybe the
best way to describe it is the feeling of avant-garde. Of course we were still following
developments in the States, but there was something nonconformist about what we
did. Our idols were Diz and Bird and Miles and those guys, and Tadd Dameron as an
arranger. And Monk, whom Dutch musicians didn't talk about then. We played pieces
by all those guys, but maybe I was the first who played at least half original material.
That was an important element. But some of my pieces must have resembled Charlie
Parker compositions, that's for sure.

"The reason I started to play soprano had nothing to do with Coltrane, but with
Lucky Thompson, who I think I'd heard before Coltrane. I absorbed a lot of Turkish
influence into my soprano. Like the zurna playing"—a double reed—"and those
recorder-like small flutes. And the fast ornamental notes I use a lot of when I improvise.

"I entered the Amsterdam conservatory very late. I was 25 already, and my experience was as a jazz musician, so it was a completely new world for me. I absorbed everything that I could get hold of, as far as contemporary music was concerned. I remember the director said to me, 'You cannot play jazz; that's forbidden.' I explained, 'I have

a family, I have a child,' so he said okay. Later on many of my fellow students said, 'It was very strange that you played jazz at that time; we talked about it.'

"I finished clarinet in about three years and composition and theory in five. When my studies were finished, I could have tried to make a kind of career as a composer of contemporary music, but I didn't feel any affinity with what was happening." Serialism was never for him. "Stravinsky and Bartok were no problem, from the first moment they were so close to me. That's not so strange since I concentrate on rhythm. When you think of rhythm, Schoenberg is not really the most interesting composer that you can imagine. Webern either. I don't mean to sound superior, but it wasn't for me. So I just continued with my jazz group."

In the early '60s or maybe late '50s, he and Nedly had Misha on piano for a minute, but only a minute. (Misha tells of helping Elstak get admitted into a hospital, to dry out, while they were working in Germany.) There was a quintet with the young Maarten Altena on bass, and Loevendie remembers a motley seven-piece group with Misha, Toon van Vliet, Arend Nijenhuis, and Surinamese trumpeter Ado Broodboom from the Ramblers—a mix of ages, styles, cliques.

"Eric Dolphy impressed me a lot. To me, what he did was an extension of Charlie Parker. That was the difference between him and Ornette Coleman, who broke with that. Dolphy rehearsed with Boy's Big Band not so long before he died. I was very impressed when he played with us, because it was a step beyond what I knew from records."

Boy Edgar, born 1915 in Amsterdam, had worked as trumpeter and arranger for numerous bands since the mid–1930s, had jammed with Hawkins and Benny Carter. Edgar was leading the Moochers in 1941 when the Kultuurkamer shut them down. After the War he had played with Kid Dynamite among others, in and out of Holland. He became a doctor in 1955: a neurologist who ended his days as a general practitioner in suburban Bijlmer.

At the end of 1960, a bunch of horn players and the rhythm section of the Diamond Five—Cees Slinger, Jacques Schols, Johnny Engels—came together as a one-shot big band for a Concertgebouw concert by Dutch jazzers including pianist Louis van Dijk. Arranger Edgar wasn't playing on the gig so they got him to conduct. Someone at VARA radio liked it enough to sign them on for monthly broadcasts which ultimately ran for a couple of years.

Edgar slid into the role of leader, although he was not so well organized. A lot of arrangements never got written down, which was no problem until someone new came in. Part of his freewheeling approach was to set up backing riffs and cue section punches on the fly—what Butch Morris later dubbed "conduction." He once apologized to guest Ben Webster for the chaos. Don't worry, Ben said, I went through this for years with Ellington. That would not have prompted him to change; Ellington was Boy's man.

Boy's Big Band was notable for his early attempt to bridge the chasm between Hilversum and the liberals—he had Toon van Vliet, studio regular Herman Schoonderwalt, and Loevendie among as many as seven saxophones, and Ramblers vets Broodboom and Marcel Thielemans in the brass.

The orchestra played with a few visiting American soloists, Johnny Griffin, Abbey Lincoln, and Nina Simone among them. And Dolphy, of course, that good-will ambassador for new music. Boy, Theo, and valve trombonist Cees Smal were the arrangers. The band recorded two albums for Artone, *Now's the Time!* in 1965, and *Finch Eye* in '66.

The former especially demonstrates how well Dutch studio musicians and other boppers could play at that time; there are no rhythm or dialect problems. Edgar's arrangements are self-effacing in the best sense, serving mainly to set up soloists, conspicuously Noordijk and the big-toned and bluesy Diamond Five tenorist Harry Verbeke. Even on "Solitude" Edgar resists Ellingtonian gestures, opting for brash, fat harmonies from melded sections. Noordijk on alto shows the side that caught Misha Mengelberg—swooping notes that owe little to Hodges or Parker—as he carves shapely swinging variations, garish excess just held in check. On the same tune Loevendie's solo on wide-open-toned soprano makes his case against Coltrane's influence (although his playing on Edgar's arrangement of "Blues Minor" from *Africa/Brass* undercuts his claim).

Swing is paramount. Boy's punchiest charts smartly call attention to drummer Engels, who kicks the band with bombs, snare chatter, and ride cymbals not unlike his friend Bennink. (Engels was still swinging hard in the mid-'90s; pointedly perhaps, he never does anything for visual effect.) The drummer's showcase is "Competitive Challenge," several versions and titles earlier, in '64, a concert vehicle for the band and guests Mengelberg, Ruud Jacobs, and Bennink.

By *Finch Eye* Loevendie was doing more of the writing. His pieces were more ambitious—sectional cross-talk, some of the simpler odd meters—but also dowdier or more bombastic. Boy kept writing the bluesy swingers, and invited young sensation Willem Breuker for one number, "2128," Edgar's reworking of Breuker's piece "28." The catchy Ellingtonian blues theme is certainly the leader's; the planar, abstract open section features Willem on fluttery bass clarinet, and future new-ager Chris Hinze on flute.

The idea of building bridges between musicians of different camps by throwing them together in one band would pay off well in Holland. Not this time though. Weeks after *Finch Eye* was taped, Boy went to America to guest-lecture at medical schools—he'd teach in the States several years—leaving Loevendie in charge. Theo had some new ideas he wanted to try, like using three drummers: Engels, Martin van Duynhoven and Han. Smal and Schoonderwalt in particular didn't like the new direction, started their own Hilversum-based Hobby Orchestra on the side, so-called because its members had real jobs in radio, and rehearsed at night for fun. So now there were two sort of rival bands with some of the same players. Tension did not abate. Noordijk balked at a Loevendie piece written for the 1967 Holland Festival, the annual June music bash. It was too much for the interim leader. With Boy's acquiescence, Theo pulled the plug. (Edgar reconsidered when he finally came home, revived the band as Boy Edgar's Sound, went on to make three more records in the '70s, including an Ellington memorial program.)

Loevendie spun off his band the Consort from here, using some of Boy's more receptive men. He tried using the three drummers there too, for a little while. But that was in the late '60s, a few years ahead.

♫

"Nedly once said to me, 'One day I'd love to have a music school.' I wasn't that fond of that idea, but. . . . The man in charge at the F.A.M.O.S., a kind of YMCA-type thing, asked me to do a workshop. It must not have been about money because I was teaching already, at the music school in Haarlem. (I taught clarinet in Haarlem, and then I replaced a teacher in the post office music school, where I gave Willem Breuker one or two clarinet lessons.)

"Willem van Manen, Arjen Gorter and Peter Bennink were members of or students at the Workshop, in the first year." Peter is Han's younger brother, a saxophonist. This is 1965. "I remember that Arjen was still in school, and about 16 or so, and played guitar. If I remember well, I did it for two years, and in the second year he played the bass. He didn't play the guitar very well, technically—some guys were much better—but I was very aware of his talent."

—The students paid only two guilders a lesson. Why'd you do it?

"Because there was nothing, there were so few musicians you could play with. I remember also that in that period I was not only dealing with chord changes, but with modal things, and a more free approach. But the things that are academic or traditional are always the easiest to teach. Now I realize that I was already interested in developing new things."

March 1967, the Theo Loevendie Three recorded *Stairs!*, one of the first albums of the new jazz from Holland. It's not on the same path as Mengelberg's quartet, but it's further into the woods. Blowing on modes and nasal soprano keening: nothing so new there; nor in the soloist deciding when to proceed from one section of a piece to the next; nor even in the Dolphian (as in "God Bless the Child") salutations and flag-waving in "Darn That Dream" for bass clarinet, an instrument Loevendie flirted with but soon gave up, one horn too many. (He also plays a little composers' piano.) "Lady Penelope," slow as a slow Ornette tune, skirls around a Phrygian melody, close to the first line of "When I Fall in Love." The bassist gives it a contemporary edge; he favored a snarling arco and flailing pizz reminiscent of Gary Peacock: Maarten van Regteren Altena, late of the conservatory, and now first-call bassist for all the weird gigs.

But what distinguishes the music is the Turkish rhythm patterns from drummer Engels, tart Morse-y tattoos: telegraphing—not talking—drums, as if paid for by the word, strong contrast to the polynoodle percussion sections on certain period works of, say, Pharoah Sanders or Hans Dulfer. Here is an early demonstration of the Dutch tendency to stamp one's music with a clear overarching idea that separates your music from everyone else's. Concentrating on rhythm over harmony, Loevendie addresses another order of organization.

His rhythms were additive not divisive: not the closed-circuit clockface but an unwinding spiral, the watchspring sprung.

Like many of the classic Dutch texts, *Stairs!* is out of print and scarce, and scarcely remembered. It won Holland's Edison Prize, so it wasn't overlooked on its release, but was eclipsed by the phenomenon of the moment, Willem Breuker.

♫

"In 1966, we went to the Loosdrecht concours and nobody was prepared for the things I did. It became a big scandal, I had big arguments, my face was on the front of the papers, I was the enfant terrible of Holland and music. Finally they found somebody they could beat up on. For my whole 23-piece band we were paid—inclusive, radio and television recording, transportation—20 guilders altogether. You couldn't even buy all the musicians a beer. So I thought, 'Next year, I won't go back.'

"But I did decide to go back and do a medley of the most famous tunes by the pretty well-known singer and concours organizer Max van Praag. I'd thought he wasn't a bad singer, but he couldn't understand what I was doing, started fighting me. So I came back, played his songs completely wrong on a two-guilder plastic flute, sang the wrong tune, made up my own words. I had a guy who couldn't play the bass, and Kees Hazevoet on piano, and Arjen Gorter playing guitar. The audience was laughing like hell. The jury was sitting there with their hands up to their eyes, 'How can a guy with a future like his do this?' It became a new scandal. 'You can't do that, it's in such bad taste.' I said, 'That's exactly what I want to prove: my bad taste. We must have more bad taste in music. You'll never get anywhere in the world with your nice taste. You think you know what art is? I'll find my own art.'"

—As if you're daring them to try and stop you.

"Yeah."

—There's a lot of anger in that.

"Yeah. I always had it in me. But there's also a special type of, maybe you could call it humor, or way of looking at life: laughing at the many things nobody can see anything funny in. Not everybody can go on stage and do a thing like that. Other people write it down or whatever, I go on stage. That also speaks to my interest in theater: How far can you go on stage? Where's the line between good and bad taste? Do you fall to the left or the right of that line?"

Willem Breuker grew up in Amsterdam East. His parents had met in a socialist choir. He was born into and in a middle-class home on 4 November 1944, just in time for the horrible last winter of the War.

"When I was born there was no food for me. Which gives you some idea about the hate some people still have for the Germans. When my brother travels he still doesn't want to go through Germany. I don't have that hate, because when I started playing in the mid-'60s I met all these German guys.

"A marching band with little flutes and percussion rehearsed in a hall across the street. And once a week a barrel organ came down the street, as did the fish man; he had a kind of yell, you didn't know what he was saying but it was a very special musical influence for me. And there were neighbors who were always having arguments, screaming at each other. This was also music for me.

On the Zeeburgerdijk we lived on the third floor, and you could see a long way up the street in either direction. When there was a fire in my neighborhood I could see and hear the fire brigade coming. It was fantastic to hear all these sounds mixed up: the fire bell, the ambulance, the fish man, whatever. It made my blood move faster."

He heard jazz on the radio when he was ten or so, remembers hearing Piet Noordijk. Around then he started taking music lessons, singing and recorder before clarinet. The story he'd tell later is, he'd read the notes till it was time to turn the page, then keep improvising in the same style. One day the teacher put on the wrong side of a record by mistake, and Willem heard Bartok's *Music for Strings, Percussion and Celesta.* He bought it soon after with his paper-route money; it was one of his first records.

"I bought a little record player. My parents said, 'Don't play that music so often when we are at home, because we can't stand it so much.' I was listening to the string quartets of Schoenberg and Bartok, but also Count Basie. I was very well-informed about many things. I like all types of music, never got fixed on one thing, but I didn't like rock and roll that much, and in that sense I didn't have too much connection with the other children in school. So I was a little bit alone. On the other hand, I had a very big mouth, and the teacher always set me apart from other pupils, because I demanded so much attention."

One night on the radio he heard Ives's *Three Places in New England.* "I was really knocked out, because I knew music like this had to exist somewhere, but where? Unbelievable."

—The second movement especially, with the clashing orchestras?

"The third movement, where he builds up and then goes back to nothing: 'The Housatonic at Stockbridge.' The whole thing is a masterpiece. And I was very much interested in the Dutch avant-garde music; whatever happened in Holland was very important to the musical environment.

"And then you got the movement—Ornette Coleman, Cecil Taylor.

"When I was 15, 16 years old, I saw an announcement that they needed a bass clarinet player in a harmonie in Tuindorp-Oostzaan, across the harbor. They had a bass clarinet I could play. Fantastic. You could take it with you so you could practice, but I never did, I played for myself. On holidays, you get to go out with the band, to walk in the streets in your uniform, but the bass clarinet is hard to carry, so they gave me a tenor saxophone, great. My first tenor.

"They threw me out when I played at the Loosdrecht jazz festival, and they saw me on television. It was on a Sunday night. Monday night, three guys from the orchestra came to my house—I was still living with my parents at that time, we'd moved next door, to Zeeburgerdijk 80—and took back the instrument. It was a big scandal.

"Later on, when the Stedelijk Museum had a celebration, I organized the music, and invited them to come over and play the Charles Ives ideas: two harmonie orchestras, walking around clockwise and counterclockwise, playing different music. Fantastic. They didn't have the slightest idea what it was about. But now they are so proud of me. Nobody talks anymore about what happened that night.

"I wanted to go the conservatory in Amsterdam, but they said to me, 'Go away, you have no talent for music.' So then I decided, 'Okay, if there's no future for me the way they want to make music, then I will become a schoolteacher.' I went to night school for a year, but at that point I was already becoming a professional musician."

He was composing from 1960—a piece a year for wind trios, often clarinets. He mixed genres early; Breuker's four compositions from '63 include an adagio for trumpet, piano, bass, and drums, and "seven epigrams" for solo bass. Also "Composition No. 7 in Black and Gray."

"At that time I gave each piece a title, a number, and a color, or a double color. I was also very much interested in painting, theater, whatever. I was just finding out what's happening in this world. I felt some connection with Paul Klee, Kokoschka, maybe the brutal Karel Appel; I had to find my own thing, and sometimes other disciplines help a lot. Literature is also important because it reveals the mentality of people, how they think about what's happening in the world.

"I was also interested in people's daily lives, how mad they are. Take normal radio tunes: I liked the originality of certain pop music, like songs from the Jordaan." That's an Amsterdam neighborhood with more than its share of singalong bars, the karaoke of the '50s. "Nothing to do with jazz or improvisation or art, or good taste. In the songs of the very famous singer, Johnny Jordaan, there was an underlying humor I liked very much. Later he went to Belgium because he owed so much in taxes, he'd spent all his money. I thought, 'This is very interesting.' Because you always think people who know how to do one thing know how to deal with the other aspects of life, but they don't. I was always taught how to spend and save your money, how to be a normal human being, a good citizen. That was my home education."

Breuker began playing at the jazz concourses—Amsterdam, the Hague, Loosdrecht—and came to the attention of judges Loevendie and Mengelberg. "Most of the time I won first prize as soloist, although the guys I was playing with were nothing. They heard something in my playing that suggested future potential, a little talent. I was always playing my own compositions, not copying anyone. I didn't want to play bebop or postbebop."

He always had an ear out for musicians he could play with; he'd collar people at a concours, invite them to rehearse. His friend the photographer Pieter Boersma brought his cello, and his brother-in-law, a classical bassoonist. A ballet-orchestra french hornist, Jan Wolff, started hanging around—Willem now living in the garden apartment under his parents—and brought in trumpeter Eddie Engels, who had studied with Wolff's father. Willem ran jam sessions at a local church hall; one night Arjen Gorter came in, asked if he could play, came back an hour later dragging electric guitar and amp.

Breuker started going to Arnhem, in the east, to improvise with drummer Pierre Courbois, who'd been playing his own rambunctious (but not yet recorded) music with a band called Original Dutch Free Jazz Group, from 1961. Courbois introduced Breuker to German vibraphonist/bass clarinetist/multi-instrumentalist Gunter Hampel. Hampel always stood a bit apart from the German free-jazz mainstream, but he was fond of Dutch talent. Except for Hampel the band that recorded ESP 1042, *Assemblage/New Music from Europe* in December '66 was all Dutch: Breuker, Courbois, Piet Hein Veening on bass. Breuker played soprano, alto, tenor, clarinet and Hampel's borrowed bass clarinet, which he used whenever possible until he could buy his own.

Breuker always had lots of energy, but it wasn't Han Bennink's childlike exuberance. He had a sinister quality that comes across in photographs: the scrawny kid of 22 with the nerd's glasses and a serial killer's dead-behind-the-baby-blues glare. You can see the chip on his shoulder.

By the summer of 1966 Amsterdam had become an early outpost for youth revolt. The police had begun clamping down on activities of the Provo (as in -cateur) movement. A construction worker died (of a heart attack, it turned out) at a heavily policed demonstration on 13 June. Riots broke out the next day.

At Loosdrecht, within weeks, Breuker presented *Litany for the 14th of June, 1966*, for 23 musicians. He came in second. "When I wrote the piece for orchestra, singers, dancers, all that shit about the fighting in Amsterdam, that was the first time anybody put politics or movements in the streets into music. That was very strange for a jazz musician, who is very apolitical, overlooking the black power fist. I had to continue with that."

Overlooking the black power fist—that's a lot of overlooking, of Max Roach's *We Insist! Freedom Now Suite*, and Mingus's "Fables of Faubus," both with acerbic verbal commentary, 1960. Let alone Archie Shepp at Newport '65. But for Holland, *14th of June* was plenty strange. Breuker revised it before a second performance at another festival, and a third time before recording it in September as the title track to his debut album. The vinyl version has a good crazy quilt texture: planned chaos, a reading of newspaper clippings about the riot, opera singing one second, flaky acoustic guitar the next. Also shrieky big-band chords akin to New York's Carla Bley–Michael Mantler Jazz Composers Orchestra. The score: straight notation on some staffs, unflagged black notes on others, or jagged, pointillistic, or scribbly graphic outlines (the piano gets huge blots). Partly that was 'cause many of his musicians couldn't read. But also, like Walt Whitman, he wanted to embrace it all, yoke it all together for synergetic effect.

Breuker's music was Happening as well as happening. In the sunny '60s, the multimedia Happening was an outgrowth of the bourgeoisie-booting (and partly Cage-inspired) Fluxus movement—movement so-called, Fluxus being looser than Unitarianism. Mengelberg's Fluxus connection is often cited, but his involvement was short-lived. The Fluxists were real internationalists. Mengelberg had met founder/ringleader George Maciunas while he was traveling around Europe—he first visited Amsterdam in 1963, a year after some Fluxus works had been exhibited at an Amsterdam gallery—but Misha himself didn't travel, was involved only with Fluxus Holland, whose few concerts included a big one in Scheveningen '64. Also on the bill was the absurdist and writer Wim T. Schippers.

Misha: "I made a piano piece that I performed on Fluxus concerts, which concerns the suicide of a good friend, composer and actor Hans van Sweeden, a very nice flamboyant person. You could say the piece had something to do with the later so-called minimal style, but aside from one gong piece by La Monte Young, I didn't know anything about that. Maybe there was a relation with Cage music, but it had a kind of tonality. It was an endless repetition of possibilities within that tonality. A nonfunctional tonal piece, you could say: leads nowhere, comes from nowhere, starts somewhere but could have started in any other place, and ends when the time is up. I played it for one and a half hours somewhere—too much, I think. Then I played versions of three minutes, too short. I ended up with something between 15 and 20 minutes, the right length."

A six-minute excerpt was released on the soundtrack to a film about van Sweeden. Misha has said it was about the nagging questions a suicide's friends ask. It's an endless cycle in more or less steady time, the only swerves apparently inadvertent. First and third beats of the bar pingpong a tonally ambiguous flat five, midkeyboard.

Sandwiched between, on two and four, splanky treble chords, so compressed their harmonic function is indeterminate, resolution always thwarted. You can't tell which chord is "home." La Monte Monk.

Fluxus had the same appeal as Taoism. It was hard to break the rules. Mengelberg told John Corbett: "Fluxus was nothing. Fluxus was a bunch of idiots who all did their things and saw at a certain point that some other people were working in similar amorphous directions. A little glass jar filled with words: instant poetry, shake well before reading. That's a very good concept, I think. It's amusing. And you can also reflect that in other areas. . . . But you couldn't say that it is a direction poetry could take."

Misha liked many Fluxers including Tomas Schmitt (who'd later do a whimsical cover for ICP 010). "But it was never meant to be something that would be like a flag or something that we all assembled behind. Nothing like that. There was a moment when we met and did some things together, and then we said goodbye and went our own directions." It does echo in his music theater, but that's for later.

Art student Bennink was less enchanted. "I never saw a Happening. I didn't like them. It's either happening or it's not happening."

♫

Willem Breuker started recording in the second half of 1966; the results were scattered over five albums released over the next few years. In September, he plays on Boy Edgar's *Finch Eye*. In December, he's the lone Dutchman in Berlin pianist Alex Schlippenbach's first recorded Globe Unity Orchestra, 14 players including Hampel and tenor saxophonist Peter Brötzmann. With eight horns, two basses, and two drummers (one with orchestral chimes), it makes *Ascension* sound dainty, a sign of things that had come. Schlippenbach had a nice way of marshalling his forces, with scant thematic material that provided an overlay of structure on the free blow, but compared with the inclusive *Litany* it sounds a bit narrow.

Two weeks later, Hampel's ESP date is recorded in Holland. On 27 December, Breuker records some short themes for a documentary about the artist Lucebert. The band was Surinam-born Victor Kaihatu on arco bass, oboist (and later Hague-school composer) Gilius van Bergeijk, and another new acquaintance, Han Bennink. There are echoes of Spanish music: groaning flamenco, swingtime variation on same, a squawky oboe theme over 2/4 martial drums.

In October, Breuker had recorded his aforementioned debut *Contemporary Jazz from Holland/Litany for the 14th of June 1966*. The 17-piece band on the first side had Courbois, cellist Boersma, hornist Wolff, trumpeter Engels, van Bergeijk, concours regular Hans Dulfer, Willem's reeds teacher Ab van der Molen—and Arjen Gorter, who came with an acoustic bass, explaining, I play this now.

The music besides *Litany* is in the same kaleidoscopic vein; operatic vocal with text from a letter from an arty American girl: "Over-stuffed America is belking and blowing her mind up, blinding her own eyes out with a churning tongue"—*belking* how the singer pronounces "belching." Mike de Ruyter's notes say part of "Time Signals and Sound Density Five" is a game, pitched battle between stereo-separated orchestra halves, an Ivesian conceit largely lost on record. Breuker remembers no details.

The other half of the album was for quintet: Courbois on drums, Kaihatu and Dick van der Capellen on basses, Misha on piano, Willem on soprano, alto and baritone saxes, and bass clarinet. He recorded the whole LP on two consecutive days; Mengelberg as usual took his time. Breuker's "Composition 30" could be played on prepared piano; Misha spent half an hour preparing: tinfoil, a gong, cymbals, Coke bottle, all but inaudible.

His playing reflects Cecil Taylor's shakeup, though Mengelberg was never one for lightning-bolt glisses. The way the pieces rest on little motivic constructions is Cecilesque too, but a conscious influence on Breuker the composer is unlikely. Anyway as Willem's composing goes these are baby steps.

"I think Pierre was the first guy who played free in Holland. His band in Arnhem was different from what we did in the west of Holland. Also a guy like Martin van Duynhoven"—another drummer from down east—"had a way of playing a little bit different from normal bebop, more open or whatever. Pierre was one of the first guys who wasn't playing time anymore. That was one reason I had a trio with him and Victor Kaihatu. But when I met Han, it was clear what to do. Han also had had enough of playing time all the time.

"We had known about each other from reading *Jazzwereld*. One day he had an exhibition of his paintings in Amsterdam, and I went over to see them and to say hello. He said, 'I'm gonna play tonight for the opening, if you'd like to join me, bring your horn.' That night we played together, and we couldn't stop. For awhile Han came over to my place every afternoon to jam, when I still lived with my parents.

"I called Misha, said I had the chance to do a recording, went over to the Hague where he was living, showed him my music and ideas, and he said, 'Nice, I'll do the recording with you.' Misha came over to my place one afternoon, brought his music, mostly graphic stuff, and I showed him my notes, and we tried to play. That was the beginning. Very small ideas, maybe just a couple of bars, then you can improvise from that, then we go on to the next phrase, and so on, and maybe combine them. Discover the music.

"I remember a figure of three 8s going all the time, against the beat in 4/4. He liked it, but he couldn't stand it because he always made mistakes. He tried over and over.

"You know Misha's first record? I've heard them play that Herbie Nichols–type music better than that, but that was what they played. When I met Misha and Han, they moved over. I think they asked me to play with them to go completely out of the Monk-Herbie Nichols-bebop-timekeeping music. There were other things going on in that period, and a day comes when you either choose to do it, or you'll never do it.

"With Victor Kaihatu and Pierre, we didn't play time at all. We could make it through the whole night, just playing free. I think Han and Misha were a little bit jealous that we had done it already."

Breuker's right—he was the catalyst, stating the possibilities so strongly they couldn't be ignored.

KLM had comped Mengelberg's quartet to Newport, and decided to back him again, flying Misha and his band to Libya to play a party for airline employees, the same October. For this he brought Han, Willem, and Victor Kaihatu. Breuker: "The KLM idiots were expecting completely other music; it was a disaster." Misha: "I think they were not so interested in the Dutch avant-garde."

Flush with this failure, Misha then tried adding Willem to his established quartet, and immediately the band began tearing in half. Han Bennink: "Rob Langereis couldn't stand Willem. When we played 'Green Dolphin Street,' Willem was not playing the right chords. It sounded like Albert Ayler with the Danish rhythm section. Piet Noordijk was sort of aping Willem, but playing all over the horn, so that was not a good combination."

Misha: "Willem did things I was really more interested in at that time than Piet Noordijk, who tried to play Charlie Parker music. It wasn't bad, but it was also not very inspiring."

—Did Piet try to sound like you Willem?

"I don't know. Piet tried to play like Dolphy. He was very unfriendly, but that was the typical studio musician attitude, 'Okay, fuck you, while I play I look at my watch, and if I play an extra solo I need another hundred guilders.' Typical radio and studio system we have all over the world. It's their profession, but maybe they have an aquarium and would rather play with their fish. The music makes no impression on them anymore."

Noordijk is 12 years older than Breuker. "Piet was 20 years older than me, a very respected musician, and I was just coming from nothing. He always called me Willem Kreukel, that means . . . "—he grabs a sheet of paper and crinkles it. "He was never able to make a living out of what he was famous for; he was sitting in the radio orchestra and playing in bands and doing a little film music, whatever he could get. Not making a fist for the music."

The conceptual dysfunction—bebop and the new thing trying to stand side by side—was like the situation in the SOSA-Band, only much worse. The quintet lasted only a few gigs. Toward year's end Misha was awarded the Wessel Ilcken Prize; at the presentation he passed out baby firecrackers to the audience, like the ones thrown about on stage during performances of that Newport piece "Paper Tiger," now redubbed "Vietcong." It was their unrecorded hit, got them some notoriety gigs.

It was more than enough for Rob and for Piet, who split, making no secret of their displeasure, and taking the band's bebop fans with them.

The Mengelberg Quartet kept going with Maarten Altena on bass. They played a couple of European festivals in 1967. Han drove his new car, weighted with bass and percussion, 23 hours straight to the Juan-les-Pins festival in Antibes on the French Riviera. He was so dazed he banged the car up. The band was bummed when the first person to congratulate them after their set was Dave Brubeck.

Maarten Altena: "Misha has always had this pubescent attitude, he likes to provoke people, and Willem was a perfect vehicle for that. Piet Noordijk had this beautiful alto sound, kind of an undercivilized Phil Woods, and from that Misha went to Breuker with his blurps and things, and his ability to camouflage his lack of knowledge of chord progressions, by doing crazy things coming from another world.

"In the beginning there was always this 4/4 or whatever in the bass, this objective rhythmic underlayer, as in jazz music. But there were free parts in there, because Willem brought his things with him. So there was this jazz-layer thing, and what I would now call insults and arguments against it. Misha would call it dialectics."

As they drifted further left, however, the bassist's own role eroded; of what use is the instrument supplying the harmonic undergirding if harmony is sliding away?

Bennink: "Maarten Altena left because Misha was not interested in playing time at that particular moment, after the quartet with Piet Noordijk. So we carried on as a trio, Willem, Misha and myself." That did not work so smoothly either.

🎵

It was almost guaranteed not to. Han and Willem are men of action; Misha is the contemplative man. Couch-potato laziness is a big part of his schtick; he's the guy who keeps his father's hours, is always late, who'd said (in '71) that three gigs a month is plenty to keep you in shape. One thing he contemplated was what he'd come to think of as the death of jazz, around 1960. Here is Misha the van Baaren pupil: for Kees, the end of the harmonic tradition in European art music came when all the possibilities had been touched on, and the rules had become fixed. For Misha, something very like it had happened to jazz. The music had run through its harmonic possibilities fast, growing ever more complex in the bebop period till harmony broke wide-open, in flat modal blowing, or early Ornette's tune-by-tune reshuffling of triadic progressions, or aharmonic free jazz. Beyond all this, reasoned Misha, must be some other music. "It was obvious that when we would do something, it would be something related to European tradition more than jazz."

The world was changing; jazz was being torn down, and so were parts of the old city, a trend that grew critical by the 1970s. Amsterdam neighborhoods would be leveled to make way for roads leading to the new harbor tunnel, and a new opera house where the main Jewish neighborhood had been before the War, and a subway line, which is a weird thing to build if your city is criss-crossed with canals and below sea level to boot. The protests and street skirmishes to come were partly a fight over preservation, and about who the city really belonged to, the people or corporate money. That battle is still being fought.

At the Concertgebouw, however, not much had changed. The Orchestra remained committed to old music, even if the Italian new-music champ Bruno Maderna had successfully guest-conducted.

In 1966 five drinking buddies and ex–van Baaren students banded together in hopes of changing that a little: Andriessen, Mengelberg, Peter Schat, Jan van Vlijmen, and the slightly younger Reinbert de Leeuw. Maderna, who had shown an interest in their music (and van Baaren's, and Earle Brown's, and improvisation), was coming to Amsterdam in June to conduct Schat's theatrical *Labyrinth* at the Holland Festival — the riots Breuker would memorialize interrupted a rehearsal. The five mounted a campaign in the press to get Maderna appointed the Orchestra's permanent second conductor, with programming input. Management was unamused, Maderna ambivalent about such advocacy, and for now nothing came of it except increased rancor on both sides.

The Notenkrakers, as the five came to call themselves—pun: *Notekraker* = Nutcracker, but *noten* means musical notes—kept their campaign simple, uncluttered by side issues. However some of the same folks also became involved in lobbying for better money for commissioned compositions. Misha remembered his father writing a concerto for horn and orchestra for something like 400 guilders. Most composers supported themselves by teaching, reviewing for a newspaper or whatever.

Mengelberg wrote a souvenir wind quintet accompanied by dadaist slide show, *Omtrent een componistenactie* (Concerning a composers' campaign). Part of it is elegant chamber writing with a light touch, and part is heavy lifting, borrowings from quintets by Schat among others. The nub of *Omtrent* is speech rhythms set to music, a denatured mock transcription of several committee meetings in which composers and/or culture ministers discuss commission fees. Kabuki-like, certain specific sounds symbolized specific events: a telephone call has its own musical signature.

As far as the horn talk goes, the Mingus-Dolphy dialogues had far more colloquial zip. On that score *Omtrent* suggests how little Misha then thought of such jazz sources when composing his chamber music.

Still, he did consider some parallels. In improvising all the same musical smarts came into play as in composing, but with even less prestige. So: if improvisers were low-ranked because they just made it up as they went along, a conceptual shift was needed. Misha began referring to improvising as "instant composing," by analogy with "instant coffee"—something he would never drink, he notes. He didn't know it, but guitarist Jim Hall had used the same term for the same idea in the notes to Jimmy Giuffre's clarinet and strings suite *Mobiles* in 1958.

While Misha thought, Han and Willem did. The drummer kept doing his zillion disparate gigs; Willem was writing, doing film scores, playing with all sorts of people at home, and with Hampel and the other Germans on the road. Breuker, Bennink and Altena had a trio, and the first two also had the New Acoustic Swing Duo. They'd played a bunch of gigs, it was happening, they felt it should be documented.

"So Han and I did the duo record, and—well to be quite honest, at that period, we didn't like to play so much with Misha. He made too many restrictions on the things we did. He had a commentary on everything, was the so-called intelligent guy who knew exactly what the future would be. But we just wanted to play, not look over every note ten times, 'Is it a good note? No, well maybe tomorrow it's a good note.' Fuck it—play it and see afterwards if it's worth anything.

"Han came over every afternoon to my parents' place to play, just to develop the music, see what we can do. Sometimes Misha promised to come over—I had a piano—but he never did. He was off playing chess or whatever.

"When Han and I made the first record, we called the label Instant Composers Pool, ICP, and Misha said to us, 'I also belong to the Instant Composers Pool.'"

The three became equal partners in the enterprise of making new music. One man, one vote. What could be better?

In Holland as Americans discover to their horror, frites—French fries, chips—are served with mayonnaise. There is also something called *patatje oorlog*: fries with ketchup, and mayo, and satay sauce, three big globs and raw onions sitting on the taters. The logic is plain, kid logic: these toppings obviously don't go together, but let's see what happens anyway.

Oorlog means war.

Chapter Three
Border Crossings

"I was just coming from art school, becoming an artist. I did lots of work on the covers, night after night, making little drawings, all different, all by hand. I'd put a little screw through one. I'd cut them, put strange stamps on them. I walked over them with ink on my feet.

"Then I had to post them myself, did it for years and years. I'm sick of doing it now. I like contact with people, like it when they come to you and say they appreciate a concert. But selling records afterwards, I don't want to do that anymore.

"In the Stedelijk Museum we had a Saturday afternoon concert of the New Acoustic Swing Duo. We brought about four or five boxes of these records. We sold like 68 at that one concert, incredible. But we sold them for only ten guilders; for that people got a record and a drawing by me. I later found out one gallery owner bought 35, and then resold them for enormous prices in Japan." Welcome to the marketplace. ICP reissued the *New Acoustic Swing Duo* LP in '84 with a mass-produced Bennink cover: photo of an ear with a toothpick-flag sticking out of it, territory claimed by these explorers.

This isn't *Driekusman*, or even *Stairs!* This is really something new. First off, note the trend-bucker name: swing was rarely a stated priority for period free improvisers. (Not swinging, that was a priority.) Bennink doesn't abandon swingtime, but he sets it aside sometimes, keeping a little distance. Between that tack and the short motives the duo often play from, they stumble on their own nervous rhythm, far from the open flow of the Coltrane–Rashied Ali *Interstellar Space* duets of the same year.

On "Music for John Tchicai" Bennink is at the tablas within three minutes (thanks to a cut // early ICP records are / big on / blatant cuts/)—tablas being a favored new toy of Han's. (He played them with Nina Simone, on a Boy Edgar TV broadcast.) Over the top, Breuker's quiet musing on subtone tenor gives way to small staccato honks made more banal with every repetition, as if he's trying to wear out himself, the audience, and especially that fucking tabla player. Three minutes after that starts, Han is back at the kit with a heavy jazz barrage under petulant huffing saxophone, Breuker clinging to uninteresting motifs like a kid clutching a favorite toy at bedtime.

The sidelong tenor and bass clarinet roast "Gamut" offers more in that vein: furious blowing with a double edge. Squalling was the saxophone style of the time, and Breuker obviously wants the listener to place him in that power-blower context. It's the foundation for the joke. As the solo wears down, and the paucity of thematic ideas is cast into bold relief, the hearer begins to suspect that maybe this person can't play at all—that maybe free-jazz musicians really are a fraud, a laugh. Bennink's a perfect foil because he makes you see being a laugh can be okay.

There was something about the infamous Max van Praag incident Breuker didn't mention, which Mike de Ruyter touched on in a brief item in his bi-monthly *Jazzwereld* column. In the travesty of melodies Willem played on his kid's flute, de Ruyter heard a critique of the avant-garde audience: they couldn't tell free-jazz passion from ineptitude.

This is a good close reading, especially for 1967. De Ruyter may have been the first to recognize ironic distance as a Breuker keystone. That said, be clear that for all the talk of irony to follow an ironic stance in jazz is of course no Dutch invention. Jelly Roll Morton, Fats Waller, Earl Hines, Ellington, Jimmy Rushing—they knew something. But the Dutch were especially sensitive to the idea of authorial distance. A few years later Misha would speak of a Sonny Rollins concert at the Concertgebouw, where Rollins would play a phrase, then reply to it, as if conducting a dialogue, yet would also seem to stand apart from both roles. Misha said it was like there was one Rollins playing on the bridge, one under the bridge answering him, and one on a boat on the river, eavesdropping.

De Ruyter aside, abundant later evidence makes it plain Willem's real target was not free-jazz listeners but free-jazz musicians: the jitter-fingered saxophonists he stood next to on stages.

Ironic distance, role-playing on one's instrument, deliberate mistakes: these ideas would prove enormously important in Holland. They can also all be found in the music of Charles Ives.

"Nobody played the bass clarinet at that time. Joachim Berendt liked my bass clarinet playing so I was often invited over to play it in different orchestras in Germany. The other reason I worked a lot there was screaming long and loud on the tenor." The Germans already had one guy who did that, guy from Wuppertal named Peter Brötzmann. He did an awful lot of it, for years. The huffing puffing big bad wolf of European improvised music sometimes displayed the swing and blues feel of a trout, and so slowly acquired mythic boogie-man status for jazz conservatives as the typical 'that ain't jazz' European. Such folks had the same reaction to Brötzmann as to early Archie Shepp: if this is what happens when musicians drift from jazz, better we don't look too closely. But it would be a mistake to think that's all Brötzmann did, even then; he might also slip into a surprising early-jazz vibrato, betray an unexpected taste for catchy melody.

Anyway, where fierce blowing was concerned, two saxes were better than one. Competition was inevitable however. "I could play louder and longer than Brötzmann, and I could drink him onto the floor. But we got along very well, for a long time." Of course, it's hard to remember things well when you're that plotzed.

Leo Cuypers, pianist and alcohol-consumption expert, who started hanging around this crowd in 1969: "Willem can play louder, harder, and longer than Brötzmann, but not drink him under the table. Brötzmann was the total winner. But Willem was the winner the next day, out making records and deals while Brötzmann was still in bed."
—Are Dutch and German improvising styles different Leo?
"Yes. The Dutch are more intellectual: "'Before you start, know your ideals.' The Germans: 'I go into the deep. Follow me.'"

∮

Peter Brötzmann: "Did I drink him on the floor, did he drink me on the floor, I don't give a shit. None of us had any money in those days but there was always a bottle of schnapps and beer around. But playing was always more important.

"I was coming to Amsterdam in those days, and met the musicians quite early. Han and Willem and I had a very funny trio for a short time. We played a few gigs but I was busy with these Fluxus guys then, just helping them out. I came to Amsterdam for their festival, and that's where I met Misha. I stayed in touch with Han and Willem, but with Misha, the connection came back later.

"I liked Willem Breuker's parents very much, and when I came to town I'd stay with them a couple of days. Later I went my way and he went his with the Kollektief—but even later we did this funny tenor tour, him and me and Frank Wright. I wanted Han for it but he was busy—but I still feel Willem and I are good friends, and that's important to me.

"Around the same time I met those guys I met the piano player Fred van Hove in Antwerp. I had some connection—the Wuppertal bass player Peter Kowald's first wife's brother played alto with Fred. They had no drummer in Antwerp, so I said, 'I met this drummer in Amsterdam recently.' Belgium was different then; you could work more. There was a guy in radio there who was interested in new possibilities.

"The first chance I had to play at a German festival, in Frankfurt, there was a little money, so I invited my friends: the Wuppertal crew, the Amsterdam guys, and Peter Kowald had good connections to London, so I invited Evan Parker. It was a time of big exchange, German guys going to Holland, Dutch to Germany, we went to London and met the South African guys. Everyone was organizing little things. We had friends in Edinburgh so we worked there a lot. And there were two radio stations in Germany, Radio Bremen, and Sudwestfunk where Joachim Berendt was making programs. He had the most money, and started the Baden-Baden Jazz Meeting, which was really happening in those days. For me it was also quite important that I had good connections early to black American musicians: Cecil Taylor, Andrew Cyrille, Don Cherry, and a little later, Frank Wright.

"Peter Kowald and I were organizing the Moers festival. There was no money but a lot of enthusiasm. Frank came, and the English, Dutch, and Belgian friends. Finally for me it came down to working with the trio with Fred and Han which we did for ten years. But then Fred got tired of Bennink." (Nine years, says Fred van Hove, ending in 1976: when Bennink missed a couple of gigs, and Mangelsdorff or Maarten Altena subbed, he realized how much stuff he couldn't get to with Han, who so often drowned him out. They did a couple of reunion gigs in the '80s: nothing had changed.)

Brötzmann: "I liked Fred very much, but on the other hand I like drummers very much. At the end I decided to go with Bennink for another eight years or so. But then it got to be like working with Peter Kowald. When you grow up together, you get to where you know each other's moves so well, it's enough.

"I'll tell you the truth, maybe it's a little secret. When Han really got into the theatrical things on stage, because I'm so serious, sometimes it got to be too much for me,"—Peter Brötzmann, with his long drooping mustache over a broom beard, with the remarkably out of character puppy eyes, is one serious looking fellow—"especially after we'd been doing it for a long time, and I knew his every move. We had a good time, but at the end, it really came to an end. But you won't find another guy like Han in all the world. When the Germans try to be funny, it ends in disaster."

The Wuppertal energy school gave Bennink a fresh perspective: could it be everyone else had been playing too soft? Meeting the live-hard-play-hard Germans was like being unleashed.

Brötzmann/Breuker/Bennink played the Persepolis as early as February '68. In May Brötz made the Germanic manifesto *Machine Gun* (FMP)—let's be loud for a long long time—with octet including Han and Willem, van Hove, Kowald, and Evan Parker. As part of the European convergence, the black Danish saxophonist John Tchicai (his father a Congoloese diplomat) had started working in Holland the year before with bebop pianist Piet Kuiters.

Evan Parker: "I was very keen on Eric Dolphy, so my first awareness of 'Dutch jazz' I think was listening to Misha and Han on *Last Date*. Then there was this period where John Stevens and myself went to live in Denmark, a very weird decision that still makes me laugh. Veryan Weston's sister came into the Little Theatre club one night, said 'I've just been to Copenhagen, they love this kind of music there.' And within a fortnight I think John and I had our bags packed and were off to live in Copenhagen. It was a bit of a—well it was an unqualified disaster. I think we played in public about . . . twice.

"We had some very interesting jams in the afternoon at the Cafe Montmartre; I remember one with John Tchicai, and Mongezi Feza was also living there at that time." Feza was an inspired raw-toned trumpeter, a South African Don Cherry who spread the kwela esthetic in Scandinavian jazz and English rock circles. "People in the offices nearby were disturbed by the loud music, and I think they sent for the police. We discovered that on average people really didn't like the music in Copenhagen any more than they did in London.

"John Stevens got a gig with an R&B band, just to make some money, and I gradually spent my savings and then started cleaning for an academic family whose house was so clean, as far as I can tell it was charity on their part. I'd dust floors which I'd dusted the day before.

"I came back home; John stayed on with the R&B band for a bit, and at some point he crossed paths with Tchicai playing with Misha and Han.

"At that point the music was actually in a state of flux. I suspect that the way John Stevens was playing had a liberating influence on Han. Whether you could get Han to admit that I don't know, but something happened between *Last Date* and the *New*

Acoustic Swing Duo. Of course Han was aware of Milford Graves and Sunny Murray, all of those things too. But something more specific happened. It would have happened anyway—I'm not trying to make a big important point—but when John came back to London he said he saw these guys playing with Tchicai, and he thought maybe he could do a better job, thought he was playing in a more appropriate way.

"From then on we were keeping an eye out. The first, or almost the first direct contact for me was with Willem and Han through Peter Brötzmann. I met them in Wuppertal, and we did some live recordings for the *Machine Gun* project.

"Han and Willem looked very wild to me. We were still in the throes of, should you wear a suit to play a concert? They were already wearing lumberjack shirts. Looking pretty frighteningly rough on the bandstand, the pair of them. They were a presence in a room, perhaps a touch more intense than they are now."

Bennink had a long Rasputin beard then, did look a trifle uncivilized and demented. The music was changing along with him, and sometimes it tried to put the wildman in cages. Han said later, when we played with the English guys then, we were forbidden to play time.

This was a factor in his adopting the alternative percussion set that had so disturbed Ben Webster back in Chapter 1. Han inherited his father's penchant for collecting old instruments; he's fond of odd-sized and -shaped drums, and took to loading his big Citroen full of them to go to any outski gig. One night at the Paradiso he looked at all the equipment arrayed before him and thought, this is insane. Then again (he said on recounting this at the time) before half an hour was up he'd use all of it.

Within a few years records would list him as playing "everything/anything." Sometimes the list was more exact, might include clarinet, alto clarinet, bass clarinet, Hanrinet, soft clarinet, soprano sax, banjo, violin, viola, flutes, harmonica, trombone, voice, saw, tins, vibra-pan, home-made junk—not to mention tablas, thumb pianos, gongs, Chinese cymbals, Korean court chimes, drums from Thailand, marimbas, and gachi, a huge Tibetan horn taller than he is. Everything and anything.

(Ages later he keeps all that stuff under a tarp in his studio, a converted stable not far from his boat: "Don't even look under there!" From above, its outline is almost the exact size and shape of a grand piano. It's like he'd lugged a piano to the gig every night.)

Evan Parker touched a truth: the later "junk percussion" school epitomized by Germany's Paul Lovens and England's Paul Lytton has roots in Bennink's and John Stevens's scrap heaps.

"John and me more or less, that's absolutely true. John invented this little toy set he was playing on, Japanese drums, a particular light-sounding kit. I was using more stuff like old Chinese cymbals, coming more from the history of percussion instruments." Bingo. For Han, it's about heavy sounds, as if anchor chain were being lowered onto a drum set.

Misha: "Han can take any instrument, take it to his stable for a week, then play it on the gig. But instruments that cannot be played loud don't get his real attention."

For the same reason—dynamics at the other end of the scale—Bennink's multiinstrumentism seems unrelated to the Chicago vanguard, toying with mostly quiet "little instruments" around the same time. (The Chicagoans began showing up in Europe in '69, too, Paris their point of entry: the Art Ensemble, closely followed by Leo Smith, Leroy Jenkins, and Anthony Braxton. The latter two met Breuker through Gunter Hampel.)

Han's interest in tablas, however, links burgeoning multi-axism with a period vogue for Indian instruments, usually unrelated to Indian practice. His attitude toward such devices places him closer to George Harrison's meditations than Coltrane's: it's about an object's potential to make music, not an infusion of alien consciousness but transposition. Even so, give George his due; he was no Carnatic virtuoso, but he was a very good sitar player for rock. "Norwegian Wood" is neither chumpwork nor something you'd hire Ravi Shankar for. Harrison—and the raga-rocking Yardbirds—made Indian instrumentation part of the background music of groovy zeitgeist. Give Han his due too: he was a very good tabla player for a swing drummer or European improviser. But the step from Han's or Harrison's good-hearted exploitation of Indian instruments to the lowest-common-denominator dithering of '80s world music is short.

Bad world music irons out cultural differences, a trap the European free players sidestepped.

Evan Parker: "The German thing is about the music as expression of a way of life. On-stage, off-stage, it's all one thing: an intensity of experience which has to be communicated. Obviously Peter embodies that. There's no doubt that Brötzmann was a sort of beacon or central focus for the freer approach.

"The English thing, whether you're talking about an AMM- or SME-type of approach, is in a way based on a sort of group introspection. The rationale for doing anything is determined by a kind of consensus that the group itself generates. Ideally there should be a kind of agreed ethos for music-making that underlies that consensus."

(SME is the Spontaneous Music Ensemble: Stevens, Parker, Derek Bailey, Dave Holland, Kenny Wheeler. Parker on their 1968 recording *Karyobin*: "There were a lot of questions in the air, which the music poses rather than answers. What is free improvisation, what can you do, how does it work, is this a valid approach? A lot of phrase shapes finish on an upward curve, like a question rather than a statement.")

"The situation in Holland is always much more about remarkable personalities— sort of Meetings with the Remarkable Men." A good laugh follows. "Dutch music is always about the strong idea, associated with the remarkable individual. And about clarity. In some way the musical activity serves to illustrate the idea of the remarkable man. The Dutch are not much interested in what Misha calls mood music, which is music where the musician becomes lost in the process, transported into what I understand is for Misha a grotesque, trancelike state, where all rational decision-making gets lost, and the idea becomes less important than the experience.

"Obviously we've played together quite a few times, and I think by now we respect each other's methods and positions. Sometimes we even find it interesting to attempt to reconcile our differences, but it's almost never straightforward.

"Fairly soon, those three stereotypes—they are stereotypes, this is a grotesquely oversimplified, hackneyed way of talking about the three schools, even if there is a grain of truth in each of those characterizations—very quickly started to infect one another, cross-pollinate, whatever metaphor you want, and so we start to get hybrid combinations.

"Now in a certain way the three schools have emerged again, as sort of representing distinct philosophies, but they're no longer tied to a specific place or cultural origin. So you have English people like Adam Wilkinson who in a way plays more like the Brötzmann school. Steve Beresford in a way has more in common with the Dutch approach. And so on. There are all kinds of anomalies now."

♫

In June '67, pianist Cecil Taylor came to the Holland Festival to play solo. Misha wrote a review of a Taylor concert for *Jazzwereld*, analyzing his alternation of hands and fingerings. While Taylor was in Amsterdam, Boy Edgar and Mike de Ruyter took him to a triple concert: Mengelberg quartet, and the trios of Nedly Elstak and Dick van der Capellen.

Cecil pointed out a few players he might not mind playing with; two nights later they went into a studio. He and Han warmed up for half an hour, then Taylor pulled out a couple of charts, said, "All right, let's make a piece. What instruments do we have?" Breuker's bass clarinet (squeaking), Chris Hinze's piccolo, van der Capellen's bass, and Han's drums. Cecil ran down the motives for the horns, divvied in a bass part, gave final instructions to Han—good luck to all who attempt that—and they wailed theme-solos-theme for 45 minutes. Bennink remembers a tape; de Ruyter's *Jazzwereld* column, the source of this item, doesn't. (Postscript: Bennink recorded duo with Taylor in 1988, for the FMP label; two days later he was playing with Percy Sledge. It's one of Han's favorite juxtapositions.)

November '67, Bennink won the Wessel Ilcken Prize, the year after Misha, two years after Piet Noordijk. The news disturbed him somehow, as if he doubted he deserved it. He deserved it. Around the same time, a film crew started shooting a TV film about him, *De Bezetene* (The Obsessed). (The cinematographer was Jan de Bont.) The folks in Breuker's neighborhood had already thought Han was weird, coming around in wooden shoes. When they saw him on TV, playing his wife's behind like a drum, they realized they'd underestimated how weird.

In December Bennink and Altena toured and recorded with American free altoist Marion Brown. Initially Misha was in the band but pianos could be very inconvenient: too much emphasis on playing changes and tempered scales. (Brown was coming out of pianoless Ornette Coleman.) The album *Porto Novo* is a fair reflection of the impact Ornette's trio music had at that time—Han's tough trunkrummaging and logrolling set up momentum free of Kenny Clarke connotations. Bouncing off Han's steady pulse, Brown can subdivide the beats as he wishes; he's not hurtled down specific channels like J. R. Monterose. Bennink covers a broad tonal spectrum from booming bass drum to rattling metal.

The track "Porto Novo" offers another gloss on the Rollins-Bennink combination. When Brown goes into jazz calypso groove the Dutch musicians know what to do: Surinamese music is their window on the Caribbean. Before that happens however

Han takes his turn at the tablas, and yes it slows things down even as you admire how much sound he can wallop out of them. He really bends those pitches. The album *Porto Novo* illuminates the cat-and-mouse game Han came to play with swing time at that time, in progressive settings anyway. He'd wail in the groove and then drop it cold. The music's accent slides away from American models. Encouraged to do so by Han, Altena began playing more arco solos, more European than jazzy.

♫

But what of the ICP trio, three for all? Han has the sunniest view: "There was no trouble: Misha hated Willem and Willem hated Misha, that was about it."

All three principals agree: any two of them could work together, but all three was impossible. Han and Willem, energy levels to match, would play like crazy idiots and run through various vernaculars; straight or jocular, it works either way. Misha and Willem: with their broad listening tastes in classical music, they have a frame of reference that lets them rifle lots of high-art styles and ideas. Han and Misha: drums liberate overtones à la Herbie Nichols, and the lifetime partners could always resume their endless game of ruthless chess. Han drowns out Misha; Misha plays clunky rhythms to drive Han mad, finds subtle ways to take indirect control.

But add Misha to Han and Willem and he slows them down, both on the gig and just trying to have a gig. (Misha, remember, was happy to play three times a month; they wanted to play every night.) Add Han to Willem and Misha and the china shop is smashed. Add Willem to Han and Misha and his linearity and literal-mindedness interrupt a game where reversals are constant.

The ICP trio never made a record, but they played their share of gigs. One night at Paradiso, Breuker was having problems controlling his clarinet; Han and Misha left the stage, letting him fend for himself. Breuker stubbornly plowed on. An anonymous critic for *Leidsch Dagblad* attended a concert in Leiden and concluded: If this is new, call me old-fashioned. Misha's preliminary lecture on what the audience wouldn't hear tonight didn't help. The verdict on the music: "fake jazz," "stunt business," "anti-music," "cackling chickens." Other critics were similarly impressed.

The editors and readers of *Jazzwereld*, a rather hip jazz magazine for that or any time, threw them support. The three improvisers were featured in almost every issue. (The magazine also covered the Hilversum guys, and New York, and blues and soul.) In the 1966 readers poll, Willem was voted best on tenor and miscellaneous instruments, Misha on piano—he also won best combo of the year, and album, for the Artone LP. Han was named the best drummer, Noordijk best alto, Loevendie best composer. A year later, results were similar. But protests against the new jazz continued. In a *Jazzwereld* forum, tenor Joop van Enkhuizen obsessed over whether Ayler had proved he could play changes.

Why was ICP 3 never recorded for release? Willem was always more interested in documenting his own stuff; this was Misha's business. And Misha has a tendency not to think of things like recording until it's too late—like after the gig. He has never been diligent about preserving his work. But another bassless trio fared better.

♫

John Tchicai: "My first Dutch contact was pianist Piet Kuiters; he had been married to a Norwegian painter I knew. He brought me to Amsterdam for a month of concerts at the Sigma Center, playing in a band with two drummers—a Belgian guy and John Stevens—and Dick van der Capellen on bass. Misha played at one of those concerts, and may have asked me then if I wanted to work with him and Han. I was hooked up doing tours of Danish secondary schools, and got the trio its first work. We went to Sweden, and did one or two gigs in Copenhagen. But I think I went to Holland more often than they came to Denmark. They definitely made me feel welcome. Great guys, great players, very much into the freedom aspect.

"Willem had that rough style, hard blowing—a power player. Maybe the reason I liked playing with him better than Brötzmann was, with charts Brötzmann gets a little lost."

—Was there a frivolous aspect to this scene?

"Yeah. I think the inspiration came from Misha; that was my impression. He was definitely the one who had his ideas down, on paper, in his playing, in his head.

"When you talk to the Dutch guys, ask them how come they always liked to play with me. I have my own ideas, I won't say what they are, but I'd like to know."

I asked Misha about it one day, when we were riding in his car—just before the cops pulled him over for some low-level moving violation, let him off with a lecture—and he said, because I liked his very un-Parker-like approach to the alto saxophone. "He agreed with our ideas about Africanizing the 12-tone row, as we said at that time: taking a small amount of musical material and subjecting it to all kinds of manipulation: shrinking it, blowing it up, retrograde, inversion, multiplication. But we were not too interested in departing from tonality at that time. We were anti-Schoenberg but pro-Webern." Did Tchicai being black and European give him extra cachet? Misha audibly scoffed: I've always been color-blind.

In July '67 a Mengleberg quintet with Breuker, Tchicai, Altena, and Bennink played and did broadcasts in Denmark and Sweden. In May 1968, Misha, Han and Tchicai made ICP 002: selections and //excerpts// from a two-day session. A gulf separates it from the Mengelberg-Noordijk quartet of '66, the time sense and much else changed utterly. Close intervals from the piano, a musing aspect, an aversion to too many notes: those are Monk's only spoor. Misha ruminates, his sense of space more Morton Feldman or Earle Brown than Nichols let alone Tommy Flanagan. More pedal, less crunch. Han's more open gait is partly a function of abandoning ride cymbals, ching-a-ching traded in for dry pulsation of slack-tuned skins. Timbres thud. His time is still impeccable, but he tears bigger openings in it. He trots out the tablas too. The effect is more joujouka than Krupa.

Tchicai was something new, and had New York experience. Born in Copenhagen in 1936, he had met Archie Shepp at a communist-backed festival in Helsinki in 1962, came to New York the following year and began working with him. Tchicai had turned up on Ayler's *New York Eye and Ear Control* and Coltrane's *Ascension*, developed a close partnership with trombonist Roswell Rudd in the New York Art Quartet. A version of that band—Tchicai, Rudd, South African drummer Louis Moholo and Danish bassist Finn von Eyben—did a Hilversum broadcast during a 1965 tour. Tchicai kept the name after returning to Denmark. The following year one "New York

Art Quartet" was the Dane and three Hollanders: Kuiters on piano and harpsichord, van der Capellen and drummer Glenn van Windt.

Tchicai's sound was like sucking a lemon: tart, puckered, thin but piercing, almost the opposite of Breuker's fat smeary tone and effect. He gets away from the sheer brouhaha of energy music, had a sense of proportion Mengelberg could appreciate. Which raises another parallel with as-yet unknown-in-Europe AACM musicians from Chicago; if Tchicai sounds like anyone, with his querulous pitch and slowly undulating lines, it's Roscoe Mitchell. (If Han does with his dry barrel-rolling, it's NYAQ's best-known drummer Milford Graves.)

Tchicai, Mengelberg, and Bennink sometimes abandon swingtime, sometimes turn it on its head. In one section, alto holds steady with one middle-register melodic fragment, worrying it repeatedly as piano and drums spin around it. The saxophonist plays what would normally be the bass part. The fragment is catchy, then maddening: musical water torture.

And here, finally, is a version of "Vietcong," which starts with a stuck record motif, eventually finds it way through the jungle to a simple pentatonic motif, which introduces military snare drum, the merest suggestion of programmatics or politicking. If "Vietcong" did get Misha lots of gigs, it showed how little you could do and still be seen as political. On this version there are no fireworks, literal or other.

By 1969 Evan Parker was coming to Holland to guest with ICP, in quartet or with other guests.

"I think the first gig I did was in Hilversum. They paid for me to fly in, a very small plane from somewhere in Germany. I thought, 'Well, this is the life,' and I played with Willem, Han, and Misha. Misha had a piece with an all-interval series, a 12-note row, divided up in boxes—this box here, this box there: 'Play those notes here; use these notes to improvise; now use these notes to improvise after you hear this box being used by that player.' A very clear set of ideas, as they like it, very clear. Of course it was very loosely interpreted in the end. Any rules Misha devises are certainly not binding on him. It was a very positive experience. To provide context, remember how few people were interested in playing this way then. It really was reassuring to know you weren't alone, you weren't crazy. Or if you were crazy there were other people who were just as crazy as you.

"The pre-given compositional material, everybody knew that was not the real issue. It was a certain kind of openness of attitude about how the music could sound. If you had that in common, ideas about telling one another what to do or how to do it was secondary. We had a lot of fun in those days. Willem was a very fun-inclined person."

—Spontaneous?

"Spontaneous—sort of scary, close to the same thing."

The ICPers took P for Pool seriously: you might hear a different band on any ICP gig, which might be rehearsed or not—i.e., masterminded by controlling Willem or anarchistic Misha. For Misha, encouraged by the flexibility of the New Acoustic Swing Duo, and averse to large milling crowds of screamers, and to playing any chart Willem put before him, a duo with Han became the most attractive option. Han meanwhile got deeper into the dramatically leaping dynamics that earmark his mature style. (Misha told Bert Vuijsje in '71, Han scares me not when he plays loud, but when he confronts me with something totally different at the right moment: like jumping from behind a door and yelling boo.)

This is when Han began delving into the duo format as a way of life: he hooked up with Evan's partner, splintery harmonics-oriented guitarist Derek Bailey (as on ICP 004, recorded July '69, three weeks after the meet with J. R. Monterose). Bailey plays guitar like a percussionist, so they pull together conceptually, even as the extreme disparity in volume levels pushes them apart. The music runs hard on alternating current. When Bennink enters for the first time on their 1972 *Live at Verity's Place* (reissued on CD) it's like a bomb going off in the room.

For Mengelberg, the thoughtful, questioning English made better partners than Breuker's balls-to-wall German allies. The mixed septet on *Groupcomposing* (ICP 006, recorded May '70 in Rotterdam)—Misha, Han, Evan, Derek, Brötzmann, English trombonist Paul Rutherford, and younger brother Peter Bennink on alto and bagpipes—is cluttered, the kind of record that helped foster modern Dutch resistance to large free-improvising units. Still, with Evan's sputter, Brötz's single-minded schmears and Rutherford prying open windows on droney vistas, it has something. Han continues to find a personal momentum somewhere between swing and surprise assaults: feints, bobs, roundhouse punches and rope-a-dope, and the clang of the bell at the end of the round.

Through it all Mengelberg sounds remarkably unaffected. As in chess, you shut out distractions. Let the group be a group, he's composing.

He makes music not with but in spite of his fellows, a turning point. Experience with Han had taught him how to play or at least appear undistracted by the most severe disturbances. He tries not to jump when he hears Boo. The pianist keeps his parts lean if not linear: he'll unleash those overtones, pedal down, but won't let them cloud over à la McCoy Tyner. He also hammers metallic reinforcement to nattering reeds' logjammed difference tones (overtones caught in interference waves). And he can take his lines into hyperjump that recalls Cecil Taylor, a source suggested more by the rhythmic flow than the harmonic density, which could just as easily come from modern composed music.

The ICP international small groups peak on *Fragments* (ICP 005), from March '71: Han, Misha, Tchicai, Derek. Less milling around, more focus. It's a classic of European improvised music. Jazz gestures are few, almost incidental.

Han's perfect time and quasi-clumsy clattershotstumble are perfectly balanced; he's become very good at BOO! He'll play possum, then hurtle into the heart of action. Such patterns of tension and release are a swinging drummer's lunchmeat, but here it's shorn of conventional swingtime, no tripleting. His line is like charcoal scribble on paper. (His outfit includes steel pans, played with no discernible Caribbean references.) As noted above, his timing and Derek's were compatible, and both liked flinty timbres and attacks. Bennink is spare, which is Derek's usual style, and Misha's, so Tchicai has room to maneuver.

This kind of free music is about Flow, and it flows beautifully, but there's more to it than sensitive English-style interplay, listening and responding. Evan Parker hit it: it's also about strong ideas personified by remarkable individuals. Each also deals with his own stylistic or conceptual obsessions.

Bennink and Mengelberg each savor one sweet memory of the quartet's nine-gig tour: the holistic Tchicai and ideologically constricted Derek couldn't stand each other, sometimes wouldn't eat at the same table. Misha grew enamored of such conflicts, later would throw together incompatible players so the music would feed off their personal tension. This idea isn't peculiar to music, of course. (Didn't Scorsese tell De Niro to get on Jerry Lewis's nerves when they were making *The King of Comedy*?)

For Bailey free improvisation has no memory, is always a matter of reacting to the musical moment. Recapitulation and thematic development have no place (for himself; he'd still invite rule flouters like Misha and Steve Beresford to his improviser-hoedown Company weeks). Tchicai, with his sinewy alto timbre and undulating dynamics, slips through the sonic hedges sideways. But his concept may clash with Bailey's. As on ICP 002, he may latch onto a lick or phrase and keep at it: unflinching practical minimalism. You take a pattern and burn it into the listener's brain; it exists outside of what happens around it, the more so as no one else takes it up. (Breuker: "He had this minimal repetitive thing going on before we had heard about minimal music.")

Somehow conflicting impulses gets lashed together through ten long and short improvisations, from half a minute to over ten. The most obvious creative tension is between Han and Misha. The second part of the Tchicailess Fragment "h"—a self-contained adventure that erupts out of the end of an aimless guitar-drums amble—is classic Mengelberg. He jumps in with an almost fully formed idea: sprinting single-note right-hand line which circles plainly through easy-to-track chords, spinning onto the tonic periodically and then off again, slowing just a hair as he scales a summit; there's less breathing room than in "Hypochristmutreefuzz."

One presumes this is a preconceived idée fixe, not least from Han's reaction. The instant he hears it begin, he does all he can to squash it. He tries drowning it out, then plays aggressively against it, then stomps on Each Of Misha's Beats To Show How Dull The Whole Thing Is, before finally relenting enough to put the sequence through the tumbler cycle. His moderate barrage encircles Misha, who keeps going and going, placidly. Mengelberg triumphs: wears Bennink out, renders Bailey's little (tonal) comments irrelevant. It's instant composing as composing on the gig.

This isn't Ives's clash of sounds occupying the same space. This is a war of wills. Three weeks later at Amsterdam's modern-art Stedelijk Museum, Mengelberg and Bennink recorded their first duo LP, untitled ICP 010 with Tomas Schmitt's cover. Whapping cymbals onto heads, clomping piano chords: slam chess.

On all their half-dozen or so duo records you hear the sport, musicians joyously pulling against not with each other. However there are spaces for Misha's musings too. On ICP 010, the Monkish balladry and rippling 19th-century romanticism are reintegrated. The music breathes deep, feeds on the impure air. For a few minutes Misha's heard on a newfangled keyboardless Putney synthesizer. In practice, the Dutch got over their anti-jazz phase pretty fast. (The Germans were slower, and retained more of that initial resolve.) Jazz no longer dominated, but it got factored in.

A note on the cover of ICP 010 says it's available by mail, like all the label's LPs. (Five guilders in Europe, $10 postpaid outside.) Once an ICP record's modest pressing sold out, it was gone for good; profits were used to finance the next one. Peter Bennink took care of the mail orders, became ICP's accountant.

Two duo sets received the catalog number ICP 013. The first, from March '72, is one of anyone's stranger issues ever: "een mirakelse tocht door het scharrebroekse eskeorberrahcs teh rood thcot eslekarim nee," strict retrograde: a (fake) palindrome. It was one duo session, spread over six 7-inch 33- rpm flexidiscs, sold by subscription, in installments, each sleeve a mailer hand-addressed/designed by Han. They are beautiful to look at, and all but unlistenable. Flexidiscs wear out appreciably with each play, and these were recorded at ridiculously low volume. The surface noise about drowns out even Han. The product self-destructs, pushing the envelope of planned obsolescence. (The other ICP 013, also by the duo, was an LP recorded in 1977.)

Meanwhile Han and Willem continued their treks into Germany. Brötzmann's octet had boiled down to the working trio he mentioned earlier, Brötzmann/van Hove/Bennink. Between 1970 and '75 they recorded eight records for the German free-music label FMP, half of them adding German trombonist Albert Mangelsdorff. (The trio plus can be heard on a two-CD FMP set; the Brötzmann/Bennink duo made two FMP LPs.) The trio had an interesting balance, for one thing because they'd break down into subgroups. Dense freneticism (Bennink on clarinet sometimes, to thicken the reed roiling) might give way to episodes of surprising calm, for van Hove's more melodic or harmonic musings. Han got to all his stuff—full-tilt bully to spare implied swing—as did his mates, which made the band engagingly evasive: tyrants one minute and puppy dogs the next.

Willem kept working with Gunter Hampel till 1971. From '68 on he had company on the long trips to Germany; he'd brought in his jam session discovery and Loosdrecht sideman Arjen Gorter, born 2 January 1948, Amsterdam.

Han Bennink: "I met Arjen via Willem at the Bohemia Jazz Club. He was 17 years old, playing on a plywood bass, sounding something like Scott LaFaro. It was amazing, really a shock. He's still an incredible bass player, very very underrated."

"I grew up across the canal from the Heineken Brewery, on the outer ring of the canals. My parents listened over and over to things I started to dislike enormously and still can't hear: Kathleen Ferrier, or the *Matthew's Passion*. I played some accordion between the ages of seven and nine. Accordion players were sort of common on the streets on Amsterdam, and I liked the guys who came by; you'd throw them a quarter. My father had a wholesale instruments business, so he brought one home. It had a piano keyboard, only 12 little basses, so you had to reharmonize things. I played it for two years, performed for old ladies who came to visit my grandfather. I didn't like the music I got to play, and when the teacher got ill I forgot about it.

"I listened to the Dutch Swing College Band with Sidney Bechet when I was 12, Blakey when I was 13. By 14, I knew I was crazy about jazz. The new pirate radio station Veronica, which started out as a ship at sea, was broadcasting jazz then, and on Saturday afternoons I listened to Michiel de Ruyter. It was incredible. I heard some tune, I think it was by Dizzy, and Mike de Ruyter explained they didn't play the theme, they were just improvising. I thought, 'That's pretty crazy. I didn't know there was such a thing as a theme, and now they don't have one and still play.' So that provoked some curiosity.

"Five years after playing accordion I picked up an old guitar and started fumbling along with jazz records. I didn't play chords at all. Playing single-line stuff, I found out the tuning was impractical. It was uneven, with that third in there. So I tuned the top two strings up a half step, which made it all fourths, so every pattern would work everywhere. It was tuned like a six-string bass an octave higher, but I didn't know it.

"I played at dances with high school bands. We played anything: all the tunes from the Oliver Nelson–Dolphy *Blues and the Abstract Truth*, and mixed up 'Twist and Shout' and 'La Bamba' and a couple of other tunes which were all the same tune anyway. A bass player came to one rehearsal at my place, left his bass and never came to pick it up. He called like half a year later. My grandmother had left me some money, so I bought it. One hundred and fifty guilders, a Czech plywood bass.

"It was like playing the four bottom strings on the guitar, and it was fun. I just tried to imitate other bass players, watching them at concerts, and listening to all kinds of things. For me *Sketches of Spain*, Ornette, Dolphy, Charlie Parker, Mingus, all came in at the same time. I heard Albert Ayler's *Spiritual Unity*. The role models were pretty much always American then. Ayler and Sunny Murray were too weird to really handle, but Peacock's bass playing hit me like"—snaps his fingers.

"So I just sort of fell right into it. I had already played with Willem at that time. I'd gone one day to play guitar at a session at a youth hangout in the east of Amsterdam. You could look up when; we played in memory of Winston Churchill, who had died that day or the day before." January 1965. "It didn't amount to much. I was playing guitar then still.

"There was a little club where I went to jam, when I was playing guitar even. De Groene Kalebas—the Green Calabash—a cellar with a '50s French bohemian atmosphere: an artists hangout, with jazz. I played there occasionally with some really good guys. The drummer died a few months later from heroin. My mom took me there in the car, with my guitar and amplifier. I was 15. On the break I'd be the only guy at the bar, drinking a Coca-Cola. The other guys would be somewhere in the back, doing whatever. Then we'd meet on stage and play some kind of bebop.

"There was also the F.A.M.O.S., near the Leidseplein, where I went when I could, even crawled through the window once when a concert was sold out. Around '64 they started having jazz every Sunday afternoon. Louis van Dijk's trio with John Engels and Jacques Schols: I heard them a lot, even heard the old Workshop Quartet with Theo Loevendie and Nedly Elstak. They had these little jazz contests, where I first heard Willem play in '62. I think he fainted against the piano, he was so nervous. He didn't win, but he did two times afterwards. That first time, he was trying to fold Coltrane and Dolphy into one, with piano, bass and drums.

"Willem invited me to play guitar on his first album. I had brought guitar and bass to rehearsals, but only played the bass on the recording. From then on I was a bass player.

"Something else important: the workshops, as they were called—they were more like a course—given by Theo Loevendie at the F.A.M.O.S., their other building on the Vondelstraat. You had to audition for Loevendie to be admitted. I think I played a couple of choruses of 'Straight, No Chaser' on guitar, with him on the piano. I did one season with guitar and one with bass. He'd be at the blackboard, writing down scales, chords. . . . There was no jazz theory book then, nothing, so I didn't know any of it. I didn't read much at all, but I wrote down all the notes, copied out every chord. Theo just kept going, didn't care if everybody understood or not.

"I went back during the week. You could reserve the piano, and sit there as long as you wanted. I'd bring what I'd written down, and figure out how everything sounded, relating it to stuff I had already heard. 'Hey! So that's what you call that!' I think learning should always be like that: discovering things first, and then learning their names.

"There were about fifteen people. There was a trio that came from Eindhoven, 120 kilometers every week, with the bass on top of the car. That's where I met Willem van Manen, who had been playing dixieland till that time. Then Theo stopped after two semesters, and Nedly Elstak continued it, teaching and having one hour of playing. By then I was already gigging everywhere, but I'd keep going back till 1969 or '70, to play his tunes or just to play. That's where I met Rob Verdurmen and Bob Driessen. Apart from three months studying the bass with Maarten Altena, that was my formal education.

"This was the crazy '60s. Somebody had inherited a lot of money, and bought or rented a theater on the Kloveniersburgwal, made it the Sigma Center for the contemporary arts, communication, whatever. The Living Theater came over and stayed half a year or so: Judith Malina, Julian Beck, the whole crew, with a few musicians. Around the corner, even a little earlier, was a cracked old building being used by Piet Kuiters, a very weird piano player, and his Free Jazz Incorporated. He got a bunch of guys to hang out there and play free jazz all day, and switch instruments for the hell of it. I heard later there were 20,000 hits of LSD stashed in a refrigerator there, but I never got close to that. I hung out there a lot, there was a bass I could play. And at the Sigma Center there was a drummer who needed somebody to play with.

"In 1966 Tchicai and John Stevens came to play with Piet Kuiters. They sort of rehearsed there for a month; nobody knew why. It made a big impression on me. One day I brought over my plywood bass you couldn't hear anyway, and got on stage with them. Tchicai asked, 'What are you doing here?' I said, 'Just play something, please.'

"So I taught myself on stage and did a lot of jamming at the old Bohemia Jazz Club, near the Concertgebouw, a Sunday afternoon hangout where people were always jamming. That's where I learned to play changes, practicing on stage. I played with Herman de Wit, met Han and played with him for the first time, and also with Don Byas.

"I was invited to join Gunter Hampel. I think Willem got me that. It was very strange; my first real serious gig, playing free jazz at the jazz festival in Ljubjana, with Gunter, Pierre Courbois and Willem. I must have joined December of '67. Nobody worried if I couldn't play. I could play anything, it didn't matter. We did the Wergo record, that's nice; I like it better than *8th of July 1969.*"

The untitled Wergo—by "Gunter Hampel Group + Jeanne Lee," April '68—was more intense, Breuker blowing his top. But the July '69 recording for Hampel's Birth label (on CD with alternate takes) is the one people remember, as historic meeting of Germans and Dutch and Americans: Hampel, Breuker, Gorter, Lee, and two

Chicagoans now based in Paris, new arrival Anthony Braxton on alto and soprano saxes and contrabass clarinet, and drummer Steve McCall, who'd come to Europe the year before, and had already played awhile with Pim Jacobs and with Don Byas. Save for Hampel's chunky piano chords on "We Move," it wears very well, main point of interest being the contrast between Lee's cool vibratoless voice and the broiling reeds of Braxton and Breuker. (Hampel sticks mostly to vibes.) They waft between cool and impassioned, light and dense textures.

The horn men were a good fit, given their penchants for playing any woodwind, their multiphonics, staccato articulation, curiosity about all sorts of music. Breuker, competitive, cranks it up a notch, plays a scarifying multiphonic tenor solo on Hampel's otherwise spacious "Crepuscule," the kind of tempoless atmospheric piece the Chicagoans liked. If Breuker's a cappella solo is the twilight of anything it's Adolphe Sax's conception of what his instrument was for. Time stands still for his seizure. At that time Dewey Redman was one of few others singing through the saxophone with comparable through-the-windshield impact. Gorter is a hotdog.

A musician's starter instrument is often significant. Hawkins played cello, and you can hear it in his sonorous tenor. From playing the chair Han Bennink learned about the drums' dry textures. Gorter plays bass with a guitarist's sense of the possibilities. No wonder he reminded Bennink of LaFaro.

"I started using an amplifier with the bass quite early, because it didn't make sense to be a mime. It's an eternal conflict, but I've always taken the position it's better to be heard than to be authentic. I always experimented; taking apart microphones, hooking them up to weird amplifiers, blowing up my home stereo speakers on a gig, because they were the only thing that sounded good. My father was a big shortwave amateur broadcaster, so I always saw this stuff around. I knew what a plug looked like and how to solder a cable but I never knew the theory behind it.

"I didn't play that much in Holland with Willem. He had started using Maarten Altena, because he was the reader, and classically trained. The things I did with Willem were mostly in Germany, with Gunter and Pierre Courbois. I think Braxton just did that one recording with us, no gigs. Gunter always had an incredible talent for finding the right people at the right time. That session was where Willem and Braxton met, definitely two kindred souls. It was a funny confrontation, the two coming from such different backgrounds, but still quite comparable in a way.

"For a little while, as a sideline Gunter had a rock band he hooked up with in Antwerp, where he was living at that moment. He was sort of predicting jazz-rock, which wasn't really happening yet. So he took a break from the band with Willem, went to London and got a very nice drummer, Laurie Allan, and an out of work guitar player tired of being on the road with Tom Jones who looked like Che Guevera and played hell out of the guitar, John McLaughlin. Gunter brought me over from the other band. We'd come to a place, and sometimes during sound check we'd ask if someone had a bass guitar. Otherwise I'd play the upright. There were no heads, mostly, just improvisation, going and going for it. We had a sound guy who dabbled in electronics; he'd build tone generators and strange noises would come out. Strange noises would come out of the PA once in awhile, made by things like soldered-together transistors.

"John and Laurie had a very tight time-feel between them. They were used to playing with bass players like Dave Holland or Danny Thompson, so that was like one big learning experience for me. That quartet lasted about half a year. Then John got the call to make his record *Extrapolation.*" That was the beginning of 1969. On that album the 11/8 "Argen's Bag"—the spelling corrected on reissue—is for Gorter, who used to beat out that rhythm on drums for something to do.

"I was hanging out in Paris around the time all the BYG recordings were made. Gunter had a place, Jeanne Lee was staying there. She was going to record 'Sophisticated Lady' with Archie Shepp the next day, and I was figuring it out on the piano, accompanying her." This was August 1969, the summer an awful lot of free-jazz records were made for the BYG/Actuel imprint—none by Dutch leaders, incidentally, unless you count American expat Burton Greene. "I hung out, going from one studio to the other, one for rehearsing, the other for recording. This big cluster of people would record in all these weird combinations. Somebody just threw a bag of money in there, and nobody knew what was going to happen with all these recordings. They just kept the tapes rolling. Incredible.

"Around 1970, Gunter's band with Willem sort of reformed, mostly without drums. Louis Moholo might join us, but we played some things just with Willem, and Willem van Manen, and Gunter and me. That's when I blew the hi-fi speakers, playing without drums. I thought I could play rhythm.

"Finally we split up because of business matters. We did a recording with Hans Werner Henze, who'd written a piece for brass quintet, the Japanese percussionist Stomu Yamashita"—and the Fires of London, and voices, in May '71—"with big graphic scores written by hand, and a giant climax before the end, and then the conductor gave the signal and everything stopped. Only the bass went on, because I wasn't looking. It's still the best-paying gig I ever had." But then the Dutch guys discovered Hampel pocketed part of their share. That ended that.

"I was not a very outgoing person, but the music always made me want to go places and play. Willem and I had already gone to London with some artists, to play in the streets. Later I went back, must have been '68. I went to the Little Theatre Club: John Stevens, Trevor Watts, Evan Parker. This was just after *Karyobin.* I went to Ronnie Scott's old place, jammed with the South African piano player Chris McGregor. He grabbed the bass from me, 'This is how you do it.' Getting up on stage and getting kicked off, I had that kind of schooling.

"A year and a half later I played two gigs with Chris and the Blue Notes at the Paradiso, December '69. Johnny Dyani had just left the band or something; I guess Hans Dulfer called me. Mongezi Feza, Dudu Pukwana, Chris, Louis Moholo and me, unamplified. That was incredible. I said to Chris. 'We met before.' 'Yes, I remember.' A couple of months after we did a trio concert, three one-hour sets, all up-tempo, with Chris and Louis Moholo. I have a cassette; the bass isn't even there.

"In the early '70s I also worked out of the country quite a bit with Irene Schweizer and Rudiger Carl and various drummers." He recorded one album with them in 1974 for FMP, *Goose Pannée*: Schweizer on piano, Carl on tenor, Heinrich Koch on drums. "There was so much going on in those few years it was hard to imagine."

—Did you have a sense of an emerging European style distinct from the American?

"Yes. Willem's first record in '66 was definitely a turning point. After that there were some very theatrical things, involved with big groups, actions, happenings, events, total theater. That was pretty original I thought. I remember reading in *Down Beat* about Joseph Jarman and the AACM doing theatrical stuff in Chicago, and thinking, 'Huh, we've been doing that for years.'"

He's laughing. "It's crazy, but it's true. We did all kinds of weird things, and on occasion it worked. Once in a while radio would give Willem a gig. I remember one piece was conducted by one of those little glass dipping-birds that look like they're drinking from a glass of water. The band was conducted by the bird, for radio—a one-off event nobody could see!"

⚕

Willem Breuker: "When I came up with my first tango, we had an orchestra playing at a festival in Frankfurt or someplace, and I made a composition especially for them. I had to write most things in graphic notation because they were unable to read a note, or refused to read a note. When I brought this very silly tango, Brötzmann got mad. 'How can you play a tango when you are a free-jazz player?' He couldn't play it at all.

"I'd sit at his table till seven in the morning, arguing. 'We have to develop this music, can't stay with this free playing and blowing and screaming, because in a few years nobody will want to listen to us anymore.' You always have to be a step ahead. But that's a political discussion.

"The reason I could play so well with Han for a long time was, he was also able to play any style of music. If I played a tune in time or did a ballad, or broke it down in the middle of the tune, he understood and he'd follow. I could also break down his tabla playing. We didn't need to discuss it.

"Then we had the trio with Han and Maarten Altena. We played on changes sometimes, and we invented our own compositions on the gig, which we'd remember sometimes at the next concert. I can also remember playing 'This Nearly Was Mine' and 'My Foolish Heart' and lots of tunes I'd always had in mind, I don't know why. But Maarten couldn't play the chords very well, and they couldn't hear what was 16 bars, 24, 32—no idea.

"At a certain moment, I had other ideas, and it became very hard for Han. He was always on time, he'll rehearse, but at the concert he won't play what you rehearsed. The moment you're on stage, he'll play completely different, played so loud, had no sense of what you'd been speaking about all day, just did what he had in mind at the moment."

Han is still notorious for this.

"That made it not so easy. Plus, now he's playing tabla, the thumb piano, the whole range of things which would engage his attention for two minutes or whatever. If you played your composition, he'd just follow his own line. He didn't like to be organized in a certain way.

"I wrote my first theater pieces, text and music. For economic reasons you have to repeat it more then ten times. He didn't like having the same music and text every night. 'Okay, we make something, we sell it to the people.' That's not possible with Han.

"When I started putting other kinds of music into the theater things I had in mind, a lot of people didn't understand. Don't forget, most jazz musicians, or free-jazz players or whatever, had never heard about Schoenberg, Varese, any other type of music. They just knew Charlie Parker, Miles Davis, Sonny Rollins, that whole thing. Some liked what I was doing, but some didn't understand it at all. So there was trouble immediately."

—Did you get any education in how to write a score?

"None. I learned all by myself, by listening and trying it. My best school was writing for theater—writing it down, and asking questions. I need an oboe, I'll call up an oboe player and ask him what's possible. I learned by doing it over and over, and looking in books and at scores, and listening. Composers would get special sounds, I'd think, 'This is beautiful, how do you get that?' My ear was developed in a certain way but I still might not know exactly how something was done, because it's also a matter of how you record it. If you put a mike over here and the French horn is over there, that gives you a completely different sound than if you put the mike near the horn.

"It was also good that I had a lot of connections with classical musicians. I think that's one of the most important reasons the music developed so well in Holland, compared to other countries. Maybe because people like Misha and Theo Loevendie and some others studied at the conservatory, we knew guys our own age who went into symphony orchestras, and they all knew each other. So if you want to write something for the other discipline, you know the musicians, and they know you, and they're prepared to do things they never did before.

"At the end of the '60s, the classical musicians, who couldn't improvise at all, were more interested in playing what you wrote for them than most of the jazz musicians. There were just a handful of new improvisers, and the rest were still fighting us, playing bebop or whatever.

"So, let's start again, thinking about how to make music. Like Albert Ayler did. I started just playing Christmas songs, or the 'Marseillaise' or whatever, very easy tunes, very badly done in a way: very easy harmony, nothing happening, Sunny-Murray-no-beat-anymore. Fantastic. What the hell, who wants to listen to swing music? You can if you want, but there are so many other possibilities.

"Sometimes I organized my shows along a timetable. This was like '67, '68. 'At nine, you play this solo by Varese. Seven minutes after nine, we do an improvisation on that. Then you classical guys play your Schubert piece, and I'll improvise straight through Schubert.' The concert started at 8:30, and at 11 it was over. Nobody knew exactly what was happening. I put in all the ideas I had in mind, to combine kinds of music, do stupid things with music. I'd take some music of Beethoven or Mozart, and remove page two, save page three, rip out page four, make a new combination. Turn the paper upside down, whatever. People were very interested in these evenings. They were a kind of Happening. People could go out and come in again, sit or drink or smoke, whatever they liked. Everybody had a very good night.

"In '64 or '5, we learned a little bit about John Cage. Gilius van Bergeijk wrote a piece for the big barrel organ at the Stedelijk Museum. He took a Bach piece in 4/4, but only used three of the four beats per bar. He made it, but it's still a Bach piece.

"I wrote a piece for Misha Mengelberg in 1967. The score was a giant card sitting on the piano, and he has to match numbers on the card with the notes below them on the keyboard. He has to look for number 1—looks, finds it, plays the note, *bong*, then looks for number 2 . . . , number 58 . . . , number 84. There is a kind of system in it, but if you don't know it in the beginning, it takes some time. Misha did it on a live radio recording, took him seven or eight minutes. 'Ah—number eight!' At the end there's a little nothing"—Breuker sings a light oompah line—"and then the piece is over.

"It was the period to find out what can you do with music. You find out what works, what helps you a little bit, or else you think, 'Forget about that.' You have to think about the implications for your next experience. People asked me to write for them, and I wrote whatever I had in mind: a concert for three barrel organs in the Dam Square, pieces for carillon, for mandolin orchestras, for harmonie orchestras.

"There was money for it. It had been 20 years since the Second World War, and there was a kind of climate in this country, after the Provo movement. We wanted to set up something else. There was the May Revolution in Paris in '68, but that same shit had happened here in '64 or '65. Such things have a lot to do with forming the mentality to do something different here from other countries."

Breuker's *Lunch Concert for Three Barrel Organs*—a Cagey and disorienting experience for anyone who knows the usual gurgling barrel organ sound—is ICP 003. His first real showcase as a composer is ICP 007/008, the "chocolate box": two LPs in a round cardboard box, credits inside the lid, strip of purple felt around the rim. It was recorded before Breuker turned 26.

He was a born conceptualist, itching to hear his ideas played. Maybe that's a reason he wrote so much and Misha so little; anything Mengelberg thought up he could hear in his head. (Misha, asked if he was suspicious of his first impressions of music: No, I trust my ear more than that.) Willem, conservatory-proof, practiced architecture without an engineering background as it were, needed trial and error to whip his ideas into shape. In the chocolate box you can hear him learning to score: on "Grüsse aus Berchtesgaden," for five winds, organ (doubling glockenspiel) and Han's percussion, he doubles a brass line with glock, his brass-band legacy coming out, and even wasting a staff this way, makes the band sound bigger than it is.

He really would try anything, given an occasion: 19 mandolins (with lots of room echo) faking Ligeti, made popular by Kubrick's current *2001*. "Serendipity" is for septet including Han and Peter Bennink on drums and bagpipes, trombonist Bert Koppelaar, and Misha in his best shaggy style, but the composer upstages them all with a chain of shotgun weddings: a bagpipe and mandolin intro, a bass clarinet and tabla duo, an ending where mandolin and accordion volley an angular faux-serial melody in short irregular bursts. He made good use of Peter's droning pipes, and caught bagpipes' sound on his own token duet with Tchicai, for alto and bass clarinet.

January 14, 1969 was the last time Misha and Willem were caught on record until 1989, with Schlippenbach's Berlin Contemporary Jazz Orchestra.

The music in the chocolate box is culled from nine sources, August '68 to March '70. (At the session for Gunter Hampel's *8th of July 1969* he got Jeanne Lee to sing a stupid song in German, and the whole band to play it.) Most of it is theater music, some pedestrian, more often fetching. The tango "Francois Le Marin" sounds oddly medieval, Han clippityclopping like horses; sour organum chords from four mixed winds underpin Willem's melancholy clarinet melody, decorously played, chalumeau, no vibrato. The piece is no less effective for his leaning hard on the melody. (Still, Breuker has always had a problem not overdoing a good thing, harps on the tune to lesser effect elsewhere.)

"Introduction and First Entrance of the Horsemen" (written for a play by Aristophanes in '68) more than anything here anticipates the Breuker Kollektief to come: blunt section writing countering solo clarinet, and an incremental structure. It's built brick by brick, a few bars at a time. "Fascinating Appie," an upbeat blues with fiddle and flute—too slick to sound more rustic than Canned Heat—is a forerunner to the Kollektief's umpteen rock and roll parodies, and like them is just tin-eared enough to betray Breuker's lack of interest in that music. Dutch boogie roots echo in Rob du Bois' rolling eights on piano, only a whiff, no stab at being authentic. But it goes on too long, the material too threadbare. Overmilking is Willem's tragic flaw.

Two performances take a side of an LP each. One is three excerpts from a Stedelijk concert. Taken together, they're a nice example of Breuker's song travesties—he sings the sentimental old "Grandfather's Clock" with naughty (clock or cock?) lyrics, then stomps the melody with Aylerized tenor and the Gorter-Bennink free-jazz rhythm section. Just when you think he's playing tenor from the heart, Breuker slides into a bathetic lower-register melody that cribs from "Gloomy Sunday" six bars at a stretch. From the same concert, he also works the can-he-play-or-can't-he routine, so radically out of tune (think Von Freeman) he looks ahead to countryman Ab Baars' '80s radicalism.

Whatever the trio had rehearsed, Han is surely not playing it—he sails past the dramatic full stops, comes to his own halt a second later, in striking contrast to his typically impeccable microtiming. That's what lets him get away with missing his cues: Han's lagging behind is his version of Pres or Von Freeman leaning way, way in back of the beat. His tectonic layer slides out of sync with the surface. He staggers the form.

There is also a 25-minute excerpt of theater music, "Song of the Lusitanian Bully," on which Breuker does not play. It's for Peter Bennink's bagpipes, Willem van Manen's trombone, Rob du Bois on organ and Han on his giant Tibetan horn, the gachi.

This marathon announces something new whose impact is still strong in Holland: minimalism, the new drone from America. The Bully's song sounds derived from both thundering Himalayan horn choirs and some key early minimalist works: La Monte Young's organ drones, Steve Reich's phased tape loops, and Terry Riley's 1964 staggered-phrasing masterpiece *In C.*

Riley's piece opened a lot of ears as soon as it appeared on record in 1968. Dutch musicians heard minimalism's great weakness—bland harmony—and worked to roughen it up, damage the goods. On "Bully" the organ drone is a constant, the bagpipe's pitch wavering in and out of sync with it, as farting/bronxing gachi and trombone go in and out of phase with each other. It's vigorous but crude, barely digested, and far too long in the context of this sampler, but minimalists are not miniaturists.

No composer on the Euro free scene kept so tight a rein on improvisers; in the circles in which Breuker traveled, only Schlippenbach marshalled similarly large forces. Willem sometimes used composer Rob du Bois as Misha's surrogate on piano; he was no world-class improviser, but he'd rehearse, and knew the other pianist's style. (Breuker and du Bois used to perform one of Misha's pieces, the latter at the keys, the former under the piano, pounding its underbelly.) Du Bois plays a fine, funny pastiche of Mengelbergisms at the end of "Tussen de dijen van 'n mokkel" (Between the thighs of a broad)—so convincing, Han tries to squash him like the real thing. This short piece has the dippy, fake-medieval feel of a Renaissance Fair—despite or because du Bois plays organ on most of it—stemming from Breuker's moronic recorder lead, piping staccato eighth notes up and down the scale to a maypole beat.

By now Breuker has become Holland's ambassador to the Eurojazz scene, a face in the crowd on one international record date after another—with Brötzmann, and Hampel, and Henze, and Tchicai's orchestra Cadentia Nova Danica, and with Don Cherry and Krzysztof Penderecki and, at the end of 1969, with the Baden-Baden Free Jazz Orchestra directed by Lester Bowie. That was Willem's first encounter with the guy on prepared piano, Leo Cuypers, who'd been recommended by Pierre Courbois when Joachim Kuhn dropped out.

"Leo came and it was clear: he was the guy I could work with. We just had to play together. He had the same ideas, was very open and not so stiff or religious about music. And he liked melodies. Melodies were forbidden at that time. Leo is a percussion player, and he loves cabaret and easy tunes. He knows nothing about music, actually. If you give him changes, he can't read them. He doesn't want to learn, so he makes fantastic mistakes. He does everything by ear, not knowing how to name it.

"In that period you could always get a good response in Holland by screaming and making a lot of noise for one hour, and then the next set, doing it again. But Leo came with melodies, and when you played with him you never had the idea you were in a straitjacket. What I had with Misha after awhile was more of a straitjacket.

"For a time Leo and I were a composing team. If someone wanted music for a little television series, or a theater group needed some: 'How much? Five thousand guilders, OK we do it.' We set up a kind of composers' factory. It worked out pretty well, because he was just the opposite of me. I had more influence in making the harmonies, and he made melodies or whatever, which I wrote down. A very good partnership."

"Willem Breuker says, 'Leo's music sounds like it's made in a nightclub.' I like that. I never lost my ideal, to make music with the feeling of the best jazz in the world, which came from America. But I never tried to play like Oscar Peterson or Monk. I'm also not into the academic Dutch style, giving guttural names to pieces that don't swing. Those musicians know Schoenberg and Ives, but I never liked that stuff. If it sounds like real jazz, fantastic."

Cuypers was born December 1, 1947, grew up in Maastricht, in the Netherlands' far south, remote from the flat historic Holland where most of our action takes place. He still lives in the south, still sits on the floor in the lotus position when he wants to get comfortable, now as ever enjoys a laugh, a smoke and a drink. He is a character: natty, owlish, stoned, irresistibly likable. Also someone who knows a good story can be a thing independent of history. (Since there's so much first-person testimony in this book, it helps to remember how your own stories get better the more you tell them.)

"The first music I heard? Classical, classical, classical, till I was 7. My granddaddy composed church music. A lovely old man with long gray hair; we loved him. He used to play a game with the six of us kids when he came to visit. He'd play some Bach or

Mozart, then cut it off within a minute, and we would all pick it up, start singing fake Bach or Mozart. We became totally sharp on styles.

"I started to study piano at age 6, but always had to sit through the lessons of my two sisters and a brother first. By my turn, I had memorized the music, would pretend to read. They found out I couldn't read when they gave me a piece to play, and the sheet music was upside down.

"The first jazz I heard was Miles and Dave Brubeck. Then Blakey, and I immediately heard the difference between East Coast and West Coast. I never liked one more than the other. What really switched me to the avant-garde was George Russell's *Ezzthetic* with Dolphy. I had that when it was brand new." He'd have been around 15; it was recorded in 1961.

"I was a little afraid of Ayler. The first time I heard *Spirits Rejoice*, I didn't get it. Then I smoked some pot: it was fantastic! Such revelations don't happen anymore."

He played some drums as a kid, which really left its mark on his piano. Cuypers went to the Maastricht Conservatory for three years. His boozing was so bad, the dean would sniff his breath every morning, checking for fumes. "Not being able to read gave me great problems at the conservatory. I played pieces with two index fingers, like Lionel Hampton on piano, but in machine-gun rhythm."

He has told the story that he was tossed out when caught playing inside the piano with drumsticks. He told it in an interview published in 1980, where he also said, "I always saw the piano as a set of 88 tuned drums. I played completely from the wrist."

Listening to Leo's piano, then or now, primary influences are easy to spot, if rarely mentioned: Dave Burrell's neo-rags (same two-beat feel without march form), Paul Bley's keyboard version of Ornette Coleman's free tonality, and especially Capetown's Dollar Brand, now called Abdullah Ibrahim. The influence of South African music on Dutch jazz is great, and Leo was an early and major conduit for it. The resemblance folks usually mention is to Keith Jarrett, who also follows Bley. Like Bley or Jarrett he spins well-turned, hornlike melodies with his right hand, but more weight rests on Abdullah-like hypno-ostinati in the left hand: endless rolling 8s in the bass, unvarying repetition suggesting vast savannah or polder more than the fevered recreation of logging-camp boogie-woogie or a minimalist's counting show.

"I heard Dollar Brand's first solo record *African Piano* on ECM." (It was the JAPO subsidiary, actually.) "He never made a better one. There's no Keith Jarrett record like that. A great influence." Leo starts singing "Bra Joe from Kilimanjaro." "But I was never really exposed to South Africa. Later I heard about the Brotherhood of Breath and Louis Moholo, but Abdullah was about the only one I actually heard. I did work later with the South African bass player Harry Miller, but the way we hooked up was personal. I met him, I liked him, and when I won the Wessel Ilcken Prize in 1973 I invited him to play on the concert, although I'd never heard him play.

"When I heard Keith Jarrett on the radio, I thought it was me. I was already playing that way. I'm a jazzman, I don't like to be influenced by anybody, although "Back to Johannesburg"—the piece on my CD *Songbook* dedicated to Harry—sounds like Dollar Brand to me. But I like Jarrett more than Dollar Brand.

"Dave Burrell I know very well, met him in Baden-Baden. We played together on one cut on the album: The Art Ensemble of Chicago, 18 other world famous musicians, and me. Dave Burrell was in his most mellow mood then; when I met him later, he was a little guarded."

—Are his rags an influence?

"I can imagine that: soft, nice personality. But Bobby Few is a piano player I feel I share something more with."

—Paul Bley.

"Finally you name someone who impressed me—which is not the same as being influenced.

"I had played at Loosdrecht in 1969, and won as soloist. I met Willem Breuker around then, but he thought I was a rich man's son, an intellectual creep, somebody not from the same background. When I walked into the hotel lounge in Baden-Baden, Arjen Gorter and Willem Breuker were sitting there. Arjen invited me to their room, and Willem smoked pot for the first and last time. He saw I wasn't a creep, and I thought the same of him.

"Three months after Baden-Baden I was the busiest pianist in Holland. I joined Willem Breuker's and Theo Loevendie's bands the same day, playing at one of those many festivals they had in Amsterdam. Loevendie asked me as a one-time guest: I was hip and new and he wanted it. I played with him three years, always as a guest. One time he organized a gig without the guest and it was over. It had become obvious I had other interests than Theo. But I like him—lively, different, honest: a complete man."

Cuypers made only one record with Loevendie, 1972's *Chess!* With Breuker he would make a bunch. Leo never did learn to read very well, a vexing thing to the increasingly control-conscious Willem, but he could be steered, could play a tune, and was interested in composing, on a tunesmith level at least. And he was very, very funny: a straightman with good timing, who knew the act. Because of him, their two duo LPs are among Breuker's best. Leo can steer as well—like Misha in his duo, finding ways to manipulate his partner undetected.

Those duo albums are from the mid-'70s, when the pair had been together for years. By 1974's Breuker/Cuypers *Live in Shaffy*, all on-the-job training is long completed. First thing you notice is the clear clangor of piano: spare, hard, repetitive yet playful, with a bias toward an 8th-note feel. He has the percussive attack of a pile driver, reminder of his early love of drumming. The pounding bass on "Churchy" is more boogie-woogie than Baptist. He sounds crisp even with the pedal down.

Cuypers' steady time focuses Breuker's phrasing; his hollering down the barrel of the tenor has more of a rhythmic edge, more bite. He doesn't bog down on comically dowdy phrases as elsewhere, keeps moving to stay a step ahead of Leo's revolving door. Willem pulls out and pulls off the free-jazzman-whose-lips-give-out and mangled-tune gambits on his tango "Ham and Egg Stango." (It is jazz*men* he's spoofing. Specifically: he highlights the macho posturing in power-blowing.) On "Stango" he plays squeaky E-flat clarinet, which also laughs in the early-jazz or klezmer style; Dutch Jews may have vanished, but Breuker has a feel for that East-European reed-talking. In a way, it's been part of his vocalized conception from the start.

"Once There Was" is Leo's adaptation of a bizarre Dutch children's song, "Once There Was a Little Girl Lost"—she dresses as a boy, runs away to sea, climbs the big mast, reveals herself to the captain her true love. Cuypers' rolling-sea Abdullah

Ibrahim major chords grease the way for bass clarinet. It rolls on and on, makes its minimalist case for the power of repeats. Breuker takes a strong falsetto chorus toward the end. His circular soprano motion at the top of Leo's "Bouquet melancolique" sounds suspiciously like a jab at Evan Parker.

The duo's *Live in Shaffy* (not to be confused with a Cuypers' group record, same title, recorded the same week) is one of Breuker's monuments as improviser, made at the time he began focusing almost all his attention on a fixed large group, the Kollektief.

You have to wonder a little at a guy who has been playing variations on the same can't-play schtick his whole career. That schtick has always been a knowing joke Breuker shares with the audience over the heads of his fellow free-jazz musicians: you're in the audience, and I'm on stage, but neither of us are really fooled by this bluster are we? The joke relies on placing it in this broader context. On the other hand, telling the same joke over and over, Breuker treats the audience as if it has no memory: no context.

In Holland, a lot of musicians look at repeating a joke that comes up on the stand as like trying to repeat a good solo: unthinkable for a real improviser. Breuker defies them all.

In 1978, he and Cuypers made a sequel in Berlin, *Superstars* for FMP, where the subject of travesty/deconstruction is "There's No Business Like Show Business."

"Willem may not be the best saxophone player but he is the funniest. His improvising brings tears to your eyes. He's more powerful than Rollins and Coltrane together, and you can print it. (Yeah, I love them too, but better to love your neighbor than a hero over the ocean.)

"*Live at Shaffy* is good for me, but *Superstars* is a deception. We had to make lots of cuts, unlike *Shaffy*, where everything is just as played, no cuts. Berlin, we had to use the less bad pieces. It's a sign the alchemy between us was running out. The formula was running out of pepper.

"I can never work with Willem again. I would like to, but old veterans can't fight their battles over. But we can drink wine together very well."

Chapter Four
Actie = Action

"At the second Lionel Hampton concert at Apollo Hall, so many people were dancing, the floor collapsed. The Notenkrakers was nothing compared to that."

J. BERNLEF

Louis Andriessen: "At that time it was very clear that my generation of composers and jazz musicians were really close together, in seeing what music had to do with politics, and how we needed to change the government's attitude about spending money on art and music. Peter Schat and Jan van Vlijmen and Misha and I, and Willem Breuker, and all the other ones, banged on the doors of the establishment, and nowadays, that money is divided differently. We supported very strongly the emancipation of improvised music, or jazz or whatever.

"I can't really remember the first time I heard Willem play, but it was long before all the Happenings and theater things. He was very young, and you went to his concerts because he was fantastic. He played very noisy bass clarinet solos. We had heard Eric Dolphy of course, but I found that use of classical instruments for this terrible noisy playing to be a big step forward, I liked it a lot.

"In the late '60s there was a cello player in the Concertgebouw Orchestra who wanted to do something about Vietnam, Edith Neumann. So she called all her musician friends, and they called their friends, and there was this large marathon concert in the Frascati Theater, an old building which had been empty. It was the first concert ever held there. It went eight or nine hours, everything from Renaissance music to avant-garde pop, and it was called Musicians for Vietnam. Out of this marathon we got the idea of the Inclusive Concerts.

"There was no charge to get into these concerts, that was one of the ideological ideas: you could walk in and out. Things like this had never been done before. All the musicians got good salaries, and had only to play 15 or 20 minutes, and then the next group came. Bang bang bang. It was very expensive. We put them on till the money ran out.

"Around this time the classical avant-garde composers started doing the quotation stuff, to get out of the cage of 12-tone music. My teacher Luciano Berio did this

66

famous piece *Sinfonia*, where he quotes all kinds of musics, brings them together in an elegant way. It was very hip in the second half of the '60s to write pieces that suddenly had a pop song in there somewhere."

Andriessen had given Berio the idea to use the Swingle Singers on *Sinfonia*, begun in 1968. Louis had already dropped a nicely incongruous spy-movie interlude into his *Anachronie I*, 1966–67, dedicated to Ives, style-quotation's grandpa.

"When we talk about this period I keep coming back to Willem Breuker, who had this kind of lousy Dutch wooden-shoe timing, which has never changed. He never really had any rhythmical. . . . I don't mean this as a negative thing. In fact it has a very strong positive side, very helpful in developing the musical language of Holland, Willem's lousy timing."

—And maybe a certain roughness of texture?

"Yeah, roughness is a crucial word, which we also used a lot in the time of Volharding and the Kollektief."

Musicians for Vietnam and the first Inclusive Concerts were in 1970. But in late May and early June '68—when the student revolution hit France—Louis Andriessen, Misha Mengelberg and Peter Schat had put on the "Political-Demonstrative Experimental" concert for which each had written pieces. It was presented in four Dutch cities; the first was held at the big old Carré circus theater then slated for demolition, on the banks of the Amstel River. (Preservationists won that battle; it still stands.) The place was papered with images of Fidel Castro and Che Guevera, which would not have been Misha's idea. The police surrounded the building, just in case.

In the bulky program book—photos on the cover show the masterminds huddled around a typewriter—Schat went on about the mechanics of his *On Escalation* and its pro-Che, anti-imperialist stance. Misha briefly explicated his "Hello! Windyboys," not very clearly, inviting the audience to join in when the musicians play a certain hopping rhythm. Andriessen took some potshots at the Concertgebouw establishment, and wrote about the new Studio for Electro-Instrumental Music—STEIM—organized to take possession of the PA equipment and electronic hardware the composers were accumulating from various projects. That stuff had been purchased with grant money. (The composers' campaign was beginning to pay off, a little: the squeaky wheels were getting greased. The compositions on the concert program were commissioned by the Dutch government, the city of Amsterdam, and VPRO radio.)

"Hello! Windyboys" is a friendly competition between two wind quintets, who variously try to trip each other up or persuade their rivals to cooperate. "Game pieces" were in the air. By 1962 Xenakis had two works for dueling orchestras. In '64, Mauricio Kagel had staged "Match" as a competition between two cellists, with a percussionist as referee. In different ways, Ives' clashing village bands and Cage's many pieces that consist of instructions rather than a score are also precedents, and Christian Wolff and Morton Subotnick had already devised pieces in which a certain move by one musician triggers a specific response from another: a cascade effect. (Peter Yates 1967 on Subotnick's "Play": "The rules are as definite of those of Parcheesi.")

As described in the last chapter, Breuker had already recorded his sparring-subgroups "Time Signals and Sound Density Five" and written Misha that hunt-and-peck piano treasure hunt. In 1966, Mengelberg had devised for TV "Parafax," a competition between the X's and the O's, two imaginary tribes who occupy the light and dark spaces on a video screen, and communicate with each other in a language of 28 musical phrases, each representing a verbal phrase. The X and O parties' binary opposition is predigital, their culture pre-PacMan: they climb ladders, and have something like ionic sex: the "ahh" state. (A concert version was performed, but it never made it to television.)

"Hello! Windyboys" breaks with at least some precedents in that it's fun to play, ingeniously simple (despite its initially daunting six pages of instructions, in Misha's typically colorful Dutch) and—given the politicized context in which it first appeared—defiantly light. The two quintets are physically separated—at the Carré, one group played inside a transparent, inflatable dome—and can hear each other only through amplification, so they can be isolated from one another. In the aforementioned "hopping" subgame each quintet plays a staccato rhythm at a tempo of its own choice, without hearing the other group. Once the amplification is switched on, the two groups must arrive at a common tempo, through unspecified means; they have to try to seduce each other, but may also prolong the battle by deliberately swerving out of each other's way, a musical game of tag. The sound of the quintets gradually moving into sync with each other curiously (and doubtless accidentally) resembles Steve Reich's phasing pieces from the same period.

"Hello! Windyboys" has a strong sense of rhythm; the other main part of the game is a call-and-response between quintets, several chords volleyed back and forth, and held either for a very long or very short time. There are complex rules about which chord held for what duration can follow another. If you make a wrong move, your quintet has to perform, as penalty, a lively little melody played hocket style, each instrument assigned a different note on each repeat. (Typically perverse, Misha makes it a six-note melody, so it's always played gap-toothed, with a rest in place of the missing note.)

About those traded chords: Gilius van Bergeijk has noted that the criss-cross chart indicating permissable permutations resembles Misha's graphic analysis of Cecil Taylor's alternating-hands patterns, observed on Taylor's '67 visit, and published in *Jazzwereld*. This appears to confirm Mengelberg's view that hearing Taylor helped him hear how his jazz and nonjazz could cross-pollinate after all.

Other aspects of the game: a rhythmic "talking code" à la "Parafax" by which the quintets can send each other simple messages: we're starting; we're stopping; hurry up; play that again; let's go to the other section; you goofed—play the penalty tune.

One elegant aspect of "Windyboys" is that, limited as players are to three or four basic routines, performances are unified and self-regulating. There's no referee, no formal means of determining a winner (although at the Carré the composer picked one, gave them a bottle of champagne) and no specified length, but because it only takes a few minutes to cycle through all the subroutines, it doesn't take long for musicians to decide enough is enough.

The score calls for a little electronic sound processing too, but the first performance was an early example of STEIM equipment fizzling on the job.

The players were drawn from the Nederlands Blazers Ensemble, a.k.a. Netherlands Wind Ensemble. Clarinetist (and now composer) Geert van Keulen drew up a worksheet to clarify Misha's sometimes vague procedures. Oboist Werner Herbers: "It was great fun to play because it was completely different from what we had learned at the conservatory. Such anarchism in music was new, and we were open for it."

The audience took Misha's instructions to join the hopping as license to hoot straight through the whole performance. VPRO broadcast an abbreviated collage of excerpts that destroyed the piece's organic unity, and even Misha writes it off now. ("I thought it would be fun to do it at that time, and then I decided it was not so much fun.")

In 1996 van Bergeijk instigated a revival, played by a mostly student ensemble, which confirmed how much fun "Windyboys" could be to play and listen to—and to follow if you know the rules. (They made no attempt to deal with the electronics, for one thing because no one could quite figure out what Misha had had in mind. He habitually blows off all questions about how his compositions should be performed.) Clarinetist Barre Bouman, who organized the quintets, a few days before the gig: "At our first rehearsal we had to concentrate on doing it right. By the second rehearsal it was easy—it was hard to do it wrong, so we weren't getting to the penalty part. So now we think we'll make it faster and more spontaneous, so we can make more mistakes."

Some have claimed the old group of five van Baarenites, The Notenkrakers, simply wanted to get their own pieces performed, but Andriessen and Mengelberg deny it. Louis says that even without Maderna on staff, the orchestra had already performed works by Andriessen, Schat and van Vlijmen. Now the Notenkrakers wanted to make the orchestra democratic: wanted its musicians to have input into repertoire; the progressives among them would surely loosen up the programming. Orchestras devoted exclusively to 20th-century music struck Louis as segregationism.

Anyway, the opposition had handed them a loaded gun: a Concertgebouw Orchestra press release boasted of its role as culture-pawn of the corporate class: "It is not without significance that when our national airline wants publicity of a certain kind in America, they choose our orchestra to underline it." The Five threw that line right back at them—literally, in an "action bulletin" dumped from the Concertgebouw balcony the night the Notenkrakers made history.

On 17 November 1969, Andriessen, de Leeuw, Mengelberg, Schat and some 35 others (Jan van Vlijmen passed, but he'd take heat for it anyway) disrupted the orchestra's regular evening concert just as Bernard Haitink raised his baton to begin a flute concerto by 18th-century German composer Johann Joachim Quantz. Half the pranksters used cheap little tin-strip clickers, the kind painted to look like frogs. The kid-stuff banality of the sound was a desperate comment on Quantz and company. Unfortunately, this tack reminded some older folks in the house of how fascists silenced opposition speakers in the bad old days. The audience was generally unamused, and some people hooted the protesters down.

Misha: "I felt, 'Anything would be better than how it is now,' but I also thought, 'This won't help, what we do here.' And it didn't."

Not long afterwards, while the Orchestra gave a private concert to guests of KLM at the Concertgebouw, a Notenkrakers Ensemble gave a surprise concert at a KLM office. The following year the Notenkrakers led a brief sit-in at the Concertgebouw, were arrested and stood trial. This is when they really found out what they were up against. The judge was a member of the orchestra's board.

That seemed to cap discussion of a democratized orchestra. But gradually, a smattering of new smaller ensembles populated by symphony musicians did begin cropping up, and liberalizing the concert repertoire after all. They became a permanent part of the musical landscape. Partly that was a matter of generational change; a few such groups, notably the Asko Ensemble, started in the '60s and '70s as student chamber units.

For all their continued shenanigans, the Notenkrakers hadn't alienated everyone. Backtrack: the Netherlands Opera had commissioned the five to write an opera, for performance at the Carré during the June '69 Holland Festival. The unwieldy result, and the group's one concrete achievement, was *Reconstructie* (Reconstruction, subtitled "A Morality"), an exercise in myth-making in which the death of Che Guevera is reconstructed as a Mozartian operetta, and in which a 36-foot-tall statue of Che at attention is constructed. The book was by writers Harry Mulisch and Hugo Claus. The characters include Don Juan and his servant Erasmus—*the* Erasmus—and Martin Bormann, alive and well in South America, and several representatives of the American Total Corporation, and their sexually frustrated wives, and the seven workmen who assemble the statue, bit by bit, over the course of alphabetical sections "A is for America" through "T is for Time."

As the audience entered, they saw a girl in a blood-stained wedding dress lying on the bed: Cuba.

Mengelberg was the gadfly of the group—the pain in the ass. "They thought they could politicize music. I thought, 'I don't agree with that completely, but I can go along with certain elements of it.' The music was worked and reworked, until finally we didn't know anymore who composed what. Jan would come with a piece, and I'd take it home and rewrite it, things like that. Louis was very good at instrumentating other people's ideas. We divided the music into different ensembles. There were four chamber orchestras, one for Reinbert, one for Louis, one for Jan, one for Peter. Sometimes they played together also. I hated conducting, so I mixed the live sound at the theater."

DON JUAN: Your lips are the leaves / Of the Mahogany tree.

BOLIVIA: I spit as the llama.

DON JUAN: Your eyes gleam like tin.

BOLIVIA (speaking, not singing): My eyes are the striking tin mines of Siglo XX / Where in 1965 the trade union leaders were deported / And a hundred and fifty miners executed.

DON JUAN: Yes, you undulate as the Amazon.

◦⅛

An explanatory note in the libretto which came with the recording—there are dozens of them, one listing 36 versions of the Don Juan story—says one Mozartian bit went through eight drafts. Dick Raaijmakers, the guru of Dutch electronic music, assisted STEIM in making or procuring contact microphones and simple distortion devices. In performance, the electronics were Mengelberg's domain; in one section he renders the sound of a contrabass recorder unrecognizable. Elsewhere there are some nice quasi-shortwave effects, under a walkie-talkie duet. Misha also had five-minute tape loops of unvarying "mood music" he could float under the action at will.

The music is referential and inclusive: rewritten motifs from *Don Giovanni* are central, but there are also pop pastiches (albeit slightly snooty ones. A note explains the parodies of commercial jingles and radio pop in "C is for Culture" are in fact more musically sophisticated than their models). Compositionally, Misha's fingerprints are hard to discern—and he's no help in sorting it out—but there is circumstantial evidence. Don Juan has an aria assembled from bits of patriotic American songs plus Monk's beloved hymn "Abide with Me." The puckish melody and euphonious saxophones of "M is for Moonlight" sound like M for Mengelberg, but only for a minute—as if the manuscript paper had been snatched from his hands.

Looking back Misha sees *Reconstructie* as a total loss. "I think they wanted us to have a forum for what we stood for, what we wanted. But we were no group. We didn't stand for anything." Four years later he'd do a music theater piece that trumped its construction of a monumental statue: with a circular saw and a power drill, he'd turn a wooden kitchen chair into a camel.

◦⅛

The three Bolivians place a statue in the shape of North America in front of the feet of the statue. Applause for the departing workmen.

◦⅛

Reconstructie was overblown on every level: Too heavy, too long, too many explanations, too many cooks. It ends with a three-minute D-major crescendo, modestly followed on record by five minutes of applause.

And yet in its yearning inclusivity *Reconstructie* aims at the heart of Louis's critique of music-making: If different styles of music have class associations, the yoking together of various classes' signifiers will have a greater-than-symbolic effect, because the actual musicians, the labor, get to meet and interact. Performers included an opera choir, a children's choir, Herbers and Breuker in the reeds, Han Bennink—briefly detectable here and there on drums—and lots of classical musicians.

But even as workers of two worlds commingled, Andriessen himself felt left out. He wrote in his diary that the gulf between the composers and musicians was little different than with a symphony orchestra. He had walked in his enemies' shoes, and didn't like the fit.

The Inclusive Concerts were an instant hit, however. (Subsidized, too—as Andriessen says, they lasted only as long as the money.) Breuker's timetable pieces deal in a way with the same idea, as did the STAMP concerts Loevendie started a little later, ditto de Leeuw's Rondom and the '90s Rumori concerts. Those series mostly followed the same basic idea: easy access, lots of music crossing genre lines. If certain musics attract a narrow audience, mix them up and the audiences will mix too, maybe discover what they have in common. Dulfer's blend of American jazz stars and home-grown improvisers at rock palace Paradiso is not so far off the same mark.

The Notenkrakers never got what they wanted, but the related composers' campaign paid off. The Notenkrakers had quit the Dutch composers union when that organization denounced them, but before long that organization took up the cause of more lucrative commissions. By the mid-'70s, city and federal government had got used to the idea of public money for the arts. (It was one way to court the youth vote.) They paid painters to paint, so some painters painted bad paintings just to get paid, paintings the government put in art libraries few folks borrowed from. From there to subsidizing composers and instant composers was a short step.

♻

Willem Breuker: "We organized ourselves in this country. That's my socialist background: you have to organize yourselves, to come up with your own situation.

"In 1970 we took over the Stichting Jazz in Nederland, by accident actually. The SJIN already existed, but only as a name. They got a little government money to fund the Dutch Jazz Orchestra playing their own bebop-type music, and they gave the Wessel Ilcken Prize to somebody once a year. That was all they did." The SJIN is the Dutch Jazz Foundation; actually they funded the Dutch Jazz Orchestra's forerunner the Hobby Orchestra, with funds from the national culture ministry.

"I had the idea to go down there one night, with Willem van Manen, Maarten Altena, and Peter Bennink. I'd asked Rudy Koopmans where the next meeting was, and warned him we were coming. Rang the doorbell, 'Here we are, I'd like to ask something: What do you plan to do for us in the future? We want to make a living from this music.'

"'What?!'

"They'd always thought, 'If you want to play this kind of music, do it on the weekend, and the rest of time play in a radio orchestra, or teach. But to make a profession out of it is stupid.' The problem was, at that time if you made that kind of music, for sure you had no diploma. In another artistic discipline you go to school for five years, and get a diploma you can show to the government. 'Okay, you gave me the chance to learn, now give me some money and give me work.' But a jazz musician—he's coming from the gutter, he's nothing.

"So they became angry, said, 'Okay, you know better, we resign, and you can take over the foundation.' Maybe they thought we'd say, 'Oh no, please not.' But no. 'We know exactly what we want; you are not the future, we are the future.' Hopefully."

SJIN treasurer Jaap de Rijke, who found himself in sympathy with the rebels, recalls the board members were motivated to quit because Breuker, Bennink and van Manen were quite nasty about the whole business.

"So then we were sitting there with nothing. We had to set up our own thing. We needed solidarity on many points."

De Rijke and much-admired critic (!) Rudy Koopmans stayed on to help the musicians set up the new SJIN. Later the foundation would be lightly redubbed, Stichting Jazz & Geïmproviseerde (improvised) Muziek in Nederland: more inclusive. Breuker wanted it to be for everybody, but the Hilversum guys resisted: who wanted an alliance with these assholes? (The fact that the money previously earmarked for the Hobby Orchestra wound up going to van Manen's new workshop orchestra Boventoon didn't help.) The progressives gathered 'round though. With help from a sympathetic bureaucrat, Breuker and van Manen wrote an elaborate plan for jazz subsidy, with input from among others Misha and Dulfer. They called for two kinds of subsidies, one that goes to musicians to support their creative activities generally, one to supplement low fees from venues who couldn't afford to pay musicians a standard minimum fee: the so-called Pool Plan and Podium Plan.

The rebels got their way. Like the composers campaign, it was an idea whose time had come: affordable now that Holland was rolling in cash, and appealing to Dutch iconoclastic sentiment and national pride. Besides which, the improvisers like the Notenkrakers were always ready and able to be a nuisance. If you were sitting on some commission and had to deal with the likes of the glaring Breuker or van Manen or windy-when-he-wants-to-be Misha, you'd give them money just to go away.

The city gave in first, embarrassed the ministry of culture into anteing up the following year.

The details were always quite complicated—from the beginning explanatory articles were accompanied by complex flowcharts—and subject to endless fluctuations, and ceaselessly denounced as imperfect.

And yet the subsidy system is the engine that has powered the triumph of Dutch improvised music. On paper the major players were the SJIN and the BIM, the Union of Improvising Musicians. The SJIN became the conduit for money to the BIM. (The musicians thought indirect funding would make it easier to criticize the government without reprisals—to bite the hand that fed them.) As in any community in which a recognized common need exists, a few people wind up doing most of the work. Misha, as ever, was more inclined to discuss than to act, but was prevailed upon to become the first chairman of the BIM, set up late in '71.

Through means subtle and otherwise, by 1975, nine musicians received a stipend from Amsterdam city. The 34 classical and improvising musicians who got stipends from the culture ministry included Altena, Han Bennink, Breuker, Loevendie, saxophonist and Breuker aide Herman de Wit, a promising young pianist named Guus Janssen, and trombonist Willem van Manen.

⚬⟊⚬

"Willem Breuker and I played together a lot then, so we talked over our ideas. Willem, Hans Dulfer and Misha, who's very unreliable and lazy, but a good philosopher, came up with lots of ideas, and I used some of them. I wrote the original plan, about 30 pages, in 1970 or '71. We got the first subsidy from the government around 1974.

"I had started playing trombone by accident. When I was 12 or 13 I played piano in a dixieland school band. When I was 15, the trombonist emigrated to Canada. Nobody knew another trombonist, but I had a friend who played piano. I'd never played trombone before, but I liked it, somehow.

"I was already a jazz fan in high school. I first played modern jazz on flugelhorn, in a quintet. We played mostly West Coast tunes, by Bill Holman and Bill Perkins. For me at 15, that'd be 1955, the Jazz Messengers were too far out, technically too. Chet Baker, Shorty Rogers, Conte Candoli were technically not so complex as Dizzy, Lee Morgan or Clifford. West Coast harmonies, Mulligan and Baker, are not so advanced as Diz and Bird. I could relate the collective improvising and rhythmic feel of Mulligan and Baker to dixieland.

"I studied at F.A.M.O.S. with Theo Loevendie and met Arjen Gorter there. The course was mainly about bebop harmony, but that's a very good thing to know. When I got out of high school, I had to make a little money, so I went back to dixieland, played trombone in a good orchestra oriented toward Bix, Red Nichols, Miff Mole, those guys. They played that style in a very pure way. The trombone plays the lead into the next chord, a third or a seventh pointing the way.

"Of the trombonists of my generation, I think I'm one of the most developed in this respect, that I've played all the styles from dixieland to free jazz, and thanks to Loevendie I'm well equipped in general jazz theory. By 1969 or '70 I was in all the major bands in Holland, because there weren't any flexible trombonists around.

"By the time I met Willem Breuker I was already playing more free stuff. I had heard Ornette Coleman and John Tchicai. In '67 or '8 I played at some festival in a quartet with baritone, bass and drums. No piano, we didn't want that. Willem Breuker played with a large group on the same festival. I didn't like the way the music was played, but his anarchism and ironic approach appealed to me. It was already a theater show, a little. It reminded me of the humor which is supposedly typical of Amsterdam.

"Later he called me. I was already playing with Dulfer and Loevendie. Theo's Consort, seven or eight pieces, made two of the best Dutch jazz records, I think, *Mandela* and *Chess!* The band was influenced by the Mingus approach. Theo is brilliant but a little chaotic. I remember we had to play this piece commissioned by a dance company, and he had forgotten to bring the music, so we played the score by heart. It sounded okay. The dancers got confused now and then.

"Dulfer, Maarten Altena, Han and me were sort of the house band at the Paradiso. Our live album is a very bad recording, but it catches the atmosphere of those concerts. We'd play 50 minutes, then after the intermission there'd be some famous other band, Lucky Thompson, Dexter, Ben Webster, Don Byas, or some famous Dutch musicians. We played more advanced stuff than the main program. The visitors didn't quite get what we were doing, but they couldn't say much, because Dulfer was the organizer. John McLaughlin came by one night and sat in. He wasn't famous yet, but he had a very big ego on stage. His solos were much too long. He said, 'I'm going to New York in two weeks to play with Miles Davis.' 'Ha ha,' we said.

"I had some nice experiences in Boy's Big Band, playing with Benny Bailey, Oliver Nelson and others. The band was mostly studio guys, with a few Amsterdammers and a few youngsters who came from a different musical world. Those older guys started out idealistic, too, but after 30, they went into the studios. Willem Breuker, Hans Dulfer and I were convinced we'd never wind up there.

"Boy Edgar was very disorganized but he had a good sense of sound. He could write an arrangement in an afternoon, in the Ellington way. He'd come in with some riffs,

8 or 12 bars, try to make something out of it in rehearsal. A workshop-like practice you could say. The money was always badly organized, too. I liked him a lot as a person, but he was an amateur working with professionals. Most of the musicians were ashamed that with all this talent, we couldn't get a better result.

"I played in Peter Brötzmann's quintet, three hours, no intermission, backs to the audience. The German audiences loved it. There was enormous social polarization then, and our music was seen as on the good left side. Musical anarchy was very politically correct. You could be unpolished and impolite and they'd love it all the more. Once Buschi Niebergall was hitting his bass with his fist, punched a hole in it, and sat weeping for the rest of the concert. It was enormously fatiguing. Saxophone you can play for two hours, but not the trombone. My lips begin bleeding on the inside.

"Gunter Hampel always said, 'I like the people from Holland, they have an open mind 'cause they live near the sea.' He had that theory about the Dutch, and good taste in talented younger musicians. That was my first time working with a singer who used voice as an instrument in a free way, Jeanne Lee. Very beautiful. I liked that we'd play without drums; that made the sound very open. Two or three years of that was great. But Gunter always took leader money, a double share, an American tradition we're not used to in Holland. We broke up over the money.

"I must say I'm less Calvinistic than Willem, or Han, or Guus Janssen. It probably has to do with my family. My grandmother was a French piano player, and I was always very interested in French classical music, Fauré, Saint-Saëns, Debussy, Ravel, Les Six. Honegger I like very much. For me, it's more spiritual than a clean, Calvinistic approach."

Willem van Manen is a stocky guy, wire-rim glasses, huge white eyebrows, wild hair to match, slow to smile, a slow talker whose delivery can throw listeners off. You don't expect him to be funny, but he can crack up an audience. The first five albums he plays on, beginning in 1968, were Breuker's chocolate box, the Hans Dulfer/Han Bennink quartet's *Live in Paradiso* he refers to above, Loevendie's *Mandela*, an LP by an international Brötzmann tentet live in Frankfurt, and Hampel's drumless *People Symphony*.

The Dulfer quartet fronted by tenor and trombone shows the lingering influence of the New York Art Quartet. *Jazzwereld* had a habit of getting musicians to review records, and van Manen had praised Roswell Rudd heavily, in a five-star review of an Archie Shepp LP. (Dulfer named his band Heavy Soul, Inc., after a record by his idol Ike Quebec, to which he'd given five stars.) Editor Bert Vuijsje liked Dulfer, gave him the first of his many magazine columns in which he fired dum-dum bullets at whatever target was at hand.

The sound quality on the Paradiso quartet album is indeed terrible, a hallmark of Dulfer's Heavy Soul Music LPs. The sketchy themes, just enough to get things under way, are mostly van Manen's. The players had so much room just to hang back and blow, it stands in marked contrast to Breuker's determinism, Misha's theorizing and German forays into the deep. It satisfied Han's craving for unfettered expression better than any of those settings, each adversarial in its way. This was a band that sounded like it worked together, instead of being pulled along or pulled apart. It also had Dulfer's hustler esthetic all over it.

♫

"When Albert Ayler and Sunny Murray first came over in 1964, I was their volunteer tour manager. Hearing them, I wanted to dance every night. Listening to Sunny and to African music I get the same feeling, of a strong rhythm based on pulse.

"I always wanted to find an audience for the music; it seemed to me bringing the music to the audience was easier than vice versa.

"When the Paradiso started, I saw a chance. At first they resisted, thought jazz was old-fashioned, but after a couple of months I succeeded, had concerts going by the end of '68. The first night, my own band and some other musicians, we had 1000 people. Everyone said, 'Jazz is booming again,' but it wasn't—they were just coming because it was the Paradiso.

"I ran that one night a week completely on my own; my wife was in the box office, my father-in-law at the door. We charged a guilder, and paid the musicians out of that. We tried to pay them well: a hundred guilders each for the Dutch guys, a hundred dollars for the Americans. That was a lot of money for that time." That means the Dutch made roughly half as much as the Americans.

"Han, Willem Breuker and some other musicians always made a lot of noise on behalf of it too. Every Sunday Han and Masje would come to our house, and address and stuff 1500 envelopes. Some of the American musicians couldn't believe their eyes when they walked in. Lockjaw Davis opened the door, saw the crowd, and wanted to run away; he was worried the National Guard would show up. Everyone was there: hippies came to see Don Byas and Willem Breuker. We had a real mix, and that's good.

"I was selling cars on a lot in the '60s: General Motors, Opels and Pontiacs. Whenever I had to pick up a musician I'd drive a brand new Opel. I loved that job. Selling a customer is like building a solo: you get them dancing, then cool them down, then bring them up again. As soon as the guy's sold—'I think I'll buy the car'—I say, 'Shouldn't you think about it?' The way you succeed is more important than success itself.

"Sun Ra had been one of my heroes, and I'd heard he was playing in Barcelona. He was difficult to reach by phone, but I found him. 'How much money will you need to come and play?' 'For you, $10,000.' I said, 'Jesus, no.' He said, 'What can you do?' 'Two thousand guilders.'" Dulfer pauses for effect. "'Okay.' He showed up with 35 musicians, and made a lot of trouble for the radio people; he wouldn't play on stage.

"What was nice was, soon there were all these little Paradisos cropping up in Holland, and they had to have jazz too.

"It ended badly. It was very successful, but I hadn't been paying taxes, and one day the tax man showed up. He wanted a hundred thousand guilders. The Paradiso dropped me.

"In the '60s, Willem Breuker, Theo Loevendie and me also played on the pop scene, and at Vietnam rallies. We were part of the far-out culture. If something was happening, we were invited.

"The Hilversum guys trusted me a little. We could start the BIM because I brough in these people who said avant-garde wasn't real music. That was my job, to bring in people like Cees Slinger. But later everything changed, and became more isolated. As usual

"The idea behind the Podium Plan was to get the musicians out of Amsterdam. If you just play here, there's no money.

"When I hear my records, my reaction is usually the opposite of how I felt on stage. I'll think I'm very good when I'm on stage, but when I listen back, it's awful.

"You're interviewing me, but I'm not part of Dutch jazz history." Typical Dulfer.

Theo Loevendie could always make room for such windy boys. On *Mandela*, 1969, his core band is Dulfer, van Manen, Nedly Elstak on trumpet, Altena, and dual drummers John Engels and Martin van Duynhoven. The Consort was Loevendie's jazz workshop after Boy's band broke up, and had some of the same better-or-worse looseness. The horns' intonation can go slack, but as usual he's good at setting up tumbling polyrhythms. The Turkish turns sound unforced; the drummers don't yammer on. The music breathes easier than *Stairs!*

Whatever Nedly was he wasn't chopsy; you hear the air escaping around his mouthpiece. Still, he and Dulfer lead an Ayler-brothers cavalry charge on "Pepy." Big smeary trombone comes out front for "Mandela." Those broad horns offset Loevendie's pinched alto. If he sounds like anyone it's Tchicai. He doesn't give too much away.

In Loevendie's band or Dulfer's, Hans and Willem van Manen make a good pair: the streetwise blusterer who plays *out* while thinking of Ike Quebec, and the trombonist who can be truculent as Rudd but may also by slide and plunger and falsetto and slippery strategies be hard to pigeonhole.

In 1971, Breuker was hired by the Will Spoor mime troupe to supply live music for a three-act "opera," *The Message*. His quartet was the same crew who'd stormed the SJIN the year before: himself on clarinet and tenor, van Manen, Altena, Peter Bennink on alto and soprano. "At that time I had the idea, I can't go on any longer with the terror of Han Bennink. I want to write compositions and perform them without a drummer who's too loud and not listening."

The Message (ICP 009), recorded live, agreeably mixes improvisation and chamber music, an idea around since before the War—Artie Shaw's first Gramercy Five with harpsichord was 1940, for example—and a '50s fashion on either coast: Mingus, Serge Chaloff, Shorty Rogers. (A decade later, Altena would have a bass, alto sax, trombone and oboe quartet.)

Breuker's band had a folksy Euro-homegrown flavor of its own, a fugue state far from MJQ's *Blues on Bach*. His harmonic knowledge has grown enough so he can blend and juggle four voices with authority: somber chorales, homespun counterpoint, pulsing 8th notes—about which much more, shortly—and on "Telephone Song," ziggurat horn lines in dissonant close harmony, Monkish, over bumblebee bass. One of Altena's conspicuous strengths was his ability to get freakish sounds with a bow. He's overtone-rich.

There is new assurance in the way Breuker handles musicians as well as materials. The players complement each other: Bennink's alto may lay sweet and straight, lining out four-note arpeggios, while Breuker plays with characteristic open-throated rasp on tenor or heavily featured clarinet, confirming his rep as a guy who can play any single-reed. His big sound betters many full-time clarinetists. He also plays some showstopping sputtural tenor, cackling chickens slight return, cutting any "nonidiomatic" free player short of Evan Parker.

The Message reveals Breuker's growing concern with overall form, in a self-conscious "Ouverture" less than the penultimate "Ominous," with its allusions to themes and motifs heard and still ahead. But the old jokes resurface—peeping clarinet clubfoots Ayler's "Ghosts." There is some forced humor: a Breuker vocal on "Suicide Song" where he bellows in a barbershop tenor, and yodels, and gargles, and scales scales like an opera singer, and strains for notes he can't hit, and splits into a male-female duet, and generally wears you down. But there are new wrinkles.

"Collision Stomp" is Breuker painting a mustache on a dixie warhorse, W. C. Handy's "Farewell Blues." Van Manen catches the leader's mocking spirit exactly, with up a harrumphingly authentic two-note chorus he may've known by heart from apprentice days, all barnyard licks and spent lip. Breuker plays buffoon another way: cheerleading bandleader yelling encouragement to his soloists, himself included. During Altena's slap-bass feature, he says (the routine's in English, dixie's mother tongue) "We need some nice accents," then counts off a staccato hit for the horns, which they bungle repeatedly, coming in too early, before nailing it in a small but satisfying way. The joke's payoff serves a straight musical function. He practices conduction even as he mocks it.

"Final" ends with a sound of things to come, the actors joining in on vocals: something sing-song for untrained voices, nothing complicated.

♫

"Louis Andriessen came to the concerts, said hello. He came from a famous family, everybody knew him, and he was always a nice guy to to talk to. But very Catholic, so you never know what he really thinks.

"Louis wrote a piece for the 1970 World Exposition in Japan, a piece for me and Han as guests with the Nederlands Blazers Ensemble. (Han didn't go, maybe he asked for too much money.) I thought it was fantastic, to go to Japan with all these classical guys. I knew a lot of them already because we had played together in the series with the timetable pieces. Then Louis asked me for a new arrangement for the Holland Festival: 'Can you take this piece we played in Japan, and with the improvisers make a new piece out of it?' I made a new score out of his material, called *Spektakel*." The large ensemble—winds, percussion, electronics—included Han, Gilius van Bergeijk, Willem van Manen, Maarten Altena, and Breuker himself.

"Then I had the quartet with Peter Bennink, Willem van Manen and Maarten. We did *The Message* and a lot of concerts. Everybody could play and find out what he wanted with music. Then, I got an invitation to write and perform street music for the opening of the Holland Festival. There were some acrobats, and we had to perform eight times a day, going from one spot to another, a 15-minute performance. So I wrote a 15-minute piece—idiot, it's much too long, but I had so many ideas. For that I needed some drums, and afterwards I thought, 'Okay, we can play a bit with this quintet.' Peter, Maarten, Han, Willem van Manen and me.

"Also Terry Riley had come up with his piece *In C*, which was a shock the way Albert Ayler was. Terry Riley invented music again, building something from nothing. That's the way I think about it. I played *In C* with a workshop band I led every Thursday night at that time—an open workshop, no musical theory. We don't play jazz, we just play music." Riley's piece came to Breuker's attention in summer 1969, around the same time composer Frederic Rzewski turned Andriessen on to it. Other folks would play it too; Maarten Altena performed it as a bass solo.

"Louis discovered minimal music, and got completely away from symphony orchestras, and serial music, whatever he wrote. He wrote a piece for me, for two pianos and solo saxophone, and another piece where I had to play a saxophone solo. He wrote notes down for me, but I could play throughout the piece, as free, loud and long as possible. That was at the beginning of the '70s.

"One day he called me up and said, 'I want to make an orchestra with good involved musicians, can you help me find the woodwinds?' Okay, so I came up with Willem van Manen, Bob Driessen, Herman de Wit, and Maarten, all the guys who were already playing with my ICP band. That was the beginning of De Volharding.

"One of the first pieces we played was an arrangement by Louis of *La Creation du Monde*, the great work by Milhaud. But that has percussion. I said to Louis, 'No percussion, please, no percussion.' The terror of percussion."

We assume this is basically true, however the band was together a little while before *The Creation* entered Volharding's repertoire.

Steve Lacy has said about influences, the things you run away from are as important as the things that attract you. Omitting drums from Volharding is a prime example. Thus (if Breuker's to be believed) did Han Bennink playing consistently too loud help fix Volharding's permanent lineup. Looking back, you can also see that Breuker's modern life—life year in and out with his ten-piece Kollektief—began in a way with that phone call from Louis Andriessen.

—Do you hear jazz influences on your early piece for Volharding, "Dat gebeurt in Vietnam," Louis?

"Yeah, certainly. It's meant to be a kind of parody of big-band music. Use the army of your enemy was the idea."

—An affectionate parody?

"To answer your question in a very philosophical way, I think one of the most brilliant ideas of Volharding was not having a drummer. That immediately took out almost all the automatism, and all the things that did not interest me about pop music. For me, without drumming, it can't really be jazz, even though it has a lot to do with it.

"What I tried to do in the beginning was cross borders, and to have a kind of equality of classical and jazz musicians, together. That specifically interested me, to find out how that worked. And it has had a lot of results on a broader scale.

"Now when we look back on this first growing period, it was very difficult. Kids have to bang around in order to become a real person. But looking back I think we didn't have that many accidents growing up, that we did a good job, both Willem and I. And why? Simply because we think the music is the most important thing there is. You shouldn't make too many victims, because it's not good for the music. But now I sound a little like a pastor."

Now or then. From the orchestra's 1972 brochure: "De Volharding starts with the advantage that it can deploy a number of musical techniques because its members consist of both classically-trained musicians and jazz musicians, each representing different musical disciplines associated with different social classes. A prerequisite for working with De Volharding is that the musician be totally committed to both the repertoire and the audience. Both are permanently open for discussion, within the group and with outsiders. . . .

"The members of the group debate the reasons for playing or not playing on a particular occasion. More than one engagement has been turned down after longer or shorter discussion.

"Once a week we work on the specifically musical problems of an entirely new repertoire, without referring to other people's opinions. For example: notation. A jazz musician will play a certain notation differently from a classical musician. The same goes for rhythm. *The Creation* is filled with passages where the two ways of playing have influenced each other in the course of many rehearsals."

Orkest de Volharding—the Perseverance Orchestra—brought the music to The People: factories, school assemblies, neighborhood centers and festivals, anti-War and anti-nuke rallies. The orchestra's second gig was at the last Inclusive Concert, 12 May 1972, at the Carré, playing Andriessen's *De Volharding* with great spirit and sloppiness. They blared. With its racing 8th and 16th notes, slowly shifting patterns with voices emerging and subsiding, flexible duration dictated by how fast the players advance from one section to the next, and its wandering into related keys from a C major start, it's a raunchy remake of Riley's 1964 *In C*, with some sudden discontinuous moves for spice.

Riley's recording for Columbia released in 1968 created a sensation. It was minimalism's calling card, major introduction to a new way of making music whose processes were clear to the ear. It was transparent in the best sense: you got the point right away, and could hear and see what the materials were. The complete score was printed inside the sleeve of the first issue (if not all subsequent editions). It consists of 53 short notated phrases, to be repeated as often as each player wishes, before moving on to the next, till everyone has arrived at the last figure. Everyone starts in one place, inches unequally toward the same goal, one measurable position at a time: a board game.

It is central to Andriessen's conception of *In C* (and by extension Volharding) that he immediately connected it to Riley's jazz background. Andriessen had met him at Darmstadt in 1962: "He was basically a crazy jazz musician who played very nice soprano saxophone solos." Around the time he wrote *In C* Riley had supported himself playing ragtime or jazz piano in bars—and many years later referred to *In C*'s "really strong developmental quality, a lot of variation and permutation of motives."

Anthony Davis once said there would be no minimalism without R&B. Composer David Dramm cites James Brown's 1956 "Please, Please, Please" as primary evidence.

Louis Andriessen: "The cosmic, holistic, dull side of minimalism is not interesting to me, but the original forms like *In C* are very interesting, and rigid and loud. I also like those rigid and aggressive early Steve Reich pieces, throwing the microphones"—in an arc past the PA, feeding back whenever they swing past the speakers: Reich's "Pendulum Music," 1968.

De Volharding is Dutch dissonant minimalism in the tradition of Breuker's "Song of the Lusitanian Bully II." But in place of that '69 piece's droning, Andriessen injected a certain staccato phrasing for saxophones that stems only partly from Riley, and which instantly became Volharding's signature. It's the way Louis most always writes for saxophones, and the way Volharding's saxes came to phrase collectively.

Volharding on that '72 Carré concert was three classical trumpeters, Breuker, Loevendie and Herman de Wit on saxes, van Manen and two classical trombonists (one named Bernard Hunnekink), and Andriessen on piano. As the concert recording makes clear, some folks hated it—you can hear them whooping derisively—but overall they were a hit.

De Volharding was orchestra as demographic and democratic laboratory. In its early years they played arrangements of revolutionary anthems from Spain, Vietnam and Chile, arranged by Andriessen, van Manen or Altena, or Breuker sideman Jan Wolff, who joined up before long, or Misha Mengelberg, who didn't. (Loevendie was the first to quit: "Politically speaking, I didn't think it was very efficient, but that's not a comment about the music.") The orchestra also played Louis's "Volkslied" (Folksong) in which the Dutch national anthem slowly gives way to the "Internationale"; his *On Jimmy Yancey*, which we'll get to later on; a Weill *Threepenny Opera* suite arranged by Breuker; Steve Lacy's '74 *Precipitation Suite*—a bouquet of pieces with weather themes—with the soprano saxophonist as guest.

But all that stuff that was permanently open for discussion? De Volharding drove each other nuts—everybody was on the same side, sort of, but all the socialists, communists, anarchists and none-of-the-aboves could sure split hairs. Volharding in the '70s was one of the most hagglesome orchestras ever. Should we have different repertoires for different audiences, and if so, do we play easy populist pieces for workers and hard stuff for concertgoers or vice versa? Are we for or against construction of the Amsterdam subway, which creates jobs but destroys neighborhoods? If we accept an offer to play in Chile, will that be seen as defiance of or compliance with a right-wing regime? (They went.)

De Volharding specialized in playing fortissimo, out of tune; somehow the blend of classical and jazz musicians resulted in intonation that was outside the norm for either. Part of their philosophy was that conductors are authoritarian, so there was no one to tell them to tune up. There is also a trace of the esthetic of George Ives, Charles's father, who as choirmaster preferred blaring enthusiasm to prim perfection.

Breuker was gone by '75: too many schedule conflicts, too many scene-stealing moves, too many disappearances to the bar when there was politics to be discussed. Personnel kept changing. By 1977 the saxophones were Bob Driessen and two newcomers from the Rotterdam Conservatory, Mariëtte Rouppe van der Voort and Ab Baars. Andriessen ducked out himself that same year, but by then Volharding had a momentum and life of its own, a leaderless band with several de facto frontfolk: van Manen, Hunnekink, Wolff.

"The two main reasons I gave for leaving: in the first place I thought I'm not a real musician, I don't like to sit three hours in a car, play a concert in Enschede and drive three hours back. The other reason was, as a composer, I had written everything I had to tell for those instruments. It was 20 years before I wrote another large piece for them.

"I never did a gig with Willem Breuker for the play *Baal*. I'm on the recording, but probably because somebody was unavailable. I played on his 'Monk in Groningen' and some other things I can't remember but I was never in his band." (On that last, from 1974, you can hear Louis trying to do Monk, via chiming repeats, but it's like Dick Hyman doing Cecil Taylor: not so precisely observed.)

"When Leonard Frank was a young director doing interesting things, he asked me to write music for a play, and I advised him to ask this Willem Breuker. When Leonard started the theater group Baal, Willem was his first composer. *Baal* was the first play they did as a group. I started writing for Leonard about six years later, but that had nothing to do with jazz, but with Bach and Stravinsky."

In the early '70s, the ICP collective ran smooth as a schismatized Church with two Popes. For Misha one facet of improvising as (instant) composing was, every piece is a fresh start; you choose the instrumentation every time. The Pool is a pool to draw from and swim in.

Willem's pool was a motor pool: guys to get his vehicles up and running. He wanted a band that would rehearse and play a repertoire, in concert or for the theater. By the early '70s, a Breuker ICP gig likely involved Altena, van Manen, Peter Bennink, Cuypers, and a newcomer with a flair for working with the first wave of commercial synthesizers, Michel Waisvisz. They worked in Belgium and Germany as well as Holland.

Breuker thought any regular participant in ICP gigs should enjoy full voting rights. He challenged Han and Misha to extend the franchise. Nothing doing; that would hand control to Willem's bloc. He could do what he liked on his own gigs, but ICP would remain a three-way partnership.

Willem van Manen: "Willem wanted me and Maarten admitted to ICP, and Misha refused, said, 'You are not on the same level as us.' But that was to protect his own interests. Later, when I asked him to play a couple of duo pieces on a record, he paid me great compliments."

Leo Cuypers: "Me and Misha liked each other 'cause we came from the same background; my grandfather was also a composer. He'd never say anything bad to me. 'I can recognize your style from 100 meters.' Occasionally we'd play two pianos, in one of Breuker's theater productions, or I'd play in bands Misha organized. So he was a little inconsistent: 'We three are the inventors.' But I didn't take it personally. Willem had such a big heart and mind, he saw he needed more people, but Han and Misha regarded everyone who came into that circle as a threat."

Willem Breuker: "We got an invitation to play at a festival in England. Misha said 'If you go with your five guys I have to be in the group too because I'm also in the Instant Composers Pool.' It was a big disaster of course. He went, no rehearsal, nothing. I tried to play some of my compositions. He had the notes but he didn't play the notes. I have the greatest respect for Misha. Even when he makes mistake after mistake, and everything goes wrong, I still think he's a great guy. But don't forget he's a big artist, he's also proud of the things he does. In a certain way he wants you to think he doesn't care at all, but he cares more than you think."

—Did you think he tried to sabotage your gig?

"Yeah. He always said to me, 'You go too far.' When I wrote the *Baal* music, he was very mean about that. 'All these tunes—what do you want with that?'

"Never forget, I was very involved with theater, brought it on stage with ICP and the Kollektief. Han and Misha didn't like that, didn't want to rehearse or think about it. If you want to repeat a joke that works the next day for another audience, why not? It's my joke, I might like to tell it again a couple of times."

—Repetition and live theater go together.

"If you can draw an audience by combining this stuff with improvisation, let them come, please, otherwise why do it? I'm not afraid of repeating a joke or repeating a piece."

Starting late in the '60s, Breuker and Mengelberg founded two strains of a nebulous and woefully underdocumented phenomenon, what the Dutch call music theater.

Misha's absurd productions reveled in disjunctive content and nice music, however little one may have had to do with another.

Breuker concentrated on an ingenious hybrid of psychodrama and fraternity skit. He got people to play types based on their own personalities and histories. That makes it easy for your players to improvise in character. It also allowed Willem to mess with their heads a little bit.

In ICP's first music-theater production *The Life of Wolfgang Amadeus Mozart*, 1969, Misha played the former child prodigy/composer/pianist, details of his life taken from a coffee company's promotional comic-strip biography. Panels from that strip were projected on a wall behind the action.

Writing in 1975, Rudy Koopmans saw the roots of Willem's music theater in his furious free-jazz parodies. "The methods used by Breuker toward the end of the sixties can practically all be described as alienation techniques. . . . Breuker's affinity with Brecht's plays and Eisler's music was no doubt a significant factor here as well."

Koopmans, on the mark, distinguished between the ritual nature of performances by Sun Ra or the Art Ensemble of Chicago, and the critical nature of Dutch music theater: Brecht and Eisler triumph over Artaud.

In time Breuker's productions became revenge therapy. For one, he shot home-movie footage to compare the swank homes of Hilversum musicians with his own crew's squalid digs. Usually the targets were nearer at hand. In Breuker and Lodewijk de Boer's 1972 *Cain and Abel*, the unrehearsable Han played a caged primitive in Alley Oop garb striking drums with tree trunks. A year later for *Oltre Tomba*, a sort of mock-Restoration comedy about a medieval cutting contest—note the potent ICP subtext: musicians working against not with each other—Bennink was a peripatetic snare-drummer bedecked with a plumed hat, kilts, and a huge ornamental collar that could have come from Sun Ra's closet. Han didn't dig all that dressing up.

In '74, Herman de Wit played the lead in *De achterlijke Klokkenmaker* (The retarded Clockmaker). His character, who makes one entrance swinging on a rope from the
balcony, echoes Victor Hugo's hunchback, but his stoop and bald-with-a-fringe skull-
cap made him look a little too pointedly like Misha. That's alienation technique.

(These techniques still echo through the occasional Dutch production. In Teo
Joling's 1997 show *Teerr en Feer*, from a Poe story about inmates running an asylum,
the cast was mostly musicians, who played Michael Moore's score and used their
instruments as props. Playing inmates, Han Bennink and Ernst Reijseger pulled many
of the same tricks they normally do on a gig.)

There's a recording of *Klokkenmaker* that suggests other ways these plays could be out-
rageous. The musicians paraded through the audience chanting Pharoah Sanders' "The
Creator Has a Master Plan," breaking it up with sabre rattling and fake zulu war whoops.
The band's one black member, flutist Ronald Snijders, was conspicuously featured.

By then Breuker's partnership with Han and Misha was over. ICP had been getting
subsidized, but subsidy money was always short and late in those days. Compounding
the problem was Peter Bennink's double duty as ICP business agent and as bookkeeper
at the electronic studio STEIM, which had its own cash-flow problems. Willem says
this made for even more tardy payment of ICPers. He also says it came to his attention
that Peter was telling folks who'd called to book Breuker that he was too busy with film
and theater projects, but that a Misha group was available instead.

"Finally came the point where we had to break up. I wrote the music for ICP, did
the theater pieces and concerts, all these activities. As a result we had our subsidy doubled; it went from 30,000 to 60,000 guilders, because of my work. Then Misha said,
'Okay, we split it three ways: me, Han and you.' I'd already spent 30,000 guilders of my
own money. So I said, 'Okay. ICP is not for me anymore.' Maybe I should have realized that earlier, and not been so faithful to the organization I put all my energy and
loyalty into. But I still had a lot of respect for Han and Misha's music.

"We had a meeting to decide who would stay with me and who with Misha. Han
of course made no decision. Most of the guys stayed with me, except Maarten Altena."
Andriessen says this also put Altena and Breuker in different political factions in
Volharding, increasing tensions there.

"So I stayed with the same guys, and the same things we'd been doing. I called my
band the Kollektief, the Collective. It's a nonsense name from the '60s, a little bit
socialistic. On the other hand, everybody in the band can say what he wants, and
everyone earns the same. Maybe that's why the band exists over 20 years, with a couple of guys from the beginning. The books are open. I take no salary, because I have
money enough from my royalties and commissions."

You ask Han if there were money problems with ICP, he says: The money is always
short in this business. You ask Misha about Breuker's allegations—that he sabotaged his
gigs, that he screwed him over the double-subsidy split, that he repeatedly criticized
Willem's choice of musicians—and he demurs: Yes, something like that may have happened. But he objects if you aver his behavior was shabby somehow: Not at all.

Misha could point to Willem's counterantagonism. But as when questioned about
how a piece should be played, or when he's attacked for being frivolous, he chooses
not to explain himself.

After I'd known Misha a couple of years:
—I'm very grateful for all the kindness you've shown me.
"You've never given me a reason to behave otherwise."

As the breakup drew near, Willem had kept recording with various groups. A mixed classical/jazz septet (with van Manen, Altena and Han Bennink) cut two tangos—Breuker was quite interested in tangos at the moment—for a TV production of Büchner's *Woyzeck* in January '72. (The problem for once is the drummer; Han cookie-cuts the beat, back in the cage.) Later in the year a promotional mailing for an entertainment discount card, the Cultural Youth Passport, included a flexidisc, same fast-decaying format as ICP 013. "My baby has gone to the schouwburg" is Willem's best AM-radio send-up—almost as if he'd heard *The Who Sell Out*—a boogie blues with Michel Waisvisz playing harmonica like it's a sine-wave generator. (Like the tangos it's on a Breuker grabbag CD, his picks, *De Onderste Steen*.)

Gradually, out of his many many sessions, a blueprint for a band sound began to emerge. Except for the name and the rhythm section, the Kollektief was up and running by 1973. The Willem Breuker Orchestra recorded in Berlin in March '72 had Peter Bennink, Herman de Wit and Willem van Manen on horns, Maarten Altena on bass, Waisvisz on synthesizer, Rob du Bois on piano or organ and Leo Cuypers on piano or drums.

In terms of Breuker's maturing sound, a watershed is his music for theater group Baal's production of Brecht's *Baal* in 1973. Conceptually it's wedged between the try-anything pragmatism of the chocolate box and the Kollektief's signature fat horn voicings. Tonny Pels plays local-color mandolin, as on ICP 007/008, except the written lines have a snap missing in '69. (The album was all-instrumental, but in the play many pieces were sung.) Breuker has found his groove, even with a one-shot Andriessen-Altena-Bennink rhythm section. Besides the pianist and bassist, trumpeter Cees Klaver, hornist Jan Wolff, de Wit, altoist Bob Driessen and trombonist Bernard Hunnekink came over from De Volharding. (The CD *Baal Brecht Breuker Handke* also contains 1974 music for a Peter Handke production, for octet with several Volhardingites, and Loek Dikker on keyboards, and Martin van Duynhoven on drums, no bass.)

Baal is by Breuker the melodist, who can take a hook and develop it, who can recycle a phrase the way he does old jokes or Han old drumsticks, measuring out his materials as if on a tight budget. It's a test of ingenuity. If his choices are sometimes simple— trumpet lead for the first four bars, French horn for the next four—he'll also sandwich a lot of subthemes and diversions into a single piece, trusting to rhythmic momentum for cohesion. Han helps there.

In much of Breuker's music, his many fanfares and marches especially, there's an archaic element, fallout from the '70s fashion for playing old music on original instruments. (In the show *The Trojan Horse Goes on Vacation*, a quartet played antiqued instruments that looked suspiciously like garden tools.) He self-consciously kids his European roots the way the Art Ensemble of Chicago's ritualized use of little percussion respectfully/humorously nods to Africa. Breuker's atavism reveals itself in *Baal* via use of harpsichord and recorder. Andriessen, brought up on Bach and church music, is at home behind organ and harpsichord as well as piano.

Breuker's European sources come from all over. The voracious listener and record collector had discovered Ennio Morricone, his ear-popping spaghetti western scores in particular. Breuker got into him heavily around 1972; the day he bought his first Morricone record, he bought four of them, one a sampler with the '65 "For a Few Dollars More" theme in leadoff position. The merry stepping of a harpsichord–bass clarinet–tuba trio on one piece smacks of Morricone's influence, but the smoking gun is "Lethe," with its tolling funeral bell and a descending minor chord chimed on celeste. A near-identical celeste figure wafts through *For a Few Dollars More*.

"I was one of the first guys who had Morricone records in Holland. I thought, 'How is it possible that a contemporary composer writes this music?' It shocked my mind. 'This guy is no asshole taking the easy way. Unbelievable, tricky professional.'"

Breuker to interviewer Henk de Boer 1982: "When you happen to know his music, you are quite willing to go to Doctor M's consulting hour, when looking for solutions . . . at the moment you're stuck. If that happens you can try the soldier's manual but you might as well consult Morricone. He has proposed beautiful and at the same time remarkably peculiar solutions. . . . Figuratively speaking: it's as if he wants to throw a ball in a basket, not directly, but by hitting the wall first. In the end, it isn't important whether the ball has or hasn't actually got into the basket, because the roundabout route has already achieved in interesting effect."

That said, "Lethe"'s main theme, two-beat circus melody with alto lead, is straight out of Nino Rota's Fellini scores. So is the horn charge that alternates with a happy-trails mandolin lope under a prim mute-trumpet melody on "Als de zachte bleke zomer" (Like a soft pale summer). The cyclical folk dance of "Ik begin een nieuw leven" (I begin a new life) sounds Italian in this context too.

There are other odd influences and juxtapositions. "Orge" breaks up a light rewrite of "White Cliffs of Dover" (mandolin again) with horns blaring the first four notes of "London Bridge." Han dons his wooden shoes to clog on one piece.

But what strikes one more than any single gesture is Willem's ever-growing mastery of his materials. He's able to get more stuff in one piece than ever. The wrap-up "Slotkoraal" is almost a compendium of everything he'd learned about music on the job.

Meanwhile the Kollektief's characteristic saxophone-section sound is unveiled on "Poenduet," throaty parallel lines in close harmony.

Allan Chase chairs the jazz department at the New England Conservatory, is a founder of Your Neighborhood Saxophone Quartet, has a keen ear for saxophone writing. In New York, Chase played with bands led by Joel Forrester and Phillip Johnston, who in the '80s ran the Microscopic Septet, a sax-heavy band that wore funny hats, endlessly repeated jokes, and played tangos and marches. I asked Chase to listen to *Baal* and some other Breuker music. He sketched out a couple of pieces, and made some impromptu comments.

"All those two-bar sequences that keep coming back, the chords in blocks—it's like a building with the plumbing on the outside. All the structure is blatant and undisguised.

"Generally I don't hear anything that sounds like jazz harmony. The harmonic language is more like Kurt Weill: a modernized, dissonance-enhanced version of 19th-century classical and folk and/or light popular-music harmony. Monk tunes like 'Skippy' are another precedent, the triads creeping up and down the scale. The chordal motion, the voice leading, is sort of Slick Barbershop. He'll wander into some weird chords—like an E-flat minor in the key of A major—led there by notes in the previous chord.

"I hear strong similarities to Carla Bley—not a matter of influence, I'd guess. Too contemporaneous. But on the 'Ouverture' in particular, the chromatic shifts remind me of Weill, and the modular repeated sections and repetitions of little kernels remind me of Carla.

"The similarities to the Micros are real too, but not necessarily the result of influence. It's easy to arrive at the same general effect by applying American pop-song, ragtime, early jazz and film-score chord progressions to a sax section. I think the similarity is mainly a mutual lack of the typical jazz voicings one would expect given the instrumentation. Both Breuker and the Micros write lots of plain triads, some plain major sixth chords, diminished sevenths, augmented triads, and other relatively simple chords in the context of a fairly modern, dissonant, ironic, sometimes free-jazz context. Everyone else uses either atonal or very chromatically complex pitch collections with nearly none of the old chord sounds—Sam Rivers, Cecil Taylor, Julius Hemphill—or else they use the advanced bebop harmonic vocabulary of Herbie Hancock, Wayne Shorter or Andrew Hill, with lots of mildly dissonant voicings, in intervals of adjacent seconds and fourths, and using seventh chords with 9ths, 11ths and 13ths added. By contrast the chords and progressions within a phrase that Breuker (or the Micros) use are the same as what the Andrews Sisters, Johann Strauss and Scott Joplin used.

"For instance on 'Evelyn Roe' from *Baal*, one phrase ends with a typical early-jazz cadence—with a blue minor third in the melody, over a dominant augmented triad—that for me conjures up singers with megaphones. Then the bridge has a secondary dominant—something you find in every other bar of bebop, but rare on this CD.

"The upshot is, I think this music doesn't sound like Breuker because of any unusual way of putting chords together or voicing horns. (They're voiced in unremarkable ways—big instruments playing low notes, etc.) But when I say 'simple,' I don't mean it pejoratively. Actually I think the almost total absence of bebop or postbebop harmony and of modern classical harmony is remarkable for a new music group."

A Kurt Weill craze hit the country in the early '70s. One spark was Lotte Lenya coming to the 1971 Holland Festival to sing his music. Orkest de Volharding's interest in political composers was another. And Weill is logical enough to study if you're writing music for Brecht plays—especially if, as in the Baal group, your actors do the singing. Misha Mengelberg is a great one for letting other people take credit for developments he helped nurture, but when Breuker's interest in Weill comes up, he says, I may have had a hand in that.

"The illness of Weill the musicians call it—Weil is also a liver illness. Even before I wrote music for *Baal* people said, 'Your music sounds a little like Kurt Weill,' but I didn't know his music. My first Weill LP had on it *Seven Deadly Sins,* of which I'd arranged two movements for a TV show. I thought, what marvelous, human music.

"If you have to write for actors who can't really sing, you have to put all your melodies in one octave, more or less. Don't make it too complicated. But why make it complicated anyway? If you have to say something, say it with the easiest words or musical devices you can." (In 1997, Breuker co-produced a 24-hour radio series devoted to Weill's music, and played his music in concerts as a tie-in.)

Chase is not the first to note the resemblance to Carla Bley's Weill and tango-laced saxophone-heavy music, with its repeating kernels and short sections. Bley and Breuker disavow mutual influence. However, like other musicians, artists, writers or joke tellers, Willem does not always remember which of his good ideas were originally someone else's. That's not dishonest, it's how the mind works.

Willem van Manen says Bley's partner Michael Mantler once told him the ICP co-op was a model for their decision to make their own records and produce their own concerts. (ICP distributed Bley's three-LP set *Escalator over the Hill;* mingling jazz, rock and world musics, it's *Reconstructie*'s American cousin. Bley and Mantler also distributed ICP discs in the US.)

In the January 1970 *Jazzwereld,* Breuker reviewed Charlie Haden's *Liberation Music Orchestra,* which Bley had arranged. Willem gave it three stars out of five. He liked a few things, chiefly the soloists, but he questioned the whole deal—thought Americans had more pressing wars to oppose than one fought in the '30s. (In the States, the unstated parallel was plain.) He was also critical of the arranging: Spanish guitar is too obvious in this context, "We Shall Overcome" is played too straight. Of course the LP might have grown on him later—critics change their minds like anyone else—but he may also have absorbed its ideas unconsciously. Whatever it's worth, this review is as close to a smoking gun as we get.

♫

Willem van Manen: "In 1974, Willem decided to start the Kollektief, and I helped him ask for subsidy. The nucleus was Willem, Leo and me, and I interested some other people, who came from the Boventoon, a workshop big band of talented amateurs I had then—Boy Raaymakers, Rob Verdurmen, Martin van Norden and Bob Driessen. I wrote the music along with Herman de Wit, who was playing tenor. It had been my idea to have an orchestra where the players would come and go. That was also the problem. The best would leave to become professionals, and we'd have to start over."

(Boventoon means Overtone. That orchestra was another instance of Loevendie- and Elstak-style community education. So is the Oktopedians, a workshop band for less advanced players which de Wit founded in the early '70s, at the Oktopus youth center, and which continued on even after de Wit died in 1995, Monday nights at the BIMhuis. The players tended to be more eager than equipped. As de Wit said in 1977, "Even if someone can only play three notes on his whistle, I'll find some way of letting him lay his egg—that's my strong side. I don't lose heart when their playing is terrible: I take the long-term view.")

Breuker had been looking for loyal guys, and some loyal guys had been looking for a competent visionary. Trumpeter Boy Raaymakers—handsome man then hiding his dimples behind an absurd Russian-anarchist beard—came from Nijmegen in the south, where he was born in '44, same year as Breuker. He'd gone directly from playing dixieland to free music—thought he and his buddies were the only people anywhere free improvising, was surprised when musicians would come up after gigs and say, we do this too. Afterwards he joined drummer Pierre Courbois's Free Music Quartet, an unruly quintet by the time they recorded *Free Music One and Two* for ESP in 1969. When he met Breuker and saw him in action, Raaymakers thought, that's the guy I've been waiting for. Twenty-odd years later he is still there. So is drummer Verdurmen who's no Han but who can read and follow orders.

So is Bernard Hunnekink.

"I started playing in a harmonie orchestra, near the woods in the east, not far from Arnhem, where I went to the conservatory. I started at 6, played till I was 18. I was very disciplined—my father was the chairman of the harmonie—and I hated it. Other kids are playing in the street, and I'm inside practicing.

"In 1969, the year I turned 23, I came to Amsterdam, and began playing trombone with the Amsterdam Philharmonic. When I arrived at the first rehearsal there was a demonstration going on outside, and police on horseback pushed me down a flight of stairs. I wasn't political then. I was a little boy from the country. I liked playing with the orchestra—we did big tours, went to Russia and Italy. Then I met Louis Andriessen, and he asked me if I was interested in playing a piece of his called *De Volharding*. First we rehearsed it at his house, then we discussed if and where we should play it publicly.

"De Volharding was the beginning of my political education, and also where I met Willem Breuker. We talked about various stuff, and he asked me to play in a music theater piece. So I went to the head of the orchestra and asked for a half-time job. He wouldn't agree—there were only two times a year you could quit, and I was under contract. So I went on strike. When we went to Groningen to play at a party for right-wing students, I refused to play the national anthem. So I got permission to leave. That was in 1975.

"Volharding was a very important orchestra then. Louis was a famous composer, so everyone on the classical scene was listening. The conservatives were furious; it was fortissimo from beginning to end. They had never heard saxophones played so loud. The jazz musicians didn't want to hear about pianissimo, but it made them think about composition, and using some new ideas in their own work. And I liked Louis's music very much.

"I stayed until 1978. With all the commissions and subsidies we started getting, I got the feeling I was back in the symphony orchestra. So I've stayed with Willem ever since.

"I'm not a real soloist, a real jazz musician like Boy Raaymakers or Alex Coke, looking for some place to play in the middle of the night. But I can make some comments on trombone, that's my way."

The first album under the Kollektief banner was *The European Scene*, produced by Willem's old patron Joachim Berendt, and recorded at the Donaueschingen Festival in October 1975. The band was Raaymakers and Jan Wolff on brass, Breuker, Driessen, van Norden and de Wit on saxes, Ronald Snijders on flute, van Manen and

Hunnekink on trombones, and the rhythm section of Cuypers, Verdurmen, and Arjen Gorter, another guy still on the payroll more than two decades later.

This is the first Breuker album a lot of non-Dutch jazz fans heard—MPS Records had pretty good U.S. distribution then—and it definitely grabbed one's attention. The music pops out of the speakers. Part of it is the band's increased size: more doubling of parts, more power. From Volharding Breuker learned the joys of pile-driving, but this band was as tight as that one was not. After years of struggle, the workers have united.

In a way, Breuker used the Volharding principle in reverse. Louis's orchestra used jazz musicians to energize composed music; Willem used classical musicians Hunnekink and Wolff to nail the charts in an improvised music setting. (This was back when you could count the jazz French horn players on one hand and still have enough fingers free to hold a cigarette.) The writing is more or less the same as on *Baal*, but better integrated. The sound is more massive, with Gorter's hotdogging a significant factor. Plus, Breuker unleashes his soloists in a way theater gigs never allowed. Whoever needs blowing room gets it.

The music is drawn from here and there: a march from Willem's soundtrack to Paul Verhoeven's early film *Keetje Tippel*, and "The PLO March" from a 1975 Johan van der Keuken documentary. (The original version—two saxes, piano and drums—has Louis Andriessen's best work with Breuker: he's good at pounding the piano till it rings, and his left hand brings out the Morricone roots that get submerged in the Kollektief version.)

Three pieces came from recent music theater productions. The show *Anthologie* was (say the LP notes by Breuker buddy Konrad Boehmer) "a cynical reckoning with the ideology of avant-garde music, whose development during the past 25 years he tells in acrimonious anecdotes." Not a new target for Willem, except that now he's funded, he includes a "March of the Subsidies," depicting grant-panelists as lunatics. Elsewhere in the show, the horn players were clad in diapers, and Wolff wore a frumpy housedress from Monty Python's closet.

♫

"Johnny Engels was the first improviser I had any contact with. He was a little older than me, but we were close. We lived on the same street when I was studying. My parents had a hotel where artists, actors and strippers stayed. We both fell in love with strippers. I'd play *La Traviata*, go home and change, meet Johnny, and we'd drive to Belgium where the girls were working. Johnny married his.

"I was born in 1941, on the Leidseplein, and had gone to the conservatory to study French horn and piano. I secretly went to the Sheherazade at night; you didn't admit you liked jazz at the conservatory in those days.

"My dad worked in the field of amusement music before the War; that had been a huge industry. He made his living playing in small orchestras in cafes or on boats, and playing for musicals, plays and revues. He worked with Han Bennink's father sometimes. Nedly Elstak studied with my father, and played with him in the Metropole Orchestra. But I was not allowed in that area of music. He decided I should choose between horn and bassoon—kind of cutting me off from jazz with those options.

"I had helped found the Nederlands Blazers Ensemble, in 1959, and was playing in the opera orchestra, and making records. People start to spot you. They knew I was talented, successful, and interested in other things. I met Willem Breuker very early. He asked me for a book on instrumentation, and asked, 'Will you play with me one day?' I said, 'Yes, but I don't improvise. I'd like to, but I don't know how.' He said, 'Do what you want.' And he promised to write me something.

"I couldn't always make his gigs—I had married, and had two kids—but I played with him at the Loosdrecht concours, the first time a free-jazz orchestra had played there. We were going to be on TV on Sunday night, and Willem said, 'You have to take a solo.' I couldn't improvise, so I took a very difficult etude by the American horn player Vern Reynolds, which I'd played all my life but couldn't really play. I played it the best I could, but I was very nervous. The next morning—I was on my way to an opera rehearsal—the milkman asked me, 'Mr. Wolff, did I see you on TV last night?' He asked me to settle my account on the spot. He had thought I was a serious musician, but now I was in another category, no longer respectable.

"In 1972, I started with Volharding. Louis thought the saxophone part on *La Creation du Monde* should sound like the jazz music Milhaud wrote about. So he got Willem to play that solo—not exactly, but it didn't matter. I had to make a lot of concessions in that band. When you bring two social strata together, everything goes back to zero, from the way you talk to each other to the way you rehearse. De Volharding didn't play or tune like classical orchestras, but I could go along with that.

"Willem and Louis had to fight something out. Louis wanted to play with Willem, but there was no place for someone with Louis's background. With Louis, it was like, 'I can't play this music after eating in an expensive restaurant.' Willem said, 'My music is political, that's enough, so I can eat where I want.' So he started his own Volharding, and he was right—jazz is more of a social commitment to the lower classes. Louis favored a palace revolution.

"Willem couldn't compose for Volharding, because the upper classes were critical of the way he wrote. He was always able to write wrong, and no one has the right to tell him any different. The stuff he wrote for horn was completely wrong, but fantastic. Together we figured out you could get a fantastic sound from horn atop two trombones. But he'd write me solos like you'd write for a saxophone. He had no burden of knowledge. Even now, he knows so much, but there are still gaps. That's good—please don't fill them.

"Early in his career, he didn't know how to transpose. But within two rehearsals he'd know exactly what he wanted to hear, and could demonstrate it, and within a few he'd get something very close to it. That's what makes him a composer. I didn't mind him changing something six or eight times, because he had vision. He learned very quickly how to express himself.

"The Kollektief's theatrical period really got started in 1975. Because I grew up around circus people, I'd been juggling and balancing objects since I was 13. I'd always done crazy things with Willem, even in the '60s. Later, Laurel and Hardy were a big influence. Simple Dutch humor."

—Leo Cuypers says, "Willem van Manen and me were the inventors of the theatrical jokes."

"Leo gives himself too much credit. I did a little. But most of the comic impulses came from Willem Breuker. They think they made the jokes, but he would typecast people—give them a character based on how he really saw them. (Except me, because I could do other things he didn't expect.) By the time the show premiered, they didn't realize they'd been typecast. He dressed Leo as the little prince, and coaxed Willem van Manen into playing the banjo. Willem also knew what ideas to take and not take from people.

"We played the show *La Plagiata* with the Baal group." Breuker co-wrote it with Leonard Frank, 29 performances, 1975. "The Kollektief played and acted, had several roles—they were the orchestra, and they played an Orchestra. In one scene, there was a demonstration, and the Orchestra played, looking very awkward, nervous and out of place. It was a satire on Volharding, which as you know had a lot of the same people in it. Someone yelled 'Actie!' and I called 'Taxi!'"

Chapter Five
Organization Is Not Hierarchical

"My father Jacques was an amateur radio operator, and had all these shortwave receivers at home, discarded military equipment that he rebuilt to match his desires, and to communicate with his friends. It was their internet."

— You heard all those burbles and squeaks.

"I played with them. I wasn't allowed to, but finally I hid a radio in the room I shared with my younger brother, and we listened to it secretly in the evening. All those sounds were fantastic. When we were three or four years old my father would take us on his knee and explain that these sounds came from very far away. That wasn't a concept we really understood, so he explained the sounds were coming from behind the factory on the other side of the street. When I got to be a little bit older, I started looking behind that factory, and discovered that the people over there made the same sounds as on our side. You could say I've been looking to recover those sounds ever since.

"When I was six my parents invited the guy who plays the bells in the local church to be my piano teacher. He was so loud I got scared. I had four or five lessons and it was over. So that's all for serious training.

"The first things I remember my father listening to were by Louis Armstrong. I think at that time he didn't quite take to *Bells* by Albert Ayler, which was really the first record that I had. I made a little bed in my room so I could listen to *A Love Supreme* by Coltrane with my eyes closed. I dropped out of school around the same time, when I was like 14, and I played the trombone for a little while. I listened to those jazz musicians, but I listened much more to Messiaen. I loved *L'Ascension*, the organ version. Also my father had built me an early Theremin, the first pure electronic instrument that I played.

"Then I started using contact microphones in old pianos, and playing in Happening-type events that I organized. For awhile I also played a harmonium too. Around my 15th, 16th birthday, when I got back into sound music, the early shortwave stuff, my father came to one of my first concerts, and it reminded him of being scared

93

while fighting in the War, surrounded by the noises of rockets and bombs. We haven't always been friends, but I think we both trained each other to become what we are. Now of course in the jazz business in Holland he's considered the hippest old man."

You see Jacques Waisvisz, who has a Prussian mustache and wears suits, sitting in the front row at gigs, with his old cassette recorder, hand-held microphone extended, taping in mono. It's hard to see the resemblance to Michel—born 8 July 1949 in Leiden—who comes on like an affable talking bear. Very talky in fact. In the '70s Jacques became programmer of the SMØR concert series in Delft, founded in '63 and still going. Michel did some of his first gigs there in 1969.

"We had concerts where we brought in people just to eat an onion, while someone played free jazz, and a violinist played Bach. It was very much like what would now be called postmodern, and then was called a Happening: a big mess. But for me it was just trying to make my own music, from a very mixed background of classical music, and some Indonesian stuff I heard early, because both my father and my stepmother grew up in Indonesia. I didn't relate very much to jazz at that time, but for several periods I've gotten back into it with the interest of a person who plays his own music. That big ego thing that's always in jazz, sometimes I hate it and sometimes I admire it.

"I did some concerts at the Free Academy in the Hague, using contact microphones. I also destroyed pianos, stripped them down to the frame to use their insides, do preparations. I think I refined the art that Cage started, because we used all kinds of little engines and drivers for the strings that you could get much more from. He still wanted a person to use the keyboard. With my brother and later some other people, we developed electromagnetic drivers for the strings. We discovered if you had a set of headphones, and removed the little plate you found inside an earpiece at that time, you'd find a little electromagnet which vibrates that thin plate in response to a change in the electromagnetic field. If you removed the plate and stuck the electromagnet under a metal string, and then fed signals through the headphone, the strings would start to resonate in response to speech or whatever. We discovered a lot of stuff like that, but I don't think I ever used it really well.

"Then I read that Dick Raaijmakers had developed something similar. I called him and he let me into the Royal Conservatory's electronic music studio, literally through the back door. He's a fantastic guy, a kind of mentor. Whenever I wanted to know something, he'd say, 'I don't want to be your teacher; find out for yourself.' It made me mad because he would explain everything to certain stupid composers, but later I felt almost honored that he didn't explain anything to me.

"He had an influence by being very negative about teaching. At some point I'd thought, maybe I should learn to read, and he said, 'You shouldn't learn.' He didn't say that to other people. I worked for half a year in that studio, and used Moog equipment and some beautiful old stuff Dick had there, and also some electromagnetic things they had developed in that period.

"I'd also put sounds on tape, and manipulate them in various ways. For a piece called 'Gulliver's Travels,' I recorded voices over the phone and then treated them, made tape loops from them and would pull them over playback heads of a tape recorder on a stand in front of me, by hand, in rhythm." He mimes rowing a small boat. "There was also a TV program where I recorded the voice of the announcer and immediately played around with it—the same stuff I'm doing now, only now the technology is more interesting.

"About 1969, at the Free Academy in the Hague there were engineers who made fucked-up transistor radios where you could touch the wires and make some very wild squeaky sounds. And partly through Dick Raaijmakers I worked on *Reconstructie*, building electroacoustical instruments like I described, such as little drivers for strings: contact-microphone technology.

"I bought this VCS–3, the Putney synthesizer. It was the first synthesizer I really liked because it sounded like a transistor radio, compared to the Moog." It looked a little like a telephone switchboard, cords and plugholes. "It was so nice to program, and I discovered that if you break the pins, take out a resistor and just stick your finger in the hole to make that same connection, you would complete the circuit.

"You become the thinking part of the machine.

"Then I took off the lid, stuck my fingers in the backside. I rebuilt the machine, with extensions, and with that I did some solo concerts.

"I think Willem Breuker showed up at a concert in the Stedelijk Museum, and he invited me to join his big ICP group. It was very nice, because all of us brought in ideas, and Willem took the responsibility for coordinating, putting a program together. Later it gradually changed into the Willem Breuker Kollektief, but in the beginning it really was a collective, which just came together for a few weeks a year. That was explosion time, the time of the Inclusive Concerts.

"I was very lucky: Gunter Hampel sort of picked me up from Willem's band, and I went on a little tour and worked in Germany. Suddenly a tape from a rehearsal became a record." Waisvisz is on the May '71 B side of Hampel's *(Ballet) Symphony No. 5/Symphony No. 6*—a duet where he plays modified Putney, and Hampel soprano, vibes and ocarina. Michel's in the background, but he creates a nice atmosphere. "Through that connection I met Steve Lacy, another person I really liked to work with."

"I came to STEIM as a customer in '73, to make the first crackle boxes. The Putney was too big. I wanted that same idea, but using dedicated hardware. I wanted a synthesizer you could carry with you like a normal instrument, and that made really wild electric sounds. I developed them with Nico Bes, and Peter Beyls, a Belgian guy, and Johan den Biggelaar.

"The crackle box idea started with the shortwave stuff. The disadvantage of shortwave receivers is that all you can do is tune in and tune out. Once you're tuned to a specific frequency you get the sounds that are there. They can be beautiful, it can be a radio station that tells you a story, it can be Telex sounds which were beautiful too, but you couldn't really change the sound.

"With the crackle box there's a direct motoric link between finger movements and the electronics. The more you squeeze, the way you change pressure on the contact points, has an incredible influence on modulations and things like that. The envelopes of sounds, like loudness and pitch, change, and sound much more natural, because your little twitches are also translated. I don't know how to decode all those little twitches, but they reveal something about me, about my physical abilities, about my character."

When it comes to art in Holland's big-spender years, STEIM looks like the kind of brainiacs' boondoggle watchdog zealots and yahoo legislators trash on several continents. In earliest days STEIM had little more than a few electric pianos, a Hammond organ and some amplifiers. That inventory had grown by 1972, when the studio set up house at 25 Groenburgwal, a picturesque canal frequently postcarded.

The early principals were the *Reconstructie* five, and Dick Raaijmakers (who ran the Hague conservatory's electronic studio thanks to Kees van Baaren, and would help set up the school's music-theater department) and a German immigrant composer who could unspool political rhetoric the way kids throw toilet paper on Halloween, Konrad Boehmer.

Discussion-wise, Volharding was a Friends prayer meeting next to STEIM. Should one construct equipment first and then build a performance around it, or conceive the show and then the gear? What's the political role of electronic music? Et cetera. STEIM was ideologically driven from the git-go: it was anti-computer, anti-synthesizer, pro-distortion (of existing sounds or simple electronic waveforms), and not so interested in the burgeoning use of electronics in pop.

Wigged out or no, the STEIMers were classical composers, had their own frame of reference. To them, Cage and David Tudor sticking toothpicks or piano strings into phonograph cartridges to make tiny noises loud and raunchy was more fun (and more hands-on) than the bonks and squeaks laboriously realized in megabuck university music labs. One early STEIM engineer insisted digital processing was the way to go, but he was hooted down. The STEIM idea was to make music in real time—or make an object that could do that. Computer music took forever, and computers were far too big to take to gigs.

But there were problems: a lot of the original equipment, much of it hand-me-down from Holland's computer-music central, Utrecht's Institute of Sonology, didn't work so well; money was always late in the early days of music subsidy; STEIM was trying to serve two functions, and didn't have enough equipment to go around. That last point prompted another debate: is our principal mission to develop new devices in the laboratory or make glorified PAs available for live performances? (As STEIMers liked to say, the loudspeaker is just another instrument.)

Execution in the field was dicey. Peter Schat's pet project was the so-called STEIM Quartet which evolved into Amsterdam Electric Circus, whose equipment included a large translucent plastic balloon. For one heavily promoted performance they tried to project a light show inside the sphere; a few feeble colors could be dimly seen by the audience, whose view of the orchestra was obscured. AEC tried playing inside the balloon, but the acoustics were terrible.

To underscore the idea the studio was the five's toy chest, the STEIM Quartet's weaponry included six five-foot tall spinning tops, Incredible Shrinking Man props, that emitted a thin wobbly drone. They were invented for and make a cameo appearance in Schat's *To You*, 1972, cantata vocal over a busy rock ensemble. The tops don't do much, but three bubbling bass guitars curiously pre-echo Ornette's electric Prime Time.

Yet, somehow things got accomplished. Even ideological wrangles yielded specific equipment, ideas made material by STEIM's working class. In *Reconstructie*, all the electronics came through one mixing table. Was that ethical? A policy group including

Mengelberg and Andriessen studied the conflict between anarchy and representative democracy; engineer Nico Bes's response was to devise "cassette tables"—modular mixers that can be detached or plugged into the circuit, so each musician got a piece of the pie. With additional help they got refined into a serially-connected "black box" system.

The research vs. field-service debate eventually set Schat and Mengelberg at odds. By '72 Misha had triumphed, and had become artistic director. (He'd checked Schat, he says, by banishing the giant spinning tops to deep storage.) But no one praises Misha's day-to-day organizational skills, and he didn't lessen confusion by involving ICP accountant Peter Bennink.

A hand-drawn family tree from a 1976 article bears the legend, typed in as an afterthought: THE ORGANIZATION IS NOT HIERARCHICAL!

Another ideal: educating the public. Around 1974, two first-year students at the Amsterdam conservatory saw a posted notice that Misha was teaching a course at STEIM.

Guus Janssen: "The first evening there were about 20 people there who wanted to know things about electro-instrumental music. Misha didn't say anything, it was completely boring. The next week there were only four left, I think. Then he de-iced, he said, 'Now we can start.'"

Paul Termos: "Everybody had to improvise something. I played classical guitar, a pathetic improvisation with classical technique, and he said, 'Is that your own?' Immediately I could see his point. After that we had a jam and I took my clarinet, somebody had an electric bass, there was piano and all kinds of percussion, and we did a kind of free improvisation with Misha playing electronics and doing all kinds of things. It lasted an hour and a half or something. Misha liked very much what Guus and I did on piano and clarinet."

Janssen: "The project was very strange, it was about making a kind of absurd theater piece. Typical Misha I think, especially in the '70s. It was quite impressive; a part of my personality liked dealing with this absurd approach very much."

Mengelberg: "I found out that with the Putney you could make sounds that were similar to words. It could say 'OW!' So we did something in which 'Ow' played a role. Guus slipped on a banana peel, there was 'Ow,' and then the ambulance came. I asked Paul Termos to somehow make with the Putney the sounds of Guus being taken by ambulance to the hospital, that little voyage." Siren, traffic, beeping monitors.

Janssen: "So we did this completely absurd piece—it was about nothing, stupid—and we went to the Hague to perform it for the music pupils. The piece was completely uninteresting, it really was. Guys in the audience were upset—'We have to sit through this shit?' And then Misha started to discuss it with them. He really succeeded in explaining that this completely boring and uninteresting theater piece was very interesting, worthwhile and meaningful. That's Misha at his best, eh?"

♬

Misha insisted anyone wanting to use STEIM had to have a specific goal. You can make your dream real here, but please dream it at home first. STEIM's founders thought like composers, but the place was strangely improviser-friendly. The stated goal was for composers/inventors to perform their own music on stage, shaping materials on the spot.

That was the climate when Waisvisz came to develop the crackle box, the great STEIM success story: the people's synthesizer, no bigger than two packs of cigarettes. With due resect to the several engineers who sweated the details, if you compare Michel's work on modified Putney before STEIM with the sounds his cracklers produced, it's clear the artistic conception was very much his.

Waisvisz and company eventually cranked out a range of whimsical crackling devices, some more for exhibition than performance. There was a crackle bicycle, and a crackle tea service—tea poured from wired pot to wired cup made the connection—and an elaborate crackle synthesizer.

But the original crackle box was the conceptual hit—another example of smaller-is-better from compact Holland—and STEIM's one successful mass-production item. Waisvisz had looked into trying to patent the technology, but the process was too expensive, and still wouldn't prevent ripoffs. The more prudent course was to saturate the market. Beginning in the mid-'70s, hundreds of them were sold out the door, first for 25 guilders, then 35, not much to pay for an electronic music instrument. We're talking around 15 or 25 bucks. Waisvisz estimates they moved about 3500. Nice to think of them adding to the local ambience, the Jetsons' miniature barrel organ.

Six exposed metal strips—laid out close together to facilitate short-circuiting—lie exposed on the lid of a small wooden cigar box, about the size of a period transistor radio. Sometimes, in fact, faint radio signals emerge from its tiny built-in speaker, fueling the (inaccurate) rumor it contains the guts of a transistor radio, but it's a dedicated device: basically, an unstable oscillator.

Because it's small, your fingers can approach the pads from any angle; hands can get as knotted as legs playing Twister. Holding it the way it feels most natural, cradled in one or two hands, the thumbs gravitate to the keys. It's as ergonomic as and rests in the hands oddly like an mbira, an African thumb piano.

Playing it as well as listening to it, the twitch factor is a big part of its appeal: it's as sensitive to tiny movements as an electric guitar string or soprano saxophone reed—and may sound rather like either instrument at times. Wiggle a finger or shake the box, you get vibrato as immediate and personal as you'd get with Strad or Strat.

But all parameters are unpredictable: speed of attack or portamento, loudness (its dynamic range is disarmingly great), purity or makeup of tone. It crackles, it swoops, it makes surprised little outbursts as if you goosed it. Lean gently on a strip, barely making contact, you can lead it in and out of split tones. Clicks may speed up and blur into discernible pitch; the box may emit a brief speedy seemingly coherent line, or may bounce between two competing sound patterns. Adding one pad to a combination may change a note a half step, or several octaves, or cut off the sound completely, or have no effect.

The idea, always, is to celebrate instability rather than control it. Like a cheap keyboard, it sounds raunchiest when its 9-volt battery is about to die.

The best thing about a crackle box is, it's good for nothing except improvising: you can't even be sure some fingering will produce any sound at all, let alone the one you got last time you tried it, yesterday or two seconds ago. (Sometimes it takes 30 seconds of touching this and that before you get a peep out of it; sometimes it'll keep whooshing after you've put it down.) A combination that works when made with the fingers of one hand may not work if you use two hands, because the resistance pattern is different. You can be wailing along deftly, and suddenly you'll touch the wrong pad, and the box will withdraw into silence from which it cannot be coaxed. But not hearing it doesn't mean it's not working; its high notes can soar out of human range. You'll be trying in vain to get a response while a dog down the block goes berserk.

So you start over looking for another happy combination, or lick a finger or two and try your luck that way. A crackle box is very susceptible to moisture, may work very differently on dry and humid days. The more moist the day or pads, the grainier the sound may become.

Yet the crackle box is a real musical instrument, because you still have enough control to establish a style. It can make anyone with fingers an electronic improviser who—by nature of the box's size and self-containment, its more-or-less reasonable volume level, its human twitches—can blend into an otherwise acoustic ensemble. It is great fun to play, so oracular in its mysterious pronouncements, so small and light and handy, you begin to understand why almost no one who bought one can locate it anymore. Did I see that in the attic a couple of years ago—or did I give it to my nephews when they were 5? Kids do love them—unless the shrill sound makes them hold their ears.

It is not, however, well represented on record. Even for Waisvisz, it was a little too indeterminate. For his own concert use he went on to develop the crackle synthesizer, same basic idea, but more sophisticated, with three oscillators, and greater control. It has a 12-key pushbutton board—each key independently knob-tunable—besides the crackle-box-like exposed pads, and an "exciter"—a contact point you touch for wildcard effects. The synthesizer is much bigger, but still completely portable: the size of a small suitcase, battery powered, with its own speaker in the detachable wooden lid (and a jack to connect to an amp). A few of these were sold too, but not many; they were expensive, not a toy.

It was also a little alien to the spirit of the original: a high-tech low-tech device, dead-end technology out of Terry Gilliam's *Brazil*.

The synth's showcase is *Crackle!* (SAJ), recorded live (with some overdubs) in '76 and '7, graphic demonstration of crackling's haywire sonorities and expressive limits. Part of its charm is hearing Waisvisz grappling with riffs and rudimentary song forms. But the synthesizer also does what makes every crackler interesting: puts out raw, barely bridled sound.

Backtrack: Waisvisz's modified Putney is all over 1974's *Lumps*, ICP 016, by Steve Lacy's "Dutch quartet" with Maarten Altena and Han Bennink. (Michel had also been on Lacy's fine, obscure *Saxophone Special*, from Emanem Records, 1971: four saxes, modified Putney and Derek Bailey.) On *Lumps*, Lacy as ever hugs his own style: flexible-rubber soft-reed timbre, ambling, unhurried time, tunes full of sing-song repeats. His band supplies ironic running commentary. They taunt each other a little, cozily. When Altena bows an exercise figure, Steve immediately runs up and down a scale.

Waisvisz contributes audio Rorschacht: variable-speed drill, creaking floor, chirping birds frogs monkey (or Lacy), arcs of raw sound, the eloquence of Cousin Itt. Michel gets some great sounds, and wields them with amazing restraint, or perhaps humble acceptance of lack of control. He never wears out a particularly striking/swooping gesture, doesn't/can't repeat it where or as often as you'd expect: his oblique strategies are a nice counterpoint to Steve's carefully ordered statements. (The same year Waisvisz joined a trio with Altena and the German guitarist/instrument maker Hans Reichel, whose later daxophone—an amplified plank of wood played like a violin—can sound a lot like a crackler.)

Altena was still developing his rude bass sounds; he has a strong pizzicato attack, and coaxes out strong high overtones with his bow. His rasp reinforces Michel's coarse texture and Lacy's squeezed harmonics. The surface has a garish sheen, the more so where Han plays clarinet, sorry "hanrinet"; it may take a second to identify who is making what awful sound. When Lacy emerges into his typical la-la cadences, he stands out in bold relief.

Bennink by then had many ways of dealing with the rhythmically intransigent. When everyone else goes to long notes, he reaches for ashcan school disruption, in rhythm. On the piece "Lumps" he seems to dump his whole trash pile of percussion at the end of each Lacy line, caged-caveman version of Edward Blackwell punctuating Ornette. The record's a vivid example of what Bennink brings to a group in overall style and attitude. *Lumps* was a typical ICP record in the occasional crudeness of the cutting. "Snips" begins with the sound of snipping scissors, followed by bald cut to a noisy Bennink intro in progress.

♫

"The first time I came to Holland was probably with Carla Bley's Jazz Realities group in 1966, with Aldo Romano, Kent Carter and Michael Mantler. In '68 I came to Holland and Germany with a quintet from New York: Kent, Paul Motian, Irene Aebi and Enrico Rava. We had a few gigs, but nothing much materialized, so I went to Rome.

"Somewhere around '66 I first came to Amsterdam, met Louis Moholo and John Tchicai. A cute place: winning, user-friendly, fun. There were good musicians around, and people who liked music, and everyone was hip to everyone else. In a flat land there's no place to hide, and everyone lives in a goldfish bowl, but they're not goldfish, they're another kind of fish. I got to know Han and Misha, and they were good." Steve Lacy doesn't remember meeting Han in New York in '61.

"It's a very important corner of the world jazz scene. A keystone, a crossroads, a corner, a niche, a place where musicians could cross paths. An interchange. People coming through and collaborating with the local scene are very important I think. It's still that way. You can't just go anywhere in Europe and show up. But if you can play you can do that in Amsterdam.

"I didn't start to use the Dutch landscape until the early '70s, when I started coming up a lot from Paris and collaborating with Dutch musicians. I think I did one of the first concerts at the BIMhuis, a piece called *Garden Variety*, with a dancer, taped Roman street sounds, and a mix of players from Paris and Amsterdam. I did some theater things with Han, Misha and Michel Waisvisz, made a few records, did some solo concerts. I appreciated the mix of jazz, theater, literature, painters, canals. Refreshing. That theater-of-the-absurd, ridiculous Dutch humor: there were some talented actresses and such, and it was an important part of the scene, but I don't speak Dutch so I don't know what they were talking about.

"At the time, there were a lot of programs mixing classical, jazz and electronic music. It didn't really work. The musicians didn't like each other, the people only liked some of it, and the seats were mostly empty. There were a lot of empty concerts in those days. With the subsidy scene, that was not an issue, but I'd prefer to starve if nobody comes, because of my old Greenwich Village experience. If no one comes and you're paid anyway, then you're beholden to the government. I don't know if there'd still be a scene if it wasn't for that, but the government bought all these terrible paintings no one wants; they wound up subsidizing bad art.

"I worked in Germany and England in the '70s too. Back then there was a common parlance in free music, it was possible to collaborate with people from all over the world. I like the English musicians, they have a more pastoral tradition. The Germans are a little more intellectual. The Dutch style has more humor, is less stodgy than the German. There's too much marching in Germany. In Holland it's too crowded. You have to turn, walk, cross a canal—there's no marching to be done. All the scenes are interesting, but there are limitations. There's no place like New York in the '50s, when there was a whole world of possibilities. Paradise is lost.

"I learned a lot from Han and Misha. Misha was the head and shoulders of the scene as far as mind power goes. He had the conception. He had instant composing going in the '70s, was using some techniques that we all learned." By now the term 'instant composing' has acquired a new meaning: conducting improvisers.

"In the '70s we were poor in the pocket but it was a very rich time. I call them the scratchy '70s 'cause we were all scratching. It was all about research and survival. So many relationships got formed then, musical and otherwise. A lot of new stuff was going on. Now I don't hear much I haven't heard before. So much is accessible now—we're over-accessed. There's so much stuff you can buy in a store, learn in school, have on the screen. The vast menu: we're over-menued.

"Misha understood Monk as well as any musician I know. He wasn't fooled, knew exactly what was going on, and could do it. Misha had an uncanny lack of waste in his playing, especially rhythmically. He's one of the few Europeans whose mise-en-place is together: his time. It has a lot to do with his partnership with Han. The relationship between them is one of the fundamental strengths of this scene. Between them you had the nucleus of the whole thing. That inspired me to deepen my relationship with Steve Potts, to get to music you couldn't get by yourself. Or take Roswell Rudd. If you have the right partner, you can correct each other's faults, go further. I think this is a much-neglected subject in jazz, and elsewhere.

"I worked with Volharding, played some workplace gigs, arranged *The Precipitation Suite* for them. I'm sure Maarten Altena procured that for me. He sort of sponsored me in Holland. I knew Louis Andriessen through him, and I liked his *Yancey* piece very much. But I didn't play their normal repertoire, just my own suite, and that's been through so many versions since I can't remember what it sounded like.

"Michel had just invented the crackle box when we did *Lumps*. I'd be afraid to listen to it! That was my Dutch record, my Dutch quartet. We worked a few gigs, I don't remember the details. It was like Dutch cooking, too heavy to have every day. But those misunderstandings are part of the understanding you wind up with. It teaches you what not to expect next time. Monk was on my case like that—he'd push me for wanting the wrong things.

"Richard Teitelbaum had turned me on to the possibility of playing with someone using electronics. Michel was fun to play with, had a lot of élan, had some fresh new sounds. It was fun. He didn't have all that Japanese hardware; I hated all that crap. This had a human scale to it. I could play it myself, it was okay." You can hear Steve Lacy's crackle box blurting away, briefly, on "Tracks (Part Two)" from *Clangs* (Ictus), duo 1976 with Italian drummer Andrea Centazzo.

"Another aspect: poetry festivals. In the middle-late '70s there were lots of them, with all these poets—Brion Gysin, Allen Ginsberg, all the cats. They were held at the Milky Way mostly. Back then, those places were psychedelic, almost. A wild, almost innocent scene. A rave, a permanent rave. Everyone getting high, very free and lively. The interchange with all these disciplines, that was what I liked." The Melkweg—the Milky Way—is a big rock club on the Leidseplein.

"Later I worked with Misha and Roswell on the Herbie Nichols project. It was a revelation for a lot of people, myself included. They really started getting people to pay attention to his music. (When Roswell and I had our band in the early '60s, the idea was repertory, but at that time the idea was so radical no one would touch us. Now everyone wants to play Monk tunes, and repertory is institutionalized.) I really respected Misha's musicality, the way he reduced the material to its correct essence without bowdlerizing it. He wasn't fooled. Misha has a hell of an ear, but he's so fucking ornery you can't get him to do what you want to do. Derek was like that too: 'No, baby.'

"We had a conflict about something I wrote that Misha wouldn't look at. A misunderstanding, but we could always work again. After the Monk and Nichols records, the last time I really worked with Han and Misha we made a record I called *Dutch Masters*. I wanted a cigar box on the cover. We had a little conflict about the title; they didn't like it. I pulled a joke on them and they didn't like it!

"You always had a nice welcome if you worked with local cats. But it wasn't what I really wanted to do. I could always collaborate, but when I wanted to bring my own band it was another story. All those years, I had one gig with my own band, in Rotterdam. Frustrating. So I stopped coming in a way. But I had wonderful rich experiences with everybody."

♫

Willem Breuker recalls that when he and Willem van Manen sat on the music panel of Amsterdam's Raad voor de Kunst—the city arts council—they explained that the improvisers wanted a place of their own, to play, rehearse, congregate. As he tells it, he got the same response he got when he challenged the SJIN: slack-jawed astonishment.

"'What? Are you crazy?' The only guy who understood was Reinbert de Leeuw, the chairman at that time." The BIM proposed a BIMhuis—pronounced rather like house, which is what that means—to the culture ministry, which blew them off. "Then at a certain moment there was fast action, because the city of Amsterdam then said, 'Okay, let's have a BIMhuis. Find a place.' With the idea that we'd never succeed in that."

Who found the BIMhuis building on the Oude Schans, an old furniture warehouse with concrete floors and a long echo? Gorter says a guy with a liquor license. Breuker says van Manen and himself. Dulfer says van Manen and Misha. Misha says, whoever they say.

Willem van Manen: "Misha found it, then called me and Hans Dulfer and we organized the whole thing. Later Willem Breuker joined us, because he was then a member of the SJIN board. Misha, not very organized, disappeared quite soon. You could say that Willem Breuker handled the artistic side, Dulfer the financial, and I took care of the building, the rent and electricity."

Gorter: "A bunch of people put their money in it, together—I was with those people but didn't have any money—to sort of force the city into backing it up."

Breuker: "Then me, and Willem van Manen also, had to pay 2872 guilders a month in rent for the BIMhuis. The city government promised us the money, but they didn't pay. I was lucky to be in circumstances where I could afford it. After four or five months—we have the BIMhuis, we have concerts—finally the city of Amsterdam paid up, and the Dutch government thought, 'We can't refuse them anymore.' So they came up with 40,000 guilders, and the next year with 160,000 guilders, and I got my money back."

♪

The Oude Schans is an industrial canal a little east of the city center, one of the main links between the Amstel River and the harbor, the IJ. (In Dutch ij is one letter, jointly capitalized, sometimes spelled ÿ, pronounced like many Dutch vowels between two English ones, long i and long a.) Driving or parking in the center was punitively difficult, so an outer location made sense. It's a fine wide canal with a view of two splendid city towers, but this was not a desirable neighborhood in the '70s. It was too close to the razing of the old Jewish quarter and those controversial construction projects, the IJ tunnel, the subway, and an imposing new opera house.

Talking about the importance of the music played at the BIMhuis—by umpteen Dutch, lots of Europeans, any American of note who'd play a small hall—is like discussing the Village Vanguard in like terms. The subject is too vast, better dealt with passim.

The same principle applied to setting up the BIMhuis as to the composers' campaign, the SJIN takeover, and subsidy debates: if you hector people long enough they'll give you money to go away. Even though money was always late for everything, looking back one might suspect that city and country were tardy with payment to starve the place out. True or not—Breuker defends bureaucrats by saying they always sit on their hands then there's work to be done; he was with the housing authority himself a minute—the BIMhuis floated partly on money he and Misha had made as composers, Willem for stage and screen and Misha for various ensembles and projects of his own.

In 1974, the culture ministry came through with its first major funding: 40,000 guilders, a third of what the BIM requested for a year's programming. The BIMmers decided to show what was possible spending that amount over three months. They also declared October "Jazz Month." The BIM printed big calendars listing every jazz gig in the country in October, whether they were funded or not, giving the impression the money went further than it did. The strategy worked; in '75 they got four times the money, and things really got under way.

BIMhuis director Huub van Riel: "The idea of 'Jazz Month' and to list all the gigs even if they weren't funded was at least 95 percent Dulfer. He said, 'If you shout "October is jazz month!" then people will do more concerts even if there's no more money,' and it worked."

Willem Breuker: "Never forget the influence of Hans Dulfer and the very good work he did in the early years. He was the guy who invited the musicians to the BIMhuis, because he had long experience booking the Paradiso. He knew a lot of musicians, and agents, and how much you had to pay.

"One night there was no money, and they called me up at home. 'We need 3000 guilders.' Charlie Mingus wanted to see his money in advance; you didn't have to give it to him, but he wanted to see the green paper. Nobody else I knew had 3000 guilders at that time. I was a lucky guy.

"But what Dulfer did was fantastic. He had this job selling cars at a dealership, and sometimes he'd take 30,000 guilders out of the safe, just to pay the musicians and the expenses."

Dulfer: "My contribution was mostly daily things: cleaning the toilet, being there every day."

—And the story everyone tells about you taking money from the till?

"I took the money from the drawer, but I always repaid it before the next audit. It was risky.

"Everyone was complaining that the money was always late from the government. But I put it in out of my own money. For me that was easier. One less thing to worry about.

"At one meeting, Maarten van Regteren Altena was complaining that when the money did come in, I always got paid first. He was right, but it was my money, so I could do that."

Willem van Manen: "Then Dulfer had to stop booking the BIMhuis, because he hadn't been paying taxes, and we got fined. Dulfer is a soloist, good at the margins of things. If you need to start an organization, show what you've done and how you've spent your money, he's not at home. So after maybe a year and a half he left and Huub van Riel came in. He'd been a fan, always attended the concerts, and worked in public relations or advertising. We asked him to make a steady job of running the place. So he was there almost from the beginning."

Huub van Riel: "Probably the simplest way to describe it is that I was doing a lot of odd jobs then, thinking about going to school to study history, and I came to the BIMhuis to replace someone for a two-week vacation. Whoever showed up got dragged in to do a job. If it wasn't a collective effort it wouldn't have worked." He came on in 1976.

Another factor in his favor: From 1975 into the early '80s he also booked Tuesday night (and Sunday afternoon) jazz at the Kroeg, a dumpy bar at Lijnbaansgracht 163 in the west side Jordaan district. The Kroeg series received podium funding for booking Dutch musicians; the programming as at Paradiso mixed homegrown and imported talent at least partly because a Dutch act on the bill effectively helped subsidize American headliners. Huub's friend Dulfer played there a lot, too, so much that some people assume he ran it. To draw publicity, a Dulfer-Breuker quartet played the opening.

Huub van Riel: "It was a mess, but it drew some attention, so we did it again." The Kroeg long ago turned into a blues bar. Huub is still at the BIMhuis. It is often a thankless job. He is the conduit for every musician's complaint about anything, especially money, and a lot of Dutch musicians complain about money a lot. Part of Huub's problem is all the acronyms have offices in the modern BIMhuis—BIM, SJIN, BIMhuis, STIBEMOS (which manages the building, and for whom Manen spearheaded a massive '84 renovation) and the National Jazz Archive. Even experts may have trouble figuring out who the folks in the upstairs offices work for, let alone who runs what. Confusion was compounded because the SJIN both subsidizes and produces music, with the BIMhuis being a primary beneficiary. In early days the same SJIN commitee that fielded subsidy requests also booked the BIMhuis, officially at least. The BIMhuis and BIM are now separate organizations. The bar, the BIM Cafe, has always been under independent, changing, frequently contentious management.

Van Riel still has a soft spot for Jazz Month, thought up the BIMhuis's 1987 and 1991 improvisers conventions, the week-plus October Meetings, and the knockoff '94 October Orchestra—Mengelberg's modern ICP octet with a few ringers including Henry Threadgill, assembled for a week of gigs at the BIMhuis and in Cologne and Ghent. Funding permitting, he still books a few extra concerts for when the nights grow longer.

Misha's well-endowed commissions had included a 1973 orchestra piece, *Met welbeleefde groet van de kameel*—composers' preferred translation "With Well-Kind Regards from the Camel." This is his *Deconstructie*, where he made a camel out of a chair. Che went to the jungle. Misha (with his wife Amy) drove and ferried to North Africa, to get away and write in a new environment. They stayed two months in Morocco, down the coast from Casablanca. Some sources say he went to research Morrocan music, but he denies it. The only camel they saw was at a petting zoo, says Misha, and that wasn't really a camel, as the Dutch classify them. It had only one hump: a dromedary.

Plus, he'd worked out the central chair trick before he'd left home. Take a wooden kitchen chair, and by making eight cuts with a circular saw, reduce it to a pile of scraps, and then in a few short minutes reconstruct the remains into the recognizable profile of a bona fide camel. The seat, cut on the diagonal, makes the two humps.

—How did you ever figure the chair trick out?

"It's in the material in a more or less obvious way."

It sounds like a concerto for tools and orchestra: while the latter goes about its business, power saw makes a glissing entrance, drowns out strings and saxes with a melismatic whine, contact with wood both dipping the pitch and thickening the timbre, resistance made most audible. It glisses out, exit punctuated by sound of wood plonking onto floor, followed shortly after by the sound of a hammer, in its usual rhythm.

"Kameel" begins with a fanfare as full of wrong notes as an Ives barn dance— Purcell on a six-week bender—played absolutely straight, rhythmically. The bulk of the orchestral backdrop is a five-note phrase followed by another, almost identical but a step lower, each pecking its way down a fourth. It'd sound maypole-merry if it wasn't so somberly voiced. The howling saxophone soloist, saw's counterpart, was South Africa's Dudu Pukwana, with a glorious sea of foghorn saxes behind unlike anything else I know, the young Volharding included. That sax section part was very repetitive, and Misha told the players they could walk off when they got bored. He says by the end only Breuker was left: "That's loyalty for you."

Peter Cusack in the 1976 Dutch Issue of the English magazine *MUSICS*:

"Six evenings last November at the Mickery Theater, Amsterdam, called Een Behoorlijk Kabaal—A Lot of Noise—were an expansively long list of performers, acts, sketches, mishaps, poetry and music. There was Derek Bailey, the Brötzmann trio, various ICP groups, Louis Andriessen (sitting at the piano delivering some sort of non-lecture), Candace Natvig (singing Charles Ives), one actor and two actresses doing various sketches (all lines read from scraps of paper in the hand), etc. etc. etc., all in no apparent order or plot but during which other things might also happen. Stage dragons would appear, cabbages or newspapers would drop from above, smoke would start wafting from the chimney of an often-collapsing cottage facade, people would walk into other peoples' acts, two acts might occur simultaneously, or there might be nothing much happening at all. . . . So the audience is faced with a variety show of botched-up comedy acts to really hard improvised music, interspersed by numerous little distractions. The whole thing is certainly entertaining. The theater was full every night.

"What I found most enjoyable was that one's attention was continually changing focus. There was often more going on than you could concentrate on, so you would quickly shift from one detail or event to another. Pretty similar to the way you notice what's going on around you all the time. Some acts were very strong, demanding your normal attention, e.g., a belly dancer backed by Gilius van Bergeijk's saxophone improvisations on one note with his foot tapping a metal clacker—an excellent combination. Some were deliberately not so, and your attention kept wandering, e.g., Michel Waisvisz and a battery of technicians trying, unsuccessfully, to fit a buzz to Peter Bennink dressed as a fly. . . .

"The unity of the thing was the apparent chaos of presentation. Nobody quite knows what is going to happen. The performers, however strong, are forced to give some attention to the little things that are going on around them. Individual performances do not therefore take place without constant reminders they are performances, and that performances take place among a multitude of equally ordinary or extraordinary everyday events. It is very difficult to build up any normal performer-audience reaction. Individual acts are, of course, appreciated, but in a context where the presentation is seen to be as important as the act. . . . But there is a danger in doing these too often. It does not take long to appreciate them as just another way of performing."

The Mengelberg–Wim T. Schippers show Cusack read so discerningly was one in a series they did most years between 1974 and '82, subsidized of course.

♫

The BIMhuis had its share of theatricals too. Like trombonist Bert Koppelaar's *Tromboxing*. He'd constructed a regulation-sized boxing ring on the BIM's stage (actually the performance space was at floor level before remodeling) and got the tar knocked out of him by an experienced boxer as his band played along.

Among the more acerbic and less genial series were Waisvisz and Altena's Evenings About Jazz, which shotgunned pretty much everyone within range. The first evening began on a drawing-room set, Maarten and Michel elegantly dressed and therefore obviously not improvisers, background tweeting of birds setting the atmosphere. They had breakfast while listening to the radio: Poulenc, suddenly replaced by "Jazz in the Morning," documenting the latest developments in improvised music.

Waisvisz: "We made up all these categories some of which people adopted later, like *ongebonden muziek praktijk*—unbounded music—and distinguished between music that was partly or fully improvised, or music which isn't really improvised and still called improvised music. We would do a whole explanation and give examples. It was totally fucked up."

No one I spoke to remembers the series being funny, exactly. Listeners were given an opportunity to play along with a Steve Lacy solo, then Lacy himself walked in, playing (surprise guest, like Bob Hope walking on Carson). In the next evening, operatic singer Moniek Toebosch ladled on the nonjazz shatter-glass vibrato, and they showed Lambert, Hendricks and Ross filmclips. In the final Evening, English synthesizer explorer Hugh Davies (a temporary STEIMer) scraped the pages of a jazz dictionary across a microphone—proving all those big jazz names sound the same—then stuck around for a cozy group improvisation, with radio behind.

"Both Maarten and I were fond of jazz music, and lots of other music as well, but in the BIMhuis you'd meet real jazz addicts, and some of them didn't like at all what we were doing, kind of making fun of them and putting them into a little macho boy-scout-like jazz scene. We weren't very friendly. For me it was almost a farewell to that scene." A bridge-burning: sometimes the people being mocked were in the house.

STEIM had concerts too. Even Han Bennink got involved, playing percussion duets with a mechanical woodpecker. Most of Misha's STEIM pieces were striking for their lack of connection to electronic music. In a couple of them, objects were suspended over keyboard instruments, and then the ropes securing them had candles placed under them. In "Organum Candelabrum," small weights drop onto organ keys in chance order, until a dense cluster results. In "Wolkenbrij" (Cloud Podge) odds and ends (heavy junk, ping-pong balls, a bag of feathers) fall on exposed grand-piano strings. As in Reich's "Pendulum Music," or when Bennink behind the drums drops objects to land loudly on a beat, gravity is the ultimate cheap special effect.

Michel Waisvisz: "When I taught a music-theater class in the Hague, we taught people to fall from the stairs. Because if you can fall well, you're okay. You're flexible, you can let go. That was more important than all that brain activity. I really like that idea of falling, which Dick Raaijmakers later started using a lot in his theater pieces.

"With Moniek Toebosch I once did a show for a few weeks in the Shaffy Theater, where she would sing, and the noise would make something vibrate, which makes an electrical contact, and makes a glass fall down. That sets off a chain reaction—an electric train, a bucket of water—which goes on while we stand there. It ends with the little train: a switch has been thrown, so this time it goes up a new track, falls into a bucket, which drops and causes a piece of wood to strum an electric guitar, which makes a big incredibly loud chord. Then I jump forward and play the crackle box, and Moniek starts singing, and that opens the show. It took so much effort to make the first thing we had to improvise the rest of it.

"Moniek Toebosch and I had become a kind of duo, and could have been very well known, but then we sort of broke it up. At the end of the '70s I started to do solo theater shows again. That was also when I got slightly stuck with the crackle box and synthesizer. I toured the States with the synthesizer not long after I made that first Claxon record." Claxon would go on to put out a bunch of Altena records, one by Toebosch, and the first four by Guus Janssen. But for Waisvisz it was an ending.

"That's sort of where I stopped making records and wanted to do live stuff only. In '82 I did a show called *Waiscrack*, when I really got into trouble with all the critics here, because they thought what I was doing was bullshit, and that electronic stuff was not going to last. So I decided first of all I needed to clean up my head, and I stopped with theater."

Chapter Six
Farewell to the First Golden Era

In 1978, after their jazz-trashing theatrical Evenings, period when Maarten Altena was proclaiming independence from jazz, the Claxon Foundation—Altena and Waisvisz—got the Wessel Ilcken Prize. For the Hilversum musicians, it was another last straw. The last mainstreamer to get it had been Gijs Hendriks, in '71, and no Prize at all was given in '76 or '7. The old guard grumbled, Ilcken widow Rita Reys among them.

In 1980, the great conciliator of outcats and studio pros died, and the Ilcken was renamed the Boy Edgar Prize. (The statuette winners keep for the year—its name is John Coltrane—stayed the same.) The first Boy Edgar Prizewinner was straightahead pianist Rein de Graff. His 1979 album *New York Jazz* was hardbop with Tom Harrell, Ronnie Cuber, Sam Jones and Louis Hayes.

When it came to conceiving music theater on a grand scale, Leo Cuypers—Ilcken Prize '73—trumped everyone. "I had a nice concert in Zeeland one time, and afterwards the organizer asked me 'What are you gonna do next year?' I was feeling mellow, and said, '*Zeeland Suite*. How many islands do you have?' 'Seven.' 'Okay, I'll do seven parts.' And I used seven people, because I like septets. A year later, we raised the money from Dutch and German TV and radio. We actually played nine pieces, including one at each end of the tour.

"The TV director, the organizer and I scouted locations. I visited every island. We'd do one piece on each island, and on the last day performed the whole concert: an eight-day trip. We had 35 people on the bus, so we always had that much of an audience. One island I didn't like. We brought this caravan of cars and technicians, dragged the piano up on the dike, played one note and that was it.

They played on a beach, at a nuclear plant, on an oil derrick above the North Sea, band in hardhats. Leo had Breuker and Bob Driessen on saxes, van Manen on trombone, Gorter and Harry Miller on basses, Martin van Duynhoven on drums.

It was good television, but on record it's threadbare when piano and horns fall back on consonant vamping. When you're playing outdoors, the less paper to fly away, the better, but Cuypers dislikes sheet music even indoors. He'd rather teach musicians by ear, like Mingus among others. Leo: "When you dictate music, at the second rehearsal it's as if they'd played it five times. I teach it from the piano. If they want to write it out, go ahead."

Breuker says Gorter wrote out the changes, van Manen added his own lines, and he himself did (modest) orchestrations. Van Manen says Gorter was the workhorse. As soloist, Breuker finds some good spots. He never felt hemmed in by simple four-chord progressions, and Leo could always write a melody that sounds good blared out of tune by Willem. With elementary dialogue of soprano saxes, oboe-pinched, "Bach I" echoes the little Cuyperses improvising 'round the piano with grandpa.

"No plooi at all blues" is Leo down in the delta, going slow, hook crafted around a shameless lift from "Willow Weep for Me." He's the Hoagy Carmichael of Holland's dear old southland. That can work against him, when a hook's too bland to ripen into anything, but the rhythm section usually saves him; Gorter's bouncing pulse fits Miller's South African accent, and van Duynhoven's swing is light and crisp.

On CD *Zeeland Suite* is paired with Cuypers' *Johnny Rep Suite*, 1974, which has more of the same virtues and less of the flaws. It was originally on Cuypers' LP *Live at Shaffy*, recorded the same week as the Cuypers/Breuker album of the same name. The saxophones are Breuker, Piet Noordijk and Dulfer, and it has a little more spark: "Floris en Rosa" has overlapping intersecting saxes, more Dutch minimalism recalling Louis's then current *De Volharding*. The addendum "Cowboylied van Ome Piet" (Uncle Pete's Cowboy Song) a duet with Rob Verdurmen at the traps, has Leo drumming with sticks or mallets inside the piano.

The two *Live at Shaffys*, along with *Baal Brecht Breuker* were among the first LPs from label BVHaast (HasteInc.) which Willem still runs. BVHaast also documented Breuker's ongoing theater and film music projects, and the Willem Breuker Kollektief.

WBK hit a peak in the late '70s; Breuker at last knew the Ellingtonian joy of always having the orchestral scratch pad at his disposal. That's when he really learned to make square corners, make the legs the same size and the nails lie flat. Mostly. His men concede that his way of notating certain wrinkles is not the clearest; van Manen once told of silently correcting Breuker's scoring mistakes, because it was easier than pointing them out.

When the band made its first North American tour late in 1977 they were a sensation: those well-drilled saxophones with their massed power; strong solo voices of Breuker, Cuypers and Gorter, who's all over the bass, his rubbery amped sound too loud to miss; the jokes the music didn't slow down for.

Soon as they hit, the zany-Dutch stereotype was set, unshakable, and hardly undermined once North Americans discovered Han Bennink. Much generalizing about Those Wacky Hollanders has come from that small sample of the populace. This often surprises the Dutch, who see themselves as rather a sober lot. There are no zany Calvinists.

Willem's first major or otherwise interview in the Americas was with British-born Canadian critic Bill Smith, in Canada's jazz magazine *Coda*, April 1978.

First question: "Near Dam Square in Amsterdam is an old man with a barrelorgan. And I thought that some of the music tonight sounded a bit like some of the music that comes out of that barrelorgan. Do you feel that's true?"

Yeah, is Breuker's short answer, I know my barrel organs, but what made *you* think of that? Smith: "When the trombones and saxophones rotate cycles like that, the barrelorgan sound appears."

Smith and Breuker talked in the wee hours after the Kollektief's gig at Buffalo's out outpost Tralfamadore Cafe on December 19, 1977. In a way, that was the day the Americas discovered the Dutch—102 years after the Fisk Jubilee Singers came to Holland. Other North American critics, like the *Voice*'s Gary Giddins, tumbled to them a little later. The little magazine *Cadence* had already reviewed a few records sympathetically, but writers' facts could be shaky, and almost no one saw it.

Hereafter Breuker was usually first to bring up the sounds of the Dam and the neighborhood. Smith had fingered their export appeal: the Kollektief sounded Dutch, right off, even if North Americans had never wondered before how Dutch jazz might sound.

Yet the timing was right, culturally. The late '70s and early '80s, when Breuker's music caught the attention of American critics, fans and record buyers, coincided with a mild mania for regional Americana, chiefly in the form of food and music. In a way "Dutch jazz" was analogous to Cajun food: exotic, a piquant blend of familiar old and new world flavors, aggressively seasoned. Breuker's roasts of high art proved as unexpectedly tasty as Paul Prudhomme's blackened fish.

WBK still play through the States more than any other Dutch act—Willem is good at making contacts, and at getting people to do his bidding. (He praises his musicians highly, but manages to give the impression they'd starve if not for him—and you.)

On a 1993 trip to New York they played the same jokes as on the previous tour— someone pulled an egg out of Willem's ass when he sax-cackled; trombonists Hunnekink and Gregg Moore danced in a circle while blowing over each other's shoulders, right arms ringing each other's necks—and got slagged by the *Times*.

They came back the summer of '95, end of a long tour, the Knitting Factory where artist hospitality is unknown and published schedules gave conflicting starting times. It was hot and humid, there were hotel and limo fuckups, they were pissed off and cranky, but on stage they loosened the roof. They can still do that.

Willem Breuker Kollektief *A Paris/Summer Music* (CD on France's Marge label) shows off all the strengths of that period, plus Cuypers' creepy Marlene Dietrich vocal on Arlen and Koehler's "Let's Fall in Love"—homage to wartime Berlin?—and Willem's continuing ambitions to write straight impressionist chamber music (the pastoral "Wake Up"). But even here one may sense the solos are more routine than improvised, that Breuker the composer's old fluidity was sliding away as his band became fixed in personnel and instrumentation.

In the year and a half between the February '78 Paris record and the September sessions for *WBK 79* (BVHaast) Jan Wolff had dropped out. The rest of the regulars held firm, but the band was changing. They played Breuker's straight bandshell chart of Grieg's "Ases Death," and Weill's "Song of Mandalay" in the same (traditional) hectic tempo and feeling as the Britpop Flying Lizards' concurrent version. "Virgins House

Song" (arranged by Hunnekink, Breuker-style) is a fanfare like those of old, but the doubling of horn parts gives it Volhardingesque blare and insistence: makes the winds sound like they mean business, gives them authority and assurance. (Those blocky section chords and unisons would become a stock effect, a Kollektief cliche. Like any demanding boss, Breuker does not like to see his workers stand idle. He likes to fill up all the staves.) The piece ends with a cross fade into the theme played on barrel organ, a tip of the hat to Bill Smith.

"Waddenzee Suite," written for a '78 Johan van der Keuken documentary, centers on Cuypers' melodically simple left-hand riff—he plays it on four keys—in very slippery time. The cockeyed 13-beat pattern volleys seven- and six-beat bars that seem to alternate straight and half time, and turns the beat around to boot. That skeleton is draped with gossamer passages for horn and reeds that sound more like a mobile than a melody, despite passing resemblance to the *Godfather* theme. It calmly passes across the music's surface like a cloud across the moon, keeps going behind van Manen's hot-pepper solo: a page from Gil Evans' book.

Van Manen's "Big Busy Band" nods to Sun Ra, tribute conveyed via Driessen's lumbering bari sax riff, and sour backing brass, and a hardbop theme whose voicings (like Ra's) suggest Tadd Dameron. On "Flat Jungle" Leo shows off several boogie-busy percussive piano styles, from two-finger jackhammer to winking mangled Bach. By New Year's 1980, three months later, Cuypers was gone.

"During the early '70s Breuker and I were working like rats—that means fast—writing theater music. We'd get a script, and five days later we'd have a half hour of music. So we took the name BVHaast, and worked so much it became a firm. When he split from ICP and needed to distribute records it was obvious to call it BVHaast. I was co-owner for five years, and invented the name.

"The Kollektief was very happening in the '70s, till the repertoire changed. Willem wanted to play nice music by other composers. I don't like to play other people's music. I'm not that kind of professional pianist. Other people play Grieg much better. I don't want to play Gershwin or even listen to it.

"When Willem used to write his timetable pieces—heaven!—I was prepared, disciplined, played the parts perfectly. But all that paper the last few years made me very unhappy. I was always saved by a piano solo, but had to go through hell to get there.

"The Old Year's Concert was the first time he let Henk de Jonge play the Gershwin concerto. I had to leave the piano, and he played with the Kollektief. Willem said, 'I'll write a chimes part for you'—three notes, playing the fool on percussion. I said 'Fuck off.' The next day at the New Year's Concert at the Concertgebouw I said, 'This is the last time I'll play in your fucking band.' He said, 'Leave now.'

"When I was in the band, paying the rent was not the first consideration. That changed after I left; it became more about making money. We never spoke about pensions. We were cowboys, man.

"I was one of the inventors of the funny theatrical shit—Willem van Manen and me—but we changed it every year. I was astonished later that the jokes never changed. When jokes get the upper hand, it's very dangerous."

—Is there too much frivolity in Dutch music?

"Not enough. They're all Presbyterians now.

"The Dutch, jumping from one canal to another crossing town, were zapping before television and remote control. The day they recognized postmodernism in it was the death of Dutch music. Because postmodernism has nothing to do with the material. The way people think about music can change it as much as the musicians do. Listeners, writers—they invented postmodernism, not the musicians. I couldn't cope with that philosophy, so I sat out for four years, till it was dead."

He's optimistic about pomo's passing, but Cuypers' canal–TV channel analogy makes sense. Even word derivation argues for it. In Amsterdam, on foot or bicycle as much as on the water, you can think of getting around in terms of streets, or according to which canals you want to weave alongside, avoiding wherever possible streets that don't follow the water. You develop a double-consciousness, two ways of reading the cityscape, dry and wet. And conceptual canal-jumping is all the more resonant in a city where streets or canals don't make right angles, where you're always reorienting your mental map.

⚓

Breuker never lost his taste for thumbing his nose at the arts panels and ensembles who subsidize him and his activities. When Amsterdam gave him its Matthijs Vermeulen Prize for music in '76, he refused it, partly for the thrill of spurning money. "They gave it to me for what I'd done for the music in Amsterdam, or whatever. I said to the city, 'Thank you, but you do nothing for the music, so don't give away prizes. Do something to improve the whole situation instead.'"

He still gets regular commissions from orchestras, chamber groups and soloists but they may end badly. He misses deadlines (one choral work took its text from the director's frantic letters, demanding the score), and skips the premieres, and the piece may never be played again, but, says Willem, his name on the list of commissioned composers helps validate the patron's hipness. It's a curious way to allow oneself to be used.

At first the Kollektief was just one of his projects, but once it started touring heavily, Willem focused on it more and more, and small-group activities faded. In the '80s WBK started putting out one or two albums a year, too many. He became determined to prove the band could play any style, any music that catches his ear. This came to include works by '20s composers who edged toward jazz from their own classical or theater backgrounds, among them Gershwin and Ferde Grofe, both championed by Paul Whiteman, whose leviathan band swallowed up jazz soloists, and who remains steadfastly unfashionable despite all rehab attempts.

—Do you see a parallel between your orchestra and Whiteman's?

"Oh yeah."

—A direct inspiration?

"No."

—He's considered square in the States.

"Oh yeah, a really big square. But I like his sound, I like violins anyway, and the combination of improvisers and readers."

Breuker's celebrated covers of Gershwin or Morricone miss their marks for better or worse. The brilliance of Morricone's "The Good, the Bad, and the Ugly" is in the wacko details as much as wacko melody. In Breuker's 1982 version, no grunting voice, no whistling, no Beatles-psychedelic-effects break; it goes wrong from the opening moment, Verdurmen's clapped drums no substitute for gentle slaps on the face of an acoustic guitar, a chord softly humming on impact. (And the tempo's wrong, too fast.) The total effect is like listening to a piano reduction of an orchestral score, or looking at a reproduction. The brushstrokes get lost. It's closer to Marlboro Man cliches than to Morricone's spoof of them.

Rhapsody in Blue (from the same '82 session with added strings) is a complex case for American ears, like hearing the Gettysburg Address with a Russian accent. The opening clarinet part, beginning with that famous upward gliss—emblem of jazz's influence on classical music—as played by Breuker comes out pure Jewish street music, klezmerized. Benefit of doubt: he puts in so much Jewish soul to make up for how much of same Amsterdam lost forever. He's so sensitive to the sounds of the neighborhood, he can hear its echoes.

Leo's defection was a turning point, but it's too simple to say the band went sour soon as he left—the 2-fer *In Holland* (BVHaast '81) with Henk de Jonge is one of the Kollektief's better documents—or right after van Manen bolted in 1982. But by the end of the '80s it was atrophying.

One shouldn't fault Breuker for maturing early. By the time the Kollektief had pretty much touched on all its possibilities, Misha Mengelberg was only beginning to figure out what his miniaturized orchestra could do. Breuker also kept working on worthwhile projects outside the band. He displayed a nice feel for period touches, scoring Brecht's play *The Resistible Rise of Arturo Ui* in 1983. And he's maintained his knack for eye-popping covers: The 1989 CD *To Remain* comes inside an LP sleeve, peeking out through a stylized gash in the front cover. The 1991 CD *Heibel* came in a round cheese box, a shrunken update of the old ICP chocolate box.

WBK still have hot nights, absolutely, but you might still wish that once in awhile Breuker would get a trio, go out on the road and blow the pads off his bass clarinet. For him and for us.

Arjen Gorter: "The year I joined the Kollektief, '75, for a very short time I had a quartet with Maarten van Norden, Rob Verdurmen, and alto player Ron Rem, now a saxophone repair man. I don't know why I never pursued that any further. I guess you have to be a composer to lead. At various times I've tried to write things, but I'm never satisfied with them. If there's always five ways to do anything, one of them must be better than what I just wrote. If you're playing, that's okay, you can try again next time. Writing is so definite. But at some point during the '70s I did realize that composition made a lot of sense, that improvising alone was not for me.

"Back then I still played gigs with all kinds of people, all kinds of bands. Roswell Rudd came here for a Theo Loevendie project, to play in a big Consort, a radio recording of compositions by Theo, which were incredibly beautiful, in my memory. About a 15-piece band, with Roswell as the featured soloist. I told the radio guy to put at least three microphones on him. The guy looked at me as if I was crazy. But Roswell spent the whole concert moving his bell around. He blew at the ceiling, toward the floor, side to side, everywhere but in that one microphone, so sometimes you hear 'wwwOOOWWwww' as he passes by. The recording sounded like nothing. Roswell is an amazing guy. Theo later wrote a piece called 'No Devils,' because he was always talking about devils, all kinds of weird shit.

"While he was here, Hans Dulfer lined up some gigs, and one of them, a Sunday afternoon, was recorded, and put on a record. I heard it lately; I thought it was awful. Toward the end of the first side, Hans and Martin van Duynhoven and me are playing like idiots, up-tempo, and all Roswell keeps playing is 'Three Blind Mice.' I never caught on till now! Great!"

BVHaast, already diversifying a little, put it out: *Maine*, quartet at the Kroeg, 28 November 1976. It's bumpy, has a real Dulfer so-sue-me sloppiness, bleary heads followed by long blowing, but the rhythm section cooks. It's better than Arjen thinks, for Roswell alone. He has his fun in the barnyard, quoting everything he can think of up to and including "Praise God from Whom All Blessings Flow."

The man at the far end of the BIMhuis bar, tall, thin, natty dresser—he gets away with wearing clown-sized checks, which anyone must admire. He's hovered at the edges of the story so long you risk never meeting at all: Boy Edgar Prizewinner 1984, Martin van Duynhoven.

One thinks of him in the next wave of drummers after Bennink, but he was born just two months later, 13 June '42. Chalk it up to Han blooming early and Martin living far from the action. He's from Boxmeer in the extreme east. Like Han he's a visual artist: a graphic designer for the free monthly paper full of entertainment listings, *Uitkrant*. But where Han always goes for broke, not least dynamically, Martin is Mr. Restraint. He doesn't lack power but he keeps it close.

"Boxmeer is on the river Maas, a Catholic village. The first music I heard was as an altar boy, in a nuns' cloister. Also Catholic processions with music, major funerals, 50th anniversaries, and also harmonie orchestras playing at festivals. I was two or three when the War ended, and suddenly there were festivities in the village. These things got me interested in music that's close to the lives of the people. When I was four I decided: 'This is what I have to do.' Later my father would let me and my brother Fred, who's also a drummer, stay up to hear jazz on the radio between ten and midnight.

"At school I picked up music easily; I could play a snare drum before I could carry it. I also had a talent for drawing, made drawings of all the school kids. Later when I went to high school, I could never decide between art and music. That's still true. I'm in my studio this morning, but at one p.m. I'm a graphic designer.

"Sometimes I have the feeling I'm describing the same ideas with music and art. Like: I might make a poster that's mostly gray, with one bright outstanding part. Or take the cover I did for Theo Loevendie's *Orlando*."

The background is a washed-out pale green detail of an intricate symmetrical (almost kaleidoscopic) coarsely woven blanket—Turkish? Navajo?—with a snapshot-size black-and-white photo of the band in action all but popping out of the middle, an oddly vivid effect considering the drab color. It's easy enough to apply such ideas to drumming: uniform textures with dramatic interruptions, but not too garish. But he also likes loud conflicting colors—the cover for his 1996 CD *Uitkrant* has brilliant pink vibrating against bright yellow, op-art, not unlike the shimmer of sustained polyrhythms on the disc.

"When you play the drums, and in particular when you take a solo, you have to order your ideas, like a visual artist or architect, or else it's boring. When I started writing music, I was influenced by the way it looks on the page. You can look at a score and see if the music is busy or not."

"The first jazz I played was in Den Bosch, where I went to school, and at a club in Arnhem. I went to art school and the conservatory at almost the same time. More things came to me at art school. There they were up on all the latest developments, but the conservatory was conservative.

"I had heard Michiel de Ruyter on the radio explain the difference between Ornette Coleman and Eric Dolphy, before Dolphy came to Holland and became so influential. I made my choice for Ornette and his rhythm sections. I'll love Billy Higgins as long as I listen to music. I thought what Ornette was doing was a simple thing to understand, like Ayler. Nobody else was trying to do anything in that line, except maybe Willem Breuker. And Loevendie was into certain kinds of folk music, as Ornette was.

"I moved to Amsterdam in 1963 because a guy I knew from art school who was involved with Fluxus said, 'If you like this stuff, you have to come to Amsterdam.' I got a job as a graphic designer in an office, and played drums at night, the same as now. I was around for the demonstrations. In a couple of photography books, you can see me in photos of Provo actions. And I got involved in a lot of Fluxus performances. I remember one piece by Nam June Paik. A player sits at a piano; a vase of flowers is placed on top of it, then removed." He seems to refer to "Piano Piece 1962," by George Brecht. "Another piece, for violin and cleaning tissue: clean the violin. Take off your shoes, and take a running jump into the audience. I met Misha then. I didn't understand a lot of their ideas or principles then, but I was good at playing those things.

"In 1966 I went to this festival in Vienna, and in two or three weeks learned about everyone important in developing the new jazz. Musicians from all over the world came and met and played with members of the jury: Ron Carter, Mel Lewis, Cannonball Adderley. You could play with anybody you wanted to, like a bigger, better October Meeting. I never played more in my life, from ten a.m. until three in the morning. I noticed strange things: every country had a specialty. There were four English drummers, three great Czech bass players including Miroslav Vitous, but Holland had a small delegation, with one of everything.

"It's funny; in competition, Barry Altschul, who had already recorded with Paul Bley, didn't make it past the first round. He was playing in the same style he got famous for later. I liked him; I didn't let the jury or anyone else sway me from doing what I want.

"After Vienna, my career really started happening. I arranged to be at every festival where the Americans were. I played with them, got gigs, put together certain combinations. For a long time I did yearly tours with Mal Waldron. I played with Don Byas, and Ben Webster, and Dexter Gordon, who was in Amsterdam a lot although living in Copenhagen. Just staying here, you could play with lots of people. At the Paradiso, the drummer was either me, Han or John Engels. (Dulfer would say, 'I can't play saxophone, but you can't stop me.')

"Johnny Engels is very tasteful, but I don't feel his influence. With Han I do, how visual ideas are reflected in his dynamics, his ideas about playing and not playing. He's a master at performing in that way. Maybe his visual thing is as influential as his music is.

"I had played with Roswell Rudd in New York before I did it here. The first time I went there to visit the Latin Percussion factory, to advise the owner. Then there was that funny week in New York with Boy Edgar. He was a great admirer of Duke, had visited him as a consulting physician, and they became good friends. We were staying at the same hotel on 42nd Street as Duke's band." The Edgar band played at Carnegie Hall on a so-called Ellington birthday concert, 26 April '74. In combination with Duke's band they also played on one of Ellington's Sacred Concerts at St. Peter's Church. Duke himself was in the hospital, close to the end.

"I was in New York again in 1976, called Andrew Cyrille—I found him in the phone book. I figured, now I can study with someone I admire, and really hear about creative music. The first thing he gave me was 'Manteca,' Dizzy's big-band score. I had to learn how to play it from a tape with Andrew playing very softly, so I could play along. We talked about it every three weeks. I learned a lot from him, but he didn't say one word about free-improvised music.

"I think I've played with pretty much everyone in Holland, but on stage I can't get along with a few no matter how I tried. Whenever I played with Ruud Jacobs on bass, we really had to work at it. A professional gig, nothing more. But with Wilbur Little, it took maybe 20 seconds to know we could play together: two heads, one heart." The American bassist moved to Amsterdam in 1977, died there a decade later.

"I got to be well known with traditional people and in the free world. I'd play with Breuker during the day, play a studio gig in Hilversum that night. Once I did gigs the same day with Theo Loevendie and a heavy metal band. That's no problem, except the rock band was twice as loud.

"Years ago I was a specialist in odd rhythms, but not now. Brubeck had success playing in 5/4, but those rhythms have never been a big influence in jazz music. Theo Loevendie is an exception, with his interest in folk music in general and Turkish music in particular. There are systems to learn the classical beats of Turkey, Mali or Peru, and books you can now buy, but you have to be careful. If you want to have a personality on your instrument, don't try to cover every style and background. You should be careful to develop your own thing. I like Han's approach; he doesn't copy the rhythms of Burkina Faso perfectly, but he gets the feeling of it.

"Nowadays, for me, less is more. I like a bass drum with a deep feeling and fast decay, so you can play rock, and get an almost mechanical sound."

—Your overall timbre is very dry.

"It has to do with my taste in tuning. It's been developing for over 20 years, and is still going on."

Martin van Duynhoven is on every Loevendie jazz record to date since *Mandela* 1969, on which Johnny Engels joined him. From '69 to '77, so was his running buddy

Dulfer. Elstak, Cuypers, Dulfer: Loevendie may be straitlaced but he likes outsize characters, can harness their energy.

On *Chess!* from '72 the rhythm section is Cuypers, Gorter and van Duynhoven, plus van Manen on trombone and the jazz/legit saxophonist Leo van Oostrom on baritone and clarinet. (It was the only record issued under the BASF label's BIM imprint, and it wasn't out long. A second BIM album recorded in '72, solo *Leo Cuypers*, was sent to critics for review but never released.) Unruly horns give some of it *Ascension*-like sprawl, and Cuypers gets into his hypnotic cycles (which don't sound like boogie but have the same mandala appeal). "Brasilia" begins with a dippy episode for wood flutes reminiscent of Breuker's ersatz early music; more interesting is the first waxing of Theo's touchstone "Lap Sang Sou Chong" (that's a Chinese restaurant tea) where fat saxophone voicings anticipate Julius Hemphill's overdubbed solo projects of the mid-'70s, and his later writing for the World Saxophone Quartet.

Loevendie really comes into his own with his quartet—Dulfer, Gorter, van Duynhoven—heard on two live LPs, 1974's *Theo Loevendie 4tet* (Universe Productions) and '77's *Orlando* (Waterland). In this band the composer's penchant for organizing music rhythmically takes over; they play on cycles rather than chord progressions.

Loevendie's pianoless quartet is out of Ornette in sound, akin to Coleman's hyper-charged *Crisis!* of 1970, which has the same lashing intensity tethered to audible form. Theo's catchy melodic kernels bear a lot of twisting without losing their identity. (This idea crept into his formal composing too—see Chapter 11.) On *4tet*, everyone plays at the top of his form and (usually) energy level. Loevendie gets alto-sized sound on soprano, and his alto has his soprano's sinuous vocal sound. His phrases are now shorter, more jagged and iterative—more in the direction of Coltrane, whom he still doesn't sound much like. But his improvised variations aren't as short as Dulfer's hectoring tenor bursts, which counter the flow of shapely hookish melodies yet reinforce the leader's mutative, variational method. It's a can't-lose deal: the more Dulfer repeats himself, à la mid-'60s Shepp, say, the more he sounds focused on the material. And he shares Loevendie's affection for a big saxophone sound: heavy tenor.

Gorter's hellzapoppin bass grabs your ears. He and van Duynhoven played together a lot, and sounded it. But you only have to compare Dulfer, Gorter and van Duynhoven with Loevendie in the 4tet and with Rudd on *Maine* to hear how much compositional sense Theo brings. On *Orlando* Loevendie pulls the bottom end into even tighter focus—really puts the Turkish in it. It's the clearest realization of his concept.

Loevendie in the liner notes: "Often there are no explicit tonal or modal implications though, in practice, one or more tonal centers emerge in a natural way." But then that pretty much always happens. "The complexity of the patterns differs strongly. In 'Destebeter' there is a relatively simple 10-beat cycle but the pattern in 'Orlando' consists of 147 time-units."

These complex cycles play neither like Don Ellis's 19/4 counting exercises nor minimalism's endless repeats. "Orlando" takes many turns, keeps halving and doubling its pulse, but the drums especially keep it limber, uncorseted, dancing. The fast "Bayram" has the rhythmic beauty of expert telegraphy, that pre–crackle box fingertip music. The crispness and fast decay time of van Duynhoven's kit, Gorter's pliable patterns dancing in and out of the cracks the drums leave: their focus keeps this keening-soprano band clear of late Trane billowing.

Dulfer got generous space as usual, and was never better used. "Sou Chong" (on three albums in a row) had become his feature, and he grew into it, playing longer, more lyrical and more internally varied lines (and a few passing quotes, Rudd-like). His personality as a tenor player comes across more clearly than almost anywhere else.

Between these two albums, just after he studied in New York, van Duynhoven made his first and for two decades only album of his own, his Percussion Ensemble's *In A.M. N.Y. '76 (Live at Frascati)*: four drummers including Harry Piller, and two saxophones—Maarten van Norden and newcomer Sean Bergin—and banjo. Mostly it's patterns for trap sets. Everyone has the same light pulse to play, same tempo, with single stylized hits for punctuation. But the patterns are different, and stagger. It's like hearing summer fireworks, irregular popping over loud crickets. It's lovely, austere, radical: indebted to minimalism's interlocking repeats, but not mistakable for it. It puts van Duynhoven on the map as another Dutch improviser with a singular viewpoint.

Michel Waisvisz: "I think Misha is one of the best people here to set up new organizations. He was at the beginning of STEIM, and the beginning of the Fund for the Creation of Music, and the BIM and SJIN, and things like that. Whatever people have said about his role, that he's an anarchist and that he doesn't do anything—he is an absolute anarchist but he is also the first one to tell people you should organize yourselves or you'll get crushed. But the trouble with Misha is, he likes to set up something, make a few rules, and then let it go.

"I have hated him at some points for letting STEIM almost drop dead. At the end of the '70s, STEIM came under attack by people from traditional music. They thought STEIM was getting too much money—it wasn't getting much, but it was too much for them. At some point, some really nasty people discovered that Misha was an easy target, because he was also criticized in other areas. Someone made a very negative report about STEIM for the city council, a serious attack. At that moment the engineers basically saw their jobs about to disappear. They became angry that Misha did nothing to stop it. He said, 'Well, STEIM is a typical '60s institution and should die organically, maybe.'

"That was at the moment when Johan den Biggelaar and I started working with computers at STEIM, which Misha also didn't like. Computers were a sort of synonym for stupid music. But at the end of the '70s we saw personal computers coming in, and I saw all these young kids who had no problems at all with them.

"So there was a revolution without bloodshed. Misha left and nobody else wanted the job so they finally got me. 'I'll do it, but only for two years.'" It took Michel about 15 years to extricate himself.

Misha doesn't remember the transition that way—for him STEIM problems were more a matter of personality conflicts than a worker bees' revolt—although he still likes to say "I wanted to run STEIM from my bed." He had helped shepherd it through several funding crises in the '70s, some of which were at least partly of his own making.

But wanting to see STEIM die—no, he says. Nico Bes, who then as now likes to be left alone to do his work, says he didn't think the place was in dire peril, although his fellow engineers honestly did. It is true that Misha had become a target; he stepped down as BIM president around 1980 also, after public flaps with Dulfer and Loevendie. His ICP band was in a shambles too: Misha was in the dumps, and his prospects didn't look good.

♫

The fuse on the bomb was lit early in the subsidy years when a decision was made to let the chickens watch over the chickens: to let the musicians review each other's SJIN subsidy requests.

Misha: "We started that in the '70s, because we thought that if the musicians couldn't deal with that in a detached and rational way, then we don't know what else to do. You need some expertise in order to decide which groups should get money and which do not, and we were the ones well-informed about the subject. Now the government only wants to give that authority to people not actually involved in the field—people with a general interest in music or theater. Generalists, they are called. We were called specialists. The generalists are unstoppable at this point." Yes, but: The generalists are entrenched at the SJIN, but musicians still review grant applications at, say, the Fonds voor de Scheppende Toonkunst, the Fund for the Creation of Music.

"From the beginning, Dulfer was opposed to specialists deciding such matters: 'We should never have a system where musicians decide other musicians' stipends.' But even into the '80s, it didn't go so badly with musicians on the board. I agree it sounds a little funny to give that power to other musicians, but it's not the same as installing corruption or cronyism.

"Initially, we had some reservations about funding solely jazz-related music. Money was not given to musicians who were already surviving by other means—it was not for Pim Jacobs and Rita Reys—but for those playing what was called something like 'authentic improvised music.' I think that was the correct thing to do at the time. Of course, deciding what's authentic or not, that's a different question. We knew what was meant, a little bit. But perhaps this initial way of letting the committees function was overdone. It became clear to me you cannot condemn people on stylistic grounds alone. You should really concentrate on the quality of whatever it is."

The Dutch scene's history is littered with acts of lunacy and idealism, but no idea was more idealistic or lunatic than thinking musicians could judge each other without severe repercussions. The same musicians serving on SJIN and BIM boards or committees at various times didn't help either.

By 1980, the national culture ministry had been pressing the SJIN for reforms—one group getting automatic annual funding turned out not to exist—and more musicians stepping up to the trough meant more winnowing was necessary.

As Mengelberg explained it to Bert Vuijsje at the time, a SJIN advisory committee had recommended three categories for applicant groups: ones whose subsidy would stay unchanged; promising ones to be coaxed along with more money; groups to be warned they were in danger of losing funding. But, Misha said, the recording secretary misunderstood the intent, and wrote an inaccurate draft statement which basically challenged certain musicians to demonstrate their worth. And since Misha the bed-side administrator didn't get around to opening his mail that month, the first he knew of it was when that statement was leaked and caused a ruckus.

It looked an awful lot like the SJIN with the BIM's complicity was setting up a hier-archy of styles. The A group, most favored, was indigenous improvised music, like that made by our heroes. On the B list were more jazz-oriented guys like Loevendie and pianist Loek Dikker. Straight-ahead jazz musicians were ranked lowest. Problem was that in the BIM and SJIN, the A folk were the empowered and the Cs were the already disaffected. It looked bad on the face of it.

Misha told Vuijsje, in a small country it's unavoidable the same people do all the jobs at one time or another, and so find themselves in awkward positions occasional-ly. Besides, in any group with common goals there are people who raise their hands and there are shirkers. Plus, he added lamely, committee members did recuse them-selves when their own music was up for consideration.

What is so galling to the sympathetic observer is how poorly those administering the system defended themselves. In the '80s persistent critics like neo-boppers Jarmo Hoogendijk and Ben van den Dungen (who were cropping up in Holland as they were in the States, and for the same reason: jazz goes to the conservatory) were among the best-funded musicians.

♯

"You should never divide musicians, trying to tell someone their music is 'not jazz' or 'old-fashioned.' Who says what's old or new? Is LOOS jazz? I'd say no, but that's just my opinion. If they play at a jazz venue, that's good enough for me.

"I played ten years with the Theo Loevendie 4, very nice, good music too. I sud-denly realized, I can't play with them anymore. They're not as free as they think. Looking back, it was a waste of time, if not for listeners, for me.

"I decided to go a different way. Jazz for me was always close to pop music, influ-encing each other. Bebop was pop played in a different way. If you're going to play jazz now, you should play the pop of today in a different way.

"At the Groningen festival in 1983, at the time of my troubles with the BIM, no one wanted to play with me. So I played with a trumpeter and a very big boom box. Set it on stage, and played along with Public Enemy."

Dulfer's recordings had been all over the map from early on: fierce ones with Han or Roswell (or, in '71, tenor Frank Wright, pianist Bobby Few and drummer Muhammad Ali) to whatever dance music was handy. He became known as a white guy fronting a black band, but give him credit: he was about the only musician on the BIM scene building bridges to the Surinam/Antillean music community and the sup-ple rhythms they had on tap, even if he was just blowing over the top of their tunes à la playing along with Public Enemy.

In 1970 he'd made his first record with his group Ritmo Naturel—heavy on per-cussion, and with Dutch rock star Jan Akkerman guesting on guitar—and the album *Candy Clouds*, named for his baby daughter, which combines heavy grooves not unlike period Pharoah Sanders, except with big studio reverb on his tenor. In 1977 Dulfer recorded a minor hit version of his chant "Red, Red Libanon," named for a popular hashish available in Dutch coffee shops. He did that one with his band Perikels, featuring musicians from Curaçao (guitarist Franky Douglas) and Surinam (including drummer Eddy Veldman).

Around the early '80s Dulfer was known to boast he had turned his back on jazz. "I needed a change of address," he'd tell folks, a remark that got around.

"I was really popular with my group, didn't need so much money. Then I got a letter from the SJIN saying that because my music had changed so much, I couldn't ask for subsidy anymore, at a time when I wasn't even asking for it. Instead of saying, someone else needs the money more.

"I was informed I was no longer a member of the jazz scene. That made me mad. It's a big mistake to discuss what jazz is with me."

Dulfer's memory fails him on a few points. In March of 1984 the SJIN programming board did write him to say his band Reflud would no longer be subsidized in its present form. It was, say folks around then, pretty much an unexceptional R&B band, in contrast to trendy free-funk units like Ornette's Prime Time and Shannon Jackson's Decoding Society. But Reflud did have some upcoming gigs for which venues had requested funding. When Dulfer asked for an explanation, Huub van Riel, writing back on behalf of the board (although he wasn't a member himself), explained they saw Reflud as wandering over the border into pop without saying anything new. The only reason the SJIN had funded it before, he wrote, was Dulfer's personal reputation—the board had hoped the band would amount to something. Even so, as Dulfer was claiming the decision had done him material harm, the board offered to make funds available for those pending gigs anyway. Dulfer spurned the offer: give me a real subsidy or nothing.

The exchange of letters lasted for months. But two weeks after the board's first letter arrived and discussion had barely begun, Dulfer was in the papers talking about the SJIN board as "a sort of Kultuurkamer"—the old Nazi-occupation arts organization— alluding to Will Gilbert's wartime list of forbidden musical practices, concocted with the stated aim of promoting indigenous European music.

It was as malicious a charge as one could make—yet you have to give him credit for making an ingenious connection.

Dulfer also gave inflammatory interviews in which he had a tendency to wildly underestimate the amount of funding he'd gotten all along. In 1983, Huub reminded him in one letter, Reflud had received 12,000 guilders from the SJIN through venue funding and 10,000 more from the culture ministry—which put him in the top ranks of the subsidized. In search of allies, Dulfer reached out to the Hilversum crowd who'd never shown him much respect before.

(A couple of years later, some of those folks announced their alternative to the SJIN, SJPN, Foundation for Jazz Production in the Netherlands. This eventually gave rise to the jazz wing of the booking agency Nederlands Impressariat, which gets funded by the same sources as the SJIN but positions itself as a more conservative alternative.)

Dulfer also used his columns in one magazine or another to attack the SJIN—and the BIMhuis, which wasn't involved in the dispute, and whose programming has always been far more diverse than critics aver. The new Kultuurkamer became his pet riff: a decade later he'd still be invoking it to spite his old pals. Dulfer made it cool to belittle new improvised music. But at least one of his former pals never could bring himself to hate him. Huub van Riel says all the damage Dulfer has done may equal but not outweigh the good he did early on.

Huub van Riel: "In any subsidy system there always are and always will be disputes about money. It did work very smoothly the first few years, and the difficulties in the early '80s were also about increased applications for money without much of an increase in funding.

"Having the same people filling multiple roles on different committees helped people see all sides of an argument. But it was not a good organizational model."

♫

Wednesday nights in the fall of 1995 Dulfer looks pretty much the way he did over 20 years ago—breaking surf of blond hair spilling over his forehead—and plays at the Cafe Alto, classic tourist trap off the Leidseplein. There's no cover, it's always jammed, and the bartender starts soliciting your drink order the second you squeeze in the door.

Way in the back on a raised platform under the rafters Dulfer and a misfit band— another tenor, rhythm section including electric bass—hold forth in one of those peculiar situations where the same people who cheer the music loudly talk straight through it. He plays sets of 20 minutes or so, blues, ballads and lockhorn battles he always wins. For the finish Dulfer balances the tenor on the tip of his nose—as he does on the cover of his book of collected articles *Jazz in China* (Dutch jazz wars described as Maoist power struggle) and ends his last set walking through the house, to play his final choruses from behind the beer taps: familiar variant on the age-old custom of walking the bar.

The Alto is not a subsidized venue; these are working conditions the subsidy system has worked to protect musicians from.

One endearing thing about Dulfer: he criticizes himself before you can. He says he knows his mid-'90s CDs like *Big Boy* where he blows over lame hiphop loops are rubbish, but for the moment at least he's big in Japan, where these records originate.

"What I really like, is to come back from playing dance music on the road and do four sets at Cafe Alto—instead of one or two, which is never enough—playing straight bebop, getting in touch with the audience."

—From the audience side, the Alto is a bad place to hear music.

About face, not missing a beat: "I'm playing for me. I like to be free on stage. And you get to play for different people: Archie Shepp. The bassist from Megadeth. Liza Minelli reserved 40 tables.

"Walking the bar is so important in music. Those R&B guys were supposed to play commercial, but when you're walking on the bar, they can't sell drinks.

"When you do what you want, you're killing them.

"You'll get my coffee?"

Dulfer fired off the last over his shoulder, running out the door to his next appointment. We had spoken at the IJsbreker on the Amstel. Jan Wolff had converted that old bar in 1980, after he left Volharding, turning it into a venue to do for new composed music what the BIMhuis had done for improvising. One difference, a sign of universal double standards about jazz and classical music: the IJsbreker gets more than triple the funding the BIMhuis does.

In 1979 while still with the Kollektief Willem van Manen made a nice record, eponymous: solos; duos with old adversary Misha at the BIMhuis; trio with bassist Harry Miller and van Duynhoven at the Kroeg. It had a great cover, suggested by Teo Joling. The front shows a trombone bell (Willem's face in distorted reflection), the inner sleeve the matching slide against the same background. You slip the inner sleeve in and out to mime playing along.

That same year van Manen put together his first big band, Springband, so called 'cause it came together once a year. By 1983 some of its members were Louis Lanzing and the American Jeff Reynolds on trumpets, trombonist Joep Maessen, Harry Miller and Maarten van Norden. They were driving back to Amsterdam from a gig down south, on a bad road, early on the morning of November 27, when Maessen's VW bus went off the pavement. He and Reynolds died in the crash. Miller died of injuries December 16. Lanzing and van Norden survived, but their recovery was slow. Van Norden was back in action for a tour with Leo Cuypers' septet Brullband by the end of '84.

Leo's career skidded after he left Breuker: few recordings, not too many gigs, persistent health problems aggravated by drinking and smoking. But the LP recorded on that tour is a strong one, *Leo Cuypers Brullband* (VARAJAZZ). All the tunes are by other bandmembers, but it's saturated with his personality just the same, starting with lively grooves from a cruise control rhythm section—van Duynhoven plus newcomers Jan Kuiper on guitar and Ernst Glerum on bass—which subtly adjusts to or engineers changes in terrain. The melodies are catchy, the cross-riffs just intricate enough to tickle the ear and boot a soloist. It's light but not insubstantial—not unlike the South African kwela that makes its presence felt. (The other half of the live program was Cuypers' Miller-dedicated "Back to Johannesburg.") It's evidence that with Leo, good feeling is yoked to good craftsmanship.

September '95, Leo has a gig at the BIMhuis, plugging his BVHaast CD *Songbook*. (No hard feelings between him and Willem; Breuker had even played on and put out Cuypers '81 *Heavy Days*, quartet with Gorter and Bennink.) He seems tentative the first set, not really in focus, his eagerness to resolve all musical tension within a few bars stopping development before it can start. But when he slips into his Abdullah Ibrahim–tinged style, slides onto rolling barrelhouse basses, droning harmonies with stepwise modulations rippling through here and there, the man from the South sounds as comfortably at home as if sitting cross-legged on a carpet.

The road accident that claimed Harry Miller and friends palled the scene, and was especially tough on van Manen; it was a fluke he wasn't in the van himself, and there were families he felt responsible toward. He dissolved Springband, didn't do much in music for a year. Overseeing the BIMhuis renovation kept him occupied.

In 1985 he put together Contraband—same once-a-year concept, but touring in the autumn. Their *Boy Edgar Suite* (1991, the year van Manen got the Edgar Prize) is less an explicit homage than declaration of his own interests: fatter less redundant chords than Breuker's girders, some latin rhythms perhaps relayed via the American West Coast, glimpses at a Catholic hymnal. One movement alludes to Andriessen's "Hymne" for Milhaud, from Volharding's first LP. And there are moments which, but for the drums, could sound like Volharding itself.

As Orkest de Volharding turned 25 he was still there, de facto leader of a leaderless band. It now has a conductor—mostly to ease rehearsing, van Manen says. It still has no drummer, still favors an aggressive attack and (often) casual intonation. On a September '95 program at the IJsbreker, more than one commissioned piece seemed to be about tuning up, one way or another, but the tendencies noted are more ensemble quirks than shortcomings at this point.

Volharding's cachugging power saxes can still make other composers' music sound like Louis Andriessen's, and Louis's ideas about ensemble playing have been forged by that collaboration as much as the band's have. (Compare the unsubtle pop/jazz evocations in an early Andriessen piece like *Anachronie I* to deft post-Volharding works like *De Stijl.*) That saxophone sound has become so much a part of Dutch musical life, so much a part of the Dutch accent, it's worth recalling again its roots in Riley and Breuker. One can hear Peter Brötzmann in there too. He was a role model for loud saxophony, as Breuker knows well, and few saxophonists take Persevering so seriously.

In the first half of '96 the Hague's monthly Thunderclaps festival features Misha Mengelberg all season; he has a gig on every inclusive concert. (The year before the featured composer was Ives; the year after, Burt Bacharach.) In February Misha's guest is Brötzmann; over dinner around the corner from the Korzo Theater they reckon it's eight years since they've played together.

On the gig Brötzmann plays more melodically and subtly than his stereotype. Their 40-minute duet is an object lesson in Misha's ability to lead a duet partner in one direction or other without appearing to steer.

The pianist immediately casts himself as accompanist, placing each of Brötzmann's scrawls or squalls in a tonal context; when Brötz gets excited, Misha lays back, feeds him consonance. The saxophonist, starting the set on alto, complies, slides into melodies frosted with heavy archaic vibrato. From here Brötzmann drifts into ballad mode—and Misha spills gravy all over it, responds with his own squalls. His partner dutifully jumps through the hoop, gets agitated again. The saxophonist plays a middle-register trill, and Misha imitates it, then begins a variation which Brötzmann duly joins.

And so it goes: Misha quietly gets him off some idea only to try to get him back on it, why not. When Brötz grabs his taragot, a wooden soprano sax, and plays one long note, Misha tries various chords behind, constantly changing the long note's harmonic function.

It's a subtle process, partly depends of course on Brötzmann's conscious cooperation, but somehow it still smacks of (benign) manipulation. When the pianist tries to pull Brötz somewhere he won't go, no problem; Misha just tries something else. Later, Peter is back on alto and blowing fiercely in one key. Mengelberg starts playing end maneuvers, chords that box him into a harmonic corral from which there's no escape, and it's over: checkmate. Afterwards, they're both justly pleased—and only then does Misha wonder if anyone taped it.

♫

Tuesday afternoons in room 213 at the Sweelinck Conservatory, formerly the Amsterdam Conservatory, the school's teacher of Palestrinian counterpoint holds an open composition workshop, "for the people of Amsterdam," he says: anyone who wishes may bring him a score or tape to give an opinion on. Some days he sits by himself an hour, goes home early. Sometimes he gets a walk-in off the street—like Vancouver jazz trumpeter and composer John Korsrud, who's studying with Louis Andriessen this year. (The professor listens to his tape, says, "Why don't you play on your own pieces?") Sometimes it's one of his own students with classroom material for review. He'll stare at pages of strict counterpoint, occasionally going over to the piano to peck out a few intervals, more often just speed-reading. The student on the hot seat looks suitably uncomfortable, but there is nothing threatening in the teacher's manner. He wears a baggy sweater with holes and old droopy jeans, occasionally dragging on a cigarette whose smoke laces across a conspicuous NIET ROKEN sign.

When he wants to challenge his students with an ear-training problem, he asks them to decode the chord—Misha calls it an "unchord"—Monk keeps chiming on "Little Rootie Tootie." He's had this job since not long after he left STEIM. He talks sometimes as if he doesn't take the job so seriously, and the great rule breaker makes an unlikely drill sergeant, but Misha figures if you want to learn a style, why not do it right.

Reading a pupil's score, he comments as he goes along: "Don't make the same turning points." "The best way to end something is making little steps. No jumps at the end." "Going back to the A is not good. It's finished already. Do something new." "These two phrases: same lengths, same intentions." He whistles the next phrase. "Better." And the next two. "No." He points his pencil at a sequence of descending fourths: "This is explicitly forbidden."

♫

December 5, 1995, the first of Willem Breuker's seasonal annuals, Sinterklaas Concert at the Stadsschouwburg, big theater on the Leidseplein. It's sort of family night; there's a storyteller, and a couple of singers, nothing shocking. But it's one of two times this month he makes me laugh with variations on his 30-year-old incompetence joke. Cole Porter's "Night and Day" is thick pea soup for winter, overblown vehicle for onetime teen thrush Greetje Kauffeld. Just when you reach for your hat: violinist Lorre Lynn Trytten, a classical musician and frequent guest with the band (which she'd join soon after), starts to solo on it. She begins to paraphrase the melody, hesitates, starts again; piano bonks out the most obvious cues, This Is Your Note, Come In Here, and still she's tangled up in the first four bars, portrait of a square classical musician trying to improvise without a clue, lost as soon as she starts.

Somehow the joke is more not less funny because she's obviously reading the whole routine off her sheet music, a reminder that she's a classical musician and therefore the butt of the joke in a real way; she's not pretending to be a nonimproviser. If she wasn't reading her solo she couldn't have this trick played on her.

Three weeks pass. Every year between Christmas and New Year's Breuker hosts five nights of his festival Klap op de Vuurpijl (literally, the Pop of the Fireworks; figuratively, icing on the cake, lagniappe, the 13th in the baker's dozen). He's been hosting it since 1975, when there wasn't much to do in Amsterdam between the holidays.

The nightly formula: inclusive concert, a jazz band or something similar (Bulgarian clarinetist Ivo Papasov one night, a rickety quartet of Misha, Ab Baars on reeds, bassist Pablo Nahar and Johnny Engels the next) then some impeccable Dutch modern-music chamber ensemble, and then the Kollektief. For some reason WBK plays mostly the same pieces every night, so you can really hear whose solos are rote, who improvises from a fixed idea, and who's really going for it.

At the Klap, Breuker's best moment is scored, again. The Xenakis Ensemble has commissioned his harpsichord concerto "Waakvlam" (Pilot Light) a nice rendering of his usual courageous voicings, plundered classical styles, maybe a little swingtime for percussion where inappropriate, and deliberate blunders: a bassoon loudly stumbles in and out of a violin passage, lost. In the middle of a furious solo passage, the conductor is instructed to peer into the guts of harpsichord, and exchange helpless looks with the soloist: what's going on in here? The butt of this joke is the apparently-out-of-his-depths composer. One thing that redeems Breuker's scalding sarcasm: he doesn't spare himself.

Fake mistakes are a central theme in Part 3 of this book, and Breuker is a prime source of same. It's a key element of his legacy.

♪

The Brötzmann-Bennink duo lasted into the early '80s.

"With Peter Brötzmann I really had to work. It was all the time that loud angry thing. All The Time. After 15 years, it gave me good chops. It didn't really change my playing, though it did focus it in a certain direction. But my idea of playing is still different from Peter's."

—Because you like to move in different directions?

"Much quicker, much quicker."

—Transitions are a major part of the art for you?

"That's right.

"With Peter I was still playing lots of junk, also xylophone, and steel drum. Then I had to sell my car, and got a smaller one. Suddenly Brötzmann said, 'Are you not bringing this or that stuff?' So I said, 'Fuck you,' and I reduced and reduced and reduced. Time to think about something else."

These days, logical enough given his penchant for recycling and his love of Duchampian ready-mades, he brings less along and uses more stuff he finds on site. (Comparing Canada to Italy, two countries he plays a lot: Canadian theaters are too clean backstage; in Italy there's always lots of junk.)

So we come at last to the musical equivalent to Han's visual art, putting a spin on the everyday. He is still, in the right moment, night after night, the most inspired theatrical showman in Holland, one of the world's great drummers and most hilarious jazz musicians.

Best exit I ever saw him make: Cristofori piano showroom, cozy space where musicians sit at floor level a few feet from the audience, October Meeting 1991. Han had been mostly demolishing an otherwise quiet improvised trio set led by the young pianist Michiel Scheen, when in the middle of a barreling barrage the drummer suddenly launched himself from his chair, leapt forward over his giant bass drum, did a 180-degree turn in midair, started to fall backwards at an alarming angle as his legs tangled—and landed with improbable grace in the front row, slouching, legs nonchalantly crossed, applauding.

Thursday, a week and a half after that Sunday concert at the Hague museum five chapters ago, it is raining in Enschede near the German border. Bennink and cellist Ernst Reijseger are here to play for an assembly of incoming students at the local arts college. They improvise, they play some tunes, sometimes they swing, and sometimes Han swats imaginary flies with a towel.

The towel is a favored prop of circumstance: he sweats, soaking one of his enormous sagging tee shirts with the word SWING emblazoned on it. (Swing is a society that runs educational workshops.) Sweating as he does, he often finds himself reaching for a towel. From this evolves a grammar of drum toweling. The towel is a beater: crisp whipping sound, resonance controlled by how much of it is extended and how far from the rim of the drum it strikes. Draped on a drumhead a towel blots up sound; playing it with sticks he gets a fast decay not unlike a junk percussionist's, but broader, lower, stronger: you really have to swing that sucker to get a decent sound. Move the towel partly on and off the head, you get more timbral variety. If you want to understand how much Han Bennink knows about drum timbre, listen to what he does with a towel. This is polishing the drums with a vengeance.

Bennink and Reijseger play in a tiled gymnasium with a slabstone floor, a cold room. The drummer had arrayed his small kit on top of a flattened cardboard box. He gets down on the floor and plays the corner of the cardboard, really plays it: demonstrates how it sounds struck, and scraped, and how the sound of the scraped corner sounds different when lifted off the floor. It's not enough just to hit something, but to make it tell its own story. He animates the inanimate.

The audience doesn't get too close or look too involved—hey, this may be their first week here, but they're still art students. Han gets his first laugh with a stock bit: bounces a stick high off the floor, times the bounce so he can strike a cymbal on the beat at the moment he catches the stick with his other hand. (A bit from early jazz by way of vaudeville or vice versa.) Han times gags so precisely, audience laughter arrives exactly on time to fill a space he leaves in the texture: guffaw as ruff.

And then Han grabs a chair, nothing special, shellacked formed plywood seat and back, tubular metal frame, a few bolts, probably isn't a kid there who hasn't seen hundreds of them in classrooms over the years, and he starts to play it, with sticks. Han plays the bottom of the seat, surface and sides, then the seatback: the different pitches he gets make you aware of the wooden parts' relative sizes. Turning the chair on one side, he plays the tubing: the choked sound of the exposed elbow between back and sides, the small clicks of the hump where it rounds the back. He flips it feet up, plays the freely ringing legs, flips it again and again till every side has been inventoried and examined. Han measures the chair sonically, makes you hear and thereby appreciate its proportional construction, makes you really see this familiar object for the first time, remade like Duchamp's bicycle parts or a stupid woodland tableau someone has defaced. He deconstructs it as surely as if he'd cut it up with a power saw. It is such an amazing display you could almost forget to listen—if it wasn't so loud.

Reijseger has taped the concert. Driving home, he pops the tape into his car's deck, rewinds till he finds the chair solo.

Engineer Dick Lucas, who has spent years recording lots of musicians in this book, has said almost no recording captures the flavor of a Bennink performance, and of course he's right. (Also right when he says Han's solo *Tempo Comodo* comes closest.) Even if you've heard him on records for years, the first time you see him ON resets your ideas about him and about the possibilities open to improvisers. And yet the audible trail these visual moments leave behind is in a way enough, crucial to the implicit pact he makes with an audience: If you don't like how it looks, shut your eyes.

The chair solo: from top to bottom it's in a Brazilian march rhythm, unswerving fast tempo, no hesitation as he tosses the chair with one hand and plays it with the other. It sounds like five guys wailing hell on African xylophones.

After it's over, cello comes back, they swing into "I've Got the World on a String."

♫

"Yeah," Han says three days later. "Forget all those cases, just take a chair on the road." It's Sunday at four at the Engelbewaarder. If you remember the jazz club in the movie *Paris Blues* you have the idea: wall-to-wall tobacco smoking bohemians and tourists, jostling, drinking, gesticulating, talking very loud over the music that brings them in. Today the band is led by the Italian tenor saxophonist Daniele D'Agaro. He's hired Pablo Nahar, the American pianist Curtis Clark and Han. Daniele sounds very strong today, has the power to project over and through all the yapping; lately he's been readying some unheard or unfinished Don Byas charts for performance. Curtis is playing the house's battered electric piano; his comping is always spare, but sometimes it's almost like he doesn't want to touch the thing. Pablo, his bass heavily amped, is limber, slides in a few dancing kaseko rhythms from his native Surinam. Bennink need we mention is playing straight swingtime; once in a while he still plays on records that make you blink at the lineup: Han with Major Holley?

By the time they finish the opening set, the room is stuffed with people and smoke, and within an hour the amount of both will double. The bandstand is on a raised platform in the front window. If you're at that end of the room, you might glimpse a ray of sun breaking through the clouds, dappling the canal, cutting a photogenic swath of light through the Ridley Scott haze. To the left of the stand is the door through which people keep streaming. Along the wall leading away from the stand on the right is the bar; Han wants to get to a corner at the far end of it to sit with Masje, who's a Sunday regular. It takes him ten minutes. On the way he chats briefly with anyone who addresses him, has a longer conversation with a tall thin well-dressed man in glasses: Martin van Duynhoven.

Masje sits in her nook with a couple of folks including trombonist Bert Koppelaar.

He is telling someone a story, almost shouting to be heard, of how he came to play with an ICP group. He met Misha on the street one day, tried to talk him into giving him a gig. "'I want to play that tetterer,'" he says he said, miming playing trombone. "'What?' 'You know,' 'Tetterer. Tetterer. Tetterettet.'" *Tetterettet* is the name of an ICP LP he's on.

Han finally squeezes into the corner, says: "Playing sessions is easy. You just have to play the first set and the last tune. Some people just play sessions, nothing else. There are five drummers here already. You know Martin's playing? Very clean, sterile almost. I like it."

The Engel indexes how different Dutch jazz life is now than when Han started out. Today's quadrinational quartet is just the beginning. Later, another Surinamese bassist sits in, paired with a Romanian drummer. In the middle of a sentence Han cuts himself off: "Listen, he's playing some Romanian stuff."

Some of the people who pass across the stage today: Koppelaar; a trio of Breukerites, trumpeter Boy Raaymakers, authentic Texas tenor Alex Coke, Arjen Gorter; expatriate American pianist Burton Greene and drummer Clarence Becton; trombonist Joost Buis, who blasts hard enough to penetrate the crowd, and is the day's MVP. "Joost sounds great, man, gets that sound because he started playing with the post office brass band in Apeldoorn."

Bennink fills a pipe. A new set starts. He doesn't see who sits down at the piano, but after two bars, just chords: "Burton."

As the afternoon marches on, Han yaks with well-wishers—he's leaving for Japan to play solo concerts in a couple of days—and keeps up a running commentary on the music. If there's something good to be said, he'll say it. But as he listens to one drummer he says he sort of likes, he becomes visibly impatient with opportunities missed.

Before long Han is acting out his commentary, pantomimes comping at the traps—his hands fly, his right foot stomps an imaginary pedal, his head turns to one side, grimace on his face. Perfect self-parody, and great bebop drumming, no phrase left unanswered or unbooted, except he never strikes anything except the air or his leg, a favorite practice pad anytime. "POW! BOF! Give them POW! Give them something BOF! BAM! for POW! for fuck's sake POW! BOF! he's too BAM! caught up in his own BOM! listen to the bass drum nothing is BAM! Jesus Christ just BOF! BOM! POW!"

An American voice down the bar yells toward the stage: "YEEAAAAH! Yeah motherfucker!"

The ad hoc band settles into playing lame hardbop. Finally, at about a quarter to seven—early, because with Amsterdam's new noise laws neighbors' complaints can shut the music down, and even the BIMhuis has to move soon although it's been around far longer than the grumbling neighbors—D'Agaro comes over to Han, says, "We'll go back on after this; let's just play free." "Yes for fuck's sake." Five minutes from now, they'll be romping along, improvising a mock-Sun Ra processional, before they close the session swinging some standard whose name I foolishly neglected to jot down.

But before Han elbows his way back to the bandstand, guy he recognizes comes over, says hello, and they sit and huddle for a few minutes, serious conversation, heads down. Then they look up, shake hands, and the man splits. As Han eases out of the corner, he says:

"Fantastic! I just sold a piece of art."

▲ Misha Mengelberg,
Han Bennink
*BIMhuis, Amsterdam, 31
Janaury 1997.*

◀ Willem Breuker,
Arjen Gorter
*Dizzy, Rotterdam, 29
August 1997.*

◀ THEO LEOVENDIE
Paradiso, Amsterdam, 26 November 1996.

◀ IG HANNEMAN
Stedelijk Museum, Amsterdam, 27 May 1995.

▲ ERNST REIJSEGER, WOLTER WIERBOS
BIMhuis, Amsterdam, 17 October, 1996.

▲ Franky Douglas
PH 31, Amsterdam, 25 April, 1995.

▶ Sean Bergin, Tristan Honsinger, Alan Purves
BIMhuis, Amsterdam, 18 April 1996.

▶ Available Jelly
Michael Vatcher, Wolter Weirbos, Tobias Delius, Ernst Glerum, Eric Boeren, Michael Moore
Zaal 100, Amsterdam, 25 August 1995.

▲ ERIC BOEREN, AB
BAARS, MICHAEL
MOORE
*BIMhuis,
Amsterdam, 20
October 1994.*

▶ LOUIS
ANDRIESSEN,
GREETJE BIJMA
*BIMHuis,
Amsterdam, 29
September 1994.*

▲ Guus Janssen,
Ernst Glerum, Wim
Janssen
*De IJsbreker, Amsterdam,
27 March 1997.*

◄ Maarten Altena
*Vredenburg, Utrecht, 5
November 1995.*

▶ PAUL TERMOS, WILBERT DE JOODE
BIMhuis, Amsterdam, 17 March
1994.

▼ PETER VAN BERGEN
BIMhuis, Amsterdam, 13 December
1996.

COR FUHLER
Felix Meritis, Amsterdam, 7 September 1995.

TRISTAN HONSINGER, ERNST REIJSEGER, MISHA MENGELBERG, HAN BENNINK–OCP ORKES *Lokaal 01, Breda, 19 April 1966.*

Part II

Troops

Chapter Seven
Menu Options

"I needed ten years to find the people who could do all the things I wanted."

MISHA MENGELBERG

Misha Mengelberg is about to fry pork chops. He puts a heavy cast-iron skillet on the stove, turns the fire up high, and adds about a third of a pound of butter. He lets it melt and then get light brown and bubbly, and is about to slide in five thick pink pork chops fresh from the local supermarket. At the last moment he gives the pan a second look, and waits till the butter is very, hazardously brown. Now he squeezes the chops into the pan, where they crackle loudly, fat mingling with butter. In a minute the pool of hot grease is an inch deep. Hunched before the stove—without a cigarette, for once—he grabs the pan by the handle and wrenches it violently back and forth on the burner to keep the chops from sticking, clatter of metal clashing pop of pork.

If you or I were to try this, the whole kitchen would be splattered with scalding fat. Not a drop flies out of the skillet. In another life, he'd have made a great short-order cook.

While they fry he dissolves a little flour in a tumbler of white wine, and slices white mushrooms, not too thin. He flips the chops. Now that they've shrunk a little, he makes room for the mushrooms on the right side of the pan. On the left, he pours in the cloudy wine, and vigorously stirs it with a fork till the gravy thickens, not long. He shuts off the burner, carries the skillet to the round dining-room table, places the pan on a hot plate next to a pot of fluffy Indonesian rice he cooked earlier, after stirring exactly 37 times while rinsing (always a prime number, he explained, 37 if three or four are dining). Also on the table is a premixed green salad he poured out of a sealed bag and then rinsed. A few months ago, "three days before my mother died," as Misha fixes the date, he was washing salad greens from the store, and out popped a salamander, not upsetting at all, no, he insists, Amy loves animals, and now it has a home. It goes unseen for days, so every sighting is a mild event.

The pork chops: succulent. The seemingly hapless-male's touch—serving them in the pan—makes the meal. There are two distinct sauces, thick wine gravy on one side gradually giving way to the mushrooms opposite, swaddled in savory caramelized butter. They're distinct, and disarmingly tasty, and even better intermingled.

In the middle, where the marriage of flavors really happens, one imperceptibly sliding into another, is the meat.

Which might also describe the music of the modern ICP Orchestra. In 1994 and '95 that's trumpeter Thomas Heberer, trombonist Wolter Wierbos, saxophonists Ab Baars and Michael Moore, cellist Ernst Reijseger, bassist Ernst Glerum, Han Bennink on drums and Misha on piano. As much as any group anywhere, ICP encompasses a full range of modern musics: Ellington and Monk, Kurt Weill and European dance band music of a lost age, lacy Webern-y chamber music, South African kwela, free improvisation, conducted improvisation, interactive games, counterpoint and simultaneity, catchy melodies, pastel harmonies, order and built-in chaos.

Postmodern composers like to jump cut from one style to another: think Zorn. ICP's music drifts from one locus to another like the action in a dream, where the guiding intelligence may thwart rational progress. Some compositions feature glaring wrong notes or brazenly dumb ideas; no piece exists in a definitive state. Players have the option of making some willfully idiotic melody sound better or even worse. From one performance to the next, a piece may sound radically different.

ICP's mix is perplexing in the best sense: the music doesn't give up its secrets on first hearing, or second, or third. It keeps you coming back. This is jazz/improvised music at its most deft and sophisticated. The musicians treat it with the reverence usually reserved for a chewed-up slipper.

The name on the posters is Instant Composers Pool Orchestra, though it's usually an octet or nonet. In conversation, no one calls it anything but ICP. Now that others have adopted the term "instant composing" for improvisation, Misha uses it to refer to conducted improvising. That's only one thing the modern ICP does. But finding musicians who could really deal with that and related concepts marks the band's coming of age, and the apotheosis of modern Dutch style.

♧

That Misha's ideas outstripped execution was clear from his 1977 piece for Volharding, *Dressoir* (The Dresser). Its nine movements in ten minutes are largely cribbed from pieces for his first big ICP groups (among other sources: the Parisian dancehall melody that ends it begins his similarly scrappy big piece, 1973's *Onderweg* (Under Way) for chamber orchestra. That composition, in six short movements, is notable for how its development parallels his improvising: motifs interrupted and returned to; deliberately threadbare ideas treated as Mahlerian profundities; a beautiful funereal melody that devolves into practicing scales; a staccato repeated-note melody for trumpets, sometimes voiced in minor seconds, which expands unpredictably to mess up the form, and which ends abruptly even as clanking percussion blithely sails past the cutoff. That recurring percussion part is a nod to Bennink; that third movement just described sounds like an orchestration of a Han and Misha duo. *Onderweg* also has what may be another personal reference, fleeting nod to another Nutcracker, Tchaikovsky's).

Even noisy Volharding's wobbly first recording of *Dressoir* circa 1980 is miles beyond what his Tentet could do then. Volharding did a crisp early-'90s remake but Misha says he prefers the original because the pauses between sections are better timed.

Dressoir is typical of Misha's commissions for idiosyncratic ensembles—Hoketus and LOOS also—in conscientiously blocking its usual style. It boasts some of his most genteel gestures so far, is lushly bourgeois from its festive can-can opening on: the odd piece out on any Volharding program of political brickbats and barricade blasters. Mengelberg, ever at ease with conventional harmony, leads the band through off-handedly clever progressions and inventive-within-the-rules voicings, the better to set up the spilled-ink anarchy of later movements: rude soprano nattering against a proper wind chorale. (Breuker is the model for the rude saxophone sound on either version.)

Misha back then to English journalist Dick Witts: "The 'Dressoir' is the form where all these things are placed, a frame. . . . [But] you shouldn't remember what's in or up. It's one of the nice things of a dressoir that you find things hidden—a box of cookies, forgotten pound notes."

The idea of a piece as a depository for sundry scraps is especially appealing for a composer fonder of hummable fragments (which don't have to be jotted to be remembered) than long forms (which do). Hummable and recyclable: the way little melodies from one composition crop up in another is not unlike the way he'll start playing one of his whistlable tunes in the thick of free improvisation. In spanning the sounds of theater orchestra and free-jazz band, *Dressoir* is an architect's drawing of the mature ICP.

Misha's first biggish band record is *ICP-Tentet in Berlin*, April '77 for FMP's SAJ subsidiary. Till the mid-'80s personnel is an endless reshuffle, Han and Misha and the American tubist Larry Fishkind the only constants. The itinerant Radu Malfatti often played trombone, and Tristan Honsinger cello. Michel Waisvisz might play crackle box, its whirrs and zwoops like built-in heckling, an extra layer that could be there or not. Lots of saxophones passed through: Gilius van Bergeijk (also on oboe), Peter Bennink, John Tchicai, Sean Bergin, and Ed Boogaard, classical musician for whom Misha wrote a mocking saxophone concerto, Breukeresque in the way the soloist goes awry. One movement is lifted from Haydn's Clock Symphony, alto unsuccessfully essaying the viola part.

And Peter Brötzmann: "I caught the train in Wuppertal once a week at 8 a.m., for an 11 o'clock rehearsal at the BIMhuis, and usually I'd be the first one there. I think I was still an enfant terrible for some people; my stays in Globe Unity and the London Jazz Composers Orchestra were short. I always said, 'Don't write me too many notes, I can't handle it.' But Misha is a wise man. I played his pieces with discipline, but when he gave me the opportunity, I played my ass off. In ICP I was a clown, but not in the Bennink way."

And Keshavan Maslak, an American from a Ukrainian enclave in Detroit, who'd come to Europe looking for his roots, and used Amsterdam as his base. Maslak combined Brötzmann's shitstorm with Breuker's mock bluster, but his pet trick was standard '40s R&B honker: falling on his back while shrieking in the falsetto register.

Those massed saxes were good for power surges and attenuated Ayleresque dirges, and for thick smeary chords that sounded like parodies of the Breuker Kollektief. Case in point, Misha's blues "Rumbone." Beginning jazz students are advised never to begin a blues chorus on the fourth degree of the scale: since blues changes proceed in fourths, you'll sound like you're on the wrong chord, lost from the git-go. On "Rumbone," the melody starts on the fourth: playing it right, you sound wrong. The composer was not without finesse. On "Tetterettet" those sax chords curiously parallel Julius Hemphill's writing for the new World Saxophone Quartet too. But the big reed section was self-defeating, an attempt to do more with more. One ICP had four tenors, including bopper Fred Leeflang, as if the lot of them might add up to one complete saxophonist. En masse, they gravitated toward the high-energy squalling Mengelberg never really liked, no matter how much he'd kid it.

Still, this unruly big band had something. Tuba as bass let Misha get into two-beat oompah, and the Kurt Weill and tango strains Breuker had been mining. Misha too was looking for a creative European orchestra's indigenous roots. There's a rare one-shot recording from Cremona 1979, *Soncino* (ICP), where Misha, Han and Larry Fishkind are joined by six Italian horns including jazz trumpeter Enrico Rava and new-music trombonist Giancarlo Schiaffini. ("People say I have a split personality, but for me, it's not so different, Mengelberg and Scelsi.") The more consciously European the material, the more they sound like an Italian brass band. They use Misha's music to get to their own roots. It's less awkward, more settled than the regular unit.

Mengelberg wanted a large group that could improvise as flexibly as Han and him. But the players he'd used so far, whom he knew from Germany, the conservatory or the A'dam scene lacked the necessary skills. In a way English improvisers might have seemed more adaptable, with their own blend of whimsy and chops. The all-free *Company* 6 and 7, London '77 at Derek Bailey's occasional improvisers festival, included three players from the ICP tentet: Bennink, Honsinger and bassist Maarten Altena. But the anticompositional stance Bailey promulgated among the Brits may've deterred Misha from trying them.

Some concert performances from the fall of '77 were issued as *Tetterettet* (ICP), but it's no portrait vérité. To impose his will on recalcitrant players, Mengelberg aggressively edited the tapes, cutting a solo off or a head in, splicing an introduction from one tune onto another, repeating a previously heard section or drum tattoo, inventing a new cello solo by looping parts of a live one. The splices and lap dissolves are obvious to anyone paying attention, but many folks missed 'em, part of the joke. (There's a little more of same on *Soncino*.)

What Mengelberg really needed, though he didn't know it, was musicians who'd come up listening to Han and him. The process began in 1980 when Fishkind brought in a young trombone discovery.

Wolter Wierbos: "Those first years with ICP, some nice concerts, but some terrible groups. I didn't like it at all the first couple of years. The saxophone section was Keshavan, Sean and Peter Brötzmann. They were always fighting, them and Han, to see who could play the loudest."

The reed section began taking shape when Bennink recommended Michael Moore. "When I first started in the band, the other saxophonists were Brötzmann and Keshavan Maslak: sort of like two goats butting at each other. I had no idea what my role was." As when Cootie Williams joined Ellington 50 years earlier, the boss would never clue him why he was there. The only way ICPers knew if Misha liked them was if he called them for the next gig.

Moore barely makes a dent on 1982's *Japan Japon* (DIW), tentet live in Tokyo, made shortly after he enlisted; it's dominated by screamers, Bennink antics, and the decidedly nonjazzy fox-hunt fanfares and blandly resolving triads Mengelberg the composer then favored. Moore: "It seemed like Misha would hire two people just to see what would happen if they played together. Maybe they were even obviously antagonistic, they had such opposing musical ideas. He likes to see what people do in situations they're not comfortable with." As Mengelberg threw his unstable elements together, looking for some new (unstable) alloy, the explicit jazz content—jamming on changes, swinging—receded to the rear.

And then two tendencies in ICP coalesced, found their balance. The poles were: violist Maurice Horsthuis, and the stringy, high-culture decadent-phase sensibility he lodged like a bullet in ICP's spine; and Misha's old hero Monk, the surgeon with the scalpel also useful for puncturing balloons. Opposed, they interacted.

Horsthuis was in and out of the band twice in the '80s. Conservatory-trained, he already knew the posthorn/post-horn school of nonswinging Eurimprov from Maarten Altena's quartet. Horsthuis was also grounded in theater music; he wrote scores for the Baal group and had the soulful good looks of a tortured artist, readymade for Misha theatricals. He could make bold musical connections of his own too. "Lea's Lied" from his Baal score *Leedvermaak* links Weill and Bessie Smith; his chugging "In de trein" deflates Glass's *Einstein on the Beach*. Here was someone who could follow the erratic pace of Han and Misha's chess game.

The viola was a perfect instrument for ICP; it represents the Great Tradition of string literature, yet is dishonored within it. Violists are the butt of more musicians' jokes than anyone save singers and drummers, and viola parts tend to be as forgettably functional as third-trombone lines. But that low status also made the instrument a tabula rasa; its lack of literature was liberating. Its in-between tuning was useful too. The top two strings are the same as the bottom two on violin, the bottom two same as the top two on cello. A skilled player can make it pass for either, play its role or "sample" its effect.

Horsthuis was on the 1982 Japanese tour, not that you'd notice from the record—all those saxes and Han smothered him good. But when he was allowed to be heard—and especially when he and Han mixed it up, as when sawed plainsong gives way to boiling drums on "De Poezenkant," from the *Purple Sofa* suite—Mengelberg found himself with a combination of elements that hadn't been heard before. There were few parallels even in the '50s or '60s third stream movement.

Horsthuis's comrades in the Amsterdam String Trio eventually joined ICP too: first Ernst Reijseger on cello (whose in-between tuning could be used to fake viola or bass roles, when the band lacked either), and eventually bassist Ernst Glerum. When Maurice left for good, Mengelberg kept the sound of viola in his head: next he tried Ig Henneman, and then Maartje ten Hoorn (another Altena alum). When she dropped out for personal reasons in '93, Misha conceded the chair. By then Reijseger and Glerum were entrenched, ditto Horsthuis's chamber-music and organic-theatrical sensibilities. One night in Berlin, in the middle of a Krupa barrage from Bennink, the musicians fell to the stage as if shot, and lay on their backs without moving for an absurdly long time. They were playing what the boss calls "The Drop-Dead Game."

Late in 1995, Tristan Honsinger crept back into the band, making it a nonet, when everyone's available at least, restoring the old balance of strings and winds.

♩

One weekend in February 1995, ICP had three gigs around the country. Friday night, home turf, BIMhuis, but except for piano the stage is nearly bare: no Bennink, his absence the last blip of a six-week feud with his old partner and antagonist. (Han and Misha are nominal partners in ICP Records, but Misha unilaterally decided to issue his solo CD *Mix*—documenting his first two successful executions of a longtime wish, to improvise a set without a clear idea where he's going, deflecting himself whenever he detects a pattern, same goal he stated in connection with 1980's *3 Intermezzi* for the Nederlands Blazers Ensemble. Han blew up when Misha presented him with a copy, and they didn't speak for a month. They'd since patched it up, sort of—Misha: for the sake of the music—but Bennink had already accepted another job for tonight.)

It's eerie seeing them without him. As several listeners volunteer later, you could hear him anyway—could hear his strong, elegant, slightly archaic swing feel, two beats crossing four, in Reijseger's four-to-the-bar strummed chords, and even more in Glerum's walking. Han's absence doesn't upset the band's balance, it stabilizes it. He's one less powerful force tugging away. Dynamically, everything loosens up. Reijseger can be heard unamplified. Unmolested by drums, he and Glerum (and Wierbos, when he wants to, tone pure and pitch precise) tilt toward chamber music.

The first tune in the first set, which like all ICP sets is continuous, features the piano player. Gradually it reveals itself as his unofficial theme "De sprong! O romantiek der hazen" (a.k.a. "Romantic Jump of Hares"), the chords arriving after agonizing hesitations and suspensions by now as much Mengelberg as Monk. When Misha talks about Monk, he dwells on his impacted harmony, waves off questions about the specifics of attack and release, how Monk shaped each note at either end, using finger and pedal. But Mengelberg can replicate that aspect of Monk's technique as well as any pianist anywhere. Tonight, the halting melody alternately suggests Monk ballad and German rhapsody, the perceptual flipflop conveyed through subtleties of touch and timing.

Several ICPers can do this: be a chameleon changing colors as you watch. Misha the con artist plays the shambling rube so well, his own musicians may underestimate his playing.

As the theme comes into focus. Wierbos enters, playing the melody with plunger. Suddenly we're in Ellington territory, Tizol time. Behind him, Misha's harmonic rhythm, chord voicings and turnarounds reference "Mood Indigo." Rhythm cello and bass quietly join them, then the horns ooze in—long tones in close harmony, "Indigo"-style—and a phantom Bennink descends on the bandstand. The set wasn't even a tune old, and Mengelberg has already highlighted two major influences, and tacitly made the case not even Han is indispensable.

Later in the set, Mengelberg is in the middle of a snappy solo, when the horns pop up with a surprise punch. Before that rude chord has stopped sounding, he's off in a new direction, starting from scratch, happy to be thwarted.

At the break Misha announces that last number was his oldie "Where Were You?," dedicated to Han.

The band disperses. Sidestage, someone hands Ab Baars a tape of Hawkins solos he's wanted to hear. Wolter goes to the bar for a drink and a cigarette, despite his oft-expressed opinion this is the worst bar in Amsterdam. A few others retreat to the war-ren-like basement for floating conversation over bottled beer.

The second set begins with an improvised duo. Baars is on clarinet. Reijseger effec-tively plays two parts, sweet high violin alternating with bass skronks. They seize on a fortuitous finish, ending with a clean chord—so Reijseger scrapes one last below-the-bridge belch, looking a little disgusted, but whether for ending clean or spoiling same isn't clear.

Next Ab, and later Wolter, lead instant compositions. They are good at this, and Misha assigns them the job more than anyone except himself. As conductors, they use pantomime gestures to cue players in and out, draw a line in the air to suggest a melody, signal approval or disapproval, direct players to stop or keep going . . . com-mands their subjects strive to accommodate or ignore.

To a New Yorker the visual and conceptual vocabularies look familiar from Butch Morris's conductions of big bands or improvising groups, and from Zorn's elaborate '80s games like "Cobra." You can look at that game, with its complex rules and sub-rules, as codifying the shifting alliances, conflicting statements, sabotage and other skullduggery ICP make up on the spot. (Butch was conducting improvisers before he knew of Mengelberg's example—see Chapter Ten. Zorn doesn't discuss his influ-ences, but makes no secret of digging Mengelberg: he presented a program of Misha's music at the 1987 October Meeting, produced Mengelberg's trio record *Who's Bridge* in '94.)

Mengelberg: "I think I tried such things in '72 and then a modus operandi came into play with the orchestra about '75."

Wierbos: "In the early years it was always a kind of gimmick"—musicians pander-ing for applause, a pet peeve. "I didn't want to conduct in those days. Others in the band didn't even react when you gave a sign, so why bother?"

Mengelberg: "I hated conducting myself, always, very much. Maybe that has some-thing to do with my great-uncle Willem. He had a very romantic view of Bach and Beethoven and Mahler, but in my opinion that type of music is not helped by that—by bringing down the tempo, for instance." He sings a line, listing rhythmically like a drunk. "Playing the whole Fifth Symphony of Beethoven ad libitum, is a little bit too much. It circumvents the music, somehow." Rule of thumb: When some musical practice strikes Misha as reprehensible, expect him to replicate or incorporate it—tragedy relived as comedy.

So he set out to subvert the role of the orchestra leader, just as he'd undermined the myth of the romantic improviser by (belatedly) issuing a 1972 duet with Amy's parrot Eeko, three-minute flipside of the Dolphy in Eindhoven recording. (They're on the same LP because Eeko had chewed up part of the Dolphy tape.) The parrot whistles triads in triplets, clicks and zooms like a crackle box as Misha lays down low-key blues piano. The bird respects bar lines, turnarounds, solo breaks, and repeats and varies pithy motifs—Eeko's eerie.

"He hated me, tried to bite me when I came close. He was very much in love with Amy, and he saw me as somebody who always fucks up his fun. A rival. So—when I am in the house, I whistle a lot, or sing or hum, things like that." Composing, he means. "The parrot listened carefully and then imitated that. That was the reason he whistles triads and things. The whole human aspect is something he stole." Eeko was baby Bennink: fucking with him, interrupting, out to steal the audience.

Eeko died long before Amy took in the salamander.

As conductor of instant compositions Misha took Willem Mengelberg's role as crude interventionist to the next level (though you might also see it as Misha's homage to his father).

Now Wierbos is up front, facing the band and gesturing to Misha. Wolter jabs his left thumb outward; he wants bass notes from piano. Misha plays dumb—you mean your left or my left?—and starts dribbling in the highest register. Wolter reverses, staying cool but losing the musical thread he's trying to hold on to. He sticks out his right thumb, and Misha mimes, oh I see, it *was* your left, so now you must want the opposite . . . and sprinkles high notes again. Wolter gives up, laughing; whatever he'd had in mind has evaporated. At the end of his conduction he looks to Misha: you gonna cue the next piece? and he gestures back: you're the boss.

Misha: "Things like that happen all the time. I am interested in that: to put sticks into the spokes of all wheels."

Soon as the gig's over, Moore and Wierbos hop in a car to go across town to Zaal 100, to play twisted Surinam music with Franky Douglas.

♫

When Mengelberg looks at the new jazz of the 1960s, he what-ifs. What if musicians had picked up on the deep-structural implications of Monk's and Nichols' tunes (or even Ayler's, simple and transparent as nursery rhymes or Christmas carols)? What if they hadn't followed the high-energy excess of late Coltrane—which, being reprehensible, he'd replicated with the oversaxed ICP.

The Dutch scene generally what-ifs the 1980s. You look back at end-of-'70s retrospectives in American music magazines, writers saw exactly where jazz was going. The '60s was inchoate revolution; '70s solo concerts took meticulous inventory of the new techniques; the '80s would be the decade when composers like Anthony Davis were in ascendance, to marshal jazz's newly expanded language.

Then Wynton Marsalis came along, declared the last 20 years of jazz null and void, belittled innovation, and didn't begin seriously exploring composition himself until the decade was almost over (at which time he started replicating and grafting old styles very like the people he disses). Holland's homegrown Wyntons were only just getting mobilized, and in the '80s, music developed more or less as forecast. But by then "outside" music had fallen out of fashion. As American musicians went to ideological war, nobody there thought much about what was happening in Holland anymore.

Still: In the '80s the American mainstream finally embraced perennial avantist Monk, once he was dead. There was even a flurry of interest in Nichols. And by the end of the '80s, much credit to Wynton, Ellington was king. As far as all that went, Misha was in step. Beginning in 1982, he executed three long-term repertory projects—Nichols, Monk, Ellington—that would preoccupy him off and on for ten years.

After Monk died in '82, musicians all over started playing him, but few got the point Steve Lacy stresses: with Monk, the melody and the improvising should be all of a piece, a compatible package. The tune is quirky so you need to be. But when New

York's Jazz Composers Collective plays Nichols or Marsalis's Lincoln Center jazz department hosts a tribute to Monk, the musicians play the head, blow over the changes without paying much attention to the melody or weird harmonizations, and then play the head again.

Which as Misha heard it was business as usual. "In the '50s and '60s, most Monk gigs sounded as if the musicians did not understand the pieces. They seemed to avoid him at all costs. This was very true of his last quartet. Charlie Rouse never played any Monk music, I think, but reduced the material to something he knew before he went with Monk: to blues fragments, and things from his hardbop experience. But it never sounded like Monk music. He attacked that, found ways to circumvent its specifics. But there were exceptions—Wilbur Ware, Shadow Wilson, Coleman Hawkins, Lucky Thompson—who tried to cope with the specific sounds." The nicest thing Mengelberg says about Coltrane is, he never sounded better than with Monk.

In the early '80s, Mengelberg and Bennink had played some Monk and Nichols in quintet with old hands at this stuff, Lacy and Misha's fellow Nichols enthusiast Roswell Rudd. In '82 they made the LP *Regeneration*—half Monk, half Nichols, maybe the first program ever devoted to Herbie's music. In July '84 Misha, Lacy and Han recorded the sequel *Change of Season*, all Nichols this time, bassist listed as "Harjen" Gorter; George Lewis filled in when Rudd became unavailable. Next to Mosaic's box of Nichols Blue Note recordings, it was the main reason folks started remembering him.

George Lewis: "I met Misha on a Company tour with Zorn and Steve Lacy, a nice group. I played him a tape of a piece that I wrote, a quasi-concerto for chamber orchestra and trombone that had gotten a good review in New York. I asked him what he thought. He didn't like it. I said, 'I never liked it either.' I didn't know his music at all. I did some ICP concerts, and then I was at IRCAM in Paris from '82 to '85." That's the high-toned electronic-music research center, a STEIM for snobs. "I think Misha spoke to Michel Waisvisz, and he found a way for me and Joel Ryan to come to STEIM as artists in residence. I had an idea for a vocal piece, wanted to make a virtual choir, but I quickly ran into technological limits. That became a piece called *The Empty Chair*, my first really big public failure. Had I been smart, I'd have written something to fit the technology of the day. We needed eight computers; I should have known we'd get into trouble.

"I have to be honest—working with Europeans, there was a certain tension between them and Americans, especially black Americans. But I'm not into tension, so that was no problem. I played my first concert ever with Steve McCall, an international kind of guy; maybe that's part of why I came to Europe later. When I came, I didn't understand the culture, and so didn't understand the music. You see Breuker marching in the street—why is that? The way I parsed it was this: one of the things Ives was supposed to be about was scenes that evoke local American culture. In the same way, shouldn't there be a Dutch concept of improvised music?

"I came here in 1985, stayed till '87. After I stopped feeling like a tourist, I started to be interested in the culture and language. Misha and Amy helped me a lot with that. After awhile I started to see what the culture was like, and how it enters the music.

"One thing that facilitates the scene here is the distribution of wealth in Holland. There's no vast disparity between rich and poor. So there's a lot of musical movement across class lines, or race lines. There's no discussion about whether some race can't play some kind of music. For me *Reconstructie* symbolizes that fluidity: pop and classical culture are being critiqued at the same time. In France or England, those lines are more rigidly drawn. Also, the scene here is so small, people can't afford to put up divisions.

"Paul Termos is a great example of someone who writes a version of what he plays on his horn, very personal. Some of my favorite parts in ICP were when he played: so weird, so totally himself, I loved it.

"The thing about ICP—Misha serves the same function as Muhal in Chicago. Both have a lot more musical knowledge than a lot of musicians. He sees potential in people, and brings them along. When I was in ICP, he was literally teaching them Thelonious Monk. Wolter couldn't play changes when that project started. Now he can. Misha puts together his ironic stance toward European classical music and its class pretensions, with the heart of jazz and theater, and he puts it all on a Monk tune. It's a band where people can play and learn.

"If you're gonna play with Misha on a tune, it's very dangerous, 'cause he usually plays something more interesting than you. If he thinks you're ignoring him, he'll play something to throw you off. I listen to him so much, I forget who else is playing."

—You did a brilliant conduction at the Vancouver jazz festival one year. Wolter was in the audience, said 'He stole it! He stole it from Misha!'

Laughing. "Wolter's right, but he doesn't know who I stole it from. Muhal did that all the time in Chicago ten years before I got involved with ICP. There were whole sections where you go out of the chart, and Muhal would conduct the band. It was pretty wild, he's really good at it. People expected it, it was a big thing. It's different with Butch, for whom it's a stand-alone concept instead of part of something else, and who gave it a name. Muhal just did it.

"I did one of Misha's theater pieces—the title translates 'Meditation of a Shitty Dog'—where Wolter and I had to play a dog duet, wearing dog masks.

"I started reading a lot about African history here. After seeing how it was possible for Misha, Willem Breuker and Maarten Altena to have a Dutch identity, I looked for ways to make my own music reflect where I'm coming from. Then I saw it already did, I just hadn't known where to look: extreme contrasts, a lot of colors, multiple rhythms all around. Confronting their culture in a deep way made me confront my own. A typical expatriate experience I think. No one ever said I had to leave, it just became an imperative."

Those quintet albums of Nichols and Monk were nice records, but from an ICP perspective, a sideshow. When Misha was commissioned to write large ensemble music for a radio hour, he penned eight Nichols arrangements for 13 players (including Moore, Wierbos, Horsthuis, Reijseger, Bennink, Lacy and Lewis). The ensemble sounds a little top-heavy, too big, as Misha's full-blown orchestras often do. (This program has never been released commercially, although Radio Netherlands World

Service made it available to stations outside Holland, for rebroadcast.) A somewhat different Nichols set from '84, for 12 pieces, is cleaner and sharper. It's on the CD *Two
Programs—The ICP Orchestra Performs Nichols-Monk*.

For Mengelberg, Nichols' harmonic nuances had gone as unexplored as Monk's. The
best thing written about Herbie's music is Rudd's extensive notes to Mosaic's (out-of-
print) Nichols box, worth reading for its own sake, and in this context for how often his
nuts-and-bolts critique could also apply to Misha. Rudd writes of Nichols' command of
"*atmospheric* harmony" achieved via dynamics, voicings, and register, to give each tune
its own character: "Brooding, deranged, comical, quizzical, and wistful come immediately to mind. . . . " He also points out how the narrow intervals Nichols used to harmonize a melody became fused with the melody itself, so as it moves horizontally through
time it drags its vertical/harmonic baggage with it—something true of Monk as well.

Compared with the anarchic ICP records that precede it, the Nichols project in
either incarnation was a radical step forward and back. There were odd and out of
tempo episodes, but Mengelberg didn't deny the composer's nimble grace. Swinging
again, Misha and company for once sounded connected to the American third stream.
His chart of "Step Tempest," with its open woodwind voicings (Lacy's soprano,
Moore's clarinet) could be Shorty Rogers or Marty Paich. Yet West Coast cool
arrangers have had little direct influence on new Dutch music. Partly it's because
Dutch outcats associate that music with the Hilversum crowd.

Even so, it's curious this bunch overlooked Shorty; even Stravinsky was said to dig
him. (In the '50s Rogers had his own way with curious ensembles: octets with baritone
and bass saxes or five trumpets; a nonet incorporating brass quintet.) But the Dutch,
their keen ears and independent thinking notwithstanding, their love of obscure jazz
arrangers like Bob Graettinger (more later) ditto, miss some American mavericks, like
East Coast trombonist Rod Levitt, who wrote field hollers for octet. Levitt might have
penned Misha's tartly blaring ending for "2300 Skidoo"; the rest of it could be Rogers.
Mengelberg reinvents the wheel, but then jazz musicians often do.

Still, viola and cello poking through the pastels set ICP apart from other revivalists.
You could read the strings' presence as signifier of Nichols' harmonic sophistication
(or as fulfilling Herbie's wishes: he'd dreamed of hearing his pieces played by an
expanded band including strings). Mengelberg rarely uses strings for sweetening. On
the broadcast "Change of Season" he comes close, but Bennink quashes that. On
"House Party Starting," strings skitter through the head, on collision course with
squealing Lacy. Viola and cello take a smooth melody chorus on "12 Bars"; on "The
Happening," they seem to suspend time and harmony as they fall into quietly chugging a two-note interval—a quiet ambulance siren—a figure they steadily maintain
through two solos and an ensemble break. Note how Misha's arrangements play on the
titles of the last two, by dealing in the nonblue and nonhappening.

For most jazz musicians who employ them, strings are add-ons, a new wing added
to the house to display the owner's opulence and taste. For Mengelberg they're vestigial, traces of a musical world he grew up with and can't quite leave behind.

The subsequent Monk project was ICP with the training wheels off. Save for
George Lewis on two tracks, the band on the '86 half of *Two Programs* is Horsthuis and
Reijseger, Moore and Wierbos, Mengelberg and Bennink, plus newcomer Ab Baars.

By Misha's reckoning, this marks the band's maturity, and by now it really could head anywhere, fast. "Four in One" starts with a dead-on Monk piano intro, followed by the melody, brightly voiced for horns, followed by solo viola, out of tempo, very old world, first disrupted by piano accompaniment, then swaddled in encircling horns. And that's just the first 40 seconds.

Later on same, Baars takes a clarinet solo in the squeal register, above the instrument's official range, sounding very like John Carter (whom he'd study with later). Which is doubly curious, because "Four in One"'s stream of consciousness arrangement resembles little except Carter's friend and fellow Angelino James Newton's slippery, allusive recasting of "Black and Tan Fantasy," on his 1985 Strayhorn/Ellington tribute *The African Flower* (Blue Note). Newton ties Bubber Miley to stride rhythms and to Rahsaan's flute shrieks, looking forward and back. To give the white West Coast its due, Californian Moore sideswipes Nelson Riddle's "Route 66" theme on "Epistrophy" at 2:20.

Even by Dutch standards, Ab is radical; not even Misha caught on when he first heard him. In Baars, Mengelberg had found his Charlie Rouse. (Talk about your replication of reprehensible practices.) If Rouse skimmed blues chord changes, as if unaware Monk exploded doorbell depth charges behind him, then why not go all the way, improvise something deliberately obtuse?

As with most jazz novelties, there was a precedent, although Baars didn't know of it. Valdo Williams was a pianist active in New York around 1950, before moving to Montreal. As Sonny Rollins and Jackie McLean recollect, when Valdo had a 64-bar solo to play over a tune's changes, he'd improvise something harmonically unrelated, but which would end at bar 64 on the dot. Ab too. He can construct solos with a perfect, transparent logic of their own, unbeholden to the forms passing beneath. He was already on to this when he joined ICP, but Misha had been thinking about it too.

Paul Termos: "I liked playing those Herbie Nichols pieces so much, but I remember feeling very frustrated, because people like Michael Moore and Steve Lacy could play on these chords so beautifully, while Misha wanted to use me as a kind of anarchist. I understood that role, but found it very limited. He asked me to do what he now has Ab Baars for, the role Brötzmann had played before me. But at the moment he asked me to ignore the chord structure, I had just started trying to really play those pieces."

Ab Baars: "For the Monk program, I thought of the first records of Albert Ayler, where he plays with this Danish rhythm section." That touchstone again. "I studied the form and basic features of the Monk pieces, but never felt any relation to the melody. But I tried to listen for notes that would somehow fit the chords or melody anyway. Sort of like an abstract painter, who smashes paint on the canvas, instead of drawing representational things.

"At the very first Monk concert, I tried to play 'like it has to be done.' Afterwards Misha said, 'You don't have to do that; you can play your own things like you always play.' He was keen on trying to avoid a traditional pattern. He wrote a lot of material you could use to escape the traditional tune: introductions and riffs"—or the quasi-improvised, scooping shout chorus on "Criss Cross"—and he always encouraged us to use things from the introduction as a riff, or to make up our own things that didn't have to do with the material." Ab's against-the-grain soprano on ICP's "Misterioso" reveals his method, although he's in Lacy's thrall more than usual; Wierbos's heavy-breathing pitchless trombone intro is a more pure example of creative irrelevance, and illustrates how ideas spread within the band.

Baars' radicalism aside, this second reed player added to the group as Horsthuis was drifting out of it tipped the ensemble accent back toward jazz. But first Glerum joined, and the Amsterdam String Trio played within ICP for a year.

Ernst Glerum: "I felt some moving around in there, because I really knocked Ernst off of his chair, away from playing bass parts. But we had good contact, really co-oper-ated to make the transition. Also I'd already been playing with Michael, and Wolter, and Ab too. So the connection was no problem, just good understanding. The band is a great deal about understanding each other quickly."

Last of the moderns to join was Cologne trumpeter Thomas Heberer. Misha had heard him years earlier, subbing at a Berlin Contemporary Jazz Orchestra rehearsal of a Mengelberg piece. Misha told him then he'd like to use him someday, but had no opening just then. Heberer later joined the Berlin orchestra and played Mengelberg's music for real. (He's on BCJO's ECM album, where three of the four compositions are Misha's.) Then he joined ICP and really played it for real.

It's Saturday night, that weekend in February '95. ICP are in Utrecht to play the SJU Jazzpodium, a reasonably cheerful basement room where the bandstand is as far from the bar as possible, so conversation won't disturb musicians or listeners. Not that they would hear calls for alcohol tonight anyway. Bennink is back—there are mikes on stage for the strings. Still, the first set begins with a free improvisation sans drums: trumpet, cello, tenor and clarinet. It's not jazz, it's not classical music, it's suspended between, as delicate and sure-footed as ICP's composed music can be. Makes sense: free improvisation is one way a group discovers its own sound, and a leader verifies he has the right players.

Misha had tried other trumpeters—Toon de Gouw on the Nichols project, the SOSA-Band's Evert Hekkema more recently—before deciding it was worth importing Heberer for gigs. Michael Moore: "Misha's hard on trumpet players. He wants some-body with a really good sound—he wants Clifford Brown, only he can't find him. Evert was perhaps too jazzistic, not at all quick with things like visual cues and the pos-sibilities in the games, stuff like that. More a 'set it up for me and let me play a solo' kind of guy."

The SJU's low ceiling cramps one of Heberer's favorite moves, pointing his bell at the roof to call Gabriel home, consciously or unconsciously imitating Armstrong, who likely got the gesture from someone else, 50 years or more before Thomas was born in '65. Like young jazz musicians of the post-Baars generation worldwide, he studied the music in school, and looks sharp: flat-top hair, expensive unrumpled clothes. (Back home he has a regular TV gig.) But he's happy to have fallen in with bad companions.

Heberer likes phrases that begin at some odd place in a bar or scale, so they seem to hover in the air. He sounds like he'd be at home in a theater playing Weill, or in a ballroom pounding out tangos for bored aristocrats. His sound is precise, it projects, and his tone is ever so slightly tinny and remote, as if you're hearing him through a gramophone horn. This weekend he plays one solo that sounds uncannily like Brooklyn's Dave Douglas, himself a jazz educated, insider-turned-outsider Weill fan, whom Thomas had heard barely if at all. (But universes do intersect; Douglas will play the SJU two weeks from tonight.)

Opposing saxophone players have been a jazz staple since Basie pitted Lester Young against Herschel Evans. It was hardly a new idea in the '30s; trumpeters had been butting heads forever. As everyone knows, Pres and Herschel liked each other; their sparring was congenial, more about creative tension than a pissing derby. Moore and Baars ditto. Michael's clarinet tone is sweet, rapturous, warm; Ab likes extremes of register, texture, concept. Michael knows a million tunes, many far too old for someone who just turned 40 to know, and he's an artful quoter—here in Utrecht he's just touching on Duke's "Purple Gazelle" now in fact, a tune he plays in Clusone 3, with Reijseger and Bennink. If Baars sneaks a quote, you'll never spot it. Tonight he slips the opening of Hawkins' solo "Picasso" past the guy who'd given him the tape the night before.

Misha tends to emphasize the reed players' polarity. Moore is his Johnny Hodges; if it's a pretty tune with nice changes, chances are good he'll get a solo. Ab is more Paul Gonsalves. (What was Gonsalves' 27-chorus Newport marathon with Ellington except the systematic development of a rhythmic motif he supplied himself, so imposing and self-contained it eclipsed the composition that set it up?)

Ab Baars: "After Friday's concert at the BIM, my friend said that everyone in the band is growing more and more towards his own style. That is very nice to hear. That doesn't often happen, to have musicians with their own approach who can fit together very well." Well, yeah, but another longtime fan made the opposite point the same night: how much Moore and Baars have absorbed each other's ideas. It's true— Michael might play some squawky ungainly outa-left-field stuff, and Ab might tootle sweetly on clarinet, chiming on the chords. (As Misha says, sometimes playing the expected can be what's least expected.) Used to be ICP had three or four saxophonists to do the work of one. Either of the current ones can do the work of two.

Ab Baars: "I think Michael's playing has changed very much from when he first came to Holland. Within the tradition he comes from, he developed a very broad, open style. Once you hear it, you immediately know this is Michael Moore. I think that's also true for Wolter and me, and Han and Misha too. But I also think there's always the kind of interaction where we influence each other. There are pieces or improvisations that will sometimes relate more to Michael's or Wolter's playing than on other nights."

They are nearing the end of that first set in Utrecht. Reijseger, who'd been plucking in 4/4 jazz time, now crooks the head of his cello behind his neck, braces its hips with his knees, gets up and starts a Cro-Magnon duckwalk around the stage as he plays. Visual pun: walking cello.

At the half, Han is feeling good. His wife Masje came with him tonight, and they see friends they haven't run into in ages. Back in the dressing room just before the break ends, Han is sharing a smoke and telling road stories, and Misha is attentive, laughing. Band members exchange furtive looks of surprise: Han and Misha are actually *enjoying each other's company.*

Second set starts with a long, boisterous drum solo, a formal announcement of Bennink's return to ICP, and ICP's to the stage: many folks still dally at the bar. He strikes a nice balance tonight, dynamics-wise: some insiders had anticipated vindictive volume—making Misha pay—but instead he does the unexpected. Now, with the stage to himself, from the bar, where you can't see who's playing, the sound is a revelation: he could be a West African drum choir. Han Bennink will never lose the swing thing, but Clusone's tour of Mali and Burkina Faso last year added another musical dimension to his style.

This moment, you can sense a heightened social dimension too. Bennink gets the spirit as well as stylistic trappings of any specific music he evokes. His roar resonates, like a real drum choir's, with the concept of community. He celebrates his kinship with old friends at the bar, with anyone enjoying the show, with the musicians shuffling onstage as he plays, or for that matter with whatever inanimate junk he fishes out of a corner to bring to life in the course of a set.

This communal impulse is very close to what motivated jazz musicians and their audiences at the Saturday night functions Langston Hughes and Albert Murray wax on about. ICP captures that spirit a lot, although it may have little to do with Misha's scores, and nothing to do with the vexing way he can jerk his friends around. More often that impulse is tied up with the marvel of free improvisation, by definition the newest music there is, every time.

Yes, but Mengelberg wants sticks in the spokes of all wheels. Think of him as Ellington in reverse. Having assembled this cast of broadly-drawn stylists, he seeks to thwart rather than amplify their natural inclinations.

Ellington was the subject of Mengelberg's final repertory project. Each composer in the series took him further into his past. He'd discovered Nichols after Monk, and him after Ellington. (On the Monk project ICP played the first three Monk tunes Misha ever heard—"Misterioso," "Humph," "'Round Midnight.") The earlier he heard a master's music, the more he remade it in his own image. "'Round Midnight" sounds like something struggling out of deep memory, low moaning trombone like a Dutch moon rising to disappear behind a cloud.

Mengelberg's Ellington program is almost entirely concerned with prewar pieces, the ones Misha had grown up on. (The youngest tune by far in his *Ellington Mix* on *Bospaadje Konijnehol I* is 1947's "Happy Go Lucky Local," which offers an excellent example of clarinetist Baars' unanchored solo style.)

Ellington Mix is co-credited to Duke Ellington/Misha Mengelberg; he had made no such claims over the Nichols or Monk arrangements. On one hand this is simply jockeying for radio royalties when ICP's version gets played—it's not like anyone's going to cover "Happy Go Lucky Local Mix." But co-billing also acknowledges the radical shift from the Nichols project to this one. Heard back to back with the Ellington, the Nichols project *is* a Shorty Rogers record.

With *Ellington Mix*, musical games get factored in. On "Solitude Mix," a feature for Moore's alto at its most blessedly mournful, first the band plays the form straight, chords changing every bar or half bar on schedule; after the first pass, they proceed from one chord to the next only on cue from Wierbos. Sometimes he'll hold one a good long while. Which means Moore has to construct his statement with no clear idea of its harmonic rhythm, thwarting his ability to plan ahead, making him confront factors a soloist usually takes for granted.

"It Don't Mix" predictably enough, studs the melody of "It Don't Mean a Thing" with long out-of-time interludes. On record, its last couple of minutes is in fact one of Mengelberg's several "viruses": booby-traps designed to mess up any piece's structure from within. This one is called "Paardebloem" (Dandelion); on the CD you can hear Baars initiate it at 3:11, when the band is in full flail. Within ten seconds he's brought everyone to a full stop, save those players (and audience members?) who echo his constant refrain: an intermittent upward-tearing squeal—a whale whistling for a taxi. It may also remind you of freak trumpeter Cat Anderson's giddy high notes on Ellington endings. After a minute or so, the band stumbles on home with a harumphing, not-quite unison melody they'd hinted at just before that break. It sounds totally unconnected to the whale squeal, but is part of the same virus. Discontinuity is built in.

Most of both volumes of the live *Bospaadje Konijnehol* (Forest Path Rabbithole), were recorded in November 1990. They're Glerum's first records with ICP. His old high-tension gut-string jazz bass sound is a major part of the conceptual mix. Glerum is the band's quiet man, but he's one of the chameleons. He can play polite ballroom bass and still be subversive. Plucking a stock slick Latin bass riff against the rhythmic grain on "Caravan," he's the wheel and the stick in the spokes, both.

The tribute projects were acts of creative memory for Misha. The further back we try to remember, the more we fill in the blanks with elements drawn from our lives now. That's why *Ellington Mix* is by far the most radical of the tributes, the most ICP-like. The players' expressive breadth makes the octet/nonet worthy of the name Orchestra.

Misha continued his theater pieces in the '80s, albeit less frequently. The most notorious is the late-'80s' *Behang* (Wallpaper) at which audiences were confused by a half-hour of silent paperhanging. (Misha didn't tell them this was intermission.) As with all his other theater pieces, no record resulted, a shame in this case. It's got some great charging features for Wierbos and for Han, nice melodies, and a memorable episode of Misha hiphop: rhyming couplets for naturally theatrical singer Jodi Gilbert, who later disappears into a box on stage to sit out that paperhanger's half hour.

In 1990 there were concert versions of a chamber opera, *De Koeien* (The Cows) but a technical problem has so far barred a full production. He'd finished two parts—one for six-voice male choir (who play cows complaining about buzzing bugs), one for soprano and ICP. But Misha needed six mechanical cows, stylized, not unlike *Kameel's* chair-cum-camel. They had to switch their tails, lift their heads, move their mouths, sing—no problem. But getting them to walk the way a cow really walks—impossible. Without that says Misha finishing it is out of the question.

⚫︎

ICP packs up and gets out of Utrecht by one a.m. Sunday. By three that afternoon they're in Leeuwarden, an old town with a medieval street plan in the far north. It's one of the few places in Holland that feels remote from the central cities. Road signs are in Frisian as well as Dutch.

The players make their own way there; unlike the Breuker Kollektief—whose bassist Arjen Gorter subs for Glerum today, because Ernst is playing one of his occasional Bartok-for-children gigs—ICP has no bus. The idea of Misha arranging his players' transportation is absurd.

It's raining at quarter to three, when Misha steps off a side street into De Brouwershoeck, a so-called brown cafe, dark cozy pub with smoke-stained woodwork, a place with the dim luster of an unrestored Hals. He's directed to the upstairs bar, which is framed by rough heavy timbers. A few dozen people are already here, including most of the musicians. A few look as disoriented as Misha to be awake, let alone hours from home, so long before nightfall. ICP are here to play the local jazz society's weekly matinee, a vibrant if no longer common jazz institution. In Leeuwarden as in Baltimore, this Sunday ritual feels rather like the convivial rite of watching football at a local bar. Hang out, drink beer, smoke cigarettes, take in a comfortably familiar spectacle. The Sunday observance, in sports bar or jazz club or any church with music, is a muted echo of Saturday night.

Mengelberg orders a coffee, then takes a seat at a table in the back of the room. He lights a cigarette, fishes a piece of paper out of a pocket, and starts writing. This is when he does a good share of his day's work: when he makes up the set lists.

After awhile each side of the sheet bears a column of cryptic notations, five or more lines: a tune title; a musician's initials with a circle around them; another title, with one or two sets of circled initials behind it; several initials with a box drawn around them. . . . He's indicating not just the order of pieces, but also who will conduct the instant compositions; who'll be the designated soloists on a tune; who will play in the subgroups whose collective improvising will bridge or break with what comes before and after. As with any surrealist, postmodernist or film editor, juxtaposition counts for a lot; the order of events may imply connections among pieces, as in Anthony Braxton's continuous sets, connections which musicians can underscore or not.

As Misha scribbles, the patrons begin to wander over from the bar, to take their seats at long heavy cloth-covered tables facing the bandstand. The jazz society regulars are mostly men, mostly ruddy and bearded, and look more Scandinavian than their southern cousins. (The southwest tip of Denmark is 170 miles away, as the crow flies across Holland's and Germany's barrier islands.)

The broad outline of the short first set is almost a caricature of ICP intransigence. Since the audience is here to hear some jazz, Mengelberg defers their gratification until just before intermission, with the danceable and swinging "Rollo I." Somehow this final-seconds rally conveys the promise of more rollicking rhythm to come—a promise they'll make good on, later.

The first tune in that first set is Baars's "Lakschoen" (Patent Leather Shoe) kicked off by an obtusely clumping intro from the band's pianist. Misha's own role is always flexible. "I never make piano parts for the pieces I write. I can add something to what the others do, or I can leave it out. I want to be left out of the cooperative playing, because I always make mistakes. I'm not capable of performing my own music; I ask the musicians to do what I can't do myself. It's not essential for me to play at all, unless I want to fuck it up, or to make them do something else." He exercises a pianist's usual prerogative for reharmonizing, but since there are no chords written on anyone's parts except the bassist's, all the players are similarly free to hear (or mishear) the chords as they like.

"Just playing changes and staying within the chords all the time, that's completely outside my interest. Sometimes I write my name in the program, and then I play something. But most of the time it has nothing to do with the material, it's something laid on top of it.

"Ab of course has his ways to avoid playing changes at all, and he has very valid and interesting forms to substitute. He knows how to think the changes and play something that opposes them in some way. The musicians can tamper with the time also. You could take Time Out, say, 'Don't bother about time. I have to make a personal statement here that will somehow be related to what you guys are doing, but give me the time regardless of what you had in mind.'"

On the first set he sandwiches a piano solo between two rowdy free improvisations. As always, in the course of laying down atmospheric harmony more radical than Nichols', Mengelberg's playing is alternately brilliant, stupid, obvious, swinging, drivel, Ellington licks, readymades (comping for a tenor solo, he plays "Fanfare for the Common Man"), anything and everything. He doesn't need written parts because mentally the pianist and composer are one. The old divisions vanished long ago.

Wierbos steals the set's second improvised quartet with an inspired solo. He keeps pointing the trombone's bell into the air, perhaps slyly mocking Heberer: Wolter signals his strong aversion to playing to an audience via replication of reprehensible practice. A musical as well as visual joke arises out of it: every time he raises the bell, he lets the extended slide fall back into the horn with a loud *thock*. It's funny, and as rhythmic and striking as a work song. Again, jokes are okay, as long as they still work with your eyes shut.

Or when you're listening to a record. Which is mostly a moot point, since ICP makes few of them. (The most recent stuff on *Konijnehol* is from '91.) Mengelberg figures it takes pieces about a year and half to cook before they're ready for the platter. The juices run clear from the current batch, which have cooked at least that long. Between Reijseger with his portable DAT machine and Dick Lucas with his professional rig, and house engineers, a lot of gigs get recorded (like today's), but Misha only recently turned down a fairly sizable offer for a new ICP hatART CD. It may have been because he'd heard horror stories about the labels's capricious management, but even folks telling him those stories had urged him to take the deal. (He would record for hatART, without ICP, in spring '96, and with ICP in the fall of '97.)

The set ends with "Rollo I," a habanera—not a tango, Han insists, though even musicians confuse the stately Cuban and sliding Argentine versions of the same rhythmic pattern. To accent its deferred-gratification function in this context, on the set list Mengelberg calls for improvisations by the band's "jazz soloists"—Moore and Heberer—so that all the players could see at a glance where the whole set was headed. Misha may not give much explicit direction, but the musicians are good at reading between his lines. But just so even he can't be sure how things'll end up, he gives the last "Rollo" solo to wild-card Baars. He behaves.

When the set's over, your feet still feel the tune's syncopation—a four-beat pattern with a hiccup/pickup at the end to boot you into the next bar—and your ears still hear

the infectious harmon-muted trumpet melody. Mengelberg has written more intention-
ally dumb or ineptly resolved melodies than anybody, but he's also written simple, genuinely charming pieces like "Rollo I," that must delight even him when they pop out.

It puts the house in a good mood, too. Whatever they were thinking earlier, they're
in his corner now. The players are all awake by intermission, which flies by quickly. At
the bar—coffee! cognac! matches!—Mengelberg chats with a friend who drove up
from the south; Gorter's Texan-Cuban wife, the singer Estrella Acosta, keeps a coterie
laughing; Wolter has a reunion with a dancer he'd worked with in Groningen 15 years
ago.

Second set: "Kwela" a.k.a. "Tetterettet VI" a.k.a. "Kwela P'Kwana"—the titles
mutate with the music, oral tradition—which dates from way back, the '70s, when
South African rhythms heavily infused Dutch jazz. (Sean Bergin's influence is deci-
sive, but remember altoist Dudu Pukwana had worked with Misha in '73. With Han
added on clarinet, trombone and scratch violin besides drums, in 1978 they made the
rollicking/farcical *Yi Yole*—ICP 021, last issue by any ICP trio. Dudu's broad/flatulent
sound and gestures—vaulting in and out of "When the Saints Go Marching In"—fit
his partners' program.) There are heavy echoes of mbira, the rattling metal tabs of
thumb piano, in Ernst Reijseger's heavy plucked intro, this afternoon and also on
Bospaadje Konijnehol II (the most faithful representation of the modern band). That
echo is even more pronounced now, after Clusone's West Africa trip.

The centerpiece of the second set, and of the weekend's gigs, is the *Picnic* suite in
six parts, their titles given here in Mengelberg's running translation: A beautiful day /
Let's go to the river / And have a picnic / Play some badminton / Watching the clouds,
meanwhile and after / Then head for home before the sparrows start waving their paja-
mas. It's one of the Orchestra's main texts, but it backed into its repertoire. Misha had
devised its themes for an improvised theater piece, but once formalized they defeated
their purpose. So he brought it ICP, to be rescued from any fixed function.

The fanfarey opening movement is another clarion call from muted trumpet. On
this tune, everyone has to be careful to come in at different times, on different notes.
On "Picnic II," Heberer "has the potato," as the band says: the crude ring around his
initials on the set list means he's the soloist. He circles one note, melismatic, by working his spit valve; he gets himself out of it with some Rex Stewart–style half-valving on
the pistons. Then he blows air; Reijseger immediately scrapes the side of his cello.

For the second half of "Picnic II," Heberer is again in the lead. The trumpet line
accelerates toward the tonic, aiming for a big ending but overshooting it. It dives too
low, brakes and reverses, overshoots again, too high this time. And so it goes. Speeding
up when it approaches the tonic, slowing down as it moves away, the trumpet is a
roller-coaster car accelerating and decelerating through dips and humps. Heberer
finally cuts it off on some other arbitrary note. Usually this episode is long and loopy—
one could easily mistake it for a free-standing piece—but today he wraps it up fast, perhaps 'cause that spit-valve solo earlier dealt with the same idea a different way.

In ICP, as in Kansas City swing bands and other oral cultures, fads come and go. A
couple of years ago, the group had a mania for ending pieces in the wrong places—in
the middle of a solo, a bar, a riff, a rest, anywhere but on a cadence. Such thwarted
endings have evolved into a formal principle, as on "Picnic II." So has thwarted

momentum. On another section, a whirling, folk-dancing hook, designed to go on for-ever, pulls itself up short. "Picnic III" is a lachrymose descent from a sixth to the tonic by half steps, a drinking song, just misshapen enough to sound thick-eared.

Misha then leads an instant composition, as simple and content-free as a conduc-tion gets. He invites solo statements by raising his right hand in solicitation—please, help yourself—and then cuts the invited players off with a curt wave of same. Han never misses an invitation, and rarely sees Misha try to silence him. When Ab's turn comes, he plays some loud and grating clarinet squeals. Often he'll solo as if he does-n't know proper fingerings or how to get a good tone, then finish (as here) with some full-bodied and exquisite phrase, so you know he could've played pretty all along.

A little later, Wierbos takes a solo with the cracked-eggshell tone of Miles or Bill Dixon, anything but his stylistic element. At one point the helpful pianist hammers a suggested note to home in on—hey modal man, we're over here—and Wolter loudly sounds a note a half step away, like a bad free improviser who stops what he's doing to imitate someone else and gets it wrong. Within seconds the whole band pounces on the idea, and any note anyone sounds is exactly a comic half step off whatever came before it, a garbled game of telephone. It's a quintessential Dutch moment, cre-atively dense. It's very funny, and will never happen that way again. Good a time as Wolter is having, yukking it up, he doesn't even glance at the audience—this is for his amusement, and the band's. Even at gigs hundreds of miles apart, ICP never repeat a joke for an audience's benefit. This is hardly the approach Gorter's used to—he's unamplified today, by the way, a change for the better—but he's obviously enjoy-ing himself.

Not that spontaneous bits don't ever find their way into the band's routine. The last piece of the weekend is "Rollo II." ("Rollo" was Charles Ives' name for any listener who cringed at difficult new music.) The opening and pivotal line of the melody, its recurring hook, is a downward skitter repeated later in strict retrograde, skittering up. During an open section, whenever the horns play both phrases back to back (skitter down skitter up, like barbershop mirrors reflecting each other), that cues a return to the main written section, a swinging romp on standard jazz changes. A new arrange-ment mutated out of this cue during performance one day, and without discussion, the band decided to keep it. However the saxes play the cue—crisp or sloppy, very slow or very fast—the other players continue in kind. Today it's slow and sloppy, sounds like a parody of *Ascension*: sour clashing long tones.

Earlier in the set, Misha does something he only does when the room is cozy, peo-ple are listening, the atmosphere just right. He steps up to the mic, the genial host, and he sings—or, more accurately, recites in rhythm (hear "Zing Zang Zaterdag"—Singsong Saturday—on *Konijnehol II*)—his song about hares, "De sprong! O romantiek der hazen," which is also the lyric to its opening line. (It dates from the '70s, and has been recorded in solo, duo and trio versions at least. He got the idea watch-ing hares frolic on a rare visit to the country, to pick wild mushrooms.) The untrans-latable Dutch lyric could be an oblique but innocent children's story: surreal as Lewis Carroll, but without the hangups.

It's strange to see him up there, this rascal playing master of ceremonies with a lit-tle smile on his face, using his cigarette as a prop. He looks happy as a hare, there in the center ring, your confiding pal. You think how long it took him to collect these musicians, you understand why he looks pleased.

So that's how Misha spends his weekend. Tuesday night he goes to Amsterdam's Paradiso, for the premier of his *Beestebeest versus Hertie* for chamber orchestra, on a program with Xenakis, Donatoni, Stockhausen and Guus Janssen. (He'd been working on it through the winter; when deadline drew near, he used part of *Picnic* as extender. It was not a popular success, the sort of thing that discourages folks from offering him commissions at this time. His next would be over a year later, from an idea by librettist J. Bernlef: *To a Dead Man's Ears*, about a birthday party for a Beethoven-like composer.) Thursday night he cooks pork chops.

That afternoon, before he knows what he'll make for dinner—he will go to the market looking for ground beef and potatoes—he sits in his apartment on the Olympiaplein, answers questions over coffee. He's asked about ICP's sources: Weill, old dance steps—and jazz, which Misha has referred to before as a dead tradition. But one day's big pronouncement is the next day's declared lie; what does he say today? Are these musics living or dead?

"Well I try to do something to the corpses that makes them live, maybe for another five minutes. I'm interested more in life than—no, scratch that from the record."

—You're more interested in life than death, scratch that from the record?

"Yes. Hee hee hee. It's not true." He's still laughing. "Did I ever bother you with my ideas about cannibalism? I'm very interested in that. I would like to be a cannibal. With so many cars and things in cities like here or New York, you could easily have a fatal accident. I think there should be the possibility that instead of giving your meat to science, to organ banks or whatever, you could give it away to some good restaurant. Something tasty could be made out of it, from the mouse of the hand, maybe. Or an ear. Yes."

—Sometimes I think of ICP's music as like cooking: not too much of any one ingredient.

He chuckles. "Maybe that's something I could have said myself, yes."

Chapter Eight
String Section

Ernst Reijseger: "The Dutch are conscious of their dependence. They have nothing to say about world economics, because Holland is too small. They can only manipulate—get power by trading information. So they don't have big pretensions about their heritage or what they have to offer the world. Historically they were a bunch of crooks, stealing all kinds of shit from others. Gatherers, in that sense."

—Do the Dutch feel polluted by American culture?

"Influences flow in a certain direction because of the time we live in, and that's about it. My music reflects trends also, no matter how much I try to avoid them. The design of my instrument is the result of certain trends, including romantic ideas about sculpture. After the time of Mondrian, to play an instrument with a design from the end of the 1600s is like—ridiculous!"

November 1991, after playing Shostakovich in Rotterdam, Yo-Yo Ma let some friends drag him from a reception to a nearby ICP gig. When they arrived, near the end of the first set, Han Bennink was attacking the floor. Yo-Yo liked it.

At the break—this is Reijseger's version—Ernst spotted him, came over, got introduced, said, come to the dressing room, I want to show you some stuff. Ma said, I just got off work, I'm tired, let me drink my beer. Ernst said, bring your drink.

So he went, and Reijseger showed him some things he'd figured out how to do with a cello. Ma stood there, another witness says, and repeated slowly under his breath, fuck-ing in-cre-di-ble.

When Reijseger tried to hand him the cello so he could show off, Yo-Yo Ma—a very nice man, soft-spoken and modest—waved him off saying something like, Oh, I just use a bow.

They drank till four. Next afternoon, Reijseger was at the Concertgebouw to hear some Shostakovich. At the break, a man introduced himself as the Concertgebouw's director, explained Ma had an upcoming series of carte blanche concerts—a nice

Dutch tradition where you get to do whatever you want—and that Yo-Yo wanted him to play on one.

In Holland, conventional wisdom was the Dutch had no strong musical identity or towering composers until recently. The big gun was Jan Pieterszoon Sweelinck, who fine-tuned the fugue before Bach. Recent stabs at rehabilitating some 19th-century Dutch composers (via subsidized recordings) confirm that wisdom. The lieder and choral music lean toward sea shanties. Dutch folk music is bar songs, or what you sing with mom around the piano, about sand dunes and the Zuider Zee.

Which is not to imply indifference to music or its demands. Holland has a strong pedagogical tradition. Pre–conservatory level, music ed is outside the regular school system; you have to choose for it. But with little of their own worth playing, the Dutch soaked up influences and styles from without.

Then came jazz: seductive music that plays nice games with harmony and rhythm—brisk cycles of fifths, stepwise modulations, switches from 4/4 time to Latin shuffle—that skilled musicians could appreciate, and which left plenty of room for personal initiative.

Because jazz, or minimalism, or rock-and-roll came second hand, the Dutch feel no impulse to preserve it in pure form. (Oh, there are exceptions aplenty, and their music remains imitative.) The heritage is all available: Monk can be as valuable as Stravinsky.

The relatively high profile of string players in creative Dutch music is a conspicuous symptom of genre mixing. Reijseger is a paradigm: virtuoso with striking strengths and limits, able to be theatrical and musical at the same time.

He is cursed with laundry-list reviews: a roster of tricks told in visual terms. (This book is filled with laundry lists, the author concedes, but that's because so many Dutch musicians push technical frontiers.) Ernst clenches his bow in his teeth, guitar-strums the cello over his knee. He picks lead-guitar runs with the plastic tag of a hotel room key. He puts peg to the floor to scrape it back and forth, or for an episode of walking basslines, before he grabs bow and begins scraping its side across the strings. (This sound will be mentioned: asthmatic Gargantua snoring.) On looks alone it's all striking and funny—not to mention metaphor for his panoramic conception of the instrument.

What's unsaid: If you're strumming chords, over-the-knee is the most comfortable position for either hand—that's why guitarists use it; strumming cello, he plays four even beats to the bar like Freddie Green, or four-string guitarist Eddie Condon, because (like ride-cymbal ching-a-ching) a breathing four lets the time flow and advance without inhibiting a soloist—again, a practical choice. Picking with a plastic slab lets him get a snapping attack reminiscent of koto, a sound you can't get with fingertips or guitar pick; the tone he gets with it varies from nasal to full, depending on how hard or far from the bridge he picks. (He found the key in his pocket after checking out of the Barclay in Vancouver, serendipity.) While you're plucking or picking, the teeth is the closest convenient place to keep a bow you may need fast (though he'll also stick it down the back of his shirt). The modified "Reijseger bow," corrugations neatly cut along one side, let him suggest cuica, nose-blowing, Hans Reichel's sawed-plank daxophone, all sorts of stuff you can't reach with the horsehairs.

But it's not cuica, any more than strumming makes it guitar—he slides between chords, exploiting that fretless neck—or 4/4 walking gives it the heft of a bass. It's always a cello, on which he also does a lot of more familiar stuff: playing a slow pretty line that wafts under greater activity. His critics aside, he doesn't have to be the center of attention.

Also unsaid: What he does is less about ingredients than timing, getting from one idea to another without hesitation. Also unsaid, what he leaves out; he has good instincts for knowing which cultural graftings will take. When Piet Noordijk's bass player Harry Emmery starts popping strings on his acoustic like a funk bassist, it comes off like a foreign-speaker's syntactical error: doesn't work for reasons he doesn't hear.

There were jazz precedents for some things Ernst does. On an early '80s blindfold test he IDd Oscar Pettiford, Sam Jones, Ron Carter, Alan Silva and Dave Holland (all bassists first and cellists second, by the way) and he's a fan of '40s/'50s cellist Harry Babasin. In the '70s with Julius Hemphill, Abdul Wadud covered the guitar-surrogate strategies, like a Delta bluesman who wound up with the wrong instrument. But Ernst didn't know any of this when he started. He worked out all those chords on his own before finding out there were mandolin fingering charts and David Baker books he could use.

Yo-Yo Ma: "I think of Ernst as an inventor. Every time I've seen him he's so delighted to have found a new sound, a new system of improvising, a new way of making the cello more than the lyrical instrument it's usually considered to be. His imagination and invention are on an incredibly high level. For someone who thinks he knows the cello's possibilities, it's amazing to see his hundreds of other ways of doing things."

—Is there anything you've learned of practical use to you?

"Whenever you meet someone challenging or innovative, it opens up your horizons about what's possible. But I also remember one of the first things he said when we started collaborating: 'If we're going to do this, we have to be able to spend time together.' That has really stayed with me. Whenever I'm involved in crossover things that bring two people together, the one thing I ask for is time. No matter what kind of music you want to deal with, it takes time to find your way in."

Tom Cora: "I took a lesson with Ernst. The first thing he said was, 'Okay, show me all the weird stuff you've figured out on the cello.'"

"I was brought up with calculators and typewriters." His parents ran their textile business out of their rowhouse in Naarden (where Ernst was born 13 November 1954) near Hilversum. When I met his father he was 96, bedridden, oxygen mask, no English, could hardly move—he tried hard to make me laugh and didn't stop till he succeeded. (Ernst's mom is 28 years younger; they dealt with some heavy disapproval.) Ernst can't ask the time in a foreign country without first trying to get a laugh from the person he asks. He can also whoop it up in the car all the way to the gig, and on arrival cop an instant attitude toward the sound engineer cause he doesn't like a provisional microphone placement.

The digital chaos of the home office marked him; his fingers stay busy even when he's idle. Squinting a little through thick glasses, he looks like a former sickly kid, which he was. He often appears distracted when he plays—as if he doesn't even notice the odd stuff he does, or is a little suspicious of it.

"My first instrument was recorder. I started playing it at four and never stopped. I had lessons till I was 15 or 16. I saw someone play the cello at a music school, when I was seven and a half. I got one for my birthday from my parents. They had encouraged me to go for a grown-up instrument.

"When I was 13, 14, my teacher changed his attitude towards me, after I'd won a prize at school, and then another at a competition between schools. So now instead of creating a passion for the instrument, he made me really practice. I had gone through the same thing with my recorder teacher, and I got really tense and fucked up.

"My first year in high school I only knew people older than me: 16, 17. I was this dwarf who played the cello. They used me in school plays. I was already acquainted with jazz music. When I was eight or nine I'd already seen Duke Ellington—the First Sacred Concert, on German TV. The music really came through, like on a jazz and poetry night where this guy from my school read from the phone book, very artistically. That made an incredible impression. I didn't know anything about religion, but if I'd been a little older, I probably would have thought I'd seen the light.

"I heard jazz records. For my birthday my older brother gave me *Soul Trane*. My mother says I listened to it in my room, came downstairs and was really depressed. 'What's wrong with you?' 'I just heard John Coltrane, I'll never be able to play that.'

"One of my older friends was Jurre Haanstra, the son of documentary filmmaker Bert Haanstra, who was known and dug by the improvisers. With Jurre I saw an ICP group with Willem Breuker, Willem van Manen, Maarten Altena and Han Bennink at the Stedelijk Museum. I saw quite a few gigs when I was really young. Sometimes I was not allowed in because you had to be 16.

"Jurre was a drummer. His father went to India on a film shoot, and came home with a set of tabla. The only person Jurre knew who could play the tabla was Han Bennink. So when I was 13 Han came over to show us the first moves. Big beard. I'd wanted to play with him since I first saw him play, before we met. But I waited till he asked.

"Burton Greene gave me my first real gigs, last days of 1969. He'd been living in Holland, and had been to India, and was into ragas. Burton was a great guy for collecting contacts. I still love him. The band was a trio, with Daoud Amin, a percussionist from Puerto Rico who grew up in New York. He had been in Turkey for a number of years, had played with Turkish musicians, spoke Turkish. At that time I'd already been listening to Indian music, which I thought was amazing. I'd had an electric cello since I was 14, and played it with Burton. (I'd play with electric guitars, and needed something as loud as them—a problem I still haven't solved.) The only jazz pieces we played were 'Nica's Dream' and maybe one other. Those were encores. Usually it was long drones, and written-out ragas."

—On "Nica's Dream" did you play the quote-unquote bass part?

"Yeah, that's when that started. I didn't understand it at all at first, but yes. Friends of mine said, 'No man, don't try to do that, you won't be able to.' My idea was that the cello's function could be expanded, but I didn't know how. It took me a long time to figure out certain things actually are impossible.

"I will never be able to sound like a bass. The way you play changes as a bass player, with an instrument tuned in fourths—if you try to copy that on cello, tuned in fifths, you get into big trouble. You have to follow your own concept of chords, and simplify things. The bass drum and the tom and sometimes even piano or tenor saxophone will be lower than you. But the bass function has less to do with how low the pitches are than the rhythm in which you play them. You can suggest lowness, by giving it a certain kind of timing. Walking bass with a similar function already existed in baroque music. That's where I find links, because I play baroque music a lot. But then it changes, develops, becomes something of your own.

"At 17 I played an English tour with Burton and a very good Indian tabla player who was a terrible person. I was driving, without a license, because they were completely drunk. I met Sean Bergin through Burton—we did some lovely quartet gigs with Martin van Duynhoven—and our duo thing started, in the Melkweg. Then we got asked to join Theo Loevendie's band, with Guus Janssen and Martin van Duynhoven. I was married to Sean musically. We practiced all the time, had a great time playing together. He introduced me to South African music. So I was practically brought up listening to kwela."

That's plain from the tunes Bergin wrote for their 1979 LP *Mistakes* (for Reijseger's Broken Records), either's debut as leader. They abstract from kwela in a hurry—cello underlines and tenor timbre unspooling, unglued—only to snap back into it. They listen closely no matter how raunchy they get, and have the internal momentum to give it some crazy kind of swing feel even where bar lines and form are suspended.

They played a few times in trio with Han Bennink also—finally, he had asked.

"Sean and Gunga—the drummer Alan Purves—had done a gig on the Festival of Fools, where I started to get really involved with clowns. Theater, music, a multimedia kind of thing. I joined theater groups, like the Great Salt Lake Mime Troupe. They were improvising clowns, but they could abstract the things they were doing. They were on to something. They weren't trying to be funny. They could be really angry. They'd steal things from people in the audience, juggle eggs over them and occasionally drop them. If they threw one at the audience, someone might catch it and throw it back. We had a lot of freedom to come up with new songs, new things to play. There were a few session-type places where you could make a little money. I joined around '76, '77, and stayed on and off about four years. That scene in places like the Shaffy Theater and the Melkweg was completely English-language, by the way, and very important to my development.

"For two years I worked for a live weekly public affairs radio program. I played music between segments, and could invite any second person I liked: Maarten van Regteren Altena, Maurice Horsthuis, Misha, Guus Janssen, Sean, Gunga, Han Bennink. That was heaven. And Sean and I did music for the Dutch edition of *Sesame Street*. We could try all kinds of things. Music for films, music with movement. We might play all day in the studio, make about 40 short items and choose the best ten."

It is hard to imagine American improvisers landing gigs like these.

With Edinburgh-born Alan Purves he made the '82 duo LP *Cellotape & Scotchtape* for Dick Lucas's DATArecords, a label run with reckless disregard of balance sheets.

Reijseger runs the checklist: pulls his low string around the side of the neck while plucking, uncorking a fine whine; strums one quote-unquote guitar line while picking another, implying different rhythms. On "Surdu & Cello" he does it all at a formidable clip. He has drummer's timing, good match for Gunga, who brings timbral and rhythmic echoes of bodhran to toms and bass drum. On thumb piano for "Shakers & Kalimba," Reijseger pops out of one meter to slide into another, may slide out of that one before you can identify it. Gunga can add and subtract rhythms much the same way. "Rekwela" reprises the three-chord bass line from Sean's kwela "For the Folks Back Home," *Mistakes*, which would later turn up in Clusone 3's book.

A couple of years earlier, Ernst's future wife Giny Busch—violin, a charter member of the Ricciotti Ensemble, another group that plays inclusive programs in streets, train stations, retirement homes—tipped him to an alto and clarinet player she'd heard: Michael Moore, fresh from the States. Reijseger had already played with Michael's brother Gregg in the Mime Troupe. Maybe being scooped up by Burton Greene made Reijseger sensitive to what foreigners had to offer; he snared guys like Sean, Gunga and the Moores almost as soon as they cleared customs.

By 1980 Reijseger, Bennink and Michael Moore were an occasional trio. When Ernst lucked into some free studio time—a last-minute cancellation—in October '80, they recorded what became the second side of *Taiming*, for Ernst's Hummeloord label. (The flipside is cello and kalimba solos, Gunga guesting.) It's nice, but only a foretaste. It wasn't till years after Reijseger and Moore had joined Bennink in ICP that they began working formally as Clusone 3 a.k.a. Trio Clusone a.k.a. Clusone Trio. In that phase it started as Clusone 4. Clusone is an Italian town that hosts a spring festival for which in '88 Ernst assembled a quartet with pianist Guus Janssen. When the gigs started getting regular, Janssen bowed out. (In 1996 trumpeter Dave Douglas joined up for a short "Plusone" tour, but it was problematic. Bennink and Reijseger got squeezed into a traditional rhythm section role they usually manage to avoid. The gigs were taped, but no CD followed.)

The trio have multiple personality conflicts, but at best it's a pretty perfect vehicle for each; Bennink and Moore share a similar background—Michael played jazz gigs with his father too—and cello and drums lock in. The trio will be blowing wide open and free, and Moore will play the first line of a tune from the book—Ellington, Nichols, Berlin, Bergin, Mengelberg, Moore—and a bar later they'll be romping full swing. Actually, it's more complicated: anybody can call any tune in the book anytime, by alluding to the melody or abruptly playing the intro, possibly at an unanticipated tempo, but the other two might blow him off. (The variable tempos, multiple menu options at any time, a willingness to confound each other and not cooperate, are standard ICP practice: Misha's ideas sifting out.)

While Moore and Bennink are romping into the second 8 of some chestnut they've played 50 times, Ernst might be leafing through the music on his stand, looking for a lead sheet. As many chords as he's figured out, he's not really a harmonic thinker. (One day when he was favoring major 7ths Misha groused about his "peppermint chords.") Moore said once, if you're playing a three-chord tune he knows well, and you modulate up a step, you may lose him. Rhythmically, he's harder to shake.

Bennink: "Ernst started coming to my house when he was a teenager, and he kept on coming, and he's still there! I play more and more often with him, and discuss rhythm with him more and more. Ernst is a frustrated drummer playing on a cello."

The pair have a way of dealing with rhythm that may seem closer to additive processes in Indian music than subdividing 4/4, jazz style. That fits: tabla brought them together. Han still has his tabla-like combinations, Ernst can cop the slick bowed microtonality of veena, but they don't go in much for explicit ethnic references or metrical patterns. They try not to be so obvious, or to stay in one place too long. With Clusone Reijseger may take the melody (bass clarinet sketching chords behind), presented without irony, until he eases toward a Stephane Grappelli sophisto veneer more corrosive than outright demolition.

On stage Moore is the hurricane's eye, gives no sign he notices his partners' mutual antics. But his rhythm is incisive too; like the others he can be tender or absurd, doing spit takes during a heart-to-heart, cheek to cheek. Dutch music is partly about a broad frame of reference, and they clock all points of the compass during a set, alliances shifting quickly as they do.

In the '90s Clusone 3 started to click as business venture: Western Canada, Norway, Mali and Burkina Faso, and in '95 Vietnam, China and Australia. Moore put out their first two (live) records on his Ramboy label; hatART made the superior third, *Soft Lights and Sweet Music*, Irving Berlin songs. Eventually Gramavision licensed Ramboy's *I Am an Indian*, and issued the '96-live *Love Henry*.

"I have some kind of deviated perfect pitch. If someone whistles a note, I can play it, but I still won't know what note it is. My analytical sense is really underdeveloped."

—You've said you had to invent things on your own, not knowing other people had invented them already.

"That basically refers to cello techniques: playing artificial harmonics by using your thumb as a movable bridge, or managing certain doublestops. There are schools and books where you can learn all the finger positions, but I took the stupid hard way to finding them, like giving myself a blindfold test." He spent two years and change at conservatories but partied them away. "When I was finally equipped to play the cello repertoire, I stopped practicing it, because I was already hooked on other musics. I never disrespected that repertoire, but I saw the two disciplines as separate, and thought that between them there was too much information to deal with.

"Because I've heard Han Bennink, I'm familiar with another approach to music that is very effective, and as enjoyable as the esthetic approach. It's not often I can convince musicians in one camp that another camp's approach can also yield great results. But Yo-Yo Ma responded quite positively, and I could play really rough sounds with Trilok Gurtu." (Ernst had passed through the Indian percussionist's band in the early '90s, plays on part of his *Crazy Saints*.)

That inclusionism fueled Reijseger's Cruise Button, a project for the 1987 October Meeting, kitchen-sink band with floating personnel including Moore and Bergin, Brooklyn trumpeter Herb Robertson, Surinam-born Eddy Veldman and New Jersey's Gerry Hemingway on drums, Curaçao-born guitarist Franky Douglas, Philadelphia's

Gerald Veasley on electric bass, East German trombonist Johannes Bauer: high-toned
dance music with cello solos.

"I've tried to apply ideas from all kinds of music in my improvising, but I also developed a strong desire to improvise without premeditated structures. In many ways it has
nothing to do with Indian music, for example; no slow this-is-how-we-feel-today
buildup, then a little faster and more intense, climax, bring it down, fade out.

"I don't see improvisation as virtuous, it's just what works for me. It's a method,
interpreting your conditioning or deconditioning: one way of concentrating, of staying
awake on the instrument. The method I often apply is definable as improvisation—I
cannot read well enough to get equally good results that way—but I condition myself
like hell. When I play for myself, I repeat something endlessly, till it gets boring, then
move slowly towards the next interesting topic to get stuck on. Sticking to my function
when it's already established—is that improvisation, or concentration? I don't know.
I'm hooked on concentrating, that's for sure.

"I have a lot of conditioned movements in my hand that I apply all the time, that
become very personal, the way someone's composing does. So for me there's no real
difference in value between what I do and interpreting written music. They're both
about how awake are you, and feeling where somebody else is as they play. Who has
the lead, whose lead do I acknowledge. In written music too, everybody has a voice,
and tries to fit in, or you can play against one another, be uncooperative.

"Playing a gig, I may forget what my possibilities are. If you ask me about the instrument, I just don't know what I know. It's weird, I've always found false harmonics on
the spot, am just able to play a melody that I hear, in harmonics, then and there. Or I
may hear other possibilities, like how I can fit into the ICP horn section, playing double-stops.

"I hate the term 'extended techniques.' A lot of what I do is common for bassists and
guitar players, for example. I reinvent the wheel sometimes, but on the other hand I
understand why it's desirable to hold your bow straight over the neck, because there
are certain things you can't control if bowing is a less conscious process.

"My teacher René van Ast was able to do certain tricks on the instrument that totally stunned me, like playing melodies and chords on the strings above and below the
left hand, circling over the fingerboard with the right hand. He strummed too. The
famous cello player Paul Tortelier used all kinds of chords, and played an encore in
the Concertgebouw where he strummed—he was famous for it—but he didn't create
an uproar, it was just cute. I'm so ignorant, I don't really know if something is new or
not. I keep inventing, and lose a lot of inventions as new ones come up."

—I haven't seen the hotel key in awhile.

He reached into a pocket, extended his hand, jingling it.

Three trios Reijseger has played with skirt the line between improvised and chamber
music. The most recent is with German pianist Georg Graewe and Gerry Hemingway.
(Reijseger, Michael Moore and Wolter Wierbos also play in Hemingway's quintet.)
Their music is free improvised. Graewe is a long-line player, a bit like Tristano on that
score; the drummer can percolate at low volume. The music is frequently introspec-

tive and contrapuntal, the voices equal in weight; early on especially they seemed to make every collective pause an ending—pulled pieces up short rather than letting them run too long. (Later, they might sail past the same opportunities, as if to avoid a schtick.) None of their records is bad, but *Zwei Naechte in Berlin* and *The Saturn Cycle* are particularly strong.

In the early '90s, Reijseger came into the extant New York string trio Arcado, with violinist Mark Feldman and bassist Mark Dresser. (With France's Trio de Clarinettes they made up Double Trio.) Ernst also plays duets with that trio's Louis Sclavis—but if we mentioned all his settings here (Derek Bailey's Company weeks, The Persons, English saxist Andy Sheppard's short-lived big band) your eyes would glaze worse.

For Ernst, Arcado's highwire balance, blurring of genres and interpersonal frictions must have reminded him of the defunct Amsterdam String Trio, with Maurice Horsthuis and Ernst Glerum. Either AST album—the LP *Dodekakania* (DATA) from 1986, the CD *Wild West* live in California 1988—displays their impeccable playing abetted by unamplified sound, and a clear ensemble personality despite disparate allusions, Bach to the 19th-century drawing room to beery back-porch jams. Their approach parallels what Tilburg guitarist Jacques Palinckx has said of his own music: the greatest moment in a concert is when the audience loses its frame of reference. (Not that they sound anything alike, Palinckx being rooted in progessive rock.) As in other Reijseger groups, there were moments of deliberate chaos, where the players seem to get their feet crossed, or forget what key they were in. This is chamber music where (to pay that dubious compliment) the line between composed and improvised is thoroughly blurred. Horsthuis can improvise, and he gets SJIN subsidies, but in AST jazz was never more than a whispering informant.

"I like melodies, nice music. I feel a little un-Dutch."

In the '90s Maurice Horsthuis leads the orchestra Amsterdam Drama—32 pieces, half of them strings, an unwieldy and expensive combination, but the size canvas he needs. Maurice is the scene's great romantic, and boy does he look the part: calling those big sad eyes puppy-like gives puppies too much credit.

Maurice Horsthuis was born in Breda, 28 April 1948, and grew up in the north, town of Meppel. After a year of recorder lessons he took up violin at 10, switched to viola at 16 or 17: the deeper sound spoke to him. He was crazy for Stravinsky by then, had driven his parents and seven younger siblings nuts listening to the *Sacre* on the family hi-fi. His parents sent him to teacher's college, but he crossfaded over to the Tilburg conservatory, which had the best (Hungarian) viola teacher he knew. He stayed four years but didn't graduate.

"It was a normal conservatory education for the early '70s. I wasn't doing what I wanted, got bored and ran away. I figured if anything was happening it would be in Amsterdam. That was 1971 or '2. (While there I also studied a year at the Sonology Institute in Utrecht, because I was interested in electronic music.)

"Somebody told me Loek Dikker was using string players in jazz music. I called him but he already had Lodewijk de Boer on viola. A week later Loek called me to do some gigs. Not too many people talk about Loek, but I'll always be grateful to him. In that band I met a lot of jazz musicians including Han Bennink. I had improvised in private at the conservatory, but this was the first time I did it with other people. I stayed in that band awhile." One 1973 octet version of Dikker's Improvisators Guild had Maurice, J. R. Monterose, German trumpeter Manfred Schoof, Arjen Gorter and Martin van Duynhoven.

"I was becoming one of the new people on the Dutch jazz scene. I was in Herman de Wit's Herbie White Combo, performing on the bill with the Amsterdam Electric Circus. Herman's band had Han and Peter Bennink, Guus Janssen, Gilius van Bergeijk and Maarten Altena. Soon I started my own group with Arjen, Guus and percussionist Peter van Ginkel, who I met through Loek. Then I had a combination with harp, and then a group with Han, Maarten, and Gilius on oboe. I was already moving toward classical instrumentation.

"Louis Andriessen asked me to play on an ironic new version of *Matthew's Passion* for the theater group Baal. I fell in love with the actress playing Jesus. After that I was Very Much Interested in theater." You can hear the caps. "I had been working as a music therapist; I stopped that and became An Artist."

He approached the AEC about doing a children's matinee: *Violen Paultje*. That was 1978. Maurice played the Little Paul of the title, "a Brilliant Young Violinist who is sent to America to further his career, and gets involved with gangsters. They gave me a violin I could shoot with too. It was a gorgeous success, so I did two more adventures the following years. I think that was my way to get the Brilliant Young Violinist out of my system."

In 1979, at the invitation of Lodewijk de Boer, now more busy directing than playing, he started writing a lot of music for Baal: numerous shows through 1987, including *Leedvermaak*. The cheery nature of some of the tunes seemed bizarre for a play about Jews and the War. He wrote mostly for small groups but one show had taped music by 24 players.

"When I was 17 or 18 I composed and conducted a piece for the music school orchestra, but at the conservatory my teacher forbade me to compose, so I would concentrate on my instrument. That was not good advice I think. Except for some little themes for my groups to improvise from, I didn't write again for ten years. At Baal I didn't feel at all self-confident even when people said they liked my work. I'd think, 'Liars.'"

He got busier; his quartet evolved into Altena's first viola/bass/oboe/alto sax quartet, where Maurice stayed a couple of years. He'd have two stints with ICP. Misha created another romantic persona for him, Mauritz Huishorst: an excellent lover who always has a pot of coffee on.

"People always ask me, 'Did you have problems with Han?' I always liked it. Han made me see that just being on stage could be more important than making music. He's loud of course, but I'd wait for the gaps when he stops playing, and then dive in. The first time I left ICP, I guess I'd had enough for the moment. After that, when Han got a carte blanche program, he invited ICP and me. I liked it, and I was back. The second time I left, in the late '80s, it probably had to do with the Amsterdam String Trio being in the band. Those were the dark years." Like other romantic artists, he could be totally charming one day, a surly drunk the next. The worst of those problems are behind him now it seems.

His early '80s theater projects included a big high-profile Holland Festival production of *Moby Dick*. There were problems, and he found himself made the fall guy in the press. No one was much interested in his version.

The String Trio with Reijseger and Glerum started up; Maurice was brimming with ideas that sparked them all. He had a genius for simple musical games, something he'd gotten a whiff of in ICP. In one, each member bows one string, then slowly turns it into a double-stop, then fades out the original note, keeping the second, and proceeds from there—shimmering slowly changing chords. There was one called "Bushalte" (Bus Stop): "A series of bars, a line you play forward and backwards, moving like a bus route." A staccato line, each note distinct. "Every note is a stop where you can get off; then you have to hold that note. When the others come back to it you can reboard or not. Finally when everyone is out of the bus, it ends on a held chord."

The most ingenious was "Andreas Fleischmann," elegant to look at and hear. It was inspired by the Fleischmann model trains he set up for his son to play with. There are three melody lines that can be read in any clef, back and forth à la "Bushalte." Except these three lines intersect in the middle, on one long whole note. Once in progress, a player can switch tracks in the middle, ride another rail back to the center, everyone converging on that whole note every 17 beats. (Railworkers call such a switch a St. Andrew's Cross—hence the title.) If a player arrives late or otherwise screws up, there is a sort of 'penalty section' as in "Hello! Windyboys." The erring player must go directly to the right border, rest till the next time the other players reach the whole note, count another half cycle until they too get to the end of a line, and then reenter, backing into traffic as it were. There is also a fourth intersecting stave, cropping out at an odd angle like a blade of a dormant windmill, that calls for steady pulsing chords or double-stops, rail-rocking in rhythm.

"Fleischmann" has giddy momentum: it races along, pauses for a dramatic whole-note chord, then moves on till it U-turns back, expanding and collapsing like Poe's universe. All the notes west of whole-note junction are on the lines of the staff, all the notes on the right between the lines. As the players pass back and forth, the tonality rocks gently like a railway carriage creeping through the yard—at least till the penalties start eroding that symmetry, as players cross from left and right simultaneously.

AST's two albums showcase Maurice's tender melodies but not the games. ("Fleischmann" is on Amsterdam Drama's first CD—the score is pictured in the booklet, alongside a muddily translated explanation—and "Bushalte" is the first part of "De Spul," The Stuff, on their second.) There is a very nice tape of a 1990 Shaffy Theater concert someone ought to issue someday.

Early on, Maurice recycled older compositions, but more and more he wrote fresh material for the trio. In retrospect, he noticed the pieces on *Dodekakania* were conventionally voiced, viola on top; on *Wild West*, cello got the nice melodies, viola often placed underneath. In the last period, all the good parts went to the bass. "Ernst Glerum was playing so beautifully—he really became a singer on his instrument. For me, that period was great; I really left classical music behind, to head to the wide open spaces."

But then the band crashed and burned. As Maurice says, he lets things build up to an explosion—not, he says, that that helps anything. AST, 1984–1990.

Orkest Amsterdam Drama came together a year later. The version heard on *Amsterdam Drama*, 1991, had Reijseger, Glerum, Michael Moore and Daniele D'Agaro in its ranks; they were all gone by the sequel *Drama in Concert/1994* (although new altoist Jorrit Dijkstra came on like Moore's understudy). By then Michael Vatcher had joined on percussion, his shambling time and unabashedness nicely offsetting the lyricism. "Schubert" there is adapted from part of the slow movement of the C-major string quintet—Schubert whose lyricism seems closer to Maurice than Stravinsky's. Dutch improvised music has few major figures whose writing can be called delicate; on that score Horsthuis surpasses even Misha or Michael Moore. He is improvised music's last 19th-century tonalist.

Each of those Drama CDs contains a cupboard composition à la Mengelberg's *Dressoir*, repository for sundry scraps; Maurice likens "Pleinvrees" (Agoraphobia) to one of A'dam's junk-filled street markets: a stained mattress, some oversize shoes, an old washing machine.

Sometimes he'd think of the band as three sections—reeds, brass, strings—but even when horns get the solos the orchestra is always about strings, including harp. He conducts the improvising occasionally, in an unsystematic way—sometimes, a section could play only when its leader did—but the CDs (like AST's) showcase the writing. Horns solo, the strings play the charts: they're Maurice's voice, counterbalancing the soloists. The orchestra recycles some older pieces, from the String Trio and theater productions, primarily *Moby Dick*—if you know the characters you'll spot most of the titles—whose music is belatedly vindicated.

The 1995 *Vreemd Hier* (Strange Here) is the pick of Drama's first three, recorded in a church on the beautiful barrier island of Terschelling, grass-covered sand dunes wild as Wyoming: the Dutch mountains. The orchestra had traveled there on two sailing ships, putting them in a suitably nautical mood for the Melville material and other bounding-main melodies (like "Plons," from another play). The apparent references to Franz Waxman or Bernard Herrmann—whose pulsing Hitchcock strings make him, in hindsight, one more ancestor of minimalism—are not conscious homages but allusions to generic film music for dramatic effect. (Even so, "Pestkop" could be a Herrmann Hitchcock theme.) Writers draw comparisons to Bartok too, but Maurice doesn't like Bartok.

Horsthuis rarely plays with Amsterdam Drama anymore—they need a conductor more than another viola. With his many writing assignments, he doesn't get much chance to play at all. But string trios stay on his mind. For the national theater's 1996 production *Céline* he wrote music for double trio: two violins, two violas, two cellos.

"When the old BIMhuis was being remodeled, Huub van Riel said to me, 'Ernst, make a program for the month of July, four concerts in a tent in the courtyard of the Amsterdam Historical Museum.' I gave myself one of those concerts, and asked Ernst Reijseger and Maurice Horsthuis, although I didn't know either of them too well. The first rehearsals were amazing. (But the concert never happened—it was raining cats and dogs. We did it a couple of months later, at the new BIMhuis I think.) Maurice had recently been cut to pieces in the press because of *Moby Dick,* and the String Trio helped him recover from that. At first I wrote some pieces, but found it quite hard to write for us. But Maurice felt like a fish in the water.

"It grew and grew; we played all over Europe, many times in Italy, went to the United States twice. Even in the wrong places it worked out great."

Ernst Glerum was born 20 April, 1955, in Deventer, in the east. He hated recorder lessons, started playing guitar at 14, Beatles and Stones. He got hooked on Dutch boogie pianist Rob Hoeke, got into piano, which he plays very well. "I traced that music to where it came from. What I got down on guitar, I put on the piano. I listened to all the records at the music library. String music: Django Reinhardt. It amazes me now how much impact things have when you hear them for the first time, all kinds of music you don't know existed." He started hanging at the local jazz cafe, a dixieland place, began playing that music in the school band 'cause the teacher was into it.

"By then I was playing bass; I think I started at 18 or 19. I'd taken one from the attic of the music school. I kept on with piano and guitar, and also played violin: Christmas Mass at the Catholic church. But I really loved the bass groove, the time. I had heard Mingus in the library; that really made an impression, that and the bass players in the jazz cafe. I had lessons for two years.

"I played in a youth orchestra: baroque music, or a flute concerto, or easy or not-so-easy overtures. I came to Amsterdam to study bass at the conservatory. The first year I practiced a lot, had nice lessons, met people, but was mainly doing classical music. I went to some of these cafes, where drummer Johnny Engels would play. The one time I sat in it was a disaster. That surprised me. I didn't know the tune. And once around 1976 I went to the old BIMhuis where Martin van Duynhoven was doing rhythm workshops, with a lot of Surinamese guys. It was very open, going on for hours. I wasn't interested At All. By now I was playing in the National Youth Orchestra, a very sociable setting, a lot of young people together. It's incredible, hearing a piece for the first time and being part of it too. To really hear a French horn, how every tone has all these sounds in it, that's beautiful.

"The improvised thing—or the jazz thing, I should say, because I feel very much a traditional jazz player—started off when I met Jan Cees Tans. He played me lots of records I didn't know, really an ear-opener. Lots of Charlie Parker, Art Tatum, Bud Powell, Gene Ammons. We made up a little quartet to play free music, with Louis Moholo, and Kees Hazevoet." J. C. Tans, bandleader, tenor saxophonist, bon vivant, Engelbewaarder barfly; Kees Hazevoet, onetime wonder boy of Dutch improvising, pianist and reeds player who burned bright than Kahoutec'd out, vanishing to become an ornithologist. Moholo was based in London but liked to visit Amsterdam.

"Jan Cees was into Albert Ayler as well as Gene Ammons. He had this thing I mentioned about French horn: in every tone there are more tones, the spectrum of sounds in one tone. He also has a hangup about tradition, connects everything back to Louis Armstrong, Tatum, Jimmy Yancey. In a strange way he's a purist. We had lots of laughs. We started this band ATO—Amsterdam Tenor Research—with Hans Dulfer and Rinus Groeneveld, who was very much into Dexter Gordon, and right he is. Dulfer was Dulfer, making kissing sounds on tenor. Sean Bergin, Maarten van Norden, some others sat in. The drummer might be Han Bennink, or Martin van Duynhoven. The music was always"—he sings a walking bass line—"boom boom boom boom—heavy. That was nice. On some other things with Jan Cees I played with Han and Harry Miller, two basses.

"The first time I really played with Han was on a tour Maarten van Norden put together, with Willem van Manen, and Curtis Clark on piano. We had 25 concerts in a row, and at all 25, Han went out of his box. Maarten had heard him play with brushes, you know how nice that is, but Han is not somebody you tell what to do, unless the material is really convincing. All these beautiful, brilliant little things Curtis played were completely demolished. I remember asking Han, why? His answer was, enthusiasm. That really puzzled me at that time."

A lot of folks passed through J. C. Tans & Rockets. (By their fourth album and only CD, they were the J. C. Tans Orchestra.) Among its many vets are Breuker's trumpeters Boy Raaymakers and Andy Altenfelder, Bergin and Baars on reeds, Wierbos and Curtis Clark. The Rockets sound like a frat band with ambition. (The CD *Around the World* has some deft moments, but Glerum was gone by then.) They played Lunceford's "Bust Out" and Sun Ra's "Brainville," a brace of Bergin and Glerum tunes. Ernst wrote some swingers and catchy vamp numbers with nice chords; for them seek out *Dance of the Tadpoles* (all the LPs were on BVHaast), his third and last Tans. "Psalm" is Glerum's change-up: chorale for acapella horns that sounds like a paraphrase of Catholic hymn "O Sacred Head Surrounded," giving way to a rock-and-roll ballad for tenor sax: a solo placed in an incongruous frame.

On the strength of his Rockets writing, NOS Radio commissioned an hour of his pieces for a 1986 broadcast. Glerum assembled the 11-piece New Klookabilities—the title a nod to Kenny Clarke—with Bergin and Moore, Wierbos and Bennink, tubist Larry Fishkind, electric guitar, and a young guy from Nijmegen on piano and celeste, Michiel Braam. There were good spots for soloists and offbeat details—a second percussionist on xylophone or orchestral bells, '30s-jazz violin, Glerum's own blues and soul licks on console organ—but no commercial recording, no follow-up save isolated pieces like "Omnibus," a quasi–Neal Hefti Basie chart with escalating rhythmic modulations.

Then as now, Glerum rode his two career tracks—he was in the Asko Ensemble, one of Holland's many (funded) chamber groups favoring new music, and plays in a trio that performs Bartok's *Mikrokosmos* for children—but he leans more on the other rail.

"I like to walk, and I like to play melodies; I'd practice Marcello cello music on the bass. Things that I encountered in classical music, I put into my jazz solos, same way I make my pieces. (I took one passage from *Romeo and Juliet*, made an introduction from it, and called the piece 'Tell Tchaikovsky the News.') With a bow, Paul Chambers plays like"—Glerum sings fast rhythmic figures—"amazing timing, almost like the bass is being plucked. I'm still working on that. Christian McBride could do that right away, he has this very solid timing like Ernst Reijseger has. Me, I have to work to get the feeling of a horn player. I find that when I improvise with a bow, I lean toward more classical-type improvising. I put in the vibrato, which I think makes for a very nice feeling in jazz music." His arco has none of the bad-cold nasality most jazz bassists get.

Guus Janssen's trio with Wim Janssen on drums best taps the bassist's technical resources, as he switches from one world to the other, crossing a bar line. Half the time on their CD *Lighter* Janssen Glerum Janssen is chamber group masquerading as a jazz band; "After AT," for one, depends on a trapeze act's precision: everyone sails through space to meet at the right place and time, or it's disaster. There are also lots of bass-piano unisons that demand precise intonation and time, and sound like Slam Stewart humming along with himself.

Janssen digs Tristano, so Glerum also gets to improvise on chord changes in swing-time, and play long unresolving walking parts up and down the neck, and serpentine arco melodies that don't come up for air, notably on "Marshcello," a line originally written for Reijseger's nimbler axe. Even more than a Tristano rhythm player, he has to keep time unperturbed by the metric displacements exploding all around him. Janssen's "Tune for F" is a slow melody played entirely in bowed harmonics, some-times double-stopped; somehow he brings out the soul of a melody he can barely inflect, fingers of his left hand barely touching the strings. On the wide-open "Taag" a steady whine like bowed cymbals is revealed to be bass only when you notice Wim Janssen is otherwise engaged. Gut strings (wire-wrapped for better bowing) give Ernst good sound across the board.

"Curtis Clark and I became friends. I dreamt about moving to the States, becom-ing a real good jazz bass player. I look upon Curtis as a real jazz piano player. He regards himself as many other things also, but he can do that *really* well. His *Letter to South Africa* is a fantastic recording, beautiful pieces, but it wasn't easy. I can play any-thing, and Curtis will stay in time, but Louis Moholo plays around the time, a lot, and plays very dense things, little accents, very free. The bass player has to be very confi-dent. To anchor the whole thing is a big responsibility you really feel.

"Now I feel more confident to trust in my own things. I know what I can do. I might get shaken up a bit by crazy accents, but I don't mind so much. That's what I learned with Han: changing a beat, or skipping one—it doesn't matter. Everybody does it. It took some time to learn that. Moholo was another good teacher for that. And John Tchicai. On that same Curtis Clark session, he told me, 'Hey man, you don't have to play all this crazy hip shit—you have to play the bass.'"

❧

The bassist on the fourth J. C. Tans disc was Wilbert de Joode, who plays all that crazy hip shit. Glerum is all dexterous elegance: a light touch combined with a blooming sound. Wilbert is more blunt, blunt as his heavy brow out of Breughel. You could almost identify the strings he uses from the dents they leave in blunted fingertips. Like Glerum's, they're wire-wound gut.

Dutch radicals agree with American conservatives: a double bass sounds better than an amplified double bass. Dutch bassists still own amps; de Joode might haul one to a gig and then not use it, if he can get away with it.

Jazz and classical players have influenced each other as long as there have been jazz musicians. Jazz bassists taught classical colleagues a lot about a ringing pizzicato. Classical bassists had the bowing chops, and stayed mindful of a woody tone, unlike jazzers whose amps let them be heard above loud drummers, but made them sound like they were plucking big rubber bands. (Remember Arjen Gorter: better to be audi-ble than authentic.) Cross-pollinators like Glerum kept striving to coax out the spec-trum of tones blooming within a single plucked note.

Wilbert de Joode's pizz is like popcorn (except when like firecrackers, strings plucked just above the bridge). Reijseger has a drummer's timing; de Joode has a drummer's attack.

His strings sit a little high off the neck so he can whack them harder. What little he loses in speed he gets back in volume and tub-thumping tone: Scott LaFaro agility meets Pops Foster articulation. He investigates the many percussive attacks possible with fingertips, dependent on how much string you grab, how close to the center of its length, whether you tug hard or strike it like a bell. . . .

His bowing is gruff; a little nasal but very well defined. He gets in and out of corners fast. Blunt, but not naive; in Ab Baars's trio he plays the changes on John Lewis's ballad "Trav'lin in Plastic Dreams": wide-fingered triads in the thumb position, high on the neck but full-sounding. His time is strong enough to let him take broad liberties; he'll let a tempo slacken and then speed up, like an overstretched cassette. He'll take drumsticks in either hand and bat them between adjacent strings, mock-bass drum rolls. He'll jam his bow into the strings and twang it, boyoyoyoyng. He never sounds at a loss, though some would wish his attack were not always so front-loaded; that legato Glerum thing isn't there. But give him a bare three-note bass line and he can harp on happily.

Wilbert has the rough steely hands of guys who shake hands too hard, but he doesn't. The frown when he's listening to someone looks engraved. Only when he erupts into a broad smile do you see how his face was made to look: sun beaming through clouds.

"The last couple of years, I think a lot about projection in music. I once played a concert with the New York alto player Jemeel Moondoc, and drummer Dennis Charles. After the rehearsal I thought, 'This will be a nice evening.' On the concert, Dennis Charles was on the ceiling. After two minutes I thought, 'I'll never make it to the end.' It was even worse the first time I played with Charles Gayle. I never got that feeling playing with Dutch guys."

As with Ernst Reijseger, his technique is homemade. His sense of urgency stems partly from lost time. He started playing in earnest when he was 24. (He's from Slotermeer, A'dam suburb where he was born 11 May '55.) Like Glerum he started with guitar—"House of the Rising Sun"—and played a little piano in school. He found an old electric bass in someone's attic. "Suddenly, I was a bass player. I bought a Fender Jazz Bass, and took off the frets because Jaco Pastorius was happening.

"I got to play in some groups, and made a lot of money in a nightclub orchestra: evergreens, easy-listening top 40 dance music; funky stuff on the weekend. I learned it all by ear, couldn't read a note. I made my own notation, a memory aide. I didn't feel like a musician at all—didn't dare to. But some people came to me, made me aware I was playing something more than was on the record. They wanted to know how I did it. It made me realize there was more in me than doing top 40, and that I had to leave that scene."

He played some fusion, aspiring to go to the conservatory. But after a year of prep work—reading, solfège, bass studies with Arnold Dooyeweerd—he never made it; family obligations intervened. He finally bought a double bass in 1982. "I wanted to improvise a little more, started going to Tuesday workshops at the BIMhuis with

Arnold Dooyeweerd. Eric Boeren was in that workshop too. I think we scared them a little. You had to come up with ideas and work them out, usually without telling anybody what they were."

Tenor saxophonist Vera Vingerhoeds and violist Ig Henneman each asked him to join their groups; he recorded with each. "Ig was the first leader I met who was really thinking about improvised music. Before that, it was all about jazz and time playing. This was an opportunity to escape from that. I still regretted entering music so late, and not having conservatory training to fall back on. But when my class graduated, I played at a lot of the parties. In a way, it was a sort of revenge.

"There is hardly anything that is new, but because I'm self-taught and haven't heard all that much music, I might play something new to me that someone has played before. I was pulling strings around the side of the neck before I ever heard Mingus on *Money Jungle*.

"Last week I finally heard David Izenzon, on an old Archie Shepp record. It was the first time I'd felt connected to another bass player since hearing Henry Grimes on Steve Lacy and Roswell Rudd's *School Days*. I liked Scott LaFaro's melodic approach, but rhythmically he never touched my heart. I did hear one bar of Chuck Israels once that really amazed me. I can't sing it, copy it, or identify it, but it had a rhythmic invention unlike anything I'd heard before. Eventually I stopped looking for it, because the memory was inspiration enough.

"Ig Henneman has been very important to my development. I'm one of the few people who can work with her without feeling like a strict mother is watching over them. In her concept, I can focus on playing just a few notes, which have their own function. I've always been able to put my own spin on them. If you just go through the motions she's not satisfied. But as soon as I make my own story out of it, she accepts it."

We had been talking one weekday afternoon in De Engelbewaarder. As often in cafes, when his hands are idle, he was twisting a coffee spoon into a pretzel, this one balanced to rock on its own bowl. A man came in, enormous head, big hair, saw Wilbert was doing an interview, and came over to draw him into a pointless conversation, just to instigate something: Jan Cees Tans.

Ig Henneman also bloomed late—made her first album under her own name at 45. Like Glerum, she came up in the system. Her family are achievers. One sister is a clothes designer, brother Jeroen a well-known painter, Maria a TV newsanchor. Ignatia (born Haarlem, four days before Christmas 1945) started testing the piano at age 4, before she can remember; that led to lessons at 5. Mom and the kids sang around the piano, Dutch songs out of a standard anthology. Jeroen, three years older, listened to Monk and Parker in his room—"But that was not for girls. That's how it was at that time." She sang in a church choir, heard French pop and Los Paraguayos, Mozart and Maria Callas. She started violin at 12. "When I wanted to play gypsy songs, or a pop tune, my teacher said, 'This is not real music.' You hear that for years, you lose track of other music a little."

She played in the Haarlem youth orchestra—"loved to play Bach and Ravel, hated Brahms and Schumann"—chose violin over piano, and moved to Amsterdam to attend the conservatory—"very old-fashioned, worse than now." She went to the Concertgebouw's progressive Sunday afternoon series—if not Andriessen, at least Berg and Stravinsky, maybe with Maderna conducting—and joined Asko in 1968, its early days as student chamber orchestra. "I enjoyed that: talking music and finding new music on your stand and discovering whether you liked it or hated it. It wasn't so dogmatic. I hated all that serial stuff I'd had to read though.

"I started playing viola in Asko; they needed it for one piece, and there was a shortage of violas then. It was an instant change: you don't have to worry about the top parts, or deal with the norms and standards set for violin. It was a more lazy sound to me. You don't have to play so many notes. You can be more of an ensemble player. It makes you more conscious of the lower parts. I'd never really listened to the bass before.

"I was a sort of sponge. It was only afterwards that I could see what I chose.

"In 1968 or '9 I met Jan Cees Tans. He forced me to listen to records—'Who is this playing?' Some things you *had* to like. For me it was very good. I learned a lot about music I'd only heard about. (Did I hear Ornette on violin? I liked it, in its own field.) We went to the Paradiso, and the Kroeg and BIMhuis later, heard everyone and everything.

"Thanks to Jan Cees I started choosing music I really liked. Ayler and Monk were the most important, I could listen to them for hours. Classical musicians think jazz musicians never practice, that it all falls from heaven. The first jazz I heard was bebop, which sounds so complex if you don't know the language. Ayler and Monk I could understand better than Charlie Parker. I could hear that playing more free music was another skill—that it was an open field anybody can enter if it suits them. One important piece for me was Ayler doing 'Summertime'"—on the record with the clueless Danes. "Of course they don't understand each other, but that gives another view of music, a better picture of how it actually goes, of what inspiration really is.

"I started to rehearse on Sunday afternoons, in a quintet, five girls, me on piano, playing standards: Cannonball Adderley, Horace Silver's 'Song for My Father.' That eventually became F. C. Gerania, which started as a jazz group but gradually became a rock band. At the end I was playing an electric piano with a string ensemble on top, and an electric viola. Lyrics, short solos, big amplifiers, a roadie. Vera Vingerhoeds was the last singer in that band, playing alto and tenor sax.

"Playing jazz, rock, I spent seven or eight years on stage without sheet music. I had been educated as a reader, and now I wanted to have ears. I took some workshops with Nedly Elstak, working with progressions so complicated—full of 11th and 13th chords—that theoretically any note would fit, if used right. Your ear has to choose. Then I was in Nedly's Seven Singers and a Horn"—which usually had three or four singers—"and his Paradise Regained Orchestra from 1981 or '2 till '84 or '5. We played a lot with guest soloists—Jan Cees Tans, or Willem Breuker, who's not so comfortable with difficult material. From Breuker I learned it's okay just to blow straight through complicated charts, do your own thing on someone else's pieces."

Harmonized voices really put Nedly's evolving complex chords into bold relief. His limited trumpet chops had fallen off even further, but he played a lot of piano now. In those same years he put out a series of four workbooks, *Praktische Jazz Theorie*, wonderfully practical in fact, taking the student from what a whole note looks like to advice on writing 12-tone melodies that imply nice chord changes.

"Suddenly I could hear more and more, could think logically about chords, could understand how people's compositions work: the same tricks over and over, always sounding the same. Writing like that works for some, but it made me feel like a bookkeeper. When it came to start my own band, I didn't want to do that anymore.

"F. C. Gerania didn't make so much of being an all-woman band at first, that was really a political decision later. I speak for myself: I was a little jealous of the boys who had a real attitude about their own taste, which I didn't have yet. Being in a women's band was one way to develop a perspective. I started to write—it took me years, developing my taste, or at least becoming more conscious of it. When we had all developed a direction, we split up." That was about 1983.

—Is it harder for women then men on this scene?

"Yes, but in everything, not just in music. It's a very complex issue, open to misunderstanding and oversimplification. I teach children a lot. Lately I teach them to write little songs with chords, use their imaginations. I notice the girls do well till they're 13 or 14, then suddenly they're watching the boys for approval before moving on. That can take five or ten years. One way to look at it: women are educated to care for others, not to be artists, who think about themselves. I'm from a generation that believed that biologically, only guys could improvise. Women artists, especially young ones, have to be self-confident, and have a good perspective on their own work, because critics will go both ways—be too positive or too negative. That can be very confusing.

"I've been interviewed a lot, and it's always about this stuff, never about the music. When I started my own band, in 1985, I didn't want to think about it anymore."

That was a quintet—the Kwintet. Their 1990 CD *in Grassetto* is exceptionally good improvised chamber music, the fruits of winnowing. She had been in no hurry—"I had made two F. C. Gerania records, so I knew what a record meant"—had tried different musicians and written and discarded lots of pieces. Clearly structured but not overdetermined, sonorous but driven by interplay, slinky melodies: she got it right the first time.

Henneman exploits the recombinant possibilities of viola, alto sax, bass clarinet, bass and drums: two reeds, two strings; two basses, two altos; three woods, one metal—or four and two when you count the drum set—or three horns and rhythm section. Three percussive voices too, counting de Joode's bass and Hein Pijnenburg's bass clarinet. Still, the Kwintet gives the impression of a string band; rather than using viola as a horn she'll use saxophone as violin, often voicing viola and alto together in close dissonance, with closely matched dynamics—and no vibrato, the better to disguise the source, and to give it a spotless surface. The last is offset by the drumming of Fred van Duynhoven, who has a heavier, chunkier sound and swing than his brother, say. Fred pushes the eight-beat backbeat on the composition "In Grassetto" evoking a Julius Hemphill blues: same pentatonic low-register string-grinding Abdul Wadud espoused. It comes off surprisingly well—think how your cheeks burn when other hip string quartets try to get down—because it treads lightly on funk gestures and doesn't stiffen up.

Bart van der Putten is an effective clean slate on alto; where a head may sound slightly reminiscent of Ornette, he avoids referents. Pijnenburg is more candid about the Dolphian origins of the goosebumping lines he reads or improvises. Dolphy by now had passed into the Dutch canon; this is the sound of Dutch jazz folding back on itself. Henneman is only four years younger than Bennink, a year than Breuker, but conceptually she's second generation, building on what the founders built.

On the CD her improvised feature is the solo viola "Violaceo," rapid strikes of the bow which bounces off the strings, letting them ring: the chirping of birds, the circularity and overtone-consciousness of Evan Parker. In its spare rapid rhythmic flutter you might also hear the rhythm of the bicycle.

"I hardly ever listen to violin improvisers, except Ray Nance; that beautiful solo on *Suite Thursday* is one of my favorites. Joe Venuti I like also. Grappelli, I hate: always the same. Lots of them go on and on because they don't have to breathe. They phrase terribly.

"I compose intuitively. For improvisers I write simple tunes I'd never write for classical musicians. If you played them very precisely, they'd sound like nothing. I like to start with something simple that's easy to elaborate on—a rhythm, an interval, a little tune, clear enough for the musicians to improvise from, and to attune listeners to what I'm looking for. The rest has to be improvised, and the variations may have no fixed length or changes. For improvisers I write as few dynamic markings as possible, so they can make the material their own, and it can be different every time. Sometimes we use different forms for the composed and improvised sections. Maybe we all start on a five-note series, then improvise on other notes. Or maybe I'll ask someone to play the pulse for a time. On 'Vijlen Blues,' we all enter separately, and each has a separate layer to play before taking off on the concept of the piece. You can't tell where the improvisation begins; I like that. I'm convinced good improvisers who really know the material can play without restriction.

"I wrote some graphic pieces for the Kwintet. But I don't like games on stage. Maybe that's nice for people to watch, once, but it's not my cup of tea. My own role in improvising groups is to watch the forms. If someone runs on too long, I'll cue them back in."

Henneman's career as commissioned composer took off when she was hired to write a score for a 1927 silent film. (Woman director, women's theme: "Yeah, I'm really a product of the second women's movement.") Composer Robert Heppener, one of her old conservatory teachers, started advising her—"my coach"—on practical aspects. She wrote for Ricciotti Ensemble plus two saxophones, a piece for eight trombones, a dance score for TV. When we spoke she was in the midst of a 20-minute piece for the popsy Metropole Orkest. When she gets a commission from someone she checks out their gigs, studies their idiosyncrasies and shortcomings. For Metropole she came up with a blues suite where the parts for strings and for saxophones fit those sections like Italian shoes.

Outside commissions do not permit working and reworking material as with the Kwintet. Subsequent projects with singers and larger groups are less settled. The strongest and weakest thing about *Dickinson*, 1993, settings of seven Emily poems sung by soprano Jannie Pranger, was its onomatoprosaics: literal tick-tock of mortality's clock on "Each that we lose takes part of us," choochoo clickclack and dopplering horns on "I like to see it lap the miles." No nods to jazz songs, though "The saddest noise, the sweetest noise" is a sort of European blues without blue notes; Mariëtte Rouppe van der Voort's plaintive alto solo is the righter for her thin '20s vibrato.

Repeat that, repeat from 1995 was better: settings of poems about birds, nine poets, several languages, the Henneman Tentet: four strings, three clarinets, Rouppe van der Voort's flute, drums and voice. The vocal settings (and Ilse van de Kasteelen's delivery) are less strained, more speechlike (and intelligible). The ensemble shifts underneath, as if disconnected, another layer. Henneman exploits the differences among Moore's, Ab Baars's and Pijnenburg's tone and phrasing on clarinet or bass clarinet, and evokes John Carter's piercing harmonics. As on *Dickinson*, there are lovely dissonant horn backgrounds—streaking long notes and held chords a speciality—and an excess of slow tempos.

"When you use lyrics, you need new structural solutions; I didn't want to use variation form. On the birds project, the improvised sections bridge the composed parts; the improvising can be free variations on something before, or something new that may or may not bend toward the next written part, or a reaction to the atmosphere or texture of a lyric. But that's up to the soloists, myself included.

"I've been influenced by Misha in a couple of ways—one of them giving the musicians a set list just half an hour before we start. With the large group, I move the solos and soloists around, so everyone doesn't always play on the same piece. With the quartet, we have a few pieces that feature specific musicians, but now when I make sets for them I don't indicate soloists; I'd rather have collective improvising where we can freely change roles."

A Sunday afternoon in the small old theater De X in Leiden. The musicians have set up at the wrong end of the room, behind all the seats—the bass player's bizarre idea, Wilbert disliking the idea of playing to a small crowd from a high stage. Henneman's concept works; her string quartet music sounds rather like an improvised version of modern barely tonal/polytonal chamber music. Well, maybe it's a little rough for that; it's thorny and dense as a briar patch.

This is that rare string quartet where slap-bass syncopations flow into or out of open improvising: no jumpcuts to such period trappings to signal how clever and eclectic it is. The music is more about simultaneities: high gentle dissonance from top strings, belches and rattles from below; long notes under fast sequences and vice versa; held harmonium chords from three arco strings, uninflected, with Tristan Honsinger improvising on cello over the top, rubato, heaving vibrato. He starts slapping his foot loudly on the floor, in some other tempo.

Busy with her writing, Henneman doesn't always practice enough. At the BIMhuis's '91 October Meeting she connected with California new music violinist/violist Mary Oliver—George Lewis had brought her—who moved to Amsterdam three years later and serves as the composer's chopsy surrogate.

As prelude to one piece Honsinger recites a Dickinson poem, stilted as Ichabod Crane. They commence, and before long he's bobbing in his chair, and a long thin mewling sound enters the room, in time with cello. He shifts his weight to his feet, crouching, begins inching around the stage, head of cello crooked around his neck, keening in a crackpot's voice. It's as if Henneman is staging her own Ayler Among the Danes: you don't put an anarchist like Tristan in your band if you're after total control. (More like draining all the water from the polder only to let some back in.) Then again, you can call attention to control issues by giving up a little. It makes amends for all the long, slow ones they play.

Concertgebouw, 31 March 1993, second set: Ernst Reijseger and Yo-Yo Ma pluck a rhythmic duo. Then they make a quartet with Michael Moore on clarinet and Trilok Gurtu on percussion, to play sometimes open, sometimes Irish, briefly South Indian music by Moore. (Michael later recycled parts into "In the Company of Angels" for Clusone 3.) Then they play two movements by Maurice Horsthuis, with Amsterdam Drama, typically insinuating string melodies, but not so much attention paid to the guests of honor. ("Celstraf" on the second Drama CD is a version of that music.)

The program was nice, if no knockout, but they found a better balance than one might expect, knowing Ma lacks improvising experience, and that any cellist who sits next to him will sound second-best judged on unextended technique. Yet they work it out: at different times each plays genial second banana. The prep time paid off.

Ernst Reijseger: "You need time to redefine yourself in different situations."

Yo-Yo Ma: "Right. To think about any kind of music, you have to start from the inside."

That same set begins with Reijseger solo. He's nervous, his first time walking down the carpeted staircase by which stars make their grand entrance. He plays an impro-vised arco solo—cellists in the house laughing as it takes off from basic finger exercis-es—then goes into the Sarabande from Bach's third cello suite, pizzicato. When he puts the cello over his knee he gets the automatic laugh. (As with Bennink, folks are often too primed to guffaw because they've heard he's funny, a bind for the performer: should one write off useful resources like gravity to avoid laughs?)

In the midst of it, a voice he knows calls out from the audience: "Hey whitey, step straight, it's after one o'clock"—South African for, you're on enemy turf, so watch out. Then another voice, quieter: "Shut up Sean." He recognizes that one too: Franky Douglas. After that, Ernst is not so nervous. At the end of the Bach he strums a two-beat vamp awhile, then stops, drops his hands, looks away bored—but the music con-tinues, seamless. A spotlight's beam creeps up the staircase, and at the top, inside the just-opened doors, there's Yo-Yo, cello over his knee, guitaring.

Chapter Nine
Travelers' Tales

From the mid-'80s until a decade later, some of the best albums made in Holland—Sean Bergin's *Kids Mysteries*, Curtis Clark's *Amsterdam Sunshine* and *Letter to South Africa*, Available Jelly's *Monuments*—were spearheaded by immigrants. The Amsterdam scene sucks in outsiders and assimilates what they bring, just as they capitalize on what they find there.

Curtis Clark, born 23 April 1950, Chicago: "When I was five my parents moved to Los Angeles, where I grew up. There are baby pictures of me playing piano. My parents said that whenever I was around one I'd play it, so they got one. After that there was always a piano in the house. My first lesson was around 12 or something. Also around 12, I started on trumpet, played it about six years. It was stolen my last year in high school—I know who you are, old rascal's probably dead now"—last words escaping as a fast snicker. "I wasn't that good. I wanted to sound like Miles, would probably have ended up imitating him.

"In elementary school, I tried to write down stuff before I could read it. I'd count the measures off—'Oh this is like, on "two and"'—and I'd write it down. The first song I wrote, with my best friend Forrest Wilson, was called 'I've Been Hurt by Love'." Curtis goes over to an electric piano and plays a bouncy blues vamp, sings, "'I've been hurt by love / She took the keys to my car and she's gone.' Very complicated song." His laugh is dry as sand. "I played piano, and we both sang. It was a big hit, in our elementary school.

"I have memories of walking to junior high school, on Cool Crisp Mornings, and hearing arrangements in my head: large ensembles, different things. I wish I'd tried to write them down. I can't remember the songs, but I remember how good I felt with all this stuff bouncing around in my head. My eyesight was better then too, so it's a memory of clarity, before alcohol, drugs and tobacco.

"I went to Garvey Junior High and Samuel Gompers High School. Donald Dustin was the music director. He turned out a lot of good musicians, Leon Chancellor, Reggie Andrews, Butch Morris—all the Morrises. Butch is my brother's age, three years ahead of me in school." One brother played trombone, another drums, another saxophone—"He was killed playing high-school football"—and a sister, violin. "I think my brothers and me played something together, but they didn't really. . . . Well my brother still had a drum set, last time I was there: He's in the LAPD, plays when he gets home from work. He says it's either that or drinking.

"In junior high school Mr. Dustin started a wind ensemble which turned into a jazz band that turned into The Shades: me and some other guys who all wore sunglasses. Daryl Clayborne the bass player was like the musical director, would show me the chords to play on piano. I learned a lot there.

"Once in high school they had a talent show, and Daryl and I played a free-jazz piece with John Carter, Jr. on oboe. We had a tape. Then John Carter, Sr. was conducting a piece for Ornette Coleman at the UCLA Jazz Festival." That was 1966. "So we were hanging around John's house, and Ornette comes in, with Charlie Haden and Charles Moffett. John says, 'Listen to what these guys did.' So Ornette gets down on his knees and puts his ear to the speaker of this old reel-to-reel tape recorder. 'Damn, Ornette Coleman's listening to us!' He said, 'Yeah, okay.' He liked it. Then I think we went to the performance, and that was—whew! More music than I can remember. After that whenever I had the opportunity I would talk to Ornette. When I was living in San Francisco for awhile, I went to the hotel with him after a concert. (This one likes to follow people around.) 'Yeah, Ornette, I could really play with you.' 'No, I don't work with piano players.' 'No, Ornette, I can really. . . . ' 'No no no.' What a lot of people liked about the way I played was that I allowed in space.

"I got my degree as a composer from Cal Arts, so now I'm officially a composer. That four-year degree took me nine years. I went to three other schools including UC Berkeley first. My mentor at Cal Arts was Harold Budd the composer. I had some very nice times there. I wrote a play for a drama student to perform, and collaborated once with an animator. It was a nice opportunity to work with different disciplines.

"After I graduated in '78, my mother died, and I was kind of emotionally fucked up. Butch Morris asked me to come to Holland to do a tour. I flew to London, and for some reason or other I wound up at the wrong airport. In the confusion I was there 24 hours. Then I got a flight to Amsterdam, and as I'm going through customs, the guy motions me over. 'What are you doing here?' 'I'm going to work, with a band.' 'How much money you got?' 'Seven dollars.' 'Okay, sit over there.' To make a long story short, I sat there all day, and then Butch and some other folks got me out, took me straight to the gig. The first thing I saw in Amsterdam was the old BIMhuis, all these guys who looked like hippies smoking these large joints. 'Damn.' LA is a little different. So after the tour I stayed, hung around for a couple of years. In that period I made *The London Concert* with David Murray." That was 1979, with Butch on cornet. Curtis knew Murray from LA, too, was reunited with him and Butch on the octet album *Murray's Steps*, New York 1982.

"In Amsterdam I worked with people like Art Taylor, Johnny Dyani, Louis Moholo. After two years I moved on to New York, worked with Billy Bang, David, Charles Tyler. I was a taxi driver, and really liked that profession. I was playing clarinet then. I used to keep it on the front seat, and at every red light I'd practice a scale. I recorded on clarinet, on a very bad album called *Phantasmagoria.*" It's from 1984. "When John Carter listened to it he said, 'Wow. I'm glad you're playing piano.'

"So I was back and forth between there and here. I got a bunch of kids here: four."

Curtis has the contradictory air of a tagalong kid brother—"This one likes to follow people around"—with an old man's crotchetiness, a likable combination in his case. He's sorta short and slight, wears old collegiate pullover sweaters. He may also wear a scowl or snicker equally demoralizing to the beholder. Curtis can be cantankerous when it would pay to be otherwise. I have also seen him act with dignity in the face of the sort of rudeness that would inspire another to fisticuffs.

Part of his first solo album *New York City Wildlife* was recorded at the BIMhuis in 1979. He made a couple of other solo LPs he doesn't care for much. *Amsterdam Sunshine* (Nimbus, November 1984) for quintet—Reijseger, Glerum, Michael Moore, drummer Don Mumford—is his first to reflect his experience in Holland, more from the musicians involved than any discernible impact on his writing.

Dutch players like Glerum took to him as a real jazz pianist and composer with his own ideas. From him they got original swinging material from the source as it were, and he got to hear players approach it from a fresh angle. The jazz they made was light, graceful, soft-edged, but never perfunctory.

Comping a couple of intervals every few beats is enough, but his spaciness is nothing like Monk's; Curtis's spans and attack are less scalding, and he likes the sustain pedal, something his general spareness lets him get away with. His grace was all the more valuable in the midst of wooden-shoe timing.

Clark's 1987 *Letter to South Africa* had the two Ernsts plus John Tchicai on tenor and Louis Moholo on drums: Amero-Dutch-Danish-South African music.

—A conscious decision, to have a united nations band?

"It wasn't so united. John Tchicai and I had worked together in Johnny Dyani's band, and he had this movable mouthpiece that let him do some really nice stuff. But on one concert he and Ernst Glerum got into some mutual antagonism, within the music. You could see it on the faces in the audience. I didn't say anything, I don't give a shit what it was about, but that's the last time Ernst Glerum and Tchicai played in my band."

This was the period in which Tchicai advised Glerum to forego the crazy hip shit. On the CD Glerum is in the pocket, swinging steady no matter where Moholo goes. The bass holds down the rhythm section so the others can float. Tchicai's mournful broad-beamed tenor and Reijseger's nimbler, narrower sound offset each other as solo voices. Curtis's lyrical tunes have lines that curve around themselves, strong shapes improvisers can use and listeners can follow when they do. His tunes sound especially fine played on tenor saxophone.

South Africa was boiling but this was an '80s civil-rights record, more about feeling than polemics: less *We Insist!* than *We Empathize.* The dark sense of drama in the solo "Twilight Union" makes its own case. (Another solo, "What Price Freedom," has heavy gospel cadences, drawing a connection to the American civil-rights movement.) With the full band the textures are more open: sun and clouds moving across the flats.

Most jazz composers filch existing chord progressions; Curtis is more likely to scavenge melodies, swerving his own way just before he gets into trouble. Thus the restful melody/vamp "Serious Wishing (For Winnie Mandela)" bows to an Abdullah Ibrahim line, "Circumstantial Blues" begins with the first eight notes as "Mr. P.C." and "Admission of Guilt" flirts with "I'll Be Around." ("Stupid Conversation," unrecorded, nods to "Girl Talk." His titles are covert confessions.) But for all their allusiveness these pieces stand on their own, move out to live their own lives.

His next CD *Live at the BIMhuis* was from a short tour supposed to feature Dewey Redman, who became unavailable and was replaced on short notice by England's Andy Sheppard, in whose big band Reijseger (and Bennink) had played. It was step back. By the mid-'90s the band had evolved into a four-horn septet: Wierbos, Australian pocket trumpeter Felicity Provan, Daniele D'Agaro and Toby Delius on tenor saxes, and rotating rhythm players: more conventional perhaps, but just as obviously reflecting a need for greater resources.

March '95, Tuesday night, Manhattan, Village Vanguard, debut of a Cecil Taylor quintet, two New Yorkers, two outlanders. Overcoated customers shuffle in, eyed furtively by the skinny guy, coat half off, smoking on the banquette by the door. Someone comes over to greet him; how does it feel to be here after so long? "Feels good." Then: "Brooklyn looks like East Berlin."

Tristan Honsinger's last visit to New York was 1979. He'd run into the English saxophonist Lol Coxhill on the flight, and when they were poured off the plane, Sunday night, they explained to the hapless guy who was to drive Lol to Baltimore, We have to play some music, Now. They drove to Soho, rang the doorbell at the Kitchen, got sent to the Ear Inn where the bartender said he guessed it'd be okay if they kept it short. They played a frantic memorable duet, Tristan's bow as ever shedding hairs faster than a cat in a heatwave. Coxhill played his usual slithery bent notes on sopranino, and Tristan indulged his habit of singing along with his cello, or not with his cello. Management signaled set's end by turning on the jukebox.

I don't think I've ever witnessed a greater need to play. A few weeks later Honsinger came through Baltimore in a trio with bassist Hal Onserud and clarinetist Perry Robinson.

This Cecil Taylor quintet has never played before—although a version of it had recorded for FMP two years before—but within the first minutes of the week's first set it's clear this is a good fit. Honsinger's keening vocal utterances dovetail with growled anacruses of Cecil's declaimed poetry. (Tristan will start the week's final set making hand farts in time with Rashid Bakr's drums and Thurman Barker's percussion.) Tristan's skittering spiccato descents bounce off the sputtery soprano of Finnish saxophonist Harri Sjöström, who crosses Coxhill with Evan Parker's brain-wave flutter.

Taylor almost never follows another player's lead, but he listens to Tristan. When he saws a clotted four-string chord, Cecil pounces the same cluster on piano. Honsinger will get inside some figure Taylor just played, and pry a new variation out of it, and branch off from it, until Taylor loops over to join in its development. Cecil always drives, but sometimes Tristan grabs the wheel a second.

Without a bass, cello and piano have the low end covered, and the great wailing center. Flushed face echoed by red sweater, mouth contorted whether sounds come out or not, Tristan sits in the crook of the piano and keeps his wary red eyes on the boss. He ignores the obvious come-ons: motifs planted for him to pick up like dollar bills on the sidewalk. When piano reaches escape velocity, Honsinger pulls back with a legato line, heavy vibrato, cello's middle register. And sometimes Tristan's right foot thumps on the wooden platform, loud as anything else on stage. He isn't just home — he's *home*.

♫

"I grew up in New England, took up cello at age nine in Springfield, Massachusetts. I was born 23rd of October 1949, in Burlington, Vermont. My first teacher was a Dutch Jew. Almost all my teachers were European immigrants. Later I went to the New England Conservatory. It was quite a good school, but I didn't feel very welcome, so I went to Peabody Conservatory in Baltimore for another year — '68 to '69. By then I'd had it, really, with the whole classical music world. I changed teachers so many times, I suppose I was confused by their contradictory advice.

"I moved to Montreal in '69, and started, slowly, to improvise. My playing was rather pseudo-classical in a certain way. I was also composing little things, on paper, not really from the cello — just writing down loads of notes, not really knowing what I was doing. I was being a composer. But once I started to improvise, I basically just did that. My girlfriend's sister played the flute, and we had been asked to do some 'improvisation.' I didn't know what that meant. But the man gave me a big joint, and I liked improvising so much, I said, 'Well, I could do this for a long long time.'

"I started off playing in the streets, because there was no one doing anything then that I knew of. A group called Jazz Lib Quebec asked me to play with them. They were into free jazz. I played with them for awhile, which wasn't very inspiring because they were more into talking about politics than playing. I'd end up playing the second set by myself. Then I met a Dutch percussionist, Peter van Ginkel, who had played with the Dutch improvising musicians. He said there was a scene here. At that time I hardly knew what free jazz was, never mind the European scene. He had the first Incus and ICP records, and I listened to *The Topography of the Lungs*" — Evan Parker 1970 with Bennink and Bailey — "and said, 'I think I can play this kind of music.'

"So off I went to Europe, in '74, came to Amsterdam. I didn't have much work, which is pretty normal. They arrested me the first time I played my cello on the street, with Peter and the American bass player Hal Onserud, and they confiscated our instruments. I had to get a lawyer so I could retrieve my cello.

"I was furious about it, so I went to Paris, played in the streets there for a time, with Hal and Peter, and a dancer who was my girlfriend. We traveled through France for six months, and then I went back to Amsterdam and it kind of took off for me. I played with Maarten van Regteren Altena, Misha, Han. I hooked up with Derek Bailey, who I'd met in Paris, and Irene Schweizer with whom I played one gig, and Globe Unity — everybody who was working at the time. Derek invited me to London to play after that.

"At that time it was pretty hardcore improvised music, as I remember. Not too much composition except for Misha; I became a part of his tentet, which brought a new aspect to my idea of improvised music. But Derek was always: 'No music, just play.' I did the first of Derek's Company records, with Maarten and Evan Parker in

1976, and that carried on for quite a few years. Free improvisation is a way of making music, a way for people from many different areas of the world to get together. It's maybe the most practical way of making music. Globe Unity had quite good musicians in it, but I found it frustrating because basically it was one soloist after another.

"By 1978 I'd gone to Italy and liked that. I had met a dancer, Katie Duck, and we decided to live in the country outside of Florence. We set up shop there for four or five years in the early '80s, and I played with quite a few people, such as Giancarlo Schiaffini, Gianluigi Trovesi, Renato Geremia, Antonello Salis. . . . I liked the Sardinian musicians, because they seemed to have their own identity, weren't so intimidated by the United States. In Italy they were more indoctrinated with mainstream jazz.

"I did get into theater in a certain way, living with Katie, because she had her own group, the Great Salt Lake Mime Troupe. I was also very interested in theater from working with Misha Mengelberg and Wim Schippers. I felt quite at home in their productions. And I started to write my own pieces, in which I included Sean Bergin and Katie. Sean didn't live in Italy very long, but it was a nice time. I also worked with many quite talented Italian unknowns, but the Italians preferred that I work with people from other countries. That annoyed me quite a lot. I couldn't get anything off the ground with the Italians who I thought were doing quite brilliant, innovative things in music theater.

"During that time I wrote a lot of songs, and made a group called This, That and the Other. It was quite successful, and included the singer Tiziana Simona, Sean, the trumpeter Toshinori Kondo, the bassist Jean-Jacques Avenel, and drummer Michael Vatcher. Because of a promoter's brilliant organizing, the group kind of fell apart. Anyway it was impossible at the time, because Jean-Jacques was living in Paris, Kondo was living in Tokyo, and Sean was in Amsterdam."

"I never really wanted to leave Italy, but the scene seemed to disappear as quickly as it had appeared. I went to England for awhile, but working there was impossible as well. So I moved back to Amsterdam.

"It was—and still is—a big problem, how to make improvised music work. I think the best way is without any talk, go up and do it. But there is also the way of trying to write for it, make different concepts to improvise with. (Which I suppose is going back to jazz, really.) That's why I named the group This, That and the Other."

The edition just named made the LP *Picnic* (DATA) at the Frascati in 1985. Like Tristan the music has its mood swings, rocketing from plaintive melody to chaos, from dense ensemble textures to naked voice, from accessible tune to inscrutable theater song where Tristan carries on like a street crazy. It reflects the composer's ambivalence about nice music; somewhat like the mature Breuker, he feels compelled to despoil his tender moments. But bass and drums and the horns make certain pieces uncommonly jazzy, for this leader. Its equally good sequel, *this, that and the other* co-billed to him and Kondo, was for the same band plus Michael Moore, and England's Steve Noble replacing Vatcher. If anything, it shows off his ingenious diatonic tunes to even greater advantage.

"I think there is a certain amount of drama involved in any good music-making. I suppose that's what I like about the American music, that it had a lot of drama in it, and theater. Armstrong, Fats Waller, the first people who were involved in developing let's say jazz, had great theatrical qualities.

"I had a kind of music-theater group about five years ago with four people including Alex Maguire from England on piano and Larry Fishkind on tuba. The choice of compositions and material to improvise with could come up in any order, so every performance developed differently. The intuitive choice of material became part of the improvised way of working. I also work in a group of Toby Delius, where we basically do the same thing. We have a map of many compositions in front of us, and we can choose the route as we go along. I now have a string quartet plus Louis Moholo, and we work this way as well. It's full of surprises, and it puts the material in context, in a certain way. It breaks down the isolation between the composed and improvised approach; a particular composition can develop out of an improvisation. The only problem is, you can run through all your compositions in ten minutes."

His 1994 CD *Map of Moods*—the string quartet has two violins (one Italian, one Russian-Spanish-English) and Glerum on bass—relies on that process. They weave through varied improvised textures and catchy tunes, which may however stand distinct from one another. The excerpts from two concerts touch on 18 Honsinger themes, some more than once.

A nine-piece This, That and the Other did a very entertaining set at AngelicA '96; that annual Bologna festival did a Dutch special that year, with multiple features for Tristan, Misha and Guus Janssen. TT&O's set had good music and loose little comic sketches—a pastiche of small-town TV programs—but its charms don't come all the way across on the resulting CD *Sketches of Probability*.

"What I think is very interesting is, people who are interested in improvisation each have a certain compositional attitude towards it. Cecil Taylor will dictate a composition to you, and then transform that material into some kind of soup that has nothing to do with what he first gave you. He mixes it all up, so it disorientates the interpreters, some of whom may be perplexed through the whole performance. He'll write a sequence, a phrase, and then disguise it to a point where no one knows where he is."

—Have you sung while you play since you started improvising?

"I have. Not very consciously."

—Like a piano player singing along with his solo?

"Like a cello player singing along. If you listen to Casals doing the Bach suites, you can hear him in the background. Not as prominently as me, but it's something I don't think is far from any cellist engaged in playing. This is a rather mystical way of saying it, but in a way the music passes through you. You get an impulse and you play the music, but the music's not yours. When you play it, it passes not just through the instrument but through yourself."

—It's not produced by a conscious process?

"It is, but that conscious process is not just an extension of your instrument. Or, your instrument is an extension of you, so the singing is a kind of natural way of making music.

"When I first improvised, it was more from a technical than lyrical approach. I was much more involved in the techniques of the cello. But I've developed into a lyrical player as opposed to a technical or graphic player. I think lyricism is an important part of music-making, improvised music especially. I feel at home in it, have no fear of adding it when I feel it's lacking.

"Someone like Sean comes out of a different area of music-making than me. He comes out of let's say popular music, and I come out of classical music. He has his own ideas of course, but he has many influences, which he likes to develop in his music-making. He's very influencable, which I like, although I'm not so influencable. I like his theatrical side also. We get along quite well together, I suppose because of our openness to anything-can-happen in the music."

Tristan Honsinger's ideas pay tribute to inescapable origins; he's a pessimistic New England transcendentalist who thinks (or so he said very late one night, leaning on a barrail) that esthetics is unethical because it teaches you to look outside yourself for answers; it erodes self-reliance.

Three days before Christmas '95, at Verkade Hall in Zaandam—Verkade one of the big chocolate manufacturers that make this wharf town smell like steaming cocoa— Tristan and Sean play duo. Before they crossed the harbor they had been half the dinner party on Sean's boat. Nat Cole had been singing "You're Looking at Me" on the box; Sean had responded to someone's witticism about shopping at the HEMA department store with, "You're a clever dick."

Tristan is skinny and Sean is fat, Laurel and Hardy. The first set is a peerless exercise in natural theatricality—no borders between the playing and the talking, equally improvised; they have their forms to work in. One moment Bergin's alto is whistling teakettle over Tristan's sped-up Gregorian chant: droney bowed chords with fleeting/phantom vocal reinforcement. The next they're a bickering couple, Honsinger in falsetto the reproachful wife, Bergin the put-upon husband who circles every grievance back to women's fault: I was late because I had to bring milk to my mother. More than any male actor I ever saw, Tristan can become an old woman on stage, sans dragshow; it's all trembling voice, meek posture, psychology.

They do Tristan's songs—Sean is a good shower-stall tenor—which have a singsong, seesaw quality, simply pleasing more than naive, with a cellistic quality that helps launch his own improvising. The wrinkle: Melody and text don't always have line endings in the same places, divided sensibility. Sean pumps a little concertina, plays alto, plays tenor, quotes "You're Looking at Me." Tristan: You get those shoes at the HEMA? Sean: "You're a clever dick."

There's nothing Dutch about it except the shifting inclusive context, nonstop drift among songs and improvisations and verbal improvisations. No props: invention laid bare for inspection.

Second set, all business: music music music. When they start talking, it's seconds from The End.

Sean Bergin: "I was born in Durban, June 29, 1948, but spent most of my youth in a small fishing town called Issipingo, south of Durban, a little colonial Peyton Place where everyone knew everyone, and everyone was having fun. There was a lagoon, with mangrove swamps and fish that jump out of the water, and a river, and beautiful beaches with rocks, and this little community of people—white people, if that makes a difference. I grew up running around outside with bare feet, put shoes on only to go to school, came back and went to the beach, fishing, swimming, catching crabs, playing on the rocks, going into the bush to collect birds' eggs. It was very free.

"My mother's family is Scottish, arrived through the shipping trade. My father was Irish, left Ireland after the War, came to South Africa and met my mother. She was working in a canteen where she also played piano. She was a boogie-woogie pianist. My father was a jazz-lover as well. They got married, my brother and I were born. I was six or seven when they split up.

"I was maybe a normal white South African, except my mother had tendencies toward the left and my grandfather was very respectful of Africans. He spoke about four African languages really well, and I was exposed to a lot of African music.

"Durban is different, the English heritage. It's a sort of Miami. We moved there when I was 13. I had started playing guitar in Issipingo, it was the guitar time. My mother had loads of jazz records, I grew up with Ella and Louis and Oscar Peterson, but she couldn't play piano anymore, she had polio. I never heard her play. I went to high school two years, got so sick and tired of it. They didn't want you to learn, just wanted to control you. Worked in a garage for a couple of years, worked on the docks as a stevedore, worked as a refrigeration mechanic.

"At the same time I was playing guitar in a few little garage bands, and was getting into the Beatles, the Hollies, that stuff. When the Beatles did 'Till There Was You,' I immediately learned the chords for that. It's an old standard, slightly jazzy, and that tickled my fancy. I started to learn blues, got into Big Bill Broonzy, John Lee Hooker, and some of the white finger-picking guys like Korner, Ray and Glover.

"When I was around 17 I'd go to the jazz club, the Blue Note, in Durban. It opened at 12 o'clock Friday night, when all the musicians got off their paying gigs. It was multi-racial. A lot of black musicians would play there, and a few white guys ran it. They'd pay the cops not to raid it. It was in an industrial area, so it wasn't disturbing anybody, a joint above a bicycle parts factory, flight of stairs going up, very seductive. The husband of the woman who ran it was named Lofty, a tenor and baritone player who worked as a lift mechanic who'd take his horn with him on the job. He'd go up the lift to inspect the motor, practice for ten minutes.

"I went to Lofty's place, and he showed me a scale on the clarinet"—he sings five descending notes—"and I played"—sings the same five, then keeps going, completes the opening phrase of "Fly Me to the Moon". "I'd never picked one up before. I borrowed it, and he gave me a lesson and a meal every week. He said, 'You gotta practice, man. Listen to Coltrane, listen to Dolphy.' One week I hadn't practiced shit, and he said 'Fuck off.' I went back the next week and played not only that lesson but the next ones too. Meanwhile I was blowing modal stuff in one scale with my buddies at night. From playing guitar I knew a bit about harmony. I got into Mingus at the same time, it was hip to listen to records like *The Black Saint and the Sinner Lady*, which sort of crept into the hip blues-pop thing.

"Then I pissed off to Cape Town one day with my clarinet. I had got in a bit of shit with the cops. I met some musicians. There was some jazz happening. I worked for about four months painting ships, and bought a tenor. I got a job in the Paddy Foote Blues Band. It wasn't much, but I could scream on the saxophone. One Sunday I was blowing at this jam session, and a guy came up, 'Hey man, we're looking for another saxophone player, are you interested?' So then for a year I played soul stuff, every night, in a joint down near the docks, whores and sailors. It was good for tone, playing long notes all night. In those days Cape Town was much more relaxed than Durban, not so segregated, a very nice scene. We were playing with colored guys, and I met a few of the jazz people, who'd played with people like Dollar Brand and the Chris McGregor big band in South Africa. I started hanging out with these guys, and they would teach me things.

"Then the scene in Cape Town folded, my saxophone got stolen, and I went on back to Durban. There I found, under the bed of some woman who knew someone else, an old tenor that was oxidized green. My old teacher Lofty fixed it for me, he was running little afternoon or weekend workshops then. We did such things as Oliver Nelson's 'Stolen Moments.' I started going back to the Blue Note, where some great musicians really helped me, like drummer Dick Xhosa, who had played with Dudu Pukwana and Mongezi Feza and all those guys. 'Sean: just blow man. If you make a mistake, I'll make it with you.' Of course he wouldn't, but he would fool me into getting up and blowing. With some friends I started a band called the Abstract Truth." He produces a photo: Sean skinny, hair to his shoulders, cocky sideways grin. "We'd travel around South Africa in a Volkswagen van, hire our own hall. We were completely against using an agent. We'd jam for an hour in D-minor. After a year I got a gig with Lofty, who'd formed a commercial band.

"I ordered a new Selmer tenor from Johannesburg, but it arrived damaged. There was a Selmer alto in the window, so I said, 'I'll take that,' traded in my old tenor, went to my organ group gig that night and had to transpose everything. Ridiculous. From then I played alto for quite awhile. For a year and a half I traveled with this show band: cocktail hour, white pants, colored shirt. It was a good experience, to learn that professional side of things.

"Lofty had said, 'If you want to get anywhere playing jazz music, get out of here, otherwise you'll end up a sad alcoholic playing bossa novas in some resort.' My girlfriend and I split to London. I had just bought a tenor. I had a couple of dates in London with some South Africans who were trying to make a demo and get a record deal. I listened to the tapes awhile ago—complete rubbish, complicated stuff with no reason behind it: like 11/8, and then we'd disguise the 11/8. We'd sit and practice it all day.

"It was the time when everyone was squatting in London: '73, '74. I went out into the streets and played 'Goodbye Porkpie Hat,' and suddenly this pound note tied up with a 20-cent coin landed on the ground in front of us. I turned to my missus and said, 'It works.'

"I played a few jazz gigs. We'd practice for three nights, play in a pub and make one pound. I could go out in the streets, have a few pints while I was at it, and come home with ten pounds. I went to night school, studied composition and basic music theory, and played in a big band run by tenor player Kathy Stobart, a great character. The singer Maggie Nicols was also a great help; she'd always inspire me to carry on. I went to a workshop of John Stevens once, and I started playing a solo, and he said, 'No solos! Workshop!' So I split. Basically I just wanted to play. I also remember seeing

Han Bennink for the first time, this crazy guy with a long beard who'd walk around the stage playing a drum. 'What the fuck's he doing?'

"I got a job with this theater group called the Friends Road Show. We went to Tunisia to play, and then they split up, and I went with one half to the States and lived for a year outside Ann Arbor, Michigan. We used to play at a place in Dearborn, run by a guy called Nick the Greek. 'How you doing Nick?' 'Another day, another dollar.' That was the Midwestern mentality; they weren't exuberant happy people. The band was very funk oriented. I'd never got into music like that before, where you have to take your time. I'd been more into the free stuff and the fast Zappa stuff, and here was something where space was just as important.

"In Tunisia we had met Jamey Haddad, a percussionist from Cleveland. He came to Michigan to visit with this friend of his, a sweet, quiet-spoken thickset guy with a beard who played tenor. He saw our show, laughed, and we went back to our house, and had a jam. This guy played the shit out of the tenor. I said, 'Hey man, teach me something.' He said, 'Well you got a nice tone, just keep practicing, it'll be fine.' I practiced like hell after that. We hung out for awhile. He'd eat these heart-attack breakfasts down at the Fleetwood Diner, pancakes with ham and eggs and maple syrup on top. That was how I met Joe Lovano.

"I met Katie Duck when I was in Detroit; she knew the Road Show people, and came to visit. So the whole spider web begins to weave itself together, like a Dickens tale.

"When all that fell through, I went back to London, where it's gray and cold. Then Friends Road Show came to Amsterdam, where they had been before. Here were people sitting in chairs on terraces, and I said to my missus, 'This is nice, eh?' She said, 'Yeah. Let's stay.' That was the end of the summer, '75.

"One of my last gigs with the Road Show was at the Shaffy Theater, 'I Was a Teenage Palm Tree,' about a guy who got turned into a half-human half-palm tree through an atomic blast. I walked outside one day with my horn, and I heard the sound of a tenor floating across the water. 'Nice.' I crossed the bridge, and headed toward a bar on the Keizersgracht. As I got closer I heard soprano, then bass and drums, and they were blowing. I took my tenor out in the street, put the case in the entrance way, walked in and just started screaming and getting into it—I was into Pharoah Sanders and Albert Ayler then. The band was Theo Loevendie, Hans Dulfer, Arjen Gorter and Martin van Duynhoven. After much huffing and puffing, I stopped. 'Nice one, where you from, blah blah blah.' Arjen said, 'You must come to the BIMhuis.' 'What kind of music do you play there?' 'Dutch music.'

"Arjen introduced me to a lot of people. Burton Greene offered me a gig, where I met Reijseger. I became a member of the BIM, got gigs with different people, like Theo Loevendie, who by then had a band with Ab Baars. This was about '78. I played a lot with Ab, and jammed a lot.

"Gregg Moore and I played in a funky band with some Surinam guys and some American military people, playing Army bases in Belgium. Around this same period I bumped into this skinny guy with a cello: Honsinger. He'd say, 'Let's play a bit.' 'What pieces?' 'No pieces, we just play.' That was the first time I got into just improvising.

"The LP with Reijseger was called *Mistakes* because we were playing, and Ernst said, 'Hey man that's a mistake,' and my Zen Buddhism came out, and I said, 'Mistakes are the best part.'

"Tristan had been playing with ICP, and Misha phoned me up. When I was first with ICP, I'd be improvising, freaking out, and Misha would come up and say, 'What do you actually mean by that?' I'd be dumbfounded by that. He also made me realize that if you like the sound that's happening, whatever it is, just use it. I'd never want to say I copied stuff from Misha, but his ideas were very strong when I started to write.

"Tristan moved to Italy, and I went down to play some gigs with him. It was the summertime, I was in love, I was sitting outside with this beautiful woman, on a hill with cypress trees and fireflies flying around, and the Tuscan landscape, and I just decided to stay. I moved in 1980 and stayed for a year. When ICP was coming, Misha would send me a letter: 'There's a gig in Pisa. Would you like to do it?' That would save my bacon, 'cause Tristan and I would be playing in the streets. We made our duo record *Lavoro* in 1981 at his and Katie's house."

—Could you hear what Arjen meant by "Dutch music?"

"Yeah: music that's experimental but not so clever, more self-searching, not just sitting there playing all the fancy songs. I learned a lot about improvising here. You had to come up with the goods; it wasn't set up so you could plan something out and then present it. I was playing once with Radu Malfatti, and he made a phrase, and I copied him, and he said, 'Hey man, that's my idea; can't you think of something yourself?' Counterpoint, not being a parrot.

"When I started to play a lot with Ernst, he would do his bass thing and stuff like that and I'd blow over the top. There was a lot more counterpoint with Tristan. Tristan's compositions are cello made. Sometimes they're pretty ridiculous to play on the saxophone—good to practice as well as nice music.

"I came back from Italy 'cause I'd got a job with the clown Teo Joling, who had seen me do some live improvised theater with Tristan and Katie. Tristan, Teo and I formed a six-piece multimedia group with Toshinori Kondo, and an American Indian named Muriel the Spiderwoman.

"I also played with Jan Cees Tans & Rockets, and got to write a lot of pieces for that group. We'd have a lot of fun. I wrote one intro the saxophones could all play with one hand, so they could also play maracas. Reijseger said, 'Why don't you start your own band.' I thought, 'My Own Band'—M.O.B., MOB. I wrote all new pieces, working into the night, got a little grant, rehearsed quite heavily. I was as impressed as some of the other people listening to it. 'Shit, this works.'"

In Cape Town or London, Bergin was too young to connect with the earlier generation: Abdullah Ibrahim, Chris McGregor, Dudu Pukwana, Johnny Dyani. Starting in the late '80s he did a few tours with Louis Moholo—they went back to South Africa: Issipingo had become a toxic dump—but eventually they fell out. Years earlier, Sean had hooked up with the only musician to rival himself in exposing the Dutch to South African strains, Harry Miller. They played together from when Harry moved to Holland in the late '70s—Cuypers' *Zeeland Suite* was his first Dutch recording—till the night of the fatal accident in November 1983.

On Miller's very good March '83 *"down south"* (VARAJAZZ) the quintet includes Bennink, Wolter Wierbos and English trumpet and alto horn player Marc Charig, then living in Amsterdam. Down deep Bergin is really a melodic jazz player—likes nice tunes, and changes, and artful lyrics he may start singing after eight beers—but here his tenor and alto are rather grainy and argumentative. Bennink sees energy doesn't flag; when the horns space out, slow and dirgey, he plays a fast pattern in opposition. The quintet is busy with horn cross-talk, but players don't feel the need to fill every cranny, and never ride one texture too long. Miller's melodies are nice and personal; only the most recent, "Mofolo," shows a heavy kwela strain. That influence, and Bennink popping the band back into the groove when they wander, and horns layered behind solos, and the driving and interlocking vamps, all anticipate Bergin's next major work.

The MOB's *Kids Mysteries*, recorded 22 November '87, was a leading indicator something good was brewing in Holland: a great Dutch record by a non-Dutchman. No album from the Lowlands is more overstuffed with good tunes, first to last. You could hear kwela in the anthemic saxophone refrains, Mingus in the low moaning brass and jostling horns and section punches, general Dutchness in "Trainride"'s pulsing-eight locomotion. Mengelberg's footprints are on the circus tunes, the remarkably delicate voicings that pop out of the maelstrom, the way bouncing themes come undone only to snap back to original form, the way melodies strong enough for two good pieces twine in counterpoint, and on the rudimentary conductions.

Yet for all that Bergin projects a consistent vision through varied content. Partly it's a matter of taking a few organizational ideas and sticking to them. Sean's cyclical melodic and harmonic forms, simple or complex, swallow their own tales, where Misha's might spit them up. Improvisations will foreshadow the next theme; a motif will be passed around from one instrument or group of instruments to another; separate themes will overlap Riley-like. "Trainride" has three train motifs, crossing like rails in a freight yard: clickety piano (sometimes doubled by low-plucked cellos—reinforcements arriving, departing, switching tracks), steamwhistle moan of South African saxes, rocking wah-wah counterpunches.

He had a blend in mind. Cellists Honsinger and Reijseger appeared together on record for the first time. Plucking or sawing, frantic or in slow-motion halftime, they offset Michael Moore's woody clarinet and Alex Maguire's lean linear piano. Sean made sparing but effective use of Jan Willem van der Ham's bassoon as melody instrument. Wierbos and trumpeter Eric Boeren are the pocket brass section, punching big-band style or playing open-vowel wahs in tandem. Extensive rehearsals paid off: the cues are as clear or sloppy as he wants them to be, intonation and ensemble balance are fine, and Bennink knows all the tunes by heart.

The chords and melodies can be very very simple—both South African themes of "Thoko's Tune" (one four bars, one eight) are pecked from an F-major scale, fitting over a three-chord four-bar pattern—but they're always strong enough to shape the improvising, so Sean can give away the solos and still make his mark. Moore steals "Beach Balls"—sweet swerving clarinet (with Maguire's constant comments) over singsong cellos—and "Tea and Scones" where he shows off his drummer's time on alto (expertly shadowed by Bennink and strumming Reijseger), diving into patterns and then flying out of them.

"Monkey Woman" is Concerto for Wolter, who makes a delayed entrance, long upward gliss rising slowly as the moon, over a most fetching bowed cello dance, discreet suggestion of tango, incantatory and persistent as airport Krishnas. Wierbos prowls for five minutes, slippery slide articulation, precise lip attacks, varied phrase lengths and timbres, gorgeous tone and surety of invention. Rarely is this great soloist given such a lovely setting, or promising role. The original title was "Donkey Woman"—Bergin likes substitution games with words as well as riffs. It was inspired by the episode in *Don Quixote* where two men seeking a stray ass bray to such perfection they keep finding each other.

Most of the pieces were inspired by memories of Issipingo: "The idea was a kids' trip to the beach, a train ride to the sea, a real English school boy story. 'Poor Poise' is porpoise, also a dolphin, a word play on Eric Dolphy"—so there are very Dolphian squeals from bass clarinet. The program explains the pieces' happy character; where Honsinger's singsongs hint at the neuroses of childhood, these kids' mysteries are sweeter, un-ironic.

It was a knockout, his best bid for the Boy Edgar Prize he deserves but never got. The MOB's 1989 *Live at the BIMhuis* had some strong kwela-soaked riff tunes— "Dudu," and "Una's Walk"—but was sloppier, less clear, and had some filler: two pieces for a wobbly Nedlyan vocal ensemble; a bleary "Old Devil Moon." For sure they were less rehearsed, and a few of the old MOB were unavailable. Only Boeren, Wierbos, Honsinger, Maguire and Glerum remained. Alan Purves was the new drummer, Toby Delius and Daniele D'Agaro among the saxes, and Franky Douglas was on guitar.

More obscure but a bit more interesting is the CD *Jazz for Freedom!* (VARAJAZZ) by Sean Bergin and Radio Freedom All-Stars, a set of South African tunes (his, Abdullah Ibrahim's "Gwinza," Mongezi Feza's Afrojazz standard "Sonia") by an 11-piece band with a double rhythm section: Bergin, Michael Moore, Wierbos, Reijseger; Franky Douglas and pianist Mervyn Africa; Paul Rogers on bass and Lesley Joseph on electric bass; drummers Moholo and Eddy Veldman; South African in England Claude Deppa on trumpet. It's a nice marriage of improvised solos and catchy dance rhythms, but it too bore the heavy burden of living up to *Kids Mysteries*.

Sean is a good-hearted bloke, but enough of a Mingus fan to like to play the big bad guy, the lumbering drunk and outcast. Usually it works against him, sometimes for. In the frequent breaks during the 1991 October Meeting, he staged mini-sets in the bar, with whoever he could sit down in front of some sheet music. Most of the first MOB got to play their old book in smaller combinations. Sean said he was forced to do these guerrilla gigs in order to be represented; Huub van Riel says he asked Sean to be on the Meeting and Bergin opted for this instead. By doing so more of his music was heard than anyone else's.

By the mid-'90s gigs for the MOB and six-piece MOBette were few, if often lovely. Once in awhile the (mostly) three-tenors Trio San Francisco—Bergin D'Agaro Delius—had a nice gig, especially when Han made it a quartet, but the main place to hear Sean and his legacy is De Engelbewaarder, where he usually runs the session, regulating the sitters-in with a firm enough hand, keeping the music more varied than it might be when five tenor players are always standing by, and where Sean's kwela tunes and South African saxophone voicings echo through even when he's out of town and saxophonist Paul Stocker takes over. You could hear Sean all over Stocker's arrangements for a 1995 CD by South African guitarist Phola Momba's group Lebombo, *Nabakitsi* (BVHaast) but Bergin was soon booted from that band for being an asshole. His bad boy reputation has kept him from getting his due from the Calvinists on the scene. In his cups he's been heard to mumble, "I never got the Prize," which long since became a self-deprecating crack. The complaint is no less just for that.

Alan Purves—or Gunga, but please not Gunga Purves or Alan "Gunga" Purves—has childhood influences too. When he was about six, in Edinburgh (where he was born 12 September 1952), he started banging on buckets with knitting needles. "I was lucky from the start—never had to wonder what I might be in life. I was always this." Once in the '80s a band asked him for a bio and he scratched out a page of formative vignettes. His dad took a stern view of his youthful stealing: "my faither would beat me to a pulp so I discovered accents like (dooff in my stomick, guff in my face and shooich when I ducked and he missed)."

That was how he developed: 12 years of knitting needles. As an apprentice black-smith, "I would sit tippy-tapping welding rods all day when the boss was away." He has not given up old ways; after more than 20 years in Holland he has a Scottish burr so thick even some Anglophones don't immediately identify what he's speaking as English. The accent is only part of the deadpan delivery which makes his conversa-tion hilarious—a quality that largely evaporates in print. He is medium-sized and shy. Behind his setup he looks a little withdrawn; he used to play a hi-hat 14 inches off the floor while sitting on a foot-high stool, an adult squeezed into a second-grader's desk on parent-teacher night.

He got some real drums when he was 18. "The first time I played 'em, the police came within minutes and threatened to confiscate 'em. So I didn't play 'em for a year after that." Then he joined a rock band with a rehearsal space. He wasn't keen to leave Edinburgh but when the other guys in Gunn Lilly moved to London, he wanted to play more than stay. The others got sidetracked by eastern religious texts but Gunga was protected; he didn't learn to read till he was 30. He persevered, went hungry, lived in a squat next door to Sean. He came to Amsterdam for two weeks, ran into Bergin. They needed a drummer for "I Was a Teenage Palm Tree." On that gig he met trom-bonist Gregg Moore, who rang him in London the following year, got him a gig accompanying dancers and clowns. He got into the theater scene, traveled widely for awhile, drifted into playing Portuguese music, did a lot of duo gigs with Reijseger.

"I have a Gretsch drum set, but I haven't used that for years. I never have a fixed set. That way I stay confused, and have to deal with the moment. When I hear the music, I get ideas about sounds to use, 'cause I have so much to pick from." On an improvised gig a few hours after he says that, he has some objects spread out low in front of him—on a sheet of foam atop two empty beer cases—a tambourine-sized frame drum, two small roto-toms on a fragment of their original rack, a couple of cow-bells and woodblocks, a tiny bell, a tiny tambourine, a tiny cymbal. He also has one small ride cymbal on a low stand, and a bell cuff on one ankle. Between pieces he keeps rearranging the stuff in front of him to try different combinations. He's said he wants to play each instrument as if on first encounter—he tests them for sounds, avoids the traditional rudiment-rooted flourishes, but he's nimble. In his small sticks and mallets and light sound you can hear the knitting needles tippy-tapping.

He also uses one Irish bodhran players' move Han is known for: hold a stick in the usual drummer's left-hand grip, and flip the wrist quickly—180 degrees, back and forth, repeatedly, knuckles up, knuckles down. The stick strikes the head from either position, damn fast.

"I see myself as a drummer, not percussionist. If Gene Krupa can be a drummer playing a matchbook, so can I playing squeaky toys, pots and pans, bits and pieces." Also the bones, Scottish standbys he plays in the approved clacking manner. He has a rhythmically intricate set piece for squeeze toys under each foot, and in each hand, one little flute in his mouth, maybe two in his nostrils. It's a hit at the children's concerts he plays with Reijseger and Wierbos.

"I've got lots of ideas for a squeeze-toy album. Sit at home, switch on the tape recorder, try lots of combinations. I have one piece called 'Ducks on the Wherepath.' Like me: I'm on a path but I don't know where. People say, 'I'm branching out.' I always saw myself as a tree and not a branch. I feel like I'm sprouting all over the place.

"Maybe every one else hears my style, but I don't hear it. Different styles of music dictate different ways of playing. Whatever music it is—rock, jazz, arty-farty—has its own philosophy, and I get into that. I don't show up with My Philosophy, My One Particular Idea.

"When I first started playing, it was just me and the boy downstairs, with an acoustic guitar. For me duo gigs are still the best. I've done a lot of good ones with Ernst, a few with Han, one great one with Misha where we didn't see or talk to each other before or after. I do much better when I don't know what's going on. With a plan, I fall to pieces. Just make the music, make harmony or disharmony together. Sitting and jamming, as they used to call it. What's the difference between jamming and improvising?"

Michael Moore, born Eureka, Northern California, 4 December 1954, who grew up in nearby Arcata: "My father played in clubs near where we lived. He'd have posters, 'Appearing at the Keg, Jerry Moore Duo.' He looked really handsome, obviously Chet Baker or somebody was his role model in those days. He played saxophone and piano, and eventually learned to play most of the instruments a bit because he became a primary-school teacher after he'd got married and had kids. He taught at elementary schools around the county, then got a couple of high-school gigs, and then took time off to go to the Eastman School of Music. We lived in Rochester two years, when I was nine and ten. Then he came back and got a better gig at the junior college in Eureka.

"I played in his college big bands, played with him in marching bands on holidays, or with all the old guys in the musicians' union band. I didn't play with my father much in small groups, and he didn't really give me any formal teaching, but there was a piano there and he'd show me things if I asked him stuff. He didn't have a lot of records but he had some really good ones. Until the early '70s he was mildly curious about the things that were going on in jazz and pop. He was into Paul Desmond, Oscar Peterson, Miles. And Kenton. He had a lot of West Coast stuff—Dave Pell, Brubeck, Shorty Rogers—but I never listened to that.

"I took some clarinet lessons at an early age, but my teacher made me cry so I stopped. In Rochester I had a teacher who got me interested again. Back in California I played it in high school, till I took up the saxophone. Mostly I was playing piano on gigs, when I was 14, 15, 16, and I had a Vox organ. I took up alto when I was around 16. The clarinet wasn't loud enough, and the girls always played better. I decided to be macho, get a saxophone.

"You play those Chicago and Paul Butterfield Blues Band riffs for a few months, then you want to know what else you can do, and eventually you gravitate to jazz. A guy named Don Sheridan—he's Don Boyd now—taught me and a friend bebop tunes, phrase by phrase. I started to write tunes when I was pretty young—15 maybe. Most of them were pretty sweet. Some of them allowed for some freebop, let's put it that way. The rhythm structure would change occasionally, and they had specific textures: a lot like the music I write now. Around then I played in a fusion band named Joint Session. Michael Vatcher was our last drummer.

"I'm a sadist; at Humboldt State I took classical piano and Marxism. I didn't grow up in a deep musical culture; it was really far away from everything that was happening. I didn't feel like I was part of something that was growing. I was listening to Dolphy, and Braxton, but didn't really start studying them till I went to Boston. But in Humboldt County there were quite a few musicians, and you could pick up a lot of different ideas about how to play, and I played four nights a week for years. (People like to go out, there's nothing else to do.) I thought that's what life was going to be like, but I've never done that since.

"At a certain point I thought, well, there's nothing more I can do here, I've got to leave. Might as well go far away. After two years of college I went to study with Jaki Byard at the New England Conservatory, so I must have had some kind of affinity with not taking yourself too seriously—or with allowing for all the possibilities. I think being around Jaki Byard prepared me for Misha Mengelberg—his ability to play anything he feels like without worrying if it's idiomatically correct. I didn't study with Ran Blake, but I played with him a lot, and saxophone with Joe Allard.

"The first year I knew no one and practiced a lot. The second year I played with big bands and didn't practice. I was still playing piano when I got there, but when I met Fred Hersch and other good pianists, I had to make a decision. I decided piano would help my saxophone playing more than the other way around. But I was always second alto behind Marty Ehrlich, who'd been there longer.

"I'd already heard Braxton's *For Alto*, and understood there were possibilities other than notes, that you could find your own vocabulary. But I never dismissed everything I'd played up to that point. I'm not that radical I guess.

"At New England Gunther Schuller had a fundraising band that played in penguin suits, dances for socialites. I started playing clarinet again—Glenn Miller lead parts, eight written-out bars of Benny Goodman. With Gunther I also played some Paul Whiteman and Ellington music. I was surprised I didn't have more solos; I could play like Sidney Bechet.

"After New England I moved to New York for about a year and a half. There were a lot of horn players there, and a lot of lofts and everything, but I didn't go to them. I played dance classes, and did some jingles, met some of the studio cats. But mostly I just knew the people that I knew from New England."

Gregg Moore, two years older, trombone and electric bass, came up in dad's bands too, took his music ed with William Fowler at U. of Utah, Salt Lake City. ("A very hip music school: restrictive societies manage to produce really creative people. I've noticed it about Australians too. The people who get weird get really weird.") He made friends with reed player Stuart Curtis, who accompanied dance classes, and who fell in with dancers Matthew Child and Katie Duck. After a performance a teacher had told those two, that's not dance that's mime. They started a company, the Great Salt Lake Mime Troupe. Stuart drafted Gregg to play bass, and after some shoestring U.S. touring—Gregg was there when Sean met Joe Lovano—they came to Amsterdam for the first Festival of Fools, summer '75. The troupe disbanded but Gregg stayed on— living with the Bergins, and playing R&B with Sean—till he hooked up with a reformed GSLMT including Gunga in 1976. For a couple of years after Gregg divided his time between Europe and the U.S. One of the many people he met in Holland was Ernst Reijseger.

Back in Utah, the mime troup band regrouped as the trio Available Jelly: Gregg, Stuart Curtis and trumpeter and drummer Jimmy Sernesky, another Arcata Jerry Moore student. They returned to Holland for the summer of '78, and Gregg coaxed his brother Michael over. Several other North Coast Californians would join for long or short periods, including clarinet and tenor bebopper Barry Block, bassist James "Sprocket" Royer on bass, and Michael Vatcher.

When Michael Moore first came over that summer, he liked what he saw enough to send for his girlfriend Jodi Gilbert (a dancer then, a singer now). He met and played with Ernst Reijseger; the following winter they went to New York for a few weeks— Ernst stopping in England to make *Mistakes*—to play with Michael Vatcher. After that Vatcher like Moore began dividing his time between Amsterdam and the Lower East Side. Each lost his New York apartment around '83 or '4 and has been a fulltime Amsterdammer ever since. (Gregg had stayed on too, stayed with Jelly, eventually joined the Breuker Kollektief in 1988.)

Michael Moore: "I knew what was happening at Melkweg and Shaffy and the Paradiso, 'cause that's where the Festival of Fools was. I'd been here maybe a couple of months before I heard about the BIMhuis.

"I saw Han and Misha at the Kroeg, which I really disliked. They were both playing violin or viola as well as drums and piano. I thought it was stupid: I had a New Yawk attitude, y'know? Later I saw them with Derek Bailey, and that was much better. It was another couple of years before I started playing with Han. Pretty soon after, Misha came to hear me play with some group, decided he wanted me in his band. Before that, for while I played with Gijs Hendriks: pretty good tenor player, big sound. He likes to invite foreigners to play with him, so I met some English people: Stan Tracey, Kenny Wheeler, Henry Lowther. There I played mostly bass clarinet.

"I worked with a lot of theater groups, and a Japanese buto dancer. In '82, I did *Leedvermaak* with Maurice Horsthuis. That was the first time I had a work permit here—my first gig under contract—and after that it was easier to get them. Right after that first run of *Leedvermaak* we went to Japan with ICP.

"Some people were curious about what I could do, because I came from a different place, and had a different musical education and different cultural references. At the same time I realized I was way behind them in terms of non-idiomatic improvisation. It was like I wasn't free enough or something. These guys have grown up just learning how to play their horns, and improvising. They didn't learn how to play in an idiom. They always knew they wanted to improvise. In America it's more like, you're either a jazz musician or a classical musician.

"So the scene here was a breath of fresh air, because it seemed to me what I knew about tradition was a burden as well as blessing. In the States you hear a lot about heritage, black heritage. You don't hear a lot about the through-line of Dutch music—not from the improvisers anyway. This is like a polder that's just been reclaimed from the water. They're taking musical impulses from everywhere."

For the next ten years Michael Moore had the cream of gigs for alto and clarinet players: ICP, Guus Janssen, Maarten Altena, Clusone 3 (along with Available Jelly, Gerry Hemingway quintet, The Persons—his old New York rock band that reunites occasionally—and various one-shot tours). He speaks very good Dutch, though it took him a few years, and has an enviable Amsterdam apartment overlooking a major canal.

His family has an interesting dynamic: wife Jodi and son Reuben are very verbal and very energetic, and a stream of out-of-town visitors passes through their guest room. The place is all bustle. Michael is the (usually) calm center, as in Clusone 3. Sometimes he seems a little remote and uncommunicative. You'll be talking to him and suddenly realize he's someplace else—someplace inside where he lives alone.

He composes a lot, when and where he can, mostly but not always for his own bands, and has an ear for good material from all over. He's a record collector with eclectic passions: Madagascar music, Burt Bacharach, Brian Wilson, Bobby Troup. (His 1995 studies for a capella horns *tunes for horn guys,* was partly inspired by the oddball music of the Croatian island of Krk.) He also knows lots of old songs with nice changes, some quite obscure.

Moore has a gift for melody, and a sweetly lyrical clarinet style: beautiful somewhat melancholy tone, especially in the lower register he's fond of; varied, rhythmic phrasing and very good intonation. He's as good as any jazz clarinetist now, would get far more credit if he lived in New York, but if he'd stayed he wouldn't have turned out as he has. His alto playing is case in point: it has many of his clarinet's strengths—if anything, on alto his timing is even more acute—but with typically Dutch doubleness. He'll shift from a finely crafted chorus to blowing rude gusts of wind through the horn, or play a sarcastic version of someone else's previous solo he didn't like. In that mood, he can be mean as a Martin Amis novel, but he's a big-hearted guy.

At times his sound may remind you of other soft-spoken and lyrical altoists. He likes Lee Konitz very much, once made a face when compared with Paul Desmond. Sometime later, after listening to some Desmond records, he said, problem is his tone never changes.

In 1986 Michael Moore was the second non-Dutch to win the Boy Edgar Prize. (The first, in '82, was the Canadian-in-Groningen Alan Laurillard.) Moore invited Steve Lacy and Jaki Byard to play on the prize concert, and Byard duetted with his quasi-doppelganger Mengelberg. Moore is a subsidized composer; at least one Dutch critic thinks Moore must be Dutch by now.

"I'm an outsider and an insider, straddling the fence."

The records he's made as leader (for his Ramboy label, baby picture of Reuben Aaron Moore its logo) are telling on this score: everyone else on his debut *Home Game* (Hersch, Hemingway, Herb Robertson, bassist Mark Helias) or third CD *Chicoutimi* (Hersch, Helias) is Stateside American. The first is free bop. *Chicoutimi*, with Moore on clarinet only, takes off from the '60s Jimmy Giuffre/Paul Bley/Steve Swallow trio. There's also a disarmingly quiet trio session with Hemingway and pianist Marilyn Crispell, another with Hemingway and Hersch.

He once fairly identified as his most Dutch record his second, *Négligé*, with Vatcher, Alex Maguire, and Reijseger—a record with traces of Misha's goofy melodic construction and the skeletal experimentalism of Shorty Rogers or Shelly Manne, all at once on "Counterpoint #1." Maguire has a drummer's timing too; there are some inventive grooves, if less overt lyricism than usual.

His main vehicle as composer remains Available Jelly, a band of outsiders. In 1984 they asked trumpeter Eric Boeren in. (Sernesky was by now touring a lot with theater and comedy groups. He'd continue to drift in and out of the band.) When Boeren joined the Americans were so far out of the loop he had to point out they could get subsidy money. He is not on their untitled anoymous-label debut LP from the same year, with Sernesky on trumpet and Curtis and Block on reeds: five horns and drums. (Gregg plays more tuba and 'bone than electric bass.) It's a souvenir of the early years, with marches, vocal chants, and Vatcher's all-too-irrepressible broadcaster voices echoing street theater roots. It was plenty eclectic: Italian and Yugoslavian folk tunes, a Nino Rota cut, "Salt Peanuts," "As Tears Go By," a James Brown cover years before that was a jazz trend, and Sean's "D.F.U.T.C." (Don't Fuck Up the Children), from *Sesame Street* days via *Mistakes*.

The Moore/Moore/Vatcher/Boeren quartet made *In Full Flail* in 1988: tunes by either Moore, and Misha, and the Beach Boys ("Catch a Wave," "Warmth of the Sun"). A year later Jelly was a sextet, adding Tobias a.k.a. Toby Delius on tenor and Eric Calmes on basses. Among the originals and collective improvisations on *Al(l)ways* for the small German label NOM: three less-played Monks ("Brake's Sake," "Gallop's Gallop," "Shuffle Boil"); Neal Hefti's "Girl Talk" (also in Clusone's book); the teenage Michael Moore's "Jinxies," slick freebop with shifting meters. It's nice, but electric bass is a sore thumb on the Monks, and there's too much noodling on melodica, that little mouth-blown organ with mini-keys and harmonica wheeze Michael uses as a pocket piano.

♫

Tobias Delius: furry post-Webster tenor sound so big and blooming you hear all the tones inside one tone, offset by modern ideas about phrasing, harmony and form; born

15 July '64, Oxford. His father is an animal behaviorist from Argentina who traveled widely, met Toby's mother in Germany. Before moving to Bochum, Germany at ten Toby had lived mostly in Durham, England, with a year in LaJolla, California. (Folks often can't figure out his 'real' nationality, since he speaks four or more languages well; the giveaway is he's a cricket fan.) He played clarinet as a boy, got into jazz at 16. He bought an old tenor, played it around a bit, was one of Georg Graewe's two students at the local conservatory.

"At 18, I went to Mexico City for awhile, where I met Francisco Tellez, who ran a music school. I visited for fun, started hanging out, started playing every night in a restaurant. That was when I decided to carry on with music."

Before Mexico he knew a little about Dutch music from hearing Michiel de Ruyter on the radio. Roundabout that led to his applying to the Sweelinck conservatory on his return. "I lasted a year and a half. Paul Stocker was my saxophone teacher. The first person I met was Daniele D'Agaro." He played in a quartet with him and a duo with pianist Michiel Scheen. "I did more and more learning outside of school, so I quit." He and Danny went to a Sean Bergin workshop, and the three became drinking buddies and musical allies.

"In 1987 I left to stay with my grandmother in Argentina. Fantastic! She cooked all day, and she was half-deaf so I could practice all day. After six months I went back to Mexico, played in that same bar every night.

"When I came back to Amsterdam, I picked up where I left off, started a quartet with Tristan, Larry Fishkind, and Han. When I won the Podium Prize in 1990"—sort of a junior-league Boy Edgar Prize awarded by Dutch venues—"we did a tour of 16 or 17 gigs. I made a big cardboard sheet with all the tunes on it, so you could point to one to jump from another. We got quite good at it, and had some creative mishaps. You only had to hint at a tune and Han was right on it." A version of this quartet, with Joe Williamson on bass, made the CD *The Heron* in 1997.

"One of the things that knocked me out about Holland was the access you had to musicians of any age or style, despite the polemics. In Germany you didn't just go up and talk to musicians—it wasn't done. Here the arguments are not really about music but about the money. People who have big arguments in committee meetings still play together the next day.

"My first and most important love on tenor was Sonny Rollins, on Blue Note. Archie Shepp became quite an influence when I heard *New Thing at Newport*. But for awhile I was quite taken with Hawkins, Chu Berry, Booker Ervin and some others, and I also love Warne Marsh and Zoot Sims; I'm not a one-style listener.

"When I came to Holland, my musical language wasn't really developed yet. I grew up in this environment. I'm influenced enormously by the music happening here, but I wouldn't call it Dutch, it's so mixed.

"With Available Jelly when it doesn't go, it really doesn't go, but the last couple of years it's been very nice. At first I came in as a guest or a sub for Gregg. I wasn't officially a member when I made *Al(l)ways*. Maybe that's true for everybody who comes in later."

Jelly's (first) masterwork is *Monuments* (Ramboy)—1993, same band plus Jimmy Sernesky, and Alexei Levin on piano and accordion. This time out, when Calmes plays electric bass he's unobtrusive, mix- and timbre-wise, and always in the pocket. True to street roots, it begins and ends with marches, neither typical, entering like Gargantua and ending with a sunset recessional. By now the band of outsiders is four Americans, a Russian, an Antillean bassist, the Argentine-German-English tenor player, and Boeren, from a part of the southern Netherlands whose borders are so ill-defined both Belgian and Dutch money are used. This is Dutch music?

Eric Boeren: "Everyone who came into the group later had the same experience as me: you have specific notes to play, but no one ever says 'This is your spot to solo' or 'Your turn next.' You have to flesh out the body, but things should take care of themselves without discussion. No one will tell you if you're doing too much or too little. Okay, sometimes after a few years I'd hear 'You're doing too much.'"

No album from Holland since *Kids Mysteries* has pieces more overloaded with catchy themes, themelets and vamps. The music is often constructed layer by intricate layer, various instruments uniting in temporary coalitions. Take Michael's ballad/blues "Shotgun Wedding" please. The quiet, not too obviously pentatonic main theme for unison tenor and trumpet is so pretty, Sernesky's plungered obbligatos ditto, it can take a couple of listens to hear everything happening behind: a bass line of alternating fifths (like "Misterioso"'s walking sixths, but backwards—root on the afterbeat) moving up and down from tonic to major third by whole steps, the upper voice doubled by alto and piano. The oompah B section, reminiscent of "Black and Tan Fantasy"'s, would seem a forced marriage, were it not for subtle echoes of the A strain: the bass line is a sort of inversion of the earlier fifths; the soft harmonized brass in back of a gorgeous (and unpredictable) alto solo a filigreed echo of the earlier alto/piano/bass line. There's also more Sernesky with plunger mute, setting himself up to take the last solo with Boeren Bubbering behind.

More often, the layering is more haphazard; as Boeren says, in this band you look for things to do. Michael Moore's gifts as composer aside, Jelly lacks a central intelligence à la *Kids Mysteries*. The motives don't interlock as much as they coalesce and spin apart, more swimming than schematic. An example of their fortuitous grace: Michael Moore's mini-suite, "Achtung Circus," beginning at 4:53: a long note Toby blows in his tenor solo triggers, from alto, a repeating (and previously heard) backing lick that starts on the same note—Michael sneaking in softly behind Toby, so you hear him only when tenor moves off it—a lick which in turn calls in its own answering figure from the brass. It sounds prearranged, it isn't, but it's just as clearly Toby's invention, shoring up the structure. (It did not work its way into the arrangement.) Sometimes a good idea is much simpler. On "Kyle," bass drum hits and plosive accents from tenor (which plays only one sustained blooming long note throughout) always coincide; they're used as one instrument. And sometimes Jelly make disparate themes go together—"Wigwam," fake Indian to cavalry charge to somber retreat—through force of will.

Boeren had also emerged as a strong writer, with an Ellingtonian raveup, "Hersinde" (pivoting on a clarinet lick very like Jimmy Hamilton's on "Ad Lib on Nippon") and a souvenir of time he spent in Peru, "Compadre Cosco" where (as on

Michael Moore's tidy arrangement of a very loose Madagascar chorale, "Remy Hira") the two trumpets sound majestic, phrasing closely apart as well as together. It is enough to make you wonder why Sernesky isn't tapped by more bands.

The Ellington Orchestra's influence is pervasive but Jelly is never really about imitation. On *Monuments* Levin's accordion somehow helps not hinders the real jazz tuncs; he has a light touch and never sounds arch or downtown. (On pipe organ, only the latter two are true.) The band never comes off hipster-slick either, even with typically eclectic material like the bluegrass lament "Kentucky" featuring tenor sax, accordion and Gregg's slide banjo. Elsewhere Gregg's tuba sounds mournful with dignity. As ever Boeren like Michael Moore can sputter or blow sour or sweet—Eric coming out of quasi-buglers Don Cherry, Butch Morris, Lester Bowie.

Gregg Moore had moved to Portugal and was (usually) out by the time they made *Happy Camp* (Ramboy) at the BIMhuis in '96. Glerum was now on bass, walking as he loves to do; Wolter Wierbos had replaced Gregg. There were two Ellington pieces, the processional "The Village of the Virgins" and "The Feeling of Jazz." The latter is a sort of octet reduction of jazz orchestra, one horn = one section.

Long before, before *Monuments*, Michael Vatcher had bloomed too, become himself. There are times when he sounds like a genial parody of a jazz drummer. Even where he plays time on the ride cymbal, he's not religious about keeping it going constantly, and his beat is more deliberately elastic than most. Like jazz only moreso: the dynamic curve of a press roll a little too exaggerated, bass drum tuned much lower than most, his bombs that much louder and maybe (like his cymbal socks) in the "wrong" place, his grooves a little drier, less cymbal-soaked.

"Because the Dutch are good with languages, including music, competition makes things change really fast here, in creative ways."

He spent his first ten years "under the shadow of Disneyland"—born Modesto, 12 November '54—before moving from Southern California to Humboldt County. Vatcher played drums in rock bands, studied in school with Jerry Moore. He knew Jerry's son only as the star alto player at another school, till he sat in one night with Michael at a session. He played a tune, stood up, Moore said, sit down. When Joint Session's drummer left he joined.

Vatcher moved to New York in 1977, reconnected with Moore before he went to Holland and came back with Reijseger. Next summer Vatcher went too, now a Mime Troupe/Available Jelly guy, and working with Michael Moore and Ernst as Nomofo Trio.

There were other drummers around of course, and he didn't always work much at first. It's difficult to find housing in Amsterdam, and for a time he had no steady pad or practice space. So he became a modest tourist attraction: weather permitting he'd haul his drums out to the harbor, set them up on a concrete tunnel embankment and accompany the passing boats. He got photographed a lot, from sea and shore: symbol of kooky anything-goes Amsterdam. He kept doing it after he got a nice apartment.

"I got my best practicing done out there. The changing patterns of the water are inspiring, and it makes me aware of the resistance in my own hands—thinking about water makes you aware of ideas you can think faster than execute: a plasma I want to break through. Plus, out there there are no distractions, no phone or fridge." That spot is now occupied by a technology museum.

"I love the sound of Philly Joe Jones or Tony Williams; the more other music I play, the more sweet and beautiful it seems. But I like to improvise in other contexts too, where you can do things you can't do in jazz. I want to get into all the corners of ensemble playing. When you hit drums or cymbals really hard, they sound different.

"I'm attracted to the conciseness of a drum set as a vehicle, but also to all the wonderful percussion sounds there are. This week I'll drop some money on some Chinese instruments for Gene Carl's Pink Chinese Restaurants project. To go from dealing with his notated material to playing with Franky Douglas and Glenn Gaddum, the inner circle of players from Surinam and Curaçao in Holland, covers a nice corner of the musical palette. On metric material those guys play just a little in back of the pulse. Franky writes a lot of rigorous metrical things, and I still have to work at trying to sound fluid on a fast uptempo seven. I also like the challenge of Maurice Horsthuis's Amsterdam Drama. You hit a cymbal, suddenly you're in the same area of the sound spectrum as 16 string players."

The cost of versatility: since California, musicians who've heard him say, I didn't know you could play jazz.

Dutch prostitutes display the goods sitting in little booths behind street-level picture windows. Vatcher lives in an old crib on the edge of a small red-light district. He soundproofed the booth, plays silent show with curtain open for the passing johns who've wandered too far. (Bennink likes to practice in a similar way, in hotel rooms: looking down at the street, playing the traffic, the way someone walks, a bird darting, a dog pissing.) The floor of his booth is usually covered with percussion instruments. So, usually, is the first room behind it: looks like the back room of a music store between fire inspections. At a former location of a dance studio where he and Moore play for classes taught by among others Katie Duck, he had a room that looked like Uncle Scrooge's Percussion Bin: rubble piles of tympany, large and small parade drums, cymbals, gongs, hi-hat stands, xylophones and other mallet boards, clappers, thumpers, dulcimers, anything hittable. He loves enormous or eccentrically proportioned bass drums, which he tunes about as low as he can get away with. ("I have a 22 inch by 22 inch drum, which means the wave is equal to the amplitude, which makes for a cavernous sound.") Like other Amsterdam drummers he also likes tall shallow bass drums that can be carried on the back of a bike.

The aforementioned hiccups in Vatcher's swing call attention to him, and the way he uses the language. (He talks that way: halting, then a rush, words racing ahead of then lagging behind his thoughts.) On drums it's all very deliberate. I once overheard him and Joey Baron spend five minutes discussing the way Joe Morello releases his stick as it bounces off the head. He can go on at greater length about Baron. It was a special treat to play with him on a John Zorn tour (and CD, *Spy Vs. Spy*) doing Ornette Coleman tunes at ridiculous tempos and volume.

He's really a live artist. You learn a lot from watching his hands: the way he'll regrip a stick, rearrange his body, so that one stroke chokes a drumhead instead of letting it ring. He manipulates the pitches of tunable parade drums as he plays them. Hit a rim hard, you jam it down further, raise the pitch. Hit the head hard a couple of times, the rim loosens again, and you can start over. He controls the pitch by adjusting the power of the rimshot.

He spends more time on the rims than other drummers; there are sets where he appears to spend most of his time cantering there. Like Gunga, or Han, or Martin, he likes little sounds too. "There are a lot of different clicks in the drum set, and a rimshot is one of the cleanest sounds I have. I think Baby Dodds said it was the driest sound in the kit. I might use it a lot when a lot of people in the room are talking; it'll still be clear."

He even sounds dry on cymbals, the kit's wettest sounds; a favorite tack is clicks of sticks on shut hi-hat. (He'll also nestle two cymbals on the same stand, to sound like a shut hat.) His clapper is a bunch of dowels strung to the top part of a hinged rack; when he whomps the top up and down, it sounds like a platoon marching on a wooden platform. He may use distinctly different brushes in each hand, and he likes multi-rods—bundles of thin sticks—and a treasured old ridged stick he scrapes loudly up a rim.

For Vatcher, lack of barriers is a blessing; in a single day he might play modern composed music with Gene Carl at a Stedelijk Museum matinee, and get to punk out with The Ex (subbing for pregnant drummer Katrin Ex) and sit in with Charles Gayle in Brussels that night. He has a good ongoing gig in Tom Cora's quartet Roof, with the extraordinary Phil Minton on vocals and Luc Ex on bass. If he has a million percussion instruments and strategies, he gets to use them all without forcing a point.

In dance classes, he watches for dancers' hiccups too: a leap on the wrong beat, midair collisions, bumps into chairs. His other serious interest is chess. He's good enough to beat Misha or learn from him when he loses. It's the glimpse of another mind that fascinates him.

Talking about improvising he drifts toward terms he gets tongue-tied defining, notably "the plasma," a state improvisers can arrive at where anything is possible. Or: "I worked with the English piano player John Law's group, and to hear trumpeter Claude Deppa and bassist Paul Rogers play, I got a sweet sense of invitation, and heard things in my own fantasy that were new: a new swing subdivision I could apply elsewhere."

The last Sunday in June '96, the two Michaels and Reijseger play the opening of an art show at a gallery in Antwerp with Franky Douglas. The music like the wine and hors d'oeuvres is meant to grease a social occasion. The band is playing in an alcove between the exhibition space and the kitchen; people walk between the musicians on the way from one room to another. A toddler plants himself on a low seat, starts kicking his legs in time, inching toward an empty wineglass someone has placed on the floor. Reijseger, who has a year-and-a-half-old daughter at home, gets off his chair and inches across the room, cello hunched over his shoulder, to move the glass out of harm's way; long as he's up he does a little two-step for the kid before wandering back to his chair. He plays a slow bass line the whole time, with that absent look he favors when performing.

Vatcher sounds very much in his element, no hiccups today: no, better say he syncs up with the composer's hiccuping meters. Franky Douglas: "Sevens, nines, tens—anything more than six works for me, except eight."

Some musicians play rhythm patterns that sound complicated but most always count out to four beats. Franky's nines and sevens are like that: sound even more screwy. His patterns falter, rush ahead, turn back on themselves, unspool at length. They breathe like swingtime and have the same buoyant effect, with these players anyway.

His melodies ride those beats rather than float above them, oddly South Indian somehow. Reijseger can relate to that. Moore too has a good ear and memory for Franky's tunes, sometimes remembers them better than Franky does. (Calling him "Douglas" is like calling Miles "Davis": affected.) On one tune Moore and Reijseger play the fast bumping line in unison, cello and bass clarinet, the melody functioning as its own bass part, or vice versa.

The leader is playing an old acoustic guitar with a pickup over the sound hole. He plays blues licks, clipped chords that pull against the meter, single notes he repeats and repeats like Morse code. He can comp around a three-chord cycle for minutes on end, and play his fancy melodies with precision. (I once heard a MOBette gig where, wires crossed, he and Ernst Glerum and Han Bennink suddenly found themselves playing three distinct rhythms. They held that unplayable pattern a good minute.)

Moore, Reijseger and Vatcher have played Franky's tunes for years, so if six bars into one of them he changes his mind and begins another, they're right on it from the third note. Still, in the midst of playing these complex dance rhythms, he can zone out completely, idly strum open strings as if daydreaming. Then he can be the most careless rhythm guitarist you ever heard.

Franky Douglas has a small head and a pleasant pebbly grin he displays a lot, as if the world is a fine place. (He's not classically handsome, but women like him well enough.) He is terminally enthusiastic; if you gave him a glass of water, a week later he'd still be telling you how good it tasted.

Franky's father came from British Guiana, moved acrossd the border to Surinam where he met and married Franky's mom. Eventually they moved to Curaçao where Franky was born, 22 October '48.

"I grew up in Palu Blancu—inland, near the refinery, in the smoke. Started playing from the radio when I was about eight or nine, by ear. I do everything by ear. I listened to the Everly Brothers, salsa, the native music. In Curaçao everyone plays and dances. It's Latin-oriented. There was no real communication between there and Surinam, which is more African-oriented.

"I came to Holland when I was 14. My mother was a piano teacher, and had a good job at a hospital, and my father had a very good one at the refinery, but they wanted to get off the island." When an older sister got a scholarship to the Hague conservatory, they managed to get the whole family over. For a year Franky lived in Groningen with his aunt. "I had culture shock, but I made friends quickly. Within two weeks I was playing Cliff Richard songs in the school band. There was nothing like jazz in my life. I was more interested in chasing Dutch girls. The cool guys started a band called The Starfighters. We went to little band contests, kicking ass in little villages.

"Meanwhile my parents had moved to Buitenveldert, a suburb of Amsterdam. It must have been 1963. The first people I met here were militant, a generation older than me, the first blacks in Amsterdam. They'd spend all day singing along with Ben E. King, Clyde McPhatter, Sam Cooke, Nat King Cole, Brook Benton. I got used to that." He started playing in Caribbean soul bands, spent about ten seconds in the conservatory. "Discipline was something I never knew existed." One band took him to Italy, where he stayed two years.

Onetime New York Art Quartet drummer Glenn van Windt turned him on to Aretha, Coltrane, Monk, Bud Powell—"and he was always talking about Louis Moholo, Sunny Murray and Pharoah Sanders." That was Franky's introduction to jazz.

"I started writing tunes. Otherwise I'd just be copying people my whole life. At 19, 20, I was still playing in pop groups, but my ideas were going more toward improvised things. I wanted to see how people reacted to my inventions. But I still don't feel like a jazz guitar player; I knew nothing of jazz history until much later. Most people playing jazz in Holland were white; the whole history of black American music seemed very distant.

"But I met Sun Ra and Archie Shepp at pianist Glenn Gaddum's place; we'd help organize places for people to stay when they came. If Shepp had a gig at the Paradiso, we'd play opposite. But I was still struggling to find a place in Dutch society.

"I started playing with Raoul Burnett, a damn good percussionist from Curaçao. We had the idea to fuse salsa with whatever was available—kind of like Santana, but we didn't know about them." He also started playing with a singer from Aruba, Robbie Schouten: "Lots of instrumentals, salsas, calypsos, pop—we started to create our own style. I tried to be the Jimi Hendrix of Amsterdam." It soured, but the rhythm section continued as Solat, a jazz-rock band.

"'Fusion' was the word then, and I wrote my first jazz-influenced songs. I was tired of people saying we sounded like Santana. I had met three American horn players who were around: Ed Neumeister, Harvey Wainapel and Frank Grasso. They really introduced me to how jazz was written out, and transcribed my stuff the American way. There was no school for jazz in Holland in those days, and to me jazz had been like something supernatural. It motivated me more to write my own tunes."

(Also passing through Solat was new arrival Gregg Moore: "I had a lot of problems, the rhythms were all difficult. But I was impressed this guy who couldn't read notes could write such good music and hold it all in his head. In U.S. music education circles, you don't come into contact with people who don't read well, but can handle complicated forms.")

"People would say, 'The music is nice—but it's too jazz.' So I went back to playing '70s hit parade material with a Latin touch—brought in my sister Mildred and a couple of other singers. It was a heavy compromise, but it got us gigs. Also Hans Dulfer had saved Solat's ass; he made us his rhythm section, called that band Perikels. Within two weeks the papers were writing about us, and we were on TV. We got arrogant, started showing up late for gigs, so he fired us. But he got us over the hump, told audiences his backing band also played as Solat.

"The whole Melkweg scene was going on, where anyone could participate, take a chance, even if they couldn't really play. It must have been around then that I met

Ernst Reijseger, raving on his cello. He reminded me of Hendrix. He listened to my songs, stimulated me to take more chances, and introduced me to Michael Moore. We'd all jam at my house. I spent years making my songs better, but not playing so many gigs. I played with Glenn, Eric Calmes, Eddy Veldman, Michael Vatcher. When I could I played with Sunchild, a septet I started in '78, including Ernst, Glenn, and Raoul.

"Through Ernst I had contact with the BIM scene, met people like Sean. I played with him on the street, which helped me very much. Sometimes I'd get a Sunchild gig at a jazz venue, but the jazz people didn't trust me, playing both funk gigs and my own music.

"I played for three or four years with Eddy Veldman and Pablo Nahar in the Surinam Music Ensemble, a nice experience with a bitter aftertaste. I started getting more gigs with Sunchild, missed a few of theirs, so they fired me. I made three albums with them, including *Dynamite Cotton Legacy*." Sunchild and SME also shared a few players: Gaddum, vibist Jeroen Goldsteen, percussionist Jogi Gillis. Franky's "Toko Toko," on 1989's *No Kiddin'* shows a Zappa influence in the snaky line, guitar breaks and time changes. "Contradiction" finds him halfway between fusion vamps and bebop turnarounds. Michael Moore guested on both tunes.

"I write on guitar, always. Piano is a nice instrument to create chords on, but when ideas get complicated, I switch to guitar. The rhythm is always the last thing: The Finishing Touch. Or else I just hear long beautiful completed melodies in my head, chords, melody, rhythm at the same time. Then I have to learn to play it; I can hear it before I can analyze it. The nicer the song, the harder it is to end it. I don't like endings. Pieces change sometimes over the years, 'cause they're never wrong, if you believe in the emotion it calls up. Sometimes I try to change an old one, and get stuck between two versions. Or sometimes I play an old one and realize I'd put the wrong chords to it. Michael Moore said to me once, 'Franky, you should learn to play your own tunes.'"

Wolter Wierbos: "Franky Douglas's music calls for a completely other sense of timing. Extremely difficult at first, but after years I now know his language. All his tunes are in guitar keys, which are difficult for the horns. His stuff is really heavy on the trombone. But with him I also invent my own lines; there are tunes where I made my own melody, which then becomes the melody. It's a completely other concept of composing; no paper, just making tapes, and a piece grows and grows. He'll come back with another line opposing the one he already had. He'll start with these long interesting basslines, like 16 bars, with few notes; when you analyze the piece it's very simple in a way. A couple of years ago there were just five or six people who knew the tunes. The circle of players who know a lot of them gets bigger and bigger."

Franky Douglas: "I've always dealt with polyrhythms, always hear different lines supporting one idea. It's a challenge to support very romantic melodies with vicious rhythms. It makes the romance less romantic, and the aggressiveness less aggressive. Even when a tune is in nine, I count everything in two, with the accent on one: '1 2 1 2 1 2 1 2 1.' But I focus on the feeling, not beautiful licks. I think the ultimate result of music should be a feeling, not a sound. It becomes music when it's collective; I've never done a solo gig, I'd miss the support. Even just working with a singer, it feels like a band to me. I need the feedback."

There is something curiously Mengelbergian in the way the band finishes his composition, as it were, and in the way he zones out while playing, like Misha paddling the keys; there's something Clusone 3–like in the way that Antwerp quartet can slip into any tune in the book within the space of a bar. Franky may not be aware of those parallels, but they're in the Amsterdam air. (Nothing mystical, just a few players spreading ideas around. In a few bands, for example, when somebody's taking a solo, one idle horn player will catch another's eye, point to a few bars on the music in front of them, and then cue it to be played once: a fleeting, usually displaced background figure. That's ICP infection.)

—What happens when you go straight from playing something very precise to something totally vague?

"Sometimes the beautiful things I think up don't come out of my fingers, and I give up. I love being lost, 'cause then you can find a new way.

"I don't really feel lost when I'm lost, but I become a little more quiet and careful." Laughing. "But I'm not ashamed to make mistakes.

"Ernst Reijseger arranged to have me play on the first October Meeting. I met a lot of people I had only heard about, like Cecil Taylor, who invited me to play in a trio with him and Sunny Murray at the BIMhuis Summer Sessions in 1990. A trio, totally free. Before we went on the only thing Cecil said to us about the music was, 'Well gentlemen, have fun.' I played all my Hendrix stuff. Sometimes it was very beautiful, soft and romantic, and sometimes loud and barbaric. We got a standing ovation, and I felt my head swell. That was when the Dutch discovered I could play jazz or something. In 1994 I got the Boy Edgar Prize. It surprised me, but it didn't make my music sound better." The SJIN asked him, what do you want? He said, gigs outside Holland. They said, can't do that.

The year before he'd recorded Sunchild's CD *The Visions Project* at the North Sea Jazz Festival, with some dozen musicians altogether. Faint praise: All his good ideas are there, but in anything but concentrated form. "Unfinished Love," waltzes in five over slick changes. On "Caribbean Beach Hotel" and "Camina" you can hear his Indian-style additive rhythms, tunes jauntily attenuated as a William Gaddis sentence. But he'll waste five winds on one unison line, and there are wet squishy synth and vibes. By comparison the Antwerp quartet was Sunchild with the water weight sweated off.

Still, in Sunchild's long modal solos and stuck-groove vamps broken up by short complex turnarounds you can hear one conduit for his Indian tendencies, rococo flourishes and leapfrogging meters: Mahavishnu-era fusion, with its fast akilter heads.

Reijseger suggests another source. Placing melody notes just before or behind the beat, changing the position of a repeating melody over the beat, tangential relationships between bass line and melody, rhythmic patterns it takes an outsider a whole tune to decode—this is the stuff of kaseko music, what Surinam and Curaçao have in common.

But then again, Surinam has Indian—and Indonesian—as well as Dutch roots, thanks to an immigrant labor force drawn from other Dutch colonies. Folks speak Hindu, Dutch and kings' English; what other country has a Nieuw Amsterdam and a Calcutta? Surinam is also a meeting ground for Latin and Anglo-Caribe and Brazilian rhythms, and there are stronger African retentions than elsewhere in the new world. Even the experts have trouble sorting out all the complex influences. Factor in all the Surinamese musicians Franky has played with—like Veldman, who phrases in six-beat cycles on 4/4 tunes—and sorting all this out becomes very unlikely. But give Dulfer credit for this much: More than anyone else to date he was intent on bringing Surinamese and Antillean musicians into Dutch jazz. In a sense, we are still waiting for the Dutch to exploit these resources, radical antidote to wooden-shoe timing.

Some people insist that Franky like other musicians from the former colonies is Dutch, fully assimilated. "I'm Dutch on paper. But after 30 years here, they don't know what I'm feeling. There's not much support for people who do what I do and aren't Dutch. Michael Moore is an exception. Sean, Daniele D'Agaro, Tristan Honsinger, everyone uses them, but they don't get the kind of credit a Jarmo Hoogendijk does. That's obvious to those of us who've been on the scene a long time."

Spring '96, word is out Curtis Clark is leaving. He has relatives in Atlanta where the Olympics are coming up, bringing a tourist boom which will mean work for musicians. He isn't so busy in Holland right now, doesn't even have a piano at home. It feels like time to move on.

One Friday night at the BIMhuis, an hour or so after the gig is over and only a cluster of musicians and other regulars sit around the tables above the pit, Curtis sneaks on stage, sits at the piano, and begins to play very quietly: a mouse's entrance, easing you into the idea someone is playing. He sounds the way you want a pianist to sound at one a.m.: slow and blue, reflective, those colorful Curtis chords. Ab Baars gets up, walks away, and a few minutes later his clarinet enters, softly, another mouse. Twenty minutes later, with the resignation of a man who has to go dig his car out of the snow, Daniele D'Agaro finishes his drink and wanders off, and then a tenor saxophone is heard as well, less mousey. He's too loud, killing the mood, but that's okay too. Five minutes later, Curtis is teaching them one of his tunes.

Two months later, he's living in Richmond, Virginia. A year after that, he's back in Amsterdam—temporarily, he says.

Two weekends after Antwerp, in the Hague it's North Sea time again—140 concerts, 13 stages, hundreds and hundreds of musicians, one extenuating circumstance being clubs like the BIMhuis close for the summer. A hundred miles south at a farm in Zonnemaire in Zeeland, Clusone 3 and the MOB play under gray skies for a few hundred folks and a pack's worth of dogs and a herd of sheep grazing nearby. It's family day: Jerry Moore is here from California, as is Eric Boeren's brother from Peru, who brings their mom. It's a strange scene. See Bennink twirling little cymbals on his drumheads, turn 45 degrees, see a sheep munching out of tempo. Look over the dike at the end of the prairie a mile away and there's the ocean.

For a MOB Sean has Boeren on cornet, Wierbos and Joost Buis on trombones, D'Agaro, Delius and Jan Willem van der Ham on reeds, Tristan, Franky, bassist Jacko Schoonderwoerd and Bennink, most of them in a chorus line spanning the makeshift stage. Out of the gate it was a photogenic mess: Franky gyrating like early Elvis and twanging like Scotty Moore, chatting with Han as he plays and then suddenly noticing Honsinger is halfway through a solo chorus. Franky turns to him smiling, not missing a beat: "Tristan, my man." It sounds like hell, but then the saxophones blend together, Han starts pulsing on snare and cymbals, trombones find their balance and rise in support as twin cellos used to, and the sea-shanty and kwela strains start coming out. One minute it's a blaring harmonie band, and then for the rest of the set it's vintage MOB.

When it's over everyone eats and has a fine time—except Bennink and D'Agaro, who hop in a car and charge off to another gig at North Sea, playing music by expat Don Byas.

Chapter Ten
Brass Bands

Dixieland is big in the south and in rural areas. So is brass band music. The sense of projection early jazz horn players prized had come (like Jelly Roll Morton's or ragtime's formal models) from brass band music. Holland, same way. Hear someone with a real sound, like Joost Buis rattling glass at the Engel on a Sunday, chances are good they came up in a brass band (cornets, alto horns and other brass + drums) fanfare (like a brass band except with trumpets and French horns + saxes) or harmonie (fanfare – trumpets + woodwinds). It's an experience about which few seem sentimental, even if such bands are among the first music future musicians get to hear—as with Breuker or Martin van Duynhoven—and help shape first conceptions of music.

The classic example is Wolter Wierbos, a great trombonist by any standard. I've heard him many times in many situations, but don't recall ever hearing him play badly—or out of tune, except by design. (He can play a quarter-tone sharp, nagging vibrato, exact sound of a Louisiana rustic on an old Folkways brass band record.) One pleasure of Franky Douglas's "Camina" on Sunchild's CD: you don't often hear a trombone play ridiculous twisty fusion tunes, especially one that takes charge by elbowing through a pack of other horns. He also regularly ignores parts written for him to come up with something better on his own—even, as on Available Jelly's *Happy Camp*, where horns coalescing is crucial to the total effect. In the midst of some dense and careful four-voice harmonization, he'll suddenly emerge sailing placidly over the top, something totally else in mind, but never forgetting to come back in at those pivot points where his written notes are essential.

Wolter's attitude as much as big sound defines him. A favorite recording is Ellington live in Fargo, 1940, and like a skilled impressionist he can do all its trombone voices: Tricky Sam Nanton's wah-wahed field hollers and frog-throated ("Chloe") or hectoring ("Sidewalks of New York") sarcasm—also the way he'll make one isolated note stand out by playing it ever so slightly off concert pitch; Lawrence Brown's elegant staccato outbursts and peaks-and-valleys dynamics ("Rose of the Rio Grande") and vibratoed bray on "Sheik of Araby"—also the way Brown sails out of ensemble to take lead on "Rumpus in Richmond," making his mark in a few bars; Juan Tizol's checked passion and melody statements. He knows those voices and strategies and many more, owes a lot to two tailgate moderns he first heard with Anthony Braxton, Ray Anderson and George Lewis. Wolter's full of bluster, the way trombone players are, but he's a nuance man too, will tailor his embouchure by the note.

English pianist, improviser and record producer Steve Beresford on his ability to be creative on an eight-bar break: "'Well, I want it with a wah, and it has to have a few wrong notes, can you make it?' If you say that sort of stuff to Wolter he just does it, and he puts in at least 50 percent of what he wants to do as well." He can also play straight when the music needs it; an almost steady diet of excess needs restraint for seasoning.

Wierbos is a quantifier. He charts his own career the most methodical way you ever saw: keeps detailed records, oversize notebooks full of graph paper, cross-indexed bar graphs detailing his working life: where he played and how many times he's played there, who with, how much he was paid. Just before going on stage with Franky Douglas one night in '95, he turned to Ernst Reijseger and said, this is our 300th gig together.

"I never had the idea I had a big sound. Because I'm standing behind my instrument, I never hear what comes out up front."

Wierbos is a compact, sturdy man, with thick Lon Chaney eyebrows. He was born in Holten, small town in the east, 1 September 1957. The local fanfare was his first gig.

"That's one of the big things in rural areas. You have a fanfare, you have an acting club, some other things. But the best orchestras come from rural areas, it's really a tradition. In big cities they're interested in other things.

"On my mother's side, almost everybody was in that band. When we were small kids they took us a lot to listen to it, and then they asked if I wanted to be a part of it. When I was around 10 or 11, I started on cornet, then changed to flugelhorn. I started the old way, some old guy from the band telling us what to do. But after a couple of months they sent all the young people to the music school for cheap private lessons. My teacher was our conductor, who lived next door, so it was kind of easy for me. We younger players were much better than the older ones who never had lessons; for them it was just for fun. So the orchestra became quite good. Six or seven years later, half the orchestra was young people. Then we became champions of Holland, competing in the highest category.

"I always was interested in improvising. When you're a little kid and have lessons, you have to study the notes, but I always hated that, the exercises they gave you are boring. Five minutes before my lesson I looked at the notes, and bzzzzzt. When I played at home, I just made up my own things, from the very start. I didn't know it was called improvising; I just played without paper. Of course I made a lot of mistakes, but I could fake my way out.

"When I was 17 I changed to trombone. It looked good, and the trombones walk in front. I liked the instrument immediately, and could play it almost immediately. I

already had the blowing technique. I had been first trumpet, but I was small and did-
n't have the power for the real high notes first trumpet had to play. I could do it for
one hour, but after that, fzzzt. The larger mouthpiece made it much easier.

"I never was interested in influences, but I admire a lot of trombone players. One
of the first I heard was Albert Mangelsdorff, on TV. In the East you could get German
TV, and they had a lot of jazz programs. I saw him play solo, and was completely
impressed with his double-tones"—multiphonics, one played, one sung, with ghost
overtones sounding like a third note: chords on trombone. "I found I could do it also,
immediately; it's not that difficult. That's how it happens, listening to players and picking up things.

"I use a technique with a lot of pressure, the opposite of what they teach you at
school. I figured out for myself what was best for me. The muscle is concentrated on
the middle of the lip, so then you can play with a lot of pressure. My lips never got
damaged by doing that. You find that you need different embouchures to get different
sounds out of your instrument, like extreme high notes. That's a technique I first saw
Ray Anderson use a long time ago. 'Why is he shifting his mouthpiece?' I figured it
must be to get some notes better. I experimented with it, and I found out another
embouchure was better for playing high notes. It was exactly what he was doing."

When he saw Ray Anderson in Groningen in the late '70s, Wolter was studying
social geography there, hadn't yet decided to go pro. "There came a point when I had
to make a decision: study or try to make a living from music? So I gave myself five years
to become a musician and make a living from it. After one year I was already doing it.
I studied till 1980, when I moved to Amsterdam." In those years Groningen spawned
a Dutch version of free funk—Ornette's Prime Time, Ronald Shannon Jackson's
Decoding Society, Defunkt and Sonny Sharrock would all play the city's fall
Jazzmarathon—centered locally around saxophonist Alan Laurillard. Wierbos wasn't
involved, but he did form a duo with trombonist Joep Maessen, whom he'd played
with in a Laurillard workshop band.

"In Groningen I played with pianist Harry de Wit." Wolter made his first record
with him, for the English improvisers' Bead label. "Harry was also in a group from
Rotterdam called The Bunker Sextet. I was invited into that group, but they were having arguments, and split up. Ab Baars and Mariëtte Rouppe van der Voort were in that
group, and decided to start a new group called Cumulus, with Harry de Wit and me
from the old group, plus Larry Fishkind and Petro Nykyruj, a drummer from Australia.
We rehearsed in Rotterdam, and had Butch Morris as a guest on one tour. That was
nice—'80, '81 I think. Then we split up again.

"Larry and Radu Malfatti were then in ICP, and when Radu couldn't make a series
of gigs, Larry proposed me to Misha. So I got a phone call: 'Oh, Misha Mengelberg
calling me!' I was still living in Groningen, which was a nice city, a lot of opportunities to play, but the circle was very small. Sean Bergin was one of the first people I met
in Amsterdam, because he was in ICP that first year, for the 20 or so gigs I did. And
then we played together with Harry Miller, J. C. Tans and the Rockets.

"In the early '80s there was a whole South African scene here. Jabula was a group
of South African players living in squat houses, having sessions, but I think they could-
n't get any work, so they went back. Harry Miller was living here, he invited me into

his quintet. We played about ten gigs, and made an album, and then he organized another tour, but he died." That was in '83. Two years later Wierbos was on *Theo Loevendie Kwintet*, LP for VARAJAZZ. "That was one of the first recordings I liked my trombone sound on, because I had control over the way it was recorded. Mostly when I play loud, the sound comes out narrow, 'cause they have compression, and the mike is mostly too close. So when I play loud I've learned to step back, and when I play soft to play close mike." He tells the engineer, don't mess with my volume level, let me do it, same thing Ernst Reijseger tells them.

"The year I learned a lot was '82, because I was doing this play with Maurice Horsthuis, *Leedvermaak*, about a Jewish family, and concentration camps. At one point I had an improvised trombone solo of a couple of minutes. Every day, I had the opportunity of checking out different aspects of my playing, and the audience reaction. I'd try to play the most terrible bullshit I could, and they still applauded. It didn't have anything to do with the music. If it's that easy to get applause, I never wanted to do it again. Some musicians think when there's applause, it's good—like Keshavan Maslak lying on the ground and playing the saxophone with ICP. For me that was kind of bullshit, had nothing to do with the group. You have to react to the players in the band, not to the audience. I never would do things like Han Bennink or Ernst Reijseger do, but with them it relates to the music. Some players don't have that kind of subtlety.

"Maarten Altena played in ICP sometimes, as a guest, and that's where he heard me. In the summer of '81 he asked me to join his quartet, with Paul Termos on alto and Maud Sauer on oboe. Everybody hated Maarten, and were warning me, 'Don't play with this guy, blah blah blah,' so I thought, 'Oh, I have to do it.' I liked it immediately.

"Maarten pushed me to write a piece for the quartet, the later version with Michael Moore and Maartje ten Hoorn, but I hated it. After we played it six or seven times, I said, 'I don't want to play it anymore.' I had decided years before I see myself more as a player than a composer. I don't like writing notes for other people. As a player I'm also composing, but without writing it down."

When Wierbos won the Boy Edgar Prize in 1995, the only substantive criticism anyone made was, it's supposed to be about leadership, and Wierbos is all sideman. By then he had made only one record under his own name, solo 1982: *Wierbos*, on DATA. It's his calling card, a Wierbos sampler: plosives and slide percussion, freak falsetto and frictive multiphonics, horsewhinnies, whaletalk, a small plane in the distance, and beautiful burnished-tone trombone playing. It's so varied from minute to minute you know he hasn't gotten to all his tricks. (You see his name on the cover of two CDs by a group he nominally co-leads, the Podium Trio—with alto saxophonist Paul van Kemenade and guitarist Jan Kuiper, the first three players to win the Podium Prize—but he stresses it's really Kuiper's group.) It took him 15 years to make a sequel, X *Caliber* (ICP). Part of it is a set from Groningen where they asked him to play half an hour. He didn't look at his watch. On CD it's 30 minutes and 26 seconds; Dick Lucas confesses they edited about one second out.

In conversation like other Dutch and non-Dutch virtuosos Wierbos can be corrosively analytical of other musicians' faults. Since he can play everything, from the fanciest technical stuff to the most rarefied improvising systems, he has no need to choose, or justify what he doesn't do. More like he wants to do it all—play dry composed music and Franky Douglas gigs and improvise collectively, and (one suspects) maybe even play music he knows he won't like just for the experience. It's as if being able to play everything counts for less than doing it.

He can be critical, but he can also be a pacifier, can break the tension that develops between musicians on the road because he has a knack for making everyone laugh at the right moment. It is one more part of being a model ensemble player.

"A band is mostly chemistry, picking up the right combination of people. Look at ICP. When I look at the list of the bands I play in, I'm eclectic. I'm not interested in one set of rules. I like it that the field is wide. Somebody like Michael Moore always had that same feeling, or Ernst Reijseger: listening to a lot of different kinds of music and using those influences in their own playing. I'm also the type of player who reacts like that.

"I'm not interested in doing just One Thing, like Peter van Bergen. I was in his band LOOS for awhile, but it was not for me as a player. I was sabotaging the whole thing all the time. He was writing these fast 16th notes, divided among the instruments, and completely unplayable. We had one great gig, and that was when he fired me and Vatcher. Because we put a kind of dixieland feel on it. I thought it was great! I thought the music was a little about dixieland, but I heard after that he was furious."

Peter van Bergen says, nothing like that happened, adding: I never fire people, I just stop calling them.

"I play solo concerts when people ask me, maybe once every couple of years, like a half-hour solo in the BIMhuis as part of a longer concert—although I'd rather play solo, opening for The Ex, than in a jazz club. I have one long solo piece only about breath: not notes but inhaling and exhaling. You can get a lot of music just doing that. A recording I made of it is like ten minutes. First I thought, 'Ah, it's boring,' but now I think it has to be even longer, to savor the quiet.

"When I make a solo album I never cut out the things I regard as mistakes. I'm not interested in the perfect recording—more honest to show how it really is. J. C. Tans likes to do a lot of takes, but on a piece where I have a solo, I'll just do it once. If you can't do it in one take, forget about it.

"I would never play in a group that only plays written music. As a player, I'm interested in a combination of the written and the improvised: how you get the piece and the improvisation to make a whole. I think improvising and composing are kind of the same. Some people, like Gerry Hemingway, really write out of that idea. He has a theme, and counterpoint, and he knows where the piece will go to, makes the connection from one written piece to another. Misha has the completely other approach: a few notes, very simple, and then you figure out yourself what to do with it.

"I think the Dutch are more open to other directions than improvisers in Germany and England. From what I see, they're very strict, defending their territory: We Are Improvisers, so we don't want to deal with other things, and blah blah blah. That attitude was here also, a little bit, but the later generations are no longer interested in that. Maybe making such connections helps your playing go even further. It's more interesting to be wide open than to be narrow minded.

"I can play free and still enjoy it a lot, but only with certain people. A lot of musicians play so soloistic, they don't relate to what's happening around them. Or they only relate to what's happening around them, because they play like a parrot: When is your idea coming? When I improvise, I have an idea about form, about where it's going. You always have to think of counterpoint. Somebody tells a story, and you have to have the answer to it, or something to add on top of it, or a contrast, but not the same story. You can do that at a certain point, to have a bit of tension, but contrasting things are usually more interesting.

"The first groups I was in didn't play any pieces, but we rehearsed a lot. We played and played. Of course in those days I also played in other groups that had written material, but mostly I didn't like them. It was too much like being back in the fanfare." Laughing. "That's what I didn't want to do."

The end of the October Orchestra tour, 1994, on the band bus (it's Breuker's—nice one: toilet, plush seats, card tables) between Ghent and Amsterdam. The New York trumpeter Ted Daniel is talking with Ab Baars. It hasn't been an easy tour—Henry Threadgill has made a point of traveling separately, showed up for the last gig minutes before it started and left at the half. He and Daniel had had a hard time getting Bennink to do anything except swing madly. (Ted: Why don't you use mallets here? Han: I don't own any.) But Daniel and Baars had enjoyed playing together. Ted takes his number, says they should do a small group sometime. He's standing in the aisle, Ab's in an aisle seat, Bennink in front of him, playing paradiddles on whatever. Talking this and that, until Ab mentions *Way Out West*. Ted's eyebrows go up, just a little.

"You know that record?"

Scoffing. "Of course."

"Who made it?"

"You're joking."

"No, come on."

Still incredulous. "Sonny Rollins."

Bennink turns around: "Ray Brown, Shelly Manne!" and plays a fast heavy turnaround on his seatback to cap the anecdote.

Baars knows his jazz sideways. He's a student of jazz tenor saxophone and clarinet players and their eccentricities, but isn't a guy who knows lots of standards and works on complex chord progressions. The players he loves most are extremists like Von Freeman and John Carter: the tenor who (like the young Rollins) pushes the boundaries of accepted intonation, playing so sharp or flat he floats out of the rest of the band's universe, apparition from another world; the clarinetist who made a science of the instrument's squeal register, extending the instrument's upward range by an octave. Like Michael Moore Baars admires Jimmy Giuffre, who went the opposite way—stayed in the lower register most clarinetists shied off, and had a wispy sound to make you wonder if a pad was leaking or he was leaning on a side key.

"My mother was raised on a farm, and had three brothers. They were all into music.

My mother played church organ; she was the only one who had lessons. These brothers never had an education, and all learned instruments by themselves. They were very good at wood-carving, creative hobbies, and one of them played saxophone and clarinet. When I was 15, I got my first saxophone from my uncle—a tenor. But it was a Belgian one, from a fanfare, and in his time the fanfare orchestras didn't use A 440 tuning; it's a little sharper. There are still orchestras in small Belgian villages that use the old tuning. I don't know why they did it; maybe, being sharper, it sounds better outside, in the cold. But I didn't know the tenor played out of tune. I only realized after I started playing with other people that something was wrong."

Put it to Ab Baars that he likes intonation as an expressive medium because his first saxophone blew out of tune (and he's right of course, sharper means brighter), he doesn't buy it. To him it's too obvious—easier for him to connect his sound with Roscoe Mitchell. Baars used to play soprano and baritone but those instrument may've been too obvious: on soprano, everyone has quirky intonation; on baritone, anyone can splat rude. On his late '80s solo CD *Krang* Mitchell's signature leaky-bagpipe losing-pressure sound echoes through "Geel and Rood" (Yellow and Red) for soprano, but the follow-up "Madang" for the same instrument goes the other way: hollow harmonics sounding long tones, a soft sho, or a melody played by distant pentatonic train whistles.

He's quiet, talks just over a mumble, looks like he's simmering inside sometimes, like when someone thinks he might not know a Rollins classic. (Really he's just shy.) Looks like Clark Kent: behind the heavy black glasses he's big, sportsman looking, jaunty lock of hair hanging. He follows football, gets depressed when Holland loses.

Baars was born 21 November 1955, in Zeeland—Sea Land—watery area where the Rhine flows into the North Sea. "As a child I had music theory lessons for seven or eight years, played piano for three or four. I was always very jealous of people who could improvise. My mother used to play at church, and then after the service, a guy would come up to play all the latest pop tunes. I'd ask, 'How do you do that?' 'Oh, I just listen to the radio, and try to figure it out.' I didn't understand how that was possible, I was so dependent on reading from paper. After that, whenever I heard music that I liked, I went to the shop and bought the sheet music, and tried to learn it by heart. So I was in between.

"Then I stopped making music for four or five years, till I was 15. I played baseball instead, was a very good first baseman, played on the Dutch national youth team, at the training stage. Then I decided to quit, 'cause I wanted to make music. I got interested in the saxophone because of musicians I heard in certain bands. The band Ekseption used to play classical music with a pop rhythm behind it. They were one of the first Dutch pop bands with trumpet and tenor saxophone. And I heard records by Chicago, which had a horn section, and there was one famous saxophone player in Eindhoven—we'd moved there when I was four or five—whose name was Bertus Borgers. He had his own band, and was very stimulating to me. But it was all more or less pop oriented. The first bands I played in were pop groups, but after I heard other music, I started improvising.

"As soon as I got the saxophone, it was clear to me I would be a musician, and nothing else. But only after playing it for three or four years did I start taking lessons. So it was the opposite of my piano experience. I started to figure out how the instrument worked, what you could do with it."

— Self-taught saxophonists tend to discover interesting things teachers discourage you from doing.

"No, I think I wanted to play it as well as possible. I started playing long notes. I was already looking for a sound. I wanted a good tone.

"After three or four years, my mother and the uncle who gave me the saxophone said, 'You should play in an orchestra, sit in a section, learn the repertoire.' I joined the harmonie from Philips, the huge company. It was a very special orchestra. They had three different uniforms, and we got paid. We would play at openings of branch offices, in Switzerland, Germany, Belgium, Austria. I think I was quite lucky. We got to see soccer games for free, 'cause we'd play at the interval. They also had a big band, and there were people in it who'd talk about jazz music, and I got free lessons. There was an alto saxophone player who was very well-known inside that world, because he had a beautiful sound, very sweet and sophisticated. I don't think he was much into jazz music, but he knew Johnny Hodges.

"I was collecting records then. There was one by Colosseum, where Dick Heckstall-Smith played an unaccompanied tenor saxophone solo. I listened to that a lot. And then I started listening to jazz music, bought records by John Coltrane and Ornette.

"It was strange, but during the period that I didn't play, I'd go to libraries searching for books on jazz music. I was fascinated by the stories, the world the musicians lived in, but I never made the connection that I would like to play this music myself. At school I made a transcription of some New Orleans music, but I still didn't play at the time. I'd try to remember what the books said about people's styles and who they played with, so when I heard their records I'd recognize them. I have an old friend who had some of the last Coltrane records, with Pharoah Sanders, and the duets with Rashied Ali, and *Let My Children Hear Music* by Mingus. He was a drummer, so we often played duos—totally open, no written or verbal guidelines. At this time Belgian radio played the music of John Coltrane every Monday, Wednesday and Friday for one hour, and I listened to that. And then I also went to concerts at Wilhelmina, the bebop-oriented club in Eindhoven. I saw Charlie Mariano, Tete Montoliu, Dexter Gordon with Maarten Altena on the bass.

"Then Niko Langenhuijsen, the piano and bass player who was very much into improvised music, had workshops every Wednesday. I think that was the first stimulating experience I had, in terms of getting information about what the possibilities were in certain material, and about records, and about improvising. He was somebody you could talk to. And now and then I joined a friend when he'd go to Amsterdam to hear concerts; I saw the very first theater productions of Willem Breuker. They were all quite stimulating experiences. It pointed me towards things I would like to do also.

"When school was over for the day I'd jump on my bike and ride home, go up to my room and start practicing. At night I would go into town and play. I was very dedicated. At that time I started doing free improvisations that had nothing to do with bebop. I was just trying to find things that would interest me.

"My father was in the army, as a profession. I got called up, but I didn't want to go in the army, I wanted to make music. So I got S5, we call it." In short, he convinced the screening personnel he wasn't military material. "My father was pretty shocked, as you can imagine. So then I decided, 'Well now I have to do something. I'll go to the conservatory.' Which was a big problem, because I never studied what you needed to pass the entrance exam. So I started working on it, and after half a year I passed the exam for the Tilburg conservatory, but they didn't know what to do with me, because I was improvising. This was long before all these Light Music courses started." That is the old patently patronizing name for things like jazz ed. "During that time I had played with Loek Dikker's big band; one of the saxophone players, Leo van Oostrom, was a teacher at the Rotterdam Conservatory, and he was looking for people like me who were interested in classical music and improvised music. The jazz music course really started two or three years after I got there, but Leo dealt with those things in his own lessons. He had me play bebop-oriented things and classical saxophone music and modern classical pieces, a bit of everything.

"Theo Loevendie taught composition at the conservatory. I was always practicing, and one day when he was in the room next door, he knocked on my door and said, 'Would you like to play in my band?' That's one of the first important bands I played in. I'd known his music, and I liked it very much. Guus Janssen was on piano, and I was very fond of his playing, because it was strange and new. After we did that awhile, Guus wanted to have his own group, and invited me. That was very important to me, because he had outspoken ideas about improvisation, and the sorts of things he wrote were very new to me.

"Until I met Guus I improvised only one way, toward a certain climax, and that was it: linear. For his band, he wrote pieces that were dedicated to John Cage, where you're given certain notes to improvise with. So for the first time I really had to improvise relating to a certain composition, another kind of structure. Those first concerts were terrible, because except for Guus nobody knew what to do. But after awhile I felt more comfortable playing things that related to certain parts of the composition, to certain rules or whatever. He'd say, 'Instead of starting at the beginning, why don't you start with this part of the theme, and try to build it up like this and this?' He's searching for things people will feel comfortable with. That was all very new to me.

"I remember being astonished that he and his brother went to discos and listened to soul music, and that he listened to medieval music. This all influenced him; he had broad ideas.

"At the same time in Rotterdam, there was a famous jazz club called The Bunker, where I started working with Wolter Wierbos, Harry de Wit and Mariëtte Rouppe van der Voort, and we played in a lot of different combinations. I think I was already using things I'd learned in Guus's band."

Mariëtte Rouppe van der Voort brought him into Volharding—he replaced Breuker's replacement—where he stayed till the late '80s, the period when the band evolved from ideologues' harmonie to concert outfit. He omits his 12 years there from his biographical squibs. Ask him what was good about it, you get an automatic answer: it expanded him, exposing him to music he knew nothing of—he arranged some Ives and some Spanish Civil War songs—and made him think about the politics of the gig. Time constraints were one factor in deciding to leave, but in the end, something soured: "It started to feel like going to the office." He doesn't hear any impact it had on his saxophone playing, but being there during his formative years must have fostered his inclination to play loud and forceful: saxophone in extremis (which is to say the Breuker legacy comes through loud and clear). And playing loud saxophone gave him the ambition to get a big sound on clarinet.

"I started clarinet at the conservatory, when I was 21 or so. You had to play a second instrument. This was the period when everybody played bass clarinet or flute, so I didn't want either of them, although I was listening to Eric Dolphy a lot and was very impressed with bass clarinet. I'd started listening to Ellington and especially enjoyed Barney Bigard, but clarinet was also related to the dixieland music I didn't like: tiny little sound, squeaks, that whole dixieland atmosphere. Nobody I knew played clarinet at that time, but I had the feeling it would fit very well in the more chamber-like music I wanted to make. Later I heard Perry Robinson, which I enjoyed very much, and John Carter. The music he wrote impressed me even more than his clarinet. Most American music I knew was written from a tradition—bebop, swing, New Orleans music—and still had that jazz stamp. I think John Carter's was the first music I heard that also related to European music, with sort of a chamber-like feeling from trumpet, violin and clarinet. It was all very open, and could go in a lot of directions.

"I quit the conservatory just before my exam. I was so much into my own music by then, I couldn't combine it with the things I had to learn at school. I was developing my own sound, and my own ideas about making music. I quit for one year, with the idea I'd finish after that, and in that year I had my own band with Butch Morris, who was living in Holland at that time, and did a lot of concerts, and a lot of writing. I think Butch has had quite an influence on a lot people in Holland, the idea of conduction.

"When I first knew him in the late '70s, he was always looking for ways to develop and change the music on stage. We did a tour with a quartet, with Ernst Glerum and Martin van Duynhoven. I'd close my eyes when I took a solo, and when I opened them and looked at my music, I'd see he had switched my parts and his. He'd do this with larger groups too: after they'd played a theme through once he'd switch the parts around. That meant some people wound up playing in strange keys, but he didn't worry about that.

"As far as I know he was always interested in visual things: he'd watch people to see how they'd get things done, how they'd react to certain things. I remember he talked a lot about how Miles Davis behaved on stage, how he could change the band's complexion with just one gesture."

That was the dawn of what Morris is now famous for, conducting improvisers. (He uses a well-developed vocabulary of about 20 hand gestures and baton moves to give directions: louder; softer; you, take a solo; you, mock that solo; everyone play a line that mirrors this zigzag I draw in the air with my baton; give me one short loud note on my mark; remember what you're playing now, because soon I'll ask you to play it again. . . .) As noted earlier, when he first started coming to Holland back then he didn't know Misha was doing something very similar if less formalized. Butch was introduced to the basics of pantomime composing in California in 1971, when he joined drummer Charles Moffett's rehearsal band. (He still uses a few gestures he learned from Moffett, including drawing-in-the-air as instant graphic notation. As George Lewis recounted earlier, Muhal was doing it in Chicago around then too.)

Lawrence D. "Butch" Morris: "When I'd do my thing, people would say, 'So-and-so used to do that.' Nedly Elstak had told me about Boy Edgar doing it. I had seen Zappa and Sun Ra do it. I didn't know about Muhal—or Lukas Foss, with his Improvisation Chamber Ensemble in the '60s. But I don't think anybody held onto it like I did; mostly they'd take it so far and no further. When I started using musicians from various areas, I saw that the range of interpretation was broad, and geographical-ly particular."

He'd get different reactions to the same gesture from jazz musicians, classical musi-cians, musicians from outside western traditions—as well as from improvisers on either side of an ocean or a national border. That inspired him to start mixing such musi-cians in one ensemble, what he sees as his major contribution to the conduction tra-dition.

Morris says he made his first breakthroughs in '77 in those workshops at The Bunker, where he met Baars: "He had his own style the first time I heard him, and it was obvious he'd blossom further. If I proposed a musical situation he'd find his own situation within it. He was one of the few who could get some distance from the mate-rial."

♪♫

"Eventually I started meeting John Carter after concerts or at festivals. I wanted to leave Holland for awhile to study. I had never had proper lessons on the clarinet, and decided I wanted to study with John. Up to then I was playing saxophone on the clar-inet, didn't have the right sound or technique. I had read in an interview that he had this Wind College in Los Angeles, and he'd talked about the ideas he had about doing workshops with James Newton, Red Callender and Bobby Bradford, and that he want-ed to invite people from all over the world who were interested in his music. So I applied for a grant from the Dutch government and after a few years I got one. It took awhile because I never did get my conservatory diploma.

"John was a very good teacher. One thing I had never thought about: he was very interested in mistakes." When he misplayed a note and got a squeak, he'd stop imme-diately, write down the fingering and determine the pitch. He wound up with what amounts to a chart of new fingerings in the falsetto range. "So he was very creative in his study. Playing exercises or scales was not a dull thing. He was always interested in what would happen if you did it like this instead of that. Everything related to a con-cept.

"I was in Los Angeles two months, but the only three things I saw were the studio, my hotel and John Carter's house. I was very serious, had a lot of money, and so—typ-ical Dutch—felt I had to work for it. I'd get up at eight or nine, have breakfast, go to the studio, practice. In the evening I would have dinner and watch television with the Carters, and then go back to the hotel.

"Now that I've played on some festivals abroad, I've found that people outside Holland always have the idea that music here is about fun and making jokes. But to me, the common thread in Dutch music is a clear awareness of form. Most musicians in Holland are very aware when they write something that it has certain implications about how it should be played. Another reason why Dutch improvised music is so specific might be that most of the important people in it are composers, or have a background which has been influenced by classical music. Misha, Theo Loevendie, Guus Janssen, Maarten Altena, they're always thinking about forms, and how to get on paper what they hear in their head. I think that also influences their thinking about improvising, and the relationship between improvisation and the written material.

"I think another typical Dutch attitude is an open mind. Not bother about the rules of a certain style but just use it in a personal manner. Once Misha and Willem Breuker and Han Bennink came on the scene, the whole tone was set: how to play music, how you could use influences from other music, how you could handle it and how you could develop it. Every kind of music is good, whatever it is.

"There are a lot of influences on my own composing, typical Dutch behavior. I relate my trio with Wilbert de Joode and Martin van Duynhoven to modern chamber music in a way. I try to write material that is easy for the musicians to understand, but has a lot of things in it they can develop. That is something I learned from Misha. His writing is never finished. There is always enough space for the musicians to finish the things he wrote, to amplify some aspect of it and work with it, make something out of it.

"It might be nice to mention the influence of punk groups The Ex and Dog Faced Hermans, whom Han Bennink and I have played with. That was a very important influence for me, because the music is so simple, direct and down-to-earth. Raw and expressive. It made me aware of the effect of simple things. From the first concerts I did with them, I played very simple things to fit the written music, and my improvisations got simpler and simpler. I think that had an influence on my writing for the trio, and also my improvising. Sometimes I do an unaccompanied solo or a duo at these concerts, for people who hardly know about improvised music."

Flashforward: As one of The Ex's several guests on 1995's —*instant*— (Ex Records)—a set of (partly overdubbed) improvisations, mostly for duos, trios and quartets—Baars plays some nice clarinet and guitar miniatures, in duo with The Ex's Terrie Hessels or Andy Moor: split tones, teakettle high notes on command, a Pee Wee Russell vocabulary of blurts and squiggles. On tenor for some pieces, his tone is brittle as Von Freeman's, but he's also going for the thick-crayon scribble of a punk's flailing lead guitar: what Ayler had been reaching for when he teamed up with Canned Heat's Henry Vestine.

Ab Baars' debut LP *Carrousel* (DATA) mostly recorded in '83 was for solo saxes (his soprano out of Steve Lacy: same tone, dry concept, no hurry) and for the trio Trebbel with Janssen on piano and Rouppe van der Voort on alto, flute and piccolo. It's cautious and undercooked, but Ab's preoccupations are in place: the dickering with pitch, the strangulated sound of a horn with a hole left open in defiance of fingering charts.

On the improvised chamber trios, Janssen's alert ears are asset and safety net. With him around, they can never screw up that bad, and so tension curiously goes out of it: no risk of a fatal plunge. But there are memorable moments: One of Mariëtte's "Five Short Forms" is a long episode for clarinet and alto, one very slowly wavering long note sliding ever so slightly out of unison and phase with itself, a study in interference patterns/difference tones and microtonal harmony. "Pauze" by Rotterdam composer Jan Willem van Mook features Volharding's barking saxophones—the Breuker connection again. (Willem knows something about mangled fingerings and playing out of tune for effect as well.)

The solo CD *Krang* was a step forward—if nowhere near as ingenious and full of contrasts as the '95 sequel *Verderame*, whose tracks include the foghorn blow "Rollins' Williamsburg Bridge." Another advance was the first CD by his trio with de Joode and van Duynhoven, *3900 Carol Court*, which was John Carter's street address. Sometimes, the eccentric parched tenor tone and squirreling away from home pitch disguise old '60s strategies. "Krang" (one of three pieces also on the first solo CD) is basically a modal blow over ostinato rhythm. Baars uses booty bluesy phrases to blast out of eddies, plays staccato cascades tumbling behind the beat like among others '60s Shepp. The best piece is their Modern Jazz Quartet cover, "Trav'lin in Plastic Dreams." Slinky clarinet melody over softly insistent tick-tock rhythm gives way to a walking-eight blowing section; Martin signs every measure with a double tom stroke on the last beat, a latin tinge. Ab gets a beautiful, sailing clarinet sound on "Glorpjes," whose birdcall lilt catches Carter.

Some grooves aim to clunk—"Kimmel," once past an elementary figure built on the pitches of Martin's cymbals, alternates a shambling backbeat with a stuck-record galumph for bass and tenor, as Martin explores the range of sounds to be coaxed from a barely opened hi-hat. This is a drummer's dream trio: arcane structures that call for a light hand, the freedom to swing in thematically open sections. Van Duynhoven carefully weighs his sounds in relation to theirs, and knows the kit's clicks as well as Vatcher or Gunga. "The Dutch Windmill," for a prizefighter, is Martin's dance around the ring, his scored hits timed like landed punches in a title bout.

"Windmill" anticipates *Sprok*, '94, which further refines their idiomatic textural sense: palpable puckered tenor, power leaping from thwacked bass cables, thin precision of sticks on drumshells and metal—thud of earth, snapping twigs. "Kuin"'s jaunty melody is etched more indelibly rather than undercut by the droll tenor tone, the seeming misfingerings, the querulous attack and vibrato, all offset by Ab's consistent big sound. The rhythm section had audibly grown together, knit like a mending bone.

The writing reflects punky simplicity. Old paradox: The barest material is often best to improvise from, because it bends most easily, and lets you hear the original shape in the bending. Punk-blunt in brevity, too, ten tracks in a defiant 39 minutes. The music is starker, the metric pieces like the rules of engagement more tightly defined, assigned parts for each player. Assigned but unconfining, letting de Joode move toward traditional jazz tactics (underscored by his natural sound). Van Duynhoven keeps up rolling momentum over or under a form where it won't fit right down the middle. There's room for long arcs of swing grooves too. This trio is one of Martin's best showcases ever. It's Dutch music as Baars characterizes it: rigor without the laughs.

A Saturday in August '96: Uitmarkt weekend. Free stages are set up on the street and in theaters and churches in Amsterdam's center, and for two days folks cram in and make the circuit, to see half-hour samples of music and theater available in the upcoming culture season. Orkest de Volharding plays in front of the royal palace in Dam Square, Amsterdam ground zero. It is not playing on sidewalks as in the old days.

They're on an enormous makeshift stage, high above and set back from the audience, who mill around or sit in distant bleachers. In a concave line stretching the huge stage the musicians look comically tiny and remote.

Their program of danceworks is like reinvented ragtime: jumping up and down on the beat like it was a trampoline, strict syncopations for relief. As one wanders around this large plaza, the sounds mingle, Ivesian spillover into real life. A helicopter zooms quickly by, in the right key, like a passing baritone saxophone. At the far end of the square in front of the Krasnapolsky hotel, a repair worker hammers on metal, in time to the music of course.

Volharding for all the changes it has been through—see the conductor beating out the simple time—still has something of the harmonie about it, the blare of horns still their signature despite piano and (usually) electric bass. Even indoors, their music reflects the outdoor-band principle: it should be forceful, clear, blunt enough to keep its shape as it bounces off the stone facades of the village square, even one this big.

Eric Boeren tells the story of every linguistic sea change he's weathered. He comes from the far south, where the landscape is curious patchwork of Dutch and Belgian territory, tethered to one nation or the other by old land grants. Boeren learned to speak the local dialect. When he began school in Breda 20 miles north, they corrected his speech, taught him normal southern Dutch. When he came north at 17 to study he found out that Amsterdammers would tolerate foreigners' half-assed Dutch but not his southern accent, and he had to learn to talk again. Then he got drafted into Available Jelly and was surrounded by English speakers. Then Jelly went to Italy for awhile and he had to deal with Italian too. Then he went to visit his brother in Peru and played with a whole other bunch of musicians speaking yet another tongue.

—Must have been really alienating to readjust so often.

No, you don't understand, he replied: every one of those linguistic shifts was like opening another door.

Eric Boeren (22 August 1959) joined the student fanfare when he was 10 or 12, because that's where the instruments were. He wanted a trumpet. First he shared a valve trombone with his brother, then both got euphoniums 'cause they were quick readers, then they got asked to play them in the adult band. After he did that awhile he swapped euphonium for E-flat tuba. "You'd have 32-bar rests and then blow one note, then another 25-bar rest till the cadenza. I was too lazy to count out all those bars, so I started listening to how the music was constructed instead." He started hearing how parts fit together and variations were made. When almost out of high school he tried his sister's flugelhorn and decided he liked that better.

Willem Breuker came to town. Eric wrote a review, sent it to the local paper, which published it. Guy who'd organized the concert invited him to ride along to that year's Groningen Jazzmarathon. He heard ICP, Braxton solo, and Butch Morris, whose cornet sound made him want to play one too.

Butch came to Tilburg to do a workshop. It was the first time anyone besides Eric's English teacher had spoken to him in that language. He figured he was the only who didn't know what was going on, and split, flustered.

He came to Amsterdam, to the university, to study sociology. He lived in an attic over a convent; he couldn't cook there but he could practice till 10. It was near the Kroeg and he heard lots of music there and elsewhere. Once he heard duets by Morris on cornet and Nedly on trumpet, which confirmed his preference for the stubbier slightly mellower horn the trumpet had all but replaced in jazz in the mid-'20s. (In Holland it's considered a horn for farmers, but he didn't mind: *Boeren* means "farmers.") Walking down the street one day, Eric found an anonymous wallet with 500 guilders in it. Being a straight arrow he took it to the police station. Nobody claimed it so he got to keep the money, bought a cornet. This ain't New York.

He went to Arnold Dooyeweerd's Tuesday night workshop at the BIMhuis. He didn't play. Dooyeweerd said, next time, you have to play. When he came back six months later, Arnold asked people to play triplets. Most didn't know how, but an old brass-band euphonium player sure did. He became a regular. "Arnold is a very cynical person, gives you a lot of shit, although he'll encourage you when you're shaky. As you get better, he'd talk about density, emptiness, getting attention, shifting from one situation to another, and how to get the theme to come back if you're lost. For me, that was fantastic. He started needling me — if you have an idea, stand up and take a solo, but if you take a solo, be clear about it. I thought, he thinks I'm a bag of shit, but when Huub van Riel asked who from the workshop should get a BIMhuis gig, he recommended me and some punk guys." They all became a quintet, got a few gigs. Eric wrote a few numbers for them — not *stukken*, pieces, but *stukjes*, little pieces. But the band kept polishing a few tunes instead of learning new ones; it died.

In 1982 he went to New York for three months, hoping to study cornet with Butch Morris or Olu Dara. He couldn't find either one. He played one gig, at Soundscape, with English art-rocker Peter Blegvad. Zorn was in the band.

Sean Bergin had heard him, recommended him to Michael Moore when Available Jelly needed a horn player. By now he had finally enrolled in the conservatory. "I never went back there after our first rehearsal." Things snowballed for him through the '80s. He got hired by Maarten Altena — but didn't stay long. Altena didn't like his high notes, and chastised him for playing a standard during a sound check. (Wolter Wierbos: "Replacing Kenny Wheeler isn't easy; even he had had problems with the written notes.") Boeren spent about five years with Jan Cees Tans; Eric brought some pieces to rehearsals but no one could play them.

By 1988 when they made *In Full Flail* Jelly was a drum and bugle corps of sorts: sometimes just drums and three horns. Boeren's playing is confident, notably on one of Misha's treacherous tunes that don't sound like much, the staccato-scaling "Kneebus," plungering with urgency and finesse, and avoiding the trap the melody sets. (Improvise from the melody, Monk-style, you may sound like you're practicing or floundering.) His sound fits Gregg Moore's approximate tailgate trombone; Eric's rawbone style bears traces of some LP heroes, especially rubber-toned bent-note Lester Bowie and Don Cherry with his failed-lip sputters and cavalry charges, but not of Butch's eerie half-valved long tones. (Eric played some trumpet then, because some leaders wanted it, but now plays cornet only.)

His and Gregg's pieces reveal their brass-band roots; Boeren's "Shaggy March" and "Waggery" have top-heavy extroverted swagger, with a hint of Ornette for lagniappe: a hiccup in the seven-beat cycle on the former, akilter turnaround and Prime Time backbeat on the latter. His "Nothing Is the Same Thing Twice" (which they play twice) is even more Coleman-stove, mimicking Ornette's playful little licks that bounce through several keys to nudge the blowing away from the modal flats, and Ornette's hurry-up-and-wait timing.

The first time he had heard Coleman was 1980, one of the old Atlantic records. He was disappointed—it wasn't free, it wasn't playing changes, it was somewhere in the middle. A couple of weeks later he put it on again and it hit him, hard. "For me, the Atlantics have Ornette's most accessible pieces—really stukjes. A few bars, a hint of a direction, but no set key: in five bars you might have two transpositions. There are lots of things to work with and from when you improvise."

Fifteen years later he was an Ornette Coleman expert.

It started, sort of, in 1993 when he and Joost Buis put together a septet to play a set of "unknown Ellington." More like fractured, as Eric describes it: a "C-Jam Blues" where the rhythm section played in one key, Tristan another, Sean another, then they moved into different tempos, then there was a a clarinet solo over the top. ("Very harmolodic: '*In C* Jam Blues'.")

A couple of years later Boeren and Buis were looking for a place to play once a week, in an informal context, something between a workshop and a concert. They wanted to open the BIMhuis on an off night but the overhead was too steep. Boeren was at a CD release party at PH31; one of the guys who booked it said he wouldn't mind having more improvised music. PH31 was one of those beneficial holdovers from A'dam's urban homesteading, a squatters rock-and-roll club in a converted stable in a well-to-do neighborhood near the Vondelpark. PH31 booked skanky rock and reggae dub and beer parties, had a big congenial bar that took up half the little performance room, a few chairs, cheap drinks, friendly staff and regulars who'd lend an ear to the music or not. The place wasn't so loud, but didn't fit the neighborhood, and the threat of demolition hung over it like stale saloon air. By summer '96, it was boarded up.

The year before, however, Tuesdays were improvisation nights, with Boeren, Buis or guitarist Paul Pallesen headlining. The first time Eric played he did his own music and attracted 10 people. Buis played Sun Ra's music and got 20. So Boeren decided to play the music of Ornette Coleman. Both leaders were on to something; before long they often packed the little place. In the spring Eric played the music of one vintage Ornette album a week: he transcribed the pieces himself, to unlock their secrets. They took the summer off—in Holland every venue seems to close up shop for the summer—but opened the BIM's season with two nights of Ornette and 11 players. (It's documented on his BIMhuis CD *Cross Breeding*). When they came back in the fall, his players knew enough Coleman (and Boeren) pieces to be able to rifle through the repertoire at will.

The band usually had de Joode on bass and Vatcher or Wim Janssen on drums, subject to availability. On alto or tenor saxophone he used Michael Moore, Paul Termos, Jan Willem van der Ham, Bergin, Baars and Tobias Delius. They treated the repertory not as sacred text but living organism.

Boeren's initial analysis was right; Coleman didn't play outside, exactly, or inside either, which makes it interesting to hear how people approach it: usually either playing the changes straight or ignoring the form once the melody's out of the way. Boeren looked for another way, not necessarily the one Ornette found.

October 3 his band is Delius, de Joode, and drummer Jeroen Blankert. They play continuous sets; the list for the first calls for "Mapa," "Unknown Artist" and "Feet Music," introduced and bridged by improvisations. While Ornette plays mostly alto, the band seemed most reliable with Delius on tenor. Partly it's just that he's so good, has such a strong way of playing across bar lines and tying remote excursions to the form, partly that his coarse deep textured sound complements the leader's farmer horn. He and Eric would rather do something than nothing, play little figures behind each other's solos to thicken the soup (a Mingus tactic, like the dialogue of bass and trumpet miming speech on "Mapa").

They dance in place. Wilbert rocks the bass. Boeren is small but wiry, always bobbing and weaving when he has the horn to his mouth, as if ducking tomatoes. Toby puts his left foot in front and right behind, shifts his weight back and forth from one to the other, sometimes pivoting on the back foot, speed of feet mirroring that of fingers.

A lot of dialogues unfold tonight. A trumpet-drums duet develops where Eric plays a phrase, picks up a mute from a small arsenal on the floor in front of him, inserts it, plays a short phrase, puts it down and grabs another, repeats, and again—unconscious echo of Misha's *17 strumenti* tuba part 36 years ago—until back-bending work-song rhythm takes on its own seductive momentum.

Wilbert has an amplifier, set so low it either doesn't distort or isn't audible, hard to say which. He can walk fast without letting the tempos dip; tonight he sounds like Scott LaFaro with a fat bottom. Ornette music is about modulations, for one thing: three-chord harmony roaming from one key to another. Wilbert can do that, also delves into rhythmic modulations; setting the pulse, he'll accelerate and slow down like a failing cassette. Tenor and bass improvise a transition from a slow "Beauty Is a Rare Thing" to a faster "Blues Connotation." But just as those two start the latter tune, Boeren cues the drummer into their own duet, at the previous slow tempo, touch of Ives. The further the old hands take it, rhythmically, the further they draw in Blankert, who's never done this gig before. He's game for the game. By the end of the night he's a full player.

When Boeren's Tuesdays resume in December, he's just returned from a project down south, with Available Jelly and Brass Band Ullicoten, his old outfit. Back at the PH, he opens his concept up. One week he has a version of his occasional band Specs: Vatcher, Mary Oliver on violin, bassist Jan Nijdam. Two weeks later he has de Joode, Vatcher and Baars, who plays mostly clarinet.

They played as many of Boeren's stukjes as Ornette's, and you could hear how he'd used Coleman's ideas to trigger his own pieces: ones that modulate through different keys and formal schemes, to increase an improviser's menu of options; one where solo traps and brief horn melodies alternated so often, you weren't sure which was foreground or background, call or response (à la "T. & T."); ones where you pop out of a groove into an out-of-tempo section and then pop back in.

The players keep finding other ways to use Ornette's constant-modulation principle, Vatcher in particular. One of the best things about those nonresonating clicks of his: you can change direction quick. But he likes long transitions too. He'll play slow time with brushes, then gradually speed up to a faster gait where he may or may not stay, but leveling off long enough to clearly establish intermediate tempos before moving on. Boeren shows off his Peruvian or bullfight sound (hear "Compadre Cosco" on Jelly's *Monuments*) one minute, then brays like an ass, coming out of a gliss to land square on the tonic, before just as quickly moving off it, in clean downward steps.

With Baars, there is a nice episode where two guys behind the bar get into a loud conversation. Cornet and clarinet fall into a heated argument that drowns those guys out, makes them self-conscious so they shut up, so deftly done no one took or gave offense.

Boeren's Ornette exemplifies another jazz paradox: the way to p(l)ay tribute to an innovator is by not being a copycat.

November is Joost Buis's month. When he put together what became known as his Famous Astronotes, he hadn't conceived it as a repertory band. "For the first gigs, I had no plan, so I brought some Sun Ra tunes, and the music took off. They're the most fertile pieces you can imagine, improvisation-wise. Before long we had 15, then 30 of his pieces in the book. I transcribed them myself, but the archeology only goes so far. I had to arrange them a little for a different lineup, and guessed at some clusters and chords. I didn't worry about it too much, because his own arrangement of a piece would change over time."

On a good night, the charts sounds very like '50s Ra's pre–space music, Dameron with wrong notes. On a bad night, pandemonium. By autumn, the sound had coalesced around the rhythm section: Cor Fuhler on battered upright piano, Paul Pallesen on electric guitar, de Joode and Alan Purves, whose not-quite jazz, n-q rock, n-q Celtic style and not-quite drumset were somehow perfect. There was also the Australian Felicity Provan on pocket trumpet, Delius on tenor, and altoist Jorrit Dijkstra. Throughout the year they kept polishing those pieces, the better to understand their arcane voicings.

Buis was born the last day of 1966 in Badhoevedorp, near Schipol airport, but grew up in Apeldoorn in the east. Like other Dutch kids he had a year of music theory before picking an instrument. He wanted trombone soon as he saw one, but his arms were too short; he started on euphonium. He joined the post office brass band's junior division, but at around 11 got bumped into the adult band, youngest member by far.

"The benefit of playing in a fanfare so young, is that you immediately learn about reading, blending, timing, tuning. You learn to play together and listen to each other in a natural way, what some musicians miss."

When he was 15 or so, he left to start his own rocky quintet, which eventually became the Big Buis Band, which played some Ellington, and begat the Buis Complex: 20 players including rockers and the local string quartet, playing Ivesian amalgams of everything he could think of. In the early '80s he went to the Arnhem conservatory ("All the brass players there came from brass bands—no one had just studied at home") but got bored before he graduated. He also took workshops with Sean Bergin, Martin van Duynhoven, Peter Bennink, Nico Bunink—"We were impressed, 'cause we were all Mingus fans"—and Vera Vingerhoeds, who drafted him into her quartet.

"The first time I played in the BIMhuis, the entire Willem Breuker Kollektief walked in, heard half a set, and then all walked out. A week later Bernard Hunnekink called, asked me to join them for a seven-week North American tour starting in Mexico. I had never been in an airplane before, now suddenly I'm in Los Angeles."

There were downsides: when saxophonist Peter Barkema was called back to Holland due to a family crisis (hastily replaced by Texas tenor Alex Coke, a friend of Gorter's who later joined the band), Buis got drafted into a comedy routine where portly trumpeter Andy Altenfelder stood on his stomach a second. There were costume changes: a tracksuit; the bare chest, suspenders and bowtie uniform of a Chippendales dancer. "I had one solo a night, wearing a black beret in the French existentialist sketch. Playing the same pieces over and over felt a bit restrictive, like I'd fallen into this giant rolling machine. They'd talk about how they didn't have time to rehearse new pieces anymore. But I learned a lot, and was amazed by their infectious energy. They'd be wrecks beforehand, go crazy on stage, and collapse afterwards."

That was 1988. He played a few gigs after the tour—they split a bill with Sun Ra once—but passed on joining formally. "Boy Raaymakers said, 'The young guys don't want to play with us anymore.'" Gregg Moore replaced him.

Only then did he move to Amsterdam, gradually came into Sean's MOB, Tilburg guitarist Jacques Palinckx's band, Guus Janssen's octet/septet, Amsterdam Drama and other groups. He often subbed for or replaced Wierbos, whom he'd first met years earlier, when he called him for a lesson.

"Wolter said, 'I don't teach, but you can come.' We played together, and he showed me all his tricks. Stupid idiot! But now I seem less and less interested in extended techniques. I always seem to like the old guys better: J. C. Higginbotham, Dicky Wells, and first and always Lawrence Brown."

Here and there he'd been hearing the two Sun Ra tunes in the fat jam-session anthology *The Real Book*; J. C. Tans played "Brainville," and "Calling All Demons" was a standard in Tilburg. When Ra's old records began coming out on CDs from Delmark and Evidence, he started scarfing them up as soon as they appeared.

♫

The PH31 series ends the night after Christmas '95. Paul Pallesen plays English folk ballads with Gunga and Andy Moor and others, and Boeren plays Ornette, with the Trio San Francisco—Delius, Bergin and D'Agaro—and then Sean lingers to use up all his drink tickets. When the Astronotes go on he drags his alto on stage, as far as possible from the leader. The big man wants to play, doesn't glance at the music, cuts across every chart, hogs all solo space, every piece a concerto for Sean. Joost's owlish face gives away nothing. A few tunes along Bergin looks up sheepishly, starts to put his horn down. Buis looks up when he stops, yells: "Yeah Sean! Go!" It's a beautiful moment, even more than the torrent of saxophone that follows. It confirms what the whole PH31 experience seemed to be about: a sense of communal music-making, an informal forum, the fanfare concept updated.

Four months later, Buis and Boeren resurfaced across town at the community center Zaal 100, in the west: different room, different faces in the house, some different musicians, same good feel.

In the fall of '96, Roswell Rudd came to Holland for a couple of weeks, and a few gigs with the Ab Baars trio. His style has a gutbucket directness, but Ab's abstruse pieces didn't faze him; it was a real quartet. This was Roswell's first time in Holland in 14 years, and everyone made a proper fuss over him. It put him in the mood to sit in — at the Engel, with Dulfer at the Alto, and two nights at Zaal 100.

He and Joost hit it off, hung out. "I think I learned more that week, standing next to Roswell when he took a solo, than in six years at the conservatory." For the next few months Buis favored the plunger heavily, played a lot of very Ruddy solos. (His slippery voicelike solo on "Jetty," from his next recording — Gene Carl's *Below Paradise*, ballet music — is souvenir of his infatuation with Roswellisms.) Then, quickly, it seemed, he digested the lump, found his own center again, but that center wasn't in the same place anymore. Hearing Rudd up close changed him more than a year studying Sun Ra. In an oral tradition, nothing works like personal contact.

Part III
Composers

Chapter Eleven

Eight to the Bar

The singer Greetje Bijma has a phonographic memory: can replicate any sound she hears, and often does. Improvising, this has advantages and disadvantages. A paradox of free improvisation is that some folks saddle it with (usually unspoken) bylaws, one of which is that you don't stop what you're doing to imitate somebody else. That's a fledgling improviser's cliche, in fact, but if you have an ear as good as hers, you can get away with it. She samples her memories of music. Bijma can do an eerie imitation of Billie Holiday in decline: the tight vibrato, choked timbre, sometimes slack articulation, and the incisive timing that never deserted her even when her voice did. Other singers imitate wah-wah brass players (who in turn are echoing voices: in jazz voices and instruments are bound in an endless loop of mutual influence). Bijma is so precise you can hear she's not just the plunger mute but also the pixie mute stuck in the bell behind the plunger: Tricky Sam Nanton, not Al Grey.

In 1980 she was inadvertently discovered by Wolter Wierbos and Harry de Wit during a gig in Friesland up north. Wierbos: "We heard these strange noises coming from someone in the audience. Greetje liked the music so much she wanted to participate, but she was too shy to come on stage."

De Wit sent her to workshop leader Alan Laurillard, who brought her into the Groningen free-funk scene. She was in his Noodband, then put together her own group using some of the same musicians, Alan included. Her Laurillard-directed 1990 CD *Tales of a Voice* shows how wide she ranges: pidgin highlife, an Yma Sumac homage, plungering, performance art or radio plays on fast-forward, and "Haden," where she nods to Charlie's "Song for Che" and restages the Spanish Civil War.

In 1990 she was the first woman to win the Boy Edgar, but she's never lived in Amsterdam and never really connected with the scene there. She did form a trio with Americans she met at the '91 October Meeting, pianist Marilyn Crispell and bassist Mark Dresser, but there her imitative gift seemed an obstacle. She did better reuniting with Laurillard in the Up There Trio with organist Klaas Hoek; they like to play in old churches, acoustics and atmosphere she can respond to.

Sometime in the late '80s Louis Andriessen came up to her after a gig in Amsterdam, paid her some compliments. Later they met again in the bar at the Frascati theater.

"She said, 'Would you help me, because I need more structure in what I'm doing.' Then I started laughing very loudly, and said, 'Greetje you don't need any composers, that could be painful, and anyway I'm absolutely the last person you should ask. But why shouldn't we play together?'

"Greetje is the only one I really like to play with, because I have no idea what she'll do next. I may try to get her into the Viennese cabaret singer, or into the birds, or whatever. There are thousands of persons or things inside her, 500 of which I don't know yet. Why I like it is, I don't have to develop a style, not at all. I can swim and flare out into all these musical worlds I like. That has a superficial aspect. But since music is a game, I think, I don't care anymore about high ideological ideas about improvisation. Enough for me that the music is improvised. You should be able to move in any direction you want."

They made a CD together, *Nadir & Zenit*, 1992, working off texts by Dutch poet Sybren Polet. It didn't quite come off, Louis messing with sampled voices as well as playing piano. This is a live not studio act, in any case: they thrive on distractions.

On stage, mostly he throws out ideas and she takes them or not. When it works, it's a humming machine: he cranks out the form, she the content. When it doesn't, you get an entertaining disaster. One way she can get him off an idea he insists on is imitate it derisively: is that all you can come up with?

As Andriessen says, he likes the voice and piano combination for its broad frame of reference—one can bounce, say, from Schubert to Stephen Foster to Bessie Smith to a Brill-Building run-through. He paints the scenery and she steps into it. As in many of his big compositions he reels out postminimal weave by the yard; a guy who writes like he does knows how to vamp. He can pick up on her ideas damn quick too. When she goes into syncopated staccato double time, a ragtime chicken, his left hand is right on it. And he knows when to leave her alone in the spotlight: a milkmaid routine where she echoes her own yodel, then walks offstage into the house and starts playing with the room echo, singing long glisses whose pitches clash with themselves on the rebound. Or she'll invent some fake ethnic music with its own specifics: Tibetan split tones whose overtones slide around, coming close to some new kind of yodel.

Saturday evening in July, rain holding off, outdoor stage in the Vondelpark, just down the path from a gazebo where he'd played long ago with Volharding. He sits down, plays a nyah-nyah motif a couple of times, but she passes. They peek at each other around the piano lid, cute couple: red-faced doughboy, jeans and cowboy boots, easy moving; white raincoat, skittish, grimaces and splay-fingered gestures, Piaf of the Valkyries.

Louis lays low till she's engaged, slides into his familiar boogie mechanique, eight-to-the-bar in a holding pattern, chord changes few and far between (very close to the boogie section he improvised for his major opus *De Stijl*). Now she gets back to the nyah-nyah he laid on her four minutes ago—no more than a courtesy call, then she's off again. The boogie turns into a familiar cow cow blues. As accompanist he knows his limitations. Andriessen plays composer's piano, feeds her four-square chords on time when she's in ballad mode (leading her, or letting the shape of her melody lead his harmonies), creeps into hypnotic backgrounds when she wails, props her up when she falters.

There are multiple rows of folding chairs out front, but the high stage is open on three sides. A few kids sit on its lip, far stage left. Roving the ring, mic in hand, she comes over and sings to the tots once in awhile. There's a classic heckling drunk in the second row. After a more than generous grace period, she works his babble into her line, without venom. She riffs on: vamps it's time to vacate, audience howls, droning plane overhead, wind rustling trees, kids paying no mind. "Listen to the birds," she sings in English—she also passes from Dutch into French, then—"Oh this is too much for me, I see too many things"—just before ending the first short set.

They play only a few times a year, and never rehearse, but like other folks who improvise together repeatedly, they have certain areas they revisit. The main one is the blues; Louis can do a credible rippling-arpeggio New Orleans R&B piano in the manner of Huey Smith (a name he didn't know when asked). On this set she sings a slowish blues, answering her own phrases with mock trombone obbligati, no mute. Louis goes into a heavy two-beat, more cabaret song than classic Bessie, then works his way back toward blues chords and fills. By now she's added a growl and a plunger to her tromboning. The heckler, drinking from his brown bag, is laughing, digging it, won over. She ends the set wailing a fraction of a blues chorus, "I had a fat bottom but it was far too small." He jumps up from the piano and gives her a squeeze. They do enjoy themselves.

This isn't Andre Previn playing "Get Me to the Church on Time." More like a two-person Inclusive Concert. Or Eeko the parrot and Misha.

♫

"In 1952 when I was young, and not yet a musician, Jurriaan Andriessen my brother, a good composer, came back from a two-year stay in New York, and brought a lot of 78s home with him. We had to buy a new record player. He came back with the Kentons, and Les Paul and Mary Ford, Nat King Cole, hundreds of them. Of all the stuff he brought back I remember very well a Kenton with Laurindo Almeida on guitar, strange experiments, and 'City of Glass' by Robert Graettinger. I must say, to this day I think he's an incredible, miraculous, strange composer, who has in a way been very important for me.

"The large block chords I write for brass are my interpretation of the organ I heard my father play in church. I think I found my way into music by moving this organ sound onto five trumpets and five trombones. At that time classical musicians didn't improvise in public, except for organists, Protestant or Catholic. It was a long tradition. There's a famous organ concours in Haarlem every year, where besides playing Bach and all that you're supposed to do an improvisation on a given theme. But I don't see any connection with the development of modern improvised music. My father had a certain sympathy for Gershwin and said good things about Ellington, but I must say in the time before the liberation there was almost no contact with American culture at all in Holland, and in general he found the culture vulgar. He's of that generation. He was from 1892.

"I had a cousin my age, and we played four hands and, when we had the opportunity, on two pianos. Boogie-woogies already ourself, when we were 14, 13, 15. The big example for me was a double LP of Pete Johnson and Albert Ammons. I must have bought that with my first pocket money, in the early '50s. Much later I heard the more original forms of boogie-woogie like Jimmy Yancey, and Pinetop Smith, who is my favorite now. But Yancey was already taking out all the notes which would later become the vulgar notes in the boogie-woogie piano sound."

(In the early '70s Andriessen picked up another Ammons-Johnson record. The flipside was his introduction to Yancey. He liked it immediately—reductive, as he says, a sort of boogie-woogie Monk—and called Misha: Now I've heard a boogie-woogie piano player. Misha: Give me three seconds to guess: "Yancey.")

"Yancey I used later as three motives, three starts of compositions, for a piece I wrote for De Volharding. That piece is the closest I've come to jazz in my composing. Because I think basically jazz and composition don't have very much to do with each other. But then in my scores you find not 'piano' but the musician's name, as Willem Breuker does. In that sense I think there's no difference with Duke Ellington at all."

—In your *Hoketus* there are alternations and swing-band section riffs, call and response.

"Antiphonal structure it's called in classical history. But it's true there is a kind of dialogue because finally the coda goes into a sort of melody, leans highly upon pop and jazz music I think. The pitches, the kind of melody—there are riffs, there are riffs, ja."

—One difficulty in looking for jazz influences on Dutch composing is assessing where certain musical strains come from, and which analogs are meaningful.

"That's exactly what you should explain to us."

—Sometimes it's useful to know a composers' intention.

"I don't have intentions, neither ideological nor any other. Most composers don't, I think. The basic reason you deal with certain musical material is because you love it, because it's part of your emotion and your consciousness. Among other reasons."

—So if I ask if the pulsing 8th notes in so much modern Dutch music is descended from boogie-woogie piano. . . .

"Well I think that pulse music mostly comes from my bad influence. I got it partly from boogie-woogie—or from jazz in general—and partly from Bach, who was the guru at home, and is guru still nowadays. Every morning I start out by playing Bach, every time.

"The return of the pulse, the diatonic, modal material, is partly the influence of American culture in Europe, which I esteem as by far the most important influence in the development of the musical language since the Second World War, on all levels. Not only, to be politically correct, the Afro-American side of it, but also the strange Cage side. That was very important for me. And I was always more interested than Misha and the others in the arranging side, the large harmonies. That was always my big thing. Big band culture."

When Andriessen was rehearsing his *De Staat* (1973–76) in Warsaw '77, he told the musicians, don't think Bruckner or Mahler, think Kenton or Basie. Not that the majestic long-note or crotchety-staccato horn writing suggests that association itself. Looking back in a '90s interview: "Now it seems that my music, ever since *De Staat*, needs an articulation that is more in touch with jazz than with classical training."

As a jazz fan Louis has always been a tiny bit square. Misha digs Monk and Nichols; Andriessen turns Berio on to the Swingle Singers. He blurs over some fine points of jazz history—has written about boogie-woogie as a simplification of ragtime, but he's confusing two piano traditions. Ragtime turned into slick New York stride piano; boogie-woogie is an independent southern blues style. But of course you can misunderstand some aspects and still profitably mine that music.

He wrote *On Jimmy Yancey* in 1973. The first Volharding version was recorded in concert the next year. The piece is in two movements, allegro and adagio. Louis plays piano, and solves the virtuosity problem—he can play but he's no Meade Lux Lewis—by slowing the pace to a manageable medium gait; it's not *so* allegro. In the first, bits of Yancey turn up whole from piano, or are transferred to Breuker's sometimes sputtery alto, or harmonized by the horns, sometimes used in opposing brass and reed sections, very jazzy. Less jazzy are the frequent interruptions of the rhythmic momentum that boogie pianists considered inviolate—even if Louis seems intent on leaving it just for the pleasure of returning, à la Bennink. A pet boogie bass figure—a fifth and a sixth of the chord humping up and down in eighth-note rhythm—is the simplest and most exploited motif.

The second movement seems to occur in slow motion, underwater: the piano plays a boogie bass figure, softly, as (sloppily massed) horns play a majestic long-note line, prefiguring much Louis music to come, *De Staat* and *De Stijl* included. Volharding's notorious inexactitude serves the music well. Think of it as a nod to the itinerant boogieist's working life, dealing with one detuned gap-toothed logging-camp piano after another. (The pianist in the itinerant Volharding, which used to bring its own upright box along when necessary, knew that experience well enough.) The only thing that sounds vaguely patronizing is the Yancey turnaround that ends each section—sounds a shade too corny. But it's a good piece, his best jazz adaptation.

In 1978 he told interviewer Dick Witts *Yancey* is a sort of fake travesty—a "mistakes" piece. "I start quoting, it does not go well, it doesn't work, let's say. Then I start my first homage in a more or less fast tempo. That stops also. Then I do it again, more slow, more serious, in another time. I feel this is a transformation of a previous part. Then the second movement, a transformation of that, even slower." Boogie-woogie submits to the laws of entropy.

De Volharding's remake, from their 1992 CD retrospective *Trajekten*, is a handy indicator of the orchestra's transformation. The alto saxophone's slightly exaggerated vibrato comes off as a studied recreation of early jazz, self-conscious in a way the blissfully loose original wasn't. The only things that sound better are those corny tags, which benefit from greater alienation from the source. But the piano on the adagio movement is far more tasteful, and lacking juice—like hearing someone who's worked hard to lose their downhome accent. Louis played it better, truer.

(Flash-forward: In 1991 he wrote the string quartet *Facing Death* for Kronos, and rearranged it at the request of the Aurelia Saxophone Quartet. It's more or less an attempt to pay tribute to Charlie Parker in much the same way, beginning with quoted Parker themes and then moving on to variations, which however have little if anything to do with bebop phrasing, timing or harmonic extensions. In either version it doesn't quite come off.)

His other pertinent Volharding piece is *Workers Union*, from 1975. Jazz reactionaries put down Anthony Braxton by claiming his (jazz) compositions sound like modern concert music, but they never cite an example, presumably because they're bluffing. *Workers Union*—the '82 Volharding recording at least—comes as close to Braxton as any formal composition I know, via independent use of a method he also employs. Andriessen refers to it as "half-composed, half-improvised." The score indicates a general melodic contour, the phrasing and the time values, but not actual notes: there are stems and bar lines, and groups of notes, but pitches are indicated only in terms of where they stand relative to the middle of the instrument's range. The composer submits a melodic contour for the band's interpretation, in thick harmolodic harmony. The resulting sound depends on instrumentation: on where the middle of an instrument's range is. Variety is built in; as the orchestra moves through various higher- or lower-register passages, different instruments cut through with greater or lesser clarity, suggesting an alternation of voices.

The momentum is hectic and headlong, the line serrated, full of shifting syncopations. Andriessen cautions the players to avoid scales, aim for dissonance and chromaticism, and play like they really mean it. (It is also, the composer says, an exploration of how jazz and classical players phrase differently, but in a way so is every early Volharding performance: "Volharding had more jazzy timing than you'd get with conservatory students.") With the saxes on the LP version especially—Bob Driessen, Ab Baars, Mariëtte Rouppe van der Voort—it can sound very like one of Braxton's fast asymmetrical pulse tracks. (Footnote: "One of my favorite later jazz recordings, where I think the combination of improvising and composing—which means thinking and organizing counterpoint—is on a very high level, is this long live recording I heard long ago by Anthony Braxton and George Lewis. Fantastic duo." No smoking gun here: The duo made the LP *Elements of surprise* for the Moers label in 1976.)

As you'd expect from a composer who uses the words BANG BANG BANG to describe some of his own music, *Workers Union* is not a subtle piece. (It also taps into Louis's Kenton side: Artistry in Overkill.) It's intended to represent workers of diverse views pulling together, and as far as that (and performers' creative input) goes, harks back to his *De Volharding*, where one section could leap into another's part, as long as each section showed solidarity by sticking together. But *Volharding*'s relentless tuttis, with no opportunities to lay out and catch one's breath, are a little like denying your workers a coffee break, making them sit at the stamping machine ten hours a day.

Volharding's recording of *Workers Union* is similarly dystopian, musicians subordinated to the process of manufacture. The Ricciotti Ensemble's live 1991 version is fuzzier, less clear than Volharding's, and less good on that score, but has amazing spirit, especially in the explosive final minutes: the workers throw off the shackles.

An entirely different false-unison piece from the same period, *Melodie* (1972–74), is no kin of jazz, but double cousin to Dutch improvised music. It is as anecdotal as any piece that ever came from the land of anecdotal music. It is Breuker's can't-play solo, soul of sarcasm, reborn, purified, as a thing of innocent beauty: Louis's Catholicism showing.

As he's told it, it began with an eavesdrop: hearing an instrument next door he couldn't identify, pale brittle high-register sound. Then he realized it was in fact two instruments: a mother giving her son a recorder lesson, doubling his notes on piano as he groped his way through a baroque sonata. Louis decided to replicate that sound, with the same instrumentation. Most of the piece is in slow unison, but unison with mistakes and capricious embellishments: "a piece without repetition which is always the same."

It is a piece, then, in which the recorder player and the pianist (Frans Brüggen and Louis on the Attaca recording) play the roles of stumbling student and occasionally impatient coach—for the pianist is sometimes moved to stark embellishments, swipes at the keys, ad libbed pickup notes. At times their interplay approaches mutual goading, as when recorder's defiantly long final note is one-upped by gratuitous piano recap. It is very beautiful, in its unblinkingly spare and simple way, with its long pauses and chaste unisons and the false unisons that result from the recorder student's rhythmic hesitations and misread accidentals.

But *Melodie* is also a bit of a cheat, as Louis departs here and there from his stated model. There are moments when the blockflutist tosses off some shakuhachi or slide-whistle bent notes a novice wouldn't conceive or execute. Composer David Dramm in his published analysis goes further, hears in one chord a third party on the set, Andriessen himself in a Hitchcock walk-on: "the only person present who could have thought of such a chord." (Dramm, a friend and protege of Louis's, also comments: "Draping the banal in elegance, this is the Louis Andriessen whose esthetic was shaped by his friend and mentor Misha Mengelberg, the prince of Dutch high mannerism.") To me that chord sounds consistent with the impatient teacher's character, a lash out (which sounds random, but hardly lays under the fingers) prompted by a frustration one may gauge from the 14 increasingly insistent A naturals hammered out before the chord is struck—and the following silence, while the teacher/pianist regains composure. Misha might like its obstinate length (26 minutes), especially with a couple of false endings.

Often recorder and piano strike out a whole step apart. The interval of a major second is a favorite of Louis's—he recalls writing a piece relying on them when he was 16, and his 1979 piece for augmented wind ensemble, *Mausoleum*, is built entirely on major seconds, down to the text sung by two lockstep voices consistently separated by a whole tone. The interval is as important to him as the minor second to Monk. (*Volharding* relies heavily on both major and minor seconds.) The whole-step interval is more stable, cleaner, tidier, finally more optimistic than Monk's perpetual quasi-gaffe. The difference of a half-step between minor second and major second makes all the difference. It's Louis leap.

Melodie is unlike any other piece of his, but looking back, it's a key link between disparate movements, Breuker's mistakes and Maarten Altena's later penchants for recorder and for loose unisons.

—Any observation about the great love of mistakes in Dutch improvising?

"It comes from Stravinsky. I advise you to read *The Apollonian Clockwork* where everything is explained. In the book we quote Monk—it may be apocryphal—who is unhappy after a gig. 'What's the problem?' 'I played the wrong wrong notes tonight.'"

True or false—likely the latter—that anecdote is a favorite bon mot.

The Apollonian Clockwork is a rambling, improvisatory 1983 book by Andriessen and critic Elmer Schönberger subtitled "On Stravinsky." (Jeff Hamburg's English translation was issued in 1989.) Stravinsky is definitely a source for some modern Dutch music, notably Altena's, but even if it's only a matter of unconscious parallels, the authors pinpoint many: pieces involving role-play (the septet in *L'Histoire du Soldat* is "not a village orchestra, but seven musicians with a diploma from the conservatory who imitate a village orchestra"), the deliberately clumsy orchestration of "Song of the Volga Boatmen" and mistimed repetition of riffs in *Danses Concertantes.* They also duly note such role-play can be traced to earlier composers like Tchaikovsky, and quote Prokofiev on Stravinsky's piano sonata: "Bach but with pockmarks." (The idea that composers deliberately mangle the ideas of their predecessors is a favorite of Louis's. From our interview: "I tell my students how even the most complex 12-tone or chromatic music is basically Wagner with a lot of wrong notes.") The authors liken Stravinsky's "corrections" of Pergolesi in *Pulcinella* to Duchamp's mustachioed Mona Lisa.

In sum, Stravinsky's influence "is the type of influence inspired by misunderstanding, the deliberate distortion, the good wrong conclusion."

So give Igor some credit for inspiring Dutch anecdotal compositions—we will encounter many more beyond this point—but remember too what J. Bernlef said about Ives's clashing orchestras and written-in mistakes: "If it happens in real life, why not in art?" No composer is more anecdotal than Ives.

The danger in assessing anecdotal pieces—pieces, defined for the moment, as onomatopoetic, or describing musical situations, or in which musicians perform in character—is that it's easy to overemphasize them because they're easy to write (or read) about. Case in point, the amount of space in the Guus Janssen literature devoted to "Brake," a fully notated piano solo which mimics a bad pianist, who goes back over a misfingered passage, a little more slowly, or whose hands churn chords madly in precarious time. It's worth bringing up here because it was written in 1974, the year Andriessen finished *Melodie,* and Breuker was in the thick of his botched-solo routines. Clearly something was in the air.

As is often the case, Misha Mengelberg wrote the anecdotal piece to beat: "Het groeit, het bloeit" (It grows, it blossoms) a piece about metaphors for music: as he plays the keys mechanical flowers bloom from inside the piano. A computer program triggers the devices when a certain note is struck a certain number of times. He hammers one key awhile to bring on the big floral finish, to the sound of piano and ratchet wheels.

In 1976, before he left Volharding, Andriessen started another band he played in at first (and whose life drifts through *The Apollonian Clockwork*): Hoketus. It grew out of a minimalism workshop he was teaching at the Hague conservatory.

"The students didn't like minimal music, because of what I called 'TV advertisement association.' I told them this music had a rigid and radical root, and started teaching them *In C,* La Monte Young, all kinds of other important minimal techniques, from Polynesia. There were also two folk musicians, who played South American Indian panpipes.

"We had rehearsed *In C*, and to avoid this TV-advertising association, we played it BANG BANG BANG BANG BANG, and it became something. We had a very clear idea of what we liked and didn't like."

Hocket techniques were Hoketus's other major subject. The band was a double sextet: panpipes, saxophones, pianos, electric pianos, electric basses, drums, all two by two. As with Volharding, the founding composer's style set the band's tone (although, commentators loved to stress, Hoketus had no political agenda), and Louis tended to group the instruments 6 by 2 or 2 by 6. Other composers who wrote for them found that pieces which broke with the formula quickly vanished from the band's book.

—Was Ornette Coleman's Double Quartet an influence?

"I was never a big Ornette Coleman fan, I have no idea why."

—Did you treat hocketing as a game, musical table tennis?

"No, I can't remember anything like that sort of lightness. Hoketus had this rigidity which you find very clearly in Peter van Bergen and Huib Emmer, they're really the kids from Hoketus I'd say." Other members included saxophonists Mariëtte Rouppe van der Voort and Jan Willem van der Ham and drummer Paul Koek.

The band's zero hour is Andriessen's *Hoketus*, Hocket 101: clinging to static clanging, stereo-demonstration ping-pong, staccato so extreme Volharding sounds legato. (Volharding: jazz :: Hoketus: rock. Think Louis, think saxophones and bass guitars.) Its beginning flashes back to Eddy Christiani slashing out the first chords of "Hilversum Express." It builds (too) gradually from an all but inert start, every move predictable, a tedious joke told by a slow talker. (This is the Louis who inspires lesser composers to write tedious music that takes forever to get going.) Loud, underpowered, slow to attain cruising speed, *Hoketus* is a VW bus, but there's a payoff. The antiphonal pattern gradually fills in, becomes more complex, until the figure emerges from the carpet in Basie/Nelson Riddle brass punches. Rhythm and cross-rhythm ignite in the blasting syncopations of that BANG BANG BANG music par excellence, boogie-woogie. It's another abstracted sequel to *Yancey*, with its own echoes of train-track clickclack. Like *Workers Union* it confirms Louis (like Yancey) as a late industrial-age composer: loom worker.

Such obviousness would drive Mengelberg crazy. After some debate Hoketus played his early '80s commission *Rokus de veldmuis* (Rokus the Fieldmouse) just once—Hoketus endlessly arguing repertoire the way Volharding did politics, no pleasure without penance in Louis's Catholic universe. It observed the hocketing and paired-instrument guidelines but subverted the BANG BANG spirit from the first bar. Hoppity-bunny melodies for panpipes or saxophones are answered by smile-faced keyboard chords, some cute syncopations in the bass, one-finger Fender Rhodes noodling, all so tonal your teeth ache. If pop inspires Hoketus, Misha gives them bubblegum, a Hoketus tune that sticks in your ear. 'Cause it's not so dumb it didn't hold Misha's attention. For the man who likes works full of untied shoelaces, it's uncommonly well-stitched—craftsmanship you can't get from a drill press.

In the first part, breakdowns into subgroups, transformations of the material into more rarefied form, bring the material to life—like improvisation, not deconstruction.

Rokus's second section is a payoff bigger than *Hoketus*'s finale; a kicker triple fugue in a bouncy 8 more pattycake than Bach or boogie, one instrumental group echoing another, four bars apart. It was nicely played too, on that one performance, broadcast but never released. An unspoken part of the Hoketus agenda was precision. (Breuker: Volharding :: Hoketus: Peter van Bergen. We'll get to him later.)

Before Hoketus broke up there was a joint project with De Volharding and singers for the 1985 Holland Festival, called Kaalslag (Demolition). For that project Andriessen wrote *De Stijl*, based on Mondrian's 1927's "Composition with Red, Yellow and Blue" in the Stedelijk's collection. Louis schematized the painting to develop his floor plan. The choice of subject is ideal for him: big blocks of primary color, internally uniform, clearly structured, carefully proportioned, squared corners. Mondrian was a jazz fan, painted to boogie-woogie in his Paris studio. *De Stijl* is way beyond *Yancey* in terms of dealing with that source. (Andriessen prefers the 1994 Nonesuch version; the timings that follow are keyed to it.) There is a boogie section 15 minutes into that 25-minute version, rolling low under a spoken excerpt from a friend's memoir. That section is prefigured from 9:00 minutes on, by grumbling bass-register piano over electric bass cross-rhythms, like a concussive's double vision of Yancey, boogie's latticework slowly coming into focus.

Andriessen has said the boogie section was improvised. "Almost all composing comes out of playing in my case. I improvise a lot." As noted earlier, he's played boogie very much like it with Bijma; it's more revealing of his jazz conception than any other vignette in his writing. It avoids blues changes for greater harmonic stasis, thus chalkboarding boogie-woogie as one source for minimalism. He characterizes the 24-bar "disco bass" line (his not so accurate term) that acts as its main theme as "a contemporary reinterpretation of boogie-woogie." The humping whole-tone interval that appears briefly at 1:32 may be taken as a nod to Yancey, but the bass line itself is more electric-bassistic than pianistic. It is enough to suggest that Louis's boogie/jazz influence, like minimalism's, descended more through R&B than bebop. That bass line begins (almost), underpins, and is varied through much of the piece, sometimes with piano shadowing less than half a beat behind for a double-vision effect. Louis makes much of digging Janet Jackson, but this staggered, hesitant line is disco or boogie with that wooden-shoe timing he diagnosed in Breuker.

There is a strong layering effect in many of Andriessen's works, this one included. Within half a minute of the piece's opening that bass line has begin to sink under strata of racing saxophones, fanfare brass and operatic voices (singing unintelligible texts by Mondrian's favorite mystical mathematician). Louis characterizes his music as homophonic, not contrapuntal. Contrapuntal in the strictest sense it isn't, nor homophonic either, but rather like boogie-woogie—always different and always the same—it is a little of both. (Like boogie, it's harmonically partial to what the composer describes as "triads with a dominant seventhish character coupled with a resolution.") *De Stijl*'s layering can be so intense, he gets to throw more of his favorite ingredients into the pot than in any other single work, perhaps. It's all here: huge chords from imperial brass or pumping saxes, four voices that sound like an apocalyptic choir, pounding tuned drums out of rock more than jazz. You can hear Bach, boogie, Riley and Breuker at the same time. (Try the passage beginning at 9:44: crisscrossing saxes, electric guitar and barrelhouse piano bass, counterpointed.) If you're looking for masterworks, this is one of Louis's, not least for his good instincts for knowing how much pressure or attention a motif will bear. He gets the proportions right.

When Louis taught a graduate composition workshop at Yale in the late '80s, the first thing he played his students to introduce them to Dutch musical culture was Misha and Eeko the parrot. To introduce members of the music department to his own music, he played them *Melodie.*

Two other pieces on that Kaalslag concert reveal much about musical influences on Dutch concert life by 1985. Willem van Manen told journalist Roland de Beer his *Mikrotoop* nods to Lennie Tristano—which it does, incidentally more than structurally, with its long snaky lines on top. Cees van Zeeland said his *Qua Kaalslag* attempts a synthesis of Messiaen and Captain Beefheart, but good luck finding the latter at least.

A decade later composer Martijn Padding could say, "For me, there are two great composers, Beethoven and Monk," and go on about Monk's impacted anti-harmonies, as if unaware Misha had parsed all this out 30 years earlier. (The declared Monkisms in Padding's "Blend" for piano, however, amount to pastiche: a hint of "Reflections," hesitant congested chords. And the Monk references are fleeting at best on his 1995 orchestra piece that sparked the above quote, *Scharf Abreissen.*) Gilius van Bergeijk's 1994–96 *Demontage* is a set of variations on Handel and Monk; it uses minor seconds for deconstructive purposes in the Handel section, then as construction material in the Monk section, where allusions to specific Monk tunes are fleeting. But then van Bergeijk can deconstruct and sabotage classics with more wicked wit than anyone.

Werner Herbers, veteran of "Hello! Windyboys" and *Reconstructie,* and Concertgebouw Orchestra oboist, founded the Ebony Band in 1990. Their first CD was of Spanish Civil War songs, but the band was named for Stravinsky's "Ebony Concerto," written for Woody Herman, and it wasn't long before Ebony began featuring the works of overlooked jazz composers and arrangers, beginning with Kentonians. Their second CD *City of Glass* has several long and short works and arrangements from the '40s and '50s by the reclusive maverick Bob (upgraded to Robert F.) Graettinger, and two Pete Rugolo pieces also written for Kenton. There was a little Dutch pride in the Graettinger revival; in 1955, Dutch critic Paul Lansink had lavishly praised "City of Glass," when many found its intricacies and high-flown rhetoric of jazz + strings indigestible: "Here the boundaries of music . . . are transcended with real genius."

Thanks to Herbers (and implicitly, Andriessen) there is a Kenton strain in Dutch concert music far more than in Dutch improvising, Monk's trinkle-tinkle vs. BANG BANG BANG.

In the 1995–96 concert season the big fad was combining diverse or disparate groups: Surinam Music Ensemble with a classical percussion group, Volharding with the Podium Trio, Ebony Band and Janssen Glerum Janssen. *Grensverleggers* it was called: Trailblazers. Ebony with Guus Janssen on piano played one Bill Russo, one George Russell, and five Johnny Carisi compositions. For the Holland Festival in June

Ebony did an evening of George Handy charts cut with a little Claude Thornhill. On the concert with Janssen, Ebony sounded out of its depth, didn't blend as well as those '50s New York studio guys who played on cool Carisi and Russell records, or as well as the Kenton band. (Ebony is a real reader's unit—orchestra masquerading as band.) On the Handy program they sounded much better with Martin van Duynhoven drafted to play traps. Playing Graettinger again months later, they sounded even better with Ernst Glerum also added.

Herbers' persistence has injected third-stream composers into Dutch concert life— not that anyone uses that term, even with Gunther Schuller coming over to conduct Ebony, and also the Dutch Jazz Orchestra doing Strayhorn, either one with fair success. By the mid-'90s jazz was part of the orchestral repertoire far more in Holland than it's ever been in the States. In 1996 the Ricciotti Ensemble promoted one program as "From Mozart to Monk."

Theo Loevendie's career stayed on two tracks. He became established as a legit composer in the 1970s, same period he was playing with Hans Dulfer. By '70s' end he had a trio with Guus Janssen and Martin van Duynhoven; his Consort had up-and-comers like Janssen, Reijseger, and briefly, Sean Bergin. His first post-Dulfer jazz LP was the 1985 *Theo Loevendie Kwintet* (VARAJAZZ), with Baars and Wierbos. Bassist Arnold Dooyeweerd had Arjen Gorter's hotdog attitude and precise articulation and his timing fits van Duynhoven. But the Turkish numbers without prescribed chords default into modal jams where Baars sounds understimulated. Ab's best showings have good changes, Brown and Da Sylva's "Sonny Boy," tenor happily lachrymose, and "B.E." for Boy Edgar, jocular Loevendie tune with a stutter, one bar which repeats verbatim several times, as if a musician reading through were trying to get it right. (Shades of "Brake.") Loevendie plays piano on both.

Wierbos, self-starter, storms the modal plains of "Camel Ride" and "Commewijne." (Loevendie identifies the latter as a typical Dutch chorale, like you'd find in Surinam; sounds a bit South African, reminder of Afrikaaners' Dutch roots.) Far behind the boss's alto on "Dam Square," the marching band vets moan a wobbly chorale like a distant fanfare, Ivesian echo of the bands Theo followed as a kid.

(It would be a decade before Loevendie made another record as improviser. In 1995 he, Janssen and van Duynhoven joined İhsan Özgen, who plays a Turkish three-string fiddle, for a few gigs jamming on Turkish themes and Loevendie tunes. The resulting CD was no more than a paranthetical for the Netherlanders.)

One sign of how little Loevendie kept up with jazz: Only after he composed his 1985 opera *Naima* did he learn there was another piece with that name. In the '90s he'd pick up a saxophone once in a while, but he obviously wasn't keeping his chops up.

Jazz still comes out in his solo piano works, distant echoes of his youthful boogies. From the barely audible bass notes it opens with, the 1976 "Strides" identifies itself as Concert Music: diffuse rhythm, radical contrasts in dynamics, sprays of treble notes, clusters. Two-thirds through, stride patterns coalesce, only to dissolve into separate bass and treble lines whose mutual disintegration ends it. All the ingredients of the first half (including a repeating high note used like a telegraph key) are also found in early jazz piano, boogie and stride. That insight makes you hear everything in a new light, makes you uncertain what his/your/its frame of reference is. One may hear some early Conlon Nancarrow player piano pieces—where boogie materials are stretched into another realm—as its precursors too. Loevendie takes his ingredients out of the box, slowly assembles them into something recognizable, then disassembles it: James P. in *Legoland*. In Loevendie's 1985 sequel, the piano solo "Walk," hints of blues and stride and walking bass coalesce and dissolve throughout, jazz traces wafting slowly across its surface, gradually coming to the fore.

Classical music derived from jazz materials: In the late '70s he began articulating a compositional method he'd been using intuitively, "curved-based architecture." Grossly oversimplified, it works something like this. Start with a short melodic fragment, and picture a zigzag line connecting its pitches. That line—the curve, or melodic contour—can be expanded or contracted at will, vertically or horizontally, to make intervals in the line greater or smaller, time values ditto, but in proportion, to preserve the (hopefully audible, albeit distorted) shape of the original. (He came to permit retrogrades and inversions also.) A handful of such forms is enough to develop an entire composition. The harmony may be derived from the notes in a particular variant—harmony, as in his jazz music, of less concern than rhythm.

Unlike serialists, he does not permit transposing pitches into different octaves, as that wreaks havoc with the curve. There are many other refinements and restricting factors we won't go into, but as system it's very unconfining. There is plenty of room for fudging, free choice and intuition in interpreting the curves. Jazz musicians work with such ideas all the time, but Loevendie applied it to music that sounds nothing like jazz. It's an improviser's idea elaborated on by a composer.

"I think that's something you find in improvising on chord changes and in free improvisation: very often it's about the contour. Because it's very difficult to transpose exact intervals when you improvise: You take a rhythmic motive, and the contour of a motive. Nobody cares about the exact intervals."

(Perhaps tired of overarching methodologies, Mengelberg came up with his *zeekip* theory of composition. *Zeekip* means sea-chicken. Imagine a music where harmony is a mirror of melody: tune goes up a third, chord goes down a third. Ah but, says Misha, when you look at a chicken sitting on the sea its reflection is in flux: sometimes you see an upside-down chicken, sometimes you see some grotesque caricature of one, and when the water is choppy you might see a dozen or more upside-down chickens, none exactly alike. So you can pretty much write any variation you please and be theoretically consistent.)

In a way Loevendie's curve-based architecture also superimposes a visual idea onto an auditory medium, not so different perhaps from *De Stijl*, or the superimposition of genres in "Strides," of two meters in his "On the Train," of two lines in the solo piece "Duo," of composition and improvisation in *Bons*.

"On the Train" is a short boogie-woogie solo, from '92, which aggressively plays duple meter in one hand versus triple meter in the other, standard boogie strategy highly exaggerated. The meters neatly avoid each other as they shift from hand to hand, and between straight and double time, hands independent enough to suggest two pianists. The effect is a little like staring out a train window at near and far objects, appearing to move at different speeds. In the simulated chaos one might detect echoes of Misha, or "Brake"'s frantic chords.

"Duo" (1987) for classical bass clarinetist Harry Sparnaay is deep in debt to Dolphy, whom Sparnaay knows as well as Loevendie does. (On the same solo CD with "Duo," he plays a transcription of Eric's improvisation on "God Bless the Child" and gets away with it.) Loevendie had played bass clarinet briefly in the '60s, and the piece has a practical reed player's perspective, in the percussive and legato attacks called for, and in recognizing a clarinet's bifurcated sound: the timbre below and above the register break can make it seem like two instruments. He alternates voices antiphonally at first, goes to a wide-interval stairstep between registers (as if "Misterioso" were an unstated theme), at last splitting the horn into two voices and/or roles, alternating so quickly they give the illusion of simulataneity, of horn accompanied by a walking bass. (The "horn" is consistently louder than the "bass"; playing solo, Braxton splits his alto into two voices using similar two-tiered dynamics.) It's an elegant puzzle for a performer to solve. Like the other solo pieces just cited, it has concision working for it. None reaches eight minutes.

Bons, 1991, is for improviser and 11 instruments, the score preceded by a caveat about what an improviser is. (Loevendie: "The soloist must be a free improviser, because the danger is, they think every studio musician can play the solo part. So I wrote—I was thinking of Wolter Wierbos—'a great variety of timbre is desirable, making use of mutes, plungers, multiphonics . . . .'") That preamble also includes line drawings of the three basic curves, with advice to the soloist on how the improvisation might be integrated into the scored ensemble part. He further suggested it might be nice to play it twice on a concert, perhaps with different soloists, so folks could hear what was fixed and unfixed.

"That forward is long and detailed because the success of the piece depends on the soloist. The score itself is not my most interesting, it's just a canvas for the soloist. What is particular to it is the combination of an improviser and classically trained musicians. There is some limited freedom at certain points, for example there are some fermatas where the conductor can direct the musicians to either hold a chord for five or ten seconds or do nothing, but it's very limited. The classical musicians complained about it! 'Why didn't you give us more freedom?'"

Free solo, cued chords: Jimmy Giuffre's 1958 suite *Mobiles*—the one about which Jim Hall used the term "instant composing"—covered that. *Bons* has not been issued commercially, but Wierbos and Baars have performed it with strikingly different results. Nice variations in tone color and some rattling percussion keep the soloists stimulated, but the backdrops are neither too busy nor confining. It's good orchestral comping. *Bons* is also a piece in which resourceful improvisers can make you hear the curves in action, make you apprehend a relationship between solo line and ensemble. They bring it to life.

"I must say when I play the solo part, I don't feel very comfortable. People often say, 'You're the composer, you know the piece very well,' but I'm so distracted by what's happening behind me.

"I think more and more I'm using elements of the jazz tradition in my work. For example I've written a piece called *Laps*, like laps of a race, which has 32 bars that are repeated and repeated and repeated. I feel like a composer improvising chorus after chorus on his own chord changes. The melody is stated only at the end; before that it's built up on every pass. (Well, sometimes it builds up and then gets more spare again.) From the beginning, I repeat these 32 bars, but with most of the notes missing. You'll have one note, and then a few bars later you'll hear another, so in the beginning it sounds very slow. The second chorus adds a few more notes. Guus Janssen said it's like one of those puzzles on a television game show, where you only see one ear, and then a brow, and then finally the whole face."

That said, aside from a moment of tailgate trombone, and a general forward thrust in the rhythm—propulsion but not "swing"—it's devoid of jazz references.

"It's a very strange piece, but I love it, it was great fun. It feels like a new development, a new approach for me, but at the same time there's a feeling of going back to the roots, to something I have done a thousand times, improvising choruses in a cyclical form."

Chapter Twelve
Boomers

"I think that the destructive element is too much neglected in art."

PIET MONDRIAN, 1943

"I had to play flute when I was eight. On the third lesson I started to scream and cry, 'I only want the drum! I want to get lessons for drums!' At the local drum band, they said, 'It's not possible; he's too young, too small.' But my father was the village doctor, so they could not refuse. That's how I got into the drum band—like a village fanfare, only just drums. Play the rolls, paradiddles, that kind of thing. It's very nice to learn that stuff at eight years old. But at that time, there were no drum teachers in the area of Heiloo. Also it really wasn't done; the son of a doctor should play piano or something. So that's one difference in technique between me and my brother Guus. At that age he got a very good education as a piano player.

"I am left-handed, but I play a right-handed drummer's set. Usually you play the swing rhythm with the right hand and the left makes the accents. The right hand has to be steady and strong, but I'm stronger with my left. Left-handed drummers usually reverse the set—like Johnny Engels, who swings with his left hand—but not me. I started doing it the other way because I didn't know any better, so some of my left-hand things are better than a right-handed drummer's are, but uptempo I have a few problems.

"We were improvising when we were 13 or 14 years old. There were six brothers and two sisters at home. Heiloo is 40 kilometers north of Amsterdam, and we were a little isolated. My oldest brother, Paul, he plays bass clarinet, clarinet, tenor and alto saxophone. He went to Amsterdam to study, and came home every weekend with records by Eric Dolphy, Han Bennink, several other things. Guus and I waited for that every week.

"On Sunday, my parents would go for a walk, and we would improvise in the music room, also with another brother who plays trumpet. At 14 Guus was already playing inside the piano. It was very nice. We developed the language together. Also Paul Termos, who played clarinet with us beginning in the early '70s.

253

"The first gig the Janssen Brothers had was in about 1968, in secondary school, a kind of jazz and poetry evening. As soon as we started to play the whole audience walked out. It was a good gig. The next day, the most popular teacher in the school defended us in front of all the pupils. He said, 'Everybody should listen to this music.' The first paid gig was in '70, I think. We played with a friend of ours, a trumpeter and big fan of Don Ayler. Immediately we started playing free jazz as loud as we could, for about two minutes, and then two stagehands in overalls came out and started rolling the piano off. Guus was walking with them as they dragged it off, playing classical music."

Sometimes, if you're lucky—because a heavy-handed player opened for him, or the tuner goofed—Guus Janssen will sit down at a piano and discover one or more notes is out of tune. He doesn't inventory the strings in any obvious way, but somehow within seconds he knows exactly what's what, and what can be done with it.

He can make that piano sound prepared: the interference patterns set up by one stray tone alter the timbre. Janssen hears so acutely the piano's acoustical properties and the fragile compromises built into the tempered scale, he hears how a single strand out of place changes the dynamic of the web. Each wayward note opens the window to a plethora of new chords and sonorities, available this evening only. After playing with its effects awhile he may then reveal the errant tone in all its glory—may peck away as the manager of the hall sinks under his seat, and the audience has a nice laugh—before moving on to whatever he had in mind when he first sat down, coming back to that clinker 20 minutes later to start a new movement. It's the kind of spontaneous problem solving he loves, and if it seems a little like showing off, it's always playful.

Listening to Guus Janssen one sometimes has the feeling music-making is a matter of detours: he says some nice intervals in his composed pieces come from flubbing a phrase while trying it out on piano, and discovering the mistake works better.

There is Monk in his harmonic conception, but not in his attack. Monk's was all flat-fingered idiosyncrasy, homemade. Janssen's is by the book, perfect curvature, fingertips like hammers, and supple enough to handle most any neo-complex score. He used to play in new-music ensembles, notably Asko. His quirkier techniques involve rethinking the possibilities. He loves to capitalize on sympathetic vibrations by using hand pedal: pressing keys down so gently the hammers don't strike the strings, but leave them free to resonate. He'll hand-pedal one or more bass notes, and then jab some keys around middle C, and the piano will sound like a gamelan. He'll silently depress a midrange chord, and strum the strings under them with his other hand, turning piano into an autoharp. Reaching under the lid again, he'll scrape some small object along a free bass string, make it yawp like a church-organ bass.

He likes crossed hands and crossed rhythms—especially rhythms that turn over on themselves so often you quickly lose track of where the original beat is, on where to tap your foot. He can strike a note so hard and true its color changes several times within two seconds of its being struck. (As Glerum would say, he finds the tones inside a tone.) He can hammer away at a repeated note until the whole piano hums to it, metallic overtones coming out you can't get any other way. He likes to whack at a key and stop the string by hand at its various nodes—points where natural harmonics ring clearest—

either before or after that note has begun to sound. He'll slam a chord with one hand on the keys, and then immediately slam the other hand onto the strings to silence it.

He can get a world of music out of the piano's clacking highest note, or from tones sounded so briefly before they're cut off, you can't ID the pitch. He also likes very small quiet gestures: he'll play an eight-note chord, and then remove the notes one at a time, one per beat, so you can hear the chord evaporate, and how different the evaporation sounds when the notes vanish in a different order. That's Janssen too—taking away materials, until what's left may bear no resemblance to what you started with.

As a composer Guus Janssen is a prime beneficiary of the founders' bequest. What Misha developed over so long a period—the culture of mistakes, the integration of improvised, composed and absurd—was in Guus's music by the time they dragged his piano off stage at that first paid gig. Unlike Misha he likes to work, and mounts major projects—like his 1994 opera *Noach* (Noah). (The Ark story is a fitting parallel to his occasional method: (genetic) material reduced as far as it can go, before reproliferating.) He is as talented a composer or improvisor as Holland has produced.

"I grew up as a classical piano player, and started to compose when I was 12 or 13. You heard part of the story from my brother Wim already. My oldest brother played the clarinet, and improvised, and would come home with all kinds of strange records like ICP 001, Albert Ayler, Eric Dolphy. The Willem Breuker stuff I liked very much, the screaming side of it, and immediately I started to imitate it. He also brought home this recent Miles Davis stuff which was completely incomprehensible to me." Guus was born 13 May 1951, two years after Wim. "I didn't understand the way Herbie Hancock accompanied Miles. Now I know the modal stuff, but still it's impossible to really grasp it, which is nice I think. It has to do with timing too, eh?"

—When you and your brothers improvised in secret, did a kind of family musical language spring up, an independent dialect?

"Yeah. Strange, because it came out of the blue in a certain sense. In the family there was a lot of music, my father played the treble recorder, my mother played the piano—not so well, but music was always there. My older brothers and one sister played instruments. The piano was there, so when I was very young, I experimented with it, as every child does: the pedals on the ground, or you lift the lid to do things on the strings. That was my first experience." Years later he'd write some student pieces for playing inside upright piano.

"I started to play piano normally, the classical stuff. The other brothers too. So it's difficult to trace the source of that family style. My older brothers played dixieland with a friend of theirs, but not me, and I was sort of jealous. Their friend played the piano, and I didn't understand what he was doing. I was already a better piano player, but this business with the chords was a completely secret language to me. So I had an urge to try something without scores. So first there was dixieland, and then the records of Thelonious Monk and Miles Davis, and then Coltrane and Ayler. In a very short period, maybe two years, there was this development from dixieland to free jazz in our house.

"That was the improvised-music side of the story. When I was 12, the local piano teacher asked me, 'What do you want to do as a profession?' I said, 'Be a composer, a musician.' 'Okay, then I'll teach you all the theoretical stuff, about chords, counterpoint, tonalities.' So that was very nice. Then he turned me on to a piece by Peter Schat, *Concerto da camera*, because he thought I should get acquainted with modern music too. I was completely shocked by it. Very strange atonal stuff, leaning a little toward Bartok, but far away too. A week later I came to the lesson with my first composition."

Schat's 1960 piano concerto forecasts some later Janssen: persistent two-handed hammering on one note; drifts from one musical language to another, including chordal cascades that kid the concerto tradition, and episodes where swingtime fitfully starts and stops; an episode where one instrument keeps interrupting another.

"There was also a record of two string quartets by Ives, which for me was amazing. At the same time Willem Breuker came along, and we got interested in that kind of music, we heard John Cage, and wanted to do a Cage kind of thing too.

"The '50s and the start of the '60s in Holland was about no dirt, everything clean. And then young people got this urge to throw dirt on it. That was on my mind too; I think our music was also this kind of reaction. We realized music was a perfect way to deal with this discontent.

"When it was time to decide what school to go to, my first thought was, 'I'll go to the Hague, because there's Andriessen, Schat, all the teachers.' And then I had a clever idea, I think. I'd read a book about 20th-century music by Ton de Leeuw, a very thorough theoretical approach to Stockhausen, Ligeti, all the guys. I liked his book, but I didn't like his music. So I decided to study with him instead. (I realized later, if I had studied with Louis, I would have become a small Louis Andriessen, because I like his music very much.) Ton de Leeuw taught at the Amsterdam Conservatory, which was very far from the Hague in those days. They had quite a duel. I had private lessons for piano, and for piano in new music, so I played all the modern stuff too. When I went to a concert it was to hear pieces by Louis Andriessen, not Ton de Leeuw.

"But with de Leeuw there are interesting parallels on the conceptual level, like his insistence on economy of means. He'd say 'Don't use too much material if it's not necessary.' I had to argue when I wanted to do it differently. I thought, 'If you want to compose a piece of mud, what good is economy of means there?' For me, the first part of the Fourth Symphony by Ives is one of the most beautifully excessive uses of mud in music. Ton de Leeuw can't handle it. To me, with my free-jazz background, it's impressive to have a big symphony orchestra screaming, for example. He'd ask—like a real Dutch grocer—'Why? What's interesting about that?' What I like about Messiaen, who was his teacher, is that there are all these moments where he's on the edge of losing control. It gets ecstatic, breaks open. That's something Ton de Leeuw lacks. A pity, because the loss of control is a very important part of music, I think.

"'Brake' has to do with that kind of ecstasy for me. It's about a piano player losing control, and trying to deal with that by putting more energy in it, and then going out of his head. Ton de Leeuw said, 'This anecdotal thing is not interesting, not musical.' But when you read music history you find a lot of examples: French composers for harpsichord who made whole battlefields in music, the sound of horses—it's all there. What the sound of horses was to them, the sound of TV zapping is for us. That's a kind of anecdotalism too.

"With Ton de Leeuw there was also a lot of discussion about improvised music. He'd attack it, and I had to defend it. In the end I couldn't win these arguments, but decided to improvise anyway. I also still think anecdotalism can play a role in music. But those discussions helped give a sharp theoretical edge to my own concept."

♫

There is a photograph, brother Thom standing with a cubistic plywood bass, Guus in shorts hunched toward the piano, music on the stand but he's looking down, at hands at work. ("I think I nearly always look at the keys when I play. I use my eyes for making decisions, apart from the ears.") He looks about nine.

Thom would grow up to be a wizard of a classical pianist, whose chops Guus concedes are better than his own.

Guus's first day at the Conservatory, this "fast-looking guy" introduced himself: Paul Termos. That night Termos went to Paradiso to see Freddie Hubbard—a Dulfer production—and there was Guus with two guys who were obviously his brothers. In those days they were as inseparable as Huey, Dewey and Louie—or Kwik, Kwek and Kwak as quacked in Dutch. Wim had come to Amsterdam to go to art school, another drummer-painter.

(The Janssens look like a Wim Janssen painting. He likes the Italian Morandi, wobbly vases, a few softly muted colors. The Janssens have pale orange-red hair, pale orange-red skin, a bit awkwardly stylized looking. Wim used to draw witty caricatures of musicians, and he and Guus also look like they could be two of those. Wim's ears protrude just a little—a drummer who keeps his ears open. Cruel irony: a mysterious virus left him deaf in his left a few years ago. Guus's balding 100-watt dome looks like the lightbulb with the idea inside.)

At Paradiso: Do you like this gig? No, not really; I prefer Han and Misha. Turned out they'd all seen a Political-Demonstrative Experimental Concert in 1968, with Mengelberg's "Hello! Windyboys." The brothers were living in the same house. A few days later Termos came over with his guitar—"They were playing amazingly good, a kind of free jazz"—and for the next few years Paul Termos became a sort of fourth Janssen Brother.

♫

Paul Termos: "I was born on the 25th of January 1952 in Hilversum, lived in Haarlem and the Hague, and then when I was 17 moved to Amsterdam with my parents. I already had ambitions to go to the conservatory, and I was already interested in the avant-garde in jazz, and Amsterdam was the place that was happening. The Notenkrakers concert happened two months after I arrived, and there were very interesting jazz concerts at the Paradiso. You'd see the Han Bennink–Misha Mengelberg duo, often with John Tchicai, who was very impressive at that time. And there was a concert of Stockhausen in the Concertgebouw, it was all starting then. Internationally it was a period of change, and there was a kind of fever in Amsterdam.

"I played guitar in rock bands, but also wanted to play classical music and jazz on the guitar, especially free jazz. I was not into bebop or anything like that. I was interested in modern music, and also wanted to improvise. I knew Mengelberg was a composer who improvised too, and that Breuker had something to do with classical players, so I saw it was possible. I wasn't that good a guitarist, but all the guitar players who applied to the conservatory were clumsy, because they all came from rock music, so the entrance exam was not as rigorous as for other instruments.

"I went there in 1970, and stayed ten years, including a year pre-class, where you're not really in the school but on the way, then three years of guitar, then clarinet for a time, and six years studying composition with Ton de Leeuw. I started playing clarinet as a second instrument, because then you couldn't play saxophone at the conservatory, and I wanted to play alto sax."

The Janssens and Termos started going to Arjen Gorter's workshops at the Oktopus. When they got a gig, Arjen called Breuker, Misha, Loevendie and others, said, check this out. That made them, sort of. On the strength of it Misha recommended them to a festival in Rotterdam. (This was before they met Mengelberg at STEIM, as told in Chapter Four.)

Paul Termos: "With the Janssen Brothers, we had it in mind to combine these things we liked in modern music with free jazz. A few years later we discovered some English people also had this idea, but with a difference. Because we were influenced by Misha Mengelberg and Han Bennink, we used all kinds of material. The whole postmodern idea which is now very common was already alive. The English guys had problems when the music became too tonal or concrete; they like to keep it very abstract. There was always a kind of polarity between the Dutch musicians and the English. It sharpened the mind."

Guitarist Peter Cusack came from London to study at Utrecht's Institute of Sonology, Holland's tweediest electronic music center, but he soon gravitated to scruffy STEIM. In the late '70s he was a most valuable contributor to England's shoestring-budgeted magazine *MUSICS*, which covered the Dutch improvising scene far better than any journal outside Holland.

"When I heard Han and Misha, I was actually shocked. They were playing tunes, rhythms, harmonies, without any embarrassment at all. The British scene at that time was hard-line free music. In Holland there was a much less reverent attitude about improvising. I realized you can take whatever musical experiences or areas you want and make them your own. The relationship with jazz is much closer in Dutch improvising than in London. It made me see how narrow the British scene was in some ways. The Dutch musicians were always more interested in playing notes, structures based around pitches—a composers' perspective—in contrast with the Londoners who (with some exceptions) were into timbres and textures.

"I started hearing about Guus Janssen right away, so I called him up. He became my main musical partner in Holland. At that time, the scene was fairly open—it's not so easy now, I think—and I got invited onto gigs quite quickly."

That was about 1975. Guus had been getting subsidy funding for the Janssen groups since '72, but now he began getting gigs away from his brothers: a Loevendie trio with Martin van Duynhoven, Herman de Wit's Herbie White Combo, the workshop orchestra De Boventoon. Guus's first vinyl appearance was a Boventoon 33-rpm 7-inch from January '75, maybe the first live record from the BIMhuis. His one solo has its playful side, but he hadn't yet figured out what could be done with a badly out-of-tune piano. By the following year Rudy Koopmans was already writing about the profound effect of his crossover mentality: composer who improvises, improviser who composes.

Sometime later Cusack proposed spending some money on a few concerts with a core cast including themselves, Termos, Tchicai, Altena, Evan Parker, German trombonist Gunter Christmann, and English drummer Paul Lytton. The series was documented on two 1978–79 LPs of concert excerpts, *Groups in Front of People* for the English label Bead. On the first, at the beginning of an Alkmaar concert, Janssen gleefully finds an out-of-tune note, and as he mines it Cusack is right there with him, picking nearby notes, net effect like a piano tuner bringing the strings under one key into unison. On the same LP Guus also does a fake delay-unit routine: keeps repeating a note at ever decreasing volume: it makes his point about how the sounds of one's era seep into the music.

The second LP (the one with Termos) gets the nod for two episodes. In one, the band deals with a hostile Delft audience by replying in kind—Cusack with an obnoxious-as-possible simulation of tuning up, finally accompanied by migraine-inducing blasts from Lytton's air horn. (The antagonists are English but the combative attitude is Dutch.) The other highlight, from Rotterdam, finds Janssen acting as composer on an improvisation—not, as Mengelberg or Steve Lacy does, playing a tune of his own while the other players blow free, but blatantly imposing a tonal order on a quiet abstract episode. He plays a recurring, twinkling, defiantly tonal run up several octaves, which the other players can bend to or resist. (Cusack does both, with chunky strummed chords that stem Guus's rhythmic tide.) It ends, there's less than enthusiastic applause, and then Guus begins again, picking up exactly as he left off. It is free music that uses the forbidden: tonality and memory. Repetition of anything was regarded as gauche by many English and American free players of that time. Not hard to see Misha in Guus's obstinacy.

(The influence of Mengelberg and his disciples was a relief to other English free improvisers who resisted codes of acceptable conduct. Pianist Steve Beresford: "The impact of the Dutch had to do with realizing how much you could wind up the other musicians without being seen as rude. You could actually play things just to fuck them up, and not aim for jewel-like perfection all the time. You might be going for some horrible mess that produces something else. Once I asked Misha how his gig was the other night. 'Oh, it was very horrible, irritating, the ideas were very weak and badly played. I liked it very much.' This sort of breaks through the moralistic bullshit around improvised music.")

Guus says of all his commercial recordings, the Bead records come closest to the flavor of the Janssen family band.

"In those days I refused to play directly on the strings, because that would have been a real easy way to connect with the sound idiom of the other instruments. I didn't want to do that, so I was stuck to the keys. It often made me very uncomfortable; the other guys had all this noise in their concept which they could bring in and I couldn't, but which I would try to imitate. When Evan Parker did overtone blowing, I would do it on the keyboard, why not? In that sense I felt sometimes like Franz Liszt, trying to imitate gypsy cymbalon and violin music on the piano, until that became the Franz Liszt technique, because the sound of real gypsy music is quite inaccessible to a classical musician. That was a kind of example to me, that there must be a way.

"It also felt uncomfortable because whenever I played with Evan Parker, for example, everything he did was drawn into a tonal context. He'd start to play, and there was a kind of let's say Jackson Pollock dripping to what he was doing. I'd play one sustaining note, and it was as if someone had drawn a straight line across the Pollock. Already I was thinking about layers, differences in idiom. If you can imagine a Jackson Pollock painting with a beautiful straight line in it, why not?"

In the same period Guus and Wim Janssen, Cusack, Termos and bassist Raoul van der Weide (who'd been playing with Wim in a Termos trio) became involved in Boventoon-alum Bert Koppelaar's Punt Uit band. (*Punt uit* means "Point made, end of discussion.") Koppelaar's gifts and liabilities are the same. He wrote interesting tunes, but many were cribbed liberally from other tunes—one lifts the bridge of the 1962 instrumental hit "Telstar" almost verbatim. Guus worked with him, transcribing and tidying up his compositions. Koppelaar was also incapable of coming in on the upbeat—which means he would sometimes come in one beat behind the rest of the band, a lag he'd rigorously maintain for the whole performance (after which he'd complain the other guys came in early). If he entered on the wrong bar, same thing. That would have made for some nice Riley/Reich phasing of parts.

There was a healthy tension between extreme order and chaos, between Bert's pop and jazz sensibility and the noise-making tendencies of Cusack or Termos. (Whenever Koppelaar threatened to fire Cusack, Guus would threaten to go too.) There are no commercial recordings, but a tape exists of a wondrous 1978 radio broadcast with obscure American singer Royal Blue, who was confused enough to start singing a blues over a nonblues structure. The band calmly sticks to its own tune, and Blue keeps searching for the chord changes to cue his next line, so his blues choruses have irregular gaps. Somehow this Ivesian disaster works out. Eventually he and the band end a chorus in the same place, and the instrumentalists go into a straight blues for him, but they like the original effect so well, they go back to playing the other tune, as Royal Blue stays his own course.

(Some of Cusack's old English colleagues didn't know what to make of his progress report *After Being in Holland for Two Years*, on Bead, with its casual quasi-amateurism and environmental-sound content. He repatriated in 1980, went on to form the band Kahondo Style, where free episodes and tunes existed side by side. He notes it had a number of non-Dutch influences, but: "I could never have come up with that group without my experience in Holland, not in a million years.")

♫

Guus Janssen *On the Line* (as in on the phone, or on a leash) from 1979 was his first record under his own name, solo piano pieces including "Brake," for Altena and

Waisvisz's Claxon label. His conservatory piano training had served him well: developed his chops without inhibiting creative use of the uncouth. He emerges matured, using stuff and displaying attitudes still in place 20 years later: prominent use of crisp high notes; acute sensitivity to piano overtones; accents that drift from one note to another in a sequence on repeats; an attack with a diamond cutter's force and precision; an archivist's knowledge of jazz vocabulary. (In one of our interviews, he said about teaching jazz at conservatories: "You do Chopin or you do Bud Powell. What's the difference, in the end? Both are a museum language, which is okay, I think.")

Janssen has mentioned Germany's Peter Kreuder as influence and guilty pleasure: pop pianist whose heyday was the '40s and '50s. Like Floyd Cramer he had some characteristics striking enough to leave their mark on better pianists. Kreuder's: unsinkably buoyant schmaltz; melodies hammered home with jabbing flourishes; frequent, near-arbitrary changes of octave and zithery sweeps up the keyboard. He hasn't much to say but says it with great conviction, and some kind of good taste. The whole is just spare enough not to be cloying. Kreuder's second-hand jazz moves are entertaining precisely for what gets added or lost in translation.

"In the '70s every now and then I'd go to the Cafe Bohemia, the jazz cafe near the BIMhuis. The guy who ran it was very much into jazz, and very interested in what I was doing. He went to my piano exam, where I played a very difficult Messiaen piece. He really liked it, and he wanted to put up the money for me to make a record.

"One time I was there he said, I'm going to turn you on to a nice record: *The New Tristano*. It was a complete shock to me. Then I had this problem; Tristano's style fit me like my pants, but then you have to wear the pants. It's like the problems a lot of turn-of-the-century composers had with Wagner: they had to defeat him before they could go on.

"You can ignore a big influence like Tristano, or transform the conception, which is what I try to do, as a composer. But you also have to deal with it as a pianist, on a physical level, which is much more difficult. I think Tristano was a kind of classical player, too: there is a lot of classical feeling in it. So then I decided to get into him: to put on the Tristano Mask, real imitation. Sometimes I still do it a little bit, but only to drop it. When I'm 70 years old I'll be able to drop it. So for me as a piano player there's more to say about Tristano than Monk.

"Art Tatum is also quite an influence, these strange jumps from one idea to another. If I put on an Art Tatum record, I'm knocked out as a piano player after one second. We go upstairs, downstairs, then we go up again. It's beautiful, but it must have been exhausting to spend all night in a club listening to Tatum.

"I used to have a record of Tristano's first recordings, where he was completely imitating Art Tatum. (Very strange also—they are both blind.) So then I realized there is a line between them. For me, that fits. But Tristano at his highest point, *The New Tristano*, has nothing to do with Tatum anymore. It's the linear thing."

Easy to hear why 1961's solo bombshell *The New Tristano* knocked him out: conceptual rigor; intricacy and order; juggling of rhythms (Tristano had set out to replicate stuff he'd done via overdub and manipulating tape speeds, using two hands in real time, and succeeded); the baroque cascades: the long, long line, the thought pursued to its extreme. "Zeven Knoesten" (Seven Knots) on Guus's 1981 LP *Tast Toe* (Claxon) out-Tristanos Tristano: not just the 8/8 walking bass under endless snaking right-hand lines draped over the changes, not just different tempos in either hand, but flexible tempos to boot, one hand sliding out of and then back in sync with the other. With Abdullah Ibrahim, independence of hands seems a trancelike feat: African drum choir complexity from a single player. With Janssen it's apt to be simulated breakdown or Brake-down.

"If I could have imagined a kind of jazz music that would fit me it would have been Tristano, with this big exception: in a way it's too restrictive. A closed idiom doesn't fit me. I need an idiom where the possibility always exists to break it open, go outside and look at it from a distance."

You could say he plays "jazz" with quotes around it, but sometimes you recognize the quotation marks without knowing who is speaking. On "Blokken" alone from *Tast Toe* there are Monkish intervals and hesitations, Andriessen-style boogie interruptus, what appears to be a paraphrase of a classical etude but turns out to be "The Third Man" theme, and the piano's highest note is used periodically for punctuation, or maybe just as tic. "Blokken" is a pun: blocks, like children's blocks, but also the verb "to plod."

Different styles rain freely, and are anchored to piano and other musico-linguistic traditions. Ragtime, with its precocious technical demands, plucked-banjo crispness of sound, cross-rhythms and other games with time, is a good precedent. "Brake" was a novelty the way ragtime was, challenge to the amateur pianist who wanted to deal with the quasi-accidental clusters and flusters and such markings as "staccatissimo" and "poco a poco rallentando." His publisher made the score available. The only problem was, it was all but impossible for anyone else to play. (Twenty years later, it sounds like a period piece itself.) On *Tast Toe* those ragtime qualities come out most strongly on "Bakkum," borrowed from the Maarten Altena quartet's book. Here and there one also hears rolling octaves, circus music, Cowell clusters, "Brake"-like contusions of time, and a little of the old BANG BANG BANG.

It was postmodernism of a sort—predating Zorn's, but then style-quotation was old pants to the Dutch by now. Yet it was so plain this was one mind (and the same two hands) at work, it didn't sound fragmented. It sounded like Guus Janssen.

Tast Toe was recorded at the '81 Holland Festival's piano masters series—the others being Misha, Steve Beresford and Tristanoite Sal Mosca, whom Guus had recommended. Janssen won the Boy Edgar that year. He was by then established as a subsidized composer as well.

"'Brake' was the moment people started to get interested—that and *Gieter*, an orchestra piece. There was a little scandal with that, as far as was possible in those days, because scandals were already out of fashion. Ton de Leeuw arranged a commission for me, with Dutch radio, but this orchestra was very conservative, used to accompanying operettas, and light classical music. There was a lot of quarreling at the rehearsals, which everyone saw because a documentary was made for TV. The title *Gieter* means watering can, which fit the subject of the piece: namely, five structures draining, one after each other. The first becomes empty in a rhythmic sense, the second part in the pitch sense, third part in the color sense, etc. The fourth part was really empty—there was something like 45 seconds of silence—and the fifth was a very short punctuation mark, the point behind the piece." That is, the period behind the sentence.

"I was warned I was setting myself up with that title, because in Dutch we have an expression, 'Go down like a watering can.' Meaning, you get bogged down in the shit and are lost. The reviews were not only negative but really polemical. The strange thing was, without having planned it—because in Holland in the conservatory in those days, there was no course for marketing, unlike now—just doing what I thought was nice started to work for me. People wanted to talk about how bad they thought my music was. So then it started to roll. But from the early years, only a couple of pieces are still played, one of which is 'Brake.'"

He's written far too much music to survey here—much of it unrelated to jazz or improvising—but there are common themes, chief among them a clear idea of what he's after. Misha's *Mix*-style amnesiac form doesn't work for him: he always has the road map in his head, and doesn't mind explaining the route if you're riding along. In a lot of his music one finds splinters in the planed surfaces: deliberately awkward gestures, time sometimes wobbly, accents exaggerated: perhaps this is a by-product of growing up playing with a left-handed drummer with a right-handed kit. Willful wooden-shoe timing and tuning are in the mix, but Guus always had his own spin. Misha ignores rules, Guus thwarts, flouts.

And reinvents the wheel, because no one can know everything. The same year as *Tast Toe* came his second string quartet *Streepjes* (Stripes) which is typical Janssen in its clear overarching concept, and in the cleverness of details which may undermine as much as reinforce the grand design. He wanted to free himself from string quartet traditions, by constructing a piece played almost entirely in harmonics, plucked or bowed without vibrato. By retuning one string on each instrument, and using four harmonics per string, he created what amounts to a single instrument with a range greater than an oboe, and a sound he likens to a glass harmonica—the rim of a water glass, set humming when you drag a wet fingertip around its edge—albeit with faster response time. Strings harmonize, or hocket single-note melodies among them. Whatever they do, *Streepjes* is rhythmically compelling; the thickets of notes and scalar skyrockets that emerge from them move fast, momentum closer to jazz than most string quartets. As much as any composer he is able to tap into the best of both worlds. The result is as clean and appealing as a Mondrian.

Only later did he discover Cage's 1949–50 string quartet played in harmonics. Janssen must have known another analog, Louis Andriessen's 1978 *Symphony for Open Strings*, which used scordatura—retuning—sans harmonics. (Given the Dutch mania for hocketing, especially with instruments limited to one or few notes, remember Mengelberg's *Musica per 17 strumenti* was ahead of them in line.) Still, Janssen took these ideas a step further, not least by breaking his own rules. In the course of writing a piece without vibrato he discovered he missed it, so at a few key junctures there is a sudden rich molto vibrato chord, played on stopped strings. Then it's back to usual business, the change-up so quick a second later you may wonder if you heard that chord at all. This is pomo Janssen-style: not cutting from one sound to another, repeatedly, but splicing a slice of something alien into an otherwise uniform texture. Guus likens it to paintings by the Belgian new figuratist Roger Raveel, with their protrusions from the surface of a flat canvas. It is an idea he would return to.

In 1983 Janssen became the second Boy Edgar/Wessel Ilcken Prize winner musician to receive the Matthijs Vermeulen Prize for composition. (You may recall Breuker had turned his Vermeulen down.) Guus won for *Temet* (Almost) for another quartet: flute, violin, cello and harp. One low harp string, E below middle C, is tuned a quarter tone sharp, departure point for the tuning problems that are *Temet*'s subject. Six basic pitches form the material.

From the composer's program note: "The exposition is a laboriously winding path from one pure octave to the next by way of a number of almost octaves. In a kind of development, the basic pitches plus rhythm are then added, creating all kinds of smaller polyrhythmic networks." The chords in the "chorale-like" closing section, he says, are in fact "sloppily played octaves."

He elaborated in an interview: "Everything which is in tune is also in rhythm, and everything out of tune is searching for regular rhythm. Whenever the tuning is lost, immediately the pulse is lost, and you get this swampy feeling. You have to look for solid ground, otherwise you sink."

There is a sort of accidental anecdotal aspect, suggested right off by the deliberate buzzy SPRONG of that low harp clunker and the repeating Es and other pitches going in and out of tune (there is frequent use of pedal glissando by the harpist) and played in perfect and imperfect octaves. You can hear it in the flurry of plucked harmonics that end the piece too. "Temet" is the sound of a giant, freshly strung guitar being tuned: guitar, whose low note is E below middle C, which is tuned to six pitches (not Guus's six, however). The rhythm-and-tuning game the piece plays is audible parallel to the visual display on an electronic tuner, which tells guitarists when they're approaching a desired pitch. It is a musical game the composer plays, solitaire, in which the sound of the piece is the rules made audible. Using bad intonation as a kind of microtonality, he shows his deeper understanding of harmonic relationships—and explores them much the way he does as improviser sitting down at an errant piano.

There are other pieces in what we might call Janssen's harmonic series: "Wandelweer," 1984, for guitar trio (the only piece that doesn't work, precisely because plinking harmonics are a guitar cliche) and "Sprezzatura," same year, for bass clarinet.

"I saw three special fingerings for a normal clarinet, in a score by the Italian composer Salvatore Sciarrino. I asked Harry Sparnaay to play those three fingerings on his bass clarinet, and he was surprised by the result: it produced these very strange ghost tones. Then I asked him to find other fingerings with other ghost tones, because the bass clarinet is three times bigger than a normal clarinet, so there are a lot more overtones, blah blah. He'd phone me nearly every day, 'I have another one, and another one.' That went on for two weeks. Then I had a whole bunch of fingerings, and I started to write. It was all my own after that. I had it in mind to have a melodic line with a lot of notes surrounding it. I realized you can play a lot of fast notes, which combined with certain trills give you a ghost tone, so you get a sustained melody note. You get a kind of polyphonic movement." The fingerings change, the trills trill, but because more than one fundamental tone may have the same overtone, a ghost tone may sustain while the lower note changes, as if divorced from it. (Interesting to note Janssen and Loevendie both wrote pieces for Sparnaay that deal with the same problem: how to play two lines in two registers at once. Ab Baars, using what he learned from John

Carter, later improvised a solo piece that did the same thing—"Verschoten Geel" on *Verderame*—a parallel which neatly illustrates how Dutch composers and improvisers think along the same lines.) Evan Parker's ghost-tone multiple-line multiple-register side-key playing is an obvious improvised-music precedent, but with "Sprezzatura" Janssen turns the free-jazz division of labor on its head: instead of melody in a lower register and squealing ornaments, it's vice versa. None of which would matter much if the ghost melody itself weren't so beautiful—he has made the dots connect, made a paint-by-numbers masterpiece.

"That's something I like: to restrict myself, and then try to find inspiration on that very narrow path."

Also in 1984 Janssen wrote *Woeha* for Volharding. The word "woeha" is the howl comic book hero Tintin's dog makes in Dutch. The piece takes jazz sectional writing to an extreme: pits the band's usual barking saxophones and brass against quiet piccolo-led chords, and then lets that separation break down: as the sound (and dynamics) of each group pollutes the other, they move to radically different tempos, so the tension remains more or less constant though the way it's established changes. It critiques the band's usual style while exploiting it.

As Janssen's writing grew more assured, as improviser he got more involved with more working groups like trio Trebbel (already noted re: Baars) and Maarten Altena's ensemble. *Guus Janssen Septet* (Claxon) was recorded in '82 and '3: Baars and Michael Moore on saxes and clarinets, Maud Sauer on oboes, Annemarie Roelofs on trombone and violin, Raoul van der Weide on bass and Wim Janssen. It's striking for its energy and the headlong rush of ideas on every track—they empty out the whole closet. Where he moves from one style to another, it's less by jumpcut than covert or dream logic: there is usually some link, often in a small detail, to justify the leap. In that way among others Janssen's midsize groups feature order masquerading as chaos. The jumbles of ideas do sort themselves out, so that no tracks sound the same even if some ideas overlap. One notable element is a seeming hybrid of Derek Bailey–style pointillist improvising and the mock-Euro-urban atmospherics of some '50s jazz pieces: the car-horns and cop-whistles intros to Brown/Roach's "Parisian Thoroughfare" and Mingus's "A Foggy Day" are implicit on "Slot." They're explicit on "Pozzuoli," where Moore works those airhorn intervals and sounds into his alto solo, which in turn leads the band into a jazz groove.

Guus's style-dicing parallels John Zorn's (though for years Janssen didn't know about the New Yorker), but he makes a bad channel zapper precisely because his ears are so good he can always make some arcane connection. (Guus has said he listens to serial music by parsing the intervals as they go by: that's a fifth, there's a triad, this bit is a children's song.) We refer again to Mengleberg's touchstone *Dressoir*, the cupboard with diverse contents comfortable with the fellow bric-a-brac and the frame. Janssen's music is obviously informed by modern concert music and jazz (and boogie-woogie, for he too has a thing for those rolling 8s), but usually steers a course between.

Janssen may be the best example of a (Dutch) musician who makes a personal music which transcends genre and resists classification. It can be jazz one minute and not the next, but no matter what musics he uses as material—including soul, disco and Mozart—or how you classify the result, it speaks to or of jazz esthetics: improvisation, rhythmic virtuosity, dirty timbre and a creative use of flexible pitch, which among other reasons he uses to make a small band sound larger, an old jazz trick. (*Temet*, come to think of it, sounds like more than four instruments.)

The problem with a composer as smart, talented and acute of ear as Guus: Is there really a place for mortal improvisers in his group music, except to do his bidding? The freewill vs. determinism question got louder on *Guus Janssen Septet 85 . . . 86* (Claxon) for several combinations, Reijseger, Horsthuis and Termos added or replacing exiting players. The compositional ideas are more in focus, which is to say the composer exerts greater control. It's tighter in both senses: trim but corseted. Yet it's more Ellingtonian in the way he writes/orchestrates around his players' strengths. There is more implicit stress on that old Dutch standby, mixing classical and jazz musicians, Sauer at one extreme, (the by-no-means-limited) Moore at the other, the likes of Baars and Wim Janssen somewhere unplaceable between. On "Plint" alone you hear the blues, two-beat, cool jazz, woodwind chamber music and rushing Volharding saxes.

Such a mix allows for some nice hairsplitting: the specificity of Sauer's Korean double-reed music on "Duw" contrasted with Guus's beyond-Hollywood "Asian" pentatonic arpeggios, something not quite the real thing playing off something not quite a travesty (because Janssen can always save himself by playing amazing piano, his jazz ears and formidable technique always on call). "Duw" begins with boogie walking 8s from piano; toward the close the pianist riffs on the *1812 Overture*.

Ernst Reijseger: "In Misha's compositions, often you're confronted with ideas that ask you not to draw on your whole array of capabilities, but to understand and recognize the hierarchical structures you may rightly or wrongly perceive in an improvisation. Often that means you serve another player's musical idea by not playing. In my view he's trying to translate compositional structures or ideas like homophony, polyphony, counterpoint and collage structures into improvised form. Guus's game pieces often had brilliant ideas that made me laugh and inspired me to almost naive enthusiasm, but a lot of them must be executed in one way only. The structure of a piece is so crystal-clear in advance, the given textures often allow little room for a personal viewpoint, only for good interpretation. On the other hand, the music is so striking, it inspires the interpreters to play everything as exactly and vividly as possible."

Take Guus's game "Pogo 1," inspired by the punks' vertical dance. Among its many features: a section where the piano plays an increasingly zigzag line (intervals and space between notes increasing, like a pogo stick aspiring to escape velocity). Each player is assigned one note in that line they can jump in on, in unison with piano; when that happens piano drops out and you get a solo improvisation—although Guus can wrest it from you by playing the next scored figure. There's another catch: there can only be one improvisation in this section, so if someone grabs their note before yours comes up, you're out of luck. There are subgames too, like stage diving: one player eye-cues another: the first plays the long slurred descent, as if leaping through the air; the other plays the SPLAT of hitting the floor. Also the pogo itself: knocking one note between two octaves; sometimes everyone can do it at a different tempo. Also head-banging: any pair of players can play a note they share, in a specified octave, according to the score—cornet and piano may sound an A together, say, and trombone and piano a G#—pairs which combine in long ensemble chords. As sometime Janssen sideman Eric Boeren points out, Guus has selected the pitches so that the chords have a consistent coloring, no matter what notes people choose.

There is a similar game in "Estampie"—horn players can sound one of three notes exclusive to each, on cue—with similarly consistent results. That one has a simpler cue game too, in which the drummer is gatekeeper for the horns, and guitar for anything with strings, including piano. At any time during a collective improvisation, the gatekeeper may sound four steady bass hits in any steady tempo. The musicians under their control must stop what they're doing on the first beat—this takes careful attention, obviously—and resume on the fourth beat, in the tempo just dictated. Sometimes the patterns overlap; when the count-off is very slow, the music gets spare to the point of pointillism.

Janssen's 11-piece Orchestra plays "Pogo 1" (and "2") on the live '88 *Dancing Series* (his first for his own Geestgronden label); on this version Reijseger "steals" the solo from piano. The band also had Jacques Palinckx on guitars, Wierbos and Americans Herb Robertson on trumpet and Vincent Chancey on French horn. All the pieces comment on dance rhythms. "Hip Hop" makes use of "Estampie"-like rhythm cues, and an identifier Janssen and (sideman) Termos have in common—the high squawk of a sustained minor second from the saxes, held for a bar, dissonant metric order— and one all Guus's own: a sleek ascending arpeggio based on the overtone series of the bass clarinet: a widely spaced triad at the bottom with a bunched 7th, 9th, 11th and 13th stacked on top—a telescoping chord that also figures in *Bruuks* for ensemble and *Keer* for orchestra, same period. "Jojo Jive" is the most puckish and jazz-based (and swinging, in 2/4) tune, colored by Ellingtonian wah-wah interjections. "Passepied" is a child-of-minimalism's 16th-note huff'n'puff; only "Mambo" takes its subject matter literally, right down to the one-chord piano break, minimalist montuno.

Next came the solo piano CD *Klankast*—wordplay: *klank* means sound, *kast* a box or case—from concerts between 1987 and '91. It's idea-rich and high-calorie, his touch precise, his ideas scalpel-sharp. "Mikstuur" shows his harmonic playfulness; the dominant chords that end a phrase never resolve to the tonic (or perhaps resolve to a silent tonic: there is always a pause after the V chord where the I chord should go). The trick, or part of it, is to always make that last chord played sound to the ear like an unresolved dominant, not the tonic itself.

"Ostinato I" has chords resolving loudly over the wrong place in bass riffs, as if two pianists lost in their own reveries were playing four hands. "Scheel" explores hand-dampened strings; on "Koprol" he rides a couch's carpet roller along the keys, arpeggios that out-arp harp. The piece "Klankast" is missing-note rather than wrong-note music: very spare, bars between single notes sometimes, like Cage's adaptations of old American hymns, from which most of the notes have been removed: spare, modern, but somehow familiar. (It could almost be "Mood Indigo" evaporated.) "Ostinato II" pits a Tristano bass line against two right-hand parts: whatever short phrase he improvises he immediately plays again in a lower register. (Then he does basically the same routine with hands reversed.) For solo piano puzzle solving, you can't do better.

"Pogo 3" turned up on the solo *Harpsichord* (Geestgronden), recorded mostly in 1991. Other improvisers had flirted with prepiano keyboards—jazz pianists would play harpsichord for a lark in the studio, Keith Jarrett made the solo-clavichord *The Book of Ways* in 1986—but Janssen's commitment to the harpsichord is long-term. He plays occasional solo concerts, and played on the recording of *Zoek*, his 1993 double concerto for piccolo and harpsichord (another piece like "Mikstuur" designed to subvert the rules of western harmony: in *Zoek* (Seek) the traditional V–I cadence always ushers in harmonic instability instead of resolution, by immediately jumping to some remote chord. It has some boogie in the bass as well).

On *Harpsichord* Janssen is particularly attracted to the guitaristic aspects of plucked strings and quick decay; when he slowly draws a metal bar along a string to change its pitch, as he does on piano, he's Ry Cooder playing a bottleneck blues. He gets under harpsichord's skin as well as its hood: uses it for a sort of esthetic time travel, returning to the aesthos of baroque improvisation, but knowing what we moderns know. He reintroduces the virtuoso improvising Bach knew well but academics long since lost, does it not to recreate a bygone style but to exploit good old ideas. He selects antiques for functionalism not quaint appearance. Janssen places baroque figurations over an insistent boogie bass on a reworked "Ostinato 1," and uses many of the same devices he does on piano: clanging dense dissonant chords, Tristanic walking bass lines, quick about-faces, modern dance rhythms ("Cha Tsja"—in Dutch, second word transliteration of the first). He brings the instrument back alive.

Nineteen ninety-four saw the premiere of Janssen's opera *Noach*, libretto in Dutch by his business manager Friso Haverkamp, designed for the stage by painter Karel Appel. (Much Dutch vocal music is written with English texts to try to attract a wider audience; Guus and company racked up points at home by using the mother tongue.) In this environmentalist rethink of the flood, Noah is the bad guy for letting too many animals die; his wife (sung by Claren McFadden) is the hero. The text exalts biodiversity—there's a lament for the dodo, picked off for sport on Mauritius by bored Dutch sailors—so it makes sense the score is as inclusive as possible. The Nieuw Artis Orchestra—Artis is the Amsterdam zoo—was a revamp of the *Dancing Series* band peppered with a few classical musicians, and supplemented by a quartet of Tuvan throat singers, the Mondrian string quartet, and tapes (Peter Cusack) and electronics worked up at STEIM. The reed and brass sections were responsible for the animal effects; Termos wasn't present, but his signature hyena cries were.

Here Janssen uses jazz and free jazz as colors, tactics, languages in the Babel of the antediluvian world. But the work holds together, feels whole, even when the roving spotlight settles on strings, saxes, Tuvans and the speaking narrator in short order. It even survives the great green cliche, the taped whalesong, partly because that sound returns transformed as a motif for linchpin reeds (Baars on clarinet, Jorrit Dijkstra and Peter van Bergen on saxes).

In a way, "Livery Stable Blues" is part of *Noach*'s cultural baggage, just as Volharding is somewhere (distant) behind the sax-dominated ensemble. There is a little bit of explicit jazz rhythm—notably just before the quietest ending in opera history, defying expectations. To be sure, he has opera singers opera singing, though the background might be bossa nova with Tuvans chiming in. But overall, there is unusually surging momentum for an opera, rhythmic punchiness and a buildup and outflow of tension outside a serialist's or minimalist's frame of reference. *Noach's* tide is jazz's benefits digested. And for once an orchestra plays the swinging bits convincingly.

♫

There was a curious situation in Holland in the '80s, where a number of musicians emerging as leaders were also busy working as sidefolk. If it seemed strange that many bands featured some combination of Baars, Michael Moore, Wierbos, Glerum, Reijseger and Guus himself, these bands did a good job of not sounding alike, tribute to them and the leaders. They brought a high level of musical intelligence to any project.

As they grew more busy with their own projects, these floaters became less available for hire work—Guus himself dropping out of Clusone 4 at least partly for that reason. In the '80s he (and Termos, and most of the above) were in and out of Maarten Altena's bands, which we'll get to. For a time in the mid-'90s Janssen had a septet with Boeren, Buis and Dijkstra on winds and Palinckx, Glerum and Wim Janssen in the rhythm section—good players for the most part, though as soloists they couldn't compete with Guus as analyzer and executor of his own compositions.

Which is why the trio Janssen Glerum Janssen—Wim's idea, by the way—is his most fully realized group to date, and *Lighter* his most perfect group record. For Guus, the piano-bass-drums trio is as classic a lineup as string quartet, one with its own traditions to work with or against. It is also a fresh format for examining old pieces, something he particularly enjoys. More than half of *Lighter* is oldies, many previously recorded. Tristano is a pet topic: "After LT" (which freezes Tristano's rapid motion into stop-action vignettes, à la early photographer Eadweard Muybridge); "Marshcello" (named for Tristano tenor Warne Marsh, and the instrument—Reijseger's —its snaky melody was written for); Tristano's own line on old chords "Lennie's Pennies," as straightforward a jazz trio performance as Janssen has recorded.

Yet his heart seems more with swing-era pianists and trios this time out. One indicator is recurrent use of piano left hand and bowed bass in unison or yoked octaves, for a groaning Slam Stewart effect. It occurs for example on the opener "Stomp," juxtaposing sturdy stamping-machine rhythm and a light paraphrase of "Stompin' at the Savoy."

"After AT" is explicit homage to the elaborate arrangements the Tatum (or Nat Cole) trios would cook up: little scored breaks, interludes, preplanned rhythm change-ups, those (sometimes minute) details that depend on careful rehearsal and crack timing. But it replaces Tatum's crush of ideas with wide-open spaces, in which unison or staggered hits are precisely placed, in time and otherwise; Glerum is assigned some exacting high notes, Wim many precise attacks (even the pitches of his cymbals are factored in). The "After . . . " series (in Dutch, "Vrij naar . . . ") also includes pieces for Monk (more precise hits, as in his comping), Erroll Garner—based on the first three notes of "Misty"—and Bill Evans and Cecil Taylor so far.

Guus had recorded "One Bar" on *Harpsichord*, where it doesn't quite come off, but on *Lighter* it does. A torturous stuck-record stutter gives way to one swinging bar, then returns to its old pattern, as if you never actually heard it, à la *Streepjes*. Once the point is made, however, the trio drop it and swing into one-bar trades for piano and drums: swing becomes its subject, not just an aside. The other Janssen standard here is "Hi Hat," built around a pet motif: the highest note on the piano played in ching-a-ching ride cymbal rhythm, complicated by an akilter counter-rhythm each player keeps going as well—highest note because it's the one on piano that most closely matches a closed hi-hat's rapid decay. It is such a favorite ploy it sometimes seems he can't go near the piano's top end without alluding to it. And he is fond of that quick-decay register; the piano's rightmost three or four notes are his traps.

Charles Ives, by the way, had imitated drums on piano while a boy.

The "Hi Hat" rhythmic figure—dotted quarter note, quarter, eighth, 3:2:1—is crucial for Janssen, turns up in several of his composed pieces, notably "Voetnoot" (Footnote) for piccolo solo, the orchestra piece *Deviaties* (Deviations) and "Klotz" for septet including hi-hat and violin. "Klotz" was written, or rather parts of "Hi Hat" and "After AT" were rewritten, for Gidon Kremer. Sometimes Guus plays the (increasingly wobbly) percussion part himself.

Janssen's jazz sources may be transformed to point of disguise: ideas developed in the mind before being returned to the instruments. The orchestra piece *Passevite*—that's a soupmaker's foodmill—in four "moments" as Janssen terms it, derives its melodic material from a six-chord sequence Tristano sometimes used to "sign" an improvisation. (Guus cites "Bud" on *New Tristano*).

"I take those six chords and put it through the mill." Going on to say he wrote it more or less in the style of maverick '50s jazz arrangers like Bill Russo and Johnny Carisi, themselves influenced by classical music, looping the loop. He adds that the percussionist's brushes-on-skins is meant to suggest the hiss of a valued old cassette you've worn out, and that the fast final moment is rewind. The way he bobbles the six chords between piano and orchestra, a cut-up scramble, is the meat of the piece; a few sunny West Coast chords pop out along the way, but not so many. But in the horns one can hear the claustrophobic rigor of a Tristano line.

And yet for all his compositional smarts some ideas come more easily in improvisation. His two-piano piece *Veranderingen* (Changes) is fitfully interesting; his every-few-years improvised piano duo with Steve Beresford is fast and telepathic—they have the same short attention span, raising and dropping ideas at the same moment—and better.

Some minds are so quick certain ideas come out fully formed only in improvisation: by the time they reach for paper it may be fading like a dream. (That's why composed music is often not as tight as improvised—gotcha, huh?) But give Guus his due, he gets the animating breath of improvisation into composition often enough to make it one of his defining traits. Instant composition's apposite opposite: frozen improvisation.

For any composer working with established units, creation is collaborative, Ellington to Volharding to Janssen. "For me working with Wim is like having a Siamese twin. There is a lot that we don't have to discuss, which is completely clear. But there are moments of irritation, because we know each other too well. The other thing is, it's always 'Guus Janssen' people speak of, while part of the conceptual rights are Wim's.

"Paul Termos dealt with the same problem. He went out of my groups in the end, and that was better for us. We can still walk on stage and improvise, no rehearsing, no thinking about it, just relying on our shared history, the tradition that we built together. Our ideas were complementary on a conceptual level. I was looking for the clear image in music, which he is also, but he can also be very dirty, despoiling, in his tone and approach. That kind of clash between concepts made for some amazing moments. But then it's always 'Guus Janssen is the leader of the band.' You can imagine how musicians can get tired of that."

When Paul Termos makes a joke he laughs hard and his body shakes; when he says something serious he may scrunch his eyes shut and furrow his brow. His compositions have always been harder to read. Take his first recorded piece, 1976's "Nieuw werk" for piano and Harry Sparnaay. It begins with a boogie-woogie bass line for bass clarinet. Then piano enters on time, same figure—only once it starts, Sparnaay pauses for one beat before his next repeat, so as soon as they begin playing together they're not together, but one beat apart, echo of Koppelaar's counting problem. (This was pre–Punt Uit, but he'd heard Bert often enough.) Is this inept minimalism, where identical lines pop out of phase with each other too quickly, or inept jazz, someone having turned the beat around? Either way, it seems someone has made a mistake, except that a composer who can pose this conundrum in the space of a few seconds knows exactly what he's doing. That's Termos: as he likes to say, he uses clear materials to ambiguous effect, gives few clues how seriously you should take the music.

"Ferdinand Bordewijk's *Karakter* is one of the best books in Dutch for me: often you don't know if he intends something to be funny or serious, or where the border between the two is, or the moment when one goes into the other. If musical humor is too explicit, it doesn't work. It's better if you're not sure. I'd rather not know myself. Better if, without intending it, I come into a situation that's open to more than one interpretation."

A deceptive simplicity is his hallmark. As Peter Cusack observed, Dutch improvisers tend to be more interested in notes than pure sound (crackle boxes aside), a compositional bias. As saxophonist Termos gets into some strange sounds, but as composer he favors an instrument's mainstream sound over special effects. He likes to convey ideas using the most reduced materials. At the outset of his 1997 Flute Concerto, a chipper repeating C-major arpeggio in fast 5/8 is undercut by a low droning D from clarinets: bitonality implied using only four pitches. That's minimalism with a vengeance.

In many ways Termos is the most typically Dutch composer in this book. He integrates clarity, gentle humor, rigor (or Benninky single-mindedness), wooden-shoe timing, game tactics, puckish grace, homophony, minimalist quilting, deliberate mistakes and sleek attractive surfaces into improvised music as thoroughly as anyone does. His compositional style works equally well in the concert hall and as improvisers' springboard.

Guus Janssen (like Andriessen) has a business head, is organized. Paul Termos (like Mengelberg) is less so. By his own admission, his composing and improvising cross each other up more than create career momentum. One discipline steals time from the other.

"Pieces that go wrong," Termos calls compositions like "Nieuw werk," mentioning the subversive rewrites of the classics by Gilius van Bergeijk and Maurice Horsthuis's anecdotalism as particular inspirations. One might also note parallels to Teo Joling's music-theater pieces, for which Termos and the Janssens worked up music in the late '80s. Termos says the shifting perspective in "Nieuw werk"—which after that opening keeps turning the same materials over and over, balancing motion and stasis with Carl Stalling–like suppleness—was influenced by visual art, like David Hockney's skewed perspective murals made up of overlapping photographs.

In the early '80s Paul's career started clicking on both tracks. He was writing for and touring widely with Maarten Altena's quartet, and playing Nichols with ICP, really working on building up his jazz chops and chord-parsing on alto. He was also writing a slew of composed works for various sized groups—including a saxophone concerto short on jazzy gestures—and won an arts prize from Amsterdam city for *Carrara*, solo piano opus Guus Janssen later recorded.

Carrara is a variety of fine Italian marble, and *Carrara* is one of several compositions Termos wrote around then that you can read as comments on Andriessen's monumental pieces like *De Staat* and *Mausoleum*, respective texts Plato and Bakunin. Termos confesses ambivalence toward Andriessen: likes the personal take on minimalism, hates the bombast. *Carrara* spoofs his monumentalism (or postmodernizes it: skeletal outline of the old marble temple constructed out of exposed beams). It takes one repeated tone (a pair of dotted eighth notes) and then bounces it around the keyboard, parading through five registers up and down the staircase. The interval they leap by is a "stretched octave," a minor ninth: the pitches are A Bb B C Db. The piece refutes the concept of octave equivalence, the idea that a note has the same function in any register. If you played *Carrara*'s pitches on adjacent keys it would come off like the rising-falling background lick on the James Bond theme. But spread out over five and a half octaves they really sound like something, albeit something obviously comical in intent, despite its hard-edged quality.

"Nothing's happening but it says 'I'm Big! Here I Am! Octaves!'"

In *Carrara* every seeming development is a blind alley. In one sequence the same trembling chord is played alternately very loud and very quiet, to glorious lack of effect. The piece makes the same imperial speeches over and over, empty rhetoric. (An awful lot of Termos's big pieces are really Big: 20 minutes where 10 would do.) Maybe it's also comment on his teacher Ton de Leeuw's insistence on economy: it squanders time as it carefully metes out its meager materials, makes them last all winter. Somehow, it avoids sounding clownish. This musical Stonehenge inhabits its own universe.

In the same period, he wrote *Fortuna* for mixed choir and chamber group, a piece which keeps going wrong—because it seems out of scale with itself, the Mormon Tabernacle Choir singing Monty Python's lumberjack song, or because the accompaniment doesn't fit, or the singers make awkward repeats like a skipping LP, or the rests are so long you don't know if or when it's over—but which also à la Mengelberg's parodic commissions contains moments of real beauty.

His most ambitious piece from the period, *Expres(s)* for eleven instruments, is a sort of summing up: unisons (particularly for two instruments blended to create a new sonority), stretched octaves (there's some all-but verbatim *Carrara* in the piano), scrambling lines taken straight off his saxophone. He also chalkboards a connection between Andriessen's pulsing and Bernard Herrmann's—he is used to folks pointing out resemblance to Herrmann's rhythmic violins, though Paul doesn't know his music—and affectionately borrows his concluding theme from Horsthuis's "Bleekgezicht." (Was its composer flattered? "Maybe he could have told me first.") A very nice piece, albeit one tied to improvised music only in its brisk flow; it is anything but minimalist in the way the basic material keeps changing like moving scenery.

"Nieuw werk" aside, these compositions were issued later if at all. Paul's reductive/ambiguous pieces got conspicuous play on Altena's quartet records, but Termos's first album under his own name in either field was *Solo 84–85* (Claxon), pieces for alto saxophone. Paul says Lacy's solo music is greater inspiration than Anthony Braxton's but Braxton's is closer kin to the way each solo composition isolates a different area to examine. That's also true of the materials themselves: wide-leaping, serrated melodies; kernels expanding and contracting, knocking beats and meters out of whack; flutter tones, multiphonics and other selected textures; dogs in the alley and Lee Konitz flotation.

There's a mild resemblance personalitywise to Braxton too: catholic in his enthusiasms, sweet disposition, a little stiff.

Termos's "For Sandy Nelson" leads off *POK* (Geestgronden) by the trio Janssen Termos Janssen, 1989 CD mostly given to trio and duo improvisations. It bridges several of Paul's interests, like Ornette's alto playing (Guus's self-explanatory "Boogie & Inversion") and Lee Konitz's ("Elliots Bag," Tristano with tempo drift) and skeletal cool jazz in general—during an interview he pulls out Shelly Manne's *"The Three"* & *"The Two,"* a useful parallel—and the forgotten pre-Beatles rock years symbolized by Sandy Nelson's surf-instrumental drums features.

Paul Termos is the first real rock and roll baby of Dutch composer/improvisers. (Andriessen's thing for Janet Jackson is about pop not rock.) For Termos the appeal of rock and roll was generational. He had always wanted to make a rebel noise; a story circulates in his family about Paul leading kids around the neighborhood, banging a drum like little Oskar. His faith in simple (and sometimes noisy) materials owes an awful lot to that background. Putting "Nieuw werk" in the very unclarinetty but very R&Ry key of more or less E-major is one fingerprint.

"I liked rock music from the pre-Beatle period, people like Phil Spector, an influence I shared with a lot of people. The books always describe this period as the lowest point of rock and roll, but I grew up with it. Connie Francis is someone I can really enjoy. Phil Spector had a more open kind of structure than the guitar sound of later rock music. Pre-Beatles, guitarists played few notes, using very simple but very comical gimmicks. Think of Dick Dale, the original surf music: it has a lot of fun in it."

"For Sandy Nelson" takes a basic surf drum break and develops it as a motif, coupled with a peppy little riff with awkwardness built in: the rests that interrupt it are just long enough to curb momentum. He had already used a variation on the same figure as rhythmic focus for *Bedankt maecenas*, 1982 composition for the Nieuw Ensemble.

"I was always inspired by things that are simple and clear and at the same moment have a kind of lucidity. I never made pop art, but pop art does look at reality in a certain way. You can listen to Sandy Nelson music or a lot of other naive rock things from that time in a similar way. Sandy Nelson as a person is not so important for me, but that surf drum pattern interested me as a kind of hallmark for that kind of music. I like to isolate such things, from pop or wherever, and make something different from it, which you still can recognize, and which still has some feeling in it."

Termos's "Pok" pits open improvisations in which short percussive POKs are a key ingredient, interrupted by a vaguely Ornetty skip-along theme which anyone can cue whenever, in any tempo. It deliberately avoids fashionable blurring of composed and improvised content, but the trio still make it whole, assembling the parts from composers' perspectives. (Wim too—he helped coin the shared language.) Still, open improvising was the trio's (and subduos') great strength; in that sense it took the two composers out of their usual element. The group lasted till the early '90s, when Wim needed a break from it, but played a reunion gig at New York's Knitting Factory in June '96. The band's successor is the Janssen Termos Bennink trio where the composers, optimists, try to get Han to play the old trio's repertoire. But with Han the parts have a tendency to slide out of sync—drums a couple of beats behind every cutoff or new direction, seismic shifting.

On *POK*, the Janssens duo "Scheel" (Squinting, or Crosseyed) sounds like a wrong-note travesty of baroque music, analog to Termos the composer's genial mangling of the virtuoso piano piece, or choral music, or string quartet (a Herrmanny one from 1987, cello's lowest note its metronome, much mighty sawing conveying little information). Termos's recorder solo "Vuoto ossesso" is like a sarcastic remake of Loevendie's "Duo" for alternating bass clarinet voices. Here one voice doodles little recordery lines and the other shrieks as shrilly as the composer could figure it. (Listen to the tape loud for a good sadomasochistic experience, he said.)

There were echoes of that split-voice duality in the flute concerto too. In that work he keeps two or three layers going, which might shift out of sync, or infiltrate, heckle or contradict the others. Seemingly ornamental details blossom into melodies; other ideas ripe for development are left hanging. Not hard to see his improvising experience in that.

Still, Termos is a real composer at heart: needs time to collect his thoughts. After 20 years in the business he'd made only four jazz records with his name on the front, and it wasn't till 1997 that he got a whole CD devoted to his compositions. A lot of his energy went into being second composer and idea-log in Altena and Janssen groups.

As composer for improvised music his major statement so far is *Shakes & Sounds* (Geestgronden) by the Termos Tentet. Members say rehearsals could be chaotic, but everyone sounds engaged and exceptionally focused on the specifics of the material. By now his pieces sound as Dutch as Copland's do American. He had Boeren and Wierbos on brass, Wil Offermans or (briefly) Anne La Berge on flute or piccolo, Peter van Bergen on tenor saxophone and contrabass clarinet, Michiel Scheen on piano, Hans Hasebos on vibes, Glerum, Vatcher and singer Jodi Gilbert. She's an excellent improviser: accurate pitch, power pipes, attentive listener, mobile; even when threatening to go over the top she stays playful. She could add a nattering Bulgarian edge too: the Balkanization of improvised vocals. Her voice is one of the band's identifiers. Another is the frictive scrape of longtone multiphonics from saxes voiced in fourths; another is Vatcher's heavy if sparing Sandy Nelsonish tom-tom hits.

The writing is most assured: a lovely waltz; a pulsing-beat piece where rude saxophone lines are repeated more smoothly by voice and brass: "Zing mij na" (Sing After Me).

Termos's rock nostalgia is more pronounced than ever, peaking with "Sam the Sham Was a Pharoa." It begins with a wobbling half-step bass line (*Jaws* theme probably an unconscious forebear) which forms the backdrop for a stately brass melody '60s relics will eventually recognize: "Wooly Bully." The joke stands up to repeated listening.

He was also writing games for improvisers, such as "La La La 1," for four duos: two improvising, two cuing. Once past the head, trombone/voice and vibes/drums perform (sometimes very) short improvisations, their length controlled by the other duos: two saxes skronking long notes turn the first improvising duo off and the second on; a more discreet signal from trumpet and flute does the opposite. Both cues are contained in the written head, which points the way. "One set of duos makes the content while the signal duos make the form. The idea is to create a kind of swing to the rhythm of the fragments, so a lot depends on the signalers." He gets what he seeks; the fixed form of the signals themselves gives the piece a call-and-response structure that focuses all the improvisers, makes them form an alliance even as the rules prevent them from ever playing together.

Termos acknowledges Zorn's influence on the games, but where the sound of "Cobra" has dead spots—where player or players stop to give hand cues or to read signals from a prompter—Termos's cues themselves are musical, so there's no interruption.

At the other extreme are his delicate, lyrical pieces almost entirely through-composed, which fit with the games on the CD because they fit the musicians so well. He's a good tailor. But one thing that made the album so good—honing the same material over time—eventually took its toll. After three years playing the same book fatigue set in, and the Tentet broke up before a second CD could be completed. The leftovers eventually came out on his next CD; by then he was off on new tangents.

"In the last few years, I've been listening to some jazz of the '50s and early '60s, thinking about it as a kind of development which never got worked through, because it was overruled by other developments. I started thinking about what would happen if you tried to pick it up from where it left off. It's like studying philosophy. You pick a philosopher and try to bring their thinking further.

"One good thing from the early free-jazz period was the use of very small themes, but that became a stereotyped kind of solution. Now we deal with more complex forms, but I think the compositions still have a kind of basic quality, to spur true free improvisation, and give that improvisation excitement and momentum. That's also the striking thing about 'La La La 1'—a more or less complicated structure built from these very short elements."

In 1995 he formed the nonet Double Express, bringing back van Bergen, Scheen, Glerum and Wim Janssen, along with Henk Bakker on bass clarinet, harpist Ulrike von Meier and on some pieces, classical sopranos Margo Rens and Janice Jackson. (Later Glerum left and the Joe Williamson came in. He's from Vancouver, was passing through town, looked around, sold his return ticket.) It's an attempt to bring all his rings under one big top, from the barbaric thumping of floor tom, Sandy Nelson thundering in the distance, to the conjoined saxes barking long notes from the Tentet period, to de rigeuer rigorous Dutch chamber music. The material is cut clean as marble. No brass and three reeds brings out the Braxton and the Volharding in his blocky repeater riffs. On their CD *Death Dance of Principles* (Geestgronden—the one with the Tentet leftovers) the reed and voice sections each stick together to a fault.

(In some pieces for Double Express there are echoes of his 1991 Volharding commission *Linea Recta*, postminimal in its static textures and thematic contrasts. Termos: "With its very objective repeats, monotonous and aggressive in a certain way, as one critic said it comes to the border of being boring. But when you do it with great intensity, that can be fascinating. There's a kind of intensity and power that comes across when you reduce the materials that far." One thinks again of *Carrara*: concentrated materials running on and on without conjuring Riley, Reich or Glass. In a way the slow pulsing repeats sound more like Bernard Herrmann than ever: *Psycho* knife slashes for the brain.)

Double Express is designed to cut a wide swath, sopranos and harp at one extreme, van Bergen's split tone squalling at the other. The saxes dominate—Termos gives himself the swinging blues break on "Death Dance of Principles"—and he solves the problem of what to do with classical sopranos on jazz pieces by having 'em sit them out (like big-band singers in this way only). When he does use them, most always in unison or harmony, they're in your face: strong voices, heavy legit vibrato. Hearing them side by side with raunchy free play makes for a bizarre effect, but on the first CD at least Double Express didn't yet measure up to the Tentet.

Still, in Termos's best work musical worlds are not discreetly separated, nor do they flow together as in a dream, but infect one another culturally. "Ensemblage" literally deconstructs Bizet's *Carmen* and Bellini's *Norma*: he has the sopranos sing familiar passages from either which however fold over each other—dueling divas—with dissonant instrumental interruptions, until it ends unexpectedly with some sort of industrial grinding. It doesn't sound slapped together only because it's so well-balanced.

The main problem with his writing for voice is his indifference to lyrics: "La La La 1" is all la-la-las for Gilbert, "Li La Lo" all li-la-los for Rens and Jackson. It may have something to do with hearing American pop on the radio as a kid; there are songs he's known forever and still likes to sing that he doesn't know the right words to. Whatever fits the meter will do.

"When I write for improvising musicians, mostly I use the kind of materials, and a way of thinking, which I'd mastered already in my development as a composer, and can apply very easily to improvisers. The kind of things I experimented with ten years ago I'm handy with now."

In a piece like "Death Dance of Principles" (where the swinging section finally breaks down, other worlds intruding) one again hears how jazz has become another part of the well-rounded musicians' background, and improvisation a normal ingredient. It's a cliche to lament that classical musicians lost the ability and desire to improvise way back when. More useful to put it back in, à la Termos and Janssen. What they do mirrors Dutch history: They assemble the little provinces into a larger and more powerful state.

"A few years ago, every reviewer and jazz critic talked about how hard it was to tell the improvised from the composed material in certain groups, like Maarten Altena's. This was proclaimed by the critics and by Maarten himself as a kind of breakthrough. But I think it's more fun for the audience to know when somebody is improvising. Improvising is more risky, and it's exciting to watch people make something from nothing in the moment, wrestling with that challenge, and doing it without making improvisation subordinate, to the point where it loses its excitement."

Chapter Thirteen
Side Exit

"But it's not jazz that we play. Not everyone seems to understand this. In what way is it jazz?"

MAARTEN ALTENA, 1994

Maarten Altena looks medieval: gaunt face, sunken eyes, haunted expression you might see staring out from a canvas in the Rijksmuseum. His toothy laugh looks a little like a grimace.

His music too: no fat on it, severe, serious or awkwardly jocular.

Maarten Altena at the BIMhuis, September 1995: bass, violin, soprano voice, recorder, clarinet, trombone, piano, electric guitar, percussion. Three years ago, almost the same lineup, recorder sounded out of place, archaic. Now, guitar seems the odd axe out. Maarten's Ensemble sounds more and more like something out of a much earlier time—especially tonight, playing arrangements of Dowland lute music, Purcell and Machaut. It fits them, somehow, more than other pieces on the program like Alison Isadora's rethink of Byrne and Eno's "America Is Waiting."

"Because the Maarten Altena Ensemble was in financial difficulties, we needed to have a very nice program in order to get it financed. So I made a list of composers I thought would like to make something for my group, and asked them to write a piece inspired by music before 1600 and after 1970, 'when music was still modern,' as I wrote to them."

He touches on a frequently groused-about by-product of the subsidy system: one sure way to get composition or touring money, or gigs, is to come up with a concept or gimmick and work it off and on for a couple of years: Dowland, John Carter, Bob Graettinger.

"Lately I'm listening a lot to really old music, far pre-baroque: early monody, Spanish things, Sephardic influences. I like it very much: the kind of one-voice music that eventually became polyphony. I see a lot of things that are similar in a way to my own writing—how a melodic phrase can stand alone, how you can make a chord by letting one note in a melody sustain in time, and then another and another. In other words I'm somebody who structures from a melodic or intervallic way of thinking in music."

How did he get here from playing with Dexter Gordon?

"The reason I like the rhythmical side of a lot of jazz music is a kind of elasticity. Kenny Clarke had it, with Monk and Oscar Pettiford, and with Bud Powell in Paris with Pierre Michelot. Or Philly Joe Jones with Sam Jones on another Bud Powell session, where the rhythm seems built up from elastic single quarter notes. It's dancing, the way one quarter leads to the other. I don't know any other music where that is so dominant as in the best jazz music.

"There's something gymnastic about the way Kenny Clarke touches the cymbal, which is not necessarily virtuosic. Like when you're on a bicycle: you get a specific cadence, and you get the feeling at some particular moment that you are thinking not in two but in three, because you'll be trying to rest one leg or the other. A specific kind of equality between the legs. Not always 1, 2, 3, 4 but 1, 2, 3, or 1, 1, 1. It's the elastic cadence I like so much, how one moment relates to another. I think in jazz terminology it's called bouncing."

No, jazz has another word for this phenomenon—flexible strings of quarter notes, duple meter with a triple feel—and it says something about Altena that the word didn't spring to mind: swing.

—Does the War seem like something that happened during your lifetime?

"Oh yes. Not like, a baby hearing bombs falling, but I have a memory of the liberation. My parents climbed on the roof, took me with them, and it was so hilarious, after all those difficulties. There were little packages dropping from Swedish airplanes, I remember that. I don't have a strong visual memory, but remember the feeling, being on the roof, and everybody being happy. I was two or something." He was born 22 January 1943.

"But the War also affected my young life, because my granddaddy died of heart trouble in a detention camp—he was taken away because the organization of artists he was involved in was not associated with the Kultuurkamer—and a lot of my parents' Jewish friends disappeared. My parents also had a kind of bar where my father sang songs with friends, composers and musicians among them, in a clandestine atmosphere.

"We lived on Vossiusstraat near the Vondelpark: high steps, third floor, the whole street designed by Berlage. Big house, a little dark, a little somber, dark brown, a lot of nice things. My father was an art historian and collector. He had gone to the academy to become a painter, but saw that he was not good enough, so he decided to study art history. So the milieu—or class, if you want to put it in Marxist terminology—was middle-class academic, very focused on the bourgeois. To a degree I tried to hate it, because it oppressed emotional feelings.

"There was always music, classical music. My father played piano—he was an amateur composer—and my mother played also. My sister still plays flute, and my brother used to play piano." It's a musical family; the Mondrian Strings' Eduard and Jan Erik van Regteren Altena are second cousins.

"I started with cello, playing music at home, and then I switched to bass when I was 16 or 17, because I liked Miles Davis, the Modern Jazz Quartet, the Gerry Mulligan quartet and Monk. Miles Davis on Blue Note was the first big love. I still think the piano playing of Horace Silver on some of those tracks is fantastic. He's someone who can express himself in a few notes, one of those composers who says a lot with little material, like Monk also. Trying to keep the best notes and throwing away the rest, that's the ideal for me. I've never liked the virtuoso side of music in any respect. So I must have already intuitively liked the elimination of the extraneous.

"I went to the conservatory in 1961, for five years. When I came to the morning solfège class, and they saw that I was tired because I'd played in a club the evening before, they'd ask me to take rhythmic dictation, write down what you hear, and I didn't do as well as I could. 'See, he's playing jazz music, he's not good enough for this.' When you said that you'd been listening to some nice piece by Peter Schat, you were out. For them music had ended with Debussy, I think. It was not very progressive. I must also say I didn't learn to play bass very well, because the method was a little outdated. So after the conservatory I went to a guy in The Hague, and he showed me better fingerings, so I had more ease with positions and combining wider intervals which in principle you're not able to do.

"After I got out of the conservatory I played in a ballet orchestra for one year, played a lot of modern music: Stravinsky, Bartok, and Ives, a composer I like very much. After that I did a lot of improvising. I played with Willem Breuker, Theo Loevendie, with Misha, and had my first meetings with Derek Bailey, Evan Parker and all those people." Already in the mid-'60s he toured a little, played one gig with an ailing Bud Powell.

"Perhaps I like certain jazz bass players—Wellman Braud, Percy Heath, Wilbur Ware, Oscar Pettiford with Kenny Clarke especially, greasy and to the point—because they contribute to the float of the music. There's a kind of independence, a layer in Ives terms, that goes together well with the percussion player. I played jazz because I loved to, but I was smart enough to accept that I would never become a Ray Brown or Oscar Pettiford. I did my best, but when Willem and Misha started with the freer forms, for me it was a relief, because I didn't have to live up to that standard I felt I could never match.

"Around 1970 I did a tour as a bass player with Dexter Gordon, Martin van Duynhoven and Cees Slinger. I did well, I did good enough"—he's laughing—"but it was not fantastic. I started to bow solos, which was strange at that time. When I hear them back, I hear myself playing variations on the melody, like a baroque variation. Very strange. So there are some seeds of something that later on became more dominant, that I acknowledge as being of myself—my musical DNA if you want.

"I liked Dexter. He had a kind of class of his own. A guy with style. I still love his incredible sound, taking something raw and natural and refining it, like Debussy, who works with very basic stuff, fantastic color that makes it rich. I remember he got one outspoken review I thought was racist. But he was very dignified. I thought, how can you have that kind of self-esteem after this racist shit, and spending the first part of your life in totally racist circumstances, and be able to play so beautifully on shit material from Tin Pan Alley?

"There are some songs that are played so often, you think you can't listen to them anymore. 'All the Things You Are' is a good example. It's a perfect vehicle for melodic improvisation or whatever. But this is low-class material, if you want to put it in Marxist terms, to the average European musicologist, compared with high-class material like the G-minor symphony of Mozart."

—In the mid-'60s, did you see European improvised music as something apart from jazz?

"Of course. I was part of that awareness, that movement. Not as much as Han, who was immediately an intermediary between Brötzmann and Derek Bailey. But I did participate in some sessions, and step by step became part of it. During the time I was with ICP, I also worked with people from other countries like Derek and Brötzmann.

"Before ICP I played with Theo Loevendie, and I remember it was a little bit square, playing with him. He was much more rooted in jazz music, there was always a fixed beat. Loek Dikker was the same, he made his own compositions on fixed rhythms, in 4/4 mostly. I would say they were more out of the American musical mechanisms. The scene had a prehistoric dimension, with these different clans talking about one another, and when you worked with both, you felt divided loyalties.

"ICP was very good PR, to put it cynically. Part of the dominance of Han and Misha was the musical product, but it's good to remember that when you organize yourself well, and can verbalize what your means are—instant composing is an expression which is still used—then you make yourself more accessible, and people can remember you better. So you fix a name to a specific musical project."

His students like Arjen Gorter or Pablo Nahar may have invented better lines, but Altena had his pick of the good gigs, not least for the plasticity of his sound. Curiosity about new music led him to new techniques and the raunchy sounds progressive composers were all for, but there was more. On Marion Brown's *Porto Novo* in '67 his pizzicato is plump and long on sustain, far from the quick-decay violinish conservatory ideal. There too, pre-Dexter, he took variational arco solos. He's not being falsely modest about his limitations—these days, for example, he doesn't play so often in the thumb position, going for the real high notes. But he found his own voice early.

"The solo projects started in the '70s. I considered that the start of formulating my own music. After I had already toured in Canada, playing solo, I took a fall on a stairs and broke my wrist." His first solo LP *Handicaps* (ICP) '73 was the result. "There was a short cast on my arm, which limited use of my hand, so I cast the bass also; somebody I knew was working in a hospital and gave me the materials." The cast covered about half the bass's neck above the shoulders. "The cast was not designed to cover specific pitch area; it was theatrical—basic medical care for the bass—to draw a parallel between the player and the object. The subject and the object, in terms of Hegel, should be the same. The cast was roughly the size of the one on my arm. It didn't move, but there was room under it so the strings could resonate. People liked it."

The bass buzzed and rattled nicely, and he managed to execute some good rhythmic effects despite double handicaps. The LP was famously Dutch in its time—helping to define the absurd national outlook—not to mention anecdotal and high-concept as it gets. (For contrast some of the pieces were recorded after the casts came off, including "Handicaps II," for which bows were wedged between the strings.) Anecdotal and high-concept also describes the title track of the 1975 sequel *Tuning the Bass* (ICP). Call it an exercise in presampling. On a trip to Los Angeles Altena had picked up session pro Carol Kaye's 2-LP instructional *How to Play the Electric Bass.* Altena made a loop out of the first item, "Tuning." In time to a slow metronome, Kaye sounds the tones of the open strings for the novice to tune to, E E E E A A A A D D D D G G G G, served very dry. Altena looped it onto a cassette which he played along with or against. His low-key scratchy sounds made a simple but effective contrast.

"I think this was the reason, or rationalization: 'This is a bass guitar, but listen everybody, I play doublebass, an entirely different world.' And it's also the most basic form of playing bass together."

The rest of Altena's LP displays his zoo of sounds: slow bowed groans, high wheezy arco, long-sustaining pizzicato, buzzing pizz, rattle of objects thrust between strings (prepared bass, if you like), rattle of bass played with a clawlike string mute, the highest and lowest strings played simultaneously, bowed from behind. "Derek, Wilbur and the Blues" features freak squeak falsetto and patented two-tier pizz: initial attack followed by a kind of aftershock, *k'ploeng!* His music definitely has a crazy momentum, especially when he plays bumblebee arco, but it's not without wooden-shoe timing. There is an opulence to the sound that makes up for his limitations.

In the '70s he played with Breuker, Mengelberg, Volharding (politics not music forced him out), the Cusack-and-Janssen pool, German trombonist Gunter Christmann, Derek Bailey's Company conclaves, Steve Lacy. After the quartet *Lumps* he and Lacy made the 1978 duo *High, Low and Order* (reissued on CD). "I've always liked improvising with Lacy very much. Looking back, I think what I must have liked was that he also has this clear melodic style, and doesn't use too many notes. Like Monk. In that duo, I had the specific role of adding expressionism to it. Or a kind of very basic, almost archaic, percussive bass style, to give his playing a frame."

Altena and Waisvisz also did their sardonic theater evenings, and five annual Claxon festivals, mostly in Utrecht (which sponsored a number of Dutch debuts, John Zorn's among them), and some trio gigs in Germany with guitarist Hans Reichel. In 1977 Altena left ICP; playing with Han, he had to amplify his bass so much, it might as well have been Carol Kaye's fretted Fender.

"That was the period I started to think about my own things. K'PLOENG was the start of organizing my own little events with people that I liked. The group was an attempt to define a specific sound, of strings and percussion and electronics." K'PLOENG was the onomatopoetic name of a pool of six players who recorded live for his new Claxon label in December '77. Selections for various combinations were drawn from three Dutch concerts. Waisvisz played mostly crackle synth; Derek Bailey was on splintery guitar, Maurice Horsthuis on viola. Terry Day—English improviser of Peter Cusack's generation—played quiet drums and some other items, spread out like junk on the floor. Maarten's sometime duo partner Tristan Honsinger was on cello. (They were supposed to make a duo CD for FMP spinoff SAJ in '76, but weren't happy with the results. Instead *Live Performances* became a split solo record, one side for each.) For a Dutch record *K'PLOENG* is pretty English, Company-like, though the microtonal blends of Day's rubbed balloons and Michel's crackle synth and "Hawaisz guitar" make one duo rather rauchier. It was very short on form, had Bailey's aversion to overarching shape.

Also starting in 1977 Altena joined Teo Joling in a few two-man music-theater shows. Maarten would play cello, he and it festooned with conifer branches, or play walking bass while walking on a treadmill; he'd wear a model battleship attached with guy wires, or hold and bow the bass horizontally, neck forward, as if carrying a canoe. In 1980 and '81, Altena and Horsthuis made live recordings for the LP *Grand DuO* (Claxon), Maarten again on cello as well as bass. In retrospect, it was his farewell to rambunctious freeplay.

Becoming a leader, these were the baby steps.

"I'm very hungry as a person, I like a lot of things. That means you have a lot of things seducing you. You have to take seductions seriously, because you're not seduced for nothing. If you take it as seriously as you think it is worth, then you have to raise yourself to the standard the seduction demands. So when I thought, 'Okay, I've heard the free music'—and it's very arrogant to say so, I only speak for myself—I knew I couldn't express myself further with it. It was finished. But I didn't regret anything; I never regret things.

"I had always liked Derek Bailey's music very much, and we often had discussions about composing. Derek sees it as a class thing, high art and low art and all that. I always said that I didn't see it that way, because I couldn't express my things without composing. (It sounds defensive when I say it like this.) But he always said that to him, it was very natural for me to do that. I remember his words: 'Some of your music has a kind of elegance to it, that I can imagine you could not express in another way.'

"But Derek and I are more similar than you'd think at first glance. The means are totally different, but we've both done only the things we really liked. My relationship with him has stayed very stable, whatever I did. I'm not a hardcore improviser anymore, but we have mutual respect for what we do."

About a year after Altena said that, he read some CD notes where I'd characterized him as a "disillusioned improviser turned composer." The next couple of times I saw him, he told me how little he cared for that. For about an hour. I never get disillusioned, he explained, I change first. On cross-examination, he did allow that he used to believe in the viability of improvising with larger groups—K'PLOENG, say—which he no longer does. The only time his current nonet walks on stage without sheet music, conductor Butch Morris is there to direct them.

Altena does have a habit of rejecting his own past—each new seduction means spurning the old love, dropped like the "van Regteren" from his name. He shucked it in this same period, seeing it as some ancestor's pretention to nobility.

Like most of us, he can forget later how far the heat of an infatuation had carried him. An example: In October 1991 Maarten told me his favorite composer was

Francesco Donatoni, for the way he'd balance order and chaos. (He went on about it so, I'd jotted myself a note about it.) Five years later he was complaining that Guus Janssen (in a just-published January '92 interview) had called him a big Donatoni fan.

Anyway: Altena played jazz early, but by the early '70s he'd rejected it in terms of hard-core improvising. As he says, he was already inching toward being a composer working up his solo programs, repeating certain ideas or titles from one program to another, even if the particulars were improvised. But that tendency toward repetition was equally true of Derek, Evan Parker, Han or Misha. By 1980 he was really thinking, and writing, like a composer.

For Joling's 1978 show *Willem de Zwijger* (William the Silent)—about William of Orange—Altena assembled a quartet: Horsthuis on viola, Termos on alto sax, Maud Sauer on oboe. The main theme co-credited to Altena and Horsthuis, with its mock antiquated gestures, was a harbinger of music to come. That unit became the first Altena Quartet, whose 1980 debut was *Op Stap* (Stepping Out) on Claxon.

Horsthuis: "I'm not sure how it happened. I had a quartet with Maarten and oboe and two years later it was the Maarten Altena quartet." Altena says looking back he can see his quartet as a logical step from Maurice's quartet, but he didn't see it that way then.

On *Op Stap* there were folk-dancey things suggested by Sauer's sometimes bagpipey tone. There were wobbly pulsing episodes, and grating close-interval dissonances. Everything sounded organized, one way or another, composers' music. There were moments recalling 19th-century concert music but virtually nothing that sounded like jazz—at least partly a reflection of Horsthuis's tastes. They are in the process of discovering their own style, but it creaks with growing pains.

"This is a problem for everybody who starts a band: You ask the people you love, from the recent past or whatever, because you have to know people a little to ask them to be in your band. But it's very difficult to get what you want, letting them be the individuals they are. I had to go through a lot of musical steps to approach what I had in mind.

"At that time, I had the idea that harsh sounds would sound even harder, more brutal, juxtaposed to the more lyrical things. I had the idea we should never be afraid of any stylistic area. We are not going to say No to anything, we can include it, with its own specifics. It could stand independently enough to defend itself, or relate to the other stylistic areas, as a clear musical object."

—There's a very self-consciously European, not-jazz aspect to the early quartet.

"There's a sort of Schubert-like attitude because it brings in Maurice with his romantic ideas. That's no reflection on my taste, but on his way of seeing the musical world. There is of course the strange Indian shenai–like aspect of Maud Sauer, who at the same time could play oboe very well. Maud was Hague-trained and up for the adventure of improvising. She wasn't used to it, but she was eager. There's a kind of tendency toward more linear and more modern composing from Paul Termos, while I'm looking for a style or whatever. So it's Nobody's Land in a way, but also in a positive way. It's a laboratory."

Paul Termos: "Maarten had heard a tape of my trio, and he liked the fact that unlike most saxophone players then, I didn't squeak in a cliched way. I was more nuance-oriented, more into textures than was common at that time. When he asked me to be in his quartet, from that point on I felt accepted. Every musician has that moment, when you're asked to be in a group by someone you admire. It's a sign you're getting someplace.

"The quartet had a very strange concept. One of the best things for me was Maud Sauer's playing. She played oboe very well, with energy, and she was classically trained, but she improvised in a childlike way in that she didn't have the same frame of reference we had. We'd listened to Steve Lacy and all those people, knew the jazz tradition. When she was at the conservatory improvisation was seen as a '60s thing, so when classical musicians had to improvise it was a little playful. But in the beginning it worked very well, because she played a lot of notes, kind of at random, not influenced by knowledge, as we say. I tried to choose my notes with care because I'm always a little bit the composer, looking for the good or most essential notes, a sense of economy I get from people like Lacy and Lee Konitz. The contrast between us worked very well. With Maarten and his brilliant route through music, and his very good melodic feeling, that makes for very good textures.

"In the last phase of this quartet—I don't think you hear it on record—Maarten and I were got into a strange sort of competition, because I was developing more and more, and my tone got broader, and I wanted to play more expansively. So Maarten played more notes and longer phrases in response, and it didn't have the openness it had at first. There were irritations, and then at a certain moment, it was finished, but I think we had five very fruitful years. I learned a lot, in terms of refining pieces and working out concepts. It was a very good quartet with a very good atmosphere.

"What I like about those records now is the clear development. The records are all quite different. Of course I'm subjective, but my choice is the first one, so anarchistic and unprofessional. It was very different for Maarten at that time: very associative, very primitive, totally unconventional—I like it."

—Straining not to have jazz references.

"True, of course, that was Maarten's obsession at that moment. And also the obsession of the time: absolutely anti-jazz. I remember when Maarten heard a tape of a trio I had, I was ashamed when he heard us playing a rhythm." He laughs nervously. "You could say it was very hip to be anti-jazz at this moment. To play it was almost forbidden."

—Did bad feeling about America enter into it?

"Nothing to do with it. It was about having an identity, and a question of improvisers having autonomy. Before that, everything had been coming from free jazz. Hans Dulfer, Willem van Manen, Leo Cuypers, they didn't play bebop—bebop didn't play a very important role at that time—but their music also had its conventions: had to be strong, macho, loud. You had to break new ground to make music with a kind of chamber-like refinement. In that sense, rejecting jazz was a very good way to make room for yourself."

The quartet did a few European tours, on the strength of Maarten's reputation. Their second Claxon was *Pisa*, recorded there in 1981. The band sounds more like a band, having developed as bands usually do, by working together. They had a good feel for staying out of each other's way without sounding timid or letting the bottom fall out (a danger when bass is all the rhythm section you've got, and the bassist not so interested in its traditional function). Horsthuis steps out more, and Termos and Sauer alternate in the roles of orderly and scrambling soloist, sometimes on the same piece. The frame of reference is more definitely chamber music, albeit unplaceable. (As Altena says, some quartet pieces only give the illusion of referring to specific composers or periods—the players rifle through evocative genres they make up themselves.) In a sense Sauer improvising like a classical musician who doesn't know what she's doing sets the tone: it's a band of conservatory types, all aware of their technical or conceptual limitations.

However the writing is more assured, has more character, is less blocky and more contrapuntal. As composers Termos and Horsthuis had the best feel for the mock-chamber style—understood how jazz's beloved playing on chords could be applied to harumphing basic cadences. Altena was getting it too. Among the more memorable items on *Pisa* are the first recordings of two tunes Guus Janssen later covered, Altena's "Bakkum" and Horsthuis's "Bleekgezicht." (The latter is on his *Harpsichord*.) "Bleekgezicht" has an oddly stridelike rhythm hocketed between plucked viola and bass, the lovely melody voiced by reeds graceful as sealhorns. The other standout is the LP's opener, Termos's "Hendrik Jan"—his pieces tended to lead off sides—with its fox-hunt hoppity gait, and tumbling phrases that don't always resolve as promptly as they lead you to expect, phrases expanding till they threaten to run away with themselves. Altena liked it enough to recap the idea and feel with "Eine Kleine Marschmusik," first track on the sequel *Veranda* (Claxon).

By the time *Veranda* was made in 1982, Horsthuis had left, to be replaced by Wolter Wierbos, which meant a new book of tunes. Actually two books, because by now Altena had an octet as well: the new quartet plus Guus on piano, Maartje ten Hoorn on violin, and two improvisers from England, trumpeter Kenny Wheeler and Lindsay Cooper on bassoon and sopranino sax.

The Octet debuted with *Tel* (Countdown) on Claxon. While Maarten was shooing jazz out the front door with the quartet it came in the back with this band, given Wheeler's reliable swingfeel and Wierbos's puckish old-timey tailgating, plus the built-in boogie bass on "Johan van Wely," whose melody paraphrases "Eleanor Rigby," and on "Tel." The latter also has spiky Dutch 16th-note passages and the highest (and lowest) key of Janssen's piano played in rhythm as surrogate drums. "Rottum" is a sleek tango, with Wierbos slip-sliding all over, never in the foreground but always tickling your ear. "C-Melody" is pastiche: generic Mozart, minimalism, modern French, Yancey blues . . . even his own pet licks, generic Maarten. He's aiming toward but not yet attaining the clarity and purity Rudy Koopmans lauds in his notes. (The Boswell of the scene died soon after; *Tel* is dedicated to Rudy's memory.)

"After I had started the Octet, I had limitations to face—I felt I hadn't come along any further as a composer. So I had to face up to the fact that I lacked the means to compose, or continue to move at crab speed as an autodidact. If you can transform self-criticism into a step-by-step process to get what you want, then you can live with it. But I had to overcome a very childish kind of pride."

He got encouragement from, among others, official composers Termos and Janssen. Maarten asked their old teacher Ton de Leeuw for lessons, but was told he'd have to reenter the conservatory after 20 years away. He passed on that sitcom scenario. Finally he arranged private lessons with composer Robert Heppener. That lasted five years, during which Altena wrote seven or eight pieces, ending with *First Floor* for the Nederlands Blazers Ensemble, performed in 1989. The Stravinsky-Andriessen-Termos lineage is plain in its halting chromatic leaps and hard unison wind attacks. It sounded a bit big and impersonal. Smaller groups and more personal intervention fit him better.

If the quartet shows his admiration for Termos's writing ("His pieces were the most outspoken; because he'd studied composition, he knew how to reduce and transform material") the Octet resonates with Janssen's good influence—graphically so on the title track of *Tel*'s sequel, the nonet and octet *Quick Step*. Janssen plays the top key of the piano in swinging-cymbal rhythm, as on "Hi Hat" and its many derivatives, which came later. Altena goes out of his way to point out he was the first to write the highest-key-as-drum idea into a composition.

Guus Janssen: "I played that 'hi-hat' lick in improvisations—I was always imitating drummers, and bass players—and Maarten used it in 'Quick Step.' He used Paul's hyena howl and some of Peter van Bergen's vocabulary in pieces also. That's okay; Ellington did the same thing. Everybody does it. More important to realize there is fertile soil in which such things start to grow. Who invented an idea is much less important than that there is a kind of mentality in which such ideas can come forth. I think that's an Amsterdam school: a group of people who have a kind of outlook which results for example in this little stupid thing on piano, or a hyena sound on the saxophone. Working with Maarten there was a conceptual awareness that let one reach for such things. That's more important than fighting over inventors' rights.

"Once Maarten made a piece that was all descending diatonic scales. I remember Paul Termos was very angry about it, because it was literally quoted from a piece of his, but done in Maarten's usual way: if you can do something in 8 bars, he wouldn't mind doing it in 120."

Even as Altena developed as composer, each of his bands was discovering its sound partly through collective improvising: the laboratory. Maybe the salient point about "Quick Step" the composition is that it sounds Janssen-like other ways too—jauntier and jazzier, less wooden-shoey, with ingenious transitions.

Quick Step the album finds the larger ensemble in transition. The '84 half including the title piece is the old octet plus Ab Baars, who didn't stay long. The pieces from '85 are by the new octet. The reshuffle was partly practical; easier to rehearse if two members don't live in England. (It was even more international before Wierbos replaced Giancarlo Schiaffini: "Maarten wanted me because my playing was more melodic than the Northern European trombonists. I was closer to his own concept: a little Stravinsky. After two or three trips to Holland he said, 'I must apologize, but you cost too much.'") With double reeds out, Boeren, Peter van Bergen and Vatcher in, and Maartje's violin less prominent, it looked and sounded more like some kind of twisted jazz band—Peter had come out of Hoketus, but had also led a band playing Monk tunes—even with a classical trombonist subbing for Wolter, and Vatcher's penchant for leaving a lot of space. He's orchestra percussionist and trap drummer both.

Twisted, or ironed out. "Bit" is built from a bar-long string of eighth notes, which repeats and adapts itself to the chord changes, but doesn't sound like a jazz riff even though it has the same propulsive comping function, and is obviously derived from jazz and blues. As much as Maarten protests against people calling his ensemble music jazz, brass and saxes riffing over piano, bass and drums is not the tradition of Schubert. (More like Basie via Riley.) There are many such stout riffs on the album.

Termos's influence was still plain, in the descending-scales "Lomo." Louis and Volharding left their mark on "Mode"'s winding staccato lines for a capella and sometimes unison horns, but even that modern concert piece eventually whirlpools into energetic riffing; "Mode" begs for revival by some smart ensemble. Altena's very catchy creeping three-step "Buona Notte," spotlighting a nicely framed Termos, is as close as the composers ever got to an Ellington-Hodges ballad. On _Quick Step_ one also detects a number of Mishan ideas, perhaps buffered through next-generation disciples Janssen and Termos, and shared sideman Horsthuis.

Altena's an amalgamator, and by the mid-'80s he was good at it. The revamped Altena-Termos-Sauer-Wierbos quartet is one of the places where the trombonist blossomed, developed his uncanny feel for playing around and against scores and ideas: inventing new harmonizations and counterlines, playing just above or below where he was expected. (He does much the same on _Quick Step_. In deliberately mangling charts, he turns "mistakes" into a way of life, justifying his stance as a noncomposer: he's a spontaneous rearranger.)

Wolter's "Buona Notte"–like woozy feature is "Veranda," from the quartet album of the same name, on which the riffs are more fluid and spirited than before. The LP also contains one tune from ICP's '70s book, Bert Koppelaar's quacky "Kwik Kwek Kwak," which fits them very well, along with four okay collective improvisations.

In '83 the same quartet made _Miere_ for France's Nato label. Altena's title track plays a game with sliding pitch and dynamics, as if each player imagines his or her sound is being picked up by a microphone swinging back and forth in front of them. This time more than half the program is improvised in a manner more "English" than "Dutch." Broad humor is out. They elaborate on the ensemble style they'd cobbled together, but in truth it's as hit or miss as other folks' free play Maarten grouses about. That said, give Sauer her due: she sounds more like a real improviser, less like a paradoxical schooled primitive; Termos's sputter and creative rigidity are in full view. Wierbos, by the way, said he never felt that heavy anti-jazz attitude, and that Maarten never criticized him for quoting standards in a solo.

Like the first quartet the second got better with time; as _Pisa_ is the best by the first unit, the final _Rondedans_ (Claxon) from '84 is best from the second. Wierbos's beautiful, discreetly walking background for Sauer's oboe solo on "Hop" is reason enough: bright panels reflecting soft light. Termos's title track is so Mengelbergian one almost hears Misha pecking it out at the keys: trotting foxhunt music to rot the aristocracy's brains. They reprise a couple of good Termos tunes from the first quartet's book, but old bald spots remain. There are enough laggard moments to suggest this band never fully found itself. Altena's pieces are frequently underpowered—the "120 bars" effect—and despite some nicely timed beat-hocketing by Termos and Wierbos, the quartet sometimes sounds like it needs more of a rhythm section.

Which is what Altena had in the larger ensemble, from now on the focus of his energy. Anti-jazz or nonjazz he may be, but by 1987's *Rif* (Claxon, reissued by hatART) his Octet was full of folks who'd played that music: Wierbos, Vatcher, Janssen; Michael Moore on reeds; the English trumpet and alto horn player Marc Charig, now living across the border in Germany. (The exception was Hague-schooled composer ten Hoorn.) Jazz is the teacher, as Misha said years before. But Moore, Janssen and van Bergen had conservatory training to draw on too. Collectively the Octet had the conceptual Full Metal Jacket: could read, could improvise, could breathe life into the rhythmic cycles and the holes: could flesh out the skeletons or at least make the bones dance.

And establish a sense of mood, even where Maarten's written themes are sketchy. That much is clear from the opening "Boa," where for once piano, bass and drums sound like some kind of rhythm section: simple half-note comping from bass outlining the static harmony, piano repeating one jittery little figure, Vatcher keeping crisp quiet time on hi-hat and what sounds like small blocks. Each of them (and sometimes ten Hoorn, with punctuating pizz chords) carries another piece of the time, meshing like gears in a watch. Aside from that, "Boa"'s written material is not much more than two melodic kernels the front-line instruments center on and revolve around, over that same rhythm. The first is a catchy five-bar tune played in weaving near unison, and embellished with light variations, as in the 14th-century monody Maarten (or reissue annotator Steve Martland) now cited. That A section quickly yields to a pop-toned tenor spot, and a rather uncharacteristic animal-sputter solo by Moore, perhaps a nod to predecessor Termos. The second kernel is a tumbling descent which, whenever it's introduced, prompts the other horns to follow, staggered, a chain-reaction cascade. On paper it's simple, but the band makes the structure dance.

So it goes with other pieces here; Altena's "Rif" and "Marre" take fetching little diatonic licks and recombine them, shifting in relation to one another like panels of Calder mobiles, Earle Brown's inspiration 30 years before. At "Rif"'s end the main themelet is stretched out of shape with uncommon levity for this band with its Calvinist outlook. Overall the mood is pretty sober.

Case in point, Janssen's touchstone "Rondo," which he's played in lots of settings. Its style-quotey vignettes—a doo-woppy I–vi–IV–V progression and an "Asian" bit—are all but totally obscured here. Only one anecdotal routine passes: the band verily grinds to a halt and then revs back up, like a gramophone winding down and being recranked—appropriately inappropriate for Claxon's only CD.

Ten Hoorn's "de Yup," with its softly undulating arco strings contrasted with jittery clarinet, is the most composerly of the pieces. Improvisation remains key. Wierbos is ever reliable—"Dek" is this disc's hooky tune over trembling background chords—and Janssen's comping is sterling but Vatcher is the real hero, punching up the time without giving pieces obvious groove, which was discouraged, and cuing or interrupting when necessary. (He's also uncharacteristically Benninky: loud crashes, clanging school bell.) His dual drummer-percussionist perspective is again ideal, and he gives the English/Andriessen-trained Martland's marchy "Re-Mix"—of baroque music by Marin Marais—a sly shambling overlay. The mixing of the composed and improvised that Altena advocates never sounded better or more balanced.

But 1988's *Quotl* came close; same band, save that the Octet had been redubbed the Maarten Altena Ensemble, and that Sweelinck grad (and former Mengelberg pupil) Michiel Scheen now sat at the piano. Scheen wrote for the band and stayed till 1997, but never put his signature on the proceedings as Guus did. The music's quieter, even less jazz-oriented—violin returns to a more prominent role—and more explicitly indebted to the Cage-Brown-Feldman New York school, with its minimal/no vibrato way to a smooth surface. These qualities come to the fore on Gilius van Bergeijk's pastoral "Scène Rurale": a single ascending arpeggio for celeste, and monodic-style embellishments of and glosses on same. The mix fosters an idiomatic improvising style Altena would find increasingly congenial.

The other conspicuous influence was Stravinsky. Maarten says the Octet was laid out two by two by design: strings, reeds, brass, percussion (counting piano). "Thinking in terms of four sections of two made it easier for me to compose, and to think about structural matters. Of course things get mixed up, but it's always nice to have a clear idea to start from." All true. But as Bill Shoemaker wrote in his notes to *Quotl*, minus piano it looks like the septet for *L'Histoire du Soldat*: "a piece brimming with folk dances, marches, tangos, waltzes and early jazz, genres that are often the stuff of Altena's compositions." Also worth recalling that Andriessen and Schönberger in *The Apollonian Clockwork* had pegged that septet as a group of trained musicians masquerading as a village band.

That Stravinskian strain also surfaces in Altena's "Rails" and ex-Hoketus American composer Gene Carl's "Roscoe Boulevard" and elsewhere. On *Quotl* as on "de Yup," the chamber-music feel can be most effectively shattered with a drum solo. Ten Hoorn brought two more pieces which show her attraction to the clarinet: Moore and van Bergen's big and little ones in rhythmic unisons on the frequently disrupted "Brokken"; the cuckoo-clock figure on "Admiraliteit," which Moore runs with, given leeway for once.

The latter is played by Altena's third quartet, with ten Hoorn and Wierbos. The quartet's three pieces here are its entire legacy, a shame: from this evidence it bested its predecessors juggling and cleanly executing austere themes and textures. If there is a severe "Hague school," as some claim, ten Hoorn was definitely in it.

On *Quotl* overall the players are held in greater check (overlooking van Bergen's squalling on "Voices"). On the Altena Ensemble's next CDs, the battle lines between composed and improvised material were more clear, even if the front kept moving back and forth.

Cities & Streets, 1989, is a retreat toward happy anarchy. No small credit goes to van Bergen, the band's most rambunctious soloist; he tears through Maarten's "Prikkel" with Brötzmann-like defiance of niceties and with incisive rhythm. "Prikkel" is a long wide-interval zigzag that spans several octaves, in deliberately crooked 9/8 time, the various instruments joining in or dropping out as the line moves in or out of their range. There is also a less eerie, more orderly redraft of "Boa," "Slange" (Snake, misspelled, deliberate mistake), and a more desultory and unruly take on "Rif."

Vatcher's enthusiastic, sometimes outsized drumming remains the band's benign id. Moore finds a few good clarinet moments, but not many; even Wierbos is mostly subdued. Although Janssen is long gone one hears his good influence in the several episodes where Scheen plays the piano's extremes in rhythm, often simultaneously—an idea Altena would stick with even in pieces written for other pianists.

Producer Werner Uehlinger had coaxed them into re-recording old pieces, a good way to mark changes in the band—ten Hoorn, Charig and Moore had drifted by 1990—but the idea got out of hand by *Code,* Altena's last hatART: another "Prikkel" and "Slange" and another oldie, "Rij," déjà entendu.

Replacements were guitarist Jacques Palinckx, skronky comper, mostly low-profile here, violinist Christel Postma and classical soprano Jannie Pranger, her pure tone used to advantage on "Prikkel," her articulation rendering Martland's huff'n'puff "Principia" text indecipherable. As ever, frayed ensemble textures are improvised within the context of orderly pieces, but sheet music was winning the war.

Maarten Altena: "My ideal is to have a repertory group that presents life as it's lived in a city: to represent not only the beauty of a new building by Frank Lloyd Wright, but also strange small neighborhoods where there are things you don't immediately understand, that are not polished. When you have both, that's fantastic. There's always a moment when I listen to a great chamber group playing Schoenberg, when I long for a chaotic or unforeseen moment. Or at jazz concerts, after the 50th chorus, I think, 'Nice, now I want to have a little Bach.' I try to do something that contains a bit of that. But of course the people you work with and your concept have limits."

Yeah but the purity and clarity he often talks about are inconsistent with vibrant urban living, which is always a bit of a mess. His musical city has its customs: music with a slightly rickety forward thrust, with few virtuoso moves, nothing too fast or overtly swinging. In short, the music sidesteps Maarten's own shortcomings as bassist or rhythmatician. Fair enough: Why lead a band if not to cater to yourself? Problems arose when the other players' inclinations led them into neighborhoods where Altena felt uncomfortable. If improvising sessions were the ensemble's town meetings, where mayor Maarten took the pulse of the people (and discovered players' idiosyncrasies and pet licks he might use in his pieces, Ellington-like), his reform administration was ever on guard against unapproved speech. Whenever Vatcher got into a good groove he could expect negative reinforcement from the boss.

There were other prohibitions: anecdotal pieces were now history. Maarten's relationship to his musicians, most rather younger than himself, has its fatherly aspects. He seeks to guide: is known not just for changing his own mind and direction but trying to get his sidefolk to do the same. Altena seems genuinely unaware that his dicta against some kind of music he's just abandoned—improvised, anecdotal, style-quoting, whatever—may be offensive to allies who might still care to play that way. And so the brain drain, as the improvisers fled the gentrified city and readers moved in. His Holland was not that of the marijuana-dealing coffee shop but the stern Calvinists. (Compare his personnel turnovers with ICP: once Misha found his optimum band he kept it together, even when gigs were few and his behavior vexing, because there was room for each musician to flourish in an environment where any prohibition is anathema.)

Maarten's piece "Code" shows how far the freedoms had been constrained: a game piece harking back to Christian Wolff's if-this-then-that cuing pieces of the '60s, and Misha's "Hello! Windyboys." Each player has a musical phone number as it were, a specific figure Scheen uses to call them in: he plays the beginning of the phrase, and the person cued finishes it. Once in, they can enter the collective improvising. Scheen also has the power to stop and restart the musicians, and can also divide these responsibilities with another player. If Misha's or Termos's games can be like school-yard games, Altena's like Janssen's are like a schoolmaster's (with Guus perhaps as a favorite teacher).

There's a different set of cues in "Code"'s second half—usually controlled by Wolter, a very good conductor by now, given his ICP experience too—to bring in background licks (Altena: "musical pepper") to stimulate or harass a soloist. The piece also has a scored beginning, middle and end.

Basically, "Code" relies on players keeping their ears open to more than one thing at a time. "It's the same as being able to speak to you, and listen to sounds in the street at the same time, and think about a telephone call that could come in also. It's like daily life, whereas most music now has nothing to do with daily life anymore." The hectic simultaneity relates to another (Kagel- Brown- Misha-derived) game, Zorn's "Cobra," which an Altena group first played with the composer in 1985, when the piece was new—although unlike most Dutch games it contains no specific pitch material. Years later "Code" was still in the book, adaptable to any lineup.

Which kept changing. HatART passed on releasing *City Music*, with Dutch texts by and read by poet Remco Campert. It went to the classical Attaca label. Improvising is really window dressing here, doily work. Peter van Bergen: "The tendency of the group was not about what you would call the sympathy and love you have for improvising musicians, but the fact that you perform modern compositions in a recognizably knowledgeable way." (Yes but, outside composers may complain the Ensemble doesn't play their pieces so well, at first especially.)

By now Altena was really finding his composer's voice, which meant placing even greater strictures on his citizens. Vibrato was on the way out, for voice and violin especially; there were more and more long notes, unisons, almost unisons. Vertical harmony gets little attention (except as derived from lines, as he described earlier: sustaining isolated notes from the melody). More and more it's about horizontals.

Back to monody. Personnel kept changing; now Alison Isadora took the violin chair; Palinckx gave way to Wiek Hijmans, solid ensemble player with a good command of noisy guitar attacks. Recorder virtuoso Walter van Hauwe was on *City Music* but was soon replaced by Michael Barker.

Altena: "The idea of parity in instruments had long ago disappeared. I liked the recorder as an archaic instrument which has many faces; liked it especially in relation to the voice."

The band was internationalizing again; Barker's originally from West Virginia, teaches recorder at the Hague conservatory; Isadora's from New Zealand, studied violin and composition in the Hague, plays in new-music ensembles. Vatcher, van Bergen and Wierbos remained.

That version of the Ensemble did a North American tour in the fall of 1992; at festivals in Toronto and Victoriaville they cut all the new-music competition in terms of ensemble precision (especially including the Toronto orchestra Hemispheres, which played two tunes from Maarten's book, "Rij" and "Roscoe Boulevard"). The following May the Altena Ensemble did two Butch Morris conductions, #35 and #36 in his conduction catalog, documented on a CD drawn from Morris's ten-disc box *A Conduction Collection*. Their playing is noticeably more detailed than any other group represented in the box—most, in their defense, one-shot aggregations.

The next one, *Maarten Altena Ensemble* (a.k.a. *Muziekpraktijk [Music + Practice]*) was on the classical Composers' Voice label, a sign, along with his occasional commissions, that Altena had successfully crossed over: he's a bona fide composer now. Not surprisingly, his career retraining had created some resentment on the part of old colleagues, who bad-mouthed him as an opportunist, going for the greater prestige and money that comes from switching allegiances.

But be fair: If your music is hard to pigeonhole, you might as well go for the hole with the most birdseed. Willem Breuker figured out the same thing—in the '90s he's funded through classical-ensemble not jazz channels—but Breuker made the switch without the fanfare. Misha might well have repositioned ICP the same way, if he weren't so obstinate, career-unconscious, contemptuous of established order, and committed to improvisation.

Asked in 1995 which album represents his maturation as a composer, Altena cited the Composers' Voice record. One hears what he means. "Figuur" (Figure) and "Lento" are typical of his new style, if that adjective may be applied to something so steeped in medieval nostalgia. Each relies on a monophonic line for voice and piano or voice and recorder, the former punctuated by trombone blasts, the latter by stark chords from conjoined piano, vibes and guitar. In each case where instruments are paired—pairs including bowed vibratoless violin and bass on "Lento"—the unisons are staggered, players moving in and out of sync with each other. Intonation is similarly inexact: the wooden endblown recorder is difficult to play in tune, not least when Barker plays it. His fortuitous wanderings off-pitch introduce harmonic tension otherwise lacking (and sometimes, oddly enough, suggest Monk's residual influence more than many explicit homages.)

"Figuur" and "Lento" both have lots of dark silence surrounding the slow horizontal line. They're spare and clean as the interiors of a Dutch reformed church, evoke stone pillars in flickering candlelight or pale winter sun. They look back to less remote ancestry too: '20s and '30s "domestic music" which brought the recorder back into temporary vogue; to Andriessen's staggered recorder and piano *Melodie*, perhaps an unconscious beacon for this sort of style. (Reviewing *Melodie* in *Key Notes*, Sytze Smit raised that church image I just stole.)

By the time these pieces were recorded, however, van Bergen and Vatcher had split, one sore point for each a project with guest composer Roscoe Mitchell. They felt some members of the band including the leader had not been entirely cooperative or taken the music seriously. A broader reason was simply that improvisation was less important than ever—a point repeatedly driven home by Jacqueline Oskamp and by Altena in her notes to the CD. What improvising remains is highly circumscribed, players being restricted to one particular sound or timbral area. "Tik" features Hijmans' guitar, but he's limited to scraping noisily along his round-wound strings. (Its bass line is boogie-derived, but it's too squared off to have headlong momentum: the boogie of *De Stijl* not Albert Ammons.)

Altena in the notes, re: restrictions: "I'm not interested in someone setting out to reinvent the music." (In contrast to Mengelberg, who is always interested in that.) Re: his new emphasis on melody and spare sound: "It's a reaction to all the improvised music I've played. . . . I don't need to hear another superfluous note for the rest of my life. I have an enormous craving for cleaning it all up." This was a year or so before he balked at the tag "disillusioned improviser."

But it was still working-band music: you'd have a devil of a time getting straight readers to play anything like certain raggedy ensembles on "ABCDE." On the other hand, severely restricted or not, for improvising you need improvisers, and the band was running out of them. In '96 Hijmans took leave to study in New York. (Butch Morris after conducting them again on a couple of gigs that fall: "They were easier to conduct three years ago.") If the Ensemble played city music, it's not a modern city that pays at least lip service to individual drive; more a medieval city where all the parties know their place.

After Vatcher left, piano, bass and percussion didn't function much like a rhythm section anymore. But vestigial traces remained of the band's old life. Despite Maarten's insistence it wasn't a jazz band, he did not refuse jazz festival or BIMhuis gigs, and it didn't stop him from soliciting a couple of pieces based on Fats Waller music for spring 1997.

You could still hear ideas he got from old sidefolk however: Vatcherly percussion strategies; piano keeping time in extreme registers à la Janssen; stark silences and crashing chords à la van Bergen's LOOS; the "stretched octave" of a ninth used in "Slow Motion"'s fabricated mode, so notes get further displaced with every octave, à la *Carrara* by Termos.

Every composer borrows or steals, but it is a jazz thing to do it from your own band. Again, consider the Ellington analogy: a major element of Duke's writing style was Bubber Miley's trumpet sound, which didn't disappear when Miley left; Duke just found someone else to play it. (Miley: Cootie :: Janssen: Scheen.) And Altena has ways of digesting ideas so the source is obscured. "Slow Motion," recorded in 1993, was inspired by one of Michael Vatcher's pet sounds: wedge a drumstick into a cymbal's center hole, then rotate the edge of the cymbal against one or more dulcimer strings; it yields a soft, eerie undulating drone, and can be played melodically. That gambit sounds throughout the piece. Behind, softly, so as not to drown Vatcher out, slow Gregorian chant–like lines move in more-or-less unisons. They re-recorded it (for the same Composers' Voice CD) after Vatcher left. The dulcimer foundation is removed, but the rest of the structure still stands.

That is a good album, only it lacks the juice and unpredictability improvising brings. It's disembodied in a way—music for people who think toe-tapping pulse and ching-a-ching (and Tin Pan Alley) are vulgar. It can be hard to hear jazz in the Ensemble's voice, but it's in its DNA. Without jazz, this nonjazz wouldn't exist. Jazz still rippled through it, so many miles and years removed from the original splash.

But circumstances conspired against it. In the first half of '97 Pranger, Scheen and new clarinetist Erik van Deuren left; Altena decided to set the Ensemble aside for a year, before reforming it—without the leader on bass, at least initially.

Maarten admits he's defensive about his pilgrim's progress, says it's clear he still believes in improvising, because his whole career is improvised: how else to explain his tacking course? Taking the best option he sees at any moment, sticking with something as long as it works and then moving on to something else, sometimes its antithesis: put it that way, it sounds like improvised music.

Chapter Fourteen
Third Generation

On their 1992 North American tour, the Altena Ensemble played Peter van Bergen's "F.021": long silences or grumbling episodes or sustained saxophone notes lying in the troughs between short and sudden clanging chords from merged piano, guitar and drums. After the gig I told Peter I liked his tribute to Count Basie. Why do you say that, he asked, looking very pleased. Because of the tight synchronization of piano and guitar was the answer. That's nice, he said, because for me the piece is about a kind of swing.

Evan Parker: "I know that Peter van Bergen loves playing free, but in a way the Dutch system won't allow him to. The Dutch system requires him to have a Strong Idea, and to illustrate it correctly and clearly and unambiguously in performance. That's what LOOS does of course, but it's been hard for Peter because there are only so many clear ideas. It's hard to come up with something distinct from what ICP represents, or Willem Breuker, or Maarten Altena, or Guus Janssen. All of these in a sense set a kind of standard for him before he arrived. It's pretty obvious Peter is now on that list. That's a remarkable achievement, to find a place which hasn't been taken by or isn't already inside the territory marked out by those other key figures. And he's done it by a method of absolute reductionism, in a way.

"Of course another characteristic of a Strong Idea is that it has to negate all other Strong Ideas. That's the great thing about the Dutch scene. You have a very small country, full of people who are attempting to render one another's work irrelevant, or obsolete. The strength of the idea is that it prevails, makes all the other ideals somehow conceptually inadequate or weak.

"Peter's music is so much the idea, especially in LOOS, but when you start to look for the skeletons in the cupboard you find out he's crazy about John Gilmore, loves Sun Ra, likes free players, likes my playing, likes all kinds of stuff which LOOS as an idea seeks to represent, while standing almost in complete opposition to it."

Misha would seem to be the grand exception to Evan's theory—unless his Strong Idea is an aversion to overarching ideas.

When Peter van Bergen joined Hoketus in 1983, one of the pieces in its book was *Bint* by Cornelis de Bondt. As noted earlier, to enter the Hoketus repertoire a new piece had to sound like the old ones, and *Bint* was in the mold of Andriessen's *Hoketus* the composition. Once *Bint* gets rolling the divided halves of the band play the same notes in slightly different tempos, mirror images sliding away from one another, a live rethink of Steve Reich's early tape-loop pieces. Before it gets rolling, though, *Bint* is all isolated short clanging chords from merged pianos, guitars and percussion, sometimes with long uninflected saxophone notes bridging the gaps between. Rather like *Hoketus* it does in 30 minutes what Eddy Christiani did in seconds at the start of "Hilversum Express" 30 years earlier, albeit without the stereo effects. (It had been too early. Late '50s stereo-demonstration records liked that kind of antiphony though; at least one featured a simulated game of table tennis.)

It's that first pre-ignition bit of *Bint* or *Hoketus* that interests van Bergen—the part where time appears to stand still. (There is an old Dick Raaijmakers performance piece where a man takes half an hour to dismount a bicycle, homage to Muybridge-like pre-motion-picture stop-action photo sequences of bodies in motion.) Peter likes to take small gestures and place them under a microscope, turn them over to inspect them at leisure, blow them up so everyone can see how they look.

BIMhuis, September 1995: LOOS—Peter van Bergen, pianist Gerard Bouwhuis, Huib Emmer on electric guitar or bass, and drummer Paul Koek, all ex-Hoketus—are joined by actor Dennis Rudge. The quartet play typical LOOSisms: clanging chord out of which one odd tone rings after the other notes have been silenced, clatter of woodblocks and other tight percussive sounds (Koek has a bunch of small objects of specific pitch arrayed on a table over his bass drum, near his rack of high-pitched bongos), occasional held split-tone from tenor sax, the hiss of a delay unit which softly echoes a staccato bark from towering contrabass clarinet, and lots of long pauses where you wait for the next chord to drop.

While this is going on Rudge, a youngish black man originally from Surinam, strikes poses: leans his head back, mouth forced open into rictus grin, and freezes. Knees and fists on floor, head down, he looks up, yells "I swear!" and freezes. His enunciation is blurry. Like many of his moves it treads close to parody of African-Americanisms, hiphop era in particular.

This is LOOS's tribute to Louis Armstrong.

Up until tenor saxophonist John Gilmore died in 1995, Peter van Bergen would call him in Philadelphia every year on his birthday, just to chat. When Peter was young— born in 1957 in Tubbergen, near the German border, an area, says Louis Andriessen, where people "were as we say very good during the War," and where Peter biked 19 kilometers each way between home and school each day—he was a very good football player, could have gone pro. He also listened to bluegrass and country music. "I liked

Eddie Peabody and the Kentucky Mountain Boys and the Country Gentleman a lot. I liked their sonority: extreme. Eddie Peabody is an extreme virtuoso on his banjo. And I liked the voice of the singer in the Kentucky Mountain Boys a lot. I wasn't a jazz record collector, but about 1981 I gave my sister Sun Ra's *Nuits de la Fondation Maeght* as a present, and she gave it back. That record has a very beautiful John Gilmore solo. What I like extremely about Gilmore is his extreme sound on tenor."

While van Bergen was studying modern saxophone at the Hague conservatory, Sun Ra came to Utrecht for a gig. Peter introduced himself to Gilmore. When he heard the Arkestra was going on to Paris for five nights, he went there, took a room at the hotel across the street from the club. He and Gilmore hit it off. Peter asked for lessons; John said ask Sun Ra's permission. Sun Ra requested a tape; he got it. Then Ra gave him a couple of three-hour lectures on metaphysical matters and band psychology.

"The next day I said, 'What about the lessons?' Sun Ra said, 'What do you want to learn?' I told him very specific things, about the way John treats rhythm as a soloist, and his conception of sound. Sun Ra said, 'Okay, you already know what you want to learn, so you don't need any lessons.'" He's laughing as he tells it. "Sometime later, when the Arkestra was in Holland I drove Gilmore around for a day, and we had several other nice meetings.

"I should mention that I like the whole Sun Ra thing a lot. Braxton and Stockhausen also. I like their ideas about futurist thinking, and new combinations of all kinds of things, although I have quite a different idea about esthetics and how to transform one thing into something else."

—Like swing.

"Swing is about music that has enough tension within itself. The tension is determined by different things: the combination of rhythm, articulation, choices of tones or tone color—I don't see these things as separate, they all have to do with one another.

"I think of my music as a transformation of several things. When it comes to swing in particular, it has a lot to do with long and short. You cannot separate it from the other elements I just mentioned, but that long-short thing, in combination with articulation and phrasing, is very important to my intention. It's also about differences in length.

"In 1982—a split-second before the earliest version of LOOS—I had my first group, Hackensack, which played about 25 concerts: all Monk music, no piano, just tenor, bass and drums. Wilbur Little was the bassist. Misha heard it once, liked it a lot, but we never collaborated. But then Monk was dying, and I didn't want to go on with it." (Almost no point to it then—after he died, everyone else formed a Monk band.) "But it was important to me, I can hear it in terms of timing in LOOS' music.

"What I like about the Monk–Sonny Rollins stuff is, they didn't fit together that well. Both had not-so-common timing. Rollins' tone-color was very bold, equal to but working against the tone of Monk. The rubbery sound of Charlie Rouse, on the other hand, is the harmonic overtone to the sound of Monk. That's why I think Charlie Rouse could play longer and better for him. I could imagine Rouse extending Monk; Rollins was more confronting rather than extending Monk."

Misha, you may remember, has another view.

"Early LOOS stuff was short funky music, very heavy. We played 16ths as short as possible, with a bass player and Willem Janssen, a very fast drummer who also played a lot of African music. Then the trio became a quintet, with Jan Willem van der Ham on alto saxophone, and a conga player. Still an early stage: fast, energetic improvised music, funk-influenced. We played at the North Sea Jazz Festival and became quite popular with that kind of music, but personally I found it quite boring. I wanted it more abstract, but not all the players agreed. They left, and I stayed with the drummer, but he couldn't live with the abstract form, he was too much into pulse and groove. Then I started to transform it into a much more abstract band, working with very small musical elements."

Pulse and groove and two-sax section work define the funky "Edge," a collective composition recorded in 1985 for the sampler *Dutch 'Difficult' Music: a selective view* (from the Tilburg label Eksakt). It's quite unlike later LOOS. Like the Noodband track on the same LP it confirms the popularity of Ornetty harmolodic fusion in Holland then. Van Bergen also mentions the Odean Pope trio—tenor sax and the Philly funk rhythm section of Gerald Veasley and Cornell Rochester—as another jittery inspiration. Peter liked funk because it's about activity at the 16th-note level, jumping ahead of and behind the beat: jazz under the microscope, quarter- or eighth-note swing in half the time or less.

At various stages Wierbos, Vatcher, Scheen, Gregg Moore, Eric Calmes and others passed through LOOS. Moore remembers supercomplicated 16th-note passages, one meter played against another, so complex the musicians couldn't tell if they were playing them right or not. (Wierbos: "There were a lot of sighs and heads hanging down in this period. But when it clicked, there were some nice moments.") Later, electric guitarist/bassist Patricio Wang, also ex-Hoketus, was sometimes added to the regular quartet.

"Into the concept I put all kinds of thoughts about what is important in jazz music, about how you deal with history as an improviser or jazz musician. I say this a lot: I think we are jazz musicians. In my concept there are all kinds of ways to transform certain ideas from jazz history.

"For instance, virtuosity is very important in jazz, but virtuosity in LOOS is not about playing long solos, or playing faster or more notes, but in quickly reacting to very small musical elements.

"The basis is the equality of the people. In LOOS, we all have to know when someone is giving a cue, and on very short notice. There are four people, each with a chord he can cue everyone to play. So you think, I'm going to cue the others, I want to play my chord—because I like it. But just as you're ready to do that, someone else may cue another chord first. So you have to be ready to shift all your energy and attention to another place, in a very short time. They might even cut in on you on purpose; that's also part of the game, and part of virtuosity in jazz music: 'See how fast I am.'"

Sort of a cutting contest for conductors. The dueling chords and if-this-then-that rules hark back yet again to "Hello! Windyboys" and other '60s composers' games. A typical LOOS score details a set of sparse chords, or short melodies, and shows the orders in which they may be played: the chord someone cues now may determine the next set of options, a chain of commands.

"A cue might suddenly send a piece off in a very different direction. It's possible to play a piece with only two small elements, a very minimalistic approach. Or it might become much more conceptual. We can all repeat our own thing, or a combination of things. When we decide to repeat a combination, we have a group idea of the direction the music should take—as in free improvised music, when the players start to go with certain material that crops up. It's a lot about the psychology of how to change your musical expectations, and how to deal with what happened one second before. So you have to be very fast in reacting to different musical circumstances, as in improvised music.

"You can hear the personalities of the players all the time, because their choices are quite different. For instance, Huib loves pauses a lot, so he will be the first to inject a pause." Silences as well as chords can be cued. "The piano player is very much into contemporary composed music, so he will try to put in certain things he's discovered there, although it's difficult for him to decide where. That's also true of free-improvised music: you try to fit in the stuff you like, or came up with while practicing.

"I think the most important thing in jazz or improvised music is or should be the personal voice. You try to develop a language, and then come to the stage to meet other people. The ultimate goal would be to have five people playing in a language in which everything you like is present. To work on that, I compose these elements."

So: it's just like free improvisation, except with restraints and conditions on all sides, and with all the options devised by Peter. LOOS's first CD _Fundamental_ from 1992 with Emmer, Bouwhuis, Koek and Wang, shows the band coming into its concept; it sounds radical compared to most anything in jazz/improvised music, but almost mild compared to how the band sounded three years later.

The CD's clinical flowchart liner notes set the right tone. ("The three fundamental building blocks are chords, silences, and improvisations." There's even a statistical analysis of van Bergen chords: minor seconds, major sevenths, major seconds and minor ninths are his favorite intervals.)

The clanky sonorities owe a lot to Emmer's high-treble solid-body guitar, coupled with stilted timing: no jazz references. (Emmer is a Hague-conservatory trained composer, who also writes for LOOS and next to van Bergen has the most influence over its direction.) That crunching guitar sounds like nothing except certain moments on Captain Beefheart's epic _Trout Mask Replica_—"When Big Joan Sets Up"—but without apparent direct influence; Emmer has listened to him but neither he nor van Bergen is a major fan. Bouwhuis's new music experience does not bring him to Monkish voicings of specified chords, but to metallic ones; he digs Xenakis and Stockhausen.

Van Bergen has mentioned stately Japanese noh plays as an influence on LOOS's timing. One might connect the way drums in kabuki theater play specific rhythms— musical formulas that convey specific information about the action or setting—to how Koek's woodblock cues may cut off or switch on some other activity. That system is also analog to (in receding order) Altena's coding, "Hello! Windyboys" yet again, and Loevendie's telegraphy. (And in the lineage of same, in reverse order: this is how ideas are transformed.)

Most of the pieces are entries in Peter's "factorseries" that spawned "F.021," pieces slow and spare as Monk's comping. Statistics? In either "F.01.5" or "F.01A2" there are seven chords/hits in the first 40 seconds; the rest is silence, maybe with one thin sustained note hanging on after a chord has been choked. Monk used to do that, sometimes, as Janssen does: unison attack, staggered release. In practice some hits are cleaner than others, which adds tension too; à la Altena, the fortuitous fuckup is part of the mix.

There are very precise strokes as well. On "F.024," yoked contrabass clarinet and percussion play a staccato pulse that might change tempo slightly the instant a chord crosses it. (You can read Braxton in those titles and the lumbering giant clarinet.) When the chords fly by relatively quickly, as on "F.002"—about as fast as on a slow "I Got Rhythm," say—you can hear them form a kind of progression, another available option. It's a little like the unfixed harmonic rhythm of Mengelberg's "Solitude Mix."

The verticals are as vertical as possible, the horizontals as flat as possible, with some basic coloration to intensify the geometric scheme: Mondrian music.

In a way, a LOOS tribute to Armstrong makes crazy sense: they have glorified, or maybe obsess over, that durable '20s device, the stoptime break: a chord cut off to let someone improvise for a few bars before the next chord arrives. (The problem with LOOS's Armstrong project was that Rudge seemed to have no clue how Armstrong moved or spoke; his performance is a caricature of the tortured twisted Louis espoused by James Lincoln Collier and almost no one else.)

Looked at one way the jazz elements are abstracted to absurdity, but to my ears it has something that, for example, Martijn Padding's Monk-inspired pieces don't: that rhythmic momentum of long and short breaths. It breathes. Which is to say it swings—this will strike some readers as the biggest heresy in the book—which is to say van Bergen brings back alive at least some of those jazz notions he talks about.

Andriessen wrote them "Hout" (Wood) in 1991, a fast rippling piece (a strict canon with the voices barely spaced) later recorded by his New York fans the Bang on a Can All-Stars, likely the world's only LOOS cover band.

In '96 Misha wrote LOOS "Enkele regels in de dierentuin" (A Few Rules of the Zoo) a stukje which like "Dressoir" or "Rokus" defies ensemble norms. A pretty long-note melody for saxophone, chord changes for guitar, a shuffle with brushes for drums, all collapse and reappear: jazz with misplaced parts. "Misha has played with LOOS; he liked the game-structure a lot, said we were the last Trotskyites." Drop-in guests like Misha (or Steve Beresford) face a sweet challenge; LOOS goes about its usual business and guests can do whatever they like.

Peter van Bergen has said his personality infuses the music so much, he doesn't need to take solos. Which is too bad because he's the band's only real soloist and an original, subjecting saxophone language to the same micro-examination as group dynamics. You could hear it developing even on his first Altena session, for *Quick Step* in '85. "Bes" (Berry) is a mini-concerto for his tenor, more Hague than H-Bomb Ferguson. He takes the honk-and-scream esthetic almost to the point of catatonia; his line is so excited it's all but inert, one of those esthetic contradictions that fascinate this guy who makes slow music about fast reactions. In doing that he bypasses the simple solutions afforded by "Bes"'s scalar riffing head.

He says all the colors of the saxophone family are available on the tenor, if you play it right. He told Jacqueline Oskamp, "I use the clarinets, on the other hand, as extensions of the various registers: the doublebass clarinet is a broadening of certain low-sax timbres, and the sound of the A-flat clarinet could be thought of as giving one part of the tenor sax's high register in isolation. If you play it 'wrong,' the A-flat clarinet can make sounds like a synthesizer."

On "Bes" you can also hear his kinship to the Breuker-Volharding-Baars overblowing lineage. He likes extremists as much as Baars likes eccentrics. Like Ab he's very loud, has real presence, not least from playing about as flat as you can get without giving the impression you've changed key. He's also in debt to Paul Termos for his jungle-mammal howls, "F.01A2" and elsewhere.

In 1990 he got a grant to study saxophone techniques with Evan Parker. Parker's reaction was not unlike Sun Ra's: You already know all this stuff. The saxophonists are a perfect pair, using molecules of saxophone technique to almost opposite ends, Parker to create a dense, continuous web of sound, several strands constantly interweaving.

"We get along very well. There's no point in copying Evan's style or language, which I think is very important, but we still have a subject to talk about: the combination of techniques, the choices. We had four years of one-day meetings of six hours, talking about techniques, and trying to discover another kind of fleeting saxophone high notes, all kinds of techniques combined with different kinds of articulation. We were thinking about writing some articles about specifics of technique, but we both like to play much more, so it's pushed away a little bit." They play together only rarely. In 1995 Parker assembled a quartet—or double duo—with drummers Vatcher and Paul Lytton for a few gigs, but nothing came of it.

The way van Bergen combines saxophone techniques from all over is all his own. Listening to him one begins to hear how the Dutch saxophone vocabulary reflects the Dutch language the way Ellington's plungered brass mirrors the syllabics of American speech. The diphthongs, the guttural attack of consonants like the notorious throat-clearing "g" and "ch" (which even some Dutch can't tell apart), and other fine distinctions in pronunciation that make the language tricky for foreigners, give Hollanders a different perspective on thick, frictive, percussive or gravelly utterances. It's the sound in their ears from birth, and maybe the sound Dutch saxophony aspires to.

He quit Guus Janssen's octet early in 1996 because there was little for him to do there, but when he guested with Guus's trio at the BIMhuis late in the year, he showed off all those LOOSy techniques in a looser format, and sounded great, timing long wavering notes to end on the next snaredrum crack, to give a microscopic example. On that gig he also played bebop on contrabass clarinet ("Marshcello") like nobody since Braxton recorded "Ornithology" in 1974.

In spring '97 LOOS—sorry, "Ensemble LOOS"—released its second CD, performing Cornelis de Bondt's *De Tragische Handeling* "for five performers and a sound engineer." Wang was the fifth. Name another group whose first record was improvised and second through-composed. It completed a circle; if de Bondt's *Bint* helped inspire LOOS, this sounded like tepid imitation of how LOOS sounds already—silences, cued hits, contrabass clarinet blips coming back on long tape delay—but with less suspenseful timing and less grating chords. It makes their improvised pieces sound that much more spontaneous.

Same season, the inherent contradictions in the band's concept (and the subsidy system itself) came to a head when van Bergen, wanting to loosen LOOS up, decided to go with different percussionists for different projects—Han Bennink had been bugging him—which meant sacking Paul Koek. But Koek and some board members of the LOOS Foundation—such infrastructure by now all but mandatory for successfully funded musicians—tried to block the move. They liked the way the band was turning into the new Hoketus, searched the bylaws to see if Peter was officially listed as the leader. He said, I've had the band 15 years, long before any of the other guys joined, you serious?

In the end, the dissenters were purged.

Another track on *Dutch 'Difficult' Music* is by singer Moniek Toebosch and Michel Waisvisz on crackle synthesizer, last gasp of the crackle era; he also plays the '80s off-the-shelf digital leader, a Yamaha DX–7. In that decade STEIM went digital with a vengeance, but remained committed to the idea people should invent instruments for themselves to play, and generally maintained an institutional bias against humdrum keyboards.

Ray Edgar shows me around STEIM, now on the Achtergracht, across the Amstel River from the Carré Theater. Ray is the son of Boy Edgar; born in 1965, he lived in the States as a tot, when his father went over to teach. Till spring '97 Ray along with Nico Bes supervised STEIM's very affordable recording studios, from a downstairs cubbyhole where they'd tinker with who knows what at their desks. Nico is still at it.

Upstairs is the workshop where designer Frank Baldé and various engineers build digital controllers to spec. Ray demonstrates his own odd MIDI-controller, Edgar's Sweatstick. He's less interested in melody than sound, likes timbres that slide across the spectrum. (Analog synths were good for that; digital ones aren't.) The Sweatstick is a meter-long aluminum rod. Actually it's two shorter rods, bridged in the middle by a heavy coil spring; you bend the instrument in the middle to trigger pitch bends— "the whammy-bar function"—though the stick fights you to stay straight. On either half is a handgrip that slides along the rod—that controls the volume, outermost position the loudest—or can be locked in place with a flick of the thumb. The player's hands fit into attached gloves; fingers rest on keypads that trigger one octave of notes; touch-sensitive keys under the index fingers control vibrato and other parameters. The handgrips also swivel around the circumference of the stick to step a note through up to ten octaves.

Giving a short demonstration using clarinet samples and other whooshing synthesized sounds, Ray Edgar looks a little like Bruce Lee in defensive mode and a little like Astaire dancing with a hat rack. As its name makes plain, the Sweatstick is designed to take some effort to play, and to look it.

"Some instruments are too easy—there's no sense of proportion between the action and the result. For me, to transform the entire sound of an orchestra by pressing one small button makes no sense. I like to feel the tension, it makes you more sensitive. Bigger movements allow for more precise fluctuations, in pitch bends for instance." That's Ray, but the sentiment is vintage Waisvisz.

We continue our tour. Among the instruments under construction is a new version of Waisvisz's Web, a sort of electronic spiderweb where touching any filament within the hexagonal frame can trigger a variety of programmable functions. This one is smaller than a hula hoop, but for one STEIM evening some young guys build one big enough to be a ship's rigging in a pirate musical. They climb on and tug at it madly.

The problem with many latter-day STEIM controllers and that oversize web in particular is that what they control isn't necessarily interesting. Or else, by the time a unit of sound has been put through the MIDI mill, it sounds rather like the academic lab music the founders detested, or like synthesizer noodling. That aside, STEIM still befriends various improvisers—like the Hague's interactive-systems saxophonist Luc Houtkamp—by helping them develop portable reliable processers for use on stage and on the road. Alas, there are no plans to resume production of the crackle box.

A lot of the devices used to run those weird digital controllers were developed for Waisvisz's major postcrackle device, The Hands. There's the Sensor Lab, a black-box sonar device to detect and respond to physical movement; LiSa, a live sampling program; the Lick Machine sequencer program. Like earlier STEIM projects The Hands went through a long period of spectacular failures before it was up and running more or less reliably.

The Hands: small keypad controllers attach to Waisvisz's hands, to allow free movement; cords connect them to the Sensor Lab affixed to his belt in the back, in turn tethered to Baldé's desktop computer off-stage. One hand unit has a microphone, so Michel can go into the audience, shove a mic in folks' faces tabloid-TV-style, and get them to say or sing things he can sample and manipulate. (At one concert in Bologna he popped open a theater's fire door to sample a thunderstorm outside.) He can repeat a sample verbatim or chop it down to a blip he can loop into a drone or a stutter. The computer can juggle some 14 voices at a time. Different samples at different pitches lie under different keys; Waisvisz can change the length of a sample by changing the distance between hands—built-in sonar measures the distance—and he can layer sounds at will.

In 1992 he used The Hands on a short European trio tour with Laurie Anderson and drummer Dougie Bowne. In public appearances three years later he seemed more intent on demonstrating the equipment than making music with it, but he got over that. Properly deployed, The Hands are fun to watch and hear. He's free to use all his prepared sequences and programs in any order.

"It's how my memory works; I'll remember short parts of a conversation but sometimes forget the big picture. In concert, I try to juggle these pieces, to try to understand what the big link is. To make it more complicated I use audience sounds, and try to integrate them into the piece I have in mind. But I don't consider myself an improviser; I think of myself as an alert composer."

♫

November '95, Diftong is on stage at the BIMhuis: Han Buhrs, Cor Fuhler, Wilbert de Joode, Michael Vatcher. Buhrs is a singer and sometimes guitarist, with the three-voices three-strings sextet Schismatics including Jodi Gilbert, Mary Oliver and Wilbert. He sings in a throaty resonant voice that reminds some folks of Beefheart, but there's a Beefheart homage by the group Palinckx, "Fat Freddy's Cat," where Buhrs succinctly demonstrates he's too much his own man to be a credible impersonator. It seems his Strong Idea is to reject musical conventions like fluid rhythm or propulsive lift. As choke-chord guitarist, he's closer to Huib Emmer than Freddie Green.

In Diftong Buhrs' wooden-shoe timing makes the other guys (over)compensate, play riffs and strong grooves as antidote. Vatcher uses an extended kit, including a zither he plays with a cymbal as on Altena's "Slow Motion," his marching-feet clapper, a big metal thunder sheet, and a 32-inch bass drum that packs a wallop you can feel across the room. (He picks up a special beater from the floor every time he wants to strike it, keeping up the flow with his other three limbs.) At one point he holds that huge drum out in front of him like a parade snare, very comic. Between pounding out riffs for the singer de Joode wedges his bow between strings and twangs it, making bass drum sounds of his own.

Cor Fuhler makes a vintage-Cage racket, though he was knocking around inside pianos long before he ever heard of Cage let alone Henry Cowell, who'd elbowed the keys and played directly on the strings by the early 1920s. Such techniques have been common among jazz pianists since the '60s, and there have been some real adepts, Guus Janssen among them, but Fuhler is the best I've seen.

Also the most involved: sometimes he's got so much junk under the hood he looks like he's tuning up a Lincoln. Not just taking a putty spreader or small metal bar and swiping it across several strings or scraping it along the length of one, or sliding it for bottleneck blues or bouzouki effects, but laying several bars across the strings and playing strings and bouncing bars with mallets. Or he'll place a thin bar across several strings exactly at a harmonic node, so a note when struck sounds an octave or other partial higher. He wedges little things between strings, throws small objects on to them, uses a mallet to play the instrument's metal frame, or to hit a little pile of junk he keeps inside the grand piano's curve for just this purpose. He can coax varied percussion sounds from different wooden planes like Bennink sounding out a chair, or make piano sound like gamelan orchestra.

But also: he uses an E-bow—a little battery-powered black box guitarists use to make a string hum, infinite sustain; has guitar pickups on the ends of cords, which he can zoom in on strings for volume-pedal effects, sometimes with wah-wah pedal or other distortion box intervening between pickup and amplifier, so the pure piano sound and the gimmicked one can shadow each other, or one can drown the other out. His devices are kin to the piano drivers Michel Waisvisz built in the '60s.

At right angles to the piano Fuhler has an old four-octave Philicorda organ, marketed for home use in the '60s, which he may play with one hand while playing piano with the other, often in unison or parallel. On the shelf above the piano keyboard he has a melodica which he blows into with a plastic tube. He often plays it in unison with organ or piano, but when he blows melodica hard it goes flat, which makes for some nice microtonal blurs. He keeps his little devices, sliders, mallets and whatnot in a little wicker basket next to the melodica—dad's toolbox with mom's homey touch.

Juggling all this stuff, he moves fast, maintaining punchy rhythm that complements the raunchy sonorities, and, maybe most dazzling, listens and reacts to everything else happening on stage.

Cor Fuhler—soft-spoken, thoughtful, a little shy but funny, looks like a bespecta-cled young Elvis—was born in 1964 in Barger-Oosterveld, Drenthe province, in the east near the border, north of where van Bergen hails from. "My granddad had a big cafe in our village, where my parents worked parttime. I practically grew up there. There was a stage in the back with a piano, the first one I ever played, an old one with some rattling broken strings. I didn't just sit and play the keys; I was always looking inside to see what was happening in there, and heard how the sound of the other strings would change when I moved the broken ones around.

"My whole family was into music. We had no TV till I was seven or so. On a nor-mal Saturday evening, we'd put a stack of ten singles on the record player; everyone could pick two. We'd talk a little, but mostly just listen. Music was something special, not just a social thing.

"I've always improvised, even when I was a kid. My uncle had an organ, but after awhile he wouldn't let me play it anymore. When I was very young—four? five? six? eight?—I'd pick three adjacent white keys and just play them, in any combination I could think of, F, G, A. Three whole notes still sound weird to me. Later I added one more, F to B. With four, there are a lot more possibilities, and I'd do it for half an hour, till someone stopped me. I was very disappointed; I wanted to go on. When I was ten I had recorder lessons, but I wasn't fascinated by the sound. At 12 I got organ lessons. I wouldn't do what the teacher asked because I wasn't interested, but at home I'd freak out on organ, get inside it, make it distort. But I'd try to be careful, and not do too much damage.

"My piano lessons were a disaster; I never did what I was told, was more into writ-ing my own things. The public library in Emmen had a good jazz and improvised music collection. I listened to instrumental music: early Chick Corea, Mahavishnu, Focus, George Antheil, Steve Reich, Art Blakey, Willem Breuker. Han and Misha were big examples. A friend had some drums, I played piano, and we played other stuff too. We didn't play very well but we had a good time.

"I remember hearing a vibes solo on a recording, and getting so fed up with all those notes, and thinking, 'I've got to find my own way.' When I couldn't finger every-thing I could think of, I decided to go to the conservatory. I wanted to study jazz, know about chords, technique, velocity, how to make my own choices. I liked the sound of jazz: the timing, acoustic instruments, good piano sound."

Rotterdam turned him down; the next year he started at the Sweelinck, studying music and carpentry in the meantime. (He's good with his hands, makes his own sim-ple instruments.) "For three and a half years I practiced seven hours a day, rehearsals aside, and then one day woke up and said, 'Not gonna do that anymore.' I decided it was time to make my own music again.

"Misha taught me counterpoint, a nice musical subject. In a way you could say he was a bad teacher—like if you need a teacher with a plan—but for me he was perfect. I made a couple of inventions the way Bach did, and then set up a new set of rules to make melodies I liked. When just the two of us were talking, Misha gave me encour-agement, helped me a lot.

"I used electronics, even in the conservatory—made a little pickup on a wagon you could roll across the strings. I made a tack piano out of my own piano"—stuck thumbtacks in the felt hammers, for a honkytonk sound—"and attached little bells to the mechanism, so they'd ring when you played a note. The guitar pickups came later, and I didn't hear about E-bows till a few years ago.

"I had a trio with Martin van Duynhoven on drums that played Wednesdays at De Engelbewaarder, and then a quintet, Wakker op Zee—Awake at Sea. I learned to organize things, and learned what sounds good and what doesn't, and how to get a good improvisation out of a person. By my fourth year in the conservatory I was sick of school. They wouldn't let me play prepared piano on my final exam—said it wasn't really piano. The day after I graduated I went to a travel agency, bought a ticket, and spent two months in Indonesia.

"I always think I can hear what's improvised and what's composed; it's like the difference between black and white. Improvisation is the most personal thing you can do: your own notes, your own timing—for me that's the most important thing to listen to. It's more honest. It's dishonest for people to say they can't improvise. Why not? They'll do it picking up the phone, but not a clarinet." He takes quiet pleasure in making classical musicians take a stab at it.

After Cor Fuhler got out of school he was in mostly low-profile bands for awhile, some of them his own. He organized a quartet for the 1991 October Meeting, with Altena, Tristan Honsinger and Wim Janssen. Before they went on Maarten was grumping that all free music sounds the same; they went out and played discreet episode after episode—would pause, then start again in a new vein.

In the '90s Cor recorded and toured Europe with Palinckx—brothers Jacques and Bert on electric guitar and acoustic bass, Joost Buis on trombone, Jim Meneses from Philadelphia on drums. Among Dutch leaders, the guitarist makes the music that sounds most Zornlike—cues and cutups, style modulation—but combined with Jacques' own heavy obsession with psychedelic mothers floyd star trek pop. (He's no jazz guy.) That band gave Fuhler a chance to revel in stupid '60s organ sounds, and indulge his own *Star Trek* fixation; he has a phone in the shape of the *Enterprise*. When asked to write a piece for the sound poet Jaap Blonk, who specializes in congested syllables, Cor wrote a text in Dutch, translated it into English, and then translated it again using an English-Klingon dictionary.

The CD *BORDER—LIVE IN ZURICH* from 1995 is a good souvenir of that Palinckx lineup. Fuhler and Buis left in 1997, aftermath of Jacques's troubled music-theater production of the previous fall, *Brian Wilson*. It had focused less on his music than on selected aspects of the Beach Boys auteur's personality; TV host and American touchstone Ed Sullivan was portrayed as a loud smooth-talking car-salesman type.

Fuhler continued playing in Buis's Astronotes, and would sit in with him or Eric Boeren at Zaal 100—taking the front bottom panel off the upright piano so he could kick the strings—and he still had Diftong and a volatile improvising trio with de Joode and Han Bennink. But some venues are leery of booking him, afraid for their pianos. Bennink likes him a lot; finding someone who can make a racket and listen at the same time and get a loud dialogue going is one thing he lives for.

Fuhler can be subtle too. His debut *7 CC IN IO* (Geestgronden), recorded in 1994 and '5, is mostly for prepared piano, abetted here and there by gurgling organ, E-bow drones ("Schoenveters"—Shoelaces) and such. It's quieter and more reflective than what he'd play with Diftong or the trio, might sound Cagelike if rhythm didn't interest Cor so. Four of twenty-two tracks are under a minute—one is eight seconds—all but forcing you to subject the program to shuffle-play, a new combination every pass. That's Cagey. Cor's puckish humor comes across. So does the influence of Indonesian gamelan music, on "Pas-pas-pas-doublet" for one.

He has been back to Indonesia a couple of times, and plays in an Amsterdam gamelan orchestra. In '96 he toured a cross-cultural music-theater production, *Wayang Detective*, metaphysical murder mystery told in the form of a shadow-puppet play, with a mixed band of gamelan musicians and improvisers (Baars, Honsinger, Vatcher and Jacques Palinckx among them). No bassist—he used big Indonesian gongs as bass instruments. The shadow play had just enough plot, and contained a twistedly lyrical (musically and visually) episode where you got to see puppets use a toilet, and a beautiful motorcycle solo for Joost Buis. It managed, somehow, to be metaphysical, trivial and funny all at once, which is to say in the grand Dutch music-theater tradition.

In that period he'd already ripened as an improviser; his composing was a little less consistent but he had his inspired moments. When the Maarten Altena Ensemble solicited a couple of pieces based on Fats Waller material, for performance early in 1997, Cor wrote them "Bitterjug." Its fragmented scalar melody was frankly derived from "Jitterbug Waltz," but phrased in the twitchy style of Altena pieces like "Prikkel"—juxtaposition of Waller rhythm and Altena rhythm reinforced by a static figure for ride-cymbal, in forbidden (6/8) swingtime. It was an ingenious piece of music that made a little fun of the band at the same time.

That's Misha's boy. And Guus's.

Cor Fuhler is not your typical conservatory graduate. The academic jazz programs beginning to crop up after Ab Baars went to the conservatory in the '70s were in full flail a decade later. By 1987 there were 1100 jazz students at ten Dutch conservatories, giving rise to the same complaints raised about jazz ed in the States: that more musicians were being trained than anyone had gigs for; that folks were being taught absolute rights and wrongs in connection with a music in which values are relative and eccentricity has its uses. (A student who sounded like Von Freeman would have a hard time in most jazz departments.) The old argument that you learn to play like someone else before you can learn to play like yourself has merit, but some musicians only a few years out of the conservatory themselves, and still aggressively imitating their role models, have already returned to school as teachers.

Lots of drawbacks, but as the good young tenor player Yuri Honing explained it, in Holland where the government subsidizes college tuition, going to the conservatory amounts to being paid to practice. In the '90s such schools had all but replaced workshops and fanfares as training grounds, and some (but not all) conservatory jazz programs offered little approval to improvised music that didn't conform to mainstream jazz models. There had always been some open-minded teachers around—in the '80s Nedly Elstak landed a conservatory gig—but in Holland as in New York, jazz conservatives were on the attack.

The Dutch conservatory system has its conspicuous successes, even in the States.

Pianist Rob van Bavel finished second to Marcus Roberts in the 1987 Thelonious Monk competition. In '96 Dutch guitarist Jesse van Ruller won it, same year pianist Michiel Borstlap won a BMI composers' competition. Bassist Joris Teepe found a niche for himself on the New York club scene. The hardbop combo The Houdini's have garnered some good reviews for their well-honed CDs. After Blue Note signed the solid Surinam-born standards singer (and Utrecht conservatory teacher) Denise Jannah, they inked the Dutch latin band Nueva Manteca. One night I caught them at the BIMhuis, their section work wouldn't have passed muster in uptown Manhattan, but Claudio Roditi says he and Paquito D'Rivera like them okay, and they know about such things. Only some of these players are hostile to new developments. Borstlap is a Mengelberg fan. Yuri Honing teamed up with Ab Baars for some gigs in 1997. The Houdini's commissioned some Ellington arrangements from Michael Moore.

Academicism breeds revivalism, not all of it bad. Buis plays Sun Ra. Boeren's Ornette project inspired another one, from Groningen tenor saxophonist Johan Huizing. Hilversum's Dutch Jazz Orchestra recorded some rare Billy Strayhorn.

Tenor, soprano and baritone saxophonist Frans Vermeerssen, ex-Noodband, has an ongoing project playing Rahsaan Roland Kirk tunes. His quintet or quartet succeeds because it does what Kirk did: makes reference to every phase of jazz history from dixie to freestyle. Slap bass, blues piano, classic breathy tenor and collective improvising intermingle. Usually his push-pull rhythm section—as on the CD *One for Rahsaan*, also with cellist Paul Stouthamer—was Vatcher, De Joode and pianist Michiel Braam. Those three also have a (very occasional) trio, playing Monk.

Michiel Braam—born 17 May 1964, two weeks before Eric Dolphy did his little tour with Mengelberg and Bennink—is everything jazz ed aspires to. Having delved into jazz history, he came up with something fresh based on it, inventive, with craft ever evident. Braam grew up in Nijmegen, inland, and got a lot of practical experience early. He played acoustic bass guitar in a folk group (for which he wrote the first tune he can remember, "A Turkish Blues"), had a dance orchestra (which made him "handy with chords" and where he learned to write for four horns), and played a lot of cocktail piano: "People like it best when you play accompaniment, even when you're alone." More recently he's played bar-band-quality New Orleans R&B covers with a quartet, and has an okay duo with alto saxophonist Frank Nielander, playing standards.

At the conservatory in Arnhem his teacher, pianist Rob van den Broeck, turned him on to Herbie Nichols: "He told me to get the double album of Blue Note stuff, and wrote out several pieces for me, and talked about his unconventional or irrational harmonies"—how Nichols could take a simple II–V–I progression and muck it up with accidentals. "I played his tunes, but I played more Monk.

"When I studied at the conservatory, it always puzzled me that people studied Michael Brecker instead of earlier music. I concentrated on Ellington, and Fletcher Henderson. To me it's one very clear line from them to Monk, Nichols and Cecil Taylor. I'm more into stride piano and Tatum than McCoy Tyner. I don't really get Tyner."

The title of Braam's self-produced solo debut, *Oeps!* (Oops) 1989, is clue to his playful approach to boogie and stride left-hand moves. The CD's charm is not so much a matter of dazzling fingerwork but of the big-man's bounce he puts into it. His stride *strides*, and he glances here and there at serial/postserial piano styles, but there's a bit too much pedal-down churning. That's also true of his quartet follow-up *Bentje Braam*—Little Band Braam—from 1990. There were a couple of moments of Ellingtonian balladry from Peter Haex's trombone, but it's audibly restless; Michiel was searching.

What he needed was a palette scaled to his expressive gestures. In the late '80s jazz musicians and critics began lining up along ideological lines to deal with the crisis conservatory jazz had presented: whether "jazz" signified an improvisational tradition or America's Classical Music, the latter a closed book like Kees van Baaren's embalmed and dissected Euroharmonic tradition. You could hear which line players took from listening to their music.

Assembling his second big band in the late '80s, the 13-piece Bik Bent Braam, he brought together musicians from both camps, straight arrows and outcats (and northerners and southerners), not out of Volhardingesque idealism—though Willem van Manen was in it a minute—but early-Kollektief pragmatism: he wanted an orchestra to nail the charts and loosen the roof. In the brass section Eric Boeren sat next to conservatory poster boy and Wyntonian trumpeter Jarmo Hoogendijk (later replaced by Rotterdam's Eric Vloeimans, polished postbopper out of Kenny Wheeler). The trombone chairs were occupied at various times by Joost Buis, Wolter Wierbos and the southland's lyrical Hans Sparla. All told Braam had two tubas (when Haex wasn't playing trombone), four saxes including Vermeerssen and Nielander, and de Joode on bass.

Bik Bent Braam's first CD, *Howdy* (1992, for Holland's mostly-mainstream Timeless label) was an encouraging field report—strong echoes of Mingus here and there, a nice take on the only non-Braam tune, Boeren's "Hersinde," and an homage of sorts to the Breuker Kollektief, which Braam had heard early, "Sire."

By 1996 and their second, *Het XYZ der Bik Bent Braam* (BVHaast), two BIMhuis-live CDs, 26 pieces from "Aardedonker" (Pitch-dark) to "Zwoerdspek" (Baconrind), Braam had really found himself. Where he found himself was the vicinity of the Cotton Club 1930: Ellington with his early, brassy rowdiness, and the helter-skelter atmosphere of hastily assembled production numbers. There are counterpunching brass and reed sections, chase choruses, stoptime breaks and other swing band devices (and also trappings of later fashion, like bongos on "Chachachtig"—Cha-cha-ish) that frankly acknowledge the points of departure—also including Lunceford and Sun Ra—without sounding like museumware. He makes the gestures a little larger than life, pushes slap bass and plunger trombone and other period effects toward the point of caricature without arriving there. Almost all his blatant references come from jazz itself. The fun is easy to spot but not strained, third-generation Dutch improvisers perhaps more sensitive than their elders to humor's strengths and pitfalls.

It swings too, and solo space is so generous you can't forget improvising is at least half of what matters. Almost every piece is designed to frame somebody's best tendencies, not least the leader's. In his piano comping there is a little of Nichols-style atmospheric harmony—gentle rumbling in the lowest register, pedal down, behind a 5/4 horn lick on "Aardedonker"—and some Erroll Garner chord-strumming in the right hand. His Monk or Ellington strains are well digested by now, though sometimes he can zone out, play something deliberately blah like Misha or Franky Douglas. He also likes to sweep either hand up or down several octaves for a flourish, part of his repertoire of theatrical comments from the ivories. His fantasias on Garner and other pianists are not as abstract as Guus Janssen's but equally affectionate and attentive to what they have to offer, much as he'd protest they are not deliberate. He is much more of a jazz cat than Guus, or Cor, or Misha. Braam is his own man on the old road.

"I'm not so interested in making something that is really new, but to use all the sounds I have heard. It's important to let the public hear something they recognize once in awhile. With a lot of avant-garde music, I'm tired after 20 minutes, need some relief: relief or I leave.

"Of course it creates problems when you mix different musicians together and write music for them, but I think a group sound is emerging out of all these individuals. I expect it'll take ten years from when I started for that to really happen."

By now Braam is also the head of the Light Music department at the Arnhem Conservatory, enjoys turning on his students to players and ideas they hadn't considered, keeps an eye out for progressive Americans coming to Holland on tour he might persuade to come down to do a clinic.

After the live XYZ came out BBB toured again, playing the same material: the solos had lost none of their edge, but the ensembles were tighter and intonation more precise, except when Braam bounced off the piano bench to conduct from out front, coaxing his players into misbehaving. As '97 dawned, he had the best working big band in Holland. At the end of the year, he got the Boy Edgar Prize.

Paradiso, December 1995. The Ex are playing their last gig for a year; guitarist Terrie Hessels a.k.a. Terrie Ex and his girlfriend Emma are leaving next week to drive to Cape Town and back, not (yet) knowing that no one sane or otherwise travels the length of Africa by car anymore. (They'll do it anyway.) Tonight, the joint is jumping. The Ex are sort of polite punks known for their impeccable politics. They should be known as rock musicians who can really improvise—not "take a solo," but play something collectively coherent. They are not virtuosi, their harmonic sense is all but nonexistent, they don't sound like they remember to tune up most weeks, but they can set up a quiet texture and maintain it, or piss all over a wall of sound.

Terrie was born in 1954, is older than he looks with his demented grin, kid's openness, and street punk reflexes. He has an annoying habit of cuffing you about the head and punching your kidneys when you talk to him. That's what he does to me anyway. His father had some Derek Bailey and a lot of jazz records; Terrie's named for Terry Gibbs, has a brother named Django.

The Ex have been together since '79, and always improvised some. "It started during the punk explosion, because it all looked so simple. Everyone started playing instruments and doing gigs, and the audience came." Once Han Bennink was doing a session at a studio they use: "He heard our drummer and became an Ex fan immediately. Our bass player Luc knew about him long before me, but I did see Han do a gig at a fancy club in Rotterdam, where he was sawing the stage. The first time we played with him was at the BIMhuis in 1991, the second time soon after at the

October Meeting. When Steve Lacy heard us, he said, 'It's demon music,' but later when he met us he said, 'You look like nice demons.'

"To play with people like Han or Ab Baars, for me that's the best music there is. I don't know any other punks interested in that scene. Our music is brutal in one sense but we've played together so long, every gig is subtly different. Ab is the same way— the little things can make all the difference. We work on that."

They weren't always as good at it as they were by the time they made their improvisation album —*instant*— in 1995. When they were recording it, sometimes they'd play some tracks they'd improvised for a guest, and invite that person to pick some pieces they'd like to add something to. A duet by guitarist Andy Moor and Michael Vatcher on steel objects sounds like gamelan of the robots. On "Exile O'Phonics," Vatcher exorcises the cymbal wheeled on zither string, retrieves it from chamber music. Other guests include Bennink, Wierbos and Tristan Honsinger. That makes sense. The Ex are heirs of sorts to their die-hard improvisers esthetic; not all the sons and daughters of the pioneers are composers. Call this music a new K'PLOENG.

The Ex have guests at Paradiso tonight. Drummer Katrin Ex is back from pregnancy leave, but her two erstwhile subs are here too, Australian Tony Buck and Vatcher, who's brought his 32-inch bass drum because, he explains, being bigger in circumference than even the bass amp and PA speakers, it has greater amplitude and so can't be drowned out. It seems to be true. Wierbos is also here, superimposing his inventions over whatever anyone else had in mind.

Bennink, invited to play solo, has brought his snare drum, but gets more involved in playing his chair, and gradually some of the thousand people enjoying the party simmer down and crane their necks to see what's going on up there: what is that noise like a dozen xylophones? Terrie's in the back, standing on a riser, huge grin. "Most of these people have never seen anything like this before!"

He's got that idealist's glow on his face. Inclusive concerts live.

Now it's January 1997. In this month's *Jazz Nu*, Dutch monthly unsympathetic to homegrown innovators, saxophonist Ben van den Dungen rails at great length against the subsidizers who have denied funding to Nueva Manteca, saying it adds nothing new to the Latin big-band genre. His retort: the band's not that big. (It's an octet, sometimes expanded.) He asks: LOOS, the folks who record for Geestgronden, the Willem Breuker Kollektief, Bik Bent Braam, Contraband—is that jazz? You know his answer. (Bik Bent Braam not jazz?) He really laces into Breuker's band; never mind that Willem doesn't call his music jazz, or solicit funding from jazz channels anymore.

If the Dutch scene teaches us anything, it's that jazz conservatives can relax, needn't worry about the harmful effects of cross-breeding jazz and other kinds of music. Because if the stuff that's happened over the last 30 years hasn't killed off mainstream jazz in Holland, it's a hardier growth than the hothouse flower its self-appointed defenders take it for.

The Breuker Kollektief still does all right for itself, funding-wise, got 271,000 guilders for 1997, paltry compared to what a ten-piece classical ensemble would get, but a lot better than what ICP got that season, almost zero. All those years of not opening his mail hasn't endeared Misha to grants panels. (In the following funding cycle, he did better, at least partly in reaction to that rebuff.)

The SJIN had suffered severe budget problems for a couple of years, having overspent itself sending a Nedly Elstak repertory orchestra on the road in 1995. Arts money in general was shrinking, partly because the Dutch economy had slowed, partly because the old excesses associated with visual-art subsidies in particular had become a Dutch equivalent of the welfare-mothers-with-Cadillacs riff. By January 1997 the SJIN was subsumed into something called the Music and Theater Network, and many subsidy applications had become so confusing some musicians no longer knew how or wanted to fill them out. And even players not given to grousing were complaining about lack of work.

In a way, things looked more bleak for Holland's improvisers than any period since the early '80s, the last time the music's death was declared prematurely.

It's a Sunday noon as I finish this. The old Available Jelly quartet was just on the weekend TV institution *Reiziger in Muziek*, playing "Catch a Wave" and "Warmth of the Sun" to promote this week's evening of Brian Wilson music at Paradiso, also featuring Palinckx, the Gene Carl Band and the Mondrian Strings. This afternoon there's an inclusive Rumori concert at Frascati, including the Palinckx quintet, Czech violinist/vocalist Iva Bittová and Ives piano music. At three o'clock in Utrecht, Paul Termos's flute concerto premiers. At four, Sean Bergin runs the session at De Engelbewaarder as usual. At 4:30 in Arnhem, the Ab Baars trio plays the first of several gigs devoted to John Carter's music. Also this week Han Bennink goes to New York to play four nights, eight duos, at the Knitting Factory. Playing with tenor Ellery Eskelin will remind him of his '67 duets with Sonny Rollins.

Two nights ago Bik Bent Braam stormed the BIMhuis. Last weekend at Frascati there was a four-hour improvised dance marathon organized by Katie Duck, improvised music from some Katie Duck regulars and a few ringers; a lovely Mengelberg duet with German drummer Paul Lovens was nicely disrupted by Terrie Ex, noisily dragging the head of his electric guitar across the floor. Weekend before that, same location, Klap op de Vuurpijl, the Breuker Kollektief sounded as good as I've ever heard them: ensembles in the pocket, good solos, welcome revival of "Waddenzee Suite," with that odd 13-beat bass line.

At Zaal 100, the Tuesday night series continues. In coming weeks, LOOS and Asko Ensemble will play Xenakis and Stockhausen, and Han and Misha will play their first duo concert in years. (Part of it will turn up on their CD *MiHA*.) A few weeks after that, Misha will have a mild heart attack, and to everyone's astonishment instantly give up smoking.

One day I telephone Ernst Reijseger, hear a slow cello blues in the background.

—Listening to one of your own tapes?

"No man I'm giving a lesson. That's my 14-year-old student Harald."

Fourth generation.

Works Consulted

[D] indicates Dutch text and a Dutch publisher. The English-language periodical *Key Notes* is published by Donemus, Amsterdam. As in the discography and index, surnames are alphabetized in the Dutch manner, i.e., under the first capitalized word; thus, for example, Roland de Beer and Erik van den Berg are found under B (and, in the index, Mariëtte Rouppe van der Voort under R).

In addition to the individual sources listed, three periodical series were invaluable:

Jazzjaarboek [D], 1–7, Erik van den Berg, Rudy Koopmans, Bert Vuijsje, et al., eds., Amsterdam: Van Gennep, 1982–88. These annual paperback collections include among other things fine profiles of Dutch musicians. Ernst Reijseger's blindfold test is in #2.

Jazz Nu [D] (various Dutch addresses) 1–212, 1978–1997. Numerous issues were dredged for information. Misha discusses subsidy woes with Bert Vuijsje in the March '82 issue; Ben van den Dungen's comments at the end of Chapter 14 come from Mark Koster's article in the last issue cited, January 1997.

Jazzwereld [D] (Hilversum, then Amsterdam) 1–43, 1965–1973. Every issue was consulted; to list every article that informed this work would take pages. Mengelberg's Newport report is in the September 1966 issue; New York correspondent Frens van der Mei's, November '66; Michiel de Ruyter on Cecil Taylor's impromptu session, July '67.

Andriessen, Bas. *Tetterettet: Interviews met Nederlandse improviserende musici* [D], Ubbergen: Tandem Felix, 1996. Essential reading, if your Dutch is good.

Andriessen, Louis, et al. Annotated English translation of the libretto in the 3-LP box *Reconstructie: een moraliteit* (STEIM Opus 001). The interpolations in the discussion of the opera in Chapter 4 are taken from here.

Andriessen, Louis, and Elmer Schöenberger. *The Apollonian Clockwork*, London: Oxford, 1989. Jeff Hamburg's translation of the 1983 Dutch text.

de Beer, Roland. "'The Awesome Symphony Orchestra': Kaalslag Presenting Four Premieres in the Holland Festival," *Key Notes* 21, 1985.

_____. "The Netherlands Saxophone Quartet: A New Culture Opened," *Key Notes* 12, 1980.

van den Berg, Erik. "Briefcase Bop and Gloss Paint," *Key Notes* 24, 1987.

Bernlef, J. "'I don't lie in my music,'" *Key Notes* 29/2, June 1994. On Theo Leovendie.

Blotkamp, Carel. *Mondrian: The Art of Destruction*, New York: Harry N. Abrams, 1995. Epigraph for Chapter 12.

Bulterman, Jack. *The Ramblers Story* [D], Bussum: Unieboek, 1973. Includes a reproduction of Hawkins' epigraph to the Prologue.

Buzelin, Françoise, and Jean Buzelin, *Willem Breuker: Maker van Mensenmuziek* [D], Zutphen: Walburg Pers, 1994. The Dutch translation of a most sympathetic biography in French (Paris: Éditions du Limon, 1992) has been expanded and improved by Sjaak Hubregste. There is also an extensive discography, a bibliography, and a directory of Breuker's film, theater, and TV music.

Cage, John. *Silence: Lectures and Writings*, Middletown, CT: Wesleyan University Press, 1973.

Calis, Hein. "Amsterdam Electric Circus" in *Key Notes* 2, 1976.

Chilton, John. *The Song of the Hawk: The Life and Recordings of Coleman Hawkins*, London: Quartet, 1990.

Cley, Michiel. "Musical Hunger: Interview with Maarten Altena," *Key Notes* 28:3, September 1994. Epigraph for Chapter 13.

Coenen, Alcedo. "Louis Andriessen's 'De Materie,'" *Key Notes* 25, 1988/89. Includes discussion of Mondrian and *De Stijl*.

Corbett, John. Unpublished interview with Misha Mengelberg, Amsterdam, 15 November 1993.

Cowell, Henry, and Sidney Cowell. *Charles Ives and His Music*, 2nd ed., New York: Oxford University Press, 1969. Told in 1946 that his music had anticipated many modern developments, Ives retorted, "That's not my fault."

Cusack, Peter, and Hugh Davies, eds. *MUSICS* (London) 7, April/May 1976. The feisty little English magazine's Dutch Issue includes Cusack articles on music theater (quoted in Chapter 5), the subsidy system, and his interview with Misha Mengelberg (quoted re: Cage at Darmstadt in Chapter 1), as well as articles by among others Maarten Altena, Nico Bes, Arjen Gorter, and Michel Waisvisz.

Dulfer, Hans. *Jazz in China en andere perikels uit de geimproviseerde muziek* [D], Amsterdam: Bert Bakker, 1980.

van Eekeren, Michael. "Juggling with melody, Mahler and Monk," *Key Notes* 30:2, June 1996. Martijn Padding on Beethoven and Monk.

Elstak, Nedly. *Praktische Jazz Theorie* [D], 4 vols., Amsterdam: Gebroeders Müller 1981–84.

Erenstein, Rob, and Joost Sternheim, eds. *Baal: 15 Jaar Toneelhistorie 1973–1988* [D], Amsterdam: International Theatre Bookshop, 1988.

van Eyle, Wim, chief ed. *The Dutch Jazz & Blues Discography 1916–1980*, Amsterdam: Spectrum.

_____ *Jazz & Geimproviseerde Muziek in Nederland* [D], Utrecht: Spectrum, 1978. This biographical dictionary of Dutch improvisers is supplemented with a chronology of Dutch jazz, Willem van Manen's account of the early history of the subsidy system, and other worthwhile features.

Feather, Leonard. *The Book of Jazz*, New York: Meridian, 1959. Source of the Wilbur de Paris quotes in the Introduction.

Giddins, Gary. "Breuker Battles the Bourgeoisie" in *Riding on a Blue Note: Jazz and American Pop*, New York: Oxford, 1981

Gilbert, Will G., and C. Poustochkine. *Jazzmuziek* [D], 2nd ed., The Hague: J. Philip Kruseman, 1947.

Griffiths, Paul. *Modern Music: The Avant Garde Since 1945*, London: Dent, 1981.

de Groot, Rokus. "Flexibility: Pitch Organization in Recent Works by Theo Loevendie," *Key Notes* 14, 1981.

Hazeldonk, Roeland. "Gerard Bowhuis on Making Music, LOOS and Boulez," in Peter van Bergen, ed., program book, *Tijdkring Contemporary Improvised Music Festival 1995*, The Hague: Hans Truijen, 1995.

Jansen, Kasper. "Bruno Maderna and Dutch Concert Life," *Key Notes* 11, 1980.

Kien, Hein. "Towards a Revaluation of the Sound Material," *Key Notes* 4, 1976. On Kees van Baaren.

de Kloet, Co, and Gabri de Wagt. *Mooi Holland: De woelige jaren van de Ramblers* [D], Nieuwkoop: Heuff, undated.

Koopmans, Rudy. "Guus Janssen—The Interaction of Composing and Improvising," *Key Notes* 7, 1978.

_____. "Hoketus—Unequivocal Music with Pronounced Contrasts," *Key Notes* 11, 1980.

_____. "On Music and Politics—Activism of Five Dutch Composers," *Key Notes* 4, 1976. On the Notenkrakers and their legacy, Misha and van Baaren, and the source of extracts from Volharding's brochure in Chapter 4.

_____. "The Retarded Clockmaker," *Key Notes* 1, 1976. An overview of Dutch music theater, referred to in Chapter 4.

_____ and Orkest de Volharding, *10 Jaar Volharding* [D], Amsterdam: Van Gennep, 1983. A long Koopman essay plus extensive documentation of the orchestra's activities and repertoire over its first decade make this a gold mine of source material and specific details that turn up in Chapter 4—like Andriessen's diary entry re: *Reconstructie.*

Kroeze, Hans, ed. *International Jazz Festival 1971–1980,* Amsterdam: Aktu & Promotions, 1981. Running accounts of the annual Loosdrecht and Laren festivals, with condensed press comments, in English and Dutch.

Leeuw, Reinbert de. *Musikale Anarchie* [D], Amsterdam: De Bezige Bij, 1973. Source for Misha's description of "Parafax."

Loevendie, Theo. "Existing Gaps Can Be Narrowed," *Key Notes* 5, 1977.

Mengelberg, Misha. "S.age T.hymes E.at I.nkfish M.mmm," *Key Notes* 8, 1978. On STEIM.

Misha Mengelberg interviewed by Andrew Timar in *Musicworks* (Toronto) 14, Winter 1981. Chapter 1's epigraph and incidental biographical details come from their October 1980 conversation.

Mertens, Wim. *American Minimal Music,* White Plains, NY: Pro/Am, 1988. A translation of the 1983 Flemish text.

Nyman, Michael. *Experimental Music: Cage and Beyond,* New York: Schirmer, 1981. An American reprint of the 1974 study.

van Oortmerssen, Jochem. "The Lost Composition," *Key Notes* 28, March 1994. On Werner Herbers and Bob Graettinger.

Openneer, Herman. *Kid Dynamite: De legende leeft* [D], Amsterdam: Jan Mets, 1995.

Oskamp, Jacqueline. "'You can hear the players thinking during the silence,'" *Key Notes* 29:2, June 1995. On Peter van Bergen; quoted in Chapter 14.

Otten, Willem Jan. "How Not to Be Trapped into Non-Art: Notes Towards a Definition of Dick Raaijmakers," *Key Notes* 20, 1984.

Pam, Max. "Leo Cuypers—Lone Wolf of the Improvised Music Scene, *Key Notes* 11, 1980.

Profeta, Alfredo. "Han Bennink's Discography (in Progress)" in Filippo Bianchi, ed., *Han Bennink: Ritratto d'artista,* Reggio Emilia, Italy: Associazione I Teatri, 1991.

van Rossum, Frans, and Sytze Smit. "Louis Andriessen: 'After Chopin and Mendelssohn We Landed in a Mudbath,'" *Key Notes* 28:1, March 1994. On jazz articulation and major and minor seconds.

Schat, Peter, and Rokus de Groot. Several articles about Schat's "Tone Clock" in *Key Notes* 19, 1984.

Schönberger, Elmer. "Louis Andriessen: On the Conceiving of Time," *Key Notes* 13, 1981.

Schouten, Martin. *Billie en de President: Over Jazz* [D], Amsterdam: Synopsis, 1977.

Simosko, Vladimir, and Barry Tepperman. *Eric Dolphy: A Musical Biography and Discography*, New York: Da Capo, 1979. This was first published in 1974.

Smith, Bill. "The Willem Breuker Interview," *Coda* (Toronto) 160, April 1978.

Strickland, Edward. *American Composers: Dialogues on Contemporary Music*, Bloomington: Indiana University Press, 1991. Source of the Terry Riley quote in Chapter 4.

Tra, Gijs. Three articles in *Key Notes* 7, 1978: "Instant Composers Pool—A Decade of Musical and Political Innovation," "De Volharding, ' . . . An Offbeat Jazz Group or a Crazy Bunch of Wind Players,'" and "Herman de Wit's Workshops."

Vermeulen, Ernst. "Kees van Baaren's Antischool," *Key Notes* 26:1, 1992. Source of some details about the Notenkraker action, Chapter 4.

Voermans, Erik. "Sympathy for the Outcast," *Key Notes* 29:2, June 1995. This Theo Loevendie profile is quoted at the beginning of Chapter 2.

Vuijsje, Bert. *De Nieuwe Jazz: Twintig Interviews* [D], Baarn: Bosch & Keuning, 1978. A double interview with Han and Misha is rife with information on their early days together.

van der Waa, Frits. "Guus Janssen," *Key Notes* 28/3, September 1994. The best précis of his music I have read.

_____ ed. *De Slag van Andriessen* [D], Amsterdam: De Bezige Bij. A collection of essays on Louis Andriessen's music. Chapter 11 is informed by J. Bernlef's article on Andriessen and jazz, and David Dramm's on *Melodie*. Dramm kindly made available his original English text.

Waisvisz, Michel. "The Crackle Project: The Need for New Instruments in Music and Theatre," *Key Notes* 8, 1978.

Weltak, Marcel, ed. *Surinamse Muziek in Nederland en Suriname* [D], Utrecht: Kosmos, 1990.

Wennekes, Emile. "LOOS: Experiment Elevated to Credo," *Key Notes* 30:3, September 1996.

Whitehead, Kevin. Interview with Steve McCall, Baltimore: 22 March 1981. Excerpted in *Cadence* 8:7, July 1982.

Witts, Dick. "On Misha Mengelberg/On Louis Andriessen," *MUSICS* (London) 18, July 1978.

Yates, Peter. *Twentieth Century Music*, London: George Allen & Unwin, 1967.

Zwerin, Mike. *La Tristesse de St. Louis: Jazz Under the Nazis*, New York: Beech Tree Books, 1985.

Discography

This is not a list of every available CD by folks mentioned, but a selection based on what's discussed in the text. Few historic Dutch recordings from the pre-CD era have been reissued, so far, but like everything connected with reissues, that's subject to change.

Sessions are generally listed under the leader's name, or the first-listed co-leader, although some appearances as sidefolk may be found under a particular musician's main listing. (Where more than one Dutch musician appears on a non-Dutch musician's CD, it's under the leader's name. However only co-leader appearances are cross-referenced.) Only such track titles and musicians worthy of special mention or not adequately limned in the main text are indicated here. Where CD sleeves contain typos or unfamiliar names for familiar pieces, they have been silently corrected.

(Full disclosure: I wrote liner notes for several discs here—almost all of which were slighted in the main text to avoid the appearance of shilling—and co-produced the two 1991 October Meeting CDs.)

Most of the labels featuring Dutch improvised music (as well as Attaca and the Breuker on Entr'acte) are distributed by BVHaast, Prinseneiland 99, 1013 LN Amsterdam NL (phone 31–20–623–9799). BVHaast's North American distributor is North Country, Redwood NY 13679–9612 (315–287–2852). Composers' Voice is distributed in the U.S. by Albany Music, 915 Broadway, Albany NY 12207 (518-436-8814).

MAARTEN ALTENA bass (see also Butch Morris)

❷ Steve Lacy & Altena: *High, Low and Order* (hatART 6069) 12/77

❷ *Rif* (hatART 6056) 8/87

❷ *Quotl* (hatART 6029) 12/88

❷ *Cities & Streets* (hatART 6082) 10/89

❷ *Code* (hatART 6094) 12/90

❷ *City Music* (Attaca Babel 9373) 1991
    Altena & Remco Campert.

❷ *Maarten Altena Ensemble* (a.k.a. *Muziekpraktijk — Music + Practice* (Composers' Voice 49) 1993–94
Ringers Cor Fuhler (harmonium) and Paul Koek (vib) make brief appearances.

❷ *Working on Time* (NM Classics 92063) 1995
Includes rewrites of Machaut (by Geert van Keulen), Purcell (Henk van der Meulen), and Byrne/Eno (Alison Isadora) as described at the top of Chapter 13, and a quiet suite by Gilius van Bergeijk.

AMSTERDAM STRING TRIO: Maurice Horsthuis, Ernst Reijseger, Ernst Glerum

❷ *Wild West* (Nimbus 506) 12/88

LOUIS ANDRIESSEN piano, composer (see also Greetje Bijma, The Busy Drone, Orkest de Volharding)

Compositions by:

❷ (Composers Voice 54) 10/94
Netherlands Ballet Orchestra, cond. Howard Williams, et al. *Anachronie I & II, Contra Tempus*, and other '60s works.

❷ *Fifty Years Holland Festival: A Dutch Miracle* (Globe 6900) 6/69
This 6-CD retrospective includes sections F through J of *Reconstructie*, by Andriessen, Mengelberg, et al., including the "Abide with Me" quotation.

❷ (Attaca Babel 9267–6) 1984 and 1986
Melodie (Andriessen, Frans Brüggen), *Symphony for Open Strings* (Caecilia Consort, cond. Ed Spanjaard).

❷ *Ricciotti Ensemble: 21 Years Stage on Street* (BVHaast 9110) 5/91
Workers Union (Andriessen), *The Unanswered Question* (Ives).

❷ *De Staat* (Elektra Nonesuch 79251) 1990
Schoenberg Ensemble, cond. Reinbert de Leeuw.

❷ (Composers' Voice 20) mid–1980s and 1990
Hoketus (Hoketus incl. future members of LOOS), *Mausoleum* (Asko and Schoenberg Ensembles et al., cond. Reinbert de Leeuw).

❷ (Elektra Nonesuch 79342) 1993–94
M Is for Man, Music, Mozart (Orkest de Volharding, cond. Jurjen Hempel), *De Stijl* (Asko and Schoenberg Ensembles, cond. Reinbert de Leeuw).
This performance of *De Stijl* is also part of *De Materie* (Nonesuch 79367), the complete megawork in four parts, sometimes very heavy on the BANG BANG BANG. The original Kaalslag recording of *De Stijl* conducted by de Leeuw is on Attaca Babel 9375.

❷ Aurelia Saxophone Quartet: *Saxophone Quartets* (NM Classics 92053) 2/95
Facing Death.

ARCADO STRING TRIO: Mark Feldman, Ernst Reijseger, Mark Dresser.

❶ *Live in Europe* (Avant 058) 1994.

AVAILABLE JELLY: Eric Boeren, Michael Moore, Michael Vatcher, et al.

❶ *In Full Flail* (Ear-Rational 1013) 6/88.

❶ *Al(l)ways* (NOM 00110/01000) 11/89.

❶ *Monuments* (Ramboy 07) 1993
   "Hersinde."

❶ *Happy Camp* (Ramboy 10) 6/96
   "Uninhabited Island."

AB BAARS clarinet, tenor saxophone

❶ *Krang* (Geestgronden 2) 1987–89
   Baars also on soprano and baritone sax.

❶ *3900 Carol Court* (Geestgronden 12) 1992

❶ *Sprok* (Geestgronden 14) 1994
   "Lakschoen."

❶ *Verderame* (Geestgronden 17) 1/95
   Very well-defined tenor and clarinet solos; includes "Verschoten geel."

HAN BENNINK drums, anything/everything (see also Peter Brötzmann, Clusone 3, Misha Mengelberg, Roswell Rudd, Collections)

❶ Derek Bailey & Han Bennink: *Live at Verity's Place* (Corti 9) 6/72

❶ *Tempo Comodo* (DATA 823) 9/82
   Han solo.

❶ Bailey & Bennink: *Han* (Incus 002) 3/86

❶ Cecil Taylor & Bennink: *Spots, Circles, and Fantasy* (FMP 5), 7/88

❶ Major Holley and the Joe [Joop] van Enkhuizen Quartet: *Major Step* (Timeless 364) 7/90

❶ Bennink & Myra Melford: *Eleven Ghosts* (hatOLOGY 507) 2/94

❶ *Irene Schweizer & Han Bennink* (Intakt 010) 1/95

❶ Bennink & Dave Douglas: *Serpentine* (Songlines 1510) 1/96
   Duo standards and improvisations. Bennink also heard on violin (played upright in his lap, cello-like) and wooden shoes.

❶ Bennink, Michiel Borstlap & Ernst Glerum: *3* (Via 992.029.2) 5/97

PETER ᴠᴀɴ BERGEN reeds (see also LOOS)

❶ King [um]Ubü Orchestru: *Binaurality* (FMP 49) 6/92
   Gunter Christmann, Radu Malfatti, Wolfgang Fuchs (reeds), Luc Houtkamp
   (reeds), Paul Lytton, et al.

❶ Van Bergen, Wolfgang Fuchs & Hans Koch (reeds): *Comité Imaginaire* (FMP 84)
   7/95

SEAN BERGIN reeds (see also Trio San Francisco)

❶ Barry Altschul: *That's Nice* (Soul Note 121115) 11/85

❶ Bergin & M.O.B.: *Kids Mysteries* (Nimbus 502) 11/87

❶ Bergin & M.O.B.: *Live at the BIMhuis* (BVHaast 9202) 4/91

BERLIN CONTEMPORARY JAZZ ORCHESTRA

❶ *Berlin Contemporary Jazz Orchestra* (ECM 1403) 5/89
   Benny Bailey, Thomas Heberer, Henry Lowther, Kenny Wheeler, Paul van
   Kemenade, Willem Breuker, Misha Mengelberg, et al. "Reef," "Kneebus,"
   "Salz" (all by Mengelberg).

GREETJE BIJMA voice (see also Collections)

❶ Five Voices: *Direct Sound* (Intakt 015) 4/89
   Shelly Hirsch, Anna Homler, David Moss, Carles Santos. Includes three Bijma
   solos and duets with Hirsch and Moss.

❶ *Tales of a Voice* (Tiptoe 888808) 10/90
   Alan Laurillard, Jan Kuiper, Gerard Ammerlaan (b, perc), Charles Huffstadt (d,
   perc).

❶ Bimja & Louis Andriessen: *Nadir & Zenit* (BVHaast 9303) 6/92

❶ Bijma, Laurillard & Klaus Hoek/Up There Trio: *Push It* (BVHaast 9607) 1994–95.

ERIC BOEREN cornet (see also Available Jelly)

❶ *Cross Breeding* (BIMhuis 005) 8/95
   Jan Willem van der Ham, Michael Moore, Paul Termos, Ab Baars, Sean Bergin,
   Tobias Delius, Wilbert de Joode, Ernst Glerum, Michael Vatcher, Wim Janssen.
   Pieces by Boeren and by Ornette Coleman include "Beauty Is a Rare Thing,"
   "Blues Connotation," "Mapa."

MICHIEL BRAAM piano

❶ *Oeps!* (B! [no number]) 3/89

❶ *Bentje Braam.* (BVHaast 9007) 2/90
   Peter Haex (tbn, tba), Ton van Erp (b), Fred van Duynhoven.

❸ Bik Bent Braam: *Howdy* (Timeless 388) 1/92
Eric Boeren, Jarmo Hoogendijk, Joost Buis, Wolter Wierbos, Frank Nielander, Bart van der Putten, Frans Vermeerssen, Rutger van Otterloo (bars), Peter Haex, Patrick Votrian (tba), Wilbert de Joode, Joop van Erven (d).

❸ *Het XYZ der Bik Bent Braam* (BVHaast 9610–11) 5/96
As above except Hoogendijk and Buis out, Eric Vloeimans and Hans Sparla in.

WILLEM BREUKER reeds

❸ *Johan van der Keuken: Music for His Films* (BVHaast 9709-10) 1966–97
Breuker Kollektief, Gilius van Bergeijk, John Tchicai, Lodewijk de Boer, Louis Andriessen, Leo Cuypers, Maarten Altena, Victor Kaihatu, Han Bennink, et al. "Monk in Groningen," "The PLO March" (both with Andriessen), "Waddenzee Suite." Some new music, and the best available glimpses of early Breuker.

❸ *De Onderste Steen* (Entr'acte 2) 1972–91
Breuker Kollektief, Michael Waisvisz, Andriessen, Johnny Meyer, Altena, Bennink, Martin van Duynhoven, et al. Another career overview including "My baby has gone to the schouwburg," "Tango I," "Tango II."

❸ *Baal Brecht Breuker Handke* (BVHaast 9006) 1973–74.

❸ *A Paris/Summer Music* (Marge 152012) 2/78

❸ *The Parrot* (BVHaast 9601) 1980–1995
Kollektief (various versions), plus strings and other readers. A so-so compilation drawn from out-of-print LPs; includes "Dance of the Knights" (Prokofiev), "The Good, the Bad, and the Ugly," "Song of Mandalay."

❸ *Gershwin* (BVHaast 8802) 1987–88
Kollektief plus strings. "Rhapsody in Blue" is out of print, but here are other representative Breuker arrangements of Gershwin and Morricone.

❸ *To Remain* (BVHaast 8904) 1983–84 and 1989
Kollektief (three versions). This is the CD stuck in an LP cover.

❸ *Heibel* (BVHaast 9102) 12/90
Kollektief, Lorre Lynn Trytten, Greetje Bijma. The "cheese box."

As composer (see also The Busy Drone):

❸ Herman Heijermans' *The Samuel Falkland Show*/Bertold Brecht's *The Resistible Rise of Arturo Ui* (BVHaast 9003) 5 & 11/89
Metropole Orkest, cond. Rob Pronk and Jurre Hanstra. Music for theater and television.

Many other recent Breuker CDs are also on BVHaast.

PETER BRÖTZMANN reeds

◉ Octet: *Machine Gun* (FMP 24) 5/68.
Willem Breuker, Evan Parker, Fred van Hove, Buschi Niebergall, Peter Kowald, Han Bennink, Sven Ake Johansson.

◉ *The Berlin Concert* (FMP 34/35) 8/71
Brötzmann, Albert Mangelsdorff, van Hove, Bennink.

MARION BROWN alto saxophone

◉ *Porto Novo* (Black Lion 760200) 12/67
Supplemented by a 1970 Brown/Leo Smith session.

THE BUSY DRONE barrel organ

◉ *The Busy Drone* (BVHaast 9603) 1981 and 1995
Includes pieces by Louis Andriessen, Gilius van Bergeijk, Willem Breuker, Guus Janssen, Misha Mengelberg.

GENE CARL piano, synthesizer

◉ *Below Paradise* (Kaztor 004) 3/97
Joost Buis, Anne La Berge, Hein Peijnenburg, Mary Oliver, Corrie van Binsbergen (eg), Tony Overwater (b), Vatcher.

CURTIS CLARK piano (see also Collections)

◉ Billy Bang (vln): *Invitation* (Soul Note 121036) 4/82

◉ David Murray (ts) Octet: *Murray's Steps* (Black Saint 120065) 7/82
Bobby Bradford, Butch Morris.

◉ *Letter to South Africa* (Nimbus 501) 1987

◉ *Live at the BIMhuis* (Nimbus 505) 10/88

CLUSONE 3: Michael Moore, Ernst Reijseger, Han Bennink

◉ *Clusone 3* (Ramboy 01) 1990 and 1991
"Debbie Warden," "Girl Talk," "Providence," "Rollo II."

◉ *I Am An Indian* (Gramavision 79505) 1993
"The Gig" (Nichols), "Purple Gazelle" (Ellington), "Wigwam."

◉ *Soft Lights and Sweet Music* (hatART 6153) 11/93
"For the Folks Back Home" (Bergin).

◉ *Love Henry* (Gramavision 79517) 7/96
"Bilbao Song" (Weill), "In the Company of Angels," "Uninhabited Island."

COMPANY

❂ *Company 6&7* (Incus 07) 5/77
Leo Smith (tpt, flt), Lol Coxhill (ss), Steve Lacy, Anthony Braxton, Evan Parker, Derek Bailey, Steve Beresford, Maarten Altena, Han Bennink.

❂ *Once* (Incus 04) 5/87
Lee Konitz, Derek Bailey, Tristan Honsinger, et al.

CONTRABAND

❂ Contraband 94: *Boy Edgar Suite* (VPRO/Eigen Wijs 9412) 5/94
Toon de Gouw, Louis Lanzing, Chris Abelen, Willem van Manen, Paul van Kemenade, Frans Vermeerssen, et al.

Two more Contraband CDs are on BVHaast.

LEO CUYPERS piano

❂ *Zeeland Suite* and *Johnny Rep Suite* (BVHaast 9307) 1977 and 1974

❂ *Songbook* (BVHaast 9502) 8/95

DANIELE D'AGARO clarinet, tenor saxophone (see also Trio San Francisco)

❂ *Lingua Franca* (Nimbus 507) 6/89
Tristan Honsinger, Ernst Glerum.

❂ D'Agaro Delius Quartet: *Byas a Drink* (NOTA 205) 3/92
Tobias Delius, Glerum, Umberto Trobetta "Gandhi" (d). "Byas a Drink," "Byas'd Opinion," "Free and Easy" (all by Don Byas).

TOBIAS DELIUS tenor saxophone (see also Daniele D'Agaro, Trio San Francisco, Collections)

❂ *The Heron* (ICP 033) 6/97

❂ Chris Abelen (tbn): *Dance of the Penguins* (BVHaast 9608) 1996
Corrie van Binsbergen (eg), Wilbert de Joode, Charles Huffstadt (d).

ERIC DOLPHY alto saxophone, bass clarinet, flute

❂ *Last Date* (Fontana/Verve 822 226) 6/64

DOUBLE TRIO

❂ *Green Dolphy Suite* (Enja 90112) 9/94
Armand Angster, Jacques di Donato, Louis Sclavis (cls), Mark Feldman, Ernst Reijseger, Mark Dresser.

FRANKY DOUGLAS electric guitar

❂ Sunchild: *The Visions Project* (Van 519938) 7/93
    Eric Boeren, Wolter Wierbos, Ronald Snijders, Michael Moore, Ernst Reijseger,
    Glenn Gaddum, Jeroen Goldsteen, Eric Calmes, Michael Vatcher, Jogi Gillis,
    Mildred Douglas, et al.

DUTCH JAZZ ORCHESTRA

❂ *Portrait of a Silk Thread: Newly Discovered Works of Billy Strayhorn* (Kokopelli
    1310) 1/95
    Cond. Jerry van Rooijen.

MARTIN van DUYNHOVEN drums

❂ *Uitkrant* (MVD 9602) 1990–1997
    Eric Boeren, Guus Janssen, Arnold Dooyeweerd, Fred van Duynhoven, et al.

EBONY BAND

❂ *City of Glass* (Channel Crossings 6394) 6/93
    Cond. Gunther Schuller.

NEDLY ELSTAK trumpet, piano

❂ *The Machine* (ESP 1076) 5/68
    Maarten Altena, Martin van Duynhoven.

As composer:

❂ *Double Eclipse: A Tribute to Nedly Elstak* (BVHaast 9210) 12/91
    Charles Green, Curtis Clark, Larry Fishkind, Arnold Dooyeweerd, Martin van
    Duynhoven, et al. Elstak pieces, many with voices, done in Nedlyan style.

THE EX

❂ *Joggers & Smoggers* (Fist Puppet 005/Ex 040/41) 6/89
    Guests include Wolter Wierbos and Ab Baars.

❂ The Ex & Guests: —*instant*—(Ex 063/064) 1995
    Guests include Wierbos, Baars, Tristan Honsinger, Han Bennink, Michael
    Vatcher. "Atoll" (Baars/Moor), "Duo Triptych Too" (Baars/Hessels), "Exile
    O'Phonics," "What Inflexibility!" (Moor/Vatcher).

COR FUHLER keyboards (see also Collections)

❂ *7 CC IN IO* (Geestgronden 15) 1994–95

ERNST GLERUM bass, piano, organ (see also Amsterdam String Trio, Han Bennink)

❶ *Elbow Room* (Via 9220322) 7/97
Curtis Clark. "Letter to South Africa" (Clark), "Psalm."

BURTON GREENE piano

❶ Klezmokum: *Klezmokum* (BVHaast 9209) 1992
Michael Moore (cl), Larry Fishkind, Roberto Haliffi (d, perc).

GUNTER HAMPEL reeds, vibes, piano

❶ *Music from Europe* (ESP Disk 1042) 12/66

❶ *The 8th of July 1969* (Birth 001)

COLEMAN HAWKINS tenor saxophone

❶ *The Chronological Coleman Hawkins 1934–1937* (Classics 602)
The Ramblers a.o. "I Wish I Were Twins," "Meditation," "What Harlem Is to Me."

GERRY HEMINGWAY drums, percussion

❶ Quartet: *Down to the Wire* (hatART 6121) 12/91
Michael Moore, Wolter Wierbos, Mark Dresser (b). "Debbie Warden."

❶ Quintet: *Perfect World* (Random Acoustics 019) 3/95
As above plus Ernst Reijseger. "The Village of the Virgins."

IG HENNEMAN viola

❶ Kwintet: *in Grassetto* (Wig 01) 5/90

❶ Tentet: *Dickinson* (Wig 02) 1/93

❶ Tentet: *Repeat that, repeat* (Wig 03) 1995

TRISTAN HONSINGER cello

❶ Honsinger & Toshinori Kondo: *this, that and the other* (ITM 971421) 1987

❶ Cecil Taylor with Tristan Honsinger & Evan Parker: *The Hearth* (FMP 11) 6/88
Improvisations.

❶ Cecil Taylor: *Always a Pleasure* (FMP 69) 4/93
Harri Sjöström, Charles Gayle, Rashid Bakr, et al.

❶ *Map of Moods* (FMP 76) 4/94
Aleksander Kolkowski, Stephano Lunardi (both vln), Ernst Glerum, Louis Moholo.

● This, That and the Other: *Sketches of Probability* (Pierrot Lunaire/Associazione di Idee 009) 5/96
  Augusto Forti (cl, vcl), Sean Bergin, Tobias Delius, Joe Williamson, Alan Purves, Katie Duck (vcl), Peggy Larson (vcl), Rick Parets (actor).

MAURICE HORSTHUIS/ORKEST AMSTERDAM DRAMA (see also Amsterdam String Trio)

● *Amsterdam Drama* (Attaca Babel 9370) 9/91

● *Drama in Concert/1994* (Cococon 96001) 1994
  "Stubb Insulted," "Waterhoogten II."

● *Vreemd Hier* (Cococon 96002) 6/95
  "Pip wordt gek," "Queequeg komt thuis."

INSTANT COMPOSERS POOL ORCHESTRA

● *Two Programs: The ICP Orchestra Performs Nichols–Monk* (ICP 026) 1984 and 1986

● *Bospaadje Konijnehol I* (ICP 028) 1986 and 1990
  Evert Hekkema, George Lewis, Wolter Wierbos, Michael Moore, Ab Baars, Maartje ten Hoorn, Maurice Horsthuis, Ernst Reijseger, Ernst Glerum, Han Bennink. *Ellington Mix, The Purple Sofa.*

● *Bospaadje Konijnehol II* (ICP 029) 1990 and 1991
  As above except: Lewis and Horstshuis out, Tristan Honsinger in. "Kwela P'Kwana."

GUUS JANSSEN piano, harpsichord (see also Collections)

● *Klankast* (Geestgronden 9) 1987–91

● *Harpsichord* (Geestgronden) 1990–91

● Janssen Glerum Janssen: *Lighter* (Geestgronden 11) 1992–95

● Janssen Glerum Janssen: *Zwik* (Geestgronden 19) 1996–97

As composer (see also The Busy Drone, Orkest de Volharding, Harry Sparnaay):

● *Piano Compositions* (Composers' Voice 8703) 1987
  "Brake" (Janssen), *Carrara* (Termos), played by Guus Janssen.

● *Guitar Music from the Netherlands* (Composers' Voice 8701) 1987–88
  Amsterdam Guitar Trio. "Wandelweer."

● (NM Classics 92041) 1993–94
  Eleonore Pameijer (picc), Janssen (hpscd), Nieuw Sinfonietta Amsterdam, cond. Lev Markiz. *Zoek.*

❶ Janssen & Friso Haverkamp: *Noach an Opera off Genesis* (Composers' Voice 42/43/Geestgronden 13) 6/94
 Herb Robertson, Vincent Chancey, Joost Buis, Ab Baars, Jorrit Dijkstra, Peter van Bergen, Jan Willem van der Ham, Jacques Palinckx, Ernst Glerum, Wim Janssen, et al., cond. Lucas Vis.

IVO JANSSEN piano

❶ (NM Classics 92028) 5/93
 Includes "Blend" (Padding), "Strides," "Walk" (Loevendie), "Trepidus" (Andriessen).

THEO LOEVENDIE reeds, piano, composer

As composer: See Ivo Janssen, Harry Sparnaay, Marcel Worms

LOOS: Peter van Bergen, Gerard Bouwhuis, Huib Emmer, Patricio Wang, Paul Koek

❶ *Fundamental* (Geestgronden 10) 8/92

❶ Ensemble LOOS: Cornelis de Bondt: *De Tragische Handeling [Actus Tragicus]* (Composers' Voice 58) 12/95

MISHA MENGELBERG piano (see also Berlin Contemporary Jazz Orchestra, Instant Composers Pool Orchestra, Orkest de Volharding, Roswell Rudd)

❶ Mengelberg, Steve Lacy, George Lewis, Arjen Gorter & Han Bennink: *Change of Season (Music of Herbie Nichols)* (Soul Note 121104) 7/84

❶ Mengelberg, Lacy, Lewis, Ernst Reijseger & Bennink: *Dutch Masters* (Soul Note 121154) 3/87
 "Kneebus," "Reef."

❶ *Impromptus* (FMP 7) 6/88
 Short piano solos (and hummed vocals), a nice complement to the two long solos on *Mix*.

❶ John Tchicai: *Grandpa's Spells* (Storyville 4182) 3/92

❶ *Who's Bridge* (Avant 038) 2/94
 "Rollo II," "Peer's Counting Song," "Rumbone," "De sprong! O romantiek der hazen."

❶ *Mix* (ICP 030) 4 & 5/94

❶ *The Root of the Problem* (hatOLOGY 504) 5/96
 Improvised duos and trios with Thomas Heberer, Steve Potts (as, ss), Michel Godard (tba,serpent) and Achim Kremer (perc).

● *No Idea* (DIW 619) 6/96
  Greg Cohen (b), Joey Baron. Mostly standards, including "House Party Starting," "The Mooche."

● Mengelberg & Han Bennink: *MiHA* (ICP 031) 1992 and 1997

As composer: See also Louis Andriessen, The Busy Drone)

● *Misha Mengelberg* (Pierrot Lunaire/Associazione di Idee 010) 5/96
  Ed Bogaard (as), Orchestra del Teatro Comunale di Bologna, cond. Ernst van Tiel. *Concerto for Saxophone and Orchestra, Onderweg,* "De sprong! O romantiek der hazen."

PINO MINAFRA trumpet

● Minafra, Ernst Reijseger, Han Bennink: *Noci . . . Strani Fruti* (Leo 176) 7/90

LOUIS MOHOLO drums

● *Exile* (Ogun 003) 1990–91
  Sean Bergin, Franky Douglas, et al. "Dudu," "Plastic Bag" (both Bergin), "Visions" (Douglas).

● *Freedom Tour, Live in South Africa 1993* (Ogun 006)
  Bergin, Tobias Delius, et al. Moholo and Bergin return to the homeland: sloppy but spirited. Includes "Dudu," "Use Less Sugar, Stir Like Hell" (Delius).

MICHAEL MOORE alto saxophone, clarinet, bass clarinet (see also Available Jelly, Clusone 3)

● *Home Game* (Ramboy 02) 10/88

● *Négligé* (Ramboy 04) 1989 and 1992

● *Chicoutimi* (Ramboy 06) 1993

● Marilyn Crispell, Gerry Hemingway, Moore: *MGM Trio* (Ramboy 09) 1994–95

● Fred Hersch, Moore, Hemingway: *Thirteen Ways* (GM 3033) 6/95

● *tunes for horn guys* (Ramboy 08) 1995
  Wolter Wierbos, Ab Baars, Frank Gratkowski (rds), Tobias Delius. "Another Day, Another Dollar."

LAWRENCE D. "BUTCH" MORRIS conductor, cornet

● *Conduction #31, #35, #36* (New World 80485) 5/93
  On #31: Wolter Wierbos, Tom Cora, Hans Reichel, Steve Beresford, Han Bennink et al. On #35 & #36: Maarten Altena Ensemble: Wierbos, Michael Barker, Peter van Bergen, Alison Isadora, Michiel Scheen, Wiek Hijmans, Altena, Michael Vatcher, Jannie Pranger.

PALINCKX: Joost Buis, Cor Fuhler, Jacques Palinckx, Bert Palinckx, Jim Meneses

- ❸ *BORDER—LIVE IN ZURICH* (Intakt 043) 4/95
  "Phase Two: Pink Floyd," "Spock sings, Kirk dies."

- ❸ *The Psychedelic Years* (Vonk 6) 12/95
  Plus Han Buhrs et al. "Fat Freddy's Cat."

ERNST REIJSEGER cello (see Amsterdam String Trio, Arcado String Trio, Clusone 3, Double Trio, Misha Mengelberg, Collections)

- ❸ Georg Graewe, Reijseger, Gerry Hemingway: *Zwei Naechte in Berlin* (Sound Aspects 049) 11/90

- ❸ Trilok Gurtu (perc): *Crazy Saints* (CMP 66) 1993

- ❸ Louis Sclavis (ss, cl, bcl) & Reijseger: *Et on Ne Parle Pas du Temps* (FMP 66) 4/94

- ❸ Graewe, Reijseger, Hemingway: *The Saturn Cycle* (Music & Arts 958) 11/94

- ❸ *Colla Parte* (Winter & Winter 910 012) 1997
  Cello solos including "Mother of All Wars" (Mengelberg).

ROSWELL RUDD trombone

- ❸ Rudd, Steve Lacy, Misha Mengelberg, Kent Carter (b) & Han Bennink: *Regeneration* (Soul Note 121054) 6/82

PETER SCHAT

As composer:

- ❸ (Donemus 19) 1970–92
  Various ensembles, cond. Lucas Vis et al. *To You.*

HARRY SPARNAAY bass clarinet

- ❸ *Ladder of Escape 1* (Attaca Babel 8945)
  "Duo" (Loevendie), "Sprezzatura" (Janssen).

SURINAM MUSIC ENSEMBLE

- ❸ *No Kiddin'* (Timeless 325) 1989
  Jarmo Hoogendijk, Gregg Moore, Michael Moore, Sean Bergin, Glenn Gaddum, Jeroen Goldsteen, Franky Douglas, Larry Fishkind, Pablo Nahar, Eddy Veldman, Jogi Gillis, Denise Jannah, et al.

J. C. TANS ORCHESTRA

- ❸ *Around the World* (BVHaast 8905) 5/89
  Eric Boeren, Boy Raaymakers, Ab Baars, Jan Willem van der Ham, Curtis Clark, Wilbert de Joode, et al.

PAUL TERMOS alto saxophone

● Termos Tentet: *Shakes & Sounds* (Geestgronden 5) 1990

● Double Express: *Death Dance of Principles* (Geestgronden 16) 1992 and 1995
    Also includes three pieces by the Termos Tentet.

As composer (see also Orkest de Volharding):

● *Piano Compositions* (Composers' Voice 8703) 1987
    Carrara (played by Guus Janssen).

● (Composers' Voice 60) 1990–97
    Concerto for Alto Saxophone and Chamber Orchestra (Arno Bornekamp,
    Netherlands Ballet Orchestra, cond. Lucas Vis), *String Quartet #1* (Mondrian
    Quartet), *Expres(s)* (Doelenensemble, cond. Arie van Beek), *Groundwork*
    (Doelenensemble, cond. George Wiegel), *Concerto for Flute and Chamber
    Orchestra* (Eleonore Pameijer, Radio Chamber Orchestra, cond. Ed Spanjaard).
    The alto saxophone part in the Concerto is so close to Termos's own style, it's
    surprising he didn't record it himself. The brass quintet *Groundwork* takes the
    first line of "Cherokee" as a prominent theme.

TRIO SAN FRANCISCO: Sean Bergin, Daniele D'Agaro, Tobias Delius

● *Prisoners of Pleasure* (BVHaast 9605) 1994

MICHAEL VATCHER drums, percussion (see also Collections)

● John Zorn: *Spy vs. Spy* (Elektra/Musician 960 844) 8/88
    Tim Berne (as) Mark Dresser, Joey Baron.

● Roof: *The Untraceable Cigar* (Red Note 4)

FRANS VERMEERSSEN saxophones

● *One for Rahsaan* (A Records 73034) 1/95

ORKEST DE VOLHARDING: Louis Lanzing, Willem van Manen, Dil Engelhard,
Maarten van Norden, Bob Driessen, et al.

● *Trajekten 1972–1992* (NM Classics 92021) 1991–92
    New recordings of old repertoire include "Dat gebeurt in Vietnam"
    (Andriessen), *Dressoir* (Mengelberg), *On Jimmy Yancey* (Andriessen), *Trajekten*
    (van Manen), *Woeha* (Janssen).

● *Hex* (Attaca Babel 9380) 1992–93
    Linea Recta (Termos).

WOLTER WIERBOS trombone (see also Collections)

● Podium Trio: *Take One* (Disckus 04) 3/91

Wolter Wierbos, Paul van Kemenade, Jan Kuiper. All compositions by Kuiper.

● *X Caliber* (ICP 032) 1995
Solo.

MARCEL WORMS piano

● *Jazz in 20th Century Piano Music* (BVHaast 9403) 12/93
"Blend" (Padding), "On the Train" (Loevendie).

COLLECTIONS

● *AngelicA 1993* (Pierrot Lunaire/Associazione di Idee 004) 5/93
Includes solos by Han Bennink and Wolter Wierbos, Bennink and Wierbos in improvised quartets, selections by the Bennink-Steve Beresford duo, excerpts from Butch Morris's Conduction #31 (see Morris above).

● *AngelicA 1996* (Pierrot Lunaire/Associazione di Idee 011) 5/96
This Bologna festival ran a Dutch special in '96. As every year, concert excerpts are edited into a montage for CD release. Represented are: Henneman String Quartet, Honsinger's This, That and the Other, Guus Janssen Septet, Jannsen Glerum Janssen, an ad hoc Misha Mengelberg group, Palinckx, plus Mengelberg (p), Janssen (hpscd), Michel Waisvisz (syn, The Hands).

● *Jazz Behind the Dikes, Part 1* ([Dutch] Philips 848 810);
● *Jazz Behind the Dikes, Part 2* ([Dutch] Philips 848 811) 1955–57
A period survey of the Hilversum scene, featuring among others Wessel Ilcken (with Ado Broodboom and Toon van Vliet), Pim and Ruud Jacobs, Rob Madna, Rita Reys, and Tony Vos (with Cees See).

● *October Meeting 1* (BIMhuis 001) 10/87
Wolter Wierbos, John Zorn (with Guus Janssen and Martin van Duynhoven), et al. "Broezimann," "G-Blues," "Number One" (a.k.a. "To John Hodjazz") (all Mengelberg).

● *October Meeting 2* (BIMhuis 002) 10/87
Ernst Reijseger's Cruise Button et al.

● *October Meeting 1991: 3 Quartets* (BIMhuis 003)
Anthony Braxton (with Misha Mengelberg, Mark Dresser, Han Bennink), Cor Fuhler (with Tristan Honsinger, Maarten Altena, Wim Janssen), Evan Parker (with Steve Beresford, Arjen Gorter, Bennink).

● *October Meeting 1991: Anatomy of a Meeting* (BIMhuis 004)
Mostly improvised trios including George Lewis/Steve Berseford/Michael Vatcher, Horst Grabosch (flgh)/Tobias Delius/Curtis Clark, Vera Vingerhoeds/ Eddy Veldman/Greetje Bijma, Ab Baars/Misha Mengelberg/Sunny Murray. Also: duo Steve Beresford/Guus Janssen; excerpts from Mark Dresser's suite *Castles for Carter* including Baars, Wierbos, et al.

Index